HOUSEHOLD HINTS & HANDY TIPS

READER'S DIGEST

HOUSEHOLD HINTS & HANDY TIPS

Published by The Reader's Digest Association Limited
LONDON · NEW YORK · SYDNEY · CAPE TOWN · MONTREAL

Contents

Getting organised

Cleaning and fixing things

Round the house outdoors

You and yours

Family health

Food and nutrition

A more beautiful home

Crisis measures

Index   page 690

Editor: Noel Buchanan
Art Editor: Joanna Walker

Contributors

The publishers wish to thank the following people for their help in creating HOUSEHOLD HINTS & HANDY TIPS

Consultant Editor Cassandra Kent

Writers
Adrian Bailey
Jane Bidder
Carolyn Chapman
Hazel Evans
Christine France
Bee Golding, BSc
Anne Johnson
Anthea Masey
Christine Parsons
Gillian Smedley
Tony Stuart-Jones
Tony Wilkins
Peter Willis
Barbara Yardley, BVSc, MRCVS

Illustrators
John Cummins
Mike Grey
Nicholas Hall
Helen Haywood
Kevin Jones Associates
Oxford Illustrators
Sandra Pond and Will Giles
Precision Illustration
Simon Thomas
Gill Tomblin
Lee Tucker
Lorna Turpin
Ann Winterbotham
John Woodcock

Specialist checkers
Pat Alburey
Peter L. G. Bateman, FRES
Jill Blake
Ivor Carroll, MIMI
Dr James Cox, FRCGP, MICGP
Linda Gray
John McGowan
Paul Messenger
Amanda Pardoe
Jane Pomeroy, BSc, B Vet Med,
    Cert VR, MRCVS
Pauline Swaine
Philip Swindells, MIHort, MISTC, FLS
Arline Usden
Jenny Webb, FInst SMM, FIHEc
Jim Williams

Photographers
Adrian Bailey
Martin Cameron
Richard Surman

Getting organised

*T*o enjoy life to the full, you need spare time. So get your household running smoothly, take control of your finances, and sort out all unnecessary family clutter. You'll be surprised at how much time is released for real living.

Sorting out your household

THE FIRST STEP IS YOU

The 'right' way Getting organised is not an end in itself. There is no right way to do things – unless it's right for you. It must fit your style, your energy, and your schedule. Whatever system helps you to function most effectively is the best one for you.

Keep it simple Beware of the tail wagging the dog. When the appointment book, the budget and expenditures records, the filing system and the master list take more time to maintain than working out the problems they're supposed to solve, it's time to revise your system. Use a simple method like the one suggested below, with a master calendar and a working list.

Start now! The key to getting things done is to start now, no matter what! If you have a call to make, start dialling. A letter to write? Start writing. If the size of a job overwhelms you, do it a piece at a time. You don't eat a loaf of bread whole; you cut it in slices. Do the same with big projects.

Body rhythms Are you a morning person or an evening person? Your efficiency may increase if you arrange your tasks as much as possible around the rhythms of your body. Try scheduling top-priority, energy-using projects during your peak hours, routine work during your 'low' time.

CALENDAR AND WORKING LIST

Family calendar To organise your family's activities and to keep track of everyone's schedule, put up a large poster-sized master calendar displaying a full year. It's called a Year Planner in stationery shops. Pin it up where everyone can see it. Enter all important family dates – birthdays, anniversaries, holidays – at the beginning of the year. Also enter all appointments, as they are made, for everyone in your family.

Notebook Buy a small notebook to carry with you. It's your working list – a continuous list that replaces those little scraps of paper. In the notebook, list appointments, things to do or buy, and items that require action. As dates approach, transfer them from your master calendar to the notebook.

The one for you Shop around in stationery and office-supply shops for the notebook that best suits you. You'll probably be pleasantly surprised at the variety available. If you'll be carrying it in a pocket, you probably won't want one with spiral wire binding. It can catch on clothing. Very inexpensive notebooks measure about 150 x 100mm (6 x 4in).

Full details Include in your notebook all telephone numbers and details needed to accomplish a job. For example: 'Call Acme customer service, 264-5000, ext. 295, re £5 overcharge on bill dated June 2nd, acc. no. 483-456-7899.'

No routine jobs Don't over-complicate your notebook by listing items that are a part of your daily or weekly routine. There's no need to list 'Do the shopping on Friday' if you always do the shopping on Friday. Save the notebook for reminders and special projects.

Lists of ideas Make a 'lists' section in your notebook – a file of ideas. For example, set aside individual pages to list books to read, videos to hire, current movies to see, places to go when people visit, recommended restaurants to try out, and so on.

Plan ahead At the start of each week – or, better still, at the end of the previous week – plan your work for several days ahead. It gives you perspective on the week, enables you to spread out the essential jobs, and prevents a frantic rush at the end of the week.

A time for fun Set aside a time for enjoying yourself and keeping up with friends – treat it like an important appointment. If you don't set aside a specific time for relaxation, your work and all those family commitments will soon take over your life.

Keep it with you Keep your list with you at all times. A list is worse than useless if you can't refer to it, because you may think that you've disposed of a matter when in fact you haven't. And you'll only start making notes on little scraps of paper again!

One unpleasant job a day Set a goal to do one necessary job each day that you really dislike. You'll have a fine sense of satisfaction each time you succeed.

Separate notebooks for complex jobs Keep a second, separate notebook to cope with complex, special situations; for example, enrolling a child in a new school, moving to a new home, or organising an annual holiday for the whole family.

Keeping a record Don't be in a hurry to throw away notebook pages that have been completed. That cooker part you ordered two months ago may be wrong when it arrives, and you may have to call the same people all over again. And if you keep the book after it has filled up, it can make fascinating reading six months later.

HOW ORGANISED ARE YOU?

1 Does it often take you more than ten minutes to unearth a particular letter, bill, report, or other paper from your files or your desk?　　YES/NO

2 Are there loose papers on your desk, other than reference materials, that you haven't looked at for a month or more?　　YES/NO

3 Has your electricity, gas, or telephone ever been turned off because you forgot to pay the bill?　　YES/NO

4 Within the last two months, have you overlooked a scheduled appointment, an anniversary, or some other date that you wanted to acknowledge?　　YES/NO

5 Do magazines and newspapers pile up unread?　　YES/NO

6 Do you frequently put off a work assignment for so long that it becomes an emergency or a panic situation?　　YES/NO

7 Do you frequently misplace your keys, glasses, gloves, handbag, briefcase or other commonly carried items?　　YES/NO

8 Do belongings gather in corners of closets, or on the floor, because you can't decide where to put them?　　YES/NO

9 Would your storage problems be solved if you had more space?　YES/NO

10 Do you want to get organised but everything is in such a mess that you don't know where to start?　　YES/NO

11 Do your children all have household jobs that they carry out quite willingly?　　YES/NO

12 By the end of the average day, have you accomplished at least the most important tasks you set for yourself?　　YES/NO

13 Are the kitchen appliances and utensils that you use most often kept in the most convenient place?　　YES/NO

14 Is your living room arranged so that family and guests can speak comfortably without raising their voices? Are there places for drinks and snacks?　　YES/NO

Score: 1 point for each 'yes' to questions 1-10; 1 point for each 'no' to questions 11-14.

If your score is:
1-3 Systems are under control. Some of the innovative tips in this section might make things even better.

4-7 Disorganisation is troublesome. Hints in 'Organising Your Household' could help considerably.

8-10 Life must be very difficult.

11 and up Disorganised to the point of chaos. Use the hints and ideas to change your life – and get to work immediately.

MAKE YOUR OWN ORGANISER

There's no need to spend a lot of money on a fancy organiser with expensive inserts that may be suited to other people's lives, but not yours. Instead, make one to suit your own personal needs. Simply buy a small loose-leaf binder in a stationery shop. At the same time, get loose-leaf paper and dividers to fit.

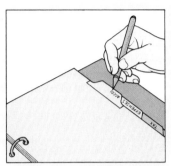

Identify the categories you wish to include in your organiser – addresses and telephone numbers, shopping, long-term projects, appointments, expenses or whatever you wish. Fill in the tabs on the dividers and insert them in the binder with paper for each section.

For the appointments section buy a small Year Planner. Alternatively, get a small calendar – perhaps the kind you get free at Christmas. Remove its outer cover and punch holes to fit the rings of the binder. Now you're ready to get your life organised.

THE FAMILY MESSAGE CENTRE

For everyone's use Establish a message centre in your home. It needn't be elaborate – it could simply be Post-it notes stuck on the refrigerator or a door, or a cork notice board with bits of paper fixed with drawing pins. Encourage everyone in the household to use it to list their plans, requirements for the next shopping trip, and – especially important – all telephone messages that they take.

Keep it up-to-date Keep the message centre current; throw away outdated notes. Take care of as many items as you can each day – or enter them in your notebook for action later.

TELEPHONE TIMESAVERS

Phone first To save time and frustration, use the telephone before making a lengthy journey by car or public transport. Phone to confirm appointments, to check if a shop has the item you want, or to find out if a showroom really is going to be open on Saturday afternoons. Don't waste your valuable weekend time making fruitless journeys.

Cutting it short Learn how to cut off time-consuming calls without hurting people's feelings. For example, it's quite all right to say: 'This is a terrible time for me, may I call you back?' (Of course, do call back later.)

A phone call instead Sometimes a phone call is more timesaving and effective than a letter. Even a long-distance call may be cheaper, when you consider how long it takes to write a letter and how busy you are.

HOW AN ANSWERING MACHINE CAN WORK FOR YOU – AND SAVE MONEY

● Use the answering machine to save you from answering the phone when you're watching TV, bathing the baby or eating a meal.
● An answering machine means you never miss a call (provided your caller leaves a message).
● Use the machine's remote control to pick up messages when you're away from home. It's handy if you're working late at the office.
● Make your outgoing message work for you. If you need to send someone a message when you're out of touch add a bit to your normal statement about returning calls – for example, 'If it's you Sarah, I can make Wednesday evening – your place at 7pm.'
● Don't be afraid of leaving messages on machines, and encourage your friends to use yours. You can keep phone bills to a minimum by making arrangements via machines and cutting out costly chats.
● Clear messages from your tape daily, keeping a pad handy as you listen to note facts and telephone numbers. If you're on holiday and expect a lot of calls, either use your remote control or ask a friend to replace the incoming message tape as often as necessary.

SHOPPING AND APPOINTMENTS

Running list Keep a running list of groceries and household supplies that you need. Add things to it as soon as you think of them. By the time you go shopping, there'll be little to add.

Monster list Alternatively, type or write a comprehensive list of all the things you ever shop for. Make lots of photocopies and before each shopping trip tick the items you need.

Several calls at once Group your calls so you can accomplish several jobs in one trip. Use a convenient shopping centre that has most of the shops, offices and services that you need. Always try to do an errand on the way to something else instead of making a special trip.

Choose the right time Whenever possible, do errands when traffic is light and queues are short. This will vary from place to place. There are likely to be long queues in a building society at Monday lunchtime in a busy office district, but not in a residential area. Supermarkets claim that Tuesday is their least busy day.

Consecutive appointments Eliminate additional trips by making consecutive doctor or dentist appointments for members of the family (or at least for all the children).

Get there first Try to get the first appointment in the morning so you won't be delayed by someone ahead of you and you'll still have most of the day left when you finish.

Fitting in an extra job Take your working list with you whenever you go out on errands. You may be able to fit in something that you scheduled for later in the week.

Help from the family Get your family to help out with errands. If a shirt has to be returned to a shop, leave it in clear sight so that anyone going to or near that particular shop can take it in. To make it easy, attach a note with instructions – credit to charge account, exchange for a different size or colour, or whatever.

USING BITS OF TIME

Most small jobs around the house can be accomplished in bits and pieces of time. For instance, while you're sitting in a doctor's waiting room, you can write cheques to pay bills; while riding on the bus you can make a shopping list. The following lists give some examples of what you can do in odd chunks of time.

What you can do in five minutes
Sew on a button.
Make an appointment.
File your nails.
Water houseplants.
Make out a party guest list.
Book tickets for a concert.

What you can do in ten minutes
Repot a plant.
Write a short letter or note.
Pick out a birthday card.
Hand-wash some clothes.
Straighten up your desktop.
Exercise.

What you can do in 30 minutes
Polish silver and brass.
Go through unread magazines and newspapers.
Work on a crafts project.
Vacuum three or four rooms.
Weed a flower bed.

YOU AND YOUR MAIL

Handle it once only Handle most of your mail only once. Immediately discard anything that needs no action, doesn't interest you or doesn't merit saving.

Making a copy of your answers When you need a copy of your reply, use carbon paper to make the copy on the back of the original letter. That way you have only one sheet of paper to file, and the chances of mislaying the copy are greatly reduced. There is no need to type to get a carbon copy either. A handwritten reply done with a ball-point pen makes a perfectly legible carbon.

Greetings cards So that you always have greetings cards for any occasion, buy extras (birthday, anniversary, get well).

ORGANISING HOUSEWORK

Everything in its place Make it a habit to return everything to its proper place and remind others to do so. If you do this daily, it takes less time than waiting until the situation is out of control. And you needn't spend time looking for out-of-place objects.

Small jobs Do small jobs as they crop up so that they occupy little time. For example, laundry left until the weekend can consume the weekend; instead, start a load before breakfast, put it in the dryer or on the line after breakfast, and it's done.

Be sensible with appliances Use labour-saving gadgets or household appliances whenever they'll *really* save time. But don't overdo it. Chopping an onion with a knife may take no longer than using a food processor and then having to take the machine apart and wash and dry it. Don't slavishly put everything in the dishwasher. Hand-wash utensils you may need again soon, such as a tea-strainer, vegetable knife or milk saucepan.

Allow for the unexpected Leave some spare time in your day for surprises, interruptions or emergencies. Some activities will take longer than expected, no matter how carefully you plan them or how much you allow for possible delays.

Preparation time Why does a half-hour job often take twice as long as you thought it would? Probably because you estimated only the actual working time and didn't take into account the preparation – getting out and putting away tools, for instance, or having to go to the shop to get some more selfraising flour.

A bit at a time Tackle the big tasks a bit at a time. Straightening every cupboard in the house might take days; but one cupboard, especially if it isn't too cluttered, may take no longer than 15 or 20 minutes to tidy.

16

VISITORS ARE COMING

High-payoff jobs Save time and concentrate on high-payoff cleaning – work on the most conspicuous areas, such as the entrance hall and living room rugs. Have you ever noticed how much cleaning you can do in the hour before visitors arrive?

Dimmed lights hide the dust If visitors are coming and things aren't quite up to par, bring out the candles, dim the lights, and serve up good food and conversation. As long as dust and disorder don't force themselves on their attention, normal people won't look for them.

Stick to priorities Once you've attended to basics, such as cleaning the bathroom, concentrate on what shows the most. Any home will pass muster if the clutter is contained, the surfaces are clean, and your best possessions are polished.

Cosmetic tricks Practise cosmetic strategies that fool the visitor's eye. Keep the white chair clean, and people will assume that the black one is also clean. If you have fringed rugs, brush the fringe so that it lies straight and neat. Your guests are then likely to assume that everything else is equally orderly.

A final once-over For a last-minute clean up of the bathroom and toilet after the family has used them, go quickly over all surfaces with a spray window cleaner and a paper towel. Give the toilet a quick scrub with the brush, and a final flush.

THE NIGHT BEFORE

Preparing for morning Cut down the chaos each morning by doing as much as you can the night before. Write absence notes, lay out clothes, fix lunches, distribute lunch money. It doesn't take long.

Setting up breakfast While you are cleaning up the kitchen after dinner, set the table for breakfast. Put out jams, cereals and other non-refrigerated items; there'll be that much less to do in the morning.

MAKING LIFE EASIER

Organise a pleasant home-coming Allow time for making up the beds and tidying the kitchen before leaving the house in the morning. It makes coming home much more pleasant – and sets an example for others in the household.

17

A shelf of their own Keep a bookcase near the front door. Assign each child a shelf on which to assemble lunch, homework, sports clothes and so on. In the morning, they can pick up everything quickly as they leave; in the afternoon, they can drop their belongings there. Designate one shelf specifically for library books and make sure your children return all books to this shelf. This can save a lot of searching.

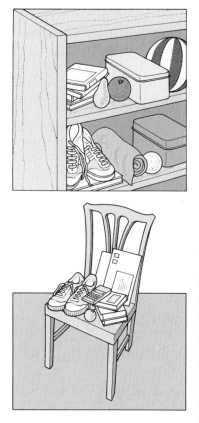

'Way station' Set up a way station where children's belongings can be temporarily left – schoolbooks, laundered clothes, toys, mail and other odds and ends. Once a day, get your children to pick up their belongings from the way station and take them to their rooms. Designate a chair, box or basket for this purpose and put it where they can't ignore it – perhaps at the bottom of the stairs so they can collect things as they go up to their rooms in the evening.

Last-minute money Keep a money dish handy for your small change so that you won't be caught short when someone going out of the door suddenly needs last-minute funds.

SHARING THE BURDEN

Finding a formula for job-sharing Try discussing the jobs that each member of the family likes least, and work around them accordingly. One person may hate to scrape dirty dishes but may not mind taking them out of the dishwasher. Rather than arguing, find something that each person doesn't mind doing.

Don't be 'boss' Avoid the boss syndrome. As soon as youngsters become proficient at a job, let them get on with it and accept responsibility for the results. Resist the temptation to keep checking up on them and pointing out the 'right' way of doing something.

Family pressure Let family group pressure maintain standards as much as possible. When some job isn't properly done, hold back for a while and give other members of the family a chance to complain and solve the problem themselves.

Adjust your expectations Be sure that you're not imposing too high a standard. When work is honestly shared, all partners are entitled to a say in how well it has to be done. If you're the only one who wants a job done better, re-examine your expectations and perhaps make some adjustments. It may then be easier to get other members of the family to work as a team.

OUTSIDE HELP

Hire someone If you can't get all your housework done in a reasonable amount of time, hire someone to help you. You'll be surprised at how much more you can accomplish with someone helping out just three hours every week.

Friends and neighbours to the rescue If you can't get professional help with household work, be creative. Possible sources of assistance include schoolchildren, college students and neighbours who might be willing to take over one or two jobs, such as house cleaning, ironing, window cleaning or grocery shopping.

GETTING CHILDREN TO HELP

A first step Include your youngest child in the housework; it may slow down progress, but it's an essential first step in helping that child feel part of the work force.

No sex divisions Assume that boys and girls will do the housework in equal amounts and without dividing work into 'girls' jobs' and 'boys' jobs'.

Train them carefully Teach your children step by step how to do whatever job you ask of them. Don't assume that the task will be completely learned by watching. Show, teach, train. Check the result when they're finished and compliment them.

Set a deadline Clearly define the time of day when a child's job is to be completed – either before school, right after school, or by dinner. Don't let tasks hang over into the evening; children are usually too tired to work after the evening meal.

Delegating work At weekends, make up a list of jobs and sort out who does what over a leisurely breakfast. Break a big job down into steps and be sure the children's ages and abilities are equal to their assignments.

Making their own beds A child as young as six can at least tidy up a bed – it doesn't have to be perfect, after all! Using duvets on beds will make the job a lot easier than if he has to struggle with sheets and blankets.

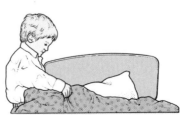

HOUSEHOLD JOBS FOR A FIVE-YEAR-OLD

- Make his own bed every day. It may be a little sloppy at first, but it'll improve in the course of time.
- Put clothes back in the wardrobe or drawer.
- Put toys back in the toy chest.
- Water houseplants.
- Feed the dog, cat or goldfish (if he's reminded).
- Set the table.
- Clear the table, one thing at a time.
- Put dirty clothes in the laundry basket.

SOME HOUSEHOLD JOBS FOR A TEENAGER

- Empty wastebaskets and ashtrays.
- Carry out rubbish bins.
- Vacuum rugs and floors.
- Clean and sweep the kitchen floor.
- Iron his own clothes and the family napkins and tablecloths.
- Polish silver, brass, copper.
- Carry in wood and lay fires.
- Vacuum the inside of the car.
- Wash the car.
- Mow the lawn.

ATTACKING THE CLUTTER

Where will it go? Before you buy something for the house, ask yourself, 'Where am I going to put it?' and make sure that you have a clearly defined place in mind.

A temporary home An 'I-don't-know-what-it-is' box can be a tremendous help. This is for orphan socks and gloves and all those important-looking but unidentifiable machine parts, nuts and bolts you find lying about. From time to time, sort the contents, tell others to claim whatever is theirs and dump what appears useless into the rubbish bin.

Grouping things Keep items used together near one another – for example, tennis rackets, balls, shoes and other tennis equipment. In the kitchen, put the carving knife, fork and sharpening steel in the same place. Don't have one in a drawer, one in a knife rack and one on a hook.

Deciding what to throw out Go through your house periodically, eliminating items you no longer want. One possible criterion: when you no longer notice a decorative object (such as a picture), it may be time to get rid of it. You might consider a trade-off system. Whenever you add a new item to the house, discard an old one.

Don't take over Caution! Do not throw out someone else's things unless they have agreed first. Suggest and encourage, but don't take over their lives. This applies to your parents, your spouse, and any children over four years old.

When in doubt . . . Be ruthless with your own possessions. Discard all unused junk. When in doubt, throw it out. It takes up space, and you'll just end up cleaning it and moving it around.

Start from the outside When the enthusiasm to clean strikes, start from the outside. Take care of the clutter scattered around the room before digging into the overcrowded cupboard. Cleaning the cupboard first makes a double mess.

Hour at a time If you're faced with an overcrowded cupboard, schedule an hour to work on it. Write it on your weekly list as a project. But don't try to finish in one session. When the hour is up, stop. Schedule another hour and then another until the job is done.

Four categories To keep mess to a minimum, before you begin cleaning a cupboard, arrange four boxes nearby to categorise those things that shouldn't go back in. Label them 'for charity', 'rubbish', 'belongs elsewhere', and 'decision pending'.

Car boot sale or garage sale Sell unwanted things at a car boot sale, or hold your own garage sale (see below and overleaf). If possible, get advice from a friend who has done it before.

Selling furniture? If you want to sell a piece of furniture, try mounting a photograph of it on a card, plus details of size and price and your phone number, and display it in a newsagent's window.

SELLING AT A CAR BOOT SALE

Car boot sales are advertised in local papers, on shop noticeboards and sometimes on homemade posters attached to lampposts. Some are held regularly, often on Sundays, others are occasional – perhaps combined with a school fete. If you can't find one locally, ring your local council or the police who should have been given information that one is to be held.

Be prepared Take a trestle table. No-one's car boot is big enough to sell from comfortably.

The right price Price your goods the night before – and keep prices low. Fill boxes with small items and mark the whole box with a fixed price. Be prepared for haggling and reduce prices accordingly.

Cash storage Wear a money belt or neck purse and take plenty of change. If you expect high takings, put a lockable cash box in your car glove box and lock that too if possible.

Worth too much Don't expect high prices. If you want to sell something worthwhile put an advertisement in your local paper or take it to an auction room.

An accomplice Take a friend to help cope with crowds and to provide company in quiet moments.

Food and drink Take some refreshments so you don't have to leave your stall tended by only one person. Don't drink too much unless you're sure there's a handy toilet.

Bring and buy Having sold your own goods, don't be tempted by a load of someone else's castoffs. The aim of this exercise is to reduce clutter in your home.

No returns At the end of the day gather up all your unsold goods and try to sell them as a job lot to a car boot sale regular. Or take them to a local charity shop.

HOLDING A SUCCESSFUL GARAGE SALE

1 Check with your local authority to see whether you need a permit.

2 Assemble items to be sold. If you don't have enough, ask friends and neighbours to participate in the sale.

3 Write an advertisement giving time, place and date. Post notices at supermarkets, bus stops, and on trees and poles if permitted by authorities.

4 Price goods with tags or tape (use different colours for different owners). When in doubt, price lower.

5 Group similar items together: put clothes on racks, books in boxes, miscellaneous items on card tables.

6 Be prepared to bargain; after all, you're trying to get rid of everything. Reduce prices during the last two hours of the sale.

7 Give any leftovers to your favourite charity. Take down all posters.

ODDS AND ENDS

Containers for small things Assign convenient permanent locations for small restless items that would otherwise end up on a tabletop or be mislaid: a hook near the door for keys that you always take when you go out; a small dish on the dressing table to collect loose change or earrings; a mug on the desk to hold pens.

Untidy housemates If messy family members are a problem, toss their out-of-place belongings into a big cardboard box. When asked where you put an item, indicate the box.

Managing the finances

KEEPING TRACK OF YOUR MONEY

 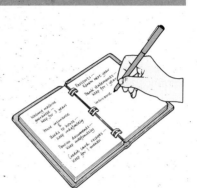

● Set aside a corner of your home for house and money management. It could be the shelf where you keep a series of box files, a desk bought for the purpose, or a specially designed household organiser which you can buy in larger stationery shops. It might be worth buying a small filing cabinet to store your paperwork.

● List the documents and records which you think you need to keep. The list will probably be long, and is likely to include such things as passports, insurance documents, bank statements, guarantees, credit card and cash machine receipts, deeds to your house and pension plan documents. Mark on each how long to keep it.

● Throw away papers when you no longer need them. This can be more difficult than you might think, especially if you are one of nature's hoarders. Just ask yourself, 'Is there any reason to keep them? Will I ever need them again?'

Using credit or cash cards

Remembering your PIN Some cards allow you to alter your PIN the first time you use it. Think of a number you could use for all your cards which you will remember, but no thief could guess from the contents of your handbag or wallet.

Security Never reveal your PIN to anyone, not even members of your own family, and never ask anyone to get cash out of a machine for you.

Dealing with card fraud You are liable for up to £50 of any loss on a credit card until you have reported the card lost or stolen. The credit card company pays any loss after that.

With debit cards and cash machine cards, banks and building societies generally follow the same policy, although they can make you liable for any loss if they think you used your card irresponsibly – if you left it lying around, and a member of your family used it to withdraw money, for example, or if you failed to destroy your PIN.

Charge card or credit card? The two main charge cards, American Express and Diners Club, give you unlimited credit but only for a very short time – charge cards must be cleared at the end of each month. There is always a yearly fee as well. Credit cards offer extended credit up to your personal limit (although extended credit is generally very expensive and should only be used in the short term) and many are still issued free of service charge.

How many credit cards can you have? As many as you like. But for security reasons, and so you're not tempted to spend too much, it's probably wise to have no more than two. Check the credit card terms, as they do have varying features. VISA and ACCESS are the principal credit cards.

Switch card Used instead of cheques, a Switch card deducts money direct from your current account. It may be incorporated in a bank card.

Make your own financial directory

● Include the names, addresses, telephone numbers and account numbers of all bank and building society accounts.

● List details of any personal advisers, such as solicitors, accountants, stockbrokers or insurance brokers.

● List all pension plans and the names, addresses and telephone numbers of the managers and/or trustees. Note the contract number, amount invested, when you entered the scheme and when you retire.

● Do the same for any life insurance or sickness insurance policies, noting when premiums are due.

● List other insurance policies, such as buildings, contents and car insurance, the sum insured and when premiums are due.

● Note the numbers of any company share, unit trust or investment trust certificates, the price you paid for them, plus any expenses. Don't forget to list the dividends and when you expect to receive them.

● Watch out for, and make a special note of, any special helplines – for reporting lost or stolen cards, for instance.

THE VALUE OF BUDGETING

Five good reasons to budget

● To keep track of where your money is going.
● To have money available to meet bills when they come in.
● To get early warning signals of over-spending.
● To see where you are wasting money.
● To set priorities so you can spend money on things you really want.

Preparing a budget

● You need to design a budget system for yourself which is quick and simple. Budgeting is best done little and often, preferably monthly. Do it as soon as your bank or building society statement arrives. If you don't already get one, ask the bank for a monthly statement.

● Records of your accounts can be kept in accounting books; on special 12-column analysis paper (with one column per month, so you can see your yearly budget at a glance); or, if you have a home computer, on a spreadsheet programme that will give you a running tally.

● The first year of a new budget is always hard as you start to save, but when you have built up a fund to cover bills, it will get easier.

Where did your money go? Use the budget planner on the next page to work out how you spent your money last year, month by month. It will show you when your gas, electricity, telephone and water bills come in. It will also reveal your heavy spending months – holidays or Christmas, for example – and where you are wasting your money.

Where would you like it to go? Now use the budget planner to plan this year's spending in advance, month by month:

● Fill in your regular monthly payments: mortgage or rent, and other bills and expenses. Allocate quarterly or yearly bills to the months in which they fall. Remember to add an element for inflation.

● List your priorities for the rest of your expenditure. Some may be long term (such as planning your retirement) whereas others could be shorter term (saving for a new car or a holiday). You may also need to spend money immediately on new furniture or clothes, or on urgent house repairs – a leaking roof, for example, or a new boiler.

● Allocate the expenditure to the month in which you want to spend it: new summer clothes might fall in May, for example.

● Work out how much you should set aside each month to meet the bigger quarterly bills. Put together the money to cover these bills and the commitments you have already identified, and you now know how much you should be putting aside each month.

Is it working out? Check your expenditure once a month to make sure you are keeping to your budget.

MONEY QUIZ: DO YOU NEED TO BUDGET?

Do you consider yourself well paid?... Yes/No

Do you often find you have no money in your wallet
   or purse? .... Yes/No

Do you often think that people in similar jobs have
   nicer cars, houses or clothes than you? .... Yes/No

Do you pay interest on your bank account
   or credit card?... Yes/No

Do you often forget when the big bills are due? .... Yes/No

If you answered 'yes' to more than three of these questions, start budgeting *now*.

Short cuts to easy budgeting

Check statements Check your bank or building society statements against your cheque book stubs for any banking mistakes – they sometimes overcharge you. Any credit card bills should also be checked against receipts and filed away if you want to keep them.

Monthly bill payments See if any of your regular bills can be paid monthly, but make sure you check first that there is no penalty. Insurance companies, for example, charge more for monthly payments as it is a form of borrowing. You're better off putting the money in a savings account and paying yearly.

Remember that gas, electricity and telephone bills are paid in arrears. If you go over to monthly payments, you effectively lose three months free credit.

Filing systems Keep a monthly file into which you place all bills, cash machine receipts, shop receipts and credit and debit card counterfoils accumulated during the month. Fill in your cheque stubs, and make a note of anything big you buy with cash. When you finally come to sort them all out at the end of the month, you will find that you have an accurate record of where your money has gone to.

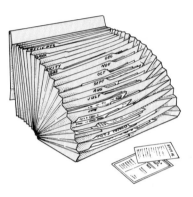

Interest-paying savings accounts Think about opening a new interest-paying bank or building society account to help save for irregular bills. This may be better than going over to monthly payments or opening a special bank budget account, which can be expensive to run and encourage you to go into debt.

Avoid credit Use your credit cards wisely. Choose one without an annual fee and don't use the credit, which is normally expensive. Clear the account at the end of each month. If you clear your account regularly and buy something immediately after your statement is sent to you, you may get up to 56 days in which to pay for it free of interest.

Do not buy small items on credit if you can possibly avoid it. It may be tempting at the time, but you will probably end up paying a third as much again. It's better to save up first in an interest-paying account.

BUDGET PLANNER

INCOME   £

Income from employment:
 PAYE earnings (enter amount after tax and
  National Insurance)   ....
 Freelance and self-employed
  earnings (enter amount before tax)   ....

Income from savings and investments:
 Income taxed at source – such as building
  society, bank and company dividends
  (enter amount after tax)   ....
 Income not taxed at source – such as
  National Savings (enter amount before tax)   ....

Any other income:
 Child benefit and other state benefits,
  alimony or child maintenance payments   ....
 Income from investment property   ....

Total income: £ ....

BUDGET PLANNER (cont)

EXPENDITURE   £

Essentials:
    Food ....
    Mortgage/Rent ....
    Local taxes ....
    Water rates ....
    Electricity ....
    Gas ....
    Other fuels ....
    Telephone ....
    Tax and National Insurance to pay on
        earnings and investment income not
        already taxed ....
    Pension contributions ....
    House maintenance ....
    Buildings and house contents insurance ....
    Travelling to work ....
    Child care ....

Total essential expenditure: £ ....

Non-essentials:
    Holidays ....
    Drink and cigarettes ....
    Entertaining and meals out ....
    Presents ....
    Car maintenance ....
    Car insurance and road tax ....
    Petrol ....
    Travel not already allowed for ....
    School fees ....
    Home improvements ....
    Housekeeping ....
    Professional fees ....
    Trade union dues or
        professional subscriptions ....
    Life insurance ....
    Savings plans ....
    Other investments ....
    Clothes ....
    Newspapers, books and periodicals ....
    TV/video rental and licence ....
    Hobbies ....
    Loan repayments ....
    Bank and credit card interest ....
    Children's pocket money ....
    Your own pocket money ....

Total non-essential expenditure: £ ....

Total expenditure: £ ....

Excess (or otherwise) of income   £ ....
    over expenditure:

PROTECTING YOUR WAY OF LIFE

Insuring your house contents

Your movable possessions can be protected by contents insurance. You can make a claim on the policy if any possessions are damaged by a range of disasters – from storms to fires – or they are stolen.

New for old Choose a policy which offers 'new for old'. It allows you to buy new items to replace those that are stolen or damaged. 'New for old' policies are more expensive than 'indemnity' policies which only pay secondhand values.

What are they worth? Working out the value of all your possessions can be difficult. Some companies use a formula depending on the number of rooms in your house. Or contact the Association of British Insurers (Aldermary House, Queen Street, London EC4N 1TT, tel. 071 248 4477) for their leaflet which contains a useful checklist.

The risk of 'averaging' Beware of underinsuring your possessions. It can lead to 'averaging', when the insurance company scales down your claim in proportion to the amount you are underinsured. Say you are underinsured by a total of 20 per cent, and your television is stolen. The insurance company has the right to deduct 20 per cent from the cost of replacing it.

Shop around Insurance premiums (the amount you have to pay) vary enormously from company to company. Insurance companies rate each area for risk, and an area rated high risk by one company may be rated lower by another. Urban areas are usually the most expensive.

Look out for discounts Make sure you are getting any discounts that are available. There may be a reduction if you live in a Neighbourhood Watch area, if you have a burglar alarm or secure locks, or if you are over 55. Some companies are now offering no-claims discounts if you don't make a claim.

Inflation Most companies automatically increase your insurance cover in line with inflation each year. This puts up the cost, but it means less risk of underinsurance. Check that your company does this, but every couple of years make sure the coverage is still enough.

What's an accident? Most policies pay for accidental damage – for example, if a picture falls off the wall and the frame and glass break. But what is and isn't insured varies a lot. Check that the policy gives you what you want. If you have a computer, you may not be covered if you pour coffee into it. If you keep a well-stocked freezer look for a policy which covers you if the contents are ruined by a breakdown or power failure.

Valuable items Make a separate list of all items of value, such as antique furniture and jewellery. If you haven't had them valued recently, it may be worth doing so. And take photographs of them as proof of ownership. The amount of cover on 'valuables' is normally restricted to half the total. If it comes to more you may have to pay more.

'**All risks**' Get an 'all risks' extension for items like cameras, jewellery or musical instruments which are regularly taken out of the house.

Cash If you keep cash at home, check the amount of cover in the policy and restrict yourself to that amount.

Personal liability You get automatic personal liability insurance with contents insurance. This pays out if you are sued because someone or something in your house has caused damage, or has injured or killed someone. Look for policies which provide cover of at least £500,000.

Are you an employer? If you employ people – a cleaning lady or a nanny, for example – check that the policy has employer's liability insurance which covers you if a person working in your house is injured or killed.

Insuring the house itself

Anyone who owns or is buying their home needs buildings insurance. This insurance pays out if your home, or the fittings in it, are damaged. If you are adequately insured, buildings insurance always pays the full cost of repairs. There is no adjustment for wear and tear.

Most misfortunes are covered, including fire, storm, flood, subsidence and theft. There are some exceptions though, such as storm damage to fences and gates. Nor are subsidence claims met in full. Most policies require you to pay the first £500 of any claim.

● Make sure you aren't underinsured, and even if the policy is index-linked check the level of insurance every couple of years. Shop around for value for money and get any discounts that are offered.
● Remember to maintain your house. You will not be covered for damage caused by your neglect.

● Your policy won't automatically cover you for accidental damage to your home. If you want to insure against any sort of household accident, be it the possibility of dropping a hammer in the wash-basin or burning a hole in the worktop of your fitted kitchen, you must ask for additional accidental damage cover when you arrange the policy, and you will pay extra.

● You can reduce the cost of accidental damage cover by offering to pay the first £50 or £100 of any claim that you make.

A MORTGAGE COMPANY'S INSURANCE ISN'T COMPULSORY

Most people take the buildings insurance offered by their mortgage lender. But you don't have to. Your mortgage lender may charge you a fee if you go elsewhere, but you can still save money by shopping around. But remember to keep previous insurance policies. If you do swop insurers, they may refuse a claim for subsidence if they think it started while you were insured with a different company. If this happens, you will need to make a claim on your old policy.

Guarding against sickness

Sickness insurance, often called permanent health insurance, protects your income if you can't work or have to take a cut in pay because of illness.

● Choose a policy which takes inflation into account so that you receive an increasing income if you are ill for a long time.

● Avoid policies which cut off your benefit if the insurance company thinks you can go back to work in a lesser capacity.

● If you are a woman thinking of starting a family, choose a policy which pays out if you continue to be ill after giving birth. Pregnancy itself is not covered.

● Some policies provide for partial disablement. They make partial payments to people who can return to work for less pay, or get another job which pays less than they used to earn.

● Don't overinsure. To encourage you to go back to work, insurance companies won't allow you to claim full pay if you fall ill. Even if you are insured for more, most offer no more than 75 per cent of your earnings, less an amount for state benefits.

● Housewives beware. Only a handful of companies will insure the value of work done in the home by a non-working partner. Look for a company which doesn't restrict cover.

Reducing the cost of sickness insurance

Shop around The cost of sickness insurance varies enormously from company to company, so shop around.

High premiums for women Women in particular need to search for value for money. Insurance companies claim that although women live longer they fall ill more often than men and for longer. Women can be charged up to a half more for sickness insurance than men.

Company benefits Check what sick pay you'll get from your employer, including state benefits. Some firms keep employees on full pay for the first three months, six months or even a year of an illness. Check your company pension plan too; you may be entitled to retire early on a reduced pension.

Deferring the payment Depending on your firm's sick pay, you can choose when the payment from sickness insurance should start. A policy which starts paying after six months is cheaper than one which pays immediately. Most companies offer four-week, three-month, six-month and one-year deferment periods.

Life insurance: protecting your family

Life insurance protects your family's standard of living if you die prematurely. But you need the right kind of life insurance. Don't confuse the life insurance which offers protection with the type which calls itself life insurance but is really a savings plan. Go for a policy that offers a high level of cover for a low premium.

There are two types of life insurance designed to give protection – term insurance, which pays a tax-free lump sum, and family income benefit, which pays a regular tax-free income. With both types, you get nothing if you outlive the policy.

Term insurance

● You choose the number of years, or term, the policy is to run. If you insure your life for £100,000 over 15 years, you only pay premiums for 15 years, and the policy only pays out the £100,000 if you die during that time.

● The insurance can be for any term you want – just a year or 25 years or more. The amount of insurance, and the premiums can be increased each year – increases of three and five per cent are common.

Family income benefit

● If you insure for £10,000 a year for 15 years and you die while the policy is in force, your family gets £10,000 a year for the rest of the 15 years. Like term insurance if you survive the policy you get nothing.

COVERING YOUR MORTGAGE

Mortgage protection insurance is a cheap form of term insurance for people who have opted for repayment mortgages. The term of the policy matches the length of the mortgage, and the sum that you are insured for decreases as the size of the loan falls.

Who needs life insurance?

Single people So long as no one depends on their income, single people don't need life insurance. Some mortgage companies insist on life insurance to cover a loan, but it's not strictly necessary. If you are single and don't want to leave your house to someone, find a mortgage company which doesn't insist on life insurance.

Couples If only one partner works, life insurance is necessary – particularly if the non-working partner could not get a well-paid job. Use term insurance or family income benefit up to retirement age, and put any surplus cash into a pension.

Couples with children A lot of life insurance is needed. Use term insurance and family income benefit up to the time you expect the children to finish their education. Insure the value of a non-working partner if you depend on her (or his) work at home. Would you need to pay a housekeeper and someone to look after the children if she wasn't there?

Applying for life and sickness insurance

● Answer all questions honestly or your insurance may be invalid.
● You may be asked to go for a medical check-up with your own doctor in which case you have the right to see the report before it is sent to the insurance company.
● If you are taking out a lot of insurance, the insurance company may send you to one of its own doctors. In that case you can't see the report.
● If you are refused insurance or the normal premium is increased, the insurance company may put you on the Impaired Lives Register. This is kept by the Association of British Insurers (Aldermary House, Queen Street, London EC4N 1TT, tel. 071 248 4477), and is open for inspection by other insurance companies. For a fee, you have the right to see what is written about you, and have any errors corrected.

Do you have enough life insurance?

● Make sure your family would have an immediate lump sum to pay funeral costs, and to replace a company car, if you have one. Use term insurance for this and have the policy written in trust so it can be paid out immediately rather than having to wait for probate. If your employer provides life insurance, this is normally paid immediately as well.

● Use the budget planner on page 26 to work out how much your family would need each year if your income stopped.

● Make an allowance for what your employer will provide. Most companies pay a lump sum of between two and four times your yearly salary if you die while you are still at work – enough to provide an income if invested in a bank or building society – and a spouse's pension too.

● If you have a mortgage, it is likely to be covered by insurance, so deduct mortgage payments from your calculation.

● Check if other loans are covered by life insurance.

● Now make sure your family would have enough to live on by taking out a family income benefit policy.

● You should also have sickness insurance (page 30). You are likely to need more sickness insurance than life insurance because you won't be able to deduct your personal expenses from the family budget.

DEVISING A SAVINGS STRATEGY

● Aim to save at least ten per cent of your take-home pay.

● Save first for an emergency fund, which can be used for items not covered by insurance: the car breaking down, major repairs to your roof, or a sick mother who needs home nursing. Two or three months' take-home pay should be enough.

HOW INFLATION AFFECTS YOUR POCKET

Savings plans can easily be blown off course as inflation reduces the purchasing power of your money. For example, 7 per cent inflation halves the value of money in ten years. The following table shows how £100 is reduced in value year by year by different rates of inflation.

AFTER	INFLATION RATE			
	2%	5%	7%	10%
1 year	98	95	94	91
2 years	96	91	87	83
3 years	94	86	82	75
4 years	92	82	76	68
5 years	91	78	71	62
6 years	89	75	67	56
7 years	87	71	62	51
8 years	85	68	58	47
9 years	84	65	54	42
10 years	82	61	51	39
11 years	80	59	48	35
12 years	79	56	44	32
13 years	77	53	42	29
14 years	76	51	39	26
15 years	74	48	36	24
16 years	73	46	34	22
17 years	71	44	32	20
18 years	70	42	30	18
19 years	69	40	28	16
20 years	67	38	26	15

● Don't put all your savings in one place. Aim for a good spread of different types of savings.
● Don't put all your savings into buying your house. House prices can fall as well as rise.
● Use a standing order to pay a regular monthly amount into a savings account.
● Look for a long-term savings scheme which makes it difficult to withdraw money, or which imposes an interest penalty.

Which scheme is right for you?

Once you have a savings strategy, you are ready to decide which savings schemes are right for you.

Bank and building society accounts

Instant access accounts The best place to keep at least some of your emergency fund. Accounts can be opened with as little as £1, and most pay higher rates of interest the more you have invested. Some accounts give you access with a cash card.
● Interest is taxable. Basic rate tax is deducted at source, but if you don't pay tax, arrange for the interest to be paid with no deductions.
● Interest is paid six-monthly or yearly. With larger amounts you may be able to get monthly income.

Term and notice accounts With term accounts you agree to invest money for a set period (one or two years, for example) and you lose interest if you withdraw the money early.
With notice accounts you agree to give notice of any withdrawal, usually 30 days or 90 days beforehand. You lose interest if you don't give notice.
● Interest rates are higher than on most instant accounts. Minimum investment varies, but is generally between £500 and £2000.
● Interest is taxable, and is paid every six months or year.

TESSA (Tax Exempt Special Savings Account) A tax-free savings scheme available from banks and building societies. There is no tax to pay if the scheme stays in force for five years. Within certain annual limits, money can be deposited in a TESSA on a regular or irregular basis.
● Suitable for anyone who is prepared to save for five years.
● Tax free if kept for five years.
● Interest can be taken as income or reinvested in the plan. Tax is deducted at source if you take income, but is returned in the form of a bonus if the plan is kept up for the five years.

National Savings accounts

Ordinary accounts Available from post offices, the first £70 of interest is tax free. You can open an account with £5 and withdraw up to £100 on demand.
● Suitable for higher rate taxpayers only, as better interest rates are available elsewhere.
● Interest is paid gross yearly with no deductions; taxpayers must declare interest to the Inland Revenue.

Investment accounts Available from post offices, one month's notice must be given for any withdrawal. You can open an account with £5.
● Particularly suited to non-taxpayers who don't need immediate access to their money.
● Interest is paid yearly, with no tax deducted; taxpayers must declare interest to the Inland Revenue.

Certificates Available from post offices; terms vary according to the issue. The rate of interest increases the longer you hold the certificates, which run for five years.

Index-linked certificates, also available, increase in value in line with inflation once they have been held for a year, with an additional payment of interest.

You buy savings certificates in blocks of £25. The maximum you can invest depends on the issue.

● National Savings Certificates are tax free, so they are often good value for higher rate taxpayers.

● Any interest is added to the value of the certificate.

Capital bonds Available from post offices, capital bonds last for five years and the interest increases the longer you hold the bond. You buy capital bonds in blocks of £100-£1000.

● Most suitable for non-taxpayers.

● Taxpayers pay income tax each year, even though the interest is only paid when the bond is cashed in or matures.

Income bonds Available from post offices, income bonds pay a monthly income with no tax deducted at the time. The interest rate is variable and you must give three months' notice when you want your money back. If you hold the bond for less than a year, the interest rate is reduced.

Income bonds are £1000 each and the minimum amount that you can hold is £2000.

● Suitable for non-taxpayers who need to boost their income.

● Interest is taxable and is paid monthly – either into a bank or building society or by cheque.

Life insurance savings plan

A regular savings plan based on endowment life insurance is designed to run for at least ten years, and offers a small element of life insurance. Safe and dependable, the minimum investment is around £10 a month.

● Suitable for higher rate taxpayers who don't want income.

● Tax free if the policy is held for at least ten years, or three-quarters of the term if less.

● There may be capital gains tax to pay if you cash the policy any earlier.

SAVINGS QUIZ: ARE YOU A RISK TAKER?

1 Do you enjoy spending money on yourself?	Yes/Sometimes/No
2 Do you know how much money you have in your bank account?	Yes/Sometimes/No
3 Do you think playing the stock market is only for the super rich?	Yes/Sometimes/No
4 Do you think taxes are too high?	Yes/Sometimes/No
5 Do you dread the expense of Christmas?	Yes/Sometimes/No
6 Do you worry about losing your job?	Yes/Sometimes/No
7 Do you think gambling is a stupid waste of money?	Yes/Sometimes/No
8 Do you worry about money?	Yes/Sometimes/No

If you answer 'yes' to all or most of these questions, you have a cautious nature. For peace of mind put your savings in schemes that are safe.

If you answered 'sometimes' to most of the questions, you may be prepared to take some risks with your long-term savings.

If you answered 'no' to most of the questions, you are one of nature's risk takers; take care not to risk everything.

BE TAX EFFICIENT

Couples where one partner doesn't have an income, or where one partner pays tax at a higher rate, should transfer savings to the more lightly taxed partner to take advantage of separate taxation.

Non-taxpayers should put money in accounts which don't deduct tax from interest payments, or where the tax can be reclaimed.

Higher-risk schemes

Unit and investment trusts Available from unit trust managers, and some life insurance companies, banks and building societies. Unit trusts invest in a selection of companies quoted on the stock market. You buy units in this collection of investments.

The price of units goes up and down depending on the value of the unit trust's investments. Unit trust prices are quoted in most of the quality newspapers.

Investment trusts are similar, except they themselves are also quoted companies and can be bought and sold. They can be bought through any share-dealing service, such as a stockbroker, bank and some building societies as well as directly from the managers.

The minimum lump sum investment for both ranges from £250 to £2500; minimum for regular savings, £25-£50 a month.

● Suitable for risk takers hoping for a high long-term return.
● Basic rate tax is deducted at source, but non-taxpayers can claim it back. Higher rate taxpayers have extra tax to pay.
● There can be capital gains tax to pay when you sell your units or shares.
● Income is normally paid out every six months; some high-yielding funds offer monthly payments.

Personal Equity Plans (PEPs) A tax-free stock market plan available from investment managers, unit trust and investment trust groups, and some banks and building societies. Part of the plan can be invested in unit trusts or investment trusts.

The maximum investment is usually raised each year in the Budget. Minimum investment ranges from £500 for lump sums and £25 a month for regular savings.

● Suitable for risk takers planning a large portfolio of shares.
● Dividends are paid every six months and PEPs are tax free.
● There is no capital gains tax on PEPs.

PLANNING FOR RETIREMENT

To provide yourself with a financially secure retirement you need to save some of what you earn during the years you work in order to give yourself an income later.

● If you are employed, find out what you will get from your firm's pension scheme.
● Find out what you will get from the state pension schemes.
● If you are self-employed (or your firm doesn't have a pension scheme), take out a personal pension.
● If your firm's pension falls short of what you need, put more money towards your pension. Either add it to your firm's scheme, or start a separate scheme run by an insurance company.
● You may prefer to invest some of your money in a long-term savings scheme (see page 32) rather than tying it all up in a pension.

WHAT YOUR STATE PENSION PROVIDES

If you work solidly for 40 or more years and regularly pay your National Insurance contributions, your combined state basic and SERPS pension will be just under 50 per cent of average industrial wage. For most people, this means a huge drop in living standards. So if you've got big plans for your retirement start organising additional funds for your old age.

What state pensions might you get?

If you would like to know what state pensions you are entitled to, and what they are likely to pay when you retire, you can request a pension forecast. Ask for Form BR19 at your local social security office.

The state basic pension

You get the basic pension if you have paid, or been credited with, National Insurance contributions for at least 90 per cent of your working life (defined as 49 years for men and 44 for women). The state basic pension is around a quarter of average take-home pay.

NOTE Women who have an incomplete National Insurance contribution record are only entitled to a reduced pension. In this case, married couples will be better off claiming the married couples pension rather than two individual pensions.

State earnings related pension scheme (SERPS)

SERPS started in 1978 and provides the top state pension. You pay higher National Insurance contributions if you are in SERPS, and are automatically included if:

● Your employer has no pension scheme and you haven't opted out of SERPS with a personal pension scheme.
● Your employer has a pension scheme, but the benefits are not good enough to allow the scheme to be 'contracted out' of SERPS.

NOTE You can't be in SERPS if you are self-employed and pay Class 2 or Class 4 National Insurance contributions.

HOW SERPS WORKS

A SERPS pension is an additional earnings-related pension that tops up your state basic pension. The more you earned while you were working, and the more you paid into the scheme, the higher your pension. It is only paid to people who work as an employee.

The amount you get is calculated from your earnings while you were working. All earnings between a lower and upper earnings limit are added up for each year after 1978, the year the scheme started. Your yearly SERPS pension is $1\frac{1}{4}$ per cent of this total.

Graduated pension

If you paid graduated National Insurance contributions at any time between April 1961 and April 1975 (when the scheme was dropped), you are entitled to a graduated pension when you retire – but it won't be much.

Do you have a company pension?

Company pensions are provided by your employer. You get tax relief on your contributions up to a maximum of 15 per cent of your earnings. If you invest £100, for example, it only costs you £75 if you pay basic rate tax – £60 if you pay higher rate tax.

● Non-contributory schemes mean that your employer meets the entire cost of your pension.

● Contributory schemes are where you pay towards the cost of your pension with an average tax-free deduction of five per cent.

A good pension scheme should include . . .

● Pensions linked to final pay. A pension calculated on one-sixtieth of your pay near retirement for each year you are in the scheme. This formula gives a pension of two-thirds your pay after 40 years' service. (Two-thirds final pay is the maximum pension allowed under Inland Revenue rules.) An even better scheme – based on fiftieths of your annual pay – would give a two-thirds pension after only 33 years.

● Provision for paying Additional Voluntary Contributions to the scheme to top up your pension to the maximum two-thirds of final pay.

● A tax-free lump sum on retirement in exchange for a reduced pension.

● Index-linking up to 5 per cent.

● A lump sum payment of at least three times annual pay for those who die before retirement.

● A two-thirds widow's or dependant's pension for those who die either before or after retirement. For those who die before retirement, the pension is based on the number of years the member would have worked had he or she survived to retirement.

● Provision for early or late retirement.

● Provision for ill-health retirement.

Less good schemes may . . .

● Be linked to pay but only offer one-eighteenth of your pay near retirement for each year, giving a pension of half final pay for 40 years' service.

● Operate as 'money purchase' schemes. In this case, your pension will depend on how well your firm's pension fund has been managed, and how much you and your employer have contributed. When you retire, the amount of money which you and your employer has provided for your pension, plus any growth, is invested to give you a regular income. It is difficult to predict your eventual pension.

Should you choose a personal pension?

Personal pensions are long-term savings schemes, either with regular monthly amounts or with a series of lump sum investments. Within limits, any contributions to a personal pension scheme are entitled to tax relief.

Most personal pensions are bought from life insurance companies. The money is left to grow until you retire, when you use the money to buy a pension. As with company pensions, you can take some of the money as a tax-free lump sum.

Who should consider a personal pension?

● The self-employed, and anyone else who doesn't have a company pension scheme.

● Part-time employees who may not be included in their company pension scheme.

● Employees who intend changing jobs frequently. This is often the case with younger people who are gaining experience or who are trying to find a job they enjoy.

● Women who intend taking a long career break when their children are preschool age.

Personal pensions are not suited to . . .

● Employees in good company pension schemes who don't plan to change jobs. Companies with their own schemes rarely agree to contribute to an employee's personal pension, so you would lose the benefit of your employer's contribution.
● Older employees who intend staying in the same job until retirement.

How to choose a personal pension

● Look for a consistent past performance record across a range of different types of investment.
● Check how much you have to pay the managers for running the fund. The more they take in charges, the less money is invested in your plan.
● Look for 'with profits' schemes. These provide a steady rate of growth, and bonuses are added every year which can't be taken away. A final bonus is added when you retire.
● Unit-linked pension schemes, similar to unit trusts (page 35), are a good way of saving but are not suitable for people with less than ten years to retirement. The shorter the time before you retire, the greater the effect a downturn in the stock market at the time of your retirement would have on your eventual pension.
● Deposit administration pension schemes work like a bank or building society deposit account. People in unit-linked schemes often switch into these as they near retirement to avoid the effects of a market downturn.

Useful addresses

National Association of Citizens Advice Bureaux
115-123 Pentonville Road
London N1 9LZ.
Tel: 071 833 2181.
Will advise on state benefits and pensions available.

Office of Fair Trading
Field House
15-25 Breams Buildings
London EC4A 1PR.
Tel: 071 242 2858.
Can provide information on reputable brokers.

Occupational Pensions Advisory Service (OPAS)
11 Belgrave Road
London SW1V 1RB.
Tel: 071 233 8080.
Will advise on pensions.

Pensions Ombudsman
11 Belgrave Road
London SW1V 1RB.
Investigates any complaints about pensions.

WHICH LOAN IS CHEAPEST?

Credit unions

Credit unions are small mutual banks run and owned by their depositors, and based in a community or workplace. The rate of interest which you earn if you save with a credit union is lower than with a bank or building society, but you have access to a cheap source of loans.
● Credit union loans are one of the cheapest ways to borrow.
● The interest rate can be fixed or variable.

Insurance company loans

If you have a life insurance policy with a cash value, which usually means an endowment or whole-of-life policy, many insurance companies will lend money using the policy as security. The loan can be repaid whenever you want or you can pay it out of the proceeds of the life policy when it matures or when you decide to cash it in.

● Insurance policies are often a good source of cheap loans.
● The rate of interest can be fixed or variable.

Bank gold cards

Gold cards give you unlimited interest-free credit for a yearly charge, but the outstanding loan must be cleared once a month. Gold cards also give you access to bank overdrafts at cheaper than normal rates.
● If you can get a gold card (you have to have a high income), the overdraft facility can be a cheap way of borrowing.
● The interest rate is variable.

Secured loans

If you have owned your house for a number of years, it may be worth much more than the outstanding mortgage. Many banks and building societies offer loans secured on your house, and these are a useful source of finance if you can't persuade your mortgage lender to increase your mortgage for major items like home improvements and school fees.
● The loans are generally fixed for a given number of years.
● The rate of interest is generally higher than the mortgage rate but lower than overdrafts and personal loans.
● The interest rate is variable.
● You risk losing your home if you offer it as security for a loan. Don't take out this sort of loan unless you are confident you can pay it back.

Overdrafts

If you have a current account with a bank or building society you may be able to use it to borrow money in the form of an overdraft.
● Avoid going into overdraft (becoming overdrawn) without the permission of your branch manager: this is an unauthorised overdraft and rates of interest are high.
● Authorised overdrafts, agreed with the manager, can be a cheap and flexible way to borrow, but check the charges. You may have to pay charges on all transactions over a full charging period (usually three months) even if you are overdrawn for a short while only. The rate of interest is variable.
● Many banks and building societies allow customers to borrow up to a predetermined amount without having to ask permission. This may look like a good idea, and it can be convenient, but the rate of interest is often higher than with an account that has no automatic overdraft.

Bank ordinary loans

Bank ordinary loans are an alternative to bank personal loans (see below), but they are often cheaper because the banks ask for security. You may have to discuss the matter with the manager as ordinary loans are not promoted. Each one is tailor-made to suit your circumstances. There is no fixed monthly repayment, although you normally agree to repay the loan by a given date.
● Bank ordinary loans are normally cheaper than personal loans.
● The rate of interest is variable.

Personal loans

Banks and building societies provide personal loans which you pay off with repayments spread over a fixed term (normally between one and five years). Personal loans are suitable for larger purchases: cars, television, audio equipment or furniture.
● Personal loans are more expensive than an authorised bank or building society overdraft but are normally cheaper than borrowing from a shop or a finance company.
● The interest rate is fixed at the outset, so a personal loan can be a good deal if you borrow while interest rates are low.

Credit cards

If you pay off your credit card account in full at the end of each month you pay no interest on your purchases. But you can use your credit card to borrow money up to a predetermined limit. You must repay a minimum each month, but you can pay back more if you wish.

● If you are going to clear your account at the end of each month, choose a card with no fee.

● If you take the credit option, shop around for the lowest rate of interest. It may be worth paying a yearly fee in exchange for a lower interest rate.

● The interest rate is usually higher than with authorised overdrafts and personal loans, but you have convenience and flexibility.

● The interest rate is variable.

Hire purchase

With hire purchase, you don't actually own what you are buying until the end of the so-called 'hire' period. You are required to pay a deposit, but otherwise the loan works in the same way as a bank or building society personal loan.

● Nowadays, hire purchase is normally only used for buying cars.

● Repayments are made over a fixed number of years and at a fixed rate of interest.

● The interest rate is usually higher than bank and building society personal loans, but there are occasional bargains.

● Buying a car on hire purchase or with a personal loan doesn't prevent you bargaining over the price of the car.

Store cards

Store cards encourage you to spend money in your favourite shop. Some operate just like credit cards; others offer revolving credit, where you undertake to pay a certain amount to the store each month in exchange for a borrowing facility of 12-24 times your monthly payment.

● The interest on store credit cards is usually high.

● Only take a store card if you intend clearing the account at the end of the month or the store doesn't take other credit cards.

● The interest rate is variable.

Shop credit

Many shops offer loans for larger items, arranged through finance companies. These operate like bank and building society personal loans.

● Shop credit is normally much more expensive than bank and building society loans.

● Check the annual percentage rate (see below) and compare it with other similar loans.

● The rate of interest is fixed at the outset.

● Treat offers of interest-free loans with suspicion – you may find the goods being offered are cheaper in other shops.

What to watch out for

APR: the Annual Percentage Rate of charge

● All loans and credit agreements must quote an APR. This figure, say 30 per cent, represents any interest you are paying on the loan plus charges and setting up fees. Don't sign any credit agreement until you have compared the APR with similar loans.

● APR shows the true cost of borrowing, but don't rely on the APR alone to tell you if it's a good deal. Check the total cost of credit as well. This is the amount of interest you pay. For example, if you borrow for one year you pay less actual interest than if you borrow for two years.

● With loans where there is no fixed monthly payment, as with credit cards, the APR you are quoted may not reflect how you use your card. With credit cards, the APR is worked out using the minimum monthly repayment including any annual fee.

● Current account overdrafts are calculated in the same way as an APR, but any fee is left out, which makes an overdraft rate difficult to compare with other forms of borrowing.

If you are refused a loan

If you don't know why you have been refused a loan, it could be the fault of a credit reference agency. Banks, building societies, stores and finance companies all consult the information data banks of such agencies before authorising a loan.

But they can get it wrong, and you have the right to ask for the name of the credit rating agency which was used, to see your file, and to correct any mistakes the agency has made. The Office of Fair Trading produces a leaflet which tells you how to correct a credit reference agency mistake.

WHERE TO GET INVESTMENT ADVICE

Financial consultants

There are two kinds of financial consultant – independent financial advisers (IFAs) and tied agents – both of whom sell mainly life insurance and related investment products, such as unit linked savings plans.

Independent financial advisers IFAs must survey the whole marketplace to find the best product to suit your needs. Most are paid commission by the companies whose products they sell, but some charge a fee instead. If you are charged a fee, make sure the adviser deducts any commission he earns first. To find an IFA, contact the IFA Promotion Hotline on 081 200 3000. They will send you the names of ten IFAs in your area and a list of questions to ask them.

Tied agents Attached to one insurance company, tied agents are paid commission by the insurance company and don't normally charge a fee.

If you want to use a tied agent, always check they are still connected with the life insurance company they claim to represent. You are not covered by the Financial Services Act if that connection has ended.

Banks and building societies

Banks and building societies will give financial advice on a commission basis, but most are tied to just one life insurance company. They may also have a separate in-house company offering independent financial advice. This service is not often promoted and is not usually available in the branches. If your bank or building society also gives independent financial advice, ask for the appropriate address and telephone number.

Solicitors

Some solicitors can give financial advice, but they must say so prominently on their writing paper and in their offices. Solicitors cannot be tied to any one financial services company – they must give independent advice – and most charge a fee.

If you use a solicitor when buying a house or making a will, find out if he is authorised to help you in other ways. You may need financial advice at both these times.

Accountants

Many accountants are authorised to give financial advice, and they must not be tied to a single financial services company. They charge a fee for their advice. If you don't want a written report, you can ask an accountant to give advice by interview. This can be a useful way of reducing the cost.

Stockbrokers

The main function of stockbrokers is to buy and sell shares, but many also give advice on all aspects of financial planning, from unit trusts to life insurance. Many stockbrokers, especially those in central London, may only agree to take you as a client if you have £25,000 or more to invest.

What to do if you get into debt

● Contact the companies you owe money to and see if they are prepared to accept lower payments until you get back on your feet.
● Don't borrow your way out of debt as you are likely to end up borrowing money at expensive rates of interest.
● Check you are getting all the state benefits that you are entitled to.
● Contact your local Citizens Advice Bureau – they may have a specialist money adviser – or ring the National Debtline on 021 3598 8501.

HOW TO COMPLAIN ABOUT BAD ADVICE

There are official ombudsmen and complaints services available for the whole range of financial services, but don't try to use them unless you have already raised your complaint with the company concerned. No ombudsmen take on a case until they are sure you have exhausted the company's own complaints procedure.

If a financial services company goes bust, you are entitled to compensation. There are various compensation schemes that cover areas such as pensions, investments or solicitors. The Citizens Advice Bureau may be able to help.

CHOOSING A MORTGAGE

Most people who buy a house or flat borrow at least part of the money to do so from a high street bank or building society in the form of a mortgage. This loan is secured on the property, which means that the house can be repossessed if you don't keep up your repayments. Mortgages comes in several different forms, and you will need to decide which method of paying back the loan is best for you.

Repayment mortgages

Repayment mortgages, the simplest form of mortgage, are normally repaid gradually over 25 years. In the early years your repayments are made up of mainly interest and just a small amount of capital, whereas in the last years you pay mainly capital and very little interest.

If you have a family who depend on your income, you will need to take out life insurance (page 30). This will pay off the outstanding loan if you die early. Or there are special mortgage protection policies available where the sum insured reduces along with the loan.

● The monthly payments on repayment mortgages normally work out cheaper than those of endowment mortgages when interest rates are above 10 per cent.

Endowment mortgages

With an endowment mortgage, you repay your mortgage out of the proceeds of an endowment insurance policy. This is a life insurance savings plan which gives a small amount of life insurance, the rest going towards a savings plan calculated to give at least the amount of money needed to repay the loan after 25 years.

If you die before the 25 years is up, the life insurance repays the loan. The final sum paid out is not guaranteed, but most policies pay more than the amount needed for the loan.

Don't let your mortgage lender pressure you into an endowment mortgage. Remember, they earn commission from the insurance company on each endowment mortgage they sell.
● The monthly payments on endowment mortgages are only cheaper than repayment mortgages when interest rates are below 10 per cent.

Pension mortgages

Pension mortgages are particularly suited to self-employed people and those with personal pension plans. You repay the mortgage out of a tax-free lump sum which you can take at retirement instead of part of the pension. If you have dependants, you will need life insurance.
● The monthly payments on pension mortgages are expensive, but if you already have, or need, a personal pension, this is an option worth considering.

PEP mortgages

The proceeds of a Personal Equity Plan (PEP) are used to repay the mortgage. PEPs are stock market investment schemes on which you pay neither income tax nor capital gains tax.

PEP mortgages are flexible. If the stock market does well you can cash in your plan when you like and repay some of the loan early. But there is a risk that the stock market may be in the doldrums when you are due to pay off the mortgage. If you have dependants, you will need life insurance.
● The monthly repayments on PEP mortgages are expensive.

Interest-only mortgages

Some mortgage lenders only ask you to pay the interest during the period of the mortgage: it is up to you how to repay the loan. Others may not require you to repay the loan at all; it is repaid from the proceeds of your estate when you die. If you have dependants, you will need life insurance.
● These mortgages have the cheapest monthly repayments, but if you never repay the loan, you will ultimately pay a great deal of interest. They may be a good idea if you don't earn much now but you expect to later in life, or if you know you will come into a large sum of money.

Unit-linked mortgages

You repay the loan with a unit-linked life insurance plan. It is similar to an endowment policy except the savings are linked to a unit trust (page 35).
● Unit-linked funds often do better than endowment policies, but there is a risk of having to repay your loan when the stock market is in decline.
● The monthly payments are similar to an endowment policy.

Low-start mortgages

Some low-start mortgages extend the mortgage period by a couple of years to 27 years on the understanding that you take out an endowment policy after two years. You save by having no endowment payments for the first two years. Others offer deferred interest, which add some of the interest due in the first few years to the outstanding loan. This keeps the monthly payments low but the size of the outstanding loan gets bigger, so you'll pay more in the long run.

Storing things away

CREATING STORAGE SPACE

Make the most of your available space

Single action storage Make your storage system as simple as possible. You want to be able to walk into a room, stretch out and pick up what you're looking for. You don't want to have to move four cardboard boxes before you find it.

Make it flexible Adjustable shelving is far more useful than fixed shelves. It can be altered to take any size objects, and in the kitchen several small shelves are often more useful than one or two large ones.

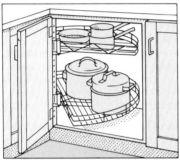

Get the best from your cupboards Fit swing-out (carousel) shelving into kitchen corner units to hold vegetables or saucepans. Make sure the hinges of the doors are strong enough to take any extra weight imposed by shelves.

Movable storage boxes To build yourself instant storage space, buy stacking cubes made of wire, plastic, wood or hardboard. Tea chests can also be used. They can be assembled to any shape or height, and are easy to rearrange.

Use your seating A trunk makes a good seat if covered with a foam cushion and attractive fabric. In front of a window, it would make a useful window seat, and can store your books as well.

Double shelves Divide a wide shelf in two by building a mini-shelf for the back. Use it to store books, cassettes or videos (page 55).

Where to store your things

● To find the best storage place for an object, take it to where it is most used in the house and find a storage spot nearby.

● Try and position the things that you use most often within easy reach. Objects that you use the least, especially in the kitchen, are the ones to store on the top and bottom shelves – such as vacuum flasks, cold boxes, picnic equipment or an ice-cream maker.

Keep objects you use more often – saucepans, food mixers, scales or the iron – closer to hand on the central shelves.

Storage cost cutters

● Finish inexpensive, DIY, unsealed pine shelving with mahogany, grey or black wood stain. Or paint them to match the existing colour scheme.
● Revive old metal office filing cabinets or industrial shelving with a coat of brightly coloured spray-on car paint.
● Buy practical, ready-made peg rails from your local DIY shop and use them to hang chairs, mirrors, small cupboards, brooms and so on. It will keep your floor clear.
● Existing kitchen units can be transformed by painting the doors a different colour if you can't afford new ones – or use a special self-adhesive plastic designed for the purpose. Contact The Kitchen Specialists Association, 8 St Bernard's Crescent, Edinburgh EHH 1NP (tel. 031 3218884) for information about replacement doors.
● A large chipboard sheet makes a practical worktable. Rest it on stacking wire mesh bins at each end.
● Make your own kitchen dresser by buying a bookshelf and a base cupboard of a similar width. Paint or stain both units to match.

Room-by-room storage

Kitchens

● Sort out your kitchen drawers so they only hold what you really need.
● Hang utensils above the cooking area on a wire mesh grid (you can drill a hole in the handle of most things) or keep them in a large-mouthed jar near your cooking area.
● Keep toasters and other everyday equipment close to hand, but pack away things used less often – a yoghurt maker, for instance.
● Store tins and jars in a single row on narrow shelves – it's easier to see what you've got. If the shelves are in a cupboard, put wire racks on the inside of the door for light things.
● Put away clean pots and pans as soon as you walk into the kitchen. It keeps your work surface clear and leaves room for fresh washing up. A wire draining rack mounted on the wall above the sink also gives more space, and cuts down on damp.
● Visit your local hardware store. They'll certainly have a selection of cheap storage items – stacking plastic vegetable trays, a kitchen utensil holder or a paper towel hanger.
● Attach fold-down racks or small drawers to the bottom of your hanging kitchen units. They can be used for knives, spices or cookbooks. And look out for any appliances that can be built into your kitchen units – a fold-away ironing board, for example, or a slide-out table.

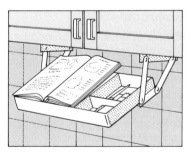

Bedrooms

● Attach a strap to the inside of wardrobe doors to take ties, belts and scarves.
● Consider fitting wardrobes with two clothes rails – one above the other – rather than just one. It's particularly practical for men's clothes and in children's rooms.
● Put a chest at the end of the bed to take spare bedding, books or magazines.
● Clothes hangers which take more than one item will save wardrobe space.

● Build a new wardrobe in a deep alcove or across the end of a small room by hanging full-length folding doors from the ceiling. Fit the interior with simple shelves and a clothes rail.

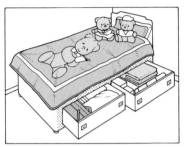

● Hang a shoe bag from the inside of a wardrobe door, or make your own simple shelves in the bottom of the cupboard to take your boots and shoes.

● Buy an ottoman bed that has a large storage space under the mattress, or a storage bed with built-in drawers. They're useful for holding blankets or shoes.

Children's rooms

● Where space is a problem in a child's room, buy a bunk bed with desk space and a wardrobe underneath it.

● It's best to use adjustable shelving for books and toys. That way, you can keep them low when the child is small and raise them as they grow.

● Keep a clothes hamper in the room, close to the cupboards, and encourage children to put their dirty clothes in it as soon as they undress.

● Use an under-bed drawer on castors to store children's toys. Later on, it can take a racing car track or train set.

● Use plastic laundry baskets or crates to keep toys tidy. Crates can double as play seats too. You'll find your small children will help to clear up more readily if they have an easy-to-fill container to put their toys into.

Bathrooms

● Build under-basin storage cupboards to hold cleaning equipment and cover any pipe work. It's easier to buy ready-made doors and build a frame to fit, rather than the other way round.

● A high shelf around the top of the bathroom can take spare towels, bath mats and flannels. It can also be used to keep cleaning materials out of the reach of small children.

● Fit a wire storage grid above the basin and clip tooth mugs or a soap rack and other containers to it with metal clips.

● Use kitchen units to create bathroom cupboards. They can easily be adapted.

Living rooms

● Use alcoves for books, records and a collection of small antiques. Build fitted shelves if you are planning to stay in your home a long time, or buy close-fitting, free-standing DIY shelves. You can dismantle them and take them with you when you move.

● If there are no alcoves, use a shelf unit as a room divider. You can cover one side or the back with wallpaper, felt, cork or hessian.

● Chests make good storage space for sewing equipment, books or drinks. Buy a thick piece of glass (with polished edges) so it doubles as a coffee table.

● Build a window seat into a window recess or round a bay. Use the underneath as storage for blankets, records, toys or games.

● Fix the television onto purpose-made wall brackets, rest it on a mobile trolley, or store it on a special unit with the video and hi-fi.

Work or general-purpose rooms

● Store heavy items, such as paint or a sewing machine, on slotted metal industrial shelving. If it's used often, keep it at worktop height.

● Fit work rooms with flexible shelving.

● Keep your home computer on a special storage unit: the screen should be slightly higher than the keyboard. If you often move your computer from one room to another, it might be a good idea to store it on a movable trolley. You can use the other shelves for storing paper.

Halls, lofts and stairways

● If your hallway is wide enough, fit narrow shelves to take books or display antiques.

● To use your loft for storage, cover the joists with 15mm ($\frac{5}{8}$in) chipboard. Don't use the loft for heavy items, though. The joists are probably not strong enough. Get the chipboard cut to a size that will fit through the loft hatch – most large DIY stores have a free cutting service.

● To keep out the dust, pack small items in closed boxes, and cover larger pieces with cloths.

● Organise a large under-stairs cupboard so that you can walk into it. Build narrow shelves along the sides and back.

● Alternatively, get a builder to remove the panelled wall from the side of the stairs, and install cupboards to your own design.

SECRETS OF MAKING SHELVES

Supporting the shelves

There are three easy ways of supporting shelves.

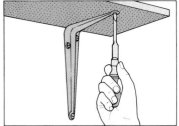

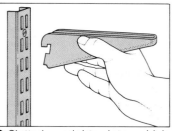

● Right-angle brackets screwed direct to the wall and the shelf. There are many different patterns.

● Slotted uprights into which brackets are fitted. The shelves can be adjusted for height.

47

● Wooden supports can be screwed to the wall on each side of the alcove beside a chimney breast. The shelf sits on the supports. Hardwood strip 12mm ($\frac{1}{2}$in) square suits most shelving.

If the shelf is to hold a heavy load such as books, put another support along the back wall.

Angle aluminium strips can be used in the same way.

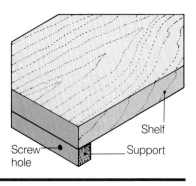

Shelf

Screw hole

Support

Making shelves with chipboard

Use melamine veneered chipboard for dependable shelves that are easy to clean. The chipboard is available in white and also a number of imitation timber finishes. There are also real wood veneers. It is sold in a range of lengths and widths – all of a standard thickness. And any cut ends can be covered with strips of iron-on edging veneer.

Applying edging veneer

1 Cut the shelf to length with a fine-tooth saw.

2 If the cut edge will be visible, lay the edging veneer along it. It has a heat-sensitive adhesive on the back.

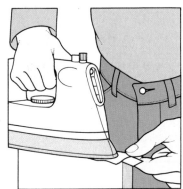

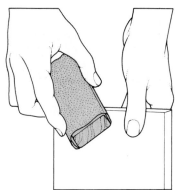

3 Run a hot iron along the veneer to stick it. Put paper on top to prevent adhesive getting on the iron. Press down with your finger while the strip cools.

4 Trim off the surplus veneer with a craft knife. Smooth the edges with fine glasspaper wrapped around a block. Work away from the veneer so you don't lift it.

DECORATIVE SHELVES MADE OF GLASS

● For decorative shelving you can use glass. It must be plate glass at least 6mm ($\frac{1}{4}$in) thick, and the supporting brackets must not be more than 400mm (16in) apart.

● For extra strength, fix supports along the back wall.

● When ordering the glass from the glazier, ask for all the edges to be ground smooth.

● To keep glass shelves in place, put small double-sided adhesive pads between the glass and the supports. The pads can be bought at a stationery or DIY shop.

Planning your shelving

Distance between the shelves When you are planning several shelves one above the other, always measure the height of items to be stored, and space the shelves accordingly. In the case of large books, it may be better to use deeper shelves and lay them flat, rather than have very large spaces between shelves.

Beware of weight Keep weight in mind too. Average bracket spacing is about 400mm (16in), but bring brackets closer for heavy loads, such as large books or big jars of cooking ingredients.

TVs and hi-fi With very heavy items like TVs and hi-fi systems, special support brackets are needed. And take great care when anchoring the brackets to the wall. Use expanding anchors rather than wall plugs. Plasterboard partitions will not take the weight.

The right materials Choose the quality of shelving to suit the location. Sheds and workshops can have very basic but strong shelving. Steel shelving units are available in kit form when appearance doesn't matter. For the lounge, timber shelves, 22mm ($\frac{7}{8}$in) thick, may be used with all-timber supports. They may be either stained and polished or painted with gloss paint.

Fitting in extra shelves Where space is limited, look for other locations. The backs of doors on the larder or pantry offer excellent storage space. Use plastic-coated wire shelving.

What sort of walls?

The way that you fit the shelf supports to the wall will be governed by the type of wall – solid masonry or hollow partitioning. Tapping the wall will usually indicate whether it is solid or hollow.

Solid wall

To find out what the wall is made of, make a fine hole with a masonry drill and examine the dust.
● First, there will be a whitish powder as the drill penetrates the surface plaster. This is never able to support any weight, and the fixing device must go well beyond it.
● Next may come a reddish powder, or sometimes yellow, both indicating that the wall is made of brick. This offers good support for shelving using wall plugs and screws.
● A light grey powder indicates lightweight building blocks, which are also good for fixing with wall plugs and screws.
● Dark grey to black in granules shows the wall is made of breeze blocks. These need special plugging because of their open texture. Use Fischer Twistlock anchors or fibrous plugging compound.

Hollow wall

● A hollow wall is usually made of plasterboard nailed to timbers.
● An internal partition may be two sheets of plasterboard separated by a honeycomb in-fill.
● Houses built before the 1920s may have lath-and-plaster internal walls. Plaster is bonded to horizontal wooden laths, which have been nailed to timber uprights.

Fixing devices Hollow walls need special hollow fixing devices even for light loads. For heavy loads, you will need to find the internal supporting timbers and use them for anchorage (see box below).

On a lath-and-plaster wall, you can support light loads by screwing directly into the laths. For heavier loads, use hollow wall fixings such as spring toggles which anchor at the back of the lath and plaster. If the plaster is thick you may need the longest toggles available. For really heavy loads, screw into the wooden uprights.

FOUR WAYS TO FIND TIMBER UPRIGHTS

● Tap the wall to find places where it sounds most solid, then push in a bradawl to pinpoint the position of the upright. In most places the bradawl will suddenly go through the plasterboard, but it will strike strong resistance from a timber upright.

● On a lath-and-plaster wall, you can locate the timber uprights by using a small metal detector that is sold for finding pipes and cables in walls. It will detect the line of nails that hold the laths to each upright. Run the metal detector along the wall, and the light should come on about every 450mm (18in) to signal the vertical line of nails.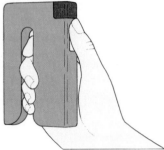

● On a plasterboard wall, use a battery-operated joist-and-stud detector which lights up when passed over the densest part of a wall. Follow the instructions that come with the tool.

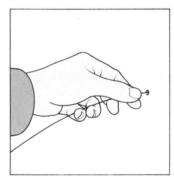 

● Use a fine masonry drill to make a small hole in the wall, angled sharply to one side. Then push in a piece of wire until it hits an upright. Hold it where it enters the wall and pull it out.

Transfer the measurement to the front of the wall and drill a hole about 20mm ($\frac{3}{4}$in) further on. It should go into the centre of the upright, and wooden shavings will come out with the drill.

Making the holes for the fixings

Drilling into solid walls

To make holes in solid walls, you'll need a masonry drill of the right size for the wall plug. And the size of the wall plug will be governed by the size of the screw.

While a masonry drill can be used in a hand-operated wheel brace, it is much better to use it in a power drill. Use a low speed, and withdraw the drill every five seconds to let the tip cool. If a wall is very hard, use a hammer-action drill.

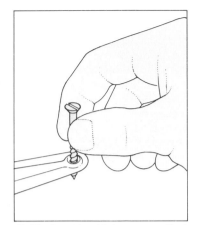

1 Find out the thickest screw that will fit through the holes in the bracket. (Screws may be supplied with the brackets.)

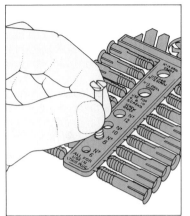

2 Buy wall plugs to match the screw size. Some sets of plugs come with a gauge to help you match them to the right screws.

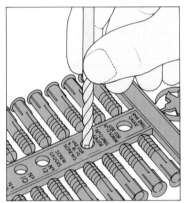

3 Get a masonry drill to suit the size of the wall plug. Again the gauge will tell you the size.

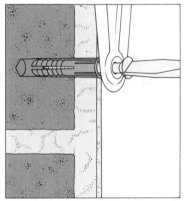

4 Make sure to drill right through the plaster and into solid masonry – at least 40mm (1½in).

Drilling into hollow walls

● Use an ordinary high-speed steel twist drill in either a wheel brace or a power drill. Apply light pressure only; pressing too hard can damage the surface of the plasterboard when the drill bit suddenly breaks through into the cavity.

● To decide the size of the drill use the same rules as 1-3 above, but larger holes are needed to accommodate some hollow fixing devices.

● If you are drilling into the timber uprights, use a high-speed steel twist drill to make a start-hole for the screws. You do not need wall plugs (see also *Understanding screws,* page 56).

Choosing the fixings

Plugs for solid walls

Wall plugs for use in solid walls are available in a number of sizes, but there is a universal plastic plug which fits 6, 8, 10 and 12 gauge screws. This will cover most jobs that you are likely to tackle around the house. Look for wall plugs moulded in sets complete with screw and drill gauge. The gauge will help you to match the screw, the plug and the masonry drill (see above).

51

Fixings for hollow walls

Cavity fixings are designed to be pushed through into the cavity, where they open out to provide rear anchorage as you tighten the screw. Some are plastic wall plugs with wings that open into the cavity.

With some types, such as spring toggles, the screw can't be taken out once the fixing is in place, without the anchor falling down inside. The toggle can be used with a hook for hanging something from a ceiling.

Others, such as Fischer nylon toggles, have special holding devices which allow the screw to be withdrawn, leaving the anchor in place. Keep this in mind when buying. It's useful if you should ever want to take the fitting off the wall and replace it again using the same holes.

Heavy loads

Check on the load that the device is designed to carry. Special heavyweight fixings are available. Items like TV shelves should not be used on a plasterboard partition unless the brackets can be screwed to the timber uprights in the wall.

Putting up the shelf

You have chosen the shelf brackets and the shelf, and decided on the spacing between the brackets. Now you need someone to help you while you fix the shelf to the wall.

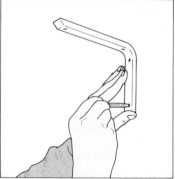

1 Get your helper to hold the shelf in place against the wall while you stand back and decide on its exact position.

2 Hold one bracket in place under the shelf and use a pencil or bradawl to mark the wall through one of the screw holes.

3 If you are drilling into a solid wall, mark the correct depth on the drill bit. Hold a wall plug against the bit so that the ends line up. Then add a few millimetres to the length of the plug and mark the position on the bit with a circle of insulating tape. The extra length allows for debris at the end of the hole.

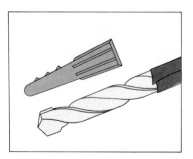

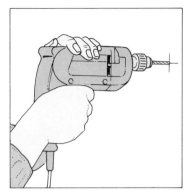

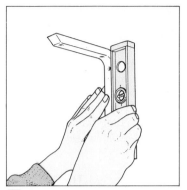

4 Drill the hole in the wall and put in the wall plug – or the cavity fixing in a hollow wall.

5 Screw the bracket to the wall with one screw only, and use a spirit level to check that it's vertical.

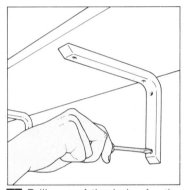

6 Get your helper to hold the shelf on the first bracket, checking with the spirit level that it's horizontal, and then mark the positions for the screw holes of the other brackets.

7 Drill one of the holes for the farthest bracket, and then secure it to the wall with just one screw. Then drill one hole for each of the other brackets and fix them in the same way.

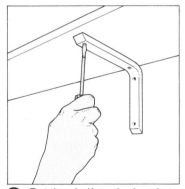

8 Make a final check that the shelf is level. Then drill the holes for the other screws, put them in and screw them up tight.

By making only one fixing in the beginning, you still have the chance to make corrections if the drill should wander in the wall or if you discover that you've made a faulty measurement.

9 Put the shelf on the brackets. Push a bradawl up through the holes in the brackets so it pierces the bottom of the shelf to make starting holes for small screws. Then insert the screws to anchor the shelf in place. But first make quite sure the screws are not so long that they will penetrate the top surface of the shelf.

10 If you are adding other shelves above or below, measure from the first fixed shelf, and always check with a spirit level that the new shelf is horizontal.

Never measure up from the skirting board or down from the ceiling. It's very unlikely that they are horizontal, particularly in an old house.

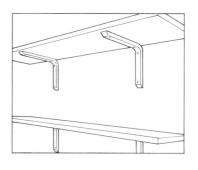

TIPS FOR CAVITY FIXINGS

● If you are fixing brackets to a hollow wall, remember to insert the screws of spring toggles through the holes in the brackets before screwing on the toggle and inserting it in the wall.

● An alternative is to use a Fischer nylon toggle which is inserted into the wall before the screw goes in.

Five ways with temporary shelves

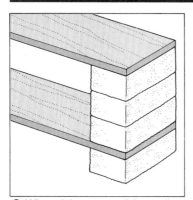

● Where it is not possible or allowable to fix permanent shelving, use house bricks painted with emulsion paint as supports.

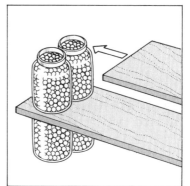

● For a more decorative effect, use glass jars filled with marbles or pebbles. Put one large jar or two smaller ones at each end.

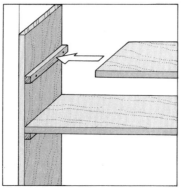

● In the alcove beside a chimney breast, make up a simple shelf unit as illustrated. If the shelves are cut to the right length, the unit will hold itself rigid and no fixing need be made to walls.

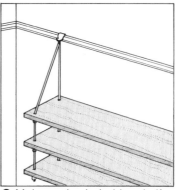

● Make a simple ladder shelf as illustrated, and hang it from a picture rail using picture rail hooks. Hold the shelves apart with wooden balls knotted in place or with plastic tube spacers.

● Where it would be possible to drill a few holes, drill the walls to take lengths of mild steel rod, then simply rest the shelves on them. Wall plugs are not needed.

Shelves to make better use of space

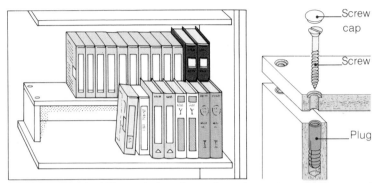

Screw cap

Screw

Plug

Small shelf units Where shelves in cupboards are too widely spaced apart, make up simple extra shelves with melamine-coated chipboard as illustrated and stand them on the existing ones.

When making the new shelves, plug the end grain so there is something firm to screw into. Special chipboard screws may also be used, but they don't make such a strong joint. The exposed screw heads can be covered with plastic screw caps that are sold for the purpose.

Tip for plugging chipboard Whenever you are putting a wall plug into the edge of a piece of chipboard, insert it so that it will expand along the length of the board when you tighten the screw. If it expands across the width, the board will split.

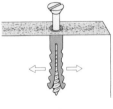

Shelf supports Extra full-length shelves can be added to a cupboard by using plastic or metal shelf supports which fit into small holes drilled in the sides of the cupboard.

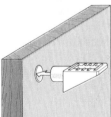

Putting up a heavy cabinet

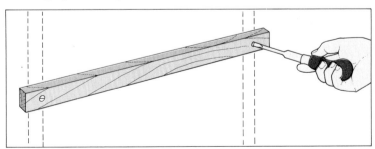

1 Plasterboard partition walls are not strong enough to support a heavy cabinet. For extra support, find the timber uprights in the wall (page 50), then screw a timber batten horizontally through the plasterboard into the uprights.

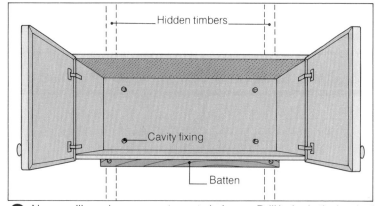

Hidden timbers

Cavity fixing

Batten

2 Now you'll need someone strong to help you. Drill holes in the back of the cabinet, at the top and bottom, then rest it on the timber batten and fix it to the plasterboard with cavity fixings. The batten will take most of the weight. The cavity fixings will merely hold the cabinet in place.

Easing drawers that stick

If drawers become difficult to open and close, a dry powder lubricant, such as Easy-Slide – which is made from the material used for coating non-stick pans – will ease them considerably. It's simply squirted from the container onto the drawer runners. It can also be used for easing sticking lock mechanisms.

UNDERSTANDING SCREWS

The size Two measurements are given to describe the size of a wood screw – the length and the shank diameter. The shank is given a gauge number – 6, 8 and 10 are the most common (10 is thicker than 6). So a screw might be called a 1in no.6 (fairly short and thin) or a 2in no.10 (fairly long and thick).

Head shapes Screws are sold with heads of three shapes, all designed for particular purposes. A screw with a countersunk head is intended to go in flush with the surface, as with most woodwork or on door hinges. Screws with raised heads are usually used on door handles and other hardware that have partly countersunk holes. Screws with round heads are used on hardware that has no coun-tersunk holes at all.

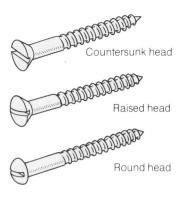

Countersunk head

Raised head

Round head

The two slot designs Screws have two main types of slot in the head – the traditional single slot, which is used with a standard screwdriver, and the cross slot. The cross-slot screw is now almost exclusively Supadriv (or Pozidriv) which requires a screwdriver with a special tip. Some foreign screws are still the old Phillips design, which are best driven with a Phillips screwdriver. But don't try to drive Supadriv screws with a Phillips screwdriver. It won't grip.

If you use a power screwdriver, choose screws with the Supadriv slot. The screwdriver locks into it, making driving much easier.

The screw thread There are also variations of screw thread. Twin-start screws can be driven in much faster than standard screws, and their sharp thread and hardened body make them ideal for use with power screwdrivers.

JOINING PIECES OF WOOD WITH SCREWS

When you are screwing two pieces of wood together, you may have to drill three holes.

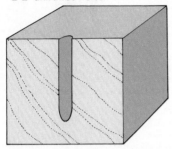

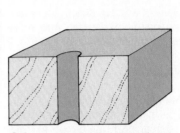

● First, a small start-hole is drilled into the bottom piece of wood so that the threaded body of the screw will be easy to drive home.

● Second, a slightly larger clearance hole is drilled through the top piece of wood to take the unthreaded shank of the screw.

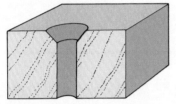

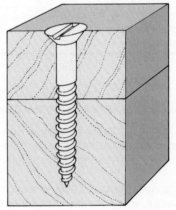

● Third, a countersunk hole is made in the top piece to house a countersunk screw head.

● The screw should fit snugly into the two pieces (see right), without needing to be driven in with any particular force.

Twist drills of different sizes and a countersink bit may be used, but a special drill, called a drill-and-counterbore bit, is available to make all three holes at one pass.

Tips for avoiding trouble

Grease the thread When inserting new screws, apply a little grease or Vaseline to the thread. This will make them easier to remove if it becomes necessary. Do not use soap. It attracts moisture which can cause unplated screws to rust.

Avoid splitting the wood Always make start-holes to avoid splitting the wood. You can use a bradawl in softwood for gauge 6 or smaller. Try to avoid a line of screws that follow the wood grain. This too can lead to splitting the wood.

Get the length right Be sure to calculate the length of screw so that it will not penetrate a decorative surface. It should finish at least 5mm (³⁄₁₆in) below the surface.

How to remove nails

Visible heads If the head of the nail is accessible, use pincers to remove small nails or the claw of a hammer for larger nails. To avoid damaging the wood, place a piece of scrap wood or cardboard between the tool and the wood.

If the nail is a long one, put a block of wood under the tool when the nail is partly out. Add more blocks after each pull. If the nail curves, the hole will become lengthened.

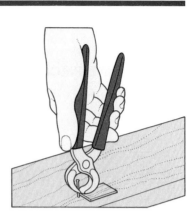

Sunken heads Where it is impossible to get a grip on the head, use a hammer and nail punch to drive the nail down to release the top piece of wood. Then the nail may be drawn from the bottom piece in the usual way.

Alternatively, chisel away the wood around the nail until you can grip it with pincers.

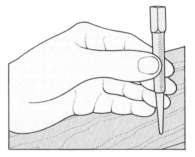

IDEAS FOR HOOKS AND HANGERS

Lightweight hooks For very light items, you can use plastic hooks held by double-sided adhesive pads, but remember that if the hook is stuck to paintwork, the bond is only as good as that of the paint.

Stronger fixing For a more secure fitting, scrape away a small patch of paint and use a plastic hook which has water-activated glue on the back. Wet the glue and allow it to soften before pressing in place. Keep it there with masking tape until the glue has set.

Hollow doors Coat hooks, called Plasplugs Hollow Door Hooks, have been designed to be fixed to a hollow door with a cavity fixing. Single hooks need only one hole in the door, while double hooks need two – one for the fixing, and one for a locating peg.

Coat racks For hanging coats, you can buy a row of plastic hooks already fixed to a back plate. They are supplied with all the fixings that are needed to attach them to a solid wall.

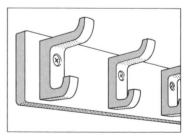

Picture hooks Hang small pictures and mirrors from a picture hook – a small brass hook and a steel pin that can be driven into masonry. As the pins are brittle, wear goggles.

Cleaning & fixing things

*E*verything in the home needs cleaning at some time – whether floors, clothes or even light fittings. Doing it the expert way saves time and can prevent unnecessary disasters. Simple repairs can keep the house and its appliances in good shape and may save you from crippling repair bills.

Keeping the house clean

GETTING YOURSELF EQUIPPED FOR CLEANING

Take a long, hard look at the contents of your cleaning cupboard. Throw out anything you don't use, and replace old items with good quality new ones as the need arises. Buy the best equipment you can afford, look after it, and you'll find it will save you time and energy in the long run.

● General-purpose dusting cloths can be made from worn-out T-shirts or flannelette sheets (page 76).

● Build up a collection of cleaning and polishing cloths to use on different surfaces. Make sure they are strong, soft, absorbent, colourfast and preferably machine-washable.

● Buy solidly made brushes and brooms which have firmly packed tufts in a smooth plastic or beechwood head.

● Use your dustpan more efficiently by having two brushes to go with it – a hard one for loose debris on carpets, and a softer one for hard floors and dusting jobs.

● A sturdy mop with a bucket that it fits into easily is essential for quick, regular mopping.

● Household (plastic) gloves give protection against grime and cleaning chemicals. Use lightweight disposable gloves when handling delicate objects as they give you a better grip than heavier ones.

CLEANING PRODUCTS YOU WILL NEED

One proprietary cleaner from each group listed below will cope with most surfaces. When you are using a product for the first time, read the label and follow the manufacturer's advice. Do a test run on an inconspicuous section and let it dry before checking the result.

PRODUCT	USES
Spray cleaners Light-duty liquid cleaners. Examples: Dettox, Flash Spray, Jif Spray 'N' Foam, Mr Muscle Concentrated Cleaner. Some kill germs including salmonella and listeria. Some trigger-action packs have a foam option for vertical surfaces.	Speedy spray-and-wipe cleaning of kitchen and bathroom surfaces. Good for worktops, wall tiles and mirrors. No need to rinse.
General-purpose liquid cleaners Thick liquids and gels for heavy cleaning. Examples: Cleen-O-Pine, Domestos Multi Surface Liquid Cleaner, Flash Liquid, Green Force Multi Surface Cleaner, and supermarket own brand products. Contain high levels of detergents. Flip-top containers are available.	Good on hard surfaces and for grease. Use diluted for kitchen surfaces, quarry and ceramic tile floors and vinyl flooring. Use neat for grease, shoe scuffing on floors and marks on walls. Rinse after using neat.

CLEANING PRODUCTS YOU WILL NEED (cont)

PRODUCT	USES

Cream cleaners
For heavy-duty cleaning. Examples: Ajax Cream Cleanser, Ecover Cream Cleaner, Jif, and supermarket own brand products. Contain detergents and mild abrasives which don't scratch. Flip-tops available.

Breaks down grease and clears stubborn dirt. Suitable for sinks, cookers (not non-stick oven linings), baths, washbasins and shower trays. Generally use a damp cloth to apply. Use a sponge on acrylic sanitary ware. Rinse well after use.

Cleaners from the kitchen cupboard

A number of cheap, readily available kitchen or DIY products can be used for cleaning, and are useful on a range of different surfaces.

Bicarbonate of soda A mild alkaline powder which neutralises acid stains, such as fruit juice, and deodorises. Use dry (on a damp cloth), as a paste mixed with water for light scouring, or as a solution in water for soaking or washing surfaces. Cleans china, stainless steel, fridges, freezers, ovens, iron soleplates and plastic furniture.

Lemon juice Used neat or added to water, the acidity of lemon juice clears tarnish on brass and copper; removes limescale, rust and stains on marble and plastic worktops; cleans chopping boards and hands; and gets rid of food smells from a microwave.

White vinegar Used neat, in a solution with water or as a paste with borax and water, vinegar cleans windows, glass surfaces, ceramic tiles and wooden furniture. It can also help to remove hard-water deposits from taps, lavatory bowls and sinks, and works as a descaler for kettles.

Household ammonia Ammonia is always used in solution with water. Windows, glass surfaces, mirrors, ceramic tiles and cooker hobs can all be cleaned with ammonia, as can jewellery.
CAUTION Never smell the bottle (the fumes are very unpleasant) and avoid contact with eyes, skin or clothing.

Domestic (or laundry) borax Borax softens water and breaks down grease, and is used dry, as a paste with water and vinegar, or in a solution with water. It's good for cleaning enamel surfaces, ceramic tiles, windows and mirrors, and for dissolving grease in sinks and drains. It will also clear tannin staining from teapots.
CAUTION Wear protective gloves if you have sensitive skin.

Methylated spirit Sold by hardware and DIY shops, methylated spirit is a form of alcohol used to clean windows, glass surfaces, mirrors and picture glass. It will also clear sticky label adhesive left after the label has been removed.
CAUTION It is highly flammable and very poisonous.

Washing soda Sold in supermarkets, washing soda softens water and breaks down grease. Used in a hot-water solution, it will clean hard floors, cooker hoods, extractor fans and drains. It will also clear green corrosion

61

on brass and copper.
CAUTION Wear protective gloves.

White spirit A turpentine substitute, white spirit is used neat to clean gilt picture frames and remove wax polish build-up. It can clear rust spots from acrylic sinks, too.
CAUTION Both turpentine and white spirit are poisonous and highly flammable.

DO'S AND DON'TS: CLEANING SAFETY

DO follow the manufacturer's advice and warnings.

DO wear protective gloves when cleaning.

DO store all products out of reach or in a locked cupboard – they are a health risk for children or those with bad eyesight.

DON'T use flammable products near a naked flame, such as a pilot light. Aerosols, cloths soaked in white spirit and methylated spirit are all flammable.

DON'T mix cleaning products unless the instructions advise you to do so. Toxic fumes could be created.

DON'T transfer household cleaners into other containers. If you do have to, never put them in containers used for drink. Label them clearly, including any warnings or instructions.

DON'T leave young children alone with cleaning products. If you are called to the phone or the door take the child (or the product) with you.

Cleaning efficiency tips

Manufacturers' instructions Keep the booklets for any new equipment and furnishings and follow the recommendations for their use and care.

Storage Try to avoid having an under-stairs storage cupboard for cleaning equipment unless you can walk in without stooping.

Storing dusters Keep dusters and polishing cloths in plastic bags between cleaning sessions. The cupboard stays tidier and fresher.

Cleaning a chamois leather After use, wash out a chamois leather in warm water with soap flakes added. Rinse it in clean water with a tablespoon of olive oil added – the oil keeps the cloth supple. Then wring it out and dry it on a line, stretching it occasionally.

Vacuuming The most effective way of removing dust from hard floors, carpets, surfaces, upholstery and curtains. Use your vacuum cleaner and its attachments whenever possible (page 135).

Two-handed dusting Fold in the corners of a duster to form a pad and work with one in each hand to speed the task.

Logical dusting Dust round a room starting from the door. It ensures nothing gets missed. Start as high as you can reach without stretching and work downwards. Drifting dust settles on lower surfaces.

The two-bucket technique When washing any surface, use two buckets: one contains a cleaning solution, the other clear water for rinsing. Rinse and squeeze out the cloth or mop in the bucket of clear water before dipping it in the cleaning solution. Change the bucket of clear water as soon as it starts to get dirty.

WALLS AND CEILINGS

Mouldings and ceiling covings Cleaning tools are more difficult to control during high-level work and can chip plaster or dent polystyrene mouldings, so take care.

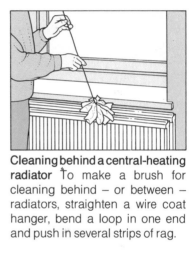

Dust Dust ceilings and walls – in that order – with the wide brush attachment on the vacuum cleaner or cover furnishings with a dust sheet and use a soft broom with a duster tied over the head.

Cleaning behind a central-heating radiator To make a brush for cleaning behind – or between – radiators, straighten a wire coat hanger, bend a loop in one end and push in several strips of rag.

Cobwebs Use a brush attachment on the vacuum cleaner or a cornice brush to remove cobwebs.

Fabric wallcoverings Vacuum lightly to remove surface and deeper dust. In general, don't hang fabric wallcoverings in kitchens or bathrooms, and protect them from furniture and food stains.

Marks and stains on walls

Marks on painted walls Put a drop of general-purpose liquid cleaner onto an absorbent cloth covering a finger. Gently rub the mark until it has gone and then rinse.

Grease splashes Act quickly. Blot firmly with a paper towel, then cover the stain with a fresh piece of paper and press with a warm iron (switched off) to draw the grease out. Change the position of the paper as the grease is absorbed. Use an aerosol stain remover such as K2r on any remaining traces. You can also try the aerosol on older grease stains.

Tobacco stains Lightly scrub with a soft brush dipped in a weak solution of washing-up liquid. Tackle them before washing the whole wall. If the room has been used by very heavy smokers, you may need to cover with a coat of aluminium sealer and repaint the room.

Dirty marks round light switches A soft India rubber will remove light marks. Wallpaper cleaning dough or crustless chunks of slightly stale bread will rub off larger areas of soiling. But take care: the surface of wallpaper is easily damaged.

Vinyl wallcoverings Never hang vinyl near a cooker. Hot grease splashes are impossible to remove.

Hardened candlewax Lift candlewax on a papered wall in the same way as grease. It's usually safe to chip it off a painted wall, vinyl or a washable wallpaper. Use your fingernail, not a knife, and clear any colour by dabbing with methylated spirit on a cotton-wool bud.

Crayon marks On painted walls and washable wallpapers, a general-purpose liquid cleaner used neat on a soft cloth may remove crayon marks. Liquid silver polish can work on vinyl. Give a final wipe with a cloth wrung out in clear water. If redecoration is the only answer for the painted surface, use a stain blocking preparation such as Polycell Stain Block or Cuprinol's Interior Stain Seal first to prevent the strong colours reappearing.
   Crayon and other indelible marks on papered walls can be disguised by covering them with a piece of matching wallpaper. Tear the patch in an irregular shape, rather than cutting it – it will be less visible (page 639).

Non-spongeable hessian As hessian can be damaged by contact with water or stain removers, try crustless, slightly stale bread on dirty marks. More delicate fabrics will probably need professional cleaning – look in the Yellow Pages under 'Cleaning & maintenance services'.

SENSIBLE PRECAUTIONS PREVENT TROUBLE

● Use a stepladder for ceiling and high-level work – standing on a stool or table is dangerous. Make sure the stepladder has wide treads, a top safety rail and a platform to hold equipment.
● Don't stretch to clean something just out of reach when using a stepladder.
● Wear protective goggles for overhead cleaning.
● Turn off electricity at the mains before cleaning with water around electric switches, sockets and light fittings.
● For any cleaning involving heavy dust, cover your nose and mouth with a dust mask.
● Mop up spills on the floor without delay: they can cause falls.

Washing walls

Painted walls Most painted walls can be washed, but do a test run on a hidden section if you are in doubt.
● Move furniture away from the walls; protect the floorcovering with polythene sheeting and dust the walls first.
● Use two buckets of water, one with a warm weak solution of washing-up liquid, the other with clear water. Start at the bottom of the wall and work upwards: dirty trickles are absorbed less by a wet surface.
● Wash by sponging and rinsing overlapping sections, and don't stop until you're finished – this avoids stubborn tidemarks. Use a sponge-head

mop for high sections if you don't have a stepladder.

● Skirting boards are the dirtiest part of the room so clean them last.

DO NOT use washing powders for cleaning painted walls. The fluorescers they contain could affect the colour of the paint.

Vinyl wallcoverings Treat in the same way as a painted wall. Don't overwet them or rub across the joins: it can cause the edges to lift.

Washable wallpaper Treat as 'wipeable' and don't rub too hard. Clean a section at a time with clear water and dry with a cloth before moving on. If the paper is very dirty, use a weak solution of washing-up liquid.

Ceramic tiles Shift a greasy film with domestic borax on a damp cloth, or with the manufacturer's recommended solution of household ammonia in hot water. Use a chamois leather to rinse and dry the surface.

Ceilings Dust occasionally – preferably with a vacuum cleaner – and repaint when necessary, but don't wash ceilings: it's too difficult.

Dealing with woodwork

Paintwork Don't let it get too dirty. Treat gloss or satin (eggshell) finishes with either a spray cleaner or a general-purpose liquid cleaner suited for use on paintwork. A cream cleaner may be necessary for stubborn marks, but use it sparingly and rinse afterwards.

Sealed wood panelling An all-purpose cleaner-polish such as Johnson's Wax Free Sparkle will brighten wood panelling, but avoid spray drifting onto a hard floor: it could leave it dangerously slippery.

Faded wax-finished panelling Clean the surface before repolishing by rubbing with steel wool dipped in white spirit. Work in the direction of the grain of the wood, never across it, and treat the whole panel.

KEEPING WINDOWS SPARKLING

Avoiding streaks Wash windows on a cloudy day. Direct sunlight dries them too quickly, leaving streaks on the glass.

Cloths A chamois leather is good for applying window cleaning solution. For normally dirty windows, add 2 tablespoons of vinegar to a small bucket of warm water. To clean greasy, heavily soiled windows, use 2 tablespoons of household ammonia or domestic borax per gallon and rinse with the vinegar solution above. Finish with a dry, lint-free cloth.

Buffing Use a pad of crumpled newspaper to buff the clean, dry glass. The printers' ink will give your windows an extra sparkle.

Spray window cleaner Practical for small panes, leaded lights and patterned and reeded glass as it evaporates without leaving a residue. Neat methylated spirit is an alternative.

Sash windows Don't take risks. Avoid sitting on the windowsill to clean the outside of a sash window, but rather raise and lower each half so you can clean each outside surface from the inside of the room.

Professional cleaning To get the full benefit from professionally cleaned windows, clean the inside of the windows on the same day.

Mould Clear dirt in the corners of window panes with an old toothbrush dipped in a fungicide such as Polycell Mould Cleaner or Rentokil Mould Cure. This stops black mould – which results from a combination of condensation and dust – from growing back so fast.

Using a window cleaning blade or squeegee

A blade or squeegee is the answer for removing water and dirt from large panes and conservatory glass. Use outdoors to avoid splashing carpets. Some squeegees such as the Bissell or Brabantia window cleaners incorporate a sponge in the head.

Using a spray container, a clean sponge or a car washing brush, wet the window lightly with cleaning solution. Wipe the squeegee blade with a damp cloth to make it glide smoothly across the glass.

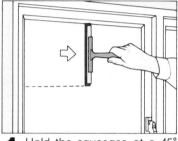 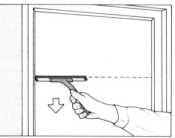

1 Hold the squeegee at a 45° angle to the glass, press one end into the top corner of the window and pull it across horizontally. Wipe the blade.

2 Starting at the lower edge of the dry strip, pull the blade down to the bottom of the pane. Remove the squeegee from the glass and wipe it.

3 Repeat across the window, overlapping the adjacent dry area. Wipe along the bottom of the window frame with the cloth.

Tackling window blinds

Clear dust from window blinds every six to eight weeks before condensation or damp weather conditions change it to a sticky film.

Venetian blinds

● To clean a Venetian blind, wear thick cotton gloves – the slats have sharp edges – and wipe with your fingers. To clean the other side, reverse the slats and repeat.

● Foam-covered tongs can be bought for cleaning the slats. Dip them in a mild washing-up liquid solution. Wear thick gloves.

● To whiten discoloured Venetian-blind tapes, use tennis-shoe cleaner. Leave the blind hanging full-length, with the slats open. Don't close until the tapes are dry in case they shrink.

● Wash very dirty Venetian blinds in the bath, but line it first with a cloth to protect the surface, and keep the blind's operating mechanism out of the water. Use a Scotchbrite pad for washing the slats. Then rinse, shake and hang the blind to dry. You may need help for this job.

● If you are renewing a blind, consider buying one with vertical slats as it will stay clean longer.

Roller blinds

● Vacuum or brush roller blinds, and use the vacuum's crevice tool to keep the roller springs free from fluff.
● Clean spongeable blinds on a flat surface. Preferably use a foam upholstery cleaner – the loosened dirt is removed by wiping so it avoids overwetting. Rehang the blind while still damp, but don't roll it up until it is completely dry or it may lose its shape.

Dusting and cleaning curtains

Fading and condensation Lining curtains will help to prevent their colours fading in the sunlight. It will also stop moisture from the windowpanes rotting the curtain fabric. Another way of preventing this is to hang the curtains away from the window glass.

Cording sets If you fit curtains with cording sets or draw rods, they can be drawn without handling the fabric. This will help them last longer, particularly with velvet.

Vacuuming and brushing Curtains should be lightly cleaned with an appropriate vacuum attachment at frequent intervals, and freshened outside on a breezy day occasionally. It lessens the need for a major clean.

Dry-cleaning Large and interlined curtains in a washable fabric are too bulky to handle at home. Get them dry-cleaned, and if possible attach a note giving details of the fibres. If you bring them home in a car after coin-op dry-cleaning, open the windows. Solvent fumes can cause dizziness if ventilation is poor.

Rehanging If curtains must be rehung at specific windows, mark the reverse of the hem with a coloured thread – one stitch for the first panel, two for the second, and so on. When you take out the curtain hooks, use spots of coloured nail varnish to indicate their positions in the heading tape – it will help when you come to replace them.

Washing curtains Shake them outdoors first and give them a cold-water soak in the washing machine or bath for about an hour, changing the water halfway through. It gets rid of a lot of the dirt. Soak discoloured polyester nets and voiles in a lukewarm solution of washing-up liquid with a few drops of ammonia added. Very dirty colourfast curtains can soak overnight in the solution.

Ironing curtains Iron lengthways, stretching them gently as you go. It helps to avoid puckered seams. If the curtains are too dry, rewet synthetic fabrics completely – it will avoid water spotting.

Keeping tracks running smoothly

● Clean the track while the curtains are down. Scrub a plastic track in the bath or sink (protecting the surface with a cloth), and soak the gliders in a bowl containing a mild solution of washing-up liquid.
● Sticking curtain gliders can be eased by spraying the track with an aerosol lubricant such as WD 40. Take care not to get it on the fabric; it is probably best to take the curtains down first.
● Wipe curtain poles with a damp cloth. When dry, rub sparingly with paste wax polish containing silicones and buff with a cloth – it will help the rings to pull smoothly.

CARING FOR FLOORS

Keep all your floors clean The whole house will stay cleaner if less dirt is carried from room to room.

Use door mats To prevent mud being brought in on shoes and boots, put mats outside both the front and back doors.

New flooring Keep a copy of the care instructions in a safe place so you can refer to it for cleaning and stain removal.

Moving heavy furniture Protect the floor when you move heavy items by using a set of slide-under castors. Just slip them under your furniture, fridge, freezer or washing machine to move them for repairs or cleaning. Alternatively, on smooth, uncarpeted floors, slip an offcut of carpet pile-side down under the piece to be moved – if it is fairly light (right).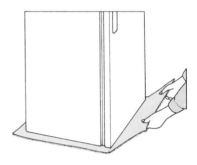

Removing dust

● Regularly remove dust from all types of flooring: it will prolong its life. If grit is left, it will work its way through to a carpet backing where it could cut the pile, or leave ugly scratch marks on a smooth floor.

● All floors should be free from dust before being shampooed, washed or polished.

● Vacuum heavy traffic areas regularly, paying particular attention to the hall and any door leading to the outside. Use a nozzle attachment to reach right into corners, under radiators and along the gap between skirting board and floor.

● If you sweep, rather than vacuum, a hard floor, use a broom with fine bristles and a hand brush to reach into nooks and crannies.

Washing floors

● Use a squeegee or floor mop with a weak washing-up liquid solution, or use one of the proprietary floor cleaners available such as Flash or Domestos.

● Avoid overwetting the floor, especially vinyl, linoleum or cork tiles. The water may seep between them, causing the tiles to lift. Eventually the water may also damage the sub-floor.

● On very dirty ceramic or quarry tiles, marble, concrete and sheet vinyl, leave the floor cleaner on the floor for up to 15 minutes. Scrub any very dirty areas, and then mop up with a cloth, rinsing it out in fresh water.

The right way to polish floors

● Always apply polish sparingly – thick applications attract dust and are difficult to buff into a shine.

● Build up the surface with two or three thin coats of polish rather than a heavy one.

● Stick to one type of polish. Different types can react with each other to leave a sticky mess.

● Apply one coat of polish to the entire floor, with subsequent coats on high-use areas only.

● Don't splash polish onto skirting boards. It is difficult to clean off.

HOW TO CLEAN AND TREAT ALL TYPES OF SOLID FLOOR

FLOORING	HOW TO CLEAN IT
Ceramic tiles	Sweep and wash, but don't polish.
Quarry tiles	Sweep and wash. Remove white patches by wiping with a solution of 1 tablespoon of vinegar in 600ml (1 pint) water. Leave to dry, then repeat if necessary. Use Cardinal Self-shine Red Liquid or Cardinal Red Tile Polish to put the colour back into tiles as they start to fade with time.
Terrazzo/ marble	Never use abrasives. Damp mop the floor in sections with a washing-up liquid solution, scrubbing stubborn marks. Rinse well. Shine the surface with a silicone wax or marble polish such as Bel Marble Polish. Use very sparingly, or thin with turpentine. Look out for a product that produces a non-slip surface.
Wood block	Sweep, damp mop and occasionally use an emulsion polish on sealed wood. To treat unsealed wood, polish the floor regularly with wax polish.
Sanded floor-boards	Sweep and damp mop for everyday care. Occasionally use an emulsion polish such as Furmoto, which has a non-slip finish, on varnished boards. Wax unvarnished boards.
Vinyl (sheet and tiles)	Sweep and damp mop with a detergent solution. Rinse well with clean water to prevent a film of dirty suds drying on the surface. Treat sheet vinyl with emulsion polish. Use a rubber on scuff marks and steel wool on stains.
Linoleum	Sweep and damp mop. Use a solvent-based polish to give a soft sheen. Remove shoe marks by scrubbing with fine steel wool dipped in turpentine or white spirit.
Rubber tiles	Sweep and damp mop with warm water and a mild detergent solution. Polish with an emulsion polish every six weeks. Strip off old polish once or twice a year using a solution of one cup each of a floor-cleaning powder and ammonia in half a bucket of cold water. Scrub and rinse with fresh water, then repolish.
Cork: sealed and vinyl-coated	Sweep and wash with detergent solution. Occasionally use an emulsion or solvent-based polish, such as Marley Floorgloss or Johnson's Wax Klear, to give a shine.
Slate	Clean by mopping with a solution of washing soda and water, scrubbing where required.
Brick and stone	Sweep and wash with a mild detergent solution.

69

Which polish to choose and how to use it

Liquid wax floor polish Solvent-based, soft polish which spreads easily and is suitable for unvarnished wooden floors, linoleum and cork. Examples are Antiquax Liquid Floor Wax and supermarket own brands liquid wax polish.

Apply it by hand with a soft cloth or with an electric floor polisher. Leave it to soak in, then buff to a shine with an old towel wrapped around the head of a broom, or with the electric polisher.

Paste wax floor polish Solvent-based polish used for the same floorings as above. It can only be applied by hand, but it leaves a long-lasting shine. Examples are Ronuk 'Lavender' Wax, Johnson's Traffic Wax and Rentokil Wax Polish.

Emulsion cleaners and polishes Water-based, easy to apply and suitable for all floors except unsealed wood, linoleum and cork. To apply, use a slightly damp sponge mop, pour a little polish on the floor and spread it out. Leave to dry then buff to a shine. Johnson's Wax Free Sparkle, Dunlop Floor Polish and Johnson's Wax Klear are all available.

An annual overhaul A build-up of old polish looks ugly, so once or twice a year remove it all. Use white spirit to shift old solvent-based polishes, or for emulsion polish use a proprietary floor cleaner with a little ammonia added. Apply the mixture generously to a small area of floor at a time. Let it soak in, and then as the wax begins to dissolve, wipe it off with crumpled newspaper. When you have removed the polish from the whole floor, finish by damp mopping it with clean water. Allow it to dry completely before applying new polish.

RUGS AND CARPETS

How to treat your rugs correctly

Getting rid of dust Shake the dust from small rugs in the garden, but don't beat them. It can damage the fibres. Vacuum them as you would a carpet, occasionally turning them over and vacuuming the back too.

Vacuuming fringes Don't vacuum the fringes of valuable or delicate rugs: they may disintegrate or get caught in the cleaner. To vacuum wool, cotton and synthetic fringes, slip an old stocking over the end of the hose attachment to prevent them being sucked up.

Avoid fading Highly coloured rugs will fade if they are left in direct sunlight. Draw your curtains during the hottest part of the day or move the rug out of the sun.

To ensure even wear Turn rugs regularly, especially those next to the bed or close to furniture.

Machine-washable rugs Small cotton rugs can usually be washed in a machine. Choose a short, low-temperature programme. If the rug still looks dirty, wash it a second time.

Oriental and handmade rugs All specialist rugs should be treated with great care. Vacuum once or twice a week with a cylinder-style cleaner, or sweep by hand with a suitable brush. Never use an upright vacuum cleaner with a beater brush/bar: it is too rough and will almost certainly damage the fibres.

● Don't vacuum silk rugs; brush them gently on the right side only in the direction of the pile.

● Never beat an antique or oriental rug by hand as you could damage the pile. Shake it gently outside to dislodge dust, then turn it over and gently tap across the back with a brush.

● To clean, send to a specialist dry-cleaner. For a local cleaner contact the Carpet Cleaners' Association (page 74).

MAKE YOUR STAIR CARPET LAST LONGER

If you move your carpet up the stairs by about 75mm (3in) once a year, you can even out the wear, making it last several years longer. Starting at the top of the stairs, lift the carpet carefully using a tack lifter. Roll it up as you go down. Pay attention to how the carpet is finished at the top and bottom of the stairs. Once it is all lifted, lay it again starting at the bottom, but turning under 75mm (3in) less at the end. The excess carpet will tuck under at the top of the stairs.

If the carpet is fitted, it's probably worth while calling in a carpet layer.

Preserving carpets

● Protect your carpet from heavy indentations made by furniture by placing castor cups under the legs.

● Change the positions of furniture from time to time to even out the wear and alter the 'traffic lanes'.

● Lift heavy furniture (with another person if necessary) rather than dragging it across the carpet.

● Protect the carpet in the doorway with a 'no-show rug', cut from a remnant of matching carpet.

● Encourage your family to wear slippers around the house. Metal-tipped high heels and crepe-soled shoes will twist and pull the pile.

Carpet care tips

To reduce fluff and dirt Spray a synthetic fibre carpet with a homemade antidust solution of 4 parts water to 1 part fabric softener. Use a plant mister to spray it evenly over the carpet.

For easy cleaning Choose a carpet with a built-in protective treatment such as Antron or Scotchgard. You can also have antistain and antistatic (for synthetic fibres) treatments applied to existing carpets. Look in the Yellow Pages under 'Carpet, curtain & upholstery cleaners'.

THROW AWAY OLD UNDERLAY

However tempting it is to keep old underlay to use again, don't – unless it is in excellent condition. The job of an underlay is to protect the carpet from irregularities in the floor below. If new carpet is laid on top of old underlay, the areas of wear will soon show through.

STAIN-BY-STAIN CLEANING GUIDE

Keep a stain-removal kit in the kitchen so you can deal with emergencies at once. It should include: a bottle of carpet shampoo, dry-cleaning solvent, carpet stain removers and a roll of kitchen paper.

Blood	Sponge with cold water and blot firmly with a towel as often as required. Finish with a carpet shampoo.
Candlewax	Once it has hardened, scrape off as much as possible. Cover what's left with blotting paper, brown paper or kitchen paper and press with the tip of a warm iron. The heat will melt the wax so it is absorbed by the paper. Don't let the iron touch the carpet – it might scorch or melt it.
Chewing gum	Place a bag of ice cubes over the gum to freeze it, break up the gum by tapping it with a hammer and then pick off as much as you can. Rub the rest with white spirit or methylated spirit on a soft cloth.
Coffee	Blot dry and treat with a carpet shampoo. When dry, use dry-cleaning solvent on any grease left by milk or cream.
Grease stains	Treat with a proprietary stain remover or dry-cleaning solvent, following the manufacturer's instructions. Or try drawing the stain out with heat – see Candlewax.
Ink	Ballpoint pen: move fast, and dab with methylated spirit on a cotton-wool bud. Fountain pen: blot with absorbent paper and sponge with cold water until it lifts. Then treat with a carpet spot-removing kit such as Carpet Devils. Felt-tip pen: use carpet shampoo on water-based inks, methylated spirit on spirit-based inks.
Jam	Spoon up the jam and wipe the area with a cloth wrung out in warm water. Clean with carpet shampoo and use stain remover on any remaining marks.
Mud	Leave mud to dry completely before you brush or vacuum it out. Sponge off any marks with carpet shampoo.
Scorch marks	Loosen burnt fibres by rubbing with the edge of a coin. Bad marks are impossible to remove, but trim off light marks with scissors or a disposable razor.
Shoe polish	Scrape off and dab with dry-cleaning solvent and then methylated spirit. Finish with carpet shampoo if required.
Tea	Blot up as thoroughly as possible and treat with carpet shampoo. Use dry-cleaning solvent on any milk stains.
Urine	Blot up with paper tissues or a towel and then treat with carpet shampoo, adding 1 egg cup of vinegar to $\frac{1}{2}$ litre (1 pint) of shampoo. A proprietary cleaner such as Petstains will deodorise the fibres.
Vomit	Scrape up deposits and blot with kitchen paper. Treat with carpet shampoo and a little disinfectant. Use a proprietary cleaner to remove the stain.
Wine	Blot fresh spills dry and then clean with carpet shampoo. Don't use salt as it might affect the carpet's colour. Try glycerine on old stains: leave a solution of equal parts glycerine and water on the stain for an hour, then rinse.

Removing stains from carpets

The secret of stain removal is speed. Always treat spillages as soon as possible with the following steps:
● Scrape off any deposit, making sure you don't spread the stain.
● Blot up any liquid by pressing hard with paper kitchen towel, a wad of tissues or a cloth. Don't add any more liquid.
● Treat water-based stains – fruit juice, beer, urine, black coffee, wine – with a carpet shampoo such as 1001, Bissell's or Carpet Devils.
● Treat grease-based stains – gravy, oil, milk, Plasticine – with a dry-cleaning solvent such as Dabitoff, Beaucaire, K2r or Thawpit.
● Rinse off any shampoo or solvent thoroughly with warm water, or it will harden, attract dust, and turn into a stain itself.

Shampooing carpets

Shampooing a stain or small patch Use a special quick-drying carpet shampoo such as 1001, Bissell's or Carpet Devils. Use just enough on a cloth to moisten the area, and turn the cloth over as it soaks up the stain. Work from the outside of the stain inwards so you don't spread it farther. Finally, cover the area with tissues and weigh them down with a heavy object or cloth. Leave overnight to absorb all the moisture.

Spring cleaning Shampoo carpets at least once a year to keep them in good condition, and to bring out their colours. Choose a day when you can leave the doors and windows open and the house won't be too busy.

Test the colour Always do a colour test on a piece of carpet that doesn't show to check that it won't run. Pick a spot under a chair or sofa.

Applying the shampoo Use a special carpet shampoo. Where carpets are lightly soiled, use the shampoo with a manual cleaner; on dirtier areas, use an electric steam cleaner. Hire one by the day or for a weekend from a local hardware store or dry-cleaners. Clean the carpet in strips, working back to the doorway. Leave it to dry and then vacuum.

Protect the wet carpet Don't put furniture straight back onto wet carpet – it could damage or stain the pile. Put strips of foil under furniture legs and castors, but if they do leave marks, sponge them off with a squeeze of lemon juice in a small jug of hot water.

Homemade dry shampoo Freshen carpets with a dry shampoo. Sprinkle the carpet liberally with salt, cornflour or oatmeal. Leave for two hours and then vacuum off. Be sure to remove all traces of salt.

Dealing with carpet problems

Flattened pile Raise indentations made by heavy furniture by using the edge of a coin to rub up the pile. Alternatively, cover the pile with a damp cloth and steam gently, but quickly, by placing a hot iron on top of the cloth.

Loose-fitting rugs For rugs on slippery surfaces, fit a non-slip backing such as Akostop or Foxi Super Plus. Or if the rug is not particularly valuable, give it a non-slip backing by coating the back with a latex adhesive. Allow the rug to dry before putting it back on the floor.

Useful addresses

A. Bell & Co Ltd
Kingsthorpe Road
Northants NN2 6LT.
Tel: 0604 712505.
Mail-order suppliers of Belsealer, a stone sealant for floors.

Carpet Cleaners' Association
126 New Walk
De Montfort Street
Leicester LE1 7JA.
Tel: 0533 554352.
Will supply the names of local cleaners of handmade rugs.

National Association of Chimney Sweeps
PO Box 35
Stoke-on-Trent ST4 7NU.
Tel: 0782 744311.
Can supply the names of local sweeps.

Textile Services Association
7 Churchill Court
58 Station Road
North Harrow
Middlesex HA2 7SA.
Tel: 081 863 7755.
Gives details of local duvet cleaning services.

LOOKING AFTER YOUR FURNITURE

Keep a copy of any care and cleaning instructions for new furniture that you buy. Check whether loose covers are machine washable, and in particular keep care labels for fixed upholstery and leather furniture.

Taking care of wooden furniture

● Keep polished furniture away from direct sunlight, which may bleach the wood, and from the heat of fires or radiators which can dry out the wood and warp it.
● Regular polishing makes old furniture look attractive, and builds up a protective layer against heat and water marks. Much modern furniture has a plasticised or varnished finish which needs little or no polishing.
● Always apply polish sparingly, building up many fine coats. Don't be tempted to switch polishes – they may react with each other and cause clouding or stickiness.

How to clean different finishes

French polish A hard, glossy surface that is easily marked by heat, solvents and abrasives.
● Before polishing, wipe off sticky marks with a cloth barely moistened with lukewarm water and detergent.
● Polish occasionally with a hard-finish wax such as Johnson's Wax Furniture Cream with Beeswax, or Traditional Beeswax Furniture Polish made by Cambridge Traditional Products. If polish builds up, remove it with a rag moistened in turpentine. Leave to dry, then repolish.

Oiled wood
● Oil reduces blemishes and nourishes wood without changing its natural colour. Teak and other hardwoods should be cleaned about twice a year with teak oil or a furniture cream intended for hardwoods.
● Prepare the wood by rubbing it clean with a cloth moistened with turpentine. Apply the teak oil sparingly, and then buff with a clean cloth.

Waxed furniture
● Use either a clear or pigmented beeswax, such as Briwax or Antiquax, to enhance the wood's natural colour.

74

● Before waxing, wipe the wood down with white spirit on a clean cloth. Apply the wax, spreading it evenly and sparingly. Leave it to dry for a few minutes, then bring out the shine by rubbing with a clean cloth, first across the grain, then along it.

● A dirty build-up of wax polish can be removed by rubbing it carefully with a very fine grade wire wool soaked in white spirit. Work along the grain and mop up the loosened polish as you go. Allow the surface to dry completely before rewaxing.

● To give shiny, waxed pine an extra gloss, wipe it occasionally with a cloth dampened with equal parts of vinegar and paraffin.

● Protect wooden furniture against woodworm with a once-yearly single application of wax polish to unpolished areas.

Painted finishes Clean painted furniture with a cloth wrung out in warm washing-up liquid solution. Rinse with clean water and leave to dry.

Sealed finishes
● Clean tough lacquered or varnished finishes on modern furniture by wiping them down with a damp cloth. If you want to buff up the shine, use a dry, soft cloth.

● Use a spray polish to give an instant but short-lived shine – but don't use it on unlacquered or matt-finish woods or you will quickly destroy their natural finish.

Treating wood blemishes

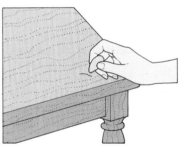

Disguising small scratches Rub a scratch on dark woods with the cut edge of a Brazil nut. On light or coloured woods, fill the scratch with shoe polish or wax crayon. Alternatively, use proprietary products such as Colron Scratch Remover or Joy Scratch Dressing.

Raising dents in solid wood Place a damp cloth over the dent and hold a warm – not hot – iron on top for a few minutes. This forces moisture into the timber, and swells the grain. Allow the wood to dry completely, and then repolish.

Shifting white rings
● Wipe with a metal polish or use Topps Ring Away or a similar brand-name cleaner. Alternatively, try one of the following:
● On dark woods, rub with a mixture of cigarette ash and vegetable oil on a soft cloth.
● On waxed surfaces, use a paste made from salt and olive oil. Leave it on overnight and then wipe off and re-wax immediately.
● On teak, sand the surface with fine glasspaper and then re-oil.
● On French-polished surfaces, rub in a mixture of 1 part turpentine to 4 parts boiled linseed oil. Leave overnight and then polish off.

Greasy marks on wood veneers
Sprinkle the surface with powdered chalk or talcum powder. Lay a couple of sheets of tissue over the top and press gently with the tip of a warm iron. It will draw out the grease.

TO MAKE A DUSTER

For a general-purpose furniture dusting cloth, soak a new duster in a mixture of paraffin and vinegar (an egg cup of each) for an hour or until the liquid is absorbed. Wring the cloth out and allow it to dry before use. Store it in a screw-top jar. Since the duster is impregnated with oil and acid, it gives a better clean, polishing as it absorbs the dust.

Looking after a piano

To remain in top condition, a piano needs:
● Room humidity of 50-55 per cent. Excessive humidity leads to rusted strings, hardened hammer felts and distortion of component parts. If you have a centrally heated house, consult a tuner about installing a humidifier as air that is too dry will make the piano go out of tune.
● A room temperature of 17-21°C (63-70°F). It should not exceed 22°C (72°F) because high temperatures cause the wood to shrink and split.
● No rapid fluctuations in temperature and humidity. Avoid opening the window last thing at night, for example.
● A position away from damp walls, windows that let in damp air, and central-heating radiators.
● Frequent use.

Cleaning pianos

● Use a damp chamois leather to dust the keyboard. Squeeze it out in a weak washing-up liquid solution to clean dirty keys.
● Use cotton wool moistened with methylated spirit on greasy keys, but don't let it trickle between the keys or touch the polished wood.
● Remove fingermarks and soiling on wooden casework with a chamois leather squeezed out in a solution of 1 part white vinegar to 8 parts water. Wipe dry with a soft cloth.
● On modern pianos with a natural veneer, use a neutral-coloured paste polish such as Antiquax or Lord Sheraton Furniture Balsam. It fills the grain without showing.
● Use furniture cream on satin or gloss finishes, French-polished or older pianos.
● A polyester high-gloss finish is best polished with an all-purpose cleaner-polish such as Johnson's Wax Free Sparkle or Mr Sheen.
● Use all polishers sparingly to avoid a smeary surface.
● Remove dust from inside the casework with your vacuum cleaner. It's best to blow the dust away if your vacuum can do that.

Preserving an unused piano

● Cover the working parts and keyboard with sheets of dry brown paper to absorb any damp.
● Put a cotton bag of paradichlorbenzene moth repellent crystals, available at larger chemists, on top of the paper to deter moths. Putting silica gel crystals on the paper in a small bag will also help to counter any humidity or damp.
● If the piano will be exposed to sunlight, cover it with a dust sheet.

Upholstered furniture

Sofas, chairs and cushions Vacuum them regularly – once a week is preferable – using low suction and a small general-purpose head. Do not use a brush attachment as it may pull out loose threads. A hand-held vacuum cleaner is ideal for this job.

To remove pet hairs Use a barely damp sponge or wide sticky tape wrapped around your hand, with the sticky side outwards. To remove hairs from Dralon and other plush fabrics, wear slightly damp rubber gloves to 'dust' the fabric, picking up stray hairs and fluff as you work over the furniture surface.

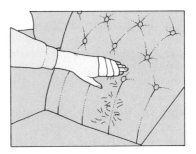

Reversible cushions Turn them regularly to restore the shape and even out the wear. Plump up cushions with loose fillings.

Avoid damaging fabrics Keep upholstery away from the prolonged, direct heat of a radiator or fire, which may scorch the fabric. Do not position upholstery in direct sunlight; after a surprisingly short time, the colours will begin to fade.

Slip covers Protect the backs and arms of upholstery with slip covers. Make simple slips from a remnant of fabric or ask for matching covers to be made when you buy your furniture.

Cleaning loose covers
● Consult care instructions to check that the covers are washable.
● Check that the fabric is colourfast by testing a hidden piece. Treat it with shampoo and dab with tissues. If the colour doesn't run, the covers are washable. If it does, have them dry-cleaned.
● If you do not have care instructions, use a low temperature programme on the washing machine. If the covers still look dirty, put them through the machine for a second time.
● If large covers will not fit into your washing machine, use the larger machines at a launderette.
● Always iron covers while they are still slightly damp – on the 'wrong' side for a matt finish and the 'right' side for a shiny one. Carefully iron the pleats and frills then replace covers while still damp, stretching them into place along the seams. They will take on the shape of the chair as they dry.
● Always remove cushion covers to wash them where possible. If you have to wash the whole cushion, never overwet cushion fillings as they may break down or go lumpy.

Cleaning fixed covers
● Treat heavy soiling or grease marks on arms and headrests with a dry-cleaning solvent such as Beaucaire or Dabitoff (page 73).
● For overall cleaning, use an upholstery shampoo, such as Bissell's or 1001. Follow the manufacturer's instructions. Upholstery shampoo is safe for most cotton, wool, linen and synthetic fabrics.
● Only use foam shampoos, never liquid ones: if the filling gets wet, it will take a long time to dry and may stain the fabric. Leave the foam to dry, absorbing the dirt, and then vacuum it off.

Leather upholstery

To check whether leather is washable Drop a spot of water onto the leather in a hidden place. If it stays on the surface, the leather is washable. If it's absorbed, leaving a damp patch, the leather must only be dusted, with an occasional wipe with a damp cloth.

To clean washable leather Use a warm soap-flake solution or saddle soap on a sponge or cloth. Avoid detergents, they can harden the leather. Don't overwet the surface, especially on the seams, as water penetration can cause distortion and mildew. Finish with a clean, damp cloth (without rinsing) and leave to dry away from direct heat.

Keeping leather supple Rub in a hide food, such as Connolly's Cee Bee or Bridge of Weir, two or three times a year to keep the leather supple.

To remove grease stains Even washable leather will stain unless treated quickly. Try covering the stain with a rubber solution, such as a bicycle puncture repair adhesive, but test it first on a hidden section for 10 minutes as its colour could cause additional staining on light leathers. Leave it on for 24 hours to absorb the grease, and then carefully roll it off. Apply hide food to the area.

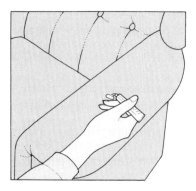

Ballpoint pen marks Swab the marks with cotton wool dipped in milk, if it's a washable surface. Then wipe with a warm soap-flake solution, leaving the leather as dry as possible.

DO NOT use dry-cleaning fluids on leather. They will not remove grease or any other stain.

Plastic and vinyl upholstery
● If a soapy cloth won't clean it, try one of the car seat cleaners sold for simulated leather. Test it on a hidden section first.
● Never use detergents, spirit-based cleaners or polishes on these surfaces. They could affect the colour and leave the surface hard or sticky.

Metal furniture

Painted cast metal furniture
● Remove dust and fingermarks by wiping with a damp cloth.
● Deal with rust spots immediately by scraping off old paint and applying a rust remover or inhibitor (see *Dealing with rust*, page 270). Then apply metal primer before touching up the paintwork.

Chrome furniture
● Clean tarnish by using equal parts of household ammonia and water. Rub it onto the metal, then rinse and wipe off. Or try a little paraffin or toothpaste on a damp cloth instead.
● Protect the surface of chrome with a thin film of silicone wax.
● Shift stubborn marks with a damp cloth dipped in bicarbonate of soda.
● If the chrome becomes pitted, clean it with a chrome cleaner from a car accessory shop.

Aluminium-framed furniture Before storing it for the winter, smear the metal lightly with clear cooking oil, but remember to wipe it off before using the furniture again the following year.

Cane furniture

To clean dirty unvarnished cane furniture Brush to clear dust. Rub the cane lightly with fine steel wool dipped in a warm washing-soda solution – add 2 tablespoons of soda to 4.5 litres (1 gallon) hot water and leave to cool before use. Rinse with a cloth lightly wrung out in cold water and leave to dry naturally, outside if possible. Sunlight helps to bleach the cane.

To tighten a sagging cane seat
Scrub both the top and the bottom of the seat with hot, soapy water and then leave the chair to dry in the open air. As the cane dries out it will shrink, and the seat will firm up again. Repeat as and when it becomes necessary.

Plastic furniture

● Clean by wiping down with a cloth wrung out in a mild washing-up liquid solution. Rinse off.
● Treat scratches by rubbing with metal polish – don't use any form of harsh abrasive cleaner.
● Move stubborn stains with a paste of bicarbonate of soda and water. Leave for two minutes and then wash off. Or use a proprietary cleaner such as Bar Keeper's Friend – an all-purpose rust, tarnish and stain remover for glass, marble, chrome, brass and plastic.

DIRTY OFFICE EQUIPMENT?

If you cut down on static – which attracts dust – you'll find your home computer stays much cleaner. Wipe all electronic equipment with an impregnated anti-static cloth or buy an anti-static foam cleaner.

Marble surfaces

Marble is porous and stains easily. In general, use a damp cloth wrung out in a mild washing-up liquid solution, wiping the surface dry afterwards.

To remove light stains Use neat lemon juice or white wine vinegar on a work surface or table top, but only leave it on for a couple of minutes. Rinse it off and repeat if necessary.

To remove stubborn stains Use a solution of 1 part 20-volume hydrogen peroxide (get it from the chemist) to 2 parts water. You also need ammonia. Pour a teaspoon of the solution onto the stain and immediately add a few drops of ammonia. As soon as the solution stops bubbling, rinse with plenty of cold water.

To remove greasy stains Rub with acetone or a small amount of lighter fuel on a cloth. Rinse well and dry with a clean cloth.

LIGHT FITTINGS

Your light fittings may appear clean, but dirt can reduce the light output by a third without even becoming noticeable. It's worth taking the time to keep them clean.

Cleaning bulbs and tubes

● Clean light bulbs at two-monthly intervals. Do a floor at a time, switching off the light and letting the bulb cool before you remove it. Hold it by the metal cap and wipe with a chamois leather or absorbent cloth dipped in a bucket of warm detergent solution and wrung out. Dry the bulb thoroughly before replacing it. Use methylated spirit on a cloth to clear stubborn fly marks.

● Take down fluorescent tubes and clean them in the same way. Kitchen tubes may need wiping with a general-purpose liquid cleaner to clear grease.

Dusting the fittings and shades

● Use a soft, dry duster only on the reflectors of ceiling-recessed light fittings: if the anodised surface is scratched, it will lose its reflective ability.

● While the bulbs are out for cleaning, use the round dusting brush on your vacuum cleaner to clean the shades on spotlights and other high light fittings. Hand dust these on table or standard lamps.

Cleaning chandeliers Chandeliers are best cleaned where they are. Turn off the electricity at the fuse box and prevent water getting into the light sockets by covering each bulb with a plastic bag secured with a twist tie. Protect the floor with polythene sheeting with newspaper on top. Using a specialised cleaner, such as Antiquax Chandelier Cleaner, spray the pendants so the dirt runs off. Leave them to drip dry.

Crystal wall lights Switch off the electricity at the fuse box. Wear dry chamois leather gloves or use a soft chamois leather to clean each pendant by gentle rubbing – it's tedious, but very effective.

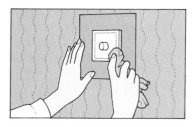

To clean light switches Make a cardboard template which fits round the light switches to protect the wall. Rub metal plates with a few spots of metal polish and burnish them with a soft cloth. Use a barely damp cloth on plastic plates.

CLEANING LIGHT FITTINGS SAFELY

● Always switch off the light before attempting to take out a bulb. Unplug table and standard lamps at the socket.

● Don't wet the metal part of a bulb during cleaning.

● If taking down and replacing a ceiling fluorescent tube, use a stepladder and get help.

● When replacing a bulb in a light fitting, never exceed the recommended wattage and always remember to check that the light is still switched off at the door or wall socket.

● If the bulb breaks while you are trying to remove it, press an old cork firmly onto the broken glass segments and twist it anticlockwise until it comes away from the fitting.

SILVER AND OTHER METALS

Silver

● Use a cleaner formulated for silver: brass polish can permanently damage a soft metal like silver.

● Don't rub the hallmarks too hard. They are easily worn away, which will affect the piece's value.

● Handle silver as little as possible. Fingermarks darken with time.

To prevent tarnishing

● Open fires and gas fires accelerate tarnishing, so keep your silver away from them.

● Display silver pieces in a glass cabinet with a vaporising tarnish inhibitor, such as the Tarnprufe Carosil Capsule.

● Store silver in Tarnprufe bags or wrapped in acid-free tissue paper. Newspaper, brown paper and elastic bands all encourage tarnishing. Then keep the silver in a dark, dry place.

● Clean silver before it becomes heavily discoloured – rubbing it too hard will remove a fine layer of silver. Treat it with a silver polish containing a tarnish inhibitor for a more lasting effect.

Minor scratches Use a cream silver polish. Rubbing with this causes particles of silver to fill the scratches, leaving the surface smooth.

Ornate items Use a foaming silver polish, such as Goddard's Long Term Silver Polish, applied on a damp sponge. Dirt and tarnish are easily rinsed off embossed and filigree sections.

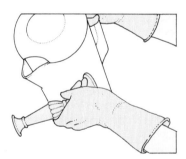 

Wax on a silver candlestick Holding the candlestick carefully in one hand, pour boiling water over the top half to melt the wax. Take care not to wet the base if it is covered with baize.

To melt the wax from the lower part of the candlestick, stand it on a newspaper. Move a hair dryer – on a low setting – slowly back and forth across the surface of the candlestick until it's clear of wax.

Silver salt cellars Stray salt grains can cause black spots, so empty and wash a silver salt cellar after use. For stubborn spots, remove the glass liner, and immerse the silver part for five minutes in a hot, strong, salt solution (1 tablespoon salt to 600ml/1 pint of water). The marks will disappear as you wash the cellar and apply silver polish to the dry surface.

Silver teapots To remove tannin staining from inside a silver teapot, fill it with boiling water and add a handful of washing soda. Leave overnight and then wash out and rinse thoroughly. This also works for china and stainless-steel teapots.

CAUTION Never use washing soda on aluminium or chromium. Use borax instead of washing soda for aluminium and wipe the inside of chromium pots with a cloth dampened in vinegar and dipped in salt.

81

Brass and copper

Regular cleaning Wash lacquered items in warm soapy water, rinse, and then dry and buff with a soft cloth. For unlacquered pieces, a tarnish-inhibiting brass and copper polish is best. Avoid dried polish deposits on ornate pieces by using an impregnated wadding such as Brasso Metal Polish Wadding.

Heavily tarnished items Use a metal polish that doesn't contain a tarnish inhibitor – it's easier. Alternatively, dip half a lemon in salt and rub over very dirty areas. Use an old toothbrush for crevices. Wash in hot, soapy water and then rinse, dry, and buff with a cloth.

Green corrosion Soak the piece for several hours in a strong, warm, washing-soda solution. Occasionally rub the surface with an old brush or cloth. Rinse, dry and polish. Alternatively, use a corrosion remover, such as Dax Chemical Brass Tarnish & Verdigris Remover.

To clear polish deposits in a patterned brass surface Treat a small area at a time. Use very fine steel wool (0000 gauge) dipped in a solution of 1 tablespoon each of vinegar and salt dissolved in 250ml (9fl oz) hot distilled water. Sponge off with soapy water and wipe dry before moving on. The solution will pit the surface if left for more than a few minutes.

Lacquering brass and copper Clean and buff the surface to a bright shine first, wearing gloves. Avoid breathing on the metal, as both fingermarks and moisture will discolour it after lacquering.

Use a transparent metal lacquer suited to brass, applying a second coat after the first has dried, in case you've missed any sections. If you are using an aerosol lacquer, watch out for spray drift. You can remove the lacquer afterwards with cellulose thinners or a proprietary lacquer stripper when the piece needs repolishing.

Long-term cleaning Clean the piece once a year with Solvol Autosol (available from motor accessory shops). Wash and dry the surface, and protect it with Renaissance Microcrystalline Wax Polish, available from some John Lewis Partnership branches.

Bronze

Regular cleaning Clean the surface with dark brown shoe polish and buff vigorously with a soft cloth. It will improve the bronze's appearance.

For stubborn marks Remove surface marks with paraffin or pure turpentine on a cloth. Burnish the dry surface with a clean polishing brush until it shines.

Bronze or spelter? Similar to bronze in appearance, spelter is a lighter zinc-based alloy which is easier to work with than bronze. It was often used for reproductions or cheaper pieces. Spelter dents and fractures more easily than bronze, and was often lacquered. It should be cleaned in the same way as bronze.

Chromium plate

Regular cleaning Wipe with a soapy cloth or general-purpose liquid cleaner. Rinse, dry and buff with a soft, dry cloth.

For stubborn marks Rub with a damp cloth dipped in bicarbonate of soda. Or use a chrome cleaner – available from motor accessory shops – or silver polish.

82

Pewter

Regular cleaning Wash with hot, soapy water, and then rinse and dry. To restore the glow, rub around the body with a soft, warm duster – don't rub at an angle, as it will spoil the light-reflecting surface.

Or use a suitable abrasive-free polish, such as Brasso Metal Polish Wadding, to give a brighter surface. Never put pewter in the dishwasher.

For heavy corrosion Rub with fine steel wool (0000 gauge) lubricated with a fine machine oil. Wipe dry and finish with polish, as above. On valuable antiques, it may be better to avoid cleaning and altering the appearance. Use an occasional application of clear wax polish to inhibit tarnish.

IN THE SITTING ROOM

To keep your main living space looking clean, give the room a daily tidying and light dusting, keep the floor clear of bits and pieces, empty the wastepaper bins and open the windows for at least an hour.

Fireplaces and chimneys

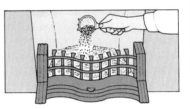

Damping down ashes You will need to clean out the fire grate and lay a new fire daily while the fire is being used regularly. Before clearing away the ashes, sprinkle damp tea leaves over them to keep down the dust.

Ceramic tiled fireplaces Don't wipe tiles while they're hot. The use of a damp cloth can cause the surface to craze.

Removing soot and tarry deposits
● Rub a stainless-steel fireplace trim with methylated spirit.
CAUTION Methylated spirit is flammable. Never use it while the fire is lit.
● It's easier to get soot off a brick fireplace if it has been treated with a brick sealing preparation such as Belsealer (page 74). Try it on a small area before treating the whole surface.
● Clean an unsealed brick fireplace by sweeping and scrubbing with clear, warm water. Don't use soap or detergent; they can leave a permanent deposit on the surface.
● Really dirty bricks should be scrubbed with neat malt vinegar. Rinse them well, using a sponge to blot the surface and avoid overwetting.
● Scrub a stone fireplace with a weak bleach solution to remove heavy soiling. Wear goggles and protect your clothes and surroundings. Rinse thoroughly and use a sponge to absorb the surplus water and grit.
● Use a grate blackener, such as Zebrite or Liberon Iron Paste, on cast-iron fireplaces.

Sweeping chimneys and flues
● Don't let soot and ash build up where it could obstruct smoke. Brush out the flues every month; if a room heater has a throatplate at the top of the firebox, remove and clean it at the same time.
● Have chimneys and flue pipes swept at least once a year, even if you are using smokeless fuel. It's advisable to employ a sweep who is a member of the National Association of Chimney Sweeps (page 74).

Cleaning ornaments

Specialist retailers and museums will advise on treating valuable ornaments. Clean them when you have the time to follow their advice fully.

Small and intricate pieces Keep them in a display cabinet to protect them from accidents and dust.

Porcelain and china figurines

Hold figures upright by the base for cleaning. Working from the top of the piece, brush off the dirt with a long-haired, soft-bristle make-up brush dipped in a warm solution of washing-up liquid – or soap flakes in the case of a matt finish. Rinse in the same way with warm water and leave to dry on a paper towel.

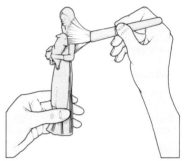

Clean larger pieces on a cloth in a plastic bowl. Use a spray bottle to apply the cleaning solution and then brush and rinse a section at a time. Don't let the ornament stand in the dirty water, as some bases are unglazed and it could be absorbed. Empty the water as it accumulates and change the cloth. Leave to dry on a towel.

Small glass and china ornaments Put them in the sink and spray thoroughly with a liquid window cleaner. To dry, move them onto a towel.

Ivory Stand an ivory ornament in daylight to keep its colour, but not near a frosty window or where it is exposed to hot sun through the glass. Extremes of temperature lead to cracking.

Blow off any dust, and clean the piece only when absolutely necessary, using a cotton-wool bud lightly dampened with methylated spirit. Never wash ivory, as water gets into minute surface cracks and can eventually discolour it.

Dried and artificial flowers

Blow dust off dried flowers and artificial flower arrangements with a hand-held hair dryer on its lowest setting. If you clean them indoors, make sure you do it before you dust and vacuum the room, or better still do it outside the window. It's surprising how dirty they can get.

Pictures and paintings

● To clean the glass on pictures and photographs, spray a liquid window cleaner on the cloth, not the glass. It prevents seepage under the frame. Alternatively, use neat methylated spirit.
● Clean the glass lightly. Vigorous rubbing could smudge pencil and pastel drawings if there is no mount.
● Most modern wood and metal picture frames need only a wipe with a slightly damp cloth, but take care with elaborate gilt frames, both old and

modern. Real gold leaf is extremely thin and easily dislodged. Use a very soft, dry brush, such as a make-up brush or a new shaving brush.

● Treat discoloured sections on less valuable gilt frames with a cotton cloth dipped in warm turpentine. Turpentine is highly flammable so don't warm it over direct heat: pour a little into a jar and stand it in a bowl of hot water.

● If a picture isn't too heavy, lift it down to clean. It's easier to work on a flat surface and there's less likelihood of damaging the wall. Dust the wall and check the picture cord and fixings at the same time.

● Use a clean, soft cloth to dust oil paintings. Winsor & Newton's Artists' Picture Cleaner can be used on less valuable unvarnished and varnished oil paintings. Varnished paintings will then need revarnishing with Artists' Picture Varnish aerosol.

IN THE BEDROOM

● Encourage your household to throw back the bedclothes when they get up in the morning. We lose up to 300ml ($\frac{1}{2}$ pint) of body moisture each night, and a bed needs at least 20 minutes to dry off before it's covered up again. Then make the bed before starting any cleaning. It creates quite a bit of dust.

Taking care of mattresses

A protective cover It's hard to remove stains from a mattress, so give it a cover of washable, unbleached calico. Don't leave on the original plastic wrapping; body warmth will cause condensation inside the bag, leading to mildew and rotting.

Turn your mattress Flip it over or reverse the head and foot ends at three-monthly intervals – more frequently when new – to keep the filling even and distribute wear.

Foam mattresses have a layered construction so shouldn't be turned, but benefit from a head-to-foot switch.

Remove accumulated dust and skin scales Use the soft-brush vacuum attachment with light suction for foam mattresses only. For interior-sprung and other mattresses, use a dustpan and brush – suction could dislodge the layers of padding beneath the cover.

Act quickly with spills Pull off the mattress and stand it on its side. Blot the stain firmly with a dry cloth or towel. Then treat as recommended for a particular stain (page 72) holding a towel against the cover under the stained area to stop the mattress getting wet. Blot frequently during treatment to keep the padding as dry as possible. Finish by feathering (wiping lightly) across the edges of the treated area with a damp cloth to prevent a water mark.

Dry all treated areas, and hot-water-bottle leaks, with an electric hair dryer – but keep it moving and don't hold it too close to the mattress so as to avoid scorching.

Pillow care

To expand the filling Choose a warm, dry day to give natural and synthetic fibre-filled pillows an outdoor airing on a clothes line.

Protective cases Always use two pillowcases for added protection. The under case stops hair and skin oils, saliva and night creams reaching the filling. Foam, in particular, is easily damaged by oil. Change the pillowcases regularly.

Clearing up spills Sponge the pillow cover quickly. If the spill has penetrated the filling, you can wash the pillow. It is not good for it, though, so only wash as a last resort.
● Use a launderette for washable pillows. They are bulky when wet and could unbalance a domestic machine. Front-loading washing machines are less likely to damage the filling.

DO NOT use a coin-op dry-cleaning machine for pillows. Toxic fumes may remain trapped in the filling, and could be dangerous.

Is it too old? A pillow won't last for ever. Check if one needs replacing by plumping it up and laying it across your outstretched arm. If it flops down on either side of your arm, it's time you bought yourself a new one.

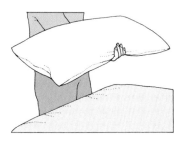

Dealing with duvets

For extra warmth Don't cover your duvet with an extra blanket – you will squash out insulating air trapped in the filling. You'd do better to put a blanket under the bottom sheet to reduce heat loss through the mattress.

Alternatively, get a two-layer duvet with different TOG (warmth) ratings. Use the lower TOG-rated layer for summer, the warmer one for the spring and autumn, and combine the two for winter.

Airing duvets Daily airing is essential for all duvets, whether made with natural or synthetic fillings. Drape them over a chair or bed rail. An occasional spell on an outside line expands a filling flattened by use.

Changing covers Choose covers which open along the width of the duvet. For easy changing, push one corner of the duvet into place and hold in position with a clothes-peg. Repeat with the other corner and shake the duvet down into the case.

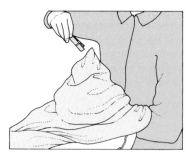

Cleaning duvets Defer full cleaning as long as possible as it can reduce the warmth of the duvet. If the duvet is properly looked after, cleaning should only be necessary once or twice in its lifetime.
● Mop up spills before they penetrate the filling. Push back the filling, tie off the stained section of the primary cover and wash it.
● Clean half of a dirty casing on a down or feather duvet at a time. Shake the filling down to one end, tie it off and wash and dry the empty half. Repeat the procedure for the other end.
● Even a single duvet is too bulky for most domestic washing machines. Use a launderette machine and tumble dryer, or have it professionally cleaned. For details of local duvet cleaning services, contact the Dry Cleaning Information Bureau or the Laundry Information Bureau at the

Textile Services Association, 7 Churchill Court, 58 Station Road, North Harrow, Middlesex HA2 7SA. Tel: 081 863 7755.

Sheets and blankets

Washing sheets and blankets Soak discoloured bed linen for an hour in a biological washing powder solution before washing, making sure it is completely immersed – there may be a colour change.

Don't wash a blanket at home unless you have checked that the dry blanket will fit into your machine; the spin-dryer, too, if applicable. If it doesn't fit, take it to a launderette instead. To get a soft, fluffy finish, dry the blanket outdoors on a warm, breezy day. If possible, hang it over parallel lines to support the weight.

Warmth without weight Use a woven blanket over a cellular one. It sandwiches the warm air in the open weave of the bottom blanket.

Storing sheets and blankets

● Avoid long-term storage of sheets and pillowcases in a heated airing cupboard – they will mark and discolour. Rotate a pile of bed linen by putting any newly laundered items at the bottom so the sheets that have been there longest are used first.

● Keep spare blankets to change with those in use – a couple of months' rest in a cool cupboard restores a blanket's condition.

● For long-term storage, seal newly washed and aired blankets in strong polythene bags or special 'blanket bags' available from most department stores. Put a moth-repellent sachet with wool or wool-content blankets that are not permanently mothproofed. Leave them in a cool, dry cupboard where they won't be crushed.

Electric blankets If you want to store an electric blanket folded up, take care – it can damage the heating element. It's better to leave the blanket on a spare bed or between a mattress and divan base, or hang it by the tapes in a cool, dry cupboard. Always follow the manufacturer's care and servicing instructions. For further tips on caring for electric blankets, see page 144.

IN THE BATHROOM

Baths and basins

Five minutes a day is all you need to restore order in a bathroom. Keep a cellulose bath-cleaning sponge and a bottle of washing-up liquid handy, and insist that everybody cleans the bath and basin as the water runs out. It makes thorough cleaning a lot easier than if soap splashes, stains and hard-water deposits are allowed to build up.

Grime and hard-water deposits Clean washbasins, bidets, baths and shower trays (except those made of glass fibre) with a cleaning product recommended for bath or general use, such as Izal Bath Cleaner or Ajax Cream Cleanser, on a bathroom sponge. Use a cellulose sponge on softer surfaces, such as acrylics, and a spray cleaner on glass fibre.

● If you can't shift stubborn tidemarks or hard-water film on vitreous-enamelled baths or porcelain, rub them with paraffin, turpentine or white spirit. Rinse off with a hot washing-up liquid solution and wipe dry.

● To remove lime scale from the spout of a tap, submerge it in a small container of white vinegar or lime-scale remover. An old yoghurt pot or a china egg cup can be supported on a towel draped around the tap. Specialist products are available, such as Oz Bathroom Cleaner &

Limescale Remover. Follow the instructions carefully and test on a small area first. Don't leave it any longer than recommended – it could eat away the surface, leaving it rough and open to staining.
● Shift soap scum and hard-water deposits round taps and waste outlets with an old toothbrush dipped in paraffin. Or use vinegar, but rinse it well after a moment or two or it could dull the glaze.

Glass-fibre baths and showers Use washing-up liquid or a general-purpose liquid cleaner. Even a mildly abrasive product can wear through the colour layer and leave a patchy surface.

Blockages and smells Use a bottle brush for cleaning the bath or washbasin overflow. Once a week, pour a small amount of thick liquid bleach down overflows and plugholes. Flush with water after 2-3 minutes.

Dripping taps Fix them (page 169). In a single day, a tap could waste enough water to fill a bath. If it has already left a grey mark that a cleaner won't budge, try paraffin, Jenolite Bath Stain Remover or Oz Bathroom Cleaner & Limescale Remover.

Damage from bath toys An acrylic bath is particularly vulnerable to damage from sharp articles. Light rubbing with a cream metal polish, such as Silvo, on a soft cloth may reduce surface scratches. For a deeper scratch, try gentle rubbing with a very fine grade of wet-and-dry abrasive paper, used wet. Don't change it as it wears smooth, but do keep it wet. Finish with metal polish to restore the sheen.

Dealing with mould If spots appear on the sealant, tackle them with neat domestic bleach on a toothbrush. Wear rubber gloves, protect your clothes and the floor, and remove any towels out of the range of splashing. Rinse thoroughly. Or use a fungicidal wash such as Dax Fungo or Rentokil Mould Cure.

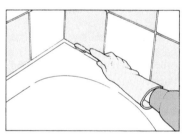

Slimy sponges Soak in 1 tablespoon of vinegar to 600ml (1 pint) water for an hour, and then wash thoroughly.

Keep plants out of the bath Don't leave your plants in the bath while you are away. Chemicals from the potting compost can cause stains.

Bathroom walls

To reduce steam Run cold water into the bath before turning on the hot tap. The reduced steam cuts down the chance of mould growth.

Clearing soap splashes on wall tiles Use a solution of 1 part white vinegar to 4 parts water. Rinse and wipe dry. A spray-and-wipe tile cleaner doesn't require rinsing and some types contain protection against mould growth, such as Rentokil's Ceramic Tile Cleaner.

Discoloured tile grout Clean with a weak solution of 1 part domestic bleach to 6 parts water on an old toothbrush, but be sure to cover the floor against splashes. Rinse well. Or use an aerosol that cleans both tile and grout, killing any mould growth, such as Mr Muscle Ceramic Tile Restorer, Rentokil Mould Cure or Dax Fungo.

A really white finish Paint over old tile grout with a thin coat of grout reviver, such as New Look White Grout Reviver or Polycell Versatile.

Shower cubicles

To keep free from mildew Wipe the shower-cubicle walls and curtain as you leave. It's the only way to keep the surfaces clean and free from mildew. Leave the curtains slightly open so air can circulate.

Hard-water film on tiles and glass panels Use neat vinegar. Give it ten minutes to dissolve the deposit before rinsing clear. Or try a spray-and-wipe tile cleaner, such as Bal Ceramic Tile Cleaner, available from tile retailers. Check that it's suited to your tiles.

Mildew-spotted curtains Soak resistant stains on plastic and polyester curtains in a solution of 1 part domestic bleach to 4 parts water. Rinse thoroughly or machine-wash where possible. Use a mould killer/inhibitor such as Cuprinol Interior Mould Killer to kill the spores and retard future growth.

Clogged shower head Unscrew it, take the pieces apart if necessary (don't lose the rubber washer) and soak them in a bowl of vinegar. Brush out any sediment or slime with an old toothbrush before reassembling.

Alternatively, use one of several proprietary shower cleaners available in hardware shops. Make up the solution in a plastic bowl and soak the shower head as instructed. Rinse thoroughly. If the problem recurs, consider installing the Hard Water Handset from the Mira Showers range. It fits most other models. Pressing the perforated plate after use pushes metal pins through the holes to clear any scale.

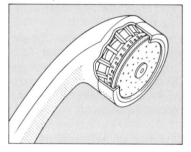

Mirrors

To remove hair spray from mirrors Wipe with a cloth moistened with neat methylated spirit.

To clean mirrors Spray window-cleaning liquid onto a dry surface; condensation stops it working so well. Or squeeze out a chamois leather in a solution of 1 tablespoon white vinegar or domestic borax to 2.3 litres (4 pints) of warm water. Don't let any liquid run between the glass and the backing or under the frame. It could cause spots on the silvered surface.

Bathroom safety tips

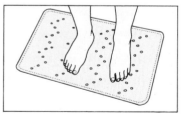

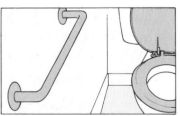

Non-slip surface Use rubber mats or self-adhesive strips to give a non-slip surface to the bottom of the bath and shower tray – essential for small children.

Wall-fixed grab rails Fit rails by the bath and shower, and maybe beside the toilet too, if there's an elderly or disabled person living in the house.

Wall-mounted bathroom cabinets Position cabinets away from basins and baths so there's no danger of dropping bottles or jars which could chip or crack them.

Ventilation Use bleach, strong-smelling cleaning products and house-hold chemicals in well-ventilated bathrooms only.

Don't mix products Never mix bleach with lavatory cleaners, household chemicals or other cleaning products. The combination of the two can produce dangerous fumes.

Storing bathroom cleaning materials Find a safe, secure place for cleaning products, out of reach of children. Bleach and disinfectant are common causes of poisoning: to a child, they look like a drink.

Door locks A locked door can be a problem if there is an accident in the bathroom. Fit the type of lock that can be released from the outside in an emergency. It will also make it easier to rescue a child that has locked itself in by mistake.

IN THE TOILET

'**Flush, brush, flush**' A daily routine is the best. It keeps the lavatory pan clean and hygienic and prevents the build-up of unsightly staining.

To remove discoloration Use a lavatory cleaner once or twice a week to leave the surface germ free. Some products, including Harpic Powder, contain a scale remover which prevents a build-up of hard-water deposit. Directable squeeze packs are good for spraying under the rim of the bowl – an area that's frequently missed in a quick clean, and is a breeding ground for germs.

Liquid bleach As long as the surface glaze is in good condition, bleach can be used to clean and disinfect a heavily stained white or coloured lavatory. Choose the thick variety, such as Domestos or Vortex, which sticks to the sloping sides. Chlorine bleaches kill germs within minutes and require only one hour for maximum effect. Repeat the treatment if necessary.

Frequent contact with neat bleach can cause the lavatory brush to disintegrate. Be sure to rinse it thoroughly after use.

CAUTION Never mix bleach with a lavatory cleaner: the acidity of the cleaner releases poisonous chlorine gas.

Lavatory bowls It may be worth your while to consider replacing a lavatory bowl that has a cracked or crazed surface. It's unsightly, difficult to clean and likely to harbour germs and smells.

To empty the pan to treat difficult staining, tie a cloth firmly over the head of a lavatory brush and use it to push the water over the trap. You may need to bale out the last bit.

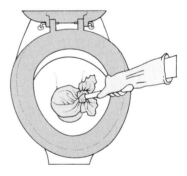

Hard-water deposits inside the bowl To clear, bale out some water and spread a paste of domestic borax and white vinegar over the deposit. Leave for two hours before brushing off the residue. A stubborn ring may need treating several times with a lime-scale remover, such as Harpic Limescale Remover or Mangers Stainex.

Antiseptic wipes A product such as Ibcol Anti-bacterial Wipes is ideal for the daily care of the lavatory seat and bowl rim and can be flushed away afterwards. Alternatively, use a spray cleaner with anti-bacterial properties, such as Dettox, with a quick-drying cloth reserved for the purpose, such as a J Cloth.

IN THE KITCHEN

Caring for plastic laminate worktops

Resistance to heat A tough laminate worktop such as Formica or Perstorp Warerite resists boiling water and fat splashes, but doesn't react well to intense heat. Be sure to put hot dishes on heat-resistant mats or pan stands.

Cleaning textured-finish laminates Never scrape the surface. A spray cleaner or general-purpose liquid cleaner copes with regular care. After rolling pastry, clean the work surface with hot soapy water and a nylon filament brush, brushing with a circular motion.

Avoiding stains Silver-plating liquid or strong dyes can permanently discolour laminate worktops. So can printer's ink on newspapers, packets and bags left on a damp surface.

Treating stains Wipe up and rinse off beetroot, blackcurrant, concentrated fruit juice and food colouring spills without delay. Rub with bicarbonate of soda or a cream cleaner on a damp cloth to clear dried stains. If the stains persist, trickle lemon juice onto the area and leave for half an hour before trying again with bicarbonate of soda or a cleaner on a cloth.

Superficial burns Rub cigarette burns with methylated spirit on a cloth. If that doesn't work, use a car-cleaning compound on a cloth held over one finger, rubbing with a circular motion.

Cleaning Corian worktops

Regular cleaning Man-made Corian looks like marble but has a smooth, non-porous surface. It's a practical and hygienic choice for fitted kitchen and bathroom tops, as it cleans with a wipe, a hot soapy rinse or the occasional use of a cream cleaner.

To remove cuts and scratches Don't chop or cut on Corian. It dulls the blades and scores the Corian. Use an abrasive cleaner, such as Ajax powder on a Scotchbrite pad, on cuts and scratches and sandpaper for deeper damage – both colour and pattern go right through.

Avoid strong heat and chemicals Very hot pans, lighted cigarettes or corrosive household chemicals such as paint strippers will damage Corian. Professional repolishing may be the only way to restore a seriously damaged surface.

Treating kitchen tiles

Specially made kitchen tiles are safe in contact with food and have high resistance to chemicals, staining and scratching. Tiles with a duller surface won't show scratches as much as glossy ones. Provided the tiles are grouted with waterproof grout and set as a level surface, they should be easy to clean with any non-abrasive kitchen cleaner on a damp cloth. Use a gentle scouring pad to remove any stubborn marks.

HOW TO GET RID OF BARBECUE STAINS

Ugly stains on the patio from last summer's barbecues? Special concrete cleaners, available from motor accessory shops, may help to shift the marks. Cover new fat splashes with cat litter, ground to a powder with your heel. Just sweep up the litter once it has absorbed the grease.

Keeping wooden work surfaces in good condition

Solid wooden worktops These need regular cleaning with a damp cloth. Wipe food preparation areas every two to three days with a light-duty antibacterial cleaner such as Dettox.

If wooden worktops look dull Use a nylon scouring pad dipped in Junckers Rustic Oil or Danish oil to wipe over the surface. Work in the direction of the grain and remove the excess with a paper towel.

Stains Rubbing in the direction of the grain with a nylon scouring pad dipped in hot water clears most stains.

Heat marks Careful sanding will clear a mark left by a hot pan or knife. Dust off and re-oil the area with sparing applications until it matches the rest of the top.

Chopping board hygiene

Keep all chopping boards scrupulously clean and free from smells and stains by washing them as soon as possible after use. Dry them naturally, standing on the long edge, and then store with the surfaces not touching. Chopping boards should not be dried flat. The underside stays damp – which can cause warping – and in warm, moist conditions bacteria multiply fast.

Wooden boards
● Natural beech or hevea wood – a tropical hardwood similar to beech from Malaysia – are good woods to choose as they have a close grain and the hard surface isn't easily scored.
● Clean a wooden board under a hot running tap, scrubbing if necessary. Use a paper towel to wipe the surface over with a sterilising solution, such as Milton 2 or Dettox (used neat), before leaving the board to dry.
● Rub wooden boards with a cut lemon dipped in a saucer of salt to clear lingering food smells and surface staining.

TO CLOSE THE JOINTS ON A WOODEN BOARD

You should never soak a wooden chopping board as it may warp and crack as it dries out. If the joints do open up on a wooden board, lay it flat and cover it with a damp cloth for several hours. This will swell the wood, helping to close the gaps.

To restore the board to its original appearance, wipe it over with a few drops of vegetable oil.

Plastic boards
● Remove the smell left by fish and onions by rubbing the surface with a cut lemon. It also helps to remove light stains.
● Most plastic chopping boards are dishwasher-proof. Use the top basket of the machine, as proximity to the heating element at the base could cause the board to buckle.

● Choose a polyethylene chopping board in preference to a polypropylene one. Both are kind to knives but polyethylene is more resistant to staining and less likely to become distorted.

How to keep sinks spotless

Using a washing-up bowl Damage from vegetable grit and wire wool embedded in the base of a plastic washing-up bowl can invalidate the sink manufacturer's guarantee. If you like using one, check if a plastic basket is made for the sink which you can rest the bowl on, or buy a sink mat that lets the water run through.

Avoid staining and other damage Prolonged contact with salt and acidic and highly coloured foods, such as salad dressing, curry sauce, beetroot, dark fruit juices and tea, will stain some sinks. Home dyes, photographic developing liquids and household chemicals are also risky. Cellulose thinners will damage an acrylic sink.

Hard-water deposits Wash the sink out daily with hot, soapy water and rinse and dry it. Clear any deposits by rubbing with vinegar or a cream or paste cleaner, such as Jif, Shiny Sinks or Astonish, on a sponge scourer. Don't use a harsh abrasive. It could dull and roughen the surface of the sink, which could then discolour.

Stainless-steel sinks
● Get rid of rust spots left by fragments of steel wool by using neat washing-up liquid or a cream cleaner on a nylon scouring pad.
● Give a stainless-steel sink extra sparkle by cleaning and polishing it with a paste made of bicarbonate of soda and water.
● Don't use silver-dip cutlery cleaner on draining boards. Splashes leave a rainbow effect on stainless steel that turns to permanent dark marking.
● Don't use bleach on stainless steel as it could cause pitting.

Acrylic sinks An acrylic surface may need soaking for about half an hour with bleach solution or white spirit to clear any rust marks.
● If aluminium pans leave silver lines on a dark-coloured acrylic sink, use a metal polish to clear them.
● Take care with hot pans. High temperatures can leave a shiny mark on a matt-finish acrylic, and hot, heavy cookware may distort it.
● Remove discoloration by filling the bowl with a weak solution of bleach – two egg cups of bleach to a sinkful of water. Leave for five minutes and then turn the plug upside-down in the plughole – that way, the solution runs out slowly, cleaning the overflow, sink and drain.

Vitreous-enamel sinks
● Don't put hot pans on a vitreous-enamel sink. The heat can fracture it.
● Remove discoloration with a weak solution of bleach, in the same way as for an acrylic sink.

Tips for more efficient washing-up

Crockery and serving dishes
● Rinse all food off plates before they are washed by hand or in the dishwasher. Use cold water for milk, egg and starch-based foods – mashed potato, for example – warm water for other types. You can loosen dried-on egg with a damp cloth dipped in salt.
● Add 1 heaped teaspoon of washing soda to the water to remove grease from crockery and pans. Rinsing in hot water will also help, but you must wear rubber gloves.

● Remove the smell of fish from plates by adding a tablespoon of vinegar to the washing water. Remove any lingering fish smells from cutlery by rubbing it with fresh lemon rind, and then dry immediately with a clean tea towel before it tarnishes.

● Don't wash a wooden salad bowl. Wipe it out with kitchen towel and then a cloth wrung out in hot water. Finish by rubbing in a few drops of oil.

Washing and storing cutlery

Wash, rinse and dry cutlery as soon as possible after use. The natural process of tarnishing is accelerated when foods with a high sulphide content, which include eggs, fish and green vegetables, are left sticking to silver and bronze items, and prolonged contact with salt and acidic foods stains all types of cutlery. Rinse the pieces immediately after the meal if washing will be delayed.

Using the dishwasher Only dishwasher-proof cutlery should be machine-washed. Remove and dry it as soon as the cycle ends. In warm, moist conditions, knife blades in particular are prone to white staining and they may soon become pitted by hard-water salts and undissolved powder detergents.

Detarnishing solutions A liquid silver cleaner is a quick way to clean lightly tarnished sterling silver and silver-plated cutlery (EPNS). Don't let it trickle onto 'stainless' knife blades or a stainless-steel sink. If it does, rinse it off immediately to prevent permanent marks.

Cleaning tissues Wipe rarely used silver or silver-plated cutlery with cleaning tissues that contain an antitarnish agent, such as Town Talk Silver Sparkle. The protective coating will survive more than one wash if you dry the pieces carefully.

Bronze cutlery Increase the stain resistance of bronze cutlery by sponging with a foaming silver polish containing a tarnish inhibitor, available in hardware stores. Low-quality bronze develops fingermarks badly after being touched and is quickly stained by acidic foods.

Storing cutlery Store less frequently used place settings in a pocketed Tarnprufe roll or a cutlery canteen.

A LARGE BATCH OF SILVER CUTLERY

Do you have silver-plated forks and spoons that need to be cleaned? Put a wide strip of aluminium foil in a plastic bowl, lay the cutlery on top so it's touching the foil, add a handful of washing soda and cover the lot with hot water until clean. An electrochemical reaction detarnishes the metal. Rinse, dry and polish the pieces.

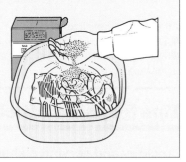

To restore stained pots and pans

● Clean a neglected roasting tin (but not an aluminium or non-stick one) by boiling it in a solution of washing soda and water. Rinse and dry in a cool oven where possible.

● To restore a burnt pan to its former glory, try one of the following: soak it overnight in a strong biological washing powder solution; boil up sliced onions in the pan and leave the solution for several hours; cover the burnt area with water, add a generous amount of salt or vinegar, bring to the boil and leave to soak overnight.

● Clear food stains from enamel pans by covering with a solution of 1 teaspoon bleach to 570ml (1 pint) of water. Leave for a maximum of two hours before washing and rinsing thoroughly.

● Clean a discoloured aluminium pan by boiling a weak solution of food acid in it – rhubarb, tomatoes or lemon peel, for example.

● Non-stick pans with food stains can be cleaned by boiling up a solution of water, $\frac{1}{2}$ cup bleach and 2 tablespoons of bicarbonate of soda for five minutes. Then wash, rinse and dry, and rub the surface with a little cooking oil on a paper towel.

Lead crystal and glass

Cleaning crystal The action of a dishwasher and detergent will etch and dull the surface of lead crystal. Hand-wash pieces singly in a warm solution of washing-up liquid, rinse in a bowl of water, and dry while warm.

Dry glasses by rotating them in a dry tea towel – a damp cloth drags a cold surface and could pull out a piece of the rim. Hold stemmed glasses firmly by the bowl as the stem is easily twisted off. And remember to remove diamond rings during washing: they could scratch the glass.

Chipped rims Provided the chip is shallow, and the glass is valuable enough to merit professional repair, have the rim ground down. But it will be shorter than the rest of the set.

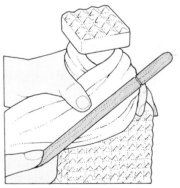

If two glasses are stuck together Fill the inner glass with iced water and repeatedly dip the outer glass in a bowl of warm water. Gradually increase the temperature of the warm water until the outer glass has expanded sufficiently for the two glasses to part.

If the stopper is stuck in a decanter Wrap the neck of the decanter in a fairly hot, damp towel, and use the handle of a wooden spoon to gently tap opposite sides of the stopper. Or pour two or three drops of cooking oil around the decanter's rim and leave in a warm place.

To remove stains in the base of a decanter Half-fill the decanter with warm soapy water and add 2 tablespoons of rice. Swirl the mixture round several times over 30 minutes, and then pour it out, rinse thoroughly and stand upside-down to drain dry.

To remove the remains of sticky labels Rub with a cloth dipped in methylated spirit. Or sprinkle on talc and rub with your finger.

Freshen a vacuum flask

Clear smells from a vacuum flask by filling it with 1 tablespoon bicarbonate of soda and hot water. Replace the stopper and leave for 20 minutes before rinsing and draining dry. Put in a couple of sugar lumps to keep it fresh and store it with the stopper tilted to allow air circulation.

Never submerge flasks in water. They never work as well again.

Keeping your cooker clean

● Before cleaning an electric cooker, hob or oven, switch off at the control panel on the wall.

● Always follow the manufacturer's care and cleaning instructions.

Cooker hob surround

Clean fat splashes from a vitreous-enamel hob surround with a cloth wrung out in hot water with a few drops of ammonia added. Wipe it regularly as a sticky hob collects other grime.

Ceramic glass hobs

Avoid scratching the surface There's no remedy for scratches. Always use saucepans with a smooth base, and before use wipe the base and hob with a clean dry cloth to remove any dust and grit. Don't slide saucepans across the hob's surface during cooking.

More than just a wipe Cleaning a ceramic hob with a dishcloth, which carries food particles and leaves a film of dirty detergent water, is not a good idea. The hob will discolour the next time it is turned on. Use the manufacturer's recommended cleaner-conditioner (preferably daily), applied on a paper kitchen towel. Rinse off the residue and dry thoroughly with a fresh towel.

Hot or cold cleaning? Wipe up fruit juice, sugar, sugar-based and acidic food spillage – jam or marmalade, for example – immediately. As sugar crystallises on a cooling ceramic hob it pits the surface, and acids can etch the glass. Turn off the heat, remove the pan and wipe the hob lightly with a clean, damp, detergent-free cloth. For all other spills, wait until the hob has cooled off.

Burnt-on spills Wait until the hob has cooled before gently prising spills off with a razor blade in a safety holder. Follow with an application of a recommended cleaner-conditioner.

Sealed (solid) hotplates

Heavily soiled hotplates Use a cream cleaner on a scouring pad if soiling doesn't come off with a damp cloth. Wipe off the residue with a clean cloth.

Avoid rust Sealed cast-iron hotplates won't rust if they are switched on briefly after cleaning, and wiped regularly with a drop or two of vegetable oil on a paper towel. Or just brush the carbonised residue off the cooled surface with a dry washing-up brush. An impregnated hotplate cleaning pad, such as Collo Electrol, gives sealed hotplates a black finish and some protection against rust.

Radiant rings

Radiant cooker rings require little cleaning. Deal with serious spillages by turning off the cooker, lifting up the hinged ring or hob top and clearing the spill from the dish or spillage tray beneath with a damp cloth. Wipe as much as possible from the ring itself; any that is left will burn off the next time you use it.

Gas burners

Deal with liquids that boil over before they burn on. Remove the pan support and burner cap for treatment with a cream cleaner or impregnated soap pad. They can go in the dishwasher, but take them out before the drying cycle and wipe off any remaining deposit: heat hardens it. Replace the parts and ignite the burner briefly to prevent rusting.

Ovens

Minimise oven soiling
● Don't use a roasting tin that's larger than necessary; fat splashes if there is too much space around the joint. Try using lower temperatures for roasting, and cover any roasting tins with foil to keep the fat in.

● Stand fruit pies and other dishes that are likely to boil over on a baking tray.

● Keep a spillage (or baking) tray permanently at the bottom of the oven to catch any drips.

● Before you cover the bottom of your oven with a spillage tray, check that it doesn't have any bottom heating elements. Covering the elements might restrict the airflow around the oven, altering temperatures and possibly harming the cooker.
● Wipe vitreous-enamel oven surfaces and glass doors while still warm with a cloth wrung out in hot water. It removes any soiling before it has a chance to burn on.

Stay-clean (catalytic) oven liners
● If you have an oven with a self-cleaning liner that isn't working as well as it should, cook at a higher temperature from time to time or set the oven at 240°C, Gas Mark 9 for an hour. Although fat splashes are continuously absorbed by the liner even on a low heat, they are only vaporised at medium and high temperatures, so you may need to heat the oven to high to keep it really clean.
● Don't wipe these surfaces or use any other cleaning methods unless the cooking instructions advise it.

For a thorough clean Use an oven cleaner approved by the Vitreous Enamel Development Council (VEDC). If your oven has stay-clean oven liners, make sure the oven cleaner doesn't come in contact with them and avoid using aerosols. Most products contain sodium hydroxide (caustic soda) – a corrosive chemical – so wear protective gloves and goggles, work with the window open, and cover nose and mouth if using an aerosol. Follow the instructions very carefully. Heavy deposits will require an impregnated soap pad.

To clean oven shelves Put them in the dishwasher, removing the top basket where necessary. Make sure the spray arm rotates freely. Take the shelves out after the final rinse – it's easier to wipe off any remaining deposit while it's still moist.

Alternatively, soak them in a hand-hot solution of biological washing powder or mild bleach to loosen soiling – but don't use bleach in a stainless-steel sink. If you have to resort to an oven cleaner, check that it's safe for use on chromed surfaces. Oven-cleaning pads or paste cleaners are easier to use on shelf bars.

Ovens with pyrolytic cleaning This special high-temperature programme automatically locks the oven door and reduces dirt to ash.

A CLEANING SHORT CUT

Use a cloth to smear a thin paste of bicarbonate of soda and water on the oven floor and other non-catalytic panels. It dries as a protective coat that absorbs greasy soiling during cooking and is easily wiped off a cooling oven when you next clean it. It may look messy, but you'll find that it's very effective.

Microwave cookers

Always switch off Unplug a microwave cooker from the electric socket before cleaning.

Maintain cooker efficiency Wipe the oven after use with a cloth wrung out in hot water. Avoid abrasive cleaners or scouring pads. Loosen stubborn soiling with steam by heating a bowl of water to boiling point on the cooker's highest setting.

Microwaving fatty foods Avoid spattering by covering the food with a paper towel, or use roasting bags for joints and poultry. Tie with string or plastic ties – metal could cause electric arcing – and pierce the bags so steam can escape.

To clear lingering smells Disconnect the microwave and leave the door open for a while. Or add a few drops of lemon juice to a basin of hot water and bring it to the boil. The steam should deodorise the interior.

Combination ovens

Wipe regularly A combination oven is more difficult to clean than a microwave because it has convected heat, and the cavity, being smaller than a conventional oven, tends to bake on the dirt. Make cleaning easier by wiping the oven with a soft, soapy cloth after each use.

A thorough cleaning Use a general-purpose liquid cleaner. Abrasives, such as powder cleaners or steel wool, could damage the metal lining.
● If you use a spray cleaner, don't spray directly onto the oven sides: it could penetrate the holes in the panels.
● Apply all cleaners on a cloth or sponge, not directly onto the surface.
● Soften baked-on fat after roasting by microwaving a large bowl of water on the high setting until boiling, then wipe off deposits.

Household pests

KEEPING PESTS AT BAY

To deprive pests of their warmth, food and shelter:
● Vacuum and clean rooms regularly, and move the furniture around.
● Remove food crumbs and loose fabric fluff as they appear and keep surfaces clean.
● Keep food in sealed containers.
● Dispose of waste and rubbish quickly and keep bins shut tight both inside and outside the house.
● Cover food and wipe away any honey, jam or preserves on the outside of jars.
● Plug gaps in doors, windows, or anywhere that pests can crawl in, and fit fly screens to open windows.
● Inspect cupboards and loft spaces regularly for nests or infestations.

Tackling your pest problem

If you have a pest problem, you can either contact the local authority pest control service, call in a pest control firm or deal with them yourself.

Local authority pest control

Contact the environmental health officer at your local council offices. The services offered vary from area to area but are likely to include:
● Control of rats and mice free of charge.
● Control of pests which are a public health hazard, such as lice, bedbugs or cockroaches, probably free of charge.
● Control of other insect pests (such as fleas and wasps) although there may be a charge.
● Free pest control for pensioners and DSS claimants.

Commercial pest control firms

Look under 'Pest and vermin control' in the Yellow Pages or a local Thompson directory. The British Pest Control Association, 3 St James Court, Friar Gate, Derby DE1 1ZU, tel. 0332 294288, will supply names of member companies who conform to a code of practice.
● Commercial companies generally offer a wider range of pest control than the local authority.
● They may treat pest problems faster than the local authority, but are likely to charge more.
● Phone around several firms for estimates before choosing.

BATS IN YOUR HOME?

Bats are harmless creatures, and they are also protected by law. If you discover bats living in your loft or roof space, and you don't like the idea, call the Nature Conservancy Council, Northminster House, Peterborough, PE1 1VA, tel. 0733 340345, who will help you deal with them.

If a bat gets into one of your rooms and you want to move it yourself, make sure that you wear a pair of heavy gloves – a frightened bat can give you a nasty nip. Lift it up gently and leave it on a wall or tree in the garden or somewhere outside the house.

ACTION CHART FOR COMMON PESTS

PEST	COMMENT	ACTION
Garden ants	Generally harmless. Attracted to sweet foods.	Locate the ants' nest and use an ant powder or spray, or an ant bait usually available as a clear jelly. Use ant pens (Vapona) to draw barrier lines around the house, or an insecticidal lacquer along skirtings and thresholds. Pouring boiling water onto the nest is a temporary measure only. It won't kill the queen ant – but it will ruin a patch of your lawn.
Pharaoh's ants	Small yellow tropical species. Nest in the building structure. Can spread disease to food.	Call in a specialist pest control company who will place baits containing methoprene or boric acid, backed up by insecticidal powder.
Bedbugs	Live in crevices, loose wallpaper and bed frames. Emerge at night to feed on human blood.	Contact local authority pest control office.
Bee swarms	Not harmful unless provoked. Some bumble bees are endangered species.	Do not attempt to remove bees yourself. Most beekeepers will collect accessible swarms as a free service – there will be a list of local keepers with the police, in the library and with the local authority.
Booklice	Feed on microscopic moulds found on the glue of book bindings, damp surfaces and food. Rapid running movements.	Ventilate and dry infested areas. Discard affected foods. Treat area with insecticide for 'Psocids' (collective name for booklice).
Carpet beetles	Mottled ladybird-like textile pests. Larvae, known as woolly bears, eat wool and damage natural fibres, leaving holes similar to moth damage.	Check loft and eaves for old birds' nests and remove. Vacuum all fluff from airing cupboards and carpets. Spray mothproofer or carpet beetle killer between floorboards, under carpets and into crevices. Clean affected blankets and clothes.

PEST	COMMENT	ACTION
Clothes moths	Adult moths don't do any damage. Larvae eat blankets, wool carpets and clothes. Some species also feed on food debris and corks. Larvae are white with brown heads.	Clean woollens and store in sealed plastic bags. Spray fabrics and carpets with a mothproofer. Put a moth repellent in wardrobes and cupboards (modern versions smell quite pleasant).
Cockroaches	Live in moist, warm, dark areas. Eat any sort of food but tend to foul more than they actually eat. Can cause serious food poisoning.	Spray insecticide into infested areas if you can find the source. Poisoned baits can work if used persistently. Call in your environmental health officer or pest control company if cockroaches persist.
Fleas	Commonly caught from cats and birds; dog fleas are rarer. August and September are problem months. Larvae found in soft furnishings used by cats.	Search for and remove any birds' nests. Treat animals by careful spraying or dusting with a veterinary insecticide (page 417). Vacuum and clean throughout the house and spray with flea killer aerosol. Wash cats' bedding and dust with flea powder, repeating when necessary.
Flies	Carry and spread gastroenteric illness and food poisoning.	Use fly spray or impregnated strips giving off insecticide vapour to deter flies. Keep food covered and bins scrupulously clean. Spray dustbins after emptying to kill eggs and maggots. Fit fly screens over windows.
Flour beetles, flour moths or weevils	Feed on stored food, flour, cereals, chocolate, dried fruit and nuts.	Clear out infested food and take it back to the shop where you bought it. Clean and dry the area well. Apply an insecticide for 'stored-product insect control'. Store fresh supplies in closed plastic containers.

101

ACTION CHART FOR COMMON PESTS (cont)

PEST	COMMENT	ACTION
Mice and rats	Damage by gnawing. They spread disease and pollute food with droppings and urine.	Consult environmental health officer. Mouse-proof entry holes with wire wool in cement or metal strips. Bait traps with chocolate, nuts or raisins placed close to signs of activity. Lay ready-to-use baits of mousekiller.
Mosquitoes, gnats and midges	Females feed on blood, biting mostly at dusk. Eggs are laid in stagnant water.	Clean breeding sites such as guttering, bird baths and water butts. Screen open doors and windows. Use a repellent on skin. Burn mosquito coils.
Silverfish	Harmless. Feed on glue and starch in paper and bookbindings. Their presence may indicate damp.	Eliminate damp: check for leaky plumbing, condensation (page 191) and rising damp. Insecticides for crawling insects will kill them.
Wasps	Attracted to sweet food and drinks. At their worst in August and September. Die naturally by end of autumn.	Close or screen windows. Spray individual wasps with a proprietary wasp killer or fly killer aerosol. Trap with jars partly filled with water, jam and a drop of detergent, covered with a punctured paper lid. For underground wasp nests, Rentokil Wasp Nest Killer is available but contact your environmental health department or pest control company for advice.
Woodworm	The larvae of the common furniture beetle. They cause round holes, 2mm ($\frac{1}{16}$in) across, in the surface of wood. Will damage structural timbers and furniture.	For small attacks, brush surfaces with two generous coats of woodworm killer. On furniture, inject the fluid into some of the holes with an applicator. Leave large outbreaks to a pest control company.

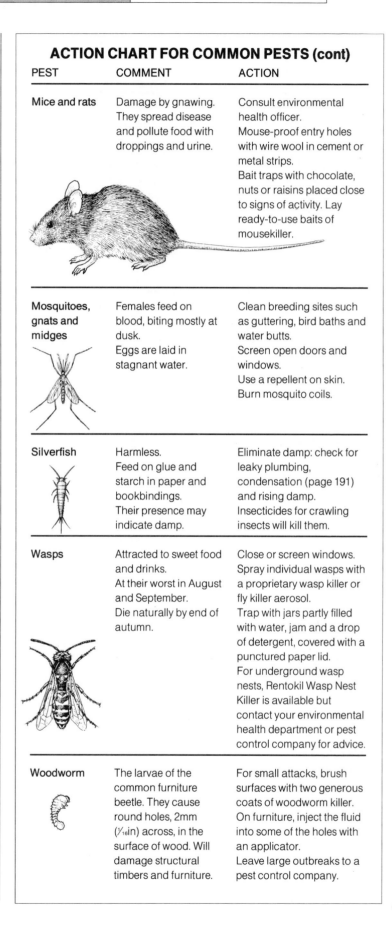

102

Secrets of cleaning clothes

NINE TIPS FOR EASY WASHING

● Wash fabrics before the dirt is ingrained.
● Act fast in dealing with stains; pretreat or soak stains before washing.
● Sort clothes carefully, according to their care labels.
● Load machine correctly. Mix large and small items. Don't overload.
● Use the right detergent (low suds for automatics) and measure it.
● Select the recommended wash code and machine programme given on the care label. It ensures the correct temperature and machine action.
● Rinse items thoroughly.
● Dry clothes at the proper setting.
● Hang clothes promptly after removing them from the dryer.

How to read care labels

When you buy new clothes and fabrics, look for the International Textile Care Label sewn into the seam. The symbols will give the best advice about washing, drying, ironing and care of the garment.

Before you buy, consider how practical the item will be to clean. If a light summer blouse is 'dry-clean only' it will spend more time at the cleaners than being worn. If the label says 'hand wash only' – and you know you will throw everything in the machine anyway – don't buy it.

DECIDING THE SETTING FOR YOUR WASH

The washtub symbol means an article can be washed safely. When a bar appears under the washtub, it indicates a reduced washing time and level of agitation for synthetics, or delicate wool and silk.

SYMBOL	WHAT IT MEANS	EXAMPLE
95	Temperature 95°C. Wash with the cotton programme. High temperature and maximum wash/spin ensure whiteness.	White cotton and linen without special finishes.
60	Temperature 60°C. Wash with cotton programme. Provides vigorous washing at a temperature which maintains fast colours.	Cotton, linen or viscose without special finishes where colours are fast at 60°C.
50	Temperature 50°C. Wash with the synthetics programme. Reduced machine action and lower temperature preserves the finish. Cold rinsing and short spinning minimise creases.	Polyester/cotton mixtures; nylon, polyester, cotton and viscose items with special finishes; cotton/acrylic.
40	Temperature 40°C. Wash with cotton programme. Cleans at low temperature to prevent colour run.	Cotton, linen or viscose where colours are fast at 40°C but not at 60°C.

103

DECIDING THE SETTING FOR YOUR WASH (cont)

SYMBOL	WHAT IT MEANS	EXAMPLE
	Temperature 40°C. Wash with the synthetics programme. Gentle wash and spin to preserve colour and shape, and minimise creasing.	Acrylics, acetates, including mixtures with wool, polyester/wool blends.
	Temperature 40°C. Wash with the wool programme. The reduced machine action preserves the colour, shape and size of machine-washable wool garments.	Wool, wool mixed with other fibres, and silk – but only if the label says 'machine wash'.
	Hand wash (DON'T machine wash).	Wool, silk, cashmere and delicate fabrics.
	Do not wash.	See dry-cleaning symbols (opposite).

BLEACHING, DRYING AND IRONING SYMBOLS

SYMBOL	WHAT IT MEANS	EXAMPLE
Bleaching	You can use chlorine bleach (household bleach).	White cotton.
	Don't use chlorine bleach (household bleach).	Coloureds.
Drying	May be tumble dried. Avoid overdrying and remove items promptly. (Where dots appear, 2 dots mean high setting, 1 dot means a low setting.)	Sheets and pillowcases, sweatshirts and tracksuits.
	Do not tumble dry.	Wool.
	Drip-drying is recommended, soaking wet.	Shirts with 'easy iron' finishes.
	Hang on a line after spin drying.	
	Dry flat.	Hand knits.
Ironing	If there is one dot in the iron symbol, the temperature should be cool.	Acrylic, nylon, polyester.
	Two dots means a warm iron.	Polyester mixtures, wool, silk.
	Three dots means hot.	Cotton, linen, viscose.
	Do not iron.	Some synthetics.

DRY-CLEANING SYMBOLS

SYMBOL	WHAT IT MEANS
◯	Dry-clean professionally, using any solvent.
Ⓟ	A circle containing a letter indicates to the dry-cleaner the type of solvent which can be used.
⊗	Do not dry-clean or press.

How to sort your washing

● Check the labels. The care symbols tell you whether an item can be machine washed and at what temperature. Make separate piles with the same symbols (see chart). Each pile can be washed using the most appropriate programme.

● Sort by colour: whites, pastels and white background prints that are colourfast should make one load and colourfast deep coloureds another load. 'Wash separately' on non-colourfast items means simply that.

● Sort items for hand washing, especially woollens.

Do's and don'ts for small batches

If there are not enough items to make up a full machine load of each type, you can mix loads with different care labels, but . . .

DO choose the programme to suit the most delicate item in the load – that is the lowest temperature shown and the gentle machine action if there is a bar under a washtub – as for synthetics, for example.

DO remember that white and fast colour fabrics need to be cleaned at the recommended higher temperature roughly every third wash, to keep their brightness.

DON'T risk mixing deep colours with light colours unless you are sure they are colourfast at the temperature you select.

DON'T mix white and coloured fabrics, especially synthetics like polyester/cotton – the result will be greying whites.

DON'T include clothes when it says 'wash separately'. The colour is likely to run and stain other clothes.

DON'T mix symbols with a broken bar with other symbols. The fabrics with a broken bar must only be washed in the minimum wool cycle.

Preparing your clothes

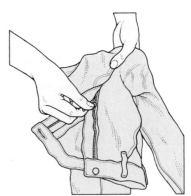

Checking each garment before putting it in the washing machine can save damage to the clothes – and to the machine from coins and other things in pockets.

● Secure zips and fastenings to prevent them snagging other fabrics. Tie any laces which may get tangled.

● Empty pockets of tissues, money and oddments. Putting a tissue through the wash can result in bits of paper on everything.

● Avoid putting in anything that is torn or frayed. Make minor repairs before washing.

● Remove things like belts or non-washable accessories.

● Brush off loose dirt, and separate any really dirty or stained garments for soaking or pretreating before they are washed. (See *Do's and don'ts of stain removal*, page 118.)

FIVE TIPS FOR EFFICIENT WASHING

● To prevent tights and stockings from tangling or snagging in the washing machine, put them in an old pillowcase or cushion cover. Small or delicate items can also be washed this way.

● Old nylon net curtains make good bags for keeping socks together or keeping fluff off dark items in the wash. Take a piece of curtain, about 1m (3ft) square. Double it over and sew across the bottom and up one side. Thread tape through the channel at the top to close the bag. Alternatively, your local market may have cheap, nylon mesh bags with zip fasteners.

● Avoid leaving damp items in a dirty-linen basket or in the machine for more than 24 hours or mildew spots may form. And mildew stains can be impossible to remove.

● Curtains and bedspreads that are dusty rather than stained will benefit from a 15-20 minute soak in cold water to loosen dirt – otherwise two washes will be needed.

● Clothes will stay looking good longer if you wash them frequently rather than letting dirt build up.

Getting the best results

● Mix large and small items in a wash load rather than, say, all the sheets together. They can move freely inside the machine and you will get a cleaner wash.

● Make sure the load is evenly distributed by alternately putting in a small item first, followed by a large one.

● Don't skimp on detergent – using less than recommended is a false economy that will leave you with dingy washing. If your machine has a mechanism to make more efficient use of the detergent, you can use less than it says on the pack. Check your machine instructions.

106

● Load the various items into the machine one at a time, rather than bundled up. They won't get so tangled.

● Before loading large things like sheets, pick them up by their middle, give them a shake, then fold them loosely. There will be less creasing and less chance of trapping other clothes in their bulk.

● Don't overload the machine. Check your instruction manual for what weight the manufacturers say is the maximum load – it will be smaller for synthetics than for cottons. You'll get a cleaner wash as a result.

● Before washing knitted fabric, jeans, corduroy or textured fabric, turn the garment inside-out.

● Also to prevent tangling, button shirt and blouse sleeves to the front buttons.

CHECKING YOUR WASH-LOAD WEIGHT

One way to find out how much your washing weighs is to use the bathroom scales: weigh yourself, pick up the washing basket and weigh yourself plus basket, then subtract your weight. Or put clothes in a carrier bag and weigh them with a spring balance. Or use the following guide:

ITEM	FABRIC	WEIGHT
Blouse	Cotton	150g (5oz)
	Mixture	100g (4oz)
Dress	Cotton	500g (1lb 2oz)
	Other	350g (12oz)
Jeans		700g (1lb 8oz)
Tee shirt		100g (4oz)
Shirt	Cotton	300g (11oz)
	Other	200g (7oz)
Duvet cover,	Polycotton	
double		1500g (3lb 5oz)
single		700g (1lb 8oz)
Pillowcase		150g (5oz)
Sheet, double		500-800g (1lb 2oz-1lb 12oz)
Sheet, single		450-700g (1lb-1lb 8oz)
Socks		50g (2oz)
Underwear		50g (2oz)
Bath towel		700g (1lb 8oz)
Tea towel		100g (4oz)

EIGHT WAYS TO CUT COSTS

● Use higher spin speeds to remove more water and reduce drying time. But synthetics only need a short spin – they could become permanently creased from a long powerful spin.

● Choose the correct setting on your tumble dryer. Long, hot cycles crease synthetic fabrics. Cool, short cycles mean little ironing is needed.

● Use cold water to rinse hand washing.

● Use the washing machine or tumble dryer during off peak Economy Seven electricity rate, if you have it.

● Dry washing on a line whenever possible, but preferably not in bright sunshine which can cause yellowing.

● Wash full loads rather than half loads. If you must wash a small load, use the half-load button if your machine has one.

● Make use of economy features on the machine, such as setting the temperature 10°C lower for each wash or selecting a quick wash for lightly soiled items. This uses less energy and water.

● Soaking heavily soiled clothes or pretreating stains before washing will ensure good results with low temperature, economy programmes.

THE RIGHT PRODUCTS FOR YOUR WASH

PRODUCT	PURPOSE	COMMENT
Detergent	There are two types of detergent: soap and synthetic. A detergent is simply something that cleans. It works by separating the dirt from the washing and holding it in the water.	Soap is less effective in hard water. It forms a scum that coats fabrics and the machine. Synthetic detergents are effective in hard and soft water.
Heavy duty detergent	Suitable for general laundry purposes.	Contains a mixture of ingredients to deal with heavy soiling and stains.
Light duty detergent	For care of delicate fabrics, hand washing and light soiling.	Simple ingredients and gentle action.
Powders	Heavy or light duty. Dispense in machine drawer or by dispensing ball placed directly in the drum.	Choose concentrated powders. You use less for each wash, they occupy less storage space and use less raw materials.
Liquids	Heavy or light duty. Dispense in machine drawer or by dispensing ball placed directly in the washing machine drum.	Easier for hand washing and soaking than powders; can be used to pretreat dirt and stains.
Biological	Liquids or powders containing enzymes which help loosen stains like blood, egg and perspiration.	Clean best at lower temperatures, therefore need less energy per wash compared with non-biological products. Good for soaking.

THE RIGHT PRODUCTS FOR YOUR WASH (cont)

PRODUCT	PURPOSE	COMMENT
Non-biological	Liquid or powder. Does not contain enzymes to which a small proportion of people are sensitive.	Less effective at removing some kinds of stains.
Automatic/low lather	For any washing machine, but especially front loading automatics. Hand washing.	Contain ingredients to prevent excessive foaming in the machine. High lather detergents must not be used in front loading and some types of top loading automatic washing machines.
Fabric conditioners	Reduce static cling, discourage dirt from settling and reduce creasing, therefore ironing time.	Liquid comes in concentrated and regular forms, or you can get impregnated sheets for using in tumble dryers. Choose concentrated and use sparingly.
Bleaches	Chlorine (household) bleach is used on stains. Oxygen bleach is used for whitening and stain removal.	Heavy duty powder detergents contain oxygen bleach, therefore separate bleaching is normally unnecessary.
Water softeners	For reducing water hardness and improving detergent performance.	Heavy duty detergents already contain water softeners. It's better to use the correct amount of detergent (see advice on pack) than to replace some of it with a separate water softener.

The 'green' way of washing

All manufactured products have some impact on the environment, but there are ways of minimising the damage.
● Use refill packs to reuse bottles of fabric conditioner.

● Use detergents more efficiently by filling a dispensing ball and placing it directly in the washing machine drum. None of the detergent is wasted. You should be able to use a little less detergent but still get a clean wash.

In a washer dryer, don't forget to remove the dispensing ball before drying the clothes. The plastic ball could melt in the heat.

● It's not so much what you use but how much of it you use. Don't just guess the amount of detergent; you may use more than necessary. Read the packet to see how much is recommended, and don't use any more.

● Choose concentrated products rather than regular. They use less resources in manufacture and distribution, and last longer.

● Try using one of the detergents formulated for the environment. To do this you need to check the information on the label (see below).

Understanding what's on the packet

'Green' washing products usually do not contain phosphates, optical brighteners or perfume.

Surfactants (another word for detergents) Remove dirt and grime from fabrics. The choice is between vegetable-based detergents or those made from petroleum sources. Vegetable detergents may break down faster or more completely than petroleum ones.

Biodegradable Means that when you rinse them away, the detergent materials break down naturally into harmless materials.

Phosphates Soften the water to improve cleaning. Phosphates are plant nutrients and if they build up in rivers and lakes, microscopic plants such as algae can use up all the oxygen in the water, overwhelming other life.

Perborate bleach Helps remove food dyes like coffee and wine. Perborate leaves boron in the environment, which can harm plants. Choose sodium percarbonate bleach which isn't harmful to the environment.

Perfume and colours Cosmetic only, with no cleaning function. They don't break down easily, can pollute rivers and affect fish.

Optical brightener Makes fabrics appear brighter and whiter (an optical illusion). Also known as fluorescers. Slow to break down.

Biological Contains enzymes to loosen stains. They clean at low temperatures so use less energy, but can cause skin reactions.

Animal testing The white rabbit 'cruelty free' symbol means the product is approved by the British Union for the Abolition of Vivisection. The product won't have been tested on animals within the last five years.

How much should you use?

For economy and efficiency, measure the amount of detergent recommended on the pack or in the instructions for your machine. Using the correct amount of washing product will help to keep the machine running, prevent scale building up and keep clothes in good condition. The right amount can vary according to:

● Load size.
● Hardness of water.
● Amount of water used.
● Amount and type of soiling.

More for: larger loads, heavy dirt and stains, harder water.
Less for: soft water, small loads or when clothes are not very dirty.

Fault-finder guide: washing

Problem	Possible causes	Action/Prevention
Whites turn grey or coloured	● Not enough detergent to deal with hard water, soiling and load size. Plus low water temperature. ● Colour run due to incorrect sorting.	● Rewash. Use half to one cup of detergent more than usual. Measure detergent into a dispensing device and put it in with the washing. ● Rewash in hottest water safe for fabric. You may need to soak whites in a colour run remover, such as Stain Devils Colour Run Remover or Dylon Run Away. ● In future, test for colour fastness and never mix white and coloured items.
Yellowing	● Using chlorine bleach on silk, wool and synthetics. ● Sun on washed items leaves yellow patches when pegged out on the line.	● Cannot be rectified. Avoid using bleach. ● Rewash the item with detergent containing oxygen bleach. ● Dry white items inside out and away from direct sunlight.
Poor dirt removal or black/brown spots appear	● Insufficient detergent. ● Grease spots from high level of soiling on garments. ● Machine overloaded.	● Rewash, increasing detergent and in the hottest water safe for fabric. ● Wash fewer items at one time. Use higher water level by avoiding 'half-load' programme.
Hard towels, stiff, harsh fabrics	● Insufficient amount of detergent in hard water allows mineral deposits to build up. ● Drying over radiators or heat source.	● Remove residues by soaking items in a solution of water softener (follow pack instructions), followed by rinsing. In future, increase the amount of detergent. Try using a liquid detergent and a fabric softener. ● Allow natural air movement or tumble dry.
White streaks or powdery residue, particularly dark fabrics	● Deposits of minerals from hard water.	● Soak items in a solution of water softener (follow pack instructions), followed by rinsing. In future, increase detergent. Try a liquid detergent and fabric softener.

111

Fault-finder guide: washing (cont)

Problem	Possible causes	Action/Prevention
Holes, tears, snags	● Chemical attack, e.g. chlorine bleach.	● Irreversible.
	● Physical damage, e.g. from unfastened zips, hooks.	● Prepare items before washing.
	● Overloading the machine.	● Wash fewer items.
	● Rust or blood stains left on fabric which can cause rotting.	● Treat rust and blood stains immediately.
	● Rotting effects of light or age and heat on fibres.	● Hand wash or dry-clean antique fabrics or curtains exposed to these conditions over a long period.
Fluff	● Incorrect sorting: washing lint-producers (sweaters, towels) with lint-receivers (synthetics, corduroys, velours and dark colours).	● Pat items with sticky tape wound round your hand.
	● Tissues in pockets.	● In future, sort items carefully.
	● Clogged filter.	● Clean washer filters by running the machine empty (quick cycle or half-load).
Creasing and wrinkling	● Incorrect cycle.	● Check the care label. Reduce temperature or choose a slower or shorter spin cycle.
	● Overdrying.	● Reduce drying cycle to cooler/shorter and remove items as soon as the dryer has stopped.
	● Overloaded washer or dryer.	● Allow free movement inside machine by washing fewer items.
Small bobbles on surface	● Abrasion from normal wear.	● Remove by gently picking off or use a fluff-removing gadget. Wash items inside-out and use a fabric conditioner.
Shrinking or felted wool	● Unsuitable for machine washing.	● Irreversible.
	● Spinning or agitation too vigorous, causing physical change in wool structure.	● Always check the care label instructions.
Shrinking or stretching of synthetics	● Temperature too high for washing or drying.	● Irreversible.
	● Spinning or machine action too vigorous.	● In future, follow care label instructions.

Washing delicate and stretchable garments by hand

If the care label on a garment says 'Hand wash', don't risk putting it in a washing machine. The general rule is that silk, wool and hand-knitted garments need to be washed by hand.

1 Dissolve detergent thoroughly in warm water before adding clothes (unless the care label says to use cold water). Wear rubber gloves to protect your hands.

2 Squeeze the water gently through the fabric. Do not rub, twist or wring, especially woollens.

3 Make sure delicate items are well supported to avoid stretching. Do not lift or allow the weight of the water to drag the garment.

4 Rinse thoroughly – two or three rinses until the water runs clear.

Drying hand-washed clothes

1 Wrap the garments in towels to remove most of the water. When the towel feels wet, unroll and finish drying flat. Or give the clothes a short, gentle spin in the machine.

2 When spinning jumpers, protect them by putting them inside a pillowcase.

3 Woollen jumpers need to be laid flat to dry. Ease them back into shape by hand patting while damp.

4 Leave to dry naturally – never use heat or sunlight.

TIPS FOR HAND WASHING

● Speed up flat drying by buying a flat-drying screen designed to fit over the bathtub.

● To avoid shrinking wool or wool mixture knitwear, treat gently and don't machine wash woollens unless the label says so. In this case, the wool fibres will have been specially adapted.

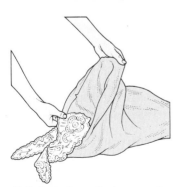

● Delicate items like lace can be hand washed inside a pillowcase to protect them. Lift and turn the whole pillowcase in warm soap suds and rinse in the same way.

● If you find that you've got too many soap suds when doing a batch of hand washing, you can get rid of them by sprinkling a little talcum powder over them.

WHAT TO DRY-CLEAN – AND WHY

● Tailored and wool suits. They crease or wrinkle as water swells the wool fibres at a different rate to the lining material.
● Any other items made with two or more fabrics – for example linings, trimmings or decoration.
● Jersey wool. The knitted fabric is likely to shrink in water but is safe to dry-clean.
● Deep-dyed or hand-painted silk, which may lose its colour or pattern during washing.
● Surface patterns and effects on fabrics such as taffeta, velvet, brocade or leather are best preserved by dry-cleaning.
● Curtains. Fabric is weakened by exposure to sunlight and daylight. Washing them could leave them at worst in shreds or, at least, shrunk.

DRY-CLEANING: QUESTIONS AND ANSWERS

The label says 'dry-clean only'. Should I risk washing it?
Not unless you're prepared to accept that if it turns out to be a disaster, you won't be able to complain to the shop that sold it.

Why are some clothes labelled 'dry-clean only'?
There are three main reasons for dry-cleaning:
Shrinkage: When some textiles are woven, tension is put on threads so they stretch. Fabric stays stretched for as long as it remains dry. But when you put it into water, it can relax and shrink.
Garment construction: Different materials may be used for the front, lining, or trimmings of one garment, each with a different weave or construction. When you wash the garment, water swells the fibres, causing them to stretch at different rates so they wrinkle, pucker and deform.
Dyes: Some colours are unstable in a washing solution, but remain fast to dry-cleaning. Dry-cleaning uses solvents and little or no water to remove dirt and stains. It has less effect than water on a garment's colour.

Do's and Don'ts of dry-cleaning

DO dry-clean matching parts of an outfit or soft furnishings at the same time, so that any colour change will be uniform.

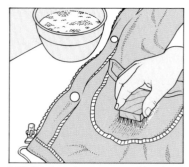

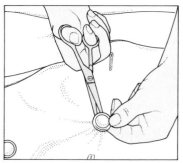

DON'T dry-clean any rubberised cotton or PVC-coated fabrics. Rubber will peel and PVC becomes brittle. Clean a raincoat made from this fabric by laying it on a flat surface and scrubbing gently with mild detergent solution.

DO watch out for leather trims, polystyrene buttons, some pigment-printed patterns and heat-sensitive interlinings. They may get damaged, so ask the dry-cleaner's advice. If necessary cut off buttons and sew them back on later.

DO dry-clean anything that's particularly old, valuable or delicate.

DO dry-clean a garment soiled with difficult or large stains. Take it as soon as possible after it is stained and tell your dry-cleaner the cause of the stain – if you know.

DO choose a dry-cleaner who observes a code of practice agreed with the Office of Fair Trading. The Dry-Cleaning Information Bureau will recommend members who do (see Useful Addresses).

COIN-OPERATED DRY-CLEANING

This is an inexpensive way of cleaning garments which don't need special care or stain removal – for example coats, curtains and loose covers from sofas.

● Don't use a coin-operated machine to dry-clean delicate clothes, leather, white or pale items or bulky duvets that will exceed the recommended weight for a load.

● Don't use a coin-operated machine if the care label symbol P or F is underlined as this indicates that the material is sensitive to some dry-cleaning processes and requires special treatment.

Useful Addresses

Dry-Cleaning Information Bureau
Textile Services Association Ltd
7 Churchill Court
58 Station Road
North Harrow HA2 7SA.
Tel: 081 863 8658.

The Home Laundering
Consultative Council
7 Swallow Place
London W1R 7AA.
Tel: 071 408 0020.
For information about care labels.

Dry-clean information hotline:
Tel: 081 863 7755.
For information and leaflets about fabric and garment care.

HOW TO TACKLE STAINS

The golden rule of treating stains is to act quickly. Don't leave the stain to set into the fabric. To avoid disasters, test chemicals or stain removers on a hidden area first. And don't treat non-washable fabrics yourself; take them to a dry cleaner and, if possible, explain what the stain is. He can then use the right chemicals.

COMMON STAINS – AND WHAT TO DO

STAIN	TREATMENT
Candle wax	Scrape off surface wax. Place brown paper or paper towel over the stain and press with a warm iron. Spot with methylated spirit to remove any colour before washing.
Collar and cuff dirt	Use biological liquid detergent as a prewash treatment by applying it gently with an old toothbrush. Then wash as usual.

COMMON STAINS – AND WHAT TO DO (cont)

STAIN	TREATMENT
Chewing gum	Freeze-harden the chewing gum by rubbing it with an ice cube placed in a plastic bag so that it doesn't wet the fabric. Scrape off the surface gum, then dab the area with dry-cleaning fluid before washing.
Chocolate	Apply biological liquid detergent, neat, to the stain. Wash, using a heavy-duty detergent containing fabric bleach. If the stain remains after washing, soak (whites only) in hydrogen peroxide solution and rewash.
Colour run	See *Dyes*.
Cosmetics (combination of wax, oil and dye)	Dab a waxy stain with white spirit or dry-cleaning fluid. Treat the dye part of the stain as described under *Dyes*. Wash in a heavy-duty detergent containing fabric bleach.
Crayon	As *Cosmetics*.
Deodorant	Sponge with a solution of hydrogen peroxide. Apply heavy-duty liquid detergent and wash. Build-up of aluminium or zinc salts may be impossible to remove.
Dyes (beer, cocoa, coffee, cola, curry, fruit juice, food dyes, mustard, pollen, preserves, spice stains, tea, tomato sauce, wine, spirits, vegetable/fruit stains. Colour run from washing)	Apply glycerine and leave for one hour. Soak or wash in a heavy-duty detergent containing oxygen bleach. If the stain remains, treat with hydrogen peroxide (page 118). Colour run from washing: use hydrogen peroxide (page 118). White fabrics: try Stain Devils Colour Run Remover or Dylon Run Away.
Grass and mud	Dab the stain with methylated spirit, then rinse in warm water and detergent. Treat with glycerine. Wash in a heavy-duty detergent containing oxygen bleach.
Ink (including ballpoint and felt-tip)	Dab with methylated spirit on a cotton wool bud. Or use Stain Devils stain remover.
Mildew	Permanent damage. Try bleaching white fabrics, or soaking and washing in a heavy-duty detergent containing oxygen bleach.
Oil, fat, grease	Damp the fabric and apply a heavy-duty liquid detergent to the stain. Wash straight away in hot water (as hot as the fabric can stand) and detergent.
Paint	Impossible to remove if the paint has dried. If it is still moist, try as follows. Oil-based paint: dab the area with white spirit and then wash. Emulsion paint: sponge with cold water then wash immediately.

COMMON STAINS – AND WHAT TO DO (cont)

STAIN	TREATMENT
Perspiration	Dab with a solution of 15ml white vinegar to 250ml water (3 teaspoons to ½ pint), and leave for five minutes. Soak in biological detergent, then wash in heavy-duty detergent. Perspiration sometimes leaves a permanent mark.
Pet stains (urine, vomit)	Use a pet-stain remover. Soak and wash fabrics in biological detergent (alternatively see *Proteins*).
Proteins (blood, egg, milk, gravy)	Soak in biological detergent and cold water, followed by washing with a heavy-duty biological detergent.
Rust	Cover with salt. Rinse, then apply lemon juice. Leave for one hour then wash. Alternatively, use a rust stain remover.
Shoe polish.	As *Cosmetics.*
Unidentifiable stains	Treat with glycerine, wash in heavy-duty biological detergent and cool water.
Wine	See *Dyes.*

Techniques of stain removal

Avoiding a ring mark When using a chemical or solvent, place the stained area over an absorbent cloth – towelling is ideal. Treat an area around the stain, then work from the outside toward the centre to avoid making a ring mark.

Dab at a stain rather than rubbing it, which may damage the surface and spread the stain.

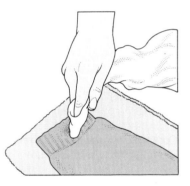

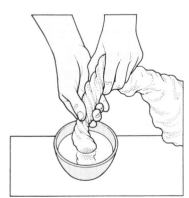

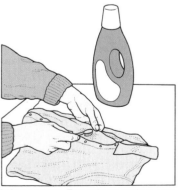

Dipping When a stain has to be dipped in a solution, hold the cloth by the stained area and twist the unstained parts. This stops the solution spreading.

Minor spots For minor stains, use liquid detergent as a prewash treatment by applying it neat with a toothbrush. Use a biological detergent on collars and cuffs.

Your own stain-removal kit

You can make up your own home kit for removing stains – then keep it handy for emergencies.

Caution Some of the chemicals suggested are poisonous or flammable, so always follow any instructions and don't work near a naked flame. Keep a window open for ventilation. Label everything, and keep the kit out of the reach of children.

Absorbent materials
Clean white cloths (handkerchiefs or an old shirt, perhaps)
Cotton wool balls
Small sponge
White paper towels

Detergents
Heavy duty liquid laundry detergent
Biological liquid detergent

Methylated spirit Try to obtain the colourless type from a chemist. Apply with a cotton wool bud. Unlikely to remove colour, but test first.

Pet-stain remover Buy any brand of stain remover intended specifically for pet stains, such as urine, and follow the instructions.

Glycerine From chemists. Lubricates and softens dried-in stains. Use diluted, 1 part to 2 parts water. Apply the mixture and leave for one hour, before washing.

Hydrogen peroxide Gentle bleaching for food and dye-based stains, sold in chemists in 'volume' strengths – ask for 20 volume strength. Test for colour fastness first. Mix 1 part to 6 parts water and soak for 30 minutes or until the stain has cleared.

Dry-cleaning fluid or white spirit Use neat, dabbed onto grease stains. Avoid using on acetates, and test on colours first.

Commercial prewash stain remover (such as Stain Devils, Vanish and Bio-tex). Follow manufacturers' instructions.

White vinegar Useful for perspiration stains. Use 15ml of white vinegar to 250ml of water (3 teaspoons to $\frac{1}{2}$ pint).

Do's and don'ts of stain removal

DO check the manufacturer's cleaning instructions on the care label.

DO try the simplest treatment first. Many stains, and heavy dirt, will respond to soaking in water and detergent, followed by washing. (See *Hints about soaking*, facing page.)

DO recheck the stain after washing. If it still remains, repeat the stain-removal treatment before tumble drying.

DON'T combine chlorine bleach with any other cleaner or stain-removal agent. It may produce toxic gases.

DON'T over-wet fabrics: use solvents sparingly.

DO consider whether the dye or surface finish of the fabric would be affected by stain-removal treatment. Test it first.

Damp the fabric where it won't show – on the hem or seam allowance. Apply the stain remover to a small area, leave for five to ten minutes and blot dry with a damp white cloth. If the colour changes or comes off, don't use the remover – consult a dry-cleaner.

Hints about soaking

● Dissolve washing powder completely in the water before putting the clothes in to soak. Try to keep items immersed. You can use the bath for bulky things.
● Soak stained items for 15-20 minutes at a hand-hot temperature of 40°C (104°F), or overnight in cold water.
● Wool, silk, leather, Lycra, flame resistant fabrics or metal trimmings should not be soaked.
● Plastic buttons may disintegrate if left to soak for too long.
● White and coloured items should not be soaked together. The dye could transfer to the whites.
● Test coloured fabrics before soaking them. Damp the fabric on the inside hem or seam allowance, and iron a piece of dry white fabric – such as a handkerchief – onto it. If any colour comes off, it's not suitable for soaking. Consult a dry-cleaner.

What to do if you're not at home

If stain happens when you're out, take this emergency action.

Grease Sprinkle with a tiny amount of talcum powder.

Other stains Dip a clean white cloth into a glass of water or soda and sponge the spot. Wash the item as soon as possible.

Not washable? If the fabric is not washable, or the item is expensive, soak up the stain with a tissue or plain white handkerchief and take it to a dry-cleaner as soon as you can.

DRYING MADE EASY

Spin drying

● Don't leave your machine running for any longer than necessary – it wastes electricity, creases fabrics and makes ironing hard work. Switch off as soon as water stops coming out.
● Don't leave damp white and damp coloured fabrics in contact. The dyes could transfer to the whites.

Line drying

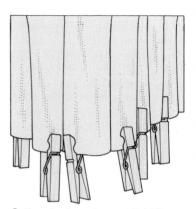

● Hang bias, full or pleated skirts from the waistband to avoid wrinkling the skirt. Clip a clothespeg to the bottom of each pleat so they'll dry in place and need little ironing.

● If you're hanging out light items of washing on a windy day, weight them down with pegs clipped to the bottom. It will stop them tangling up in the line.

● When hanging tee shirts or sweaters outdoors, turn them inside-out and dry them in the shade to prevent sunlight from fading them or turning them yellow.

● An easy way to hang sheets is to fold them in half and hang them by the hems.

If possible, peg them to two parallel lines so that they dry faster.

Tumble drying

● Choosing the wrong tumble-dryer heat may damage fibres, causing them to melt, distort or shrink. Check the care labels and the dryer handbook first.

● Avoid drying sheets with smaller items – they can bunch up and lead to patchy drying. If you must do them together, put the smaller items in a pillowcase.

● Load by bulk rather than weight. There should be a small clearance at the top of the drum when full. Overloading will cause uneven drying and excessive creasing and make it difficult to deal with those items that need to be ironed.

● To freshen bedspreads, blankets and pillows, tumble them in the dryer with a sheet of fabric softener. It will also help to prevent static electricity from building up in synthetic fabrics. But first check in the dryer handbook that the dryer will accommodate them.

● If your towels are hard and scratchy, tumble drying them will make them softer.

● Don't tumble dry light fluffy items with dark coloured ones – the fluff may be transferred.

● Clean the filters in a tumble dryer frequently to maintain the efficiency of the machine.

Green tips for tumble drying

● Remove as much water as possible by spinning first.
● Don't waste energy by drying only a couple of items.
● Avoid over-drying fabrics. It can waste energy and may make them harder to iron.

SUCCESSFUL IRONING

Work from cool to hot Sort your ironing into piles and start with items that need a cool iron, working up to those needing a hot setting. This saves you waiting for the iron to cool down between batches.

Pressing and ironing To press, lift and lower the iron with a light touch. To iron, slide the iron back and forth in the direction of the fabric grain, without putting on any pressure.

Reverse side first Press or iron on the reverse side first, then iron the other side only if necessary. Move the garment away from you as you iron to avoid leaning on the ironed parts.

Pressing cloths Use only white or neutral coloured cotton or linen fabrics as pressing cloths – an old cotton sheet is ideal.

The right temperature Always match temperatures on the iron and care labels correctly (see page 104).

Fabric shine To avoid fabric shine on some fabrics such as acrylic, iron on the reverse side. Don't iron over or press fastenings, thick sections of fabric or hems (see *Awkward and delicate things,* next page).
　　To get rid of fabric shine, soak and wring out a pressing cloth in water. Place the damp cloth on top of the shiny surface and steam press. Repeat several times. Press the area almost dry. If the fabric has a nap, raise it with a soft brush.

Reflect the heat Make ironing more efficient by slipping aluminium foil under the ironing cover to reflect the heat back up.

Steam ironing If you have a steam iron, don't set it to the steam position unless the care label has three dots in the iron symbol. If you live in a hard water area, it is advisable to use distilled (or demineralised) water – it will not scale up your iron.

The ironing board Adjust the height of the ironing board so that you can sit or stand comfortably – and have clean washing neatly piled close by.

Support large items When you are ironing large items like sheets, arrange a chair on the other side of the ironing board to support them.

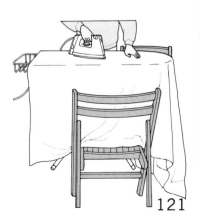

121

Awkward and delicate things

Velvet Press on the reverse through a double layer of cloth, such as a thick towel folded.

Embroidery Place a thick towel underneath to avoid crushing, then press on the reverse side to make the pattern stand out.

Pleats Iron each one separately using a pressing cloth folded double. Press inside from top to hem, then outside. If the garment is heavy, rest the surplus on a chair beside the ironing board.

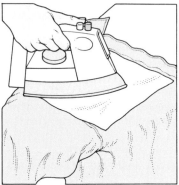

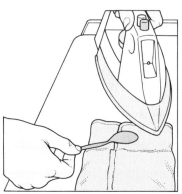

Silk Iron silk when it is evenly damp, using the 2-dot setting. Iron on the reverse side of the garment with a sheet of tissue paper on top to prevent iron marks.

Buttons If they are delicate, cover them with the bowl of a metal spoon while ironing the surrounding fabric. If your iron has button grooves this may not be necessary.

Gathers and ruffles Press on the reverse side from the outer edge towards the gathers.

Belts Press reverse side first.

Hems Press the inside of the garment; then, if the finish isn't satisfactory, press the outside lightly.

Jeans and heavy cottons Iron light-coloured material on the outside with a steam iron. Iron dark items inside out, or they might show shiny marks.

Cuffs Press on the inside, moving from the edges to the seam, then press them on the outside.

Dresses Iron as a shirt (see next page), but do the skirt area first.

Seams Smooth seams flat. Press inside the length, then outside.

Zips Don't iron over a zip. A metal zip may damage the sole plate. Close the zip and, with the garment inside-out, press the inside flaps, using the tip of the iron. Then open the zip and press lightly along the fabric in which it's set. Close it again and press on the outside. If the zip is plastic, do not touch it with the iron – the heat will melt it.

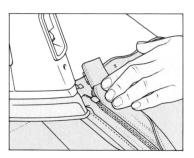

Wool Press on a damp cloth laid over the garment. Hold the iron in place for a few seconds, then lift and put it down on another section.

Pressing trousers

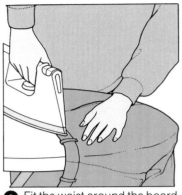

1 Start by laying the trouser pockets on the ironing board and pressing them flat.

2 Fit the waist around the board and press the top, rotating the trousers away from you.

3 Lay the trousers flat, with the side and inside seams aligned. Press the inside of the bottom leg, using a damp pressing cloth. Repeat with the other leg.

4 Press the outside of each leg, taking the creases right up to the seat at the back and to 150mm (6in) below the waistband at the front of the trousers.

Ironing a shirt or blouse

1 Iron the cuffs inside first, then outside. Iron the body of each sleeve on the cuff-opening side first, then the reverse.

2 Hook the shirt over the narrow end of the ironing board and iron the material across the shoulders.

123

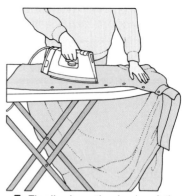

3 Iron the collar – the underside first, then the outside. To avoid getting wrinkles, work from each point to the centre.

4 Finally, iron the body of the shirt, starting with one front panel and continuing right around to the other.

Keeping that perfect finish when the work is complete

● Clothes you hang up should be placed in cupboards which are not too full, to avoid crushing and creasing.
● If possible, do not put on garments immediately after ironing – they will crease easily.
● Do not store white or light coloured linens in an airing cupboard – they may go yellow in the heat.

SIX WAYS TO AVOID IRONING

● Silk and velvet: crumples and creases will drop out of clothes or curtains made of silk or velvet if you hang the item in the bathroom while you are running a hot bath – the rising steam will help to make the creases fall out.

● Synthetic sweaters: drip-dry on a washing line using a clean pair of old tights to hang them. Thread a leg through each arm of the sweater, then pull the waist of the tights through the neck hole. Peg the tights – not the sweater – to the line.
● Drip-dry skirts and slips: hang them by their hems to distribute the weight evenly – and avoid causing peg marks by putting the pegs over a white handkerchief.
● Drip-dry shirts and blouses: hang and button up on plastic hangers. To prevent garments being blown off outdoor lines, peg the hanger hook to the line. While still damp, make sure collars are straight and neat so they won't curl or crumple.
● Synthetic fabrics such as polyester/cotton shirts and blouses may not need ironing if you remove them from a tumble dryer while they are still hot and hang them up on coat hangers. The creases will drop out as they cool. Many tumble dryers include a ten-minute cool tumble at the end of a drying cycle. If your machine is one of them, remove the clothes before the cool tumble begins.
● Buy clothes with an 'easy care' finish.

Coping with appliances

CHOOSING AND USING COOKERS

Useful features to look out for

Grills Keep an eye out for a grill pan with stops on it – they will prevent you pulling it all the way out – and a grill pan support. Dual circuit facilities are also useful for heating one half of the grill only.

Hobs Hob lights on electric hobs will warn you that the boiling area is still hot even if it has already been switched off. A useful extra is a hob guard, which prevents small children pulling hot pans off the stove.

Ovens Oven cleaning features come in two main types – stay-clean (catalytic) oven liners which carbonise splashes, and pyrolytic ovens with a special high temperature cycle which destroys any food spillage.

Fan-assisted ovens are useful as they maintain an even temperature throughout to let you make the most of the oven space (see box).

TIPS FOR USING FAN OVENS

● With a fan oven, you can use temperatures 10–20°C lower than with a normal oven. Above 200°C, reduce by 30°C.

● Cut cooking times by five to ten minutes per hour for most foods, except when the oven is full.

● When the oven is full, leave a space around dishes for hot air to circulate; stagger trays so they are not directly above or below one another.

● If you are cooking several dishes at once and recipe temperatures differ, just adjust their cooking times. Add a few minutes to those requiring a higher temperature, or cut a few minutes from those requiring a lower one.

Safety considerations in the kitchen

Is your cooker approved? Check that your model has been approved by the British Electrotechnical Approvals Board (BEAB) if electric, or the British Standards Institution (BSI) for gas. European-made cookers are tested to EN60 and EN30 standards respectively.

Glass parts Glass lids on gas cookers should have a gas cut-off device in case the lid is closed on a lit burner. All glass should be toughened to approved safety levels.

Installation of gas cookers Contact British Gas (in your phone book under 'Gas') or someone with the gas installers' register CORGI.

Manuals Keep all equipment manuals in one place and read them carefully for advice on safety.

Keeping children safe The outside of cookers can get very hot, so teach children to stay away. Always turn saucepan handles inwards to stop children pulling them off the stove. And fit a hob guard.

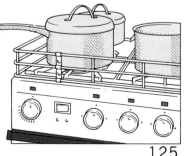

Fault-finder guide: cookers

Problem	Possible cause	Possible solution
Gas burner won't light	● Pilot light out. ● Gas supply off. ● Dirty spark igniter.	● Relight pilot (see your manual) and prevent draughts blowing it out. ● Check the gas supply is working. ● Clean the igniter (see your manual). If other burners and gas appliances won't light, call the gas service.
Gas burner flames uneven	● Clogged burner.	● Clean holes in burner with a straight pin or pipe cleaner.
Gas oven won't light, but hob works	● Pilot light out. ● Electric ignition not working. ● Oven set to come on automatically.	● Relight the pilot light. ● Check power switch to cooker is on. ● Switch automatic control to manual.
Electric elements, lights and clock not working	● No power to cooker.	● Check that the power is switched on. Check for a blown fuse or a tripped circuit breaker.
Electric oven won't come on	● Oven set to come on automatically.	● Switch automatic control to manual.
Electric oven burns or undercooks food	● Food dishes blocking air circulation. ● Temperature control set wrongly.	● Space dishes in the oven. ● Adjust temperature up or down.

For any other problems, check the manual first, then call an engineer.

SAVE ENERGY WHILE YOU COOK

● If you're using the oven, try and cook more than one dish at a time. For anything small, the grill or microwave might do.
● Put lids on saucepans and turn the heat down once the contents have boiled.
● Turn off an electric oven or hob before the food is done – the remaining heat will complete the cooking.
● Pressure cookers cook far quicker than boiling or baking.
● Pick the right size pan for the burner. If you're using gas, adjust the flame to the size of the pan.
● Fan settings on an oven will use less energy than conventional settings as cooking times will be shorter and temperatures slightly lower.

MICROWAVE OVENS

Tabletop microwaves Designed to sit on a worktop, these can be plugged into a 13amp socket. You can buy models that use microwave energy only, microwave plus a grill, or combination models which use both microwave energy and conventional energy, or the two simultaneously.

To check that a tabletop microwave is big enough for your needs, take a large cooking dish with you when you buy one to see that it fits.

Combination microwaves Can be tabletop models or the same size as a conventional oven. Full-size combination models need to be connected to a cooker wiring circuit. Combinations are suitable for most types of cooking, but especially roasting, pastry, cakes and breads. Almost all models come with a grill.

Microwave safety tips

Before you start cooking Read any instructions for cooking given on packaged foods, and check with the microwave manual.

Defrosting Make sure that food defrosts evenly, turning it if necessary. It is easy for one part to be cooking while the rest is still frozen.

Reheating As with cooking conventionally, make sure that any foods reheated in the microwave are heated through thoroughly and are served piping hot. If necessary, stir the food to make sure it is evenly heated. Never reheat something from cold more than once.

Stay nearby Some foods can unexpectedly catch alight, particularly if they have a high fat or sugar content, so it's best never to leave the microwave unattended. And never attempt to deep or shallow fry in the microwave for the same reason.

Containers Always check with the cooker manual about the type of materials or containers which are suitable to use in it. Avoid wrapping food in clingfilm, but it can be used as a covering for a container. Avoid allowing roasting bags or heat resistant plastic pouches to touch any elements in a combination model – they might melt.

Features to look out for

Electronic timer Some microwave recipes require time settings for half a minute or less. That may be difficult to get accurately on a dial timer, but electronic ones are more precise.

Turntables Turning the food during cooking helps to even out hot and cold spots although you will also need to stir the food. Try and find a model which has a turntable that can be removed. It makes it easier to clean out the microwave thoroughly and the space may be needed for large dishes.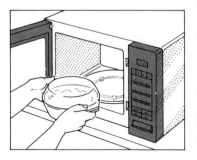

Shelf Some models have a shelf. It can be useful if you want to cook two or more things at once but you will need to increase the cooking times.

Cleaning features Self-cleaning back or top panels are available on combination models only. Smaller models should be cleaned as normal.

COPING WITH A POWER FAILURE

If a failure is likely, be prepared

● Keep matches, candles and a torch where you can find them in the dark. Make sure the torch batteries work.

● Make a list of emergency telephone numbers for the gas and electricity companies and keep it near the telephone for quick reference and advice. Look up the numbers in your local telephone directory now – under 'Gas' and 'Electricity'.

● Your central heating will probably not work during the black-out, so arrange alternative heating in one room if the weather's cold. If you have a working fireplace, set a fire. A gas heater can be lit with matches. If you have a paraffin heater, make sure you have some fuel stored nearby for use in emergencies. If you have an old electric fire stored in the loft, get it out and make sure that it works.

● If you suffer frequent power failures, keep a small camping stove for simple cooking. Follow the manufacturer's instructions carefully.

If the electricity fails

● Locate a torch.

● Turn all appliances and electrical switches off, with the exception of one light switch, so that you know when the supply has been restored. Don't leave anything on top of an electric hob, or in front of an electric fire in case the heat comes on unexpectedly.

● The freezer will stay cold for up to 24 hours if the door is kept shut. After that, cook the food and refreeze later.

● If you have a gas cooker, you can still light the hob with a match or manual ignitor. If it works from battery spark ignition, you'll be able to use that too.

● Take extra care when moving around in the dark, particularly if you're carrying a candle. If possible, leave a battery lamp on the stairs for light while the power cut lasts.

When the power is restored

● Double check that electrical appliances are off, but make sure the fridge and freezer are on.

● Electric powered clocks and automatic timers will have been affected by the cut. Reset to the correct time and instructions. The most important will probably be the central heating controller.

● Check that pilot lights on gas appliances, such as a cooker or fire, are functioning correctly.

● Check the information stored in the video – date, time, programmes to be recorded. You may need to reprogramme it.

● Look at any other electrical equipment, such as a fish tank pump, that might need adjusting.

FRIDGES AND FREEZERS

Getting the temperature right

Whether you are buying a separate fridge and freezer or a combined fridge/freezer, you need to make sure that the temperatures inside remain constant and at the right level. Some models (but very few) have built-in thermometers. For those that don't, get a fridge thermometer (they are available in most hardware stores) to give yourself an idea of the fridge's temperature.

Don't forget: in summer, you will need to alter the thermostat to keep the fridge cool as the temperature outside it rises.

Fridges There should be two different temperature levels. The top shelf should be approximately 5°C (41°F) or less. If it is, the cool section at the bottom of the fridge will be 1°C (34°F).

● Leave the thermometer in the middle of the top shelf overnight. Check the temperature in the morning without letting in too much warm air.

● Use the top shelf for yoghurt, orange juice, butter or food that doesn't need to be too cold.

● Use the bottom, cooler area for raw meat, fish, poultry or vegetables. Take care not to let raw meat juices run onto leftover foods (see also page 537).

Freezers To be safe, freezers should be kept at a temperature of −18°C (−0.4°F). A genuine freezer (as opposed to the freezer section of a fridge) is marked with the freezer symbol.

● Stand the thermometer on the edge of the top shelf (or at the front of the top basket if it's a chest freezer) on the side the door opens. Leave it for a couple of hours before reading it. If it's higher than −18°C (−0.4°F) food deteriorates quicker, so turn the temperature down. If it's lower than that, you're wasting energy.

● Try to keep the door closed as much as possible. Warm air gets in very fast and raises the temperature.

Fridge/freezers Most fridge/freezers have only one temperature control for both parts, and rarely include a thermometer. This makes it difficult to maintain the correct temperatures.

● If necessary, have the freezer slightly warmer, but get the correct temperature for the fridge – fresh food is more likely to spoil.

● Shared control fridge/freezers are often not too good at freezing. They may well take longer to freeze food than a separate freezer.

● Look for a two-control fridge/freezer with warning lights. It will give you the right temperature for both parts and show if the electricity and fast-freeze are on, and if the freezer is too warm.

DEFROSTING TIPS

● Always switch off and unplug the freezer before cleaning or defrosting.

● Load the contents of your freezer into large dustbin bags and cover the bags with a duvet or blanket. The food should stay frozen for several hours, but use a cool box for ice cream or soup which melt quickly.

● After defrosting, wash fridges and freezers with a solution of two teaspoons of bicarbonate of soda to 1 litre (2 pints) of warm water – it removes lingering smells.

● Rub the inside of your freezer with glycerine, available from chemists, after it has defrosted. When you next have to defrost it, the ice will come away from the sides more easily.

● Use a wet/dry vacuum cleaner to suck up any water left on the floor.

● Defrosting fridge/freezers is much easier with a two-control model. That way, you can use the fridge to keep foodstuffs frozen while you deal with the freezer.

● If you don't like defrosting, you can always pay more for a frost-free freezer which never needs it.

129

Replacing a worn seal

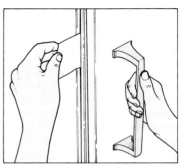

If your fridge door won't close properly, or the inside of the fridge seems warmer than it should be, the seal around the door may have gone. Check it by closing a thin strip of paper in the door. When the door is shut, the paper should be tightly gripped, and shouldn't slide easily.

If you want to change the seal (also known as the gasket) yourself, buy a new one from a stockist listed in the Yellow Pages under 'Refrigerator repairs'. Check with the shop or the manufacturers how to replace it, or call in an engineer.

IS YOUR FRIDGE GREEN ENOUGH?

One of the major causes of concern about the world's ozone layer is the use of CFCs – chemicals that are used in a fridge's insulation and cooling system. New technology has developed a non-CFC coolant, but how do you get rid of an old fridge or freezer?

● If you buy a new fridge or freezer from a major freezer centre, it will probably collect your old one free of charge and remove the CFCs safely before it is recycled.

● Sell your old fridge, don't scrap it. Or look out for notices in your area telling you who is recycling old fridges. Ask the local authority.

● If you're buying a fridge/freezer, look into how energy efficient it is. Some use more electricity than others – the manufacturers will be able to tell you how much – so compare the different models.

Refrigeration cost cutters

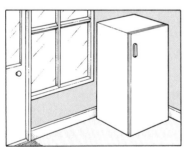

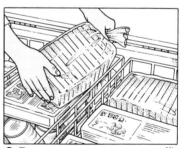

● Place fridges and freezers in a cool position – against an outside north-facing wall, for example, out of direct sunlight and away from radiators and cookers.

● Freezers operate more efficiently when they're full. Fill them up with spare loaves of bread or even old, clean towels if you don't have any food to freeze.

● Bulk buying often works out cheaper than shopping in smaller quantities, particularly if you have a freezer to fill up with cuts of meat.

● Don't open the door more than necessary, and always be as quick as possible when taking something out.

● Regular defrosting cuts running costs. Frost build-up can coat the refrigeration tubes so the fridge has to work harder to keep the inside cold (see previous page).

● Don't buy a fridge or freezer that is bigger than you need. It's a waste of both electricity and money.

WASHING MACHINES AND TUMBLE DRYERS

Y ou can either buy a separate washing machine and tumble dryer, or a combination washer/dryer. Which you choose may depend on the following:

● How much space do you have? Two machines will obviously take up more room than one, but some manufacturers make stacking kits which allow you to put the dryer on top of the washing machine.

● How much washing do you do? The drying cycle of a combined washer/dryer will usually dry approximately half a full load of washing at a time. And you won't be able to get on with the next load either.

● How easy is it to find a repair man? Combined machines generally break down more than separate washing machines or dryers.

Taking care of your equipment

Washing machines and washer/dryers

● Check the rubber seal on the door regularly for signs of deterioration and wipe it down after each wash.

● Clean out the filter regularly.

● If sharp edges develop in the drum, tears and snags will appear on your clothes. Prevent this happening by fastening buttons and zips before putting them in the machine. To get rid of sharp edges, cover your hand with an old pair of tights and run it slowly round the inside of the machine to find any snags. Then smooth them off with fine sandpaper.

● Many manufacturers recommend a particular type of washing powder or fabric softener to be used in the machine. If they do, follow their suggestions for the best results.

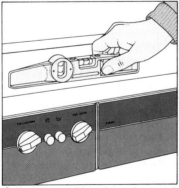 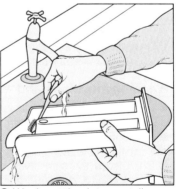

● If the machine is noisy and vibrates a lot while spinning, use a spirit level to check that it is on a level surface, and make sure that the load is evenly distributed.

● Wash out the detergent dispenser drawer regularly under a running tap, and scrub out the fabric conditioner compartment with an old toothbrush.

Tumble dryers

● Fasten buttons and zips before putting them in to dry – they could harm the drum.

● Wipe the drum with a damp soft cloth after drying anything that is starched in the wash.

● Leave the door open for an hour or so after drying clothes to get rid of any dampness in the machine.

131

WASHING TRAINERS IN THE MACHINE

If your sports shoes are made of synthetic materials and not leather or suede, you can wash them in the machine as long as the shoe manufacturer recommends it. Clean off any mud with newspaper or a knife, and remove the laces and inner soles. Wash the trainers with a pair of trousers to balance the load, and set the machine on a gentle programme, such as for wool. Hot temperatures will distort the shoes.

Fault-finder guide: washing machines

Problem	Possible cause	Solution
The machine won't fill	● The hose is bent. ● The water has been turned off.	● Unbend the hose. ● Check the water supply.
The machine won't spin	● The machine is overloaded. ● The load is unevenly distributed. ● The machine is on a programme which has no spin.	● Remove some clothes. ● Redistribute the load. ● Check the programming.
There are too many suds	● You are using a detergent which lathers too much.	● Change to a low lather detergent.
The machine won't start	● A fuse is blown. ● The machine isn't plugged in.	● Change the fuse. ● Check the plug.

Wash-day economy tips ✿

Washing machines and washer/dryers

● Low-temperature programmes will work for all but the dirtiest loads – and save on electricity.
● Only operate the machine when you have a full load. If you must wash less, use the 'half-load' option, and half the detergent too.
● Don't leave the spin dryer running any longer than necessary. It creases fabrics and makes ironing difficult.

SAFETY ADVICE

● Beware of fire. It sounds unlikely, but fires do start in washing machines and tumble dryers. Clean any fluff out of all filters, and don't leave the machine running when you go out.
● The glass doors on washing machines and tumble dryers may get very hot during a drying cycle. Keep small children away from them.
● Look out for safety approval marks when buying a new or secondhand machine – the BEAB mark on British models, the VDE mark for German ones, or the Italian IMQ mark.

Tumble dryers

● Wring out clothes as much as possible before putting them in the dryer – especially if hand washed.

● Look out for a dryer that has an economy thermostat built in. It automatically reduces the heat as the clothes dry out.

● A cool and intermittent drying programme creases the clothes less and makes ironing easier.

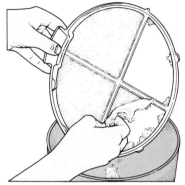
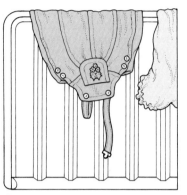

● Each time you use the dryer, clean out the filter when you have finished. A filter blocked with fluff reduces the dryer's efficiency and increases the cost of drying.

● Only use a tumble dryer when you really need to, and when you have a full load. Use radiators, clothes horses or an outside line if you can.

DISHWASHERS

Maintenance tips

● Look for a machine which uses less water, electricity and detergent than average. Compare manufacturers' information to find out.

● Try out all the programmes, especially the economy ones. Your dishes may clean just as well on a shorter, cooler programme.

● Don't put wooden, plastic or bone-handled cutlery; hand-painted porcelain; painted or lead crystal ware; old or precious china; or aluminium in the dishwasher. Wash them by hand.

● Clean the inside of your machine regularly with general purpose liquid cleaner (page 60).

● Remove and clean the filter weekly by brushing it under a running tap.

● Keep the rinse aid and salt levels topped up.

Unexplained floods?

If your dishwasher starts leaking, check the seal before you call out an engineer. When it becomes lined with grease, it lets water through. Using your fingers, run all the way around the seal, scraping off as much grease as you can. Then wipe it down with a damp cloth wrung out in a washing-up liquid solution. Try the machine again, but stay close by in case of further flooding.

What size machine will you need?

Family sized dishwashers usually hold 12-14 place settings. One 'setting' consists of a soup plate, dinner plate, side plate, cup, saucer, glass, knife, fork, teaspoon, soup spoon, dessertspoon and a few extra serving utensils. Small tabletop dishwashers hold around four to six place settings, and slimline models about seven.

133

Fault-finder guide: dishwashers

Problem	Possible cause	Solution
White spots, streaks or film on crockery	● Hard water. ● Machine needs salt.	● Increase the amount of detergent slightly. ● Top up salt and rinse aid.
Gritty deposits (like sand)	● High proportion of starchy food left on dishes.	● Scrape or rinse off excess food before loading.
Food specks remain	● Incorrect loading. ● Not enough detergent. ● Wrong programme.	● Don't overload. Allow spray to reach all surfaces of dishes. ● Increase detergent. Clean filter. ● Use a more intensive programme.
Black marks on china	● Metal marks from knives or metallic rims.	● Soak in a mild bleach solution.
Discoloured aluminium	● Minerals in water and high temperature.	● Remove cookware before the drying part of the cycle or wash by hand.
Dishwasher leaks	● Worn or soiled gasket. ● Excessive foam.	● Clean gasket and edge of door. Replace worn or loose gasket. ● Use automatic dishwasher detergents only.
Corrosion of cutlery	● Detergent grains in contact with stainless steel or silver. ● Knife blades in contact with acids such as lemon juice, mayonnaise and jam.	● Do not allow dry detergent to come into contact with metal. Take care when loading not to nest cutlery types together – mix up the spoons, knives and forks. Don't mix different metals in the same cutlery basket. ● Rinse cutlery as soon as it has been used.
Cloudy glass	● Hard-water deposits. ● Etching of surface.	● Top up rinse aid, salt and detergent levels. ● Etching is permanent; don't put delicate glassware in the dishwasher, but always wash it by hand.

BUYING A VACUUM CLEANER

Upright cleaners

● Advantages: good on large expanses of carpet and for picking up embedded dirt and animal hairs.
● Disadvantages: not convenient for corners or stairs unless used with extra attachments.

Cylinder cleaners

● Cleans rugs, curtains and a variety of floor coverings.
● Accessories available may include a power nozzle for greater suction.
● Advantages: the flexible hose is good for around and under furniture, and convenient for stairs.
● Disadvantages: often knocks into furniture as it is pulled along behind you. The suction hose also tends to kink.

Wet-and-dry cleaners

● Three-in-one cleaners that vacuum, shampoo carpet and upholstery, and suck up water.
● Advantages: good for cleaning up after floods or DIY jobs.
● Disadvantages: awkward for everyday use, particularly on stairs, and storage can be difficult as they are often bulky.

Hand-held cordless cleaners

● Advantages: wet-and-dry models are useful for minor spills, and the standard vacuum is good for minor jobs like crumbs on the floor, cleaning the car and carpet edges.
● Disadvantages: only runs for 5-12 minutes before it needs recharging, and has weak suction.

Built-in central system

● Hidden suction pipes, with outlets in each room and hallway, carry dust to a central collection bin.
● Advantages: easy to operate, as you only have to carry the hose, and it removes more dust from a room than an ordinary vacuum. Good for asthma sufferers.
● Disadvantages: expensive to install and can't be moved.

Vacuum cleaner attachments

Floor and carpet nozzle For cleaning both hard flooring and carpeting. The brush in the nozzle retracts for use on carpet to provide a hard nozzle, and is exposed for hard floors. It should have a swivel joint at the head so that it's convenient to use.

Upholstery tool For upholstered furniture, mattresses, carpeted stairs and curtains. Some have an 'insert' which fits into the tool and picks up threads and pet hairs.

Soft, round brush tool For fiddly or delicate surfaces, such as carved woodwork, picture frames or cornices. The head should swivel in all directions.

Crevice nozzle For corners, crevices in furniture, refrigerator grilles and other awkward places. Wipe it clean after use.

Dusting brush ring For cleaning bookshelves, Venetian blinds and radiators. Cover it with a soft, clean cloth to dust delicate surfaces.

Motorised or turbo power nozzle A more advanced floor nozzle, with revolving brushes. These improve the pick-up of dust and hairs. The nozzle also has wheels, so is easier to move over the carpet.

Features to look out for

● A warning signal when the dust bag is full.
● Easy-release flex on upright cleaners and self-retracting flex on cylinders.
● Handles on uprights that can be lowered to clean under furniture.
● Variable suction strengths for different surfaces and to save energy.
● The BEAB or CCA European approval marks to show it has been tested to approved safety limits.
● Easily available replacement filters and dust bags. It's probably worth buying a few extra bags when you buy the machine.
● A model which will clean close to the edges of a room or hallway without using a crevice tool.

Fault-finder guide: vacuum cleaners

CAUTION Before cleaning or repairing any parts, switch off and unplug the vacuum cleaner.

Problem	Possible cause	Solution
Motor doesn't run	● Plug not secure.	● Push plug firmly into socket.
	● Power off at socket.	● Switch on.
	● Fuse in plug blown.	● Replace fuse. If it blows again, have machine checked by a service engineer.
	● Fan obstructed.	● Unplug and remove the obstruction.
Motor runs but suction is poor	● Dust bag full.	● Unplug and empty or replace dust bag.
	● Filter dirty.	● Clean or replace filter.
	● Hose wrongly attached.	● Secure hose to the cleaner.
	● Obstruction in the hose or attachment.	● Remove the obstruction.
	● Leak in hose or attachment.	● Repair leak with insulating tape or replace part.
	● Fan obstructed.	● Unplug and remove the obstruction.
	● Worn roller brush.	● Unplug and fit new brush.
	● Worn belt.	● Unplug and replace belt.
Smell of burning rubber	● Loose drive belt.	● Fit new belt.
	● String around drive shaft.	● Remove obstruction.

FOOD PREPARATION MACHINES

Food processors

● Good points: slicing, grating, chopping, blending and puréeing.
● Limitations: whisking egg whites, mixing cakes, kneading dough and whipping cream.

Features to look out for

Easy to clean Make sure the bowl and accessories have no difficult corners to clean. Some models are dishwasher-safe.

Capacity Buy a machine that suits how you cook. If you cook in bulk, get a large bowl, but you won't be able to use it for small amounts. Some large models also provide an extra mini-bowl.

Storage Attachments for food processors can be bulky. Look for a model with a storage box – it will keep sharp blades out of the way of children.

Safety Some models provide more safety guards against touching moving parts with your hands than others. Always use the food pusher provided, and look for a model with a lid that cuts off the electricity when not properly closed. Don't overload the processor. If it stops suddenly, allow the food to settle and then remove some before continuing to process the food.

  Look for BEAB approved models: they conform to both electrical and mechanical safety standards.

Controls Look out for a pulse button, to avoid overprocessing, and different speed selections. The controls should be easy to get at while the machine is in use.

Blenders

● Good points: blending soups, puréeing fruit, making breadcrumbs.
● Limitations: chopping herbs and nuts unless recommended.

Features to look out for

Capacity If you mainly use your blender to prepare baby food, buy one with a small container. Or buy a mini-blender or hand-held model.

Controls Look for a pulse control – the food settles between bursts, and so is blended more uniformly. Two speeds are also useful.

Measurements Some blending goblets show liquid measurements on the side – useful for following recipes accurately.

Design Make sure the model you choose comes with a handle, a pouring lip and a removable section in the lid so you can add ingredients while the machine is working.

Easy to clean Some models are easier to clean than others as all the working parts dismantle.

137

Food mixers and beaters

● Good points: can take a wide range of attachments. Small, hand-held beaters are very useful for quick beating – cream, potatoes, egg whites, and so on.
● Limitations: needs more attention than a food processor to mix well, and is slower.

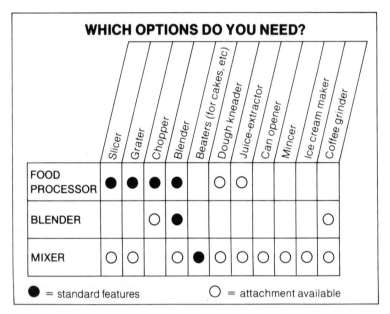

WHICH OPTIONS DO YOU NEED?

	Slicer	Grater	Chopper	Blender	Beaters (for cakes, etc)	Dough kneader	Juice-extractor	Can opener	Mincer	Ice cream maker	Coffee grinder
FOOD PROCESSOR	●	●	●	●		○	○				
BLENDER			○	●							○
MIXER	○	○		○	●	○	○	○	○	○	○

● = standard features   ○ = attachment available

To get the best from your mixer

● Use the correct speed: low for rubbing in, medium for creaming and high for whisking.
● Use a higher speed if the machine is labouring. Or mix smaller quantities at a time.
● Stop the machine occasionally and scrape the sides of the bowl with a rubber spatula, pushing the ingredients to the middle, to make sure it mixes evenly.

USEFUL ATTACHMENTS FOR A MIXER

Large mixers with a powerful motor can drive a number of useful kitchen gadgets. You may be able to buy a:

● Coffee grinder   ● Can opener
● Shredder/slicer   ● Mincer
● Juice extractor   ● Cream maker
● Fruit press

IRONS

Checklist for choosing an iron

● Do you need a dry iron, steam iron, cordless or optional cord/cordless iron? Which additional features might make ironing easier? (See *Useful features on irons*, facing page.)
● Try the irons out in your hand; one that feels comfortable and well-balanced will be less tiring to use.

● A heavy iron doesn't necessarily iron better than a lightweight one. The right temperature control, dampness and a smooth soleplate are all more important than weight.

● Check that the controls are easy to use.

Useful features on irons

Ironing safety tip A safety iron is a good idea for the absentminded, or those with children. If the iron is left sitting on its heel or soleplate, it will automatically cut out. Some models have an alarm which sounds.

Steam A steam facility takes the effort out of ironing creased or dry fabrics. Steam irons can usually be used as dry irons too.

● Variable steam output allows you to adjust the steam for different fabrics.

● An extra shot of steam provides extra dampness for stubborn creases. But the steam burst gets weaker as the water tank empties, so the tank needs frequent topping up. Look for a model with a large capacity tank or a mechanism to achieve a consistent steam output.

Antidrip device Prevents water marks on the fabric which can be caused by drips as the soleplate cools.

Coated soleplate Chrome, porcelain enamel, stainless steel and non-stick Silverstone are all better for ironing than the standard aluminium surface, although aluminium is lighter. A coated surface means the iron moves more easily over the fabric, so ironing is faster.

Antiscaling device Most irons are designed to use tap water, but will probably clog up if you live in a hard-water area. A few models have a special cartridge feature which softens the water, or use deionised or demineralised water.

Cordless irons

A mains-powered base recharges the iron, but it needs to be returned to the base regularly to keep the temperature up. Choose a model with a powerful heating element for fast recharge.

Cordless irons are convenient to use, especially for tricky corners, and are good for both right and left-handers. But look for a model that has a mains lead option – you won't spend so much time recharging.

Cleaning irons

Spray starch on the soleplate Heat the iron on a warm setting and rub it across a damp, loosely woven cloth or coarse towel which is held taut over the edge of the ironing board.

Burnt deposits of synthetic fibres Use a damp rag dipped in bicarbonate of soda or a proprietary soleplate cleaner such as Vilene Iron Cleaner. Clean steam irons standing on their heel rest.

Avoid chalky marks on fabrics Lime scale deposits can build up in the iron as tap water evaporates during ironing. To prevent the build-up, empty the reservoir while the iron is still hot and store it on its heel rest to prevent leaking. In a hard-water area, use demineralised water.

Descaling your iron Unless your iron has a descaling mechanism, you will need to descale it occasionally if you use tap water. Some models have a removable valve that attracts scale, others a removable section on the soleplate. Descale both by soaking them in white wine vinegar or by using a proprietary descaler such as Oster Steam Iron Cleaner. Wear gloves if you are using descaling crystals.

DO'S AND DON'TS WHEN USING IRONS

DO use deionised or demineralised water if you live in a hard-water area. You can easily treat tap water by buying a demineralising bottle in a hardware shop. It contains crystals which are dissolved when you fill the bottle with tap water and shake.

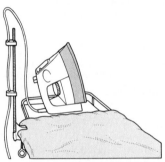

DON'T leave water in the iron after use – it will clog it up and in doing so will shorten the iron's life.

DO check the flex regularly. Repair it as soon as there are signs of fraying. A flex holder prevents wear.

DO keep the soleplate clean (see previous page).

DO always store the iron upright, on its heel, not its soleplate.

DON'T fill your steam iron with water when it's on – you should always switch it off first to be safe.

DON'T use distilled water meant for a car battery or water from the fridge in the iron – they may contain impurities.

ELECTRIC KETTLES

Before you buy a kettle consider the following:

● Do you often need to heat a full kettle? A jug kettle is usually more economical than a traditional kettle, as the heating element is smaller, and can be covered with less water – so you can heat small amounts at a time.

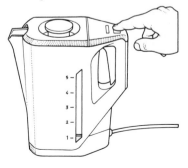

● Is it comfortable to hold? If you have weak wrists or hands, will it be too heavy when it's full?

● Would you be better off with a cordless kettle? Children are less likely to pull it over.

Useful features to look out for

Secure lid Some kettles have locking lids, a good idea if you have small children. It will stop too much water spilling if the kettle is knocked over.

Water gauge Most jug kettles have a gauge on the outside so you can see at a glance if it needs filling up.

Cord storage If the kettle doesn't have a short, curly lead, look for a model which stores the flex inside – it's much safer with children around.

Non-slip feet They keep the kettle more firmly on the worktop. The kettle is less likely to fall if it's knocked or if a child pulls at the flex.

Cool exterior A kettle gets very hot, particularly at the base, when it is boiling. Small children could reach up and touch it when you're not looking. To avoid this, some models are double skinned, with an exterior layer that remains cool even when the water is boiling.

TO KEEP YOUR KETTLE DESCALED . . .

● Cover the element with a 1:1 solution of malt vinegar and water. Bring it to the boil and leave overnight.

● Or boil the kettle and add 75g (13 teaspoons) of citric acid granules. Leave for 20 minutes, reheating once if necessary.

● Or remove the hardness from your tap water (page 168).

● Or buy a chemical descaler and treat your kettle with it. Bring a half-full kettle to the boil, add the descaler and leave for half an hour – but make sure you read the manufacturer's instructions first.

TOASTERS

What to look for in a toaster

Variable width Thicker slices of bread, muffins and baps are all toasted more easily in a model with adjustable racks.

One-side-only toasting A useful option if you toast tea cakes and muffins.

Electronic toasters Microchip electronic toasters are expensive but produce the most evenly toasted slices. More basic models often give uneven results as the elements heat up.

Infrared and humidity sensors Infrared sensors sense the temperature of the toast surface and adjust the browning accordingly. Humidity sensors monitor the degree of moisture in the slice.

Reheating facility Keeps your toast warm while you finish making the coffee or frying the eggs.

Frozen bread setting If you need to make toast from a frozen sliced loaf, this setting adds a measured amount of time for defrosting the slice first.

Crumb tray A removable crumb tray may make cleaning easier.

BEAB approval The BEAB stamp indicates that the toaster has been tested to approved safety standards.

DO'S AND DON'TS: TOASTER SAFETY

DO always unplug the toaster before you clean it. It's best if you unplug it after general use too.

DON'T allow water to enter either the appliance or the plug. Clean it with a damp cloth.

DON'T heat waffles in the toaster – they contain grease, which could clog the elements.

DON'T use anything sharp, such as a knife, to remove toast stuck in the toaster – it could harm the elements. Unplug the toaster and use a non-metallic implement such as a wooden spoon.

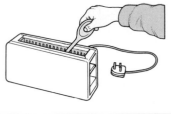

COFFEE MAKERS

If you want to use more than an ordinary household jug to make a pot of fresh, ground coffee, you have three main options – plungers, electric filter machines and espresso machines.

Plunger jugs The plunger method works in much the same way as using an ordinary jug. You measure the coffee into a glass jug, which has a metal plunger mechanism to filter the coffee grains attached to a lid. Add water that is just off the boil, stir, cover with the lid and leave for a few minutes. Then slowly push the plunger to the base.

Filter machines Easy to use and reasonably cheap to buy, filter machines make a large amount of coffee in about ten minutes. An electric element heats the water, sprays or drips it through the coffee into a jug, and keeps it hot on a hotplate. The machines use either permanent filters of stainless steel or nylon (which need cleaning after every use) or replaceable paper ones.

● An antidrip device is useful for when you remove the jug of coffee, and so is a filter holder which swivels out, allowing easy access to the coffee grounds.

● Unless your machine keeps the coffee above 80°C (176°F), you will need to add hot milk to make drinkable coffee. Many machines don't keep the coffee really hot.

● Some machines have a detachable hotplate, which allows you to take coffee to the table and keep it warm.

● Chlorine bleach is often used to bleach coffee filter papers. If you want to avoid chlorine-bleached filters, look for unbleached brands or buy a machine with a permanent filter.

Espresso machines Stove-top espresso coffee pots are made of metal, and screw together in three parts. Water is heated in the base until it escapes as steam through the coffee grounds, trapped in a central filter. More expensive electric machines use pump pressure to force the water through the coffee grounds.

● Some electric machines can also froth milk to make cappuccino. Semiskimmed milk produces more froth than full cream milk. You can also buy machines exclusively for frothing milk.

What sort of coffee do I use?

Coffee beans need to be roasted and ground before you can make coffee with them, and you will need to choose the right grind for your machine to get the best results.

● Use a coarse grind for jug and plunger coffee making.

● Filter coffee machines need medium to fine-ground coffee.

● Espresso machines need a very fine-ground coffee for both stove-top and electric models.

MAKING THE PERFECT CUP OF COFFEE

Three things are going to affect your final cup of coffee – the coffee beans, the water and the machine. Experiment to find your favourite type, roast and grind of bean. The lighter the roast, the milder the flavour. Always use freshly ground coffee within a week, or store coffee beans in the freezer but use within three months.

● Use fresh, cold water.

● Experiment with different amounts of coffee to find the strength you like. Start with 4 level tablespoons coffee to 600ml (1 pint) of water, or 1 dessertspoon of coffee per mug.

● Wait for the water to come off the boil before pouring it over the coffee grounds.

● Make the coffee fresh for each occasion and serve it straight away. Never reheat coffee as it will be bitter.

● Keep your coffee machine scrupulously clean and descale it regularly (see *Descaling your iron*, page 140).

CHOOSING ELECTRIC BLANKETS

● Make sure you pick a blanket that covers enough of the bed – tall people will need to look for a longer one.

● Do you want separate controls for each side of the bed?

● A BEAB mark means that it has been tested to a rigorous safety standard. Check that older blankets have protection against overheating, and replace if not.

Which type to buy?

Preheating underblanket Switch on an hour before bedtime, and off before you get into bed. Use it under the bottom sheet, tied to the mattress to keep it flat if tapes are provided.

Extra-low voltage and all-night underblankets Can be used in the same way as an underblanket but can be left on all night. Some are controlled electronically and react to the temperature of the room and bed.

Overblanket Use it over a top sheet and with only a light covering over the top. Designed to be left on all night.

Electric duvets Can be used all year round and incorporate protection against overheating. They will fit inside a standard duvet cover and are machine washable.

DO'S AND DON'TS: ELECTRIC BLANKETS

DO get the electric blanket serviced every two or three years.

DO follow the manufacturer's instructions for washing electric blankets. Only some of them are washable; air others, and contact the manufacturer for cleaning advice.

DON'T plug an electric blanket into an adaptor with another appliance on it. It may be switched on unintentionally.

DON'T use a blanket which is folded or creased, and don't stick safety pins into it for any reason.

Safety tips

● Don't use underblankets as overblankets. It can be dangerous.
● Avoid sitting on the bed when a preheating underblanket or an overblanket are turned on, and don't use them folded. It may cause hot-spotting and trigger the overheating protection device; you will have to return the blanket to the manufacturer. Keep pets off the bed for the same reason.
● Check frequently for loose connections, damage to the flexible cord, worn fabric and scorch marks. Hold the blanket up to the light to make sure the heating wires are evenly spaced and not touching. Return blankets to the firm if there is any sign of wear or damage.

CLEANING ELECTRIC BLANKETS

An electric blanket should not be dry-cleaned, and underblankets are not usually washable. Most overblankets can be laundered, but only when absolutely necessary.

If you want to wash it at home, and the manufacturers advise it, disconnect the mains lead (if detachable), measure the blanket so it can be stretched back to size and launder according to the care label. Use a low spin speed and don't tumble dry; it could cause shrinkage. Then spread the blanket over a table and get help to pull it carefully into shape. Hold it up to the light to check the wires are straight and not touching and dry on a line or indoors over an airer. Don't apply direct heat. Never switch the blanket on before it's dried and aired.

Electronics round the house

BUYING A NEW TV SET?

Measuring the screen The sizes of TV screens are based on the diagonal measurement of the face of the tube. Metric sizes measure only the visible part of the screen; imperial sizes measure the full screen, so there are slight discrepancies in the equivalents:
14in – 34cm; 17in – 41cm; 21in – 51cm; 25in – 59cm; 28in – 66cm.

How far away? Comfortable viewing distances are three to five times the screen size.

Screen size	Viewing Distance
34cm	1m – 1.6m (3ft 3in – 5ft 4in)
41cm	1.2m – 2m (4ft – 6ft 6in)
51cm	1.5m – 2.5m (5ft – 8ft 6in)
59cm	1.8m – 2.8m (6ft – 9ft)
66cm	2m – 3.2m (6ft 6in – 10ft 6in)

Choice of sizes If you intend to put your TV set 2.2m (8ft) away from the living room sofa, you have a choice of three screen sizes – 51cm, 59cm or 66cm.

Getting the best from stereo TV NICAM is a form of broadcast stereo for TV which is available on BBC and ITV in most parts of the country. It requires a special decoder to receive it, and stereo speakers. Both are provided in a NICAM stereo TV set.

Using your hi-fi speakers To convert an existing mono television set to stereo, you can buy a decoder in a separate set-top box. It needs to be connected to stereo speakers through your hi-fi system. In fact, it makes sense to connect even a NICAM TV set to the hi-fi system if you want to make the most of the stereo sound. Reasonable-quality hi-fi speakers are almost certain to be better than those provided in TV sets. The only problem is that the TV set will have to be positioned so that it is midway between the speakers.

YOUR LOCAL TV TRANSMITTER

The four terrestrial TV channels (BBC 1, BBC 2, ITV and Channel 4) broadcast all around the United Kingdom from several hundred transmitter masts. Each transmitter carries all four of the channels. Each channel uses a separate frequency, and to prevent cross-interference causing bad reception each transmitter uses a different set of frequencies from its neighbours.

So there are more than 40 different frequencies in use throughout the country. The broadcasting authorities give them two-figure channel numbers – from 21 to 69.

You can find out the location of your local television transmitter, together with channel numbers and aerial groups (see *Choosing the right TV aerial*, page 147), by writing to the BBC Engineering Information Department, Broadcasting House, London W1A 1AA, or to your local independent television company.

TUNING A TV SET TO RECEIVE PROGRAMMES

To call up channels on a TV set, you use the number buttons on the remote control handset, or on the TV set itself. But, first, the programme numbers have to be tuned – which means that they have to be matched up to the frequencies of the channels. This has to be done when you buy a new TV set, or whenever you move your set to a different part of the country.

On a portable set, you can use spare programme numbers to store channels used at your holiday cottage or caravan. You can then watch the set in both places.

How to tune a modern TV set

Most modern TV sets have electronic tuning. The basic procedure is the same for all sets but details vary between different models, so follow these guidelines in conjunction with the instruction manual that comes with your set.

1 Put the set into tuning mode. With sets that have on-screen display, this may be done from the handset; otherwise by a switch (probably concealed) on the TV fascia.

2 Select a programme number (1, 2, 3, 4, etc).

3 Instruct the set to search through the channel numbers until it finds a strong signal.

Alternatively if you know the channel numbers of your local transmitter (see *Your local TV transmitter*, previous page) call up the one you want (using your number buttons, and following the procedure in the instruction manual), and go to step 6.

4 Once a channel is found, decide if it is BBC1, BBC2, ITV or Channel 4. To do this, you can use the programme listings in a newspaper, or teletext if it's fitted to your set, or even another TV set.

5 Decide whether you want that channel on that number. If not, continue the search. Most people find it convenient to store BBC1 on programme 1, BBC2 on 2, ITV on 3 and C4 on 4, but if your set always goes to programme 1 when switched on, you might prefer to assign that number to the channel you watch most.

6 When you find the channel you want, store it against the programme number.

7 Repeat steps 2-6 until you have stored all the programmes you want.

8 Return the TV to 'view' mode.

Tuning older TV sets

Older or cheaper TV sets may have a limited number of preset number buttons (typically eight) and are tuned manually with a knob or wheel (usually concealed behind a cover on the control panel) for each programme.

146

HOW TO TUNE YOUR VIDEO RECORDER

Video recorders are tuned in the same way as TV sets, but first a programme number on the TV set needs to be tuned to the video recorder's output frequency so that you can see what's going on when you tune the video.

1 Connect the aerial to the video recorder's 'Aerial in' or 'RF in' socket. Connect the video recorder's 'Aerial out' or 'RF out' socket to the aerial socket on the TV set. (For an alternative means of connection, see *Scart sockets for better pictures*, page 152.)

2 Switch on the video recorder's tuning signal. This provides an on-screen signal (such as a black stripe) which shows when you have found the channel that carries the output frequency of the video recorder. Video recorders with on-screen programming will use that instead. Look in the manual to see which type you have.

3 Tune a programme number on the TV to this signal (see *Tuning a TV set to receive programmes* on the facing page, or your TV manual). Most video recorders use channel 36, 37 or 38. Some TV sets have a programme number, usually 9 or 0, pretuned to this channel.

4 Switch off the tuning signal.

5 Tune the video recorder. It makes life much easier if the programme numbers on the video recorder are the same as on the TV set.

HOW TO FIND A RECORDED PROGRAMME QUICKLY

Finding a programme on a tape usually requires either careful coordination of the tape and the tape counter or trial and error in fast-forward and rewind.

Some video recorders have a device called VISS (Video Index Search System) or simply Index Search. This automatically puts an electronic 'tag' at the beginning of a recording (it can also be added manually at any point). The machine can then be instructed to fast-forward or rewind and stop at the next tag.

A Skip Search option switches the tape from 'fast-wind' to 'play' for a few seconds at each index tag.

CHOOSING THE RIGHT TV AERIAL

● There are five types of outdoor TV aerial. The first four are known as groups A, B, C/D and E, and are each designed to receive some of the channel numbers used by local transmitters (see *Your local TV transmitter*, page 145).

Group	Channels
A	21-34
B	39-53
C/D	48-68
E	39-68

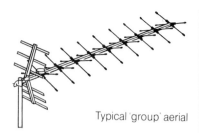
Wideband aerial

Typical 'group' aerial

● To check which type of aerial you need, ask an aerial supplier or contact the BBC or your local ITV station.

● The fifth type is a wideband aerial, which covers all channels. However it is larger, more expensive, more obtrusive, and more prone to wind deflection than a single-group aerial.

Installing a TV aerial

Direction The aerial needs to point at the local transmitter. Your neighbours' aerials will show you the general direction. Fine adjustment can be made when the aerial has been installed while somebody watches the TV set.

Horizontal or vertical? For main transmitters, the elements (parallel bars) need to be mounted horizontally. For most relay transmitters, vertically. Again, look at your neighbours' aerials.

Position In very good reception areas, it may be possible to install an aerial in the loft. Normally, though, external fitting above surrounding rooftops is necessary. A mast attached firmly to a chimney stack is the most common solution. Mounts and brackets to hold the mast in place can be bought from aerial suppliers.

Cabling Loose, flapping cabling will cause loss of picture quality, so secure it carefully with cable clips. Before the cable goes into the house, let it sag into a small loop so that rainwater drips off and doesn't enter the house.

CAUTION Only fit an aerial if you have safe access to the chimney – from a flat roof, for example. Otherwise call in a fitter.

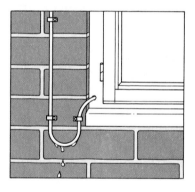

TV (AND VIDEO) IN EVERY ROOM

It's possible to use a TV set in as many as eight rooms in a house by using a small box called a distributor amplifier. It is powered by mains electricity, and can be either plugged into a socket or permanently wired into the supply.

Locating the amplifier The loft is usually the most convenient location for the amplifier. You can bring the aerial cable in under the eaves and connect it to the amplifier's input socket. But if you are first taking the cable to the video recorder, bring it into the room where you keep the video (see next page).

Cables running to each room Coaxial cable is run from each of the amplifier's output sockets to the rooms where you want TV sets. The cables can end with either a flush-mounted wall socket or a coaxial plug which goes direct into the TV's aerial socket. If you have a wall socket, use a short length of cable to connect the socket to the TV.

A WHOLE-HOUSE SYSTEM – WITH VIDEO AND SATELLITE TV

If you want to incorporate a video recorder and satellite TV into a whole-house network, run both aerial cables to the satellite receiver. Then link the satellite receiver to the video recorder. The output cable from the video recorder goes into the distributor amplifier. If you don't want satellite TV, take the terrestrial aerial direct to the video recorder.

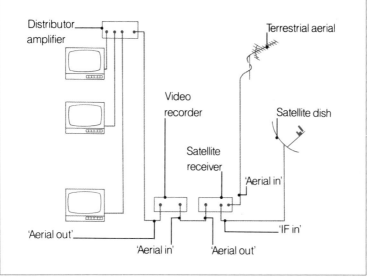

Who can see what? With this arrangement it's possible to watch any of the normal four TV channels in any room. It's also possible to send a video recording or a satellite channel to any of the rooms. But it's not possible to operate the video recorder or the satellite receiver from anywhere but the room in which they are placed. To do that you need a more complicated and expensive system.

FM radio, as well An FM radio aerial can be connected to the distributor amplifier, provided the amplifier has more than one input socket. The radio signal will share the cable down through the house without interfering with the TV. When the cable reaches a room that has both a TV set and an FM radio, fit a double socket outlet so that separate cable can be run to the two sets.

Poor reception areas If you live in a fringe reception area, TV signals from two television regions, or two transmitters, can be fed into the distributor amplifier. But you'll need two aerials.

How to connect a coaxial plug

If you want to run coaxial cable between one piece of video equipment and another, you'll need to know how to fit plugs at each end. There are male and female plugs to suit different socket outlets, so make sure that you buy the right sort from the video shop.

1 Cut off 30mm (1¼in) of outer sheath. Loosen and fold back the wire mesh 20mm (¾in) from the end. Then strip off 12mm (½in) of inner sheath.

Slide the plug cap down the cable. Fit the cable grip over the exposed wire mesh. The strands of the mesh must not touch the inner wire. You will have to open the jaws of the grip to cover the mesh and then squeeze them together with a pair of pliers.

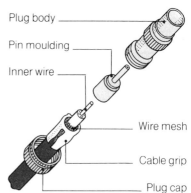

Plug body

Pin moulding

Inner wire

Wire mesh

Cable grip

Plug cap

2 Feed the inner wire into the pin moulding, then push the moulding into the plug body.

3 Slide the plug cap up over the cable grip and screw it firmly to the plug body.

HOW TO GET SATELLITE TV

To receive satellite TV, you need two pieces of equipment:
● An aerial – usually a dish, but it may be a flat plate.
● A satellite receiver – a box which contains a tuner for the satellite channels. Some TV sets have the receiver built in or it can be built into a video recorder.

Two satellites provide direct-to-home services to the United Kingdom. Astra carries Sky channels among others; Marcopolo, the former BSB satellite, also carries Sky channels, but may be given to a different programme company by the end of 1992. The two satellites need different aerials and receivers.

Installing a satellite aerial

Fitting a satellite aerial is in one way easier than fitting a normal TV aerial, because it doesn't need to be high up. But it does need a clear line of sight to the point in the sky where its satellite is stationed, avoiding obstacles such as trees and buildings.

So before spending any money on equipment, work out the line of sight. It doesn't have to be absolutely exact, and if you can take a compass bearing you should be able to do it.

Finding the right spot in the sky

● If you want to receive Astra, take a compass bearing between 148 and 158 degrees. It depends where in Britain you live. For Marcopolo, the bearing is 218-222 degrees.

Rotate the dial of a compass until the arrow on the dial lines up with the red end of the needle, then read off the bearing from the numbers round the dial.

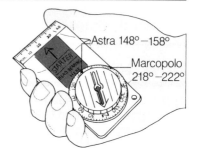

Astra 148°–158°

Marcopolo 218°–222°

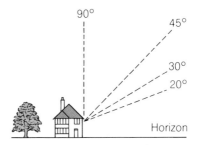

● Then you need to find the correct angle above the horizon. For Astra, this varies from 30 degrees in the south of England to 21 degrees in the north of Scotland. For Marcopolo, the angle varies from 27 degrees in the south to 19 degrees in the north. So both satellites are fairly low in the sky.

● If the sky is unobstructed in that direction it should be possible to install a satellite aerial.

Fitting the dish

● Before you start, make sure you have all the equipment you'll need, including the correct cable. Some Astra receivers need coaxial cable; others use a twin cable.
● It may help to align the dish in a temporary position on the ground, connect it to the receiver and tune in a satellite channel on the TV set before starting the ladder-work.
● Fit the dish, using the brackets that are supplied with it, and align it exactly with the help of someone who is watching the television set. Alternatively, you can use a portable TV set connected to the receiver and placed where you can see it.

LOW-COST WAY TO GET MULTI-CHANNELS

There are more than a dozen satellites serving Europe, broadcasting about 100 TV channels. Of these, more than 30 are in the PAL transmission standard (as used by Sky Television) and are not scrambled. Most broadcast in foreign languages.

To receive them, you need a movable dish. This can be motorised, and part of a system costing over £1000.

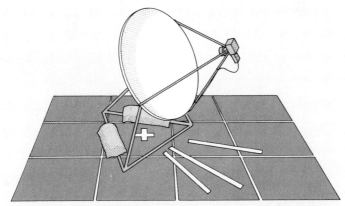

A cheap alternative is a patio dish, which is mounted on a frame and simply stands on the ground. You move it by hand when you want to change satellites.

The dish needs to be at least 90cm (3ft) in diameter. Use tape or paint to mark different satellite positions on the ground. A couple of sandbags will help to keep the dish stable in windy conditions. This type of dish can be connected to any Astra-compatible satellite receiver, provided it has user-tunable channels.

151

Connecting up the aerial

● The simplest way of connecting the satellite receiver, a video recorder and the TV set is by using their aerial sockets which may be labelled RF.
● The cable from the TV aerial leads to the RF input of the satellite receiver. The cable from the satellite aerial goes to the satellite receiver's other input, marked IF. The receiver's RF output is connected to the video recorder's aerial input, and the video recorder's aerial output is connected to the aerial input of the TV set.
● Connections are made by coaxial cable, with male and female coaxial cable plugs.

Scart sockets for better pictures

Scart sockets, which are found on most modern video equipment, provide a better way of connecting up your TV and video for satellite broadcasts. There are two types of Scart sockets – 'full' and 'restricted' and they give several advantages.
● Better picture quality.
● Freedom from cross-channel interference in both terrestrial and satellite TV.
● Sky transmissions on Marcopolo (but not on Astra) use the improved D-MAC system. Full Scart gives the benefits of D-MAC – better pictures, NICAM stereo sound and widescreen pictures (if transmitted). Restricted Scart gives PAL transmission and stereo sound. RF (aerial) socket gives PAL transmission and mono sound.
● 'Full' Scart is suitable for connecting computers to your TV set.
● It leaves some of the non-broadcast channels (35-38) free to carry other sources such as video games.

Making a Scart connection. To make the connection, join the satellite receiver or the video recorder if you've got one, to the TV set through the Scart sockets. The sockets, which are near-rectangular in shape, are also known as Euroconnectors and Peritel sockets.

Sockets and leads Full and restricted Scart sockets look identical, so look in your instruction manual. Full scart leads (European standard EN 50049) are much thicker than restricted ones and cost about 50 per cent more.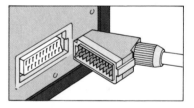

Using Scart On some television sets, programme number 0 has to be used for Scart reception. Alternatively, there may be a button marked Ext or Aux. Your TV set's instruction book should tell you.
    When you are using Scart sockets, leave the RF chain in place for making video recordings.

STEREO SOUND FROM SATELLITE TV

Many satellite receivers offer stereo sound. So do some video recorders. You can enjoy the stereo sound even if your TV set is mono. Connect the audio output on the receiver or the video recorder to an audio input (marked Spare or Tape, not Record-player or Phono) on your hi-fi system. Place the TV set halfway between the two loudspeakers.

Fault-finder guide: television and video recorder

Problem	Likely cause/Remedy
TELEVISION No power	Mains not connected. Fuse blown in mains plug.
Power but no signal	Are all RF/Scart connections in place?
Poor picture quality, characters missing on teletext (terrestrial channels).	Weak signal due to aerial deterioration or unsuitability to local reception conditions. Check aerial direction, stability and connections. Use higher-gain aerial or indoor, powered amplifier.
Ghosting (faint, repeated image on terrestrial channels)	Caused by reflected signals from hills and buildings. Check aerial installation. Try different position or height. Use a more highly directive aerial to strengthen wanted signal and reject unwanted reflections. Try receiving from a different transmitter (page 145).
Poor picture on satellite TV – usually 'sparklies' (white dashes on screen)	Can be caused by rain. Check dish has not become misaligned or obscured, e.g. by foliage. Check skew adjustment on receiver (if available) and adjust if necessary. If severe, consider a larger dish.
VIDEO RECORDER Poor picture on playback	Tape heads dirty. Clean (using a cleaning tape).
Rented video tape gives fuzzy picture and/or sound	Adjust tracking control.
Remote control doesn't work	Solid object between control and receiving 'eye'. Batteries exhausted.
Satellite signal shows through on video-recorder channel	Retune satellite receiver (or video recorder) output to another channel – if necessary, a locally vacant one other than 35-38. Retune the TV to the same channel.
'Herringbone' patterning on screen	Interference from adjacent channel (usually between video or satellite receiver and broadcast channel). Retune video/satellite receiver to another, locally vacant channel and retune TV set to the same channel.

MAKING YOUR OWN VIDEO

If you only use a video camera rarely, it's possible to rent one at a daily rate, with reductions for longer periods.

● Check the insurance position – add it to your own household insurance if it is not included in the rental. Video cameras are delicate, expensive and attractive to thieves.

● Book early for birthday parties and at peak times such as Christmas.

● Practise using the machine before the big event.

● Make sure the batteries are fully charged before you use the camera.

● If you rent a camera with a format (VHS-C or V8) which is different from your video recorder, be sure to transfer recordings to a suitable tape before taking the camera back. This is done by playing the tape in the camera, and rerecording it onto your video recorder – so you will need a suitable lead to connect the two. If you can't hire one with the camera, they can be bought fairly cheaply.

DO'S AND DON'TS OF VIDEO SHOOTING

DO reduce camera wobble by steadying yourself against anything available – wall, car roof, street furniture – while shooting.

DO seek out a moving item – perhaps a boat, a vehicle or an animal – to follow with the camera.

DO use moving vehicles to film from. But don't walk while filming – you'll create camera wobble.

DON'T produce a series of 10-second still snapshots. If your subjects won't provide motion, create it yourself by using the zoom facility on the camera or by panning – moving the camera round in an arc – while you stand in the same place.

DON'T overdo these effects, or the results will become too restless.

Staying behind the line

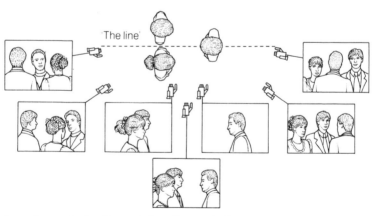

'The line'

It can be confusing if people in a film are facing one way in one shot and the opposite way in another. If you film an event – say a wedding – from all angles, that is what will happen. It's known as 'crossing the line' and you avoid it by drawing an imaginary line through the action, and working from one side of it.

Four tips for better lighting

Stronger bulbs Even using stronger general-purpose bulbs in domestic fittings will improve indoor scenes. But beware of using specialist filming bulbs in ordinary light fittings – they can overheat, or even fuse your electrical circuit.

Point the lights Use directable lighting – from table or standard lamps – to create the desired effect.

Window lights When shooting indoors in daylight, keep the window behind you.

Sun over your shoulder Out-of-doors, keep the sun behind you, preferably over one shoulder.

DON'T BE AFRAID OF THE DARK

The high spot of children's birthday parties is the blowing-out of the candles. Switch off (or dim right down) the room lights and shoot by the light of the candles. Have someone standing by to turn up the lights gently (if they're on a dimmer) after all the candles are blown out – but get him to allow a good second of darkness first. The quality won't be top-rate but the atmosphere will be magical.

Editing a videotape

Using the camcorder Videotape is edited by copying from one tape to another, using the camcorder and a video recorder. The original remains intact and you can afford to experiment without risk and at little cost.

Purpose-made console Editing consoles make the job easier, but they're costly. You may be able to get the use of one by joining a video club – or see if you can rent one.

Spare footage 'Live' sound is often spoilt by shouted conversations between the cameraman and the subject. Replacing it with music can be effective, but sometimes can seem too artificial. Try to film some footage just for the background sounds, which can be used to patch over such moments.

WHERE TO PUT HI-FI SPEAKERS

The position of speakers can greatly affect their sound. Experiment by moving them around for better results, keeping in mind the following principles:

Solid base To avoid vibration, don't just stand the speakers on the carpet. Put them on purpose-made metal frames with spiked feet that go through the carpet to the solid floor. The frames can be bought from hi-fi shops, and substantially improve the sound quality.

Soft furnishings Curtains, upholstered furniture and carpets will tend to absorb higher frequencies. This can be useful if speakers seem too

155

'bright' (high-pitched); otherwise try to place the speakers away from curtains or upholstered chairs.

Use of walls Standing a speaker against a wall tends to reflect lower frequencies, boosting the bass notes. A corner of the room will increase this effect still further. To reduce it, move speakers about 600mm (2ft) out from the wall.

Raising the height of the speakers To increase brightness (clarity in the treble range), raise the speakers on stands or wall brackets so that the tweeters (the treble cones) are on a level with the ears of the seated listener, or higher.

'Tweeters' together Should you wish to lay the speakers on their sides – on a bookshelf for example – place them so that the treble cones are closest together. Treble cones, also called 'tweeters', are the smallest cones on two or three-way speakers. They are nearest to the top of the cabinet, and can be seen if you remove the fabric cover over the front of the speaker.

Connecting separate components

The record deck Only connect the record deck to the amplifier through the correct socket (possibly marked phono, disc or gram). The socket pre-amplifies the weak signal from the cartridge.

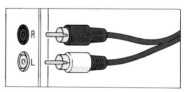

CD player If your amplifier has no CD or AUX input socket, use the socket for the tuner or tape deck. Do not use the record-player (phono) socket – it will produce bad distortion.

If there are not enough sockets, a 2-into-1 switchable adaptor may be the answer.

Just as a temporary measure, you can try routing the CD player through Line In on the tape deck. You will need to put the tape deck into record mode (either on 'Pause' or with a 'sacrificial' blank tape permanently inserted).

Lower volume for CDs A CD player has a higher output than the other hi-fi components, so you'll need to use a lower volume setting on the amplifier when playing a CD.

AN AERIAL FOR YOUR TUNER

T he best quality of reproduction available from a mid-price audio system is usually through the FM radio tuner, so it is well worth buying a good radio aerial.

The aerial can normally be mounted in the loft and you can connect it to the TV aerial cable to cut down on the number of wires that are running through the house.

Fault-finder guide: hi-fi

Problem	Probable cause/ Solution
No sound, no fascia lights	Mains disconnected. Mains plug fused.
No sound, but fascia lights on	Check speaker connections. Check 'speaker off' switch. Is the correct component (tape deck, CD player, tuner, etc) switched in?
Hum	Can be caused by components placed too close together, especially if, say, a record deck is stacked on top of an amplifier. Should not happen with matched systems. Connect components one at a time to the amplifier to identify the source of the trouble. Then try moving the component, or rearranging the connecting leads. Can also be caused by earthing problems. Try connecting a thin wire, metal-to-metal from the body of the component to the body of the amplifier. There may be a small screw provided for this purpose.
Poor sound	If from tape deck or record deck, clean tape heads or stylus. If from FM radio, make sure the aerial is secure, and check all connections. If from all sources, check the speakers. Switch them around (left-right) and listen closely to each cone. If the speakers are not faulty, the problem is probably in the amplifier and will need professional attention.
Speakers 'sound wrong' (poor stereo image)	Speakers are out of phase. To check this, select a mono source, then place the speakers close together – about 150mm (6in) apart – facing each other, and listen. Now switch round the connections of the lead at the two terminals on the back of one of the speakers, and listen again. The connection producing the loudest sound, especially in the bass, is the correct one. Note: always switch off the amplifier when disconnecting speakers.

GETTING MORE OUT OF A SOCKET

The more video and audio components you have, the more mains sockets you need – often in one corner of the room. The best solution is extra sockets, which can be added to a ring main easily by an electrician.

Alternatively, you can install some form of multisocket adaptor. The best is the fused flat-board type, with a short trailing lead. It can be screwed to the skirting board, if you wish. A block type is not recommended, because the weight of the plugs and the cables can drag it partially out of the socket.

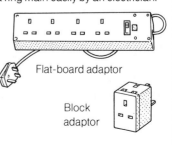

Flat-board adaptor

Block adaptor

Recording the radio when you're out

● Buy a radio-cassette recorder with a clock-timer. A few models are available.

● Use a plug-in timer. Tune the radio to the correct station, and leave it on; set the tape recorder to record. Then set the timer, plug the radio into the timer and the timer into the wall socket. (This may not work for recorders with electronic controls.)

● Try using your video recorder. Feed the sound from the radio output to the audio inputs (if any) or the Scart socket, using a lead with the appropriate connectors. On the control panel, turn the knob from 'Aerial' to 'External source'.

INSTALLING PHONE EXTENSIONS

To fit one or more telephone extensions in your house, you can buy the cable and sockets in kit form. You will need:

● A master socket (which has to be installed by British Telecom).

● A two-way converter which plugs into the master socket.

● Telephone cable and cable cleats (one cleat for every 200-300mm (8-12in) of cable.

● A wall socket for each new extension.

● Possibly a junction box.

● A hammer, a screwdriver, a trimming knife and a disposable tool for inserting wires (buy it with the sockets).

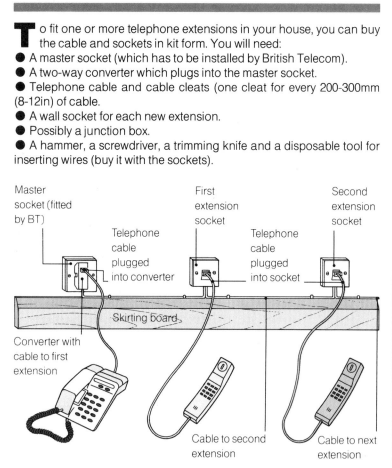

Master socket (fitted by BT)

First extension socket

Second extension socket

Telephone cable plugged into converter

Telephone cable plugged into socket

Skirting board

Converter with cable to first extension

Cable to second extension

Cable to next extension

1 Plan the cable routes and the site of the extension sockets or junction box. A junction box saves cable if it is fitted on a landing so that extensions can be run from it to more than one room.

2 Attach the converter to the end of the cable (if it is not already attached), plug it into the master socket and fix the nearest part of the cable to the wall with a cleat. Then unplug the converter.

3 Screw the back boxes of the new extension sockets and junction box into place.

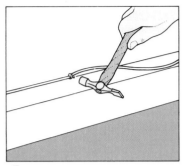
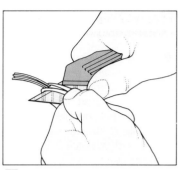

4 Run the cable to the boxes and fix it in place with cleats. It will probably look neatest running along the top of the skirting board.

5 For each socket or junction, trim cable to allow enough for attachment and strip back about 35mm (1⅜in) of outer casing.

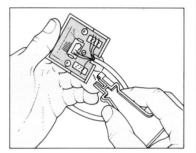

6 Insert the wires into the correct holes, using the disposable insertion tool and following the instructions that come with the kit.

7 Plug in the converter at the master socket and plug in the phones at the extensions.

How many extensions?

There is no limit to the number of extension sockets you can install, but:
● The number of phones which can be attached to one line is limited, according to a calculation based on RENs (ringer equivalent numbers). Most phones have an REN of 1. Some fax machines have an REN of 1.5. An answering machine is 1 or 1.5. The maximum number of RENs a line can support is 4.
● The total length of cable should not exceed 50 metres (55yds).

TAKING A NUMBER OF EXTENSIONS FROM A JUNCTION BOX

You may want to take more than one extension from the same place – perhaps from the landing outside three rooms, for example. A junction box is designed specially for the job. Run your cable from the converter at the master socket to a junction box on the landing. It will accommodate the main cable plus as many as three extension cables.

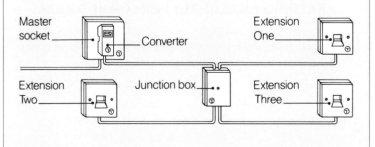

How to reduce your phone bill

● Don't rent your phone – buy one.
● Don't phone in the mornings – rates are cheaper after 1pm, and even lower after 6pm and at weekends.
● Keep calls short. Don't hold for long if an extension is engaged (unless you know there is always a problem getting through). If someone is unavailable, leave a message for them to phone you back.
● Many organisations now have Freephone numbers. Note any you come across.
● If you make a lot of long-distance calls, use Mercury – rates are lower and calls are charged to the second, not by the unit. To use Mercury, you don't need a new line, but you do need a Mercury-compatible phone. There is an annual subscription.
● Don't use your answering machine to collect messages – all those call-backs are costing you money! Leave a number at which you can be contacted on the tape, or have your calls diverted to it by British Telecom (BT Star Service).
● Making arrangements involving more than one other person can involve a lot of time and ringing back. Three-way calling allows you and two other numbers to talk together at the same time (BT Star Service).
● Don't incur charges by calling Directory Enquiries. Make sure you have up-to-date phone books. Unless a long-distance call is urgent, get the number from phone books held at public libraries. If you receive a London Community Book, you are entitled to the three central London directories without charge. Ring 100 and ask for Freephone Phonebooks.
● If family members are running up huge phone bills, consider:
— Installing a pay phone.
— Getting a phone lock or device to limit the numbers that can be called.
— Using Call Barring, which blocks outgoing calls as well as incoming ones when you're out (BT Star Service).
— Using itemised billing.

How to cope with nuisance calls

● Hang up at once. Do not start a conversation and do not give your name or address. If the calls persist, call 0800 666 700 for a recorded BT message or contact BT Customer Liaison for advice (ring operator or dial 150). Also call the police.
● Use an answering machine. Listen in to the caller and pick up the phone if you wish to speak. This can be an effective deterrent.
● Go ex-directory.
● Change your phone number – the cost is quite modest.
● Use Call Barring – putting your phone on 'engaged' for as long as you like (BT Star Service).
● Use Call Diversion – calls taken by someone else (BT Star Service).

KEEPING AN ELDERLY PERSON IN TOUCH

To avoid the risk of an elderly or housebound person having their phone disconnected because they haven't paid the bill, get them to apply for British Telecom's Protected Service Scheme.

When a final reminder is ignored (perhaps because of a long stay in hospital), BT undertakes to contact a nominee, who will be given time to sort things out. The nominee does not become liable for the bill. The service is free, but only available where the phone is essential.

Simple home maintenance

HOW TO WIRE A PLUG

All electric plugs need a cartridge fuse. Many are fitted with a 13amp fuse when you buy them, but you should make sure that the plug has the right fuse to protect the appliance. It will only need a 3amp fuse if the appliance is, say, a table lamp or a hair dryer. The more powerful 13amp fuse could damage the wiring or even cause a fire.

1 Unscrew the cover of the plug with a screwdriver, and take care not to lose the screw.

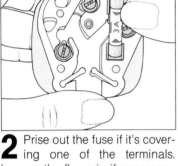
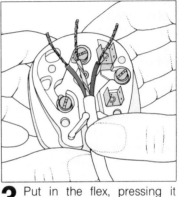

2 Prise out the fuse if it's covering one of the terminals. Loosen the flex grip if necessary. Plastic flanges grip the flex in some plugs, and they don't need loosening; but in others the flex is held by a screw-down bar.

3 Put in the flex, pressing it between the flanges. Or push it under the bar and tighten the screws. Make sure the bar grips the outer sheath, not just the wires.

If the flex has to pass through a sleeve in the cover, do it now.

4 Cut the wires to the right length to reach the terminals and strip off some insulation from each wire if necessary (page 163). Connect the wires to the correct terminals. The brown wire is connected to the terminal marked L, the blue wire goes to the terminal marked N, and the earth wire (green and yellow) goes to the terminal marked E or ⏚.

Wind the tip of each wire round the correct terminal and tighten the screw. Wind the wire clockwise

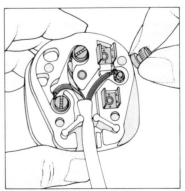

round the terminal or it will be loosened as you tighten the screw. Alternatively, if the terminal has a hole, push the wire into it until no bare wire is showing, and tighten the screw.

5 Replace the fuse if you had to remove it to reach the terminal. Make sure it has the correct amp rating.

6 Screw the cover back onto the plug.

IDENTIFYING AN OLD FLEX

The colours of the wires in a flex were changed in the 1970s. If you have an appliance with the old colours (red, black and green), get the flex changed by an electrical repair shop and have the appliance serviced at the same time.

Which fuse do you need?

3amp cartridge

Use in plugs for appliances up to 700 watts. The wattage is given on the rating plate of the appliance.

Appliances that take a 3amp fuse include:

Clock
Electric blanket
Extractor fan
Food processor/mixer/blender
Hair dryer
Hi-fi system   Lamp (standard or table)
Home computer   Radio
Iron (travel model)   Tape recorder
Slow cooker   Television (black and white)

13amp fuse

Use in plugs for appliances between 700 and 3000 watts. The wattage is given on the rating plate.

Appliances that take a 13amp fuse include:

Deep-fat fryer
Dishwasher
Fan heater
Fires (some)
Freezer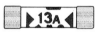
Iron (standard model)
Kettle   Toaster
Refrigerator   Tumble dryer
Spin dryer   Vacuum cleaner
Television (colour)   Washing machine

How to make a flex longer

If you need to make a flex longer, join a new piece to the existing flex with a fixed connector which can be bought at an electrical shop.

DO NOT join two pieces of flex by twisting the wires together and binding them up with tape. The join may overheat and start a fire, or it could be pulled apart by someone tripping over the flex.

When you buy the flex, take the appliance (or a piece of the existing flex) with you to ensure you get the right sort. It may not cost much more for the shop to replace the old flex with a new one of the right length. If you decide to do it yourself, prepare the ends of both flexes (see next page).

1 Unscrew the cover of the fixed connector and loosen the flex grip (the little bar) at each end.

2 Push the prepared ends of flex under each flex grip.

3 Screw the conductors tightly into place at the terminals so that the pairs match – brown to brown at one side, green and yellow in the middle and blue to blue at the other side.

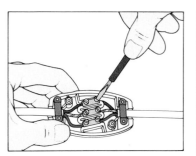

4 Tighten the flex grips securely, and screw the cover back on.

5 Fit a plug at the other end of the new flex (page 161).

Stripping the end of a flex

To do this you will need a craft knife – the sort with replaceable blades which preferably retract for safety. You'll also need wire strippers (from an electrical shop).

1 Lay the flex on a firm surface and cut through the outer sheath with the knife, making a single lengthwise cut.
   Take great care not to cut or nick the insulation on the wires. If you do, cut off the damaged piece and start again.

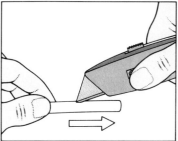

2 Bend back the outer sheath and cut at the fold to remove it.

3 Cut the individual wires to the right length so that they reach their terminals comfortably.

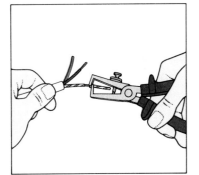

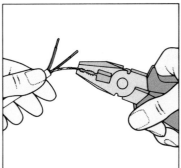

4 Adjust the hole on the wire strippers to the thickness of the wires. Use a spare bit of wire to get the adjustment right. Press the handles firmly together to cut the insulation about 15mm ($\frac{5}{8}$in) from the tip. Rotate the strippers half a turn and pull them towards the tip of the wire. The unwanted insulation will slide off.

5 Tidy up the ends by twisting the tip of each wire with pliers to wind the thin strands tightly together.
   This is done to make sure that no whiskery pieces are splaying out. There is then no danger of stray strands from different wires making contact with one another, causing the plug fuse to blow.

HOW TO CHANGE A MAIN FUSE

I f all the lights suddenly go out on one floor – or all the power sockets on one floor stop working – a fuse has probably blown at the main fuse box. It's not difficult to replace, but you should try to find out what caused it to blow. Otherwise it's likely to blow again immediately (see *Checking the circuit*, next page).

A modern fuse box (known in the electrical trade as a consumer unit) may have any of half a dozen different types of fuse. Keep spare fuse wire or cartridge fuses in the house. You'll also probably need a torch.

A rewirable fuse

1 Turn off the main switch on the fuse box and, if necessary, remove the fuse box cover.

2 The circuit protected by each fuse should be marked on the fuse carrier or fuse box – 'Upstairs lights', 'Downstairs sockets', and so on. If not, you will have to discover which fuse has blown.
● Scorch marks around the fuse carrier often reveal the faulty one.
● If there are no marks, look at each fuse wire. Take out only one fuse carrier at a time and put it back before taking out the next. The one with a broken wire is faulty.

3 Unplug all the appliances or lamps on the faulty circuit. If it's a lighting circuit, turn off all the light switches. If you don't, the fuse is likely to blow again when you turn the power back on.

4 Use a screwdriver to loosen the two screws on the fuse carrier and take out the old wire.
Cut a new fuse wire of the amp rating shown on the fuse carrier and long enough to cross the carrier and go round both screws, with a little slack. Use one strand only; don't double it.

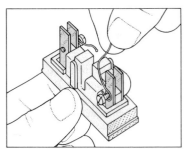

5 Wind the wire clockwise around one screw; tighten the screw.

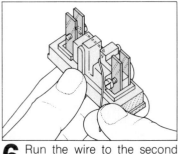

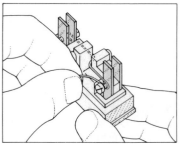

6 Run the wire to the second screw. Look at another fuse carrier to see what path it takes.

7 Wind it clockwise round the second screw, leaving a little slack. Then tighten the screw.

8 Replace the fuse carrier, close the box and turn on the main switch to restore the power.

Checking the circuit

Before plugging in the appliances or switching on the lights, do a check of the electrical circuit.
●Look for damage on the appliances, the lights and the flexes that were in use when the circuit failed. If you find one that is damaged, don't plug it back in but get it repaired. Then switch on the appliances or lights one at a time.
●Make sure you are not overloading the circuit, which is the likeliest cause of a blown fuse. A lighting circuit should have no more than ten lights, totalling up to 1200 watts. A ring (socket) circuit cannot supply more than 7200 watts – so don't try running two three-bar fires, an iron and a kettle off the same circuit at the same time.
●If the fuse blows again, don't keep trying – call an electrician.

Replacing a cartridge fuse

1 Turn off the main switch on the fuse box.

2 Replace the faulty circuit cartridge with one marked with the rating shown on the carrier.

If the fuse carriers have not been marked to show which circuits they protect, you can test each fuse on a metal torch. Remove the end of the torch, and put one end of the fuse on the battery and the other on the torch case. Switch on the torch. If it fails to light, the fuse is faulty. Purpose-made fuse testers are also available.

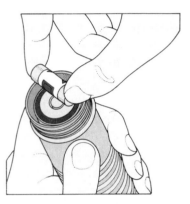

3 To prevent the new fuse blowing again immediately, unplug all appliances and lamps on a ring (socket) circuit, or switch off all the lights on a lighting circuit.

4 Replace the fuse carrier, close the fuse box and turn on the main switch to restore the power.

5 Check the circuit as described above.

Checking miniature circuit breakers

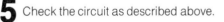

If the fuse box is fitted with miniature circuit breakers, the faulty circuit will be obvious – the lever will be in the 'off' position or the button will have popped out.

1 Before doing anything to the circuit breaker, turn off the main switch on the fuse box.

2 Unplug all appliances and lamps on the faulty circuit. If it's a lighting circuit, switch off all the lights.

3 Switch on the circuit breaker and then the main switch.

4 Check the circuit for damage or for overloading as described at the top of the facing page.

MAKE SURE A CIRCUIT IS DEAD

I f you are switching off a circuit for any reason, always double check that the right one has been switched off. If you fail to get this right, you could electrocute yourself or someone else.

● Plug a lamp – one that you know works – into a socket on the circuit and make sure it won't turn on.

● On a lighting circuit, turn a switch on and off two or three times to make sure the light doesn't come on.

● If you are not totally certain which circuit should be switched off, cut off the entire electricity supply by turning off the main switch on the fuse box.

A neat fixing for bell and phone wires

One way to keep long runs of wire from doorbells or telephone extensions out of the way is to hammer them in place on skirting boards and door architraves with plastic cable cleats. But for a neater finish you can fix them in place with a hot-melt glue gun.

● Plan the route you want the wire to follow.

● Pull the wire taut and apply a small blob of glue to the back of the wire about every 100mm (4in). Press it immediately to the wall or skirting, and the glue will grip instantly.

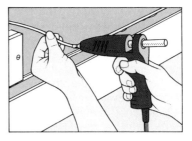

KNOWING YOUR WATER SYSTEM

M ost houses have a cold-water tank, usually in the loft, which feeds most of the taps in the house, plus the lavatory cistern. The tank is filled by the rising main.

The only tap fed direct from the rising main is usually the kitchen cold tap, which should always be used for drinking water. A washing machine and a garden tap may also be fed by the rising main.

A few prewar and country houses have all the taps, and lavatory cistern, fed direct from the rising main.

HOW TO CUT OFF THE WATER

I f you want to change a tap washer you will need to cut off the water supply to the tap first.

Taps fed from the cold-water tank Turn off (clockwise) the gate valve or isolating valve in the appropriate pipe. It may be in the loft. When you have identified it, label it so you don't forget.

If there is no gate valve or isolating valve on the pipe, you will have to drain the cold-water tank as follows:

1 Put a piece of wood, such as a broomstick, across the cold-water tank and tie the ball-valve arm up to it. This will stop the water coming in from the rising main.

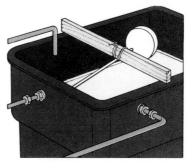

2 Turn on the bathroom cold taps until the water stops flowing, then turn on the hot taps – a little water will come out. (There is no need to turn off the boiler as the hot-water cylinder will not be drained.)

Taps fed from the rising main Turn off (clockwise) the main stopcock, then turn on the tap until the water stops flowing.

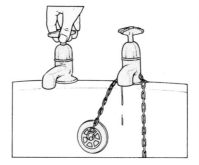

The easy way to stop the flow

Repairs to taps and other fittings are much easier if the water can be cut off by a stop valve in the pipe that is being worked on. The supply to other parts of the house is then not disrupted. Small stop valves, usually called isolating valves, are available that can be turned on and off with a coin.
● One type has a compression joint at each end. It can be fitted by draining the pipe, cutting out a small section with a hacksaw, putting the valve on the pipe ends, and tightening the joints.
● A flexible tap connector, incorporating an isolating valve, can be used to connect a tap to the pipe – very useful when a tap is being fitted in an awkward place.

The main stopcock

Where is it? In a full-blooded emergency such as a burst pipe, you need to get to the main stopcock in a hurry. So if you don't know where it is, find it now. In most houses it is where the water supply pipe enters the house. This is often under the kitchen sink or in a larder. If the house has a cellar it may be down there. In a bungalow, look in the airing cupboard.

Check that it works When you've found it, make sure it hasn't stiffened up from lack of use, and that it actually works. Turn it fully off (clockwise), and then check that water stops flowing from the kitchen cold tap.
    If water still flows out of the kitchen tap, the washer on the stopcock probably needs replacing. Get a plumber to do it as soon as possible.
    If the stopcock is hard to turn, apply a few drops of penetrating oil.

Stop it jamming To guard against the stopcock jamming in future, close and open it fully once or twice a year. After opening it, give it a quarter turn towards closure. This will stop it jamming without affecting the water flow.

167

A last resort – the outdoor stopcock

If the stopcock is jammed or doesn't stop the flow of water, it may be possible to turn off the outdoor stopcock in front of your house. It's under a small metal cover, either just inside your garden or in the pavement.

The stopcock is below ground level at the bottom of a pipe, so you need a key. If you haven't got one, buy or make one. But first check the type needed – the stopcock may have a handle with a single cross piece (a crutch handle) or a tapered knob.

1 Raise the metal cover. If it is hard to move scrape soil from around it, then lift with an old chisel.

2 Put the key down the pipe so that it engages the stopcock handle, and turn it clockwise.

MAKING A STOPCOCK KEY

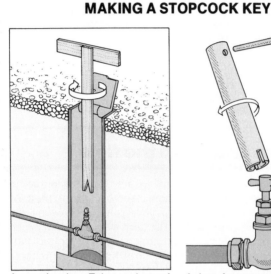

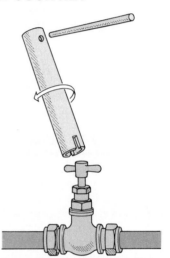

A wooden key Take a piece of wood about 1m (3ft) long, and in one end cut a V-shaped slot about 25mm (1in) wide at the opening and 75mm (3in) deep. Screw and glue another piece across the other end as a handle. It should turn a crutch handle or a tapered knob.

A key from metal tubing If the stopcock has a crutch handle, use aluminium tubing about 30mm (1¼in) diameter. With a hacksaw, cut a slot in one end of the tubing to fit over the stopcock handle and drill a hole near the other end to take a steel bar.

How to 'soften' tap water

In hard-water areas, soap won't lather and kettles and pipes fur up with lime scale. Here are four ways to make the water 'softer' for washing. Water for drinking and cooking should come from the kitchen cold tap not connected to a softener.

Direct application Use a proprietary softening powder in washing water. It will dissolve in either hot or cold water and is suitable for all fabrics.

Portable softener A water-softening unit can be connected by a hose to a hot or cold tap. The unit needs occasional topping up with a softening agent – usually ordinary salt.

Crystals in the tank A container full of crystals can be suspended in the cold-water tank. It needs replacing about every six months.

Plumbed-in softener An ion-exchange water softener can be permanently plumbed-in to the rising main. It also has to be regularly topped up with salt, which can be fed automatically into the unit.

STOPPING A TAP FROM DRIPPING

Water dripping from the spout of a tap is usually a signal that the washer needs replacing. Constantly dripping water will eventually stain the bath or basin.

Change the washer on a morning when the shops are open. You may have to go out and buy something halfway through.

When you buy a new washer, get some spares for both bath and basin taps, and store them where you'll remember to find them.

Removing the headgear

1 Before starting, turn off the water supply to the tap (page 166).

2 Turn the tap fully on, and when no more water comes out, put the plug in the hole to prevent any small parts from falling through.

3 Unscrew the bell-shaped cover. (For shrouded head taps, see next page.) This can often be done by hand, but if the cover is too stiff use an adjustable spanner or pipe wrench, padding the jaws with a cloth or chamois leather so they don't scratch.

4 Insert an open-ended spanner under the cover and undo the headgear nut by turning it anti-clockwise (when looking down on the tap).

If you only have an adjustable spanner it will probably be too thick to fit under the cover, so undo the little screw that holds the handle, then pull off the handle and lift up the bell-shaped cover.

If the headgear nut is hard to turn, don't force it. Put penetrating oil around the joint and wait for ten minutes. Then hold the spout of the tap with a padded pipe wrench and counteract the force applied to the nut by pulling in the opposite direction. You may have to make several applications of oil.

Fitting the washer

1 According to the type of tap you have, the washer will either be fixed to the bottom of the headgear or it will have stayed behind inside the body of the tap.

169

● If the washer is fixed to the headgear by a small button, prise it off with a screwdriver.

● If it's held on by a small nut, apply penetrating oil, leave it for ten minutes and then undo it with a spanner that fits exactly.

● A separate jumper stem can be held with a pair of pliers or a vice. If the nut won't come off, buy a new washer and jumper complete.

2 Fit the new washer, and grease the thread of the headgear before reassembling the tap.

3 Turn the tap off before restoring the water supply.

TAPS WITH SHROUDED HEADS

Many taps have the handle and cover in one piece, and it must be removed to get at the headgear.

● Some models have a plate on top which hides a retaining screw. Prise off the plate with a knife and undo the screw. Then lift off the handle.

● On other models the handle pulls straight off.

● Or it may unscrew by continuing to turn after you have turned the tap fully on.

● Or there may be a small screw in the head.

Once the shrouded head has been removed, the headgear nut can be unscrewed with any type of spanner that fits, in the same way as for a conventional tap.

If the drip is coming from a mixer tap, replace both the hot and cold washers.

A new washer unit for a Supatap

You don't have to turn off the water supply when changing a Supatap washer because the tap has a valve that stops the flow as the nozzle is unscrewed.

Before you start, buy a new washer and jumper unit from a plumbers' supply shop.

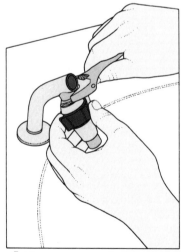 

1 Use a spanner to loosen the six-sided retaining nut at the top of the nozzle by turning it anticlockwise (it has a left-hand thread).

2 Hold the loosened nut with one hand while you turn the tap on. Keep turning it to unscrew the nozzle. The water flow will stop just before the nozzle comes off.

3 Tap the base of the nozzle against something firm – not the washbasin, or you may chip the surface. Then turn the nozzle upside-down. The antisplash device, which contains the washer unit, will fall out.

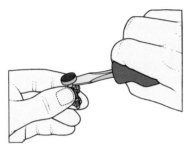

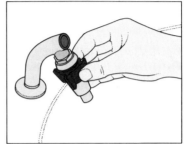

4 Prise out the washer unit with a screwdriver blade inserted under the washer plate.

5 Snap the new unit into place, then reassemble the tap by screwing the nozzle clockwise.

A LEAK NEAR THE HANDLE

When a tap leaks near the handle, the cause is a faulty gland or O-ring seal which is supposed to prevent water coming out past the spindle when the tap is turned on.

This sort of leak is most likely to occur on an old kitchen cold tap. Detergent from wet hands may have run down the spindle and washed the grease out of the gland.

Modern taps usually have an O-ring seal instead of a gland, and it rarely needs replacing. O-ring seals are also used on the spout of a mixer tap and on a shower diverter. They may occasionally become worn, or perish.

Checking the seal

Taps with shrouded heads are usually sealed with O-rings.

If your tap has a conventional cross-shaped handle, you'll need to find out if it has a hemp gland or an O-ring.

To be on the safe side, cut off the water supply to the tap (page 166) – although if it has a hemp gland there is no need to.

1 Turn the tap off and undo the small screw that secures the capstan handle. Put it in a safe place (it is very easily lost), then remove the handle.

If there is no screw, the handle should pull off.

Or the screw may be hidden under a plastic cap on top of the tap, which can be prised off with the point of a knife.

171

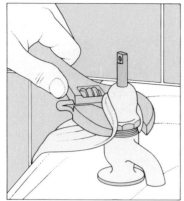

2 Remove the bell-shaped cover to reveal the gland nut – the highest nut on the spindle.

3 Use a spanner to remove the gland nut. Turn the nut anti-clockwise.

4 Note the type of seal used in the gland. In an older-style tap it may be hemp, in a modern tap a rubber O-ring. Hemp can be replaced with wool. Replace an O-ring with a new one of the same size.

REMOVING A STUBBORN HANDLE

If a conventional tap handle is difficult to pull off after you have removed the screw, turn the tap fully on, raise the bell-shaped cover, and put a wedge of wood, such as a clothespeg, on each side between the raised cover and the tap body. Then turn the tap off (clockwise).

The pressure will force the handle off. Remove the pegs and temporarily slip the handle on again to fully close the tap.

Repacking a gland with wool

1 Turn off the tap. With the bell-shaped cover and the handle removed, undo the gland nut and slide it off the spindle.

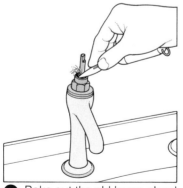

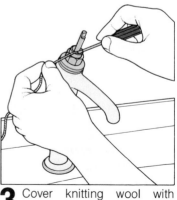

2 Rake out the old hemp gland packing in the recess with a pointed knife.

3 Cover knitting wool with petroleum jelly, then wind and stuff it into the gland.

172

4 Continue until the wool is caulked down hard, then reassemble the tap. Don't tighten the gland nut too much or the tap will be hard to turn on and off.

New O-ring on a shrouded-head tap

If you know the make of tap, a plumbers' merchant will sell you the correct O-rings before you start work. Otherwise take the old ones with you.

1 Cut off the water supply to the tap (page 166) and remove the tap handle and headgear in the same way as for renewing a washer.

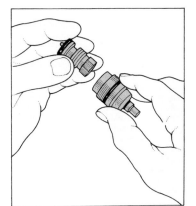

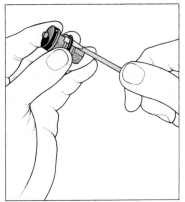

2 Hold the headgear between your fingers and turn the spindle clockwise to unscrew and remove the washer unit.

3 Use a slim screwdriver to prise out the O-ring at the top of the washer unit. Throw the old O-ring away.

4 Grease the new O-ring with petroleum jelly (Vaseline), fit it in position, and reassemble the tap.

New O-rings on a swivel spout

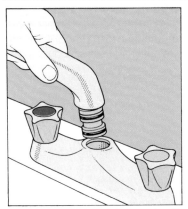

1 With both taps turned off, remove the retaining screw at the base of the spout. Ease out the spout by lifting and twisting it from side to side.

2 Note the position of the O-rings (there'll probably be two) and remove them. The new ones must go back in exactly the same place and be the same size.

3 Grease new O-rings with petroleum jelly (Vaseline) and put them on. Don't use oil. Then refit the spout to the tap.

Swivel spout held with a circlip

A mixer tap that has a shroud at the base of the spout might have a circlip holding the spout in place.

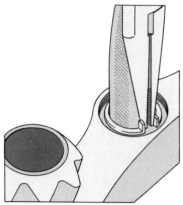

1 Unscrew or lever up the shroud at the base. There is no need to cut off the water supply.

2 Prise up the circlip and expand it with a pair of fine-nosed pliers so it can be slid up the spout.

3 Pull the spout right out of the mixer. Remove the seals in the base and fit new ones the same size. Wet the base of the spout and refit it.

New O-rings on a shower diverter

Shower diverters all have a rod and plate attached to the knob. When the knob is lifted, the plate opens the shower outlet and seals the tap outlet.

1 With the bath taps turned off, lift the shower-diverter knob and undo the headgear nut.

2 Lift out the diverter and look carefully at the position of the washers and O-rings.

174

Remove the knob by turning it anticlockwise. You may need to grip it with a wrench.

4 Withdraw the rod and plate and remove the small O-ring at the top of the rod.

5 Grease a new O-ring of the correct size with petroleum jelly and fit it in place.

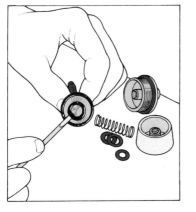

6 Replace all other rubber washers and O-rings on the base of the rod and plate. Old ones may have to be prised out with a screwdriver.

REPLACING A PLUG CHAIN

If the chain on a bath or basin plug breaks, buy a new one at a hardware or DIY shop. Make sure it will be long enough.

Use pliers to open the rings at each end of the chain. Fit one end to the bath and the other to the plug, and close the rings.

HOW TO MEND A BURST PIPE

Pipes can burst in freezing weather because the water inside expands as it turns into ice. The burst is most likely to happen in the loft where a draught of air is blowing onto an unlagged or badly lagged pipe.

While you wait for a plumber, you can make a temporary repair with a repair kit or a piece of hose.

Repairing a copper or plastic pipe

Using epoxy putty

The repair kit consists of two containers of epoxy putty which hardens within about 20 minutes of being mixed together. Drain the pipe first (pages 166-7). Then repair it, following the instructions given with the kit.

Using a piece of hose

Any pipe other than the rising main can be repaired with a piece of garden hose and two or three hose clips. But this method won't work on a joint; the burst has to be in a straight run of pipe.

1 Turn off the water (pages 166-7). Then cut a piece off the end of your garden hose to cover the pipe for at least 50mm (2in) beyond the damage. Split the hose down its length with a sharp knife.

2 Wrap the hose around the pipe so that it meets at the edges. If the pipe is a wide one and the hose will not meet, ensure that the split is thoroughly covered in all directions.

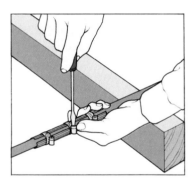

3 Secure the hose round the pipe with three or more hose clips (also called Jubilee clips). If you can't get hose clips, bend pieces of wire around the pipe and twist the ends together with pliers so that they tighten.

A NAIL THROUGH A PIPE?

If you are nailing down a loose floorboard and drive a nail through a water pipe, the first sign of damage will probably be a damp patch on the ceiling below.

Don't pull out the nail straight away; it will be keeping the leak down to a fairly slow rate.

Cut off the water to the pipe (pages 166-7) and empty it by  turning on the tap that it goes to. If you don't know the right tap, turn off the main stopcock and turn on the bathroom cold taps to empty the tank

Lift the floorboard with the nail in it and see if you can make an emergency repair until you can get hold of a plumber. Put the floorboard back in place straightaway so that no-one gets hurt.

Bandaging a lead pipe with tape

Repair kits containing two types of tape are sold for lead pipes. They make a strong repair until you can get a plumber to make it permanent. Lead pipes look silver-grey when scratched.

1 Cut off the water supply (pages 166-7) and drain the pipe.

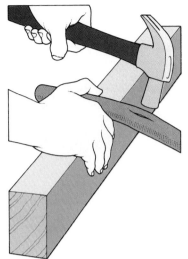
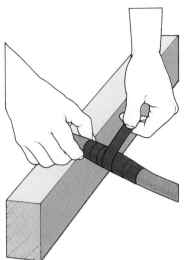

2 Hammer the sides of the split together, as far as possible. Then clean the pipe around the split with fine abrasive paper or wire wool. Make sure the pipe is dry.

3 Cover the split, and 25mm (1in) beyond it at each end, with reinforcing tape. Wind the tape around the pipe with a half overlap on each turn.

4 Cut a 150mm (6in) length of amalgamating tape and remove the backing film. Do not lose sight of which side of the tape is exposed (both sides look the same).

5 Wrap the amalgamating tape (exposed side down) around the pipe for 25mm (1in) beyond each end of the reinforcing tape, stretching it nearly three times its own length as you do so.

6 Wind a final layer of reinforcing tape over the taped area.

7 Allow two hours for the bandage to set before running water through the pipe.

8 Get a plumber to repair the pipe as soon as possible.

Five ways to prevent freeze-ups

As loft floors become better insulated, water pipes in the loft are more likely to freeze up because the air in the loft is not being heated from the rooms below. The problem is made worse if the loft is given extra ventilation to reduce risk of condensation. So pipes and tanks need to be kept warm.

Pipes on outside walls Pipes that run along the inside of an exterior wall should be protected from the cold wall surface – perhaps by a piece of expanded polystyrene. If pipes are boxed in to improve the appearance, be sure to leave the base and top open so there is always a free flow of warm air. Totally isolated pipes against an exterior wall can freeze in severe conditions.

Electric protection Pipes near the eaves, where air is blowing in, are particularly at risk. They can be protected by low-wattage heating cable wrapped around them. Ideally, the cable should be controlled by a temperature-sensitive switch. Alternatively, fit a switch outside the loft space – perhaps on a landing – with a pilot light so you can see at a glance whether the heating is on or off.

Lagging for pipes Ensure that all pipes in the loft are well lagged. The simplest way is to use foam tubes which are split along one side. They enclose the pipes and are then taped to close the split as shown on the right. Pay particular attention to all bends and joints – and include all the expansion pipes and the overflow pipes.

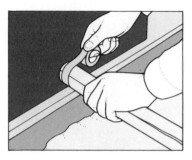

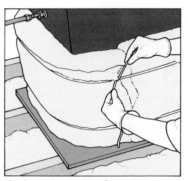

Jackets for tanks See that tanks have lagging jackets. You can buy purpose-made ones, or make them yourself out of fibre blanket material wrapped around the tanks and held by string or plastic tape.

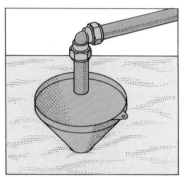

Fitting a lid A cold-water tank should have a well-fitting lid with insulation on top. If there is an expansion pipe bent over the tank, bore a hole in the lid and put in a plastic funnel to catch water.

DO NOT lay insulation under a cold-water tank. Any warmth that comes up from the room below will help to prevent the water from freezing.

UNBLOCKING A SINK OR BATH

If the sink is slow to empty, there is probably grease in the U-bend. In a washbasin or bath, hairs may be clinging below the plughole.

If the water will not run away at all, accumulated grease has built up to a complete blockage, or something such as a bone or hair grip is obstructing the waste pipe. If you cannot find an obstruction in the trap or waste pipe, check the drain (page 236).

The sink empties slowly

1 Clear hairs from the plughole by pulling them up with a bent piece of wire (a paper clip will do).

2 If the sink is still slow to empty, wait for it to drain, and pour in a strong solution of washing soda (or borax) and boiling water.

3 If this doesn't work, let it drain again and smear petroleum jelly on the rim of the plughole to protect it. Pour caustic soda or a chemical cleaner into the hole, following the instructions on the packet.

If it's completely blocked

DO NOT pour caustic soda or chemical cleaner into the water. You will just create a sinkful of caustic liquid that could give you (or a plumber) nasty burns.

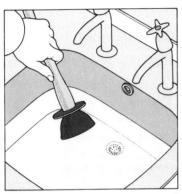

1 If the water will not run out of the sink or bath at all, place a sink plunger squarely over the plughole.

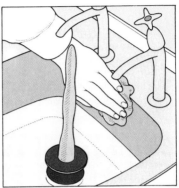

2 Stuff a damp cloth firmly over the overflow opening. This stops air from escaping when you are using the plunger.

3 Pump the plunger sharply up and down a few times. If the blockage does not clear straight away, continue pumping for a few minutes.

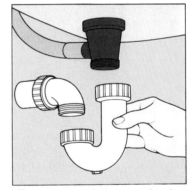

4 If plunging fails, put a bucket under the sink and unscrew the U-bend. Take off the U-bend and clean it out – but if you do it in the sink put the plug in first.

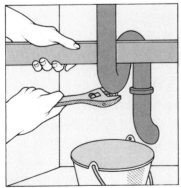

5 To undo the access nut on an old U-bend with a spanner, steady the joint with a piece of wood held in the bend.

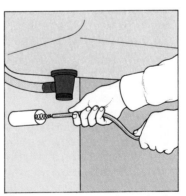

6 If the obstruction is not in the U-bend use expanding curtain wire or a sink auger to probe the waste pipe.

Vacuuming your sink

A modern way of clearing a blocked sink is to use a wet-or-dry vacuum cleaner. Put water in the basin, then place the nozzle over the plughole and suck it up. This should pull the blockage to the underside of the waste grille, and you can hook it out with a piece of bent wire.

GETTING RID OF COOKING FAT

Don't pour cooking fat down a sink. It will just go solid when it reaches the cold water in the U-bend and block the outlet. Pour the liquid fat into an old tin or yoghurt pot and put it in the dustbin when it has set. Or put it in a cup and scoop it into the dustbin when it's solid.

Clearing a bottle trap

Some modern washbasins have a bottle trap with a bottom section that can be unscrewed.

 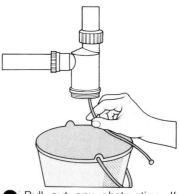

1 Support the waste pipe with one hand so that you don't buckle it, and unscrew the bottom piece of the trap.

2 Pull out any obstruction. If necessary, push a curtain wire up into the outlet from the basin and also along the waste pipe.

Replacing washers on a waste trap

If a waste trap is leaking, it probably needs new washers.

U-shaped trap Plastic waste traps have large nuts at each end. The trap will be full of water, so put a bucket or large bowl underneath. Unscrew the nuts by hand – or if they are stiff use a pipe wrench padded with cloth.

Remove the washers and take them to a hardware shop to buy new ones. Fit the new washers, screw the trap back on and run the water to check for leaks.

Bottle trap A bottle trap has three washers – one for each of the nuts and another for the removable bottom section. Replace all three.

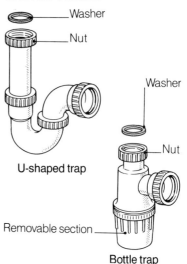

Washer

Nut

Washer

Nut

U-shaped trap

Removable section

Bottle trap

CLEARING A BLOCKED LAVATORY

When water rises almost to the rim of the bowl and drains away slowly, there is a blockage in the outlet – or in the outside drain.

● Wait until the water level is normal, then get a bucket of water and tip it into the bowl, all in one go.

● If the blockage remains, go outside and lift the manhole cover to make sure the drain itself is not blocked. If it is, see page 236.

If the drain is clear, either call a plumber or tackle the blockage yourself with a plunger or a drain auger.

Using a plunger A WC plunger has a long handle and some models have a special head to give a close fit.

Push the plunger sharply into the bottom of the bowl to cover the outlet. Pump the handle up and down several times. If that doesn't clear the blockage, you need a WC auger.

Using a WC auger An auger for WCs can be hired from a tool hire shop. Push the flexible part of the auger as far as possible into the blockage, then turn the handle and push in and out at the same time. When the blockage is loosened, wash it through the pipe by pouring in a bucket of water.

Wash the auger thoroughly in hot soapy water, and preferably some disinfectant, before you take it back to the hire shop.

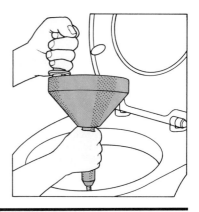

Flush won't clear the bowl

When the lavatory is flushed, two streams of water should flow around each side of the bowl and meet in the middle at the height of the rim. If they don't meet, there are three possible reasons.

Lack of water Take the lid off the cistern (it may lift off or you may have to remove one or more screws). See if the cistern fills to about 25mm (1in) from the outlet pipe. If not, adjust the water level (page 185). If it doesn't fill, clean the ball valve (pages 183-5). If that doesn't work, call a plumber.

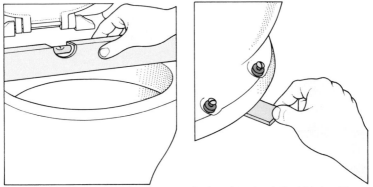

Uneven bowl Lay a spirit level across the bowl to check that it is level from side to side and front to back. If not, loosen the screws holding it to the floor and pack pieces of hardboard or vinyl flooring under it to make it level.

181

Clogged inlet If the cistern contains plenty of water, use a mirror to look at the water inlet under the rim of the bowl. If it contains rust or debris, put on rubber gloves and clear it out with your fingers, and perhaps a screwdriver if limescale has built up.

CURING AN AIRLOCK

Sometimes a tap (usually a hot one) gives a poor flow when it's turned on, then the water hisses and bubbles and stops completely. The reason is that air has got into the pipe and caused an airlock.

It usually happens after a lot of water has been drawn off for a bath. This may have temporarily emptied the cold-water tank, allowing air to get into the pipes. To cure the problem, you need a garden hose with tap connectors fitted at each end.

1 Fix one end of the hose to the faulty tap. If it's the bath tap and the hose won't fit, connect to the hot tap on the washbasin instead.

2 Connect the other end of the hose to the cold tap in the kitchen, or to any other tap fed from the mains – perhaps a garden tap.

3 Turn on the faulty tap, then turn on the mains-fed tap. The pressure of the water from the mains should blow the air out of the pipe. Leave the taps on until the rumbling of air stops completely.

Supatap

1 Take off the nozzle of the faulty tap as though you were about to change the washer (page 170).

2 Connect the hose to the outlet, then fit the other end to a tap fed from the mains and turn it on.

A kitchen mixer tap

If the hot tap has the airlock, you don't need a hose.

1 Remove the spout by undoing the little screw at the base. But first put the plug in the sink so you don't lose the screw down the drain. (Even if you do, don't worry. It will be in the U-bend.)

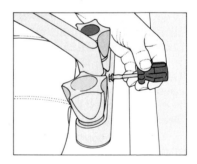

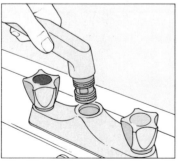

2 After taking out the screw, lift and twist the spout until it comes off.

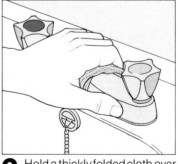

3 Hold a thickly folded cloth over the spout hole, while you turn on the hot and then the cold taps.

182

Preventing airlocks in future

If airlocks happen often, you need to find out how the air is getting into the pipes.

● Is the ball valve in the cold-water tank sticking? Go up into the loft and watch the tank as it empties while someone fills the bath. If the ball valve does not let enough fresh water in, the tank will empty before the bath is full, and air will get into the pipe. If this is happening, dismantle the ball valve and clean it (see below).

● Is the main stopcock only partly turned on? If it is, the flow into the tank will be slow.

● Is the pipe which takes water from the cold-water tank to the hot-water cylinder obstructed or too narrow? Make sure that any gate valve on the pipe is fully open, and that the pipe is at least 22mm ($\frac{7}{8}$in) across. If it is too narrow, have it replaced.

● Is the cold-water tank too small? If it's smaller than the standard 50 gallon (227 litre) size, have it replaced.

WHAT TO DO WHEN AN OVERFLOW PIPE STARTS TO DRIP

W hen cold water runs out of the overflow pipe from the lavatory or the cold-water tank, it's a signal that the ball valve, which controls the flow of water into the tank, probably needs a new washer. Or dirt might be stopping the valve from closing. Either way, you need to take the valve apart, which is not too difficult.

First, identify the type of ball valve. It will probably be either a traditional brass Portsmouth valve or a plastic diaphragm valve. Before you start the job, buy a washer for a Portsmouth valve or a diaphragm for a diaphragm valve.

Then turn off the water to the cistern. How you do that depends on whether it's a lavatory cistern or a cold-water tank (page 166). Then flush the lavatory to empty the cistern, but you needn't bother to empty a cold-water tank.

Repairing a Portsmouth valve

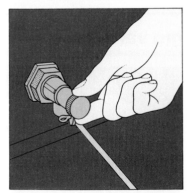

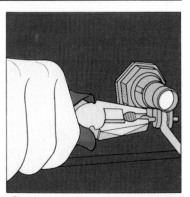

1 If there is a metal cap on the end of the valve, use pliers or a pipe wrench to loosen it (turn it anti-clockwise). Then unscrew the cap and take it off.

2 Use pliers to close the end of the split pin that holds the float arm to the valve, then pull out the pin, twisting as you pull. Remove the float arm.

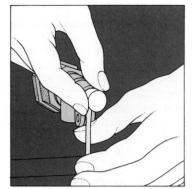

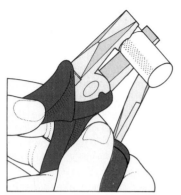

3 Insert a small screwdriver into the hole under the valve and push out the plug so that you can remove it with your fingers.

4 Hold the washer end with pliers, put a screwdriver into the slot and unscrew. (With some plastic plugs this isn't necessary.)

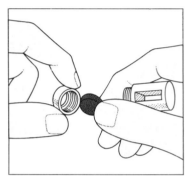

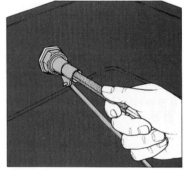

5 Push out the old washer with a screwdriver and replace it with a new one.

Smear a little petroleum jelly (Vaseline) on the thread and screw the plug back together.

6 Clean off any metal burrs or limescale from the plug with wire wool or fine emery paper. If there is limescale inside the valve casing, wrap fine emery paper around a pencil and clean it out.

7 Put the lid temporarily back on the cistern and turn on the water briefly (it comes out with a gush) to flush out any dirt.

8 Lightly smear the plug with petroleum jelly and replace it – washer end first. Reassemble the valve and turn on the water supply.

Repairing a diaphragm valve

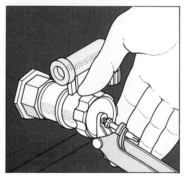

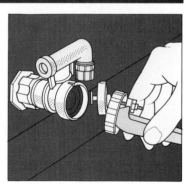

1 Unscrew the large knurled nut by hand. If it's stiff, use a pipe wrench padded with cloth. The float arm and plunger will come away.

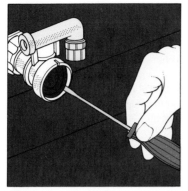

2 Use a screwdriver to free the diaphragm from the inlet, taking care not to damage it.

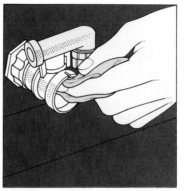

3 With a piece of lint-free rag, clean out any dirt and debris from the inlet.

4 Wash the diaphragm in warm soapy water, then rinse it. If it is pitted or damaged, throw it away and use a new one.

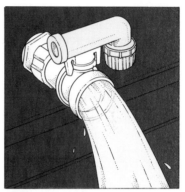

5 Turn on the water briefly (it comes out with a gush) to flush out any dirt. Then replace the diaphragm – with the rim inwards.

6 Reassemble the valve and turn the water supply back on.

A VERTICAL VALVE?

If you have an old cistern it may still be fitted with an old-fashioned Croydon valve which opens and closes vertically. The washer can be replaced in the same way as for a Portsmouth valve.

How to adjust the water level

When you have repaired a ball valve you might find that the water level in the cistern is either too high or too low. It should be about 25mm (1in) below the overflow pipe. It can be raised by raising the float and lowered by lowering the float.

Portsmouth valve

With a Portsmouth valve, unscrew the float from the arm.

To lower the water level, hold the arm firmly in both hands and bend it slightly downwards. To raise the level bend the arm slightly upwards. Then screw the float back on.

If the arm is too stiff to bend, remove it from the valve (page 183) and hold it in a vice, or under your foot, while you bend it.

185

REPLACING A BALL FLOAT

Another cause of an overflowing cistern is a faulty ball float. If a metal float corrodes, water gets in, the float sinks and the valve will not close. So the cistern overflows.

As a temporary measure, unscrew the float and empty it. You might have to enlarge the hole with a screwdriver to let the water out. Then screw it back on the lever arm and tie it up inside a plastic bag. At the first opportunity, buy a new float and fit it on.

Diaphragm valve

Different models of diaphragm valve have different ways of adjusting the float.

● If it has an adjuster at the top of the float arm, lower the water level by loosening the locking nut and screwing the adjuster forward, nearer to the plunger.

● Other models have an adjuster nut or clip near the float to move the float farther away from the valve along a horizontal arm.

● If the float is linked to the arm by a vertical rod it can be moved lower.

STOPPING AN OVERFLOW TEMPORARILY

You can easily stop an overflow until you have time to repair the ball valve. Put a piece of wood across the top of the cistern and tie the lever arm close up to it. A wooden spoon or a coat hanger will do for a lavatory cistern.

If you want to use the cistern, you will have to release the arm to fill it up again. Then re-tie the arm.

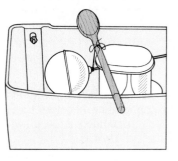

Silencing noisy pipes

A banging or humming noise from the water pipes is caused by ripples on the surface of the water as a cistern is filling. The ripples cause the ball float to bob up and down, and the valve bounces on its seating. This sets up a vibration in the pipes.

● The ball float can be stabilised with an old yoghurt pot and a piece of stiff galvanised wire. Make two holes in the rim of the pot on opposite sides. Bend the wire through one hole, then twist it tightly around the float arm near the ball float before bending it through the other hole. The pot should be underwater, a few inches below the float. A purpose-made 'paddle' can be bought to do the same job

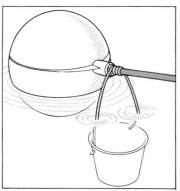

● If the noise is coming from the cold-water tank, make sure that the rising main is securely fixed with pipe clips to joists near the cistern.

● The surest way to get rid of water hammer is to replace a Portsmouth

valve with an equilibrium valve which has a flexible polythene tube that feeds water into the cistern below surface level.

● A single thump in a pipe is caused by a shock wave, produced when a tap is turned off suddenly. This has become more common with the introduction of ceramic-disc taps which require very little movement of the handle. The problem can be cured by fitting a little damping device, called a shock arrester, near the top of the mains water pipe before it enters the tank. The device contains a column of air which absorbs the shock before it can produce a noise.

Flushing lever loose?

If the lever on the lavatory cistern feels completely loose and there's no flush, the hook connecting it to the flush mechanism might have broken (the water corrodes it).

Take the top off the cistern and check. If the hook is broken, buy a new one or make one by cutting off a piece of wire coat hanger with pliers and bending it to shape.

Alternatively, tie the lever arm to the flush mechanism with thin wire until you can buy a hook.

Sealing the gap along a bath

There are three main ways to seal the gap between a wall and the bath or washbasin. But first make sure that all surfaces are dry.

Squirting sealant from a 'gun'

Silicone rubber sealant is available in various colours and is designed to be squirted into the gap from a tube fitted into an applicator gun. But getting a really smooth surface is not easy.

1 Run a strip of masking tape along both the wall and the rim of the bath, leaving a gap just the size you want the sealant to occupy.

2 Apply the sealant, following the instructions on the pack.

3 Smooth the sealant with a wet finger if you need to, then immediately pull away the masking tape while the sealant is still wet. Do not touch the sealant again until it is dry. You cannot smooth it once it has started to set.

Large gaps If the gap is large in places, fill it with strips of expanded polystyrene – such as pieces cut from an old ceiling tile. Press it well down and then apply the sealant on top.

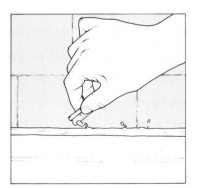

Removing dry sealant If some of the sealant dries on the tiles where it's not wanted, allow it to dry fully, then ease it off with a flexible razor blade. There is no solvent that will soften it.

Ceramic quadrant sets

You can buy sets of tile quadrant – to bridge the gap between wall tiles and bath – in a range of colours to match existing tiles. They can only be used on rigid baths made of cast iron or pressed steel. They are not suitable for plastic baths.

Stick the top edge to the wall tiles with tile adhesive, but use silicone rubber bath sealant to stick the bottom edge to the rim of the bath. The sealant remains flexible to cope with slight movements.

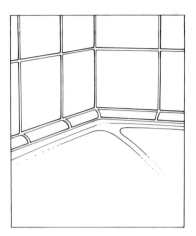

Flexible plastic strips

Press-in-place sealant Pre-formed sealants, with an adhesive back, are pressed in position and trimmed to length with scissors.

Quadrant-shaped strips Plastic strip, shaped like ceramic quadrant, is stuck between the wall and the bath, and is suitable for plastic baths. Both wall and bath must be perfectly clean and dry before applying.

PREVENTING A PLASTIC BATH FROM MOVING

A plastic bath needs far more support than heavier metal ones. When it's installed you should see that it sits correctly on the timber frame that holds it in place. Before tiling and sealing around the bath, fill it two-thirds full of cold water so it settles correctly.

If there is excessive movement, it is best to remove the bath and improve the supporting frame. You might need help from a carpenter.

REPAIRING BATHS AND BASINS

A scratched acrylic bath A great advantage of acrylic plastic for baths is that the colour goes right through, so to remove scratches use metal polish wadding such as Duraglit to gently polish out the marks. It can be a slow process, but scratches can be lost without affecting the colour of the bath. Finally, polish with a clean, dry duster.

Broken acrylic A sharp blow on an acrylic bath may knock a piece out. Recover the piece and stick it back in place with an acrylic adhesive. No other adhesive will do. Confine the adhesive to the area of the repair only, otherwise it may mark the surrounding plastic. Allow to dry thoroughly before the bath is used.

Re-enamelling a bath Re-coating an old metal bath with enamel is not something you can do yourself. But there are specialist companies which will do the job for you without removing the bath. You will find them listed in the Yellow Pages under 'Bathroom Equipment'.

A chipped basin If a washbasin gets chipped try to find the missing piece, however small, and stick it back in place with epoxy two-part adhesive. Hold the chip in place with clear adhesive tape while the adhesive sets. When it's hard, pare away any surplus adhesive with a razor blade. Then touch in the join with enamel paint, which is available in miniature tins.

REMOVING A CAST-IRON BATH

Old cast-iron baths are extremely heavy, and very difficult to remove. If the bath is being scrapped, the best way is to smash it up in the bathroom with a sledgehammer, or cut it up with an angle grinder. Both operations are difficult and best done by experts. But if you undertake the work, be sure to wear safety spectacles, heavy leather gloves and protective shoes. Flying chips of enamel are dangerous. Cover the bath with an old dust sheet to prevent pieces flying before hammering it.

If a chip is missing and you can't locate it, or it has broken up, apply enamel paint layer on layer, allowing each coat to dry hard before applying the next. Keep building up the paint until the repair is level with the surface of the basin.

A cracked basin If a basin is cracked, the best you can do is disguise the damage. It should be done quickly before dirt discolours the crack. Ensure the crack is dry, then apply enamel paint along it with a fine camel-hair brush. Apply the thinnest coat and allow it to dry. Then apply further coats, allowing each to dry, until the enamel is flush with the basin.

Putting in a shower

You will only get a reasonable pressure of water from a shower if the bottom of your cold-water tank is at least 1m (3ft) above the shower head. If the pressure is too low, you can either raise the tank or install a booster pump.

Which type of pump? Dual pumps are more powerful, and more expensive, than single pumps. A single pump, driven by a small electric motor, is fitted between the shower mixer and the shower head so that it boosts the water after the hot and cold have been mixed. A dual pump is fitted to the supply pipes to boost both the hot and cold water before they reach the mixer.

What can a pump achieve? Depending on the model, a booster pump will give a decent shower if there is only 150mm (6in) between the base of the cold-water tank and the spray head. Some dual pumps can even supply a shower sited above the tank, making it possible to put a shower in a loft which has been converted into a room.

If you want a 'power-shower', with a really strong jet of water, a booster pump will probably be necessary whatever the position of the tank.

A shower cabinet Installing a shower in a shower cabinet needs careful consideration, as the waste water has to be carried out into the drainage system. It's not always easy to find a route that allows a fall in the drainage pipe. If you're in any doubt, get a plumber's advice before you decide where a shower cabinet is to go.

HOW TO BLEED A RADIATOR

If a radiator goes cool when it should be hot, first suspect a build-up of air or gas. To remove the air you will need a radiator key, which should have been supplied with the radiator. They can also be bought at DIY shops or plumbers' suppliers.

1 Hold a rag under the square-ended valve at the top of one end of the radiator. Turn the tap anticlockwise with the key until air starts to hiss out.

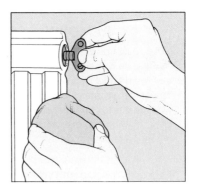

DO NOT turn the key more than about half a turn. If you turn it too far the valve may come out and you may have trouble getting it back in. In the meantime, water will be squirting out of the hole.

2 When the hissing stops and water starts to dribble out, close the valve quickly, and wipe up the water.

If you notice a gassy smell as the air comes out, and the radiators often need bleeding, there may be corrosion in the system causing a build-up of gas. Get advice from a central-heating engineer.

Avoiding corrosion in the radiators

Corrosion in a central-heating system can cause sludge to block pipes, pumps and radiators. A corrosion-inhibiting liquid can be fed into the system to protect it.

An old system An old installation should be drained down and flushed through with clean water before it is refilled and the protective liquid is added. The work is best done by an experienced central-heating plumber.

A new system If the system is new and you know the water is clean, it can be treated by pouring the liquid into the expansion tank, then draining off enough water from the system for the liquid to be drawn in. (See below.)

Three ways to prevent a freeze-up during a winter holiday

● On a gas-fired or oil-fired system, turn the room thermostat down to its minimum setting and set the programmer to come on for two periods each day if you are only going to be away for a week or so.
● For a long absence, you could have a frost thermostat installed. It will turn the system on whenever the temperature approaches freezing point.

HOW TO PUT ANTICORROSION LIQUID INTO YOUR CENTRAL HEATING

Tie up the ball valve in the expansion tank to a stick laid across the tank. Find the drain cock at the base of the boiler or at the lowest point of the pipework, and fix a hose to it with a hose clip. Lead the hose to a drain and open the cock. When the anticorrosion liquid disappears into the system, close the cock and release the ball valve.

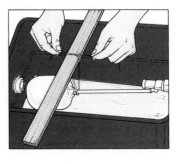

● Put central-heating antifreeze into the system in the same way as an anticorrosion liquid. The antifreeze will prevent the central heating from freezing, but will not protect the domestic water system.

Fault-finder guide: cold radiators

The top of the radiator is cold
Air or gas has probably collected in the top of the radiator, preventing the hot water from circulating fully. The radiator needs to be bled – an easy job. (See *How to bleed a radiator*, page 189.)

The radiators on the top floor are cold
Check that the expansion tank, which is probably in the loft, has water in it and that the ball valve is operating. Jiggle the ball-valve arm. If no water comes through, it will have to be repaired.

The radiators all over the house are cool
Corrosion of the metal inside the system can cause sludge to build up, resulting in poor water circulation. The radiators will be cooler than they should be. The system needs to be chemically cleaned – a job best left to a plumber with knowledge of central heating. (See *Avoiding corrosion in the radiators*, previous page.)

The radiators farthest from the boiler are cool
When the central-heating system is installed, the lockshield valve at one end of each radiator is adjusted so that every radiator gets the right amount of hot water. If the system goes out of balance – perhaps because a new radiator has been added – some radiators will get too hot and others too cold. Call in a central-heating engineer to rebalance it.

DEALING WITH DAMP AND ROT

There are two main likely causes of damp patches on inside walls: a structural problem, or condensation of damp air. The solution might involve calling in a builder or it might just be better ventilation.

Structural problems

If the patch appears on a mild but very wet day, look for something wrong with the structure of the house.
● Check for gutters leaking rainwater down a wall.
● If the damp patch is at skirting board level, the damp-proof course might have failed or it could have been covered by rubbish or a flower bed.
● On a chimney breast wall, damp could be due to rain coming down an unused flue through an uncapped chimney pot.

Remedies Gutter problems – pages 237-9. Damp-proof course – page 248. Chimney problems – page 245.

Dealing with condensation

If a patch appears on a dry but cold day, condensation is probably to blame. The moisture level in the air may be excessive, through cooking, washing or bathing, and when warm, moisture-laden air touches a cold surface, water droplets are deposited as the air cools.

Remedies

● Efficient ventilation is vital. Ensure that kitchen and bathroom are fitted with an extractor fan to remove moisture-laden air. You can calculate the size of fan from the information in extractor-fan leaflets.
● Decorate with a matt anticondensation paint.
● Insulate cavity walls to make them warmer.
● Line cold walls with a veneer of expanded polystyrene before papering. The veneer is sold in rolls and applied with heavy duty wallpaper adhesive. Ensure that seam joints on the veneer do not align with those of the new wallpaper.
● A very cold wall may also be individually warmed. Fit a black-heat tubular heater at skirting level and switch it on during cold spells. It will produce a curtain of warm air, discouraging condensation. The heater only uses about the same power as a light bulb.

Damp in wardrobes

A common problem in modern homes is the appearance of damp patches on walls enclosed by built-in wardrobes. It is usually coupled with mould and a musty smell. The cause is condensation on a cold, unventilated surface and is often linked with insufficient ventilation in steamy areas like the kitchen and bathroom.
● Fit small vents to the top and bottom of the wardrobes, to allow a flow of warm air from the room.

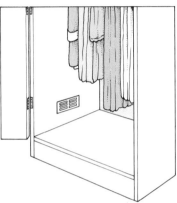

● Line the damp wall with expanded polystyrene veneer. It isolates the cold wall surface from the room air, and can be decorated with wallpaper.

● Fit a small airing cupboard heater or a short length of black-heat tubular heater against the damp wall. Switch on during cold spells. The heaters consume no more electricity than a light bulb, so are economical. Protect the heater with wire netting, or fit a slatted shelf above, so there is no risk of clothing falling on it.

Getting rid of mould

When millions of tiny mould spores in the air encounter a damp surface, some grow, forming unpleasant coloured spots. They will stain wallpapers and spoil paintwork. Window frames and cold wall surfaces are most likely to be affected.
● To kill mould, use a proprietary fungicide, diluted as recommended on the container.
● Bleach has only a limited effect, and the mould will regrow after a short time.
● Don't use fungicide over a wallpaper. Strip off the paper and treat the wall.
● When redecorating, use a wallpaper paste which contains a fungicide to give added protection.
● Improve insulation to warm up cold walls, and increase ventilation. Dehumidifiers, cavity wall insulation and extractor fans all help. Use matt, not gloss, paint in bathrooms and kitchens.

Damp in the basement

The walls of a basement often show signs of damp. It may be caused by cold walls attracting condensation. Warming the area will help. Treat small areas of damp with a transparent waterproofing sealant, which soaks into the plaster or masonry.

Where damp is extensive Hack off the old plaster back to the bare masonry, then fix dimpled damp-resistant sheeting, such as Newlath, holding it in place with masonry nails. Coat with plaster or cover with sheet plasterboard to form a new wall surface, totally isolated from the damp wall. Full fixing instructions are supplied with the sheeting.

Treating the floor Spread a bitumen-rubber waterproofing compound or a waterproofing sealant on the floor, then lay building paper before laying a decorative floor covering. If the covering is to be stuck down, omit the building paper.

Rot in timber

Wet rot Recognisable by fine whitish strands spreading over the surface of damp timber, plus softening and discolouring of the wood. The rot will die off if the source of moisture is removed.
● Treat the cause of the problem: leaking radiator or pipe; faulty guttering; rain penetrating door or window frames.
● Treat the wood with a wood preservative to prevent further trouble. If the rot is widespread, call in a builder.

Dry rot This is a much more serious problem, and is often caused by a faulty damp-proof course. Spores on damp, badly ventilated wood send out root-like strands which feed on the wood, infecting previously dry areas. Spread can be rapid, so have it dealt with as soon as possible.
   Tell-tale signs are: a dank, musty smell; cracking of wood across the grain; softening of the timber so a knife blade can be easily inserted. A large pancake-like growth is produced.
● It is not wise to treat this rot yourself. Miss the smallest area and the rot will continue to spread. So call in a specialist company, preferably a member of the British Wood Preserving and Damp-proofing Association, 6 The Office Village, 4 Romford Road, London E15 4EA (tel. 081-519 2588). Some companies offer a free survey, but many make a charge which is later deducted from any remedial work done.
● Prevention is better than cure, so use factory pressure-impregnated timbers for all new constructional or repair work. It will be unaffected by rot spores or insects.

CONDENSATION ON A TOILET CISTERN

A toilet cistern full of cold water often attracts condensation, especially when someone is bathing or showering.
● The best solution is an efficient extractor fan to expel steam-laden air as it is produced. You can buy extractor fans that automatically switch on and off as the moisture content of the air rises and falls.
● A special moisture-absorbing strip can be secured around the outside of the cistern, close to its base, with an end leading into the toilet pan from behind the seat hinge. This will ensure that no water drips onto the floor. Spontex anti-condensation strip, as used on window ledges, will do the job.

TACKLING CRACKS IN WALLS

Fine cracks in the plaster Most cracks in plastered walls are superficial. They're often caused by shrinkage of the plaster, and they're easy to repair. First, rake out loose material with the point of a trowel, and use an old paintbrush to remove dust. Then fill the crack with a cellulose wall filler, leaving it just proud of the wall surface. When it's set, use a fine abrasive paper wrapped around a sanding block to smooth it flush with the surrounding plaster.

Gaps beside woodwork Cracks alongside door frames or window frames are best filled with an acrylic sealant. The sealant remains flexible so is able to withstand slight movement or, in the case of doors, slamming. Use an applicator gun to run a strip of sealant along the gap, then smooth it in place with a wet finger or a damp lint-free rag. You can buy the applicator gun very cheaply with the sealant.

Cracks at ceiling level Cracks between walls and ceiling are quite common, and are usually caused by slight movement of the structure of the house. It is not a serious problem, but the cracks are very difficult to fill, so it's best to bridge them with coving. DIY shops sell coving made of expanded polystyrene, rigid polyurethane or gypsum plaster – all of which can be stuck in place with their own special adhesive.

Cracks that change with the seasons Occasionally a deeper crack may occur which involves the actual fabric of the house, and you may notice that the crack opens and shuts with the seasons. This is due to changes in the water content of the soil, which cause slight movement of the foundations.

It is best to bridge the crack with fine adhesive netting which is sold in DIY shops for the purpose. Then wallpaper over the netting. Even then, the paper may crease when the crack closes following a long wet spell. Filling the crack in the normal way rarely helps as the filler will be squeezed out by the great pressures involved.

Gaps that get bigger The most serious cracks involve settlement of the house. Settlement may occur because of poor foundations, because the house was built on reclaimed land not yet fully consolidated, or because of old mine workings below. If you think that a crack is continuing to open, get the advice of the Building Control Officer who can be contacted at your local authority offices.

COVERING CEILING STAINS

Stains on ceilings can be caused by leaks in the loft when water carries dirt and rust through the plaster. Applying new paint usually doesn't help. The stains just 'bleed' through.

● Before redecorating, treat the stained area with a stain-blocking coating such as Polycell Stain Block. Different coatings are designed for application with a brush or aerosol. Both types dry quickly, sealing off the stain. You can then repaint.

● The same coating can be used to cover up graffiti – such as wax crayon scribbles on walls – before you repaint.

FIXING JAMMED WINDOWS

● The most common cause of windows becoming hard to open is a build-up of paint on the surfaces that meet. Strip off the paint along these edges back to the bare wood, and check whether the window closes.

● If it is still a tight fit, use a power drill with a drum sander to remove enough wood to give an easy fit.

● If a casement window sticks in a few places, put carbon paper between window and frame, then close the window. Marks left by the carbon paper will show where the fit is too tight.

● In extreme cases, remove the window and plane the meeting edges.

Swollen and rotten wood

A more serious cause of windows sticking is damp getting into the timber.

● Strip the paint off and let the wood dry. To speed up the process use a hot air stripper. Timber rarely shrinks back fully, so you may have to sand the frame before repainting it.

● Small areas of rot can be repaired with a wood repair paste.

● If you find badly rotted timber, get a carpenter to cut it out and replace it.

When a window won't move after painting

If a window won't budge after painting, run a thin knife all round between window and frame. Next time, do the painting early in the day and leave the window ajar until evening.

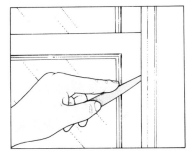

Clingfilm between newly dry surfaces prevents them sticking.

Straightening a warped metal frame

If a metal window becomes warped, you cannot correct it with the glass in place. It has to be taken out first.

1 If possible, remove the window completely from its frame. Chip out the putty, as when replacing broken glass (page 252). The glass may be held in place by small metal spring clips, which should be carefully removed and kept. Carefully take out the glass.

2 Sighting along the edge of the metal, gently twist it in the opposite direction to the warp to correct it.

3 Replace the window and check that it lies flat in the frame. When it is true, replace the glass using the metal clips and multipurpose putty.

SMOOTH-RUNNING WINDOWS

To make sash windows slide smoothly, rub a candle on all the sliding surfaces and lightly oil the pulleys. Do it at any time to ease running but make a point of doing it when the window is dismantled for repair.

Curing rattling windows

Wedges Small plastic wedges can be bought for pushing between sash windows and the frame. They stop rattles, but must be removed whenever the window is raised or lowered.

Draught excluder To cure draughts and rattles in one operation, fit a nylon brush pile draught excluder to the inside face of the staff beads – both inner and outer (see below) – so the sashes run along it.

Or fit the draught excluder to the inner face of one of the meeting rails. This is simpler, but it only stops the rattles when the window is closed. If you put the draught excluder on the meeting rail of the bottom sash, it won't show when the window is open.

Fitting a fitch catch Another possible cure is to change the window lock for a fitch catch – a fastener which draws the sashes together when closed and often stops the rattle.

Moving the bead Sash windows rattle because there is too much space around each sash. The problem occurs more often with the lower (inner) sash and is caused by the staff bead not being close enough to the sash. The remedy is to remove and refix the staff beads.

FIXING FAULTY DOORS

A door that sticks along one side

When a door jams along the opening edge, the cause is usually a build-up of paint. The problem is often worse in wet weather when the wood swells. If it is not severe, rub the edge of the door with a candle or dry powder lubricant.

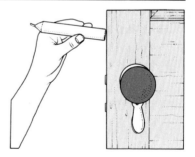

If that doesn't fix it, you will have to strip paint off either the door edge or the frame.

1 Wait for a warm dry spell, and strip off the paint (page 250).

2 If you have one, use a hot-air gun to dry out the wood.

3 Sand the stripped surface and check that the door closes easily.

4 There should be a slight gap between the edge of the door and the frame, so run a thin knife all round the edge of the door when it is closed. Where the gap is insufficient, plane the edge of the door.

5 Sand, prime and paint the bare wood. Let it dry before closing it.

A door that sticks at the bottom

If your front or back door sticks along the bottom, the problem is often caused by rain being absorbed by the bottom edge of the door which has never been painted.

1 Wait for dry weather, then take the door off its hinges and thoroughly dry the bare edge with a hot-air gun.

2 If the binding is severe, hold the door on one of its long edges in a portable workbench. Mark a line to work to, then plane downwards from the corners to the centre; this will avoid splintering the corners.

3 Prime and paint to match the rest of the door.

A door that sticks at the top

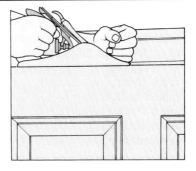

You may be able to plane the top edge of a door without taking it off its hinges. It will have to be propped open firmly while you work from a stepladder.

Plane from the end to avoid splitting the corner.

Curing a squeaking door

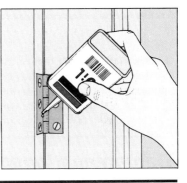

Oil the hinge pins, and work the door backwards and forwards to get the oil into the hinge, then wipe away surplus oil with a rag.

With rising hinges, lift the open door off the hinge pins and smear them with petroleum jelly. Wipe away the surplus after rehanging.

Stopping a door from slamming

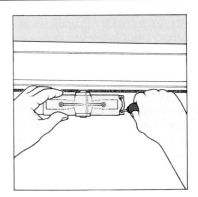

The only cure for a slamming door is to fit a hydraulic or sprung door-closer.

The door-closers are often supplied with a paper template which you can use as a guide for the fixing holes that have to be marked at the top of the door and on the architrave above.

1 If a template is not supplied, hold the door-closer in position on the top edge of the door on the hinge side, and use a long bradawl to mark the screw positions.

2 Drill pilot holes for the screws, making sure that the drill bit is narrower than the diameter of the screws. Then screw the closer to the door.

197

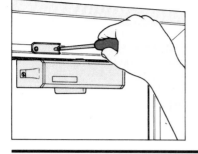

3 Chisel out a flat recess for the pivot arm fixing plate in the architrave and screw it on.

Fix the pivot arm to the body of the closer, and turn the adjusting screws on the closer so the door closes smoothly. Follow the maker's instructions.

A door latch that won't close

If a door sags a little or becomes slightly swollen, the latch bolt will be out of alignment with the striking plate and won't go into the hole. A small misalignment can be corrected by enlarging the cutout in the striking plate with a file.

Otherwise, remove the plate and refix it in the right place. If it has to be moved only a small distance, plug the old screw holes with small wooden pegs coated in glue. Drill new pilot holes for the screws. You can cut the pegs out of any piece of softwood, using a craft knife.

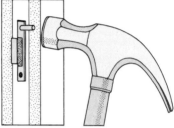

When a lock is hard to turn

● Spray an aerosol lubricant into the lock using the narrow applicator tube that usually comes with it.
● If this is not sufficient, remove the lock from the door, take off one side of the case, and lightly grease the mechanism. Before starting work, note the positions of the components so they can be put back if they get displaced.
● Do not use oil in cylinder-type front-door locks. It attracts grit. Use graphite powder or PTFE dry powder lubricant.

Tightening a loose door frame

Slamming can make a door frame loose. Make new fixings with three large screws and wall plugs, called frame fixings, on each side of the frame. The length should be the frame thickness plus 60mm ($2\frac{1}{2}$in).

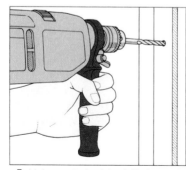

1 Using a twist bit, drill through the frame and then change to a masonry bit and drill into the supporting masonry.

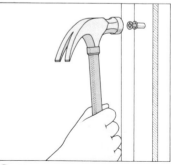

2 Hammer the frame fixing into the hole so that the plug is fully into the wall, then tighten the screw to hold the frame secure.

Fixing a hinge-bound door

A door that is difficult to close, and tends to spring open, is said to be hinge-bound.

The problem is usually caused by hinge recesses being too deep in either the door edge or in the frame. When correctly fitted the hinge flaps should be flush with, or slightly below, the surface of the wood.

1 Open the door and push a piece of wood or a thin book under the opening edge to take the weight.

2 Clear any paint from the slots in the hinge screws. You can use an old screwdriver, a nail file or a bradawl. Then remove the screws.

3 Get someone to steady the door while you lever the hinge flap out of its recess. Pack out the recess with pieces of cardboard cut to the right size, and replace the screws.

Protruding screw heads

Occasionally the hinges may not shut fully because the screw heads are too large, or have been put in askew and so hit each other when the door is closed.

● Remove the screws and replace them with screws that have heads that fit the countersinks in the hinges. One gauge size smaller should be sufficient. If they will not tighten, pack out the holes with matches or a plug of softwood coated in glue.

● Alternatively, deepen the countersinks in the hinge flaps so that the screw head will be flush with the surface. Use a high-speed steel countersink bit.

● If the screws were originally set in askew, remove them and plug the screw holes with pieces of scrap wood dipped in wood glue. Then redrill straight pilot holes.

Badly placed hinges

Binding can also be caused by hinges that are set into the frame too near to the door stop. As the door is closed, it presses against the stop, preventing it from going any further.

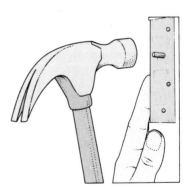

1 Remove the hinges from the door frame and plug the fixing holes with little pegs made out of bits of scrap softwood dipped in wood glue.

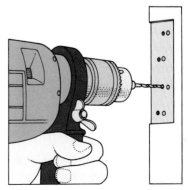

2 Redrill the hinge fixing holes so that they are farther away from the door stop.

When the door is closed the exposed edge of the hinge pin should protrude an equal distance from the face of the door and the edge of the frame.

199

Moving the door stop

On an internal door it may be possible to move the door stop as it is probably made from a separate piece of wood from the rest of the frame. Lever it off with an old chisel.

Curing rot in an outside door

If exterior doors have not been protected with paint or varnish, rot may set in, especially near the bottom and at joints.

If you catch it early, you can patch it with a high-performance filler, called a wood repair system.

1 On a warm dry day, dig out the rotten wood and allow the remaining wood to dry. Warming with a hot-air gun can help.

2 Treat the area with the wood hardener supplied with the kit, and when this has dried fill the cavity with the two-part epoxy filler. Build it up slightly above the surface, and sand it flat when it has hardened. Hardening will take about 30 minutes.

3 Drill holes in the wood around the rotted area, at intervals of about 150mm (6in).

4 Push the wood preservative pellets, which come with the kit, into the holes (right) and then fill the holes with more of the filler.

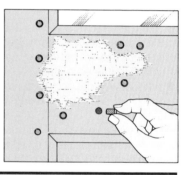

5 Repaint the area to match the door and cover the repair.

Tightening a sagging door

When the bottom corner of the door rubs on the floor, the cause is either faulty hinges or loose joints in the door. Partly open the door and lift the handle to see if there is movement at the hinges or the joints.

Faulty hinges

If the hinges are loose, unscrew them and plug the screw holes with dowels coated with wood glue. Drill new pilot holes, and refit the screws, or fit thicker or longer screws. If necessary, enlarge the countersunk holes in the hinge to take the larger screw heads, using a high-speed steel countersink bit.

If the movement is in the knuckle of the hinge due to a worn hinge pin the only cure is to fit new hinges. It may be that the hinges are not big enough to support the weight of the door. In this case fit larger, heavier hinges and perhaps a third hinge midway between them.

Loose door joints

If the door is loose in the joints, you'll need to glue and clamp them.

1 Take the door off its hinges, and try to dismantle it by gently prising the loose joints apart, or tapping with a rubber hammer.

2 Reglue the joints and put them together again. If they will not come apart, inject woodworking glue into the gaps around them.

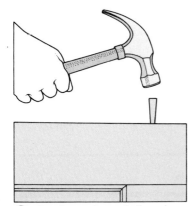

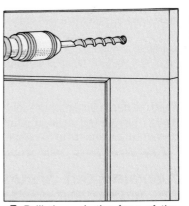

3 On the edge of the door, hammer small wooden wedges coated with glue into the ends of the tenons (the wooden tongues) to prevent the joints from opening up in the future.

4 Drill through the face of the door and through the tenon and drive a dowel smeared with glue into the hole. This will lock the tenon in place. On an exterior door use waterproof glue.

5 Clamp the door with a sash clamp, which can be hired, or with a tourniquet (page 211), while the glue sets.

6 Trim off the dowels flush with the door, then sand and repaint.

❦ KEEPING YOUR HOUSE WARM

You will get much bigger savings from some types of insulation than others. Draughtproofing and loft insulation cost little but conserve a lot of heat. Double glazing, on the other hand, can be expensive and saves very little – although it does improve comfort.

Ideally, you should try to use every form of insulation. They can save around 50 per cent of your heating bill – cutting down heavily on the burning of coal and gas, which adds to the greenhouse effect.

Insulating the loft

If the plasterboard on the floor of your loft hasn't a foil upper face, lay building paper over it. It will prevent moist air percolating up from the rooms below. Then lay the insulation on top to a minimum depth of 100mm (4in). It can be glass fibre blanket or a loose-fill, such as vermiculite or pelleted mineral wool.

Lining the roof If you can see daylight between the roof tiles or slates, fix building paper to the rafters with brass drawing pins. Work from the top down, running the paper horizontally and over-lapping each run by about 75mm (3in). Push the lowest strip out at the eaves so that any water from in-blown snow or rain runs out of the loft and into the guttering. The paper provides extra insulation.

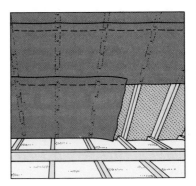

Lag the pipes Once the loft space is insulated, it will be much colder, so make sure all pipes are well lagged.

Ventilate the loft If condensation occurs in the loft, ventilation must be provided. Various types of ventilator are available for fitting into the roof covering, the eaves, or into an end wall.

Keep out damp air Apply draughtproofing strip around the trap door to the loft. It will keep out warm damp air from the house, which causes condensation and rot to the timbers.

Keeping out draughts

Use one of the many strip materials to seal gaps around door and window frames. Doors in constant use need a durable material such as sprung metal or plastic strip. But if there is too much 'spring', a door will be hard to open and close.

● If you use foam strip, choose the best quality, otherwise the foam will only last a season.

● The best material to use for sash windows and sliding doors is a self-adhesive siliconised brush strip which can withstand the wear of sliding frames.

Sealing casement windows Large and irregular gaps sometimes develop around casement windows – the type that open outwards. You can seal the gaps with a silicone rubber sealant applied with a sealant gun. The only other materials you need are a bucket of soapy water and a cloth.

1 Clean the window and frame, then squeeze a generous strip of sealant into the frame rebate.

2 Wet the closing window frame with soapy water, and shut it to its normal position – then immediately open it and allow the squeezed sealant to set. It will make a neat seal.

Insulating cavity walls

Filling the space in a cavity wall is a cost-effective way of reducing heat loss – but it is a job for the experts.

Choose a reputable, well-established contractor. You can get names from The National Cavity Insulation Association, PO Box 12, Haslemere, Surrey GU27 3AH (tel. 0428 654011). The work usually takes a day.

If you have a timber-framed house, cavity infill is not possible, but the walls will probably be well insulated already.

Insulating solid walls

On the outside If your house has solid walls, specialist companies can apply an external layer of insulating slabs. But it is an elaborate process, which can involve repositioning of downpipes, and it has to be decorated after application.

On the inside Alternatively, internal walls can be lined with insulation board, the most common of which is a plasterboard bonded with expanded polystyrene. It is either nailed to wooden battens fitted to the walls or fixed direct to the plaster by special panel adhesive. Adjustments may be necessary to skirting boards and architraves, and light switches, power sockets and wall lights have to be resited. The work is best handled by an experienced builder.

Fitting your own double glazing

There are a number of DIY double glazing systems, all of which are fairly easy to install. The simplest systems use clear plastic film or rigid sheet plastic. They provide only short-term insulation, and don't look particularly elegant – best suited for spare rooms.

Clear plastic film

You can stick clear plastic film to the window frame with double-sided adhesive tape that won't strip off the paint when it's removed. After fitting, one type of film can be shrunk with gentle heat from a hair dryer to make it taut and free of wrinkles.

Rigid plastic sheet

Sheets of rigid plastic can be fixed with double-sided adhesive tape or with magnetic strip. One part of the strip is put round the frame, the other around the edges of the sheet.

Longer-lasting double glazing

More permanent systems are sold in packs of preformed aluminium. There are length and width packs, from which pieces can be cut to form a frame. Then glass is ordered to fit. Some systems are designed to hinge open, others to slide in an extra frame screwed to the window.

How big a gap? The gap between window and secondary frame should be 18mm ($\frac{3}{4}$in) for optimum heat retention. Any less and the air buffer is too small. Any more and convection currents, which will allow cold to pass from one pane to the other, may be set up.

To cut down noise For noise reduction, the gap needs to be about 75mm (3in), and the weight of the glass should be different from the glass in the window. Otherwise vibration can occur.

For both insulation and noise reduction Triple glazing should be installed, with 18mm and 75mm gaps.

Sealed units – the pros and cons There are factory-sealed double glazing panels to fit into most windows in place of standard glass. It is a neat and simple way of providing double glazing, but because the units fit into the opening frames, they provide no draughtproofing. And most units are guaranteed for only ten years. After this time, failure of the seals will mean complete replacement. It is worth keeping in mind when buying a house. Sealed units can be an attraction – but if they're outside the guarantee period they could be a liability.

Make them openable If you design your own double glazing, always make the frames openable so any condensation can be wiped away. If you seal air in, there will always be sufficient moisture to form condensation on cold, sunny days. Using silica gel crystals to dry out the air won't help. The crystals will absorb moisture from the trapped air, but when the sun shines on them the moisture will evaporate again and condense on the glass.

FITTING A LOFT LADDER

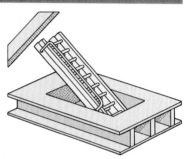

If you need to gain access to a loft, don't try to make do with a stepladder. It can be unstable – especially when you are leaving the loft. Install a loft ladder, or get a builder to do it. It will be firmly attached so it can't move, and it can be fitted with hand rails to make climbing easier.

Getting the measurements right Before looking for a ladder, check the clearance along the loft floor, and the headroom. Many ladders slide up into the loft space as they are put away, and in some cases may foul the roof. Then the ladder may rest on the loft floor, so space is important here, too. Make a simple sketch of the hatch opening and roof which you can take shopping with you, then check on leaflets to see what clearances are needed.

When space is limited There are hinged loft ladders which fold, occupying no more space than that of the loft hatch. So no clearances are involved. But you may find that your existing hatch has to be enlarged to accommodate the size of hatch cover needed. On some models, the ladder comes ready mounted on the hatch cover, making the fitting work easier.

Turning a loft into a habitable room

If you plan to use the loft for storage only, there are no regulations to worry about. And you can add roof windows without seeking permission. But if you plan to make the loft habitable there are two types of regulations.

Planning permission Only if your work changes the appearance of the roof, or is likely to interfere with the privacy of neighbours, must your local

Planning Department be consulted. But it is worthwhile contacting them anyway – many can supply printed guidance notes.

Building regulations There are strict rules about fire precautions and means of escape from the loft space.

Floors may need strengthening to support the additional load of people and furniture, and some local authorities will not accept a loft ladder as a means of access. They will insist on the addition of a staircase. As interpretations of rules vary, consult your local Planning Department before any work is done. If you employ a specialist company to do the conversion work, they will deal with the regulations.

Adding a loft window

Putting in new dormer windows is a big roofing job, but installing a modern roof window is much simpler. All the work can be tackled from inside the roof space – from removing tiles to sealing in the new window unit. No scaffolding is required, and work can be completed quickly.

An escape window To conform with building regulations, special means-of-escape windows are available, allowing easy access to the roof in the event of fire. There should be one window of this type in each room.

A staircase to the loft

Two areas are most commonly used for installing a new staircase into the loft: the open space above an existing staircase, and part of a large bedroom. This is the ideal time to call in an architect. He or she may see likely areas you haven't thought of, and will also be familiar with the staircases available – both straight and spiral – which would meet the regulations. Specialist loft companies can also advise.

TOOL-USER'S TIPS

Bolt cutting If you have to cut the threaded part of a bolt to length, screw the nut past the point to be cut, then cut through the bolt with a hacksaw. Removing the nut will straighten out any damage to the thread.

Damaged nut If a nut is impossible to grip with a spanner and does not loosen with oil, use a small tool called a nut splitter. It has a cutting blade which, when forced onto the nut with a spanner, will cut through and open up the nut without damage to the bolt thread. The bolt can be reused with a new nut.

Rusted nut and bolt Use easing oil. Give it time to work into the thread. Then try to tighten the nut before undoing. If this fails, apply heat with a soldering iron, or the pencil flame of a blowlamp. The heat should expand the nut, breaking the grip of the rust.

Cutting with a knife Clamp work to be cut to leave both hands free. If you can't clamp it, use the knife so that the blade moves away from the hand holding the work. If the knife slips, it will not injure your other hand. This applies particularly with materials like sheet vinyl, which are difficult to cut.

Drilling masonry If your drill has variable speed, start off slowly through any surface plaster, increasing speed as you enter hard masonry. Remove the drill from the hole every five seconds – keeping it running – to cool off the cutting edge. Overheating can lead to permanent damage.

If you encounter tough material, try hammer action, withdrawing the drill regularly. But never use hammer action on ceramic tiling – it will only crack the tiles.

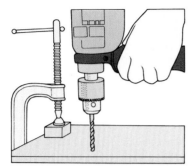

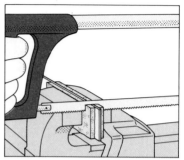

Clamps for control Whenever possible, hold work firmly to a bench with a clamp, leaving both hands free to use tools. You're less likely to injure yourself, and you'll have better control of the tools.

Cutting metal To cut thin sheet metal, sandwich it between pieces of plywood or hardboard – then cut through the lot. Use the hacksaw at a shallow angle so the teeth are not damaged by the metal.

Sawing Before using a handsaw, give the teeth a start by making a V cut with a knife where the cut will be made. Make a vertical cut with the knife on the marked line and a sloping cut to meet it on the side which is to be cut away. Draw the saw backwards first – then a gentle cut forwards.

Using a jigsaw A jigsaw blade cuts on the upstroke. So the fine surface of any material being cut should always be underneath. The same applies with a circular saw blade, which enters the wood from below.

Cutting an enclosed hole Sometimes, as when fitting a sink into a worktop, you need to cut a large hole in a board. First mark the cutting line on the board. Then drill a hole within the area to be cut away, close to the cutting line. The hole should be large enough to take the blade of a jigsaw or a hand-held padsaw.

Unlike a jigsaw (see above), a hand-held padsaw cuts on the downstroke, so have the good side of the board uppermost. Use gentle, even strokes.

With either saw, work from the hole to meet the cutting line. Take the weight of the cut piece as you near the end of the cut so that it doesn't break away unevenly.

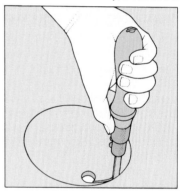

Screwdriving Always ensure that a single slot screwdriver has a clean flat-topped tip so that it sits neatly in the slot and isn't too wide or too narrow for the slot. Driving should never be hard work. Too much force can split the wood.

● Always make a start-hole, smaller in diameter than the screw thread. This is particularly important when working with hardwoods, which will split easily.

● Small Supadriv or Pozidriv screws, which have a cross-shaped slot, are best driven with a small screwdriver to ensure a snug fit in the head. The old Phillips screwdriver is not designed to drive Supadriv or Pozidriv screws, and can damage the heads.

Holding a nut To steady a nut that you're installing in a tight spot, make a

KEEPING TOOLS SHARP

A sharp tool will cut well and be safe to use. Blunt tools tend to slip and can cause a serious injury.

Chisels You can sharpen a wood chisel with a small attachment that fits onto a power drill. The chisel is gripped in a holder at the correct angle to a grinding wheel. It's much simpler to use than the traditional oilstone and honing guide.

Drills Both masonry drills and twist drills can also be sharpened with an attachment that fits on a power drill. The drill is lowered into contact with a small, enclosed grinding wheel. A chuck holds the drill at the correct angle while it is being ground.

small loop of double-sided adhesive carpet tape. Stick the tape to your fingertip and use it to pick up the nut. You can now hold the nut with one finger and put it into almost any small space. To get started, twist your wrist until the nut engages on the bolt.

How to release stubborn screws
● If a screw won't budge, clamp a self-grip (Mole) wrench to the blade of the screwdriver and use the wrench as a lever while pressing down on the screwdriver.
● For large screws use a brace with a screwdriver bit fitted. Leverage is considerable and the bit will try to jump the screw head slot, so keep it pressed in.
● If this fails, apply easing oil to the head and leave to soak until the screw will move.
● Or apply the tip of a hot soldering iron to the screw head. This expands the metal, breaking the bond.
● If a round-headed screw has a damaged head, file a new slot with a fine file – or use a mini hacksaw blade.
● If a countersunk screw won't come out, select a high-speed steel twist drill of a size that will probably equal the shank size of the damaged screw. Drill into the head until it drops away. Remove the fitting, then use a self-grip wrench to wind out the screw. This may not work on modern case-hardened screws.

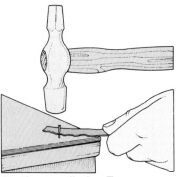

Storing screws and nails A space-saving way of storing screws and nails is to nail or screw the lids of screwtop jars to the underside of a shelf. Screw the jar containing the screws or nails to the lid when not in use and unscrew to get at the contents when you need them.

Starting small pins To save your fingers from injury when driving in small nails or panel pins, push the nail through one end of a piece of stiff paper. Use the paper to hold the nail in place while you drive it. Before hammering the nail finally home, tear away the paper.

207

Protecting surfaces When using the claw of a hammer or pincers to draw nails from a well-finished surface, slip a piece of hardboard or plywood between the tool and the timber to prevent bruising it. When knocking nails in, stop just above the surface and finish sinking the nail with nail punch and hammer.

Detecting metal Metal pipes and cables are often hidden under floors and in walls. Before doing any drilling or cutting, check with a simple metal detector to ensure there are no hidden hazards. Cable and pipe runs can be traced by running the detector slowly across the surface. It is wise to mark these runs on floors and walls as a permanent reminder.

Storing nuts and washers Loop nuts and washers of uniform sizes on pear-shaped shower curtain rings. Close the rings and hang them on a pegboard for easy access.

Hammers Always grip a hammer towards the end of the handle, and swing it so that the head is at right angles to the nail when it connects. This will ensure that nails don't bend. Lots of short sharp blows are better than one heavy one when nailing. Never hit with the side of a hammer. It has not been hardened like the hammer head and may crack. A light rub with fine emery paper on the face of the hammer head will make it less likely to slip.

Tools it's best to hire

Expensive tools that are only needed occasionally can be hired from a tool hire shop. Keep costs down by collecting and returning the tool yourself. And plan your work so you don't borrow the tool until you need it.

Take care! If the tool is new to you, get an instruction manual and read it carefully. If safety clothing is recommended, wear it. This applies particularly to dangerous tools like chain saws and angle grinders. Misuse and the lack of protective gear can result in serious accidents.

Return it clean Be sure to return the equipment in a clean condition. Cement mixers can be cleaned with a liquid called Disclean, available from builder's merchants. It will also clean spades, shovels and trowels.

A PORTABLE MAKESHIFT SAWHORSE

Lay a wooden stepladder open on its side to create a makeshift sawhorse, which you can move practically anywhere about the house. Lay the wood across the ladder and cut it. You can use the ladder in the same way for sanding, planing or painting wood.

But don't use an aluminium ladder this way – it's too light.

MAKING THINGS STICK

No single glue will stick everything, but there are different glues to cope with most household jobs. Plastics are the biggest problem. Nylon and polythene can't be repaired with glue, only by heat welding, and other plastics need their own glues. So unless you know the type of plastic, you have to use trial and error, allowing time for the glue to set before testing the join.

Some adhesives contain solvents which shouldn't be inhaled – and some are highly flammable. Always ensure good ventilation to carry fumes away and never smoke or work anywhere near exposed flames – including pilot lights of cookers, boilers or gas fires. Clothing exposed to solvents should be aired outside – never store clothes in a room with solvents.

Keep all glue well out of the reach of children.

How to do repairs with glue

● If you have several pieces of broken pottery do a dummy run to see how they fit together, then lightly number them with a Chinagraph pencil.
● Keep broken items clean. Even natural skin oils can contaminate a surface, so don't finger broken pieces. Keep them in a polythene bag until you are ready to repair them.
● Apply the glue sparingly, following the manufacturer's instructions. More glue doesn't necessarily make a better bond. Often the opposite is true, so read the instructions. Some adhesives are applied to both surfaces, others only to one. Some bond immediately, while with others you must allow the solvent to evaporate before bringing the surfaces together.
● If you're using a contact adhesive – one applied to both surfaces and which bonds on contact – let the solvent evaporate until the surfaces feel touch-dry before pressing them together. Otherwise bubbles may form between surfaces and they won't bond.

● Whenever possible, clean away surplus glue while it's still wet. Some water-based glues become water-resistant once they set. Check which solvent will clean them off. Rubber-based adhesives respond to lighter fluid – but take care when using it because it is highly flammable. Some glues, including superglues, have their own release agent.

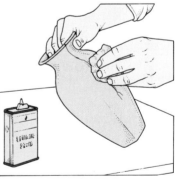

Choosing the right glue

PVA (polyvinyl acetate) A versatile glue, used for general woodwork. It will also stick paper and card; can be used as a sealer and primer before tiling; may be used as an additive to concrete or mortar to improve adhesion, and used neat on concrete to ensure a good bond between old and new. It can also be used to seal a concrete floor that gives off dust. A water-resistant building version is available for outdoor use.

Clear resin Usually sold in small tubes, it's ideal for sticking card and flexible materials like leather and fabric-backed plastics. For flexible materials apply it to both surfaces, bringing them together when the glue becomes tacky. Not strong enough for replacing cup or jug handles.

Epoxy resin A strong adhesive, supplied in two tubes – the glue and a hardener which you mix. Epoxy resin is useful for metal, china and glass, although it leaves a line. Two types are available: normal set, which takes about six hours to set, and quick set, which takes about five minutes. Not suitable for flexible materials.

Rubber-based glue There are three main types:
● Contact adhesive, for sticking sheet material like plastic laminate. Apply it to both surfaces and allow it to become touch-dry before bringing the surfaces together. It is not suitable for wood joints.
● White latex adhesive, for bonding fabrics, leather and carpet edges.
● Black rubber-based adhesive, suitable for sticking material such as canvas in exposed conditions. Once dry it is waterproof, which makes it suitable for repairs to boats and caravans.
Some rubber-based glues used for sticking floorcoverings are flammable. Ventilate the room well, turn off pilot lights, and don't smoke.

Cyanoacrylate (superglue) A fast-setting glue. Apply in the thinnest of coats to only one surface, then immediately bring them together. It bonds metals, most hard materials and synthetic rubber. But it should not be used to repair household crockery, because it softens in warm water. Although it is harmless, it can be alarming if the skin on your fingers sticks together. If this happens, immerse them in warm soapy water, then wiggle them until the glue fails.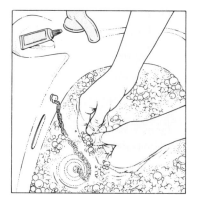

After you've used superglue, it solidifies in the nozzle, so it's best to clear the nozzle with a pin. To prevent the cap sticking, don't screw it back on too tightly.

HOW TO MAKE A GLUE BRUSH

If you need a brush to spread PVA glue, make one from the tube of an old ballpoint pen. Push a piece of coarse string through the tube and fluff out the end of the string to make 'bristles'.

When you've finished a job, cut off the used string and pull through a clean piece for next time.

PVC adhesive Repairs things like plastic raincoats and beach balls. It acts by softening the plastic, so try not to get it on surrounding areas.

Polystyrene adhesive For bonding polystyrene. It is used mostly by model-makers for aeroplane and car-kit assembly. It softens plastic so will easily mark and spoil other areas unless you are careful.

Hot-melt glue Comes in sticks which are fed into an electrically heated gun, then forced from a nozzle. Don't use it on things that become hot.

SEVEN EASY GLUING TIPS

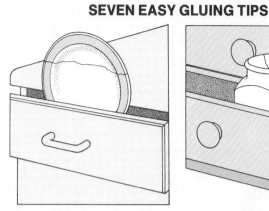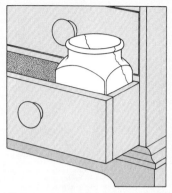

● To keep the broken edge of a plate upwards while you glue back the other piece, stand it in a partly open drawer. Apply glue and balance the top piece in position.

● To hold together broken pieces of small and awkwardly shaped objects, such as a pottery eggcup, use elastic bands or paper masking tape, as shown on the right. Long strips of rubber cut from the length of an old cycle inner tube can be used for large things.

● A partly open drawer can also be used as a clamp to hold together objects while glue is setting. Stand the object on something inside the drawer to bring it to the right height.

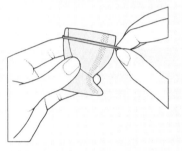

● Instead of using clamps, which may bruise furniture while doing repairs, hold joints together with a tourniquet of strong cord and a stick. Twist the cord with the stick – but be sure to place stiff card between furniture and cord to prevent bruising. An alternative is to use strips of old cycle inner tube wound around and pulled tight.

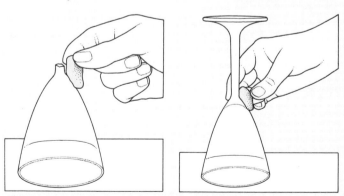

● To hold a broken glass stem upright put the rim of the glass downwards on a flat surface. Press a piece of putty or Plasticine against the bowl at the point of the break and it will support the stem. (Continued overleaf)

SEVEN EASY GLUING TIPS (cont)

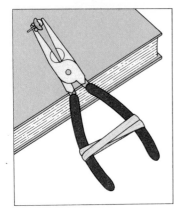

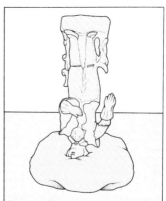

● To hold small items, place them between the jaws of a pair of pliers, and bind the handles with an elastic band. Add more turns of the elastic to increase the pressure.

● If an item has no flat surface to stand on while being repaired, press it into modelling clay or Plasticine. Or stand it in a box of fine sand.

DEALING WITH WOOD AND BOARD

Drilling large holes without damage

● To bore large holes with a carpenter's brace, use either a centre bit or an auger bit.

● In a power drill, use a spade bit (also called a flat bit).

● The danger is that when the tip of the bit breaks through the other side, it may tear the wood – or the veneer on chipboard. To avoid this, withdraw the bit as soon as its point appears through the far side. Then drill from the other side – putting the drill tip into the small hole – to produce a clean finish.

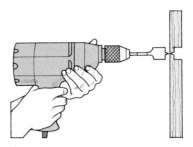

Cutting chipboard

The resins used to bond chipboard are highly abrasive and will quickly blunt saw teeth. To avoid this, use either a hard-point saw, which has hardened teeth, or a blade tipped with tungsten carbide. You can also get circular saw blades tipped in the same way.

Cutting laminate

● Cut sheet laminate, such as melamine, with a fine-tooth saw, working with the decorative surface uppermost.

● Or use a craft knife with a laminate-cutting blade. It scores the laminate on the decorative side. Then you can snap it downwards.

● If you use a jigsaw, use a fine-tooth blade and work with the decorative side downwards.

● After cutting, run a sanding block along the edge to remove any roughness.

Renewing laminate

If a laminate surface on a table or worktop is badly worn or scarred, don't try to remove it. You won't be able to get at the adhesive to soften it. Instead, stick new laminate over the old surface.

1 Roughen the old laminate with a tungsten carbide sanding block. Dust it clean with an old paintbrush.

2 Apply contact adhesive to both surfaces. When there is no tackiness, lay a sheet of brown paper over the old surface and place the new laminate over the paper.

3 Ease the paper out, pressing the laminate in place from one end to the other to expel air. Thump down hard with a fist to ensure tight contact.

Tightening loose joints in furniture

1 Joints in older pieces of furniture often work loose as the old animal glue loses its grip.

Use a rubber hammer or a wooden mallet, together with a piece of scrap wood, to knock the loose joints apart.

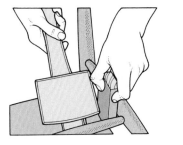

2 Clean off all the old dry glue with a knife. If the joints are dowelled, cut a V-shaped groove along the full length of the dowels. The groove will allow trapped air and surplus glue to escape – otherwise the pressure of air and glue at the base of the joint may prevent the pieces from coming tightly together.

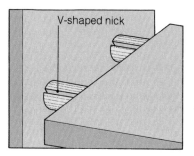

V-shaped nick

3 Apply new wood adhesive to the rim of the hole – not to the dowel. The adhesive will be carried down the hole by the dowel. Wipe away surplus adhesive with a damp cloth before it sets.

The secret of bending hardboard

To make hardboard follow a curve, damp it well and allow it to stand for 24 hours. But stand oil-tempered board for two or three times longer, because it's water resistant. Apply extra water if it gets dry.

CURING DENTS IN WOOD

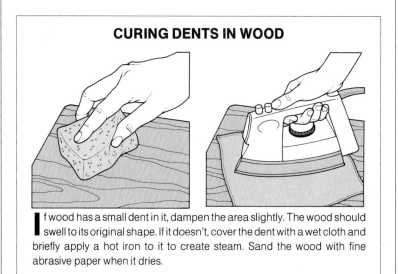

I f wood has a small dent in it, dampen the area slightly. The wood should swell to its original shape. If it doesn't, cover the dent with a wet cloth and briefly apply a hot iron to it to create steam. Sand the wood with fine abrasive paper when it dries.

Sanding wood by hand

● For general preparation when a fine finish isn't needed, use glass paper, which is made with crushed glass.
● For finer sanding, smoothing down fillers and cleaning metal, use aluminium oxide abrasive paper.
● For fine rubbing down between coats of paint, keying plastics and preparing painted surfaces for repainting, use silicon carbide abrasive.
● For removing light rust and cleaning up metal, use emery cloth.

THREE BASIC SANDING TIPS

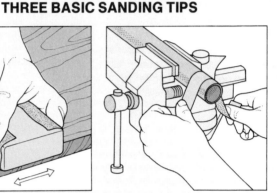

● On flat surfaces wrap a piece of abrasive paper around a cork or wood block. Some abrasives are coated on the back with adhesive for use with a sanding block.

● To use emery cloth on curved surfaces and awkward spots, tear strips from the cloth and use them rather like a belt, working the cloth back and forth.

● If you're sanding small pieces of wood, it's often easier to attach a piece of sandpaper to a clipboard, secure its other three edges with clips, and move the wood across the stationary sandpaper.

Staining and varnishing wood

Wood stains Bare timber can be coloured with wood stains, either spirit-based or water-based. Water-based stain raises the grain, so either damp the wood first and sand before staining, or sand lightly afterwards.

Try it first Try a little stain on an area that doesn't matter before you cover large areas – often the final colour is not quite what you expect.

Recolouring sealed wood If you want to recolour wood which has been sealed, use a stain varnish – the stain is mixed with the varnish. The only disadvantage is that each coat darkens the colour a little.

A natural look If you want to give wood a natural finish, choose a clear varnish suited to the job. Finish furniture with standard varnish. But floors need a coating recommended for hard wear.

Outdoor varnish For outdoors, use microporous varnish which can 'breathe' and release trapped air or moisture – usually responsible for blistering and flaking. The varnish also contains a fungicide to prevent mould, and an ultraviolet filter to counter bleaching by the sun.

A good grip To make sure varnish gets a good grip, apply the first coat with a lint-free rag, working it into the wood pores. Follow with two or more brush-applied coats – the more coats, the better the protection.

Removing a high gloss Varnish can look over glossy, so for a more natural appearance use a matt varnish. Or, if you have already used gloss varnish, remove the sheen with fine wire wool and white spirit, rubbing very gently. When the surface is dry, dust off with an old paintbrush, then finish with a clear furniture polish.

TACKLING PROBLEM FLOORS

Silencing creaking floorboards

Floors often develop creaks after central heating has been installed. The warmth dries out the wood which contracts, causing slight gaps between the boards which allow them to rub together and squeak.
● Walk over the bare boards slowly, noting where the squeaks occur.
● Screwing a floorboard to the nearest joist will often cure the problem. Tighten the screws until the heads sink into the wood, so there is no movement at all.

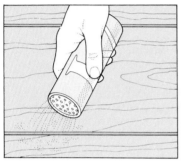

● If there isn't a conveniently close joist, puff talc or a dry lubricant between the boards until the squeaking stops.

● If that fails, try driving a screw or two down in the gap between the boards. Use screws that have the thread right up to the head.

Curing stairs that squeak

Squeaking stairs, like squeaking floorboards, are usually caused by the wood drying out and shrinking, very often after central heating has been installed.

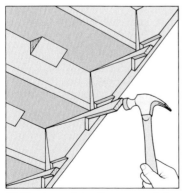

● Try to get to the rear of the stairs, where wooden wedges hold the components in place. Remove loose wedges, clean off old glue, apply fresh woodworking glue and tap them back in place.

● Alternatively, cut some triangular wood moulding into short pieces and drill holes through them, horizontally and vertically. Then screw them into the corners where treads and risers meet.

215

● If you can't get access to the underside of the stairs, drill pilot holes in the tread immediately above the riser, then drive screws down into the riser, tightening them as much as possible.

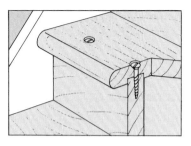

Make sure the screw heads are countersunk below the tread surface so they don't wear the carpet.

● If you suspect that squeaking is caused by wood surfaces rubbing together, inject dry lubricant such as Easy-Slide into any gaps.

Dealing with concrete floors

Stopping dust If a concrete floor produces fine dust however often you sweep it, seal it with pva adhesive. Dilute the adhesive one part pva to four parts water and work it well into the surface of the concrete. It will dry clear.

Painting the floor To improve the appearance of a plain concrete floor, coat it with floor paint which is available in a limited colour range. When dry, the paint will be water-resistant and unaffected by household chemicals. It will also withstand a lot of scuffing and prevent dusting.

Smoothing an uneven concrete floor Never put a new floorcovering over an irregular concrete floor – it will greatly reduce the life of the covering.

● Chip away small nibs of concrete with a cold chisel and club hammer. Protect your eyes from flying fragments with safety spectacles and your hands with work gloves.

● For large areas, use a self-levelling screeding compound. It's available in tubs, ready-mixed. First fill holes up to 20mm (¾in) deep. Then tip out the compound and spread it with a plasterer's float. If slight cracks develop, apply a second coat when the first has set.

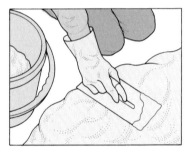

Patching a damaged carpet

If a carpet is damaged in a small area, you can patch it with a piece of matching carpet left over from when it was laid. Or you can take a piece from beneath furniture and replace that with a non-matching piece.

1 Remove the carpet tacks so that the damaged area can be lifted from the floor. Find a piece of matching carpet and cut a square larger than the damaged area.

2 Put a piece of scrap hardboard or plywood underneath the damage, between the carpet and the underlay. Then put the patch over the damage, making sure the pile and the carpet weave run the same way.

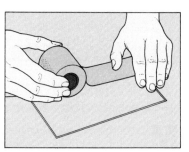

3 Hold the patch in place, and cut through both patch and carpet below with a craft knife, severing all threads. Remove all the pieces and put the new patch in the hole. It should fit perfectly.

4 Turn the carpet over and secure the patch with self-adhesive carpet tape. If the carpet is foam-backed, you can anchor the patch with a square of coarse fabric and latex adhesive.

5 Replace the carpet and work the fibres around the join with your fingers to disguise the patch.

LIFTING DAMAGED VINYL FLOOR TILES

Place aluminium cooking foil over the damaged tiles you want to remove. Slowly move an iron, set at maximum heat, over each foil-covered tile. The heat will soften the tile adhesive in about a minute, allowing you to lift each tile without damaging the wooden floor beneath.

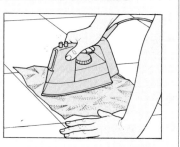

GETTING RID OF RUBBISH

Large household items Old cookers, refrigerators and furniture, and garden rubbish, can be disposed of free of charge at household waste sites, which local authorities are obliged by law to provide. Some authorities will also collect old appliances and furniture. Many waste sites also have bottle and can banks, paper recycling bins and engine oil collection tanks.

Building debris Skips are the best way to dispose of large amounts of rubble. Check with your local authority – some councils hire out skips at a cheaper rate than commercial operators. Some may even offer skips free if several neighbours are using them. If a skip is on a public road, you'll need a council permit – and it must be well lit at night and cause no obstruction.

Usable furniture Some social services departments and charity organisations will collect furniture that's reusable. Or advertise the furniture in your local newspaper – many give free advertisements for items priced less than £10.

Clothing Give unwanted clothing to charity shops or a local jumble sale. Even clothes that are no longer wearable are acceptable – they can be recycled. Rags are used to manufacture various products, such as roofing felt and carpet underlay.

Home security

CHECK YOUR DEFENCES

Most burglaries are committed by casual thieves looking for an easy way into a house. If a thief encounters well-locked doors and windows – or hears a dog inside – he will probably move onto a house where the pickings are easier. He needs a fast way in and out, and he won't climb through broken glass.

Windows

● Fit locks to all ground-floor windows and to any windows near flat roofs, drainpipes or wherever a thief can get easy access. Never leave ground-floor windows open when you go out.

● Windows that are hidden from the street and from the neighbours are particularly at risk. You can make them more secure by fitting laminated glass – a sandwich of glass with clear plastic film in between. Don't use wired glass; it's not very secure.

Doors

● Make sure that your front and back doors were really intended to be exterior doors. They must have a solid core of wood and be about 45mm (1$\frac{3}{4}$in) thick. Interior doors may be lightweight and thinner, and much easier to knock down. They shouldn't be used as exterior doors.

● Don't expect a cheap cylinder nightlatch to keep out a thief. Have a mortise deadlock fitted to the front door as well (page 220).

● Fit a good-quality two-bolt mortise lock on the back door.

Garage

A garage attached to the house can allow a thief to work on a side door totally hidden. Make sure the garage is fitted with secure locks and fit the house door with extra security (page 225).

Ladders

Keep ladders locked away. If they must be stored outside, padlock them to a wall with special brackets that can be bought at a DIY store. And buy a good-quality padlock at the same time.

Sheds

Make sure your garden shed is securely padlocked. Tools stored there could be used for a break-in. A garden spade, for example, makes a powerful lever for opening windows.

Hedges and shrubs

Avoid having high hedges and shrubs at the front of your house. They will screen a thief from the road or from neighbours, allowing him to attack windows unseen.

Marking valuables

● Print your house number and post code on valuable possessions with an ultraviolet pen. This will help police to prove they were stolen, and assist in returning them.

● Metal items can be marked with hammer-and-letter punches.

● Collect valuable items together and photograph them, showing on the photograph where they are marked.

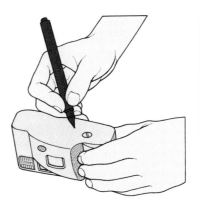

Keys

● Do not leave house keys in locks, under the mat, or hanging on a string inside the letterbox.

● Never have a name-and-address tag on your keys. At most, use your surname with a company address or the address of a relative.

● Be wary of leaving home to go and collect keys from someone who says they have found them. It may be a ruse to get you out of the house while the keys are used for entry.

● Don't carry your keys in a handbag. If the bag is stolen, letters or documents in it could tell the thief your address.

Coal chute

If you have a coal chute which you don't use any more, have it sealed up, or have bars cemented across it if you want to keep it for ventilation. Coal chutes can be an easy way to get into a house.

Going on holiday

When you go away on an annual holiday, or just for a weekend, the first rule of security is: don't advertise your absence. Try to make the house look occupied.

● Be sure to cancel milk and newspapers. Arrange for a neighbour to push in unexpected items like leaflets and free newspapers.

● If you have a glazed porch, ask the neighbour to collect post so it is not visible from outside.

● Don't write your address on luggage labels. It just announces to anyone at the airport that your house will be unoccupied for the next week or two. Put your address inside the suitcase.

● Ask your neighbour to mow the front lawn, sweep up leaves, leave footprints in the snow and generally make the house look lived in. Offer to do the same for the neighbour.

● Consider hiring a telephone answering service – you'll find them in Yellow Pages under 'Telephone answering service'. Then your telephone gives no clue that you are absent. If you already have a telephone answering machine, word your announcement as though you were merely away for an hour or two.

● Fit timeswitches (available from DIY and electrical shops) to turn lights and the TV on at night (page 231).

● If you are going away for only a short period, consider leaving your car locked outside. It may fool a prowling thief into thinking that the house is occupied. But if you will be away for a long holiday, remember that a dusty car – or one on which snow has lain for days – may itself become an indication that the house is empty.

● Tell your local police station that you will be away. They will keep an eye on the house for you.

ADVICE AND HELP FROM THE POLICE

● If you want expert advice on making your home secure, contact the Crime Prevention Officer at your local police station. He will visit the house if necessary, point out weak spots in your defences and suggest the most appropriate security devices. His advice is free.

● If you see anyone loitering in your street or acting suspiciously, do not disturb him. Call the police, then continue to watch unseen.

● Neighbourhood Watch groups, run in collaboration with the local police, are intended to encourage neighbours to work together by watching for anything suspicious in the area. They also stress the importance of protecting property and marking valuables. If you are interested in getting involved in a group, contact your local Crime Prevention Officer at the police station.

● You can have bicycles punch-marked with your post code at the local police station.

BEST LOCKS FOR YOUR DOORS

Make sure that your door frame is sound. If it's rotten get a builder to replace it. Surface-mounted locks are only as strong as the screws holding them in place. So use the length and gauge that are recommended; never use anything smaller.

Front doors

Nightlatch The traditional cylinder nightlatch, commonly used on front doors, is useful for frequent comings and goings, but doesn't have high security value. If a door has a glass panel, a thief just has to break the glass, put his hand in and open the door. You need another lock to reinforce it, or something quite different (see below).

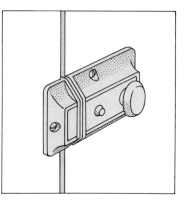

Mortise deadlock Get a locksmith to add a mortise deadlock below the nightlatch. Buy a five-lever model for best security. A deadlock can only be opened with a key.

Latchbolt If you only want one lock, buy a latchbolt (also called a locking latch) which has both a bolt and latch. The latch is opened from the inside by a handle.

Back and side doors

A sashlock has both a bolt and a latch, with handles on both sides to operate the latch. If you already have a sashlock, check if it has only two or three levers. If it does, exchange it for one with five levers which give much better security. It may be possible to convert the existing lock with an 'upgrader' unit, but make sure you get one of the right size.

French windows

On wooden French windows, fit rack bolts (see next page) at the top and bottom so that they slide into the frame. Fit them on the door which overlaps the other one.

If you have metal French windows, fit surface-mounted self-locking bolts in the same way (see next page).

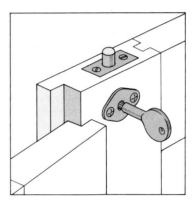

Patio doors

A small lock can be fixed to the inside door. A bolt slides into a hole in the second door. The lock can be attached to either wooden or metal doors provided you get the right screws – either wood screws or self-tapping screws for metal.

For the greatest strength fit two locks – top and bottom. This is particularly necessary on an old aluminium patio door which can sometimes be jemmied out.

SHOULD YOU LOCK INTERNAL DOORS?

When the home is empty, internal doors are best left unlocked. Once a determined burglar is inside the house he will usually not be deterred by locked doors unless they are particularly strong. He will kick or jemmy them open, causing a great deal of extra damage to the house. The same applies to wardrobe doors and to drawers, both of which can easily be forced open. Put valuables in a hidden safe, then leave all the doors and drawers unlocked.

When the house is occupied, however, ground-floor doors can be locked at night. A burglar trying to get from, say, the living room to the rest of the house will probably make so much noise that he will wake you, and you can then call the police. Fit a sashlock, as you would for a back or side door. The handles on both sides of the door will be necessary for normal use in the daytime. Whatever practice you adopt, give priority to fitting good locks to external doors and windows.

Extra security fittings to make a door even more burglar-proof

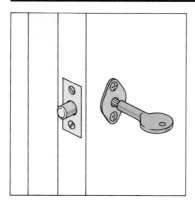

Rack bolts

On every door that opens to the outside, you should fit rack bolts to make it even harder for a burglar to force. The bolt has a key which should be kept out of arm-reach if the door has a glass panel.

Fit two bolts on each door – one in the closing edge well away from the lock, and one at the top or bottom.

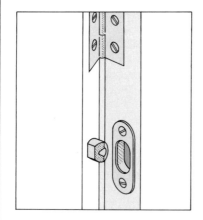

Self-locking bolts

Where a door is too thin to house a rack bolt without being weakened, fit a surface mounted, self-locking bolt. It is merely screwed in place; when fitted, all screws are concealed. Pushing the bolt end slides it into the locked position where it deadlocks and cannot be moved without the use of a key.

Hinge bolts

It's possible for a determined burglar to force a door off its hinges by levering it with a jemmy on the hinge side. To prevent this happening, fit hinge bolts – two on each door – about 75mm (3in) away from the hinges.

Door limiter

A more substantial version of the door chain (opposite page) is called a door limiter, with a sliding bar replacing the chain. When it's in place the bar engages with the retaining part of the unit, restricting the door's opening while you talk to someone outside. The door has to be closed and the bar swung away before it can be fully opened.

Door chains

To prevent an intruder forcing his way in after ringing the doorbell, fit a chain to the front door. It allows the door to be opened just far enough to speak to a caller, but the door has to be shut again before the chain can be released to allow the person in.

The strength of the device depends entirely on how well the chain is anchored to both the door and the frame, so the longest and heaviest-gauge screws possible should be used. Various patterns are available, including a simple chain, a chain combined with a sliding bolt, a chain which can be unlocked from the outside with a key, and a chain with a built-in alarm which is triggered by an attempt to enter.

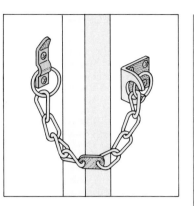

Peephole viewer

A simple lens system offers a wide-angle view of the area immediately outside the door. You can look out when someone rings the bell, but the person outside cannot see in. Install a porch light as well so that the caller on the doorstep is well lit.

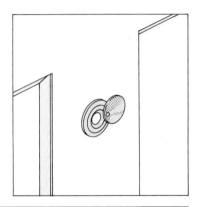

How to fit a new cylinder to an old nightlatch

If the keys of a cylinder nightlatch are lost, or if you want to be sure of security when taking over a new house, it's cheaper to replace the cylinder than to buy a completely new lock.

This can only be done with a traditional nightlatch of a well-known make. You cannot replace the cylinder on the type of nightlatch which has a locking interior handle.

Buy the new cylinder and keys from a locksmith.

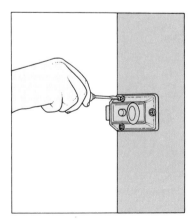

1 Working from the inside of the door, unscrew the lock cover to expose the connecting screws which hold the central cylinder in place.

223

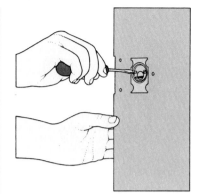

2 Unscrew the connecting screws until the cylinder can be removed. The connecting bar will come away as well.

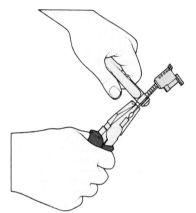

3 Hold the connecting bar of the new cylinder in a self-grip wrench or a vice and use pliers to snap it to the same length as the old one so that it's correctly housed in the handle of the lock when the cylinder is in place.

   The connecting bar is divided into several breakable segments along its length.

4 Make sure that the connecting screws are also the right length. They can be cut to length with a mini hacksaw.

5 Insert the new cylinder into the hole. Tighten the connecting screws and replace the cover, making sure that the handle of the lock connects with the bar. Finally, screw back the cover.

Protecting sheds and workshops

The flimsy hasp and staple fitted to many ready-made sheds have no real security value, and they need to be replaced with a much stronger device called a locking bar.

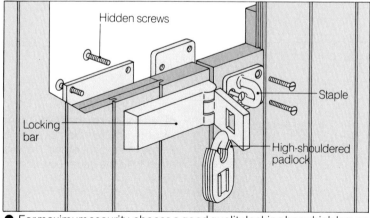

Hidden screws

Staple

Locking bar

High-shouldered padlock

● For maximum security, choose a good quality locking bar which leaves no screw or bolt heads visible when it's closed. The hinged section should have a totally enclosed pin that can't be knocked out by a thief who is armed with tools.

● Buy a five-lever padlock with raised shoulders to protect it from attack by hacksaw, bolt cutters or crowbar.

● Ideally both the locking bar and the staple should be bolted right through the frame of the building.

● If screws are used, buy clutch-head ones which can be tightened with a screwdriver but cannot be undone.

Protecting garages

Securing hinged doors

Garages with hinged doors can be padlocked with a locking bar in the same way as sheds and workshops.

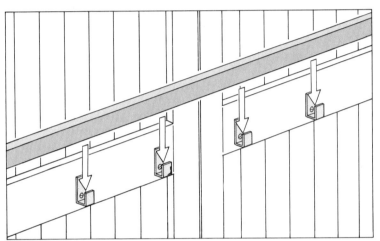

If the garage is attached to the house and there is a door leading inside, extra security is needed, because once he is in the garage a thief can work unseen. A beam made of wood or metal can be dropped into brackets fixed to the inside of the garage door and the frame, ensuring that the doors cannot be opened from the outside while you are away from the house.

Bend here for wide beam

Bend here for narrow beam

You can make your own brackets by bending one arm of a large angle bracket into a U-shape. Hold the bracket in a vice and tap it with a hammer to bend it.

Securing up-and-over doors

Up-and-over doors are normally fitted with a cylinder lock which forms part of the door handle. If the keys are lost, a replacement handle should be available from the door manufacturers.

If a garage with up-and-over doors is attached to the house and there is access from the garage into the house, put a locking bar on the inside of the door about 100mm (4in) down from the top, so that the door can be locked to the vertical frame with a padlock. Fit the hasp to the frame and the staple to the door.

Then the door can only be opened from inside. It should always be kept locked when you are away from the house.

Inexpensive lock for door or window

A cheap and easy way of locking doors and windows from the inside is to use plastic block-joints that are sold in DIY shops for joining pieces of wood together. But be careful to leave yourself a quick escape route in case of fire if you use this technique at night. Keep a screwdriver beside the doors or windows that have been fastened with the block-joints.

The technique can only be used for doors and windows that open outwards – casement windows, French windows and interior doors that you want to lock when you are in the house at night (page 221).

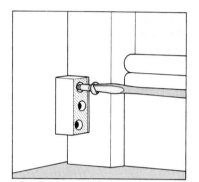

1 Fit one half of the block-joint in the angle between a door or window and its frame, and screw it to the door or window.

2 Screw the other half to the frame. On doors and long windows, use one joint at the top and one at the bottom.

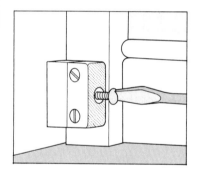

3 Once the two halves are in position, they can be left there. To undo the lock, simply unscrew the bolt that holds the two halves together.

CHOOSING LOCKS FOR WINDOWS

The most common method used by burglars to break into a house is to smash a window, reach through and release the catch on the inside. If the window is securely locked, a thief is unlikely to try to crawl through the broken glass.

Most window locks will either lock the frames together, make the handle immovable, or lock the stay arm. Locking the frames together gives the best result on both sash and casement windows.

Before buying window locks, make sure they are suitable for your particular windows. A lock for timber windows will be supplied with woodscrews. Locks for metal windows will have self-tapping screws. Also be sure that there is space on the window to accommodate the lock. A wooden casement window, for example, might have a frame that is too narrow to take a mortise bolt, in which case you should use a surface-fitted lock (see facing page).

Wooden sash windows

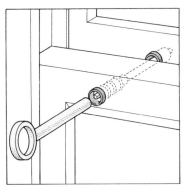

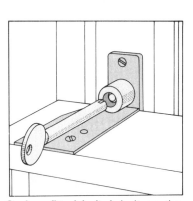

Dual screw A bolt goes through a barrel in the inner frame into the outer frame. Fit two dual screws if the window is large.

Surface-fitted bolt A bolt on the upper sash allows the window to be opened a little for ventilation. Fit two to large windows.

Wooden casement windows

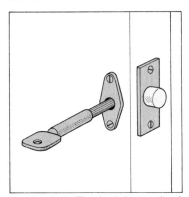

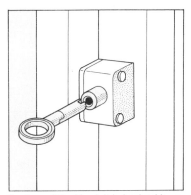

Mortise bolt The lock is mortised into the opening window, so it may be too large for a narrow frame. It's a bit tricky to install, but gives excellent security. Fit two to big windows – at each end of the opening edge.

Surface-fitted lock It is locked by a push-button action, and unlocked with a key. Suitable for narrow frames. Fit the lock close to the centre of the opening edge. On large windows fit one at the top and one at the bottom.

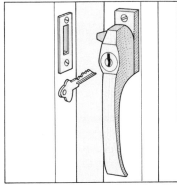

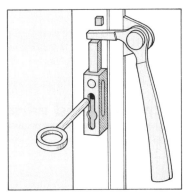

Locking handle A new handle with a lock replaces the existing handle. Once locked, it cannot be opened without the key. Make sure you buy the correct right-hand or left-hand type for your window.

Blocking bolt The lock is fitted to the fixed frame and prevents the cockspur handle on the window from being moved. Only suitable when the cockspur is on the surface of the frame, not recessed.

227

Metal windows

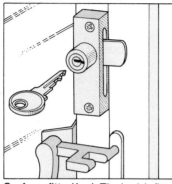

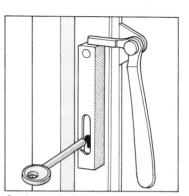

Surface-fitted lock The lock is fitted with self-tapping screws near the centre of the opening edge of the window. The bolt locks against the fixed frame.

Cockspur bolt When the cockspur handle is closed, the case of the bolt is moved up on the fixed frame and locked, preventing the cockspur from opening.

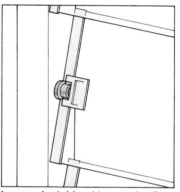

Stay bolt The device fits underneath the window's stay bar and is fixed to it. A bolt slides under the stay retainer, preventing the arm from being lifted.

Louvre lock Metal inserts for Beta Naco windows lock the glass in the holders. Or use epoxy glue to stick the glass. A blocking bolt (previous page) can lock the handle.

SAFETY WARNING

When locks are used on windows, make sure there are keys in each room so a window can be opened in an emergency.

Do not permanently screw down windows that may be needed as an escape route in time of fire.

A rarely used window

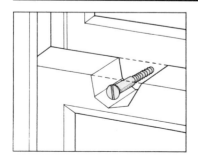

Before you spend money on window locks, think how often the window is going to be used.

Screw through frame A sash window that is rarely opened can be screwed together through the meeting rails with a long wood screw. The screw can always be removed in the future, if necessary.

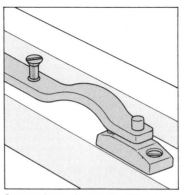

Corner-joint A casement window can be locked with a plastic corner-joint screwed to both window and frame.

Screw through stay-bar The stay-bar of a casement window can be anchored to the frame with a screw in one of the holes.

A quick answer to window security

You're about to go on holiday and you realise that the downstairs windows can't be locked. What can you do? A screw sunk into the frame beside the catch can provide effective security and give you peace of mind until you can install a permanent lock.

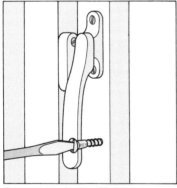

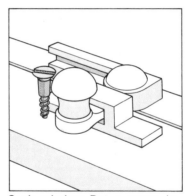

Casement window Sink the screw about 25mm (1in) into the wood beside the handle.

Sash window Put a screw in vertically, close up against the lever so that it can't be opened.

PROTECTING JEWELLERY

Once a thief has got into an empty house, locked drawers and cupboards won't stop him getting to your jewellery. If you have some valuable pieces that you don't use often, deposit them with your bank and take them out when you need them.

Alternatively, install a domestic safe in an inconspicuous place. Models are available from security shops that can be bolted to the floor, either under the floorboards or on top (see next page). You can also buy a small safe that fits into a hole in a brick wall. The front looks like a double power socket and is opened with a key inserted into one of the plug holes. There is no electrical wiring. The safe is big enough to hold money or jewellery.

If you install a safe yourself, follow the instructions precisely so that it can't be jemmied out.

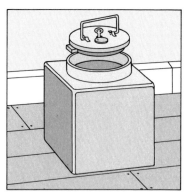

Under-floor The safe fits between the joists of a floor. It can then be covered by a carpet. It is screwed to the joists from the inside, and has a combination lock.

Above-floor The safe is bolted to the floor joists from the inside. It can be installed inside a cupboard, in the loft or in any other inconspicuous place in the house.

INSTALLING A BURGLAR ALARM

The range of burglar alarms can be confusing, so don't spend money until you have talked to your local Crime Prevention Officer about the system that is most suitable for your home.

A whole-house system

Alarm The most popular type sets off an alarm when a burglar tries to break in. Magnetic switches fitted to your doors and windows are connected to a central control unit.

Panic button You can also have a panic button fitted beside your bed or by the front door. You can then operate it by hand if someone tries to break in.

Pressure pad A pressure pad can be placed under a rug or carpet, usually inside the front door. It triggers the alarm when someone treads on it. But as it gets older you need to check it by running your hand over it to make sure the alarm is set off. Pressure pads tire with age and become unreliable.

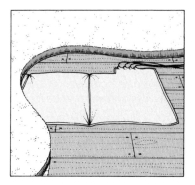

Door alarm

An inexpensive alarm, which can be fitted to a front or back door, goes off if the door is opened when the alarm is set. It works on batteries, so no electrical wiring is needed. Useful in a flat where there is only one entry door.

Acoustic alarm

A single box which is set off by noise, such as the breaking of glass or splintering of wood. An acoustic alarm is inexpensive, easy to install and quite small. It should be placed in the room which is most likely to be broken into.

Infra-red alarm

Detects the body heat of a burglar. Once the siren has begun to sound, it can only be turned off with the key. The unit can be moved around the house, or you can have several room sensors connected to a central unit.

Ultrasonic alarm

An ultrasonic alarm works by sending out continuous sound waves which bounce back to it from the opposite wall. If the wave-pattern is broken by a burglar walking past or a door being opened, the alarm goes off.

Using automatic switches

You can make your house look lived-in while you are away by using switches that turn lights, radios and TV on and off during the day. Don't just have a single hall light shining in the evening. It's more likely to betray that the house is empty. Try to have lights coming on in different rooms at different times, as though people are moving around the house.

Sunset switch The switch is installed in place of a normal light switch. A light-sensitive eye turns it on as daylight fades, and it switches off at a time that you can pre-set.

Programmable switch Also installed in place of a normal switch. It can be programmed to switch on and off as often as you want. It will also

231

memorise the times when you normally switch the light on and off, and will repeat the pattern. It can be operated manually at any time.

Automatic outdoor light An infra-red sensor switches the light on after dusk when anyone – visitor or burglar – comes within a certain distance. The light goes off after a few minutes. The unit can be fitted instead of a normal outside light.

Socket timer A plug-in timer can be used to control anything that plugs into a 13amp socket – a lamp, radio, TV or tape recorder. Models vary in the number of times they will switch an appliance on and off. Simple timers switch on up to five times a day. Electronic models can switch on 14 times a day on a weekly cycle.

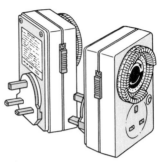

If your home should be burgled

You return home to see signs of a break-in
● If you notice or suspect that somebody is inside your home when you arrive at the gate – you see movement, perhaps, or notice an open door – avoid entering the house at all.
● If you have driven home, back out of the drive again and drive off. The intruder may think you were just turning round.
● If you are on foot, walk on down the street.
● Go to a neighbour's house at once and call the police.

You get indoors to find a prowler inside
● Ask the intruder what he wants.
● Do not give any impression that you intend to fight over money or possessions – you may get hurt. Try not to anger or provoke him.
● Memorise his appearance, and call the police as soon as he has gone.
● If you have a panic button, use it if you think it's safe to do so.

You wake up to hear a burglar in the house
● If you wake at night to hear an intruder downstairs – or if you hear someone trying to break in – put all the lights on and make a lot of noise by moving about. Most burglars will choose to flee empty-handed.
● Do not go downstairs. Dial the police from your bedroom, if possible, and press a panic button if you have one.
● If you are on your own, call out loudly to an imaginary male companion: 'Harry, there's someone in the house.'
● Look out of your window after the intruder leaves and try to note what he looks like, and what car, if any, he gets into. Then call the police.

How to give a description to the police
If you contact the police, you may need to give a description of the person you have seen. This is a checklist of useful details.
● Male/female
● Colour of skin
● Complexion
● Height
● Hair (colour, length, etc.)
● Build
● Age
● Eye colour
● Wears glasses?
● Face (long, thin, round, clean-shaven, moustache, beard)
● Marks (scars, tattoos)
● Mouth (narrow/wide)
● Dress (description of clothing)

Around the house outdoors

*A*ll the tips you need to keep your house weatherproof and looking smart. How to get a reluctant car to start, and keep the family bicycles running smoothly. And no-fuss gardening with a minimum of chemical sprays.

Looking after the outside

DEALING WITH EXTERIOR DOORS

Guarding doors against the weather

Any outside door exposed to the weather should be well protected. To repaint an old door, sand it down and apply an undercoat and two gloss coats. But to give maximum protection to a new door, follow these steps:

1 First treat the door with a clear wood preservative, applied liberally by brush.

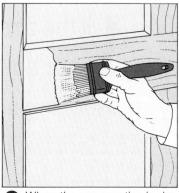

2 When the preservative is dry, coat with wood primer to seal the pores of the wood.

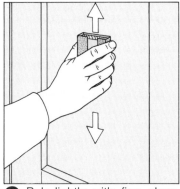

3 Rub lightly with fine glass-paper on a cork block to remove any roughness – but work only with the run of the grain.

4 Dust off the sanded surface with an old paintbrush, then apply an undercoat and two coats of gloss paint.

THE NATURAL LOOK

If you want a natural finish on a hardwood door, do not use linseed oil – it becomes gummy with age and discolours. Instead, buy an all-weather varnish made for exterior use. It contains a fungicide to discourage mould growth and discoloration. It is microporous, so the wood can 'breathe', allowing any trapped air or moisture to escape. And it has an ultraviolet filter to counter the bleaching effects of bright sunlight. The varnish must be applied to bare or stained wood to be effective.

Keeping out draughts and rain

Choose only the most durable materials for draughtproofing external doors. The best is a flexible strip of phosphor bronze or nylon which can be bent to form a seal between door and frame.

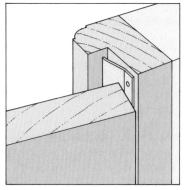 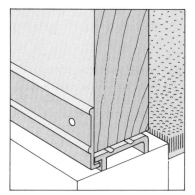

● Pin the draughtproofing strip to the door frame so that the closing door first comes into contact with the pinned edge.

● Don't put any more bend into the strip than is necessary to seal the gap – too much, and the door will be hard to open and close.

● Seal the bottom of the door with a threshold draught excluder. The best consists of two interlocking sections – one fitted to the door, the other to the threshold. It keeps out rain as well as draughts, and should be fitted if the door is not sheltered by a porch.

Weather bars Back doors, front doors exposed to the weather, and doors to sun rooms and outhouses should be fitted with an external weather bar. It is designed to deflect water away from the gap between the door and the frame at the bottom. The bars are available in metal, softwood and hardwood – usually slightly over-length so they can be cut to fit. If the door opens outwards, check whether the bar is likely to foul the door frame when the door is open wide. If so, cut the end of the bar at an angle nearest to the hinged side of the door.

DOOR STRIPPING SERVICES

Stripping a painted door back to bare wood can be a long job. It is much quicker – and not much more expensive – to let a specialist company do it for you. You'll find companies listed in the Yellow Pages under 'Furniture repairs & restoration', or 'Antique repair & restoration'.

But there can be snags Some doors react badly to immersion – joints can open up or become loose. So if you have a number of similar doors to be stripped, send one first and assess the results.

You may also be disappointed with the colouring of the door. Many cheaper doors are not intended to be seen without paint – and the individual timbers may be of different colours. It may be possible to stain to a standard colouring, but experiment before sending a number of doors to be stripped. This may not apply to high quality doors of many older properties and professional stripping can be very effective.

Caution Check with the stripping company before taking a polyurethane-painted door to be stripped. While hand-painted polyurethane can be stripped, factory-finished doors can only be done with difficulty.

CLEARING A BLOCKED DRAIN

If a lavatory pan, sink or outside gulley is slow to empty, there may be a blockage in the drain carrying waste away from the house.

1 Lift the manhole cover nearest the blockage. If the manhole is clear, the blockage must be in one of the pipes leading to it from the house. If it is full, there is a blockage farther down the system.

2 Lift the next manhole cover. If the manhole is full, the blockage must be still farther along. If it's empty, the blockage must lie between the first and second manholes. However, if the blockage lies beyond the last manhole on your property, inform your local authority – they are responsible for drainage outside your boundary.

3 Once you have established where the blockage lies, hire a set of drain rods (check the Yellow Pages under 'Hire services – tools & equipment'). You will get a number of flexible rods which screw together, plus a rubber plunger and a corkscrew head.

4 Put on rubber gloves. Screw together a number of rods and fit the corkscrew device. Feed the rods into the drain, turning them clockwise. As the blockage is breached, water will start to drain off, washing most of the blockage with it.

DO NOT turn drain rods anti-clockwise while they are inside the drain – they will unscrew and you'll lose them.

5 To clean the pipe finally, withdraw the rods and replace the corkscrew head with the rubber plunger. Run water from the kitchen and bathroom taps, then work the plunger back and forth to remove any remaining material.

6 Remove any debris remaining in the manholes, then flush with a jet of water from a garden hose.

7 Clean the grooves in which the manhole cover sits and apply thick car grease before replacing the cover. It will ensure an airtight fit to eliminate any smell.

CALLING IN A PROFESSIONAL

If possible, only call a specialist drain-cleaning company during normal working hours. You can look up a local company in the Yellow Pages under 'Drain, sewer & pipe cleaning'. While most companies offer a 24-hour service, charges can rise considerably outside office hours. Always get an estimate – your local plumber might be just as cheap.

Try to find a plumber who is a member of the Institute of Plumbing. The institute will give you the names of members in your area – but can't advise on plumbing problems itself. Its address is 64 Station Lane, Hornchurch, Essex RM12 6NB (tel. 04024 72791).

KEEPING GUTTERS WORKING

Cleaning blocked gutters

Gutters collect debris which doesn't wash away. It may include growing moss, leaves and twigs and the remains of birds' nests. Late autumn is a good time to make a thorough check to ensure gutters are clean, in readiness for winter rain.

● Use a ladder stand-off so the ladder is held out from the wall and doesn't rest on the gutter. Being slightly away from the gutter makes work easier. The top of the ladder should be well above the gutter to give you a handhold.

● Use a large wire brush to remove stubborn debris from metal guttering, although this shouldn't be necessary on modern plastic gutters.
● Then gather material with a stiff hand brush, lifting it out into a bucket with a garden trowel. The bucket can be suspended from the ladder with a metal S-hook.
● When the gutters are clear, flush with water.

Repairing leaking gutter joints

If a gutter starts to leak, repair it quickly. Water can soon penetrate the wall and damage interior decoration. Treatment for leaking gutter joints depends on the type of gutter.

Plastic gutters
● Prise off the plastic union piece holding together a joint.
● Separate the gutter sections and check the neoprene foam gasket.
● If it is displaced, reposition it and replace the union piece.
● If it has perished, take the old gasket to a plumber's supplier and buy new ones to replace all gaskets on that run of guttering.

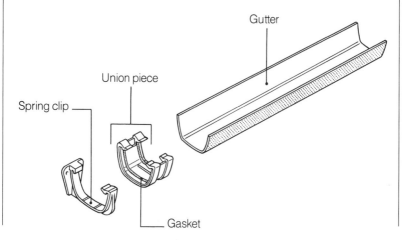

Gutter

Union piece

Spring clip

Gasket

Cast-concrete guttering

● Rake out the leaking joints of cast-concrete gutters with the point of a trowel.

● Brush out all loose material.

● Reseal the joints with a pre-mixed instant mortar that can be bought in a tub.

● Be sure to smooth the surface so there are no projections that may help to cause future blockages.

Cast-iron guttering

Older type cast-iron guttering is usually bolted together at the joints, with the gap between sections sealed with putty.

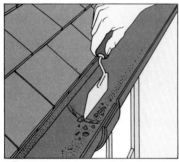

1 If the putty has perished, scrape out loose pieces. The bolts may be too stiff to undo.

2 Brush out all the debris and thoroughly dry the areas to be resealed, perhaps with a hair dryer.

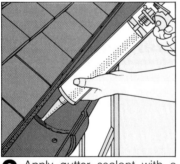

3 Apply gutter sealant with a sealant gun, and press it well into the gaps.

4 Smooth the sealant with a wet finger or a wet lint-free rag, such as an old handkerchief.

COVERING A GUTTER WITH NETTING

One way to keep debris out of gutters is to fit special gutter netting, held with clips. However, it is unwise to use netting if there are nearby trees – leaves can collect on the netting, making rainwater overflow. The water will probably soak into the wall, causing damage to the inside of the house.

Realigning a plastic gutter

Guttering usually has a slight fall towards the downpipe so that debris will be carried along with the flow of water. Sometimes a gutter will sag, perhaps because the screws holding the support brackets have come out. The gutter may then need to be realigned.

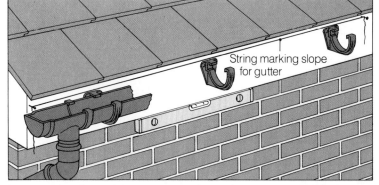

String marking slope for gutter

Before realigning or renewing plastic guttering, check with a spirit level that the fascia board is horizontal. Then mark the run of guttering on the fascia board by measuring up from the bottom of the board and creating a fall of 15-20mm ($\frac{1}{2}$-$\frac{3}{4}$in) in every 3m (10ft) run. Stretch a piece of string between two nails knocked into the board at each end of the run. The string marks the upper level of the guttering. If the fascia board isn't horizontal, use the spirit level to draw a horizontal line on the board and measure up from that.

On a particularly long run, it is sometimes best to site the downpipe centrally, with the guttering sloping towards it from each side. The downpipe can take a diagonal path down the wall to the gulley.

CLEARING AND REPAIRING DOWNPIPES

Clearing a blockage

Birds trying to nest in the head of a pipe are the most common cause of blockage. Rain will wash the nest into the downpipe, where the materials will swell and block the pipe.
● If the blockage is visible from above, you may be able to hook it out with stiff bent wire.

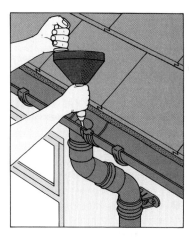

● When the blockage is out of sight, hire a Sanisnake tool from a tool-hire shop. It consists of a flexible drive with a screw device at the working end. It burrows through the blockage, which can then be pulled out through the top of the downpipe.

DO NOT push the blockage down – it will almost certainly simply shift the obstruction to a lower level and further debris will then accumulate on top of it, making the problem even worse.

● Once the obstruction is cleared, use a garden hose to flush out any remaining debris from the pipe.
● As a last resort, it is possible to dismantle plastic downpipes, but it is rarely practical with cast iron. The cast-iron brackets are usually nailed to the wall.

239

● To prevent further trouble, fit wire or plastic cages, which can be bought at DIY shops, into the mouths of downpipes. Check them occasionally to ensure there isn't a build-up of debris.

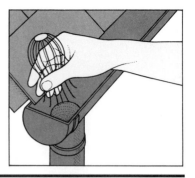

Repairing a cracked downpipe

A cracked section of cast-iron downpipe should be replaced, but a good temporary repair can be done with self-adhesive flashing tape.
● Clean the area to be covered, then wind the tape around the pipe, pressing the adhesive side firmly to the pipe. Paint the smooth outer surface to match the rest of the pipe.

● Cracks can also be sealed with a two-part epoxy repair paste. Before it has set, strengthen the repair by binding over the paste with glass-fibre bandage, then over-coating the bandage with more paste. This may be painted when it has set.

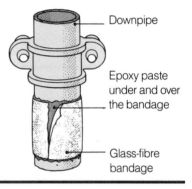

Downpipe

Epoxy paste under and over the bandage

Glass-fibre bandage

Spotting a blockage in a cast-iron pipe

If you have cast-iron downpipes, do not seal the gaps between sections. Water will flow from the gap immediately above any blockage, indicating which section needs clearing.

CHOOSING AND USING LADDERS

What type of ladder?

● Before buying a ladder, decide on the highest point on your house that it may have to reach, and allow at least three rungs above that spot. This ensures that you will always have an adequate handhold. To calculate the height of the eaves of your house, add together the ceiling heights of the ground-floor and first-floor rooms and then add on about 1m (3ft).
● Length is particularly important if your home is on a sloping site. The difference in height from one side of the house to another can be considerable.
● For DIY, aluminium ladders are the most popular – they are lighter and do not rot.
● Timber ladders should be protected with clear exterior grade varnish. Never paint them; you won't be able to see any cracks that develop.
● Whichever type you decide on, choose one with non-slip rungs.

● A double-extension ladder is adequate for most houses.
● A triple-extension ladder is more compact than a double-extension and will reach higher, but it is more difficult to put up without help – unless it is fitted with a rope system.

Stepladders

● If you live in a bungalow, a stepladder should take you to gutter height. The weight of a wooden stepladder makes it more stable.
● Choose steps with a safety grab rail so there is always something to hang onto.
● The alternative is a combination ladder, which can be converted from steps to a single section ladder if necessary. Some models can also be used as stairwell ladders – standing on two levels.

Putting up a ladder

Ideally, putting up a ladder is a job for two people – one to put a foot on the base to prevent it sliding, while the other works up the rungs from the underside until the ladder is vertical.

But it's possible to do the job on your own:

1 Lay the ladder on the ground with the base resting against the wall of the house. Have the underside of the ladder uppermost.

2 Stand at the top end of the ladder, lift it off the ground and work up the rungs from beneath until the ladder is vertical.

3 With your arms well apart on the rungs, lift the base of the ladder away from the wall. You can also carry it in this position.

Eight tips for ladder safety

● A ladder tray can be useful for holding things you are using – but clear the tray before moving the ladder. Objects, such as tins of paint, can slide off and cause serious injury.
● Never lean sideways off a ladder to reach work.

● Always secure the ladder at its base – either by placing something heavy, like a sandbag, across the base, or by roping it to a suitable point on the house or to pegs driven into the ground.

● On soft ground, such as a lawn, stand the ladder on a board pegged in place and with a batten nailed along it to hold the base of the ladder steady.

● You can secure the ladder at first-floor level by tying it to a wood batten laid across the inside frame of an upstairs window. Protect the frame with cloth.

● Make sure the ladder can't slide at the top. A ladder stand-off will help – it has rubber grips in contact with the wall and prevents the ladder resting on the gutter, which may be slippery.

● Alternatively, fix large eye bolts about every 1m (3ft) along the fascia board. The ladder can then be roped securely to the nearest eye, preventing any movement.

● Always have a helper at least within calling distance when you are working at height.

● Don't try to handle heavy items, such as a length of cast-iron guttering, that may unbalance you. Have a helper on another ladder to steady the weight.

The advantages of scaffold towers

A scaffold tower, which is supplied in kit form, is the ideal way of providing a platform for outside work on your house. It has several advantages over a ladder:

● A large platform for stowing equipment you're using.
● It allows you to work at an even distance from the wall at any height – a distinct advantage when painting.
● Narrow towers are available for interior work and on stairways.
     Tower kits can be rented on a daily or weekly basis from tool hire shops. Or, if you prefer to own a kit, you could share the cost with friends.

Using a tower safely

● The tower base must have a firm support, such as a concrete path or patio. If you have to erect it on soft ground, put a paving slab or a plank of wood under each leg.
● Check the hire catalogue for the maximum recommended height for a freestanding unit. For a standard domestic tower this is usually 3.7m (12ft) – any higher and the tower must be firmly anchored to the building.
● Some models have optional outriggers which increase stability.
● Most models have castors to make moving easy, but they must be locked when the tower is in use. Castors can only be used on a completely flat, solid surface.
● Always climb from inside the scaffolding to ensure the unit doesn't tip. Alternatively, use a separate ladder to reach the working platform.

TAKING CARE OF ROOFS

A simple roof check

To make sure your roof is in sound condition, stand at the end of the garden or across the street with binoculars.
● Look for loose or damaged slates or tiles.
● Check that all the ridge tiles are in place and that mortar is holding them firmly.
● Examine the flashings around chimneys and bay or dormer windows to see if they've pulled from the wall or if the wind has blown them up away from the roof.
● Check the eaves to see if all gaps are sealed with mortar. Birds will try to pull out mortar to gain entry to the roof space for nesting.

Getting roof work done Roof work calls for a head for heights, experience and the correct access equipment. When in doubt, call in a reputable roofing firm. Try to get recommendations from friends.

Repairs to flashings

A flashing is a means of sealing a gap between two surfaces, such as chimney stack and roof tiles. While serious damage is best left to experts, simple repairs are possible. Flashing tape is available in a range of widths. DIY versions are usually from 75mm (3in) to 300mm (12in) wide.

1 If a flashing has cracked or is lifting from a surface, clean away all loose material, including the old flashing. Then apply a flashing primer to prepare the surface.

2 Apply self-adhesive flashing tape over the primer. Use an old wallpaper seam roller, or a piece of wood with a rounded, smooth end, to press the tape firmly in place. It does not need painting.

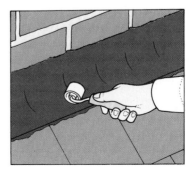

Checking a flat roof

Flat roofs often leak, usually because a bitumen felt covering has deteriorated. An ideal time to check is after a hot, dry summer and before winter rains. There are materials advertised for repairing wet roofs, but they are merely temporary, as they tend to seal in damp rather than get rid of it, and this can lead to serious rot.

● Check for cracks. Clean out and fill with a bituminous mastic.

● Repairs can be strengthened by adding a glass-fibre repair bandage, sandwiching it between layers of mastic. Roof repair kits, which can be bought at DIY stores, contain roofing compound and reinforcing fabric.

● Blisters may have formed where the felt has lifted from the roof. Cut each blister crossways and peel back the quarters. Clean out any debris; fill with bituminous mastic, then press the pieces back in place. Finish with a final coat of mastic.

● If the roof is coated with loose stone chippings, sweep them up with a stiff brush and dustpan or, if they are embedded in the bitumen, scrape them up with a wallpaper scraper before doing repairs. If the stones are sharp and too firmly embedded, lay a plank over the roof, with an old dust sheet or blanket underneath, so you don't press the stones through the roofing felt and cause holes.

● When all cracks and holes are repaired, coat the whole roof with a bitumen rubber roofing compound. It will prolong the life of the covering.

Re-felting a shed roof

Standard roofing felt does not last indefinitely; even the best felted roof can only last for about 15 years. When it shows signs of cracking up, it's quite possible to replace it yourself.

1 Remove the roofing nails and strip off the felt to the bare boards.

2 Brush clean and apply a coat of wood preservative as extra protection. Allow it to dry before re-covering the roof.

3 Buy the heaviest grade of roofing felt you can afford, plus a can of bitumen-based adhesive.

4 Unroll the felt in sunny weather and allow it to expand before transferring it to the roof.

5 Lay the first strip horizontally at the bottom of the roof, allowing for a fold over the edge of the eaves.

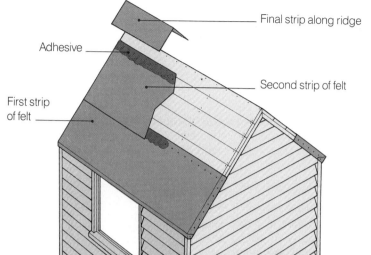

Final strip along ridge

Adhesive

Second strip of felt

First strip
of felt

6 Secure the felt with 13mm ($\frac{1}{2}$in) clout nails. Nail the top edge of the strip at intervals of 150mm (6in), and the bottom edge and the sides at 50mm (2in) intervals.

7 Then apply a 75mm (3in) strip of adhesive along the top edge of the felt for the next strip to stick to.

8 Complete both sides, then finish off with a strip that straddles the ridge, again overlapping by 75mm on each side.

9 At the corners of the roof, fold the surplus felt into a neat triangle, bend it flat and drive a nail through into the wood.

Caution Take care to hammer in nails square; if angled, they will cut into the felt. Cover exposed nail heads with bitumen adhesive.

Patching felt A small damaged area can be patched with a square of felt and bitumen-based adhesive.

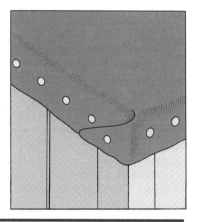

Looking after your chimneys

Check the condition Work on chimneys is best left to the experts. But you can keep an eye on the condition of your chimney, using binoculars.

Flue ventilation When a flue is no longer in use, have the chimney pot capped, either with a half-round tile, or with a purpose-made capping pot. Both will allow ventilation through the flue without letting in rain.

To ensure adequate ventilation if the fireplace is blocked off, fit a simple metal or plastic ventilator in the panel covering the fireplace.

Smoking fireplaces Do you have trouble with a smoking fireplace? If so, it might help to fit a cowl on the chimney. Cowls can deflect wind away from the chimney, preventing downdraughts. Some actually draw air up the flue. To find a chimney specialist, look in the Yellow Pages under 'Chimney builders & repairs' and 'Fireplaces'.

SEALING GAPS AROUND FRAMES

Much of the rot in door and window frames is caused by rain getting into gaps around the frames. Often these have been filled with putty or cement mortar – both of which set hard, crack away from the masonry, then allow in the damp.

1 If you find damp in the gaps, dry the area with a hot air stripping gun – sealants won't bond to wet surfaces. Keep the nozzle of the gun well back and on the move so it doesn't damage the paintwork.

2 Dig out all old material which isn't providing a proper seal. Dust the gaps with an old paint brush, then apply an exterior grade sealant. This may come in a dispensing tube, or in a cartridge for use in a simple, trigger-operated gun which can be bought with the sealant.

3 Let the nozzle force the sealant into the gap, running a continuous strip around the frame. (When you stop, remember to release the trigger first, otherwise sealant will continue to ooze from the nozzle).

4 As soon as a strip is complete, run a wet finger, or a wet piece of lint-free rag such as an old handkerchief, down the sealant, pressing it into tight contact with wall and frame, and applying a smooth finish.

Working with putty

Filling cracks Although putty in window frames may be well anchored, you may find a fine crack close to the glass. Make sure the area is dry, then force some clear silicone rubber sealant into the cracks. Smooth it with a wet finger. The sealant will adhere firmly to the glass.

To stop birds eating putty Some birds, especially tits, like to eat the linseed oil in putty. And if it is soft enough for them to peck, gaps will soon appear, allowing damp to penetrate into the frames. To discourage the birds, mix some black pepper with the new putty before applying it.

Softening putty If putty is cold, mould it in the warmth of your hands for five minutes to soften it. A few drops of linseed oil can also help.

If putty is too soft Sticky putty is impossible to work and it's hard to get off your hands. Roll sticky putty in dry newspaper, which will absorb the oil. Eventually, the putty will become workable. Dipping your fingers in water before handling putty also prevents it clinging.

Storing unused putty You can keep putty for some months as long as it is not in contact with the air. Roll the remaining putty into a ball, and wrap it closely in kitchen foil. Then place it in the tub it came in and close the lid.

DO NOT seal putty in polythene – a skin will form over it.

MAKING WALLS WEATHERPROOF

Treating porous brickwork

All bricks are porous. They absorb some rain, then dry out as the weather improves. But if they are over-porous, damp can seep through and, in the case of solid walls, can cause internal damp.

● If you suspect brickwork is too wet, wait until it is as dry as possible, then treat with a damp-proofing liquid.

● Apply it liberally so that it flows down the brickwork and is absorbed. The liquid may be slightly coloured, but this will disappear once the surface dries.

The brickwork will then repel rain, but moisture already trapped in the wall will be able to escape through the damp-proofing, which is microporous.

DO NOT coat the walls of your house with totally waterproof finishes, such as some wall coatings and most gloss paints. Every wall should be able to 'breathe'. If damp is trapped inside, it will find its way out on the inside of the house, damaging decoration and possibly leading to rot in the structure.

Fixing damaged pointing

Mortar pointing between bricks can be damaged by frost, and become loose and crumbling. This is another route for damp to seep through walls into the house.

1 Rake out all loose material to a depth of at least 15mm ($\frac{1}{2}$in), using a club hammer and narrow cold chisel.

2 Brush away the dirt with an old paintbrush, then wet around the gaps with clean water.

3 Make up a batch of mortar – ideally from a bagged ready-mix – keeping the mix very dry. It should just bind in your hands, but not be sloppy or it will mark the bricks.

4 Lift up a narrow roll of mortar on the back of a pointing trowel and press it well into the gap until it protrudes slightly beyond the surface of the brick.

5 Finish off to match the surrounding pointing.

● To make the pointing flush with the brickwork, draw the trowel along the seam of mortar, keeping it flat against the bricks. Rub the joint smooth with a piece of sacking.

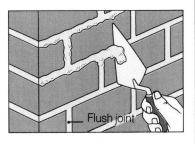

Flush joint

● If the surrounding pointing is slightly concave, get a piece of narrow copper pipe and bend it into a curve. Then draw it along the seam of mortar. Remove any surplus mortar with the trowel.

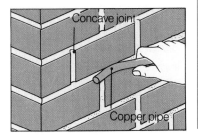

Concave joint

Copper pipe

● If the pointing on the rest of the wall slopes outwards, press the mortar in at the top of the gap and slope it to the bottom. To trim off the overhang, run the trowel along a straightedge which has a small block of wood nailed to each end. The surplus mortar will drop down behind the straightedge.

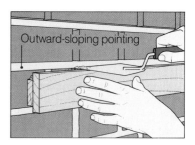

Outward-sloping pointing

6 If the mortar is of the correct consistency, any left on the brick surfaces can be brushed away.

Cleaning cement from brickwork

When a wall has been badly pointed, mortar may have spilled onto the brickwork, spoiling its appearance. It can be dissolved with an acid-based cleaning fluid called Disclean which is obtainable from most builders' merchants.

Caution Read the instructions carefully – and protect your eyes and hands against splashes.

Problems with the damp-proof course?

Unless your home is extremely old, it will have a damp-proof course about 150mm (6in) up from ground level, running around all exterior walls. It can often be identified by a black line, where a bitumen strip has been inserted during building. If this barrier is bridged in any way, damp will rise up the wall causing a damp patch inside the house.

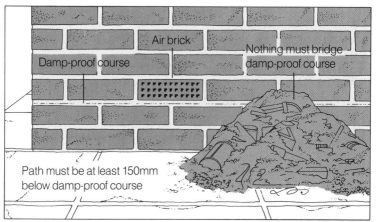

Air brick

Damp-proof course

Nothing must bridge damp-proof course

Path must be at least 150mm below damp-proof course

● Make sure that nothing is built or stored against the wall – no rockery or heaps of earth or stored sand.
● Make sure that paths close to the house – or a new patio – are at least 150mm below the damp-proof course.

Fungal growth on a wall

If you find fungus growing on an external wall, look for a source of damp. It might be a leaking gutter or a cracked downpipe. Cure the damp, and then scrape off the growth with a wire brush.

Air bricks – essential ventilation

If your house has cavity walls, you will find air bricks at the same level as the damp-proof course. They ventilate the under-floor area, protecting timbers from rot. Never block these ventilators – if there are draughts, deal with them from inside. Check the ventilation in autumn by poking a stick through the holes in the air bricks to make sure there is no obstruction.

DRIP GROOVES TO KEEP OUT DAMP

Under most windowsills or external door thresholds there is a deep groove. It is designed to stop water running from the sill back to the wall. So make sure the groove never becomes clogged with paint.

If there are no grooves on timber sills, pin a length of hardwood beading in the centre of the underside of the sill. Treat it with wood preservative, then varnish or paint it to match the sill. In future, water will drip from the beading.

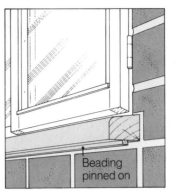

Beading pinned on

PAINTING THE OUTSIDE OF THE HOUSE

Don't assume that exterior painting always involves stripping back the surface to bare wood or metal. If the paint is in good shape but simply needs brightening – or if you want a change of colour – follow these two steps.

1 Wash it down with a solution of sugar soap in water. It removes grime and keys the surface so that new paint will grip the old. Rinse off and allow to dry.

2 If you're changing the colour, use undercoat to hide the old colour, followed by topcoat for protection from the weather. If you are not having a colour change, simply put on one layer of topcoat.

When more work is needed

● If there is slight damage to paintwork, smooth the damaged areas with fine abrasive paper. On old paintwork, use a wet-or-dry paper dampened with water. It will help to contain the dust.
● Allow the cleaned areas to dry. Then, if bare wood or metal is showing, paint it with primer followed by an undercoat.
● When dry, wash down all the paintwork with a solution of sugar soap and water, then repaint with topcoat, covering both repaired areas and sound paintwork.
● If paintwork is in poor condition, it must be completely stripped, using one of the methods on the opposite page.
● If windows or doors have too much paint and are stiff to open, strip off the paint where frames meet so they shut easily. Then prime, undercoat and topcoat the stripped areas.

PROTECTING ROOFS, PATHS AND CARS

Protect areas such as porch roofs, paths and patios with dust sheets. Move parked vehicles away when painting walls – and wipe up any splashes as they occur, as dry paint is hard to remove.

How to strip off old paint

Dry scrapers

Some flat and most convex surfaces can be stripped dry using a very sharp scraping blade called a Skarsten scraper.

● Protect your eyes from flying paint with safety spectacles.

● Protect your hands from flakes of dry paint with cotton gloves, which are cooler than rubber or plastic ones.

● If old lead paint is involved, wear a dust mask to protect your lungs.

Chemical strippers

Chemical paint stripper comes in two forms: liquid and paste. Liquids are usually clear and you can see the paint blister and soften. Depending on the age and thickness of the paint layers, it can take anything up to about 20 minutes.

Paste stripper is thicker and should be laid on generously and allowed to set before lifting away with a narrow-blade scraper. This method is useful on mouldings and carved surfaces – it lifts paint or varnish without any need for scraping or digging.

Whichever kind of chemical stripper you use:

● Read the instructions carefully – either water or white spirit is used to rinse off traces of chemicals on the wood and neutralise the stripper.

● Always wear safety spectacles and rubber, plastic or disposable polythene gloves to protect your hands.

Hot air gun

Heat is one of the quickest and cheapest ways of stripping – but it must be done carefully. It is easy to crack glass, scorch wood or damage nearby plastic.

There are various types of blowtorch, some working on bottled gas. But the safest for DIY work is a hot air gun, which looks like a large hair dryer.

● Take great care, because there is no visible flame.

● A clip-on deflector is available for working close to glass.

● Be careful if you are working near eaves. Birds' nesting materials can easily catch fire and set the roof alight.

SMOOTH AND CLEAN WITH ABRASIVES

Use abrasive papers only to smooth paintwork before repainting, or to give a surface a final clean after the paint has been stripped. Remove any resultant dust by rinsing.

DO NOT use abrasive paper to remove paint completely. It takes too long and the friction can melt the paint, which then clogs the paper.

Which paints to use

Always make sure the paints you buy for the outside of the house are suitable for outdoor work. They include:

Oil-based paint Traditional paint which comes as separate primer, undercoat and topcoat, or special primer/undercoat and topcoat. It is suitable for wood and metal.

Microporous paint A multipurpose paint – equivalent to primer, undercoat and topcoat – to use on bare wood. It remains porous, allowing air or moisture trapped in wood to escape, while preventing damp from getting in. This reduces the risk of blistering and flaking.

Matt black Suitable for wood and metal. It looks good on wrought ironwork and Tudor-style timbers.

Masonry paint For rendered surfaces. It may have additives, such as mica, sand or nylon fibre, to fill hairline cracks and crevices.

Oil stain preservative A cross between paint and stain preservative, they are for decorating and protecting wood, including cladding and Tudor timbering. No primer or undercoat is needed and the preservative will colour wood while still allowing the grain to show.

Varnish Use only varnish suitable for outdoors. The best types have a fungicide and an ultraviolet filter to combat bleaching by the sun.

DO NOT use linseed oil. Its life is limited and it becomes gummy and difficult to remove with age.

Rust-inhibiting enamel Does not need primer or undercoat. It can be applied to rusted surfaces that are free of loose material and will inhibit further rusting. Finishes that look like a hammered surface are available, as well as smooth finishes.

Wood preservatives Not strictly paints, but they can be used to preserve and decorate structural timbers, gates and doors. There are water-based versions which do not harm plants and so can be used for garden fences.

Tools to use for outdoor decorating

Any good quality paintbrush can be used for external painting – but for walls use the widest brush you can handle.
● Most masonry paints can be applied by soft handbrush – like the ones used with a dustpan.
● If you use a roller on walls, it must be of shaggy nylon, designed for outdoor use – textured surfaces are very abrasive.
● A spray gun is not advisable for DIY outdoor use. Surfaces not intended to be painted have to be carefully masked – and there is a risk of wind-borne spray getting onto nearby property or parked cars.

If your paintwork goes wrong

If the final appearance of your decorating work is spoiled – perhaps by blistered patches or insects settling on the wet paint – turn to the *Fault-finder guide* on page 646.

REPLACING BROKEN GLASS

A broken window pane has to be replaced from outside the house. Ground-floor windows are usually accessible, but if it's an upstairs window call a glazier. Carrying glass up a ladder is no job for a beginner. When handling glass, always wear heavy gardening gloves.

Laminated glass for doors If you are replacing a large pane of glass in a door or at the bottom of a staircase, use laminated glass which has a plastic interlayer. It won't shatter, so is safe if someone falls against it and will also help to keep out burglars. Toughened (or tempered) glass can also be used, but must be ordered to size.

Timber windows

Measure the height and width of the area to be glazed, and ask a glazier to cut the glass to the right size. At the same time, buy some linseed-oil putty, glazing sprigs and primer paint.

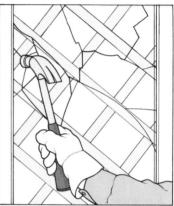

1 Lay newspapers on the ground on both sides of the window to catch any glass. Then stick several strips of masking tape across the glass and onto the frame. They should reduce flying shards.

2 Put on leather gloves, safety spectacles and thick leather shoes and tap the glass with a hammer to break it, starting from the top. Try to keep the pieces as large as possible.

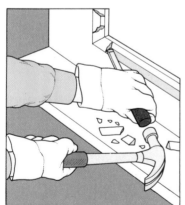

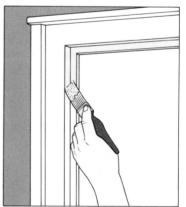

3 Remove the remaining putty and glass with an old chisel. Old glazing sprigs embedded in the putty can be pulled out with pincers or pliers. Throw them away; they will be replaced with new ones.

4 Brush all the dust from the frame, and paint the rebate with primer which should be allowed to dry. If the window has to be left overnight, cover it with polythene or plywood (page 254).

5 Mould the putty in your hands to get it soft and pliable. If it sticks to your hands, try wetting them, or take some of the oil out by rolling the putty on newspaper.

6 Hold the putty in your hand and squeeze it out between the thumb and forefinger to form a layer about 3mm ($\frac{1}{8}$in) thick in the rebate all the way round.

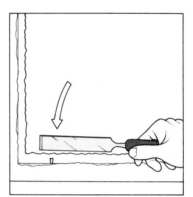

7 Press the glass carefully into the putty. Press it round the edges only, taking care not to push too hard in one place – and never in the middle of the glass. It could break and injure you.

8 Fix the glass in place with glazing sprigs inserted into the window about 250mm (10in) apart. Knock them in with the edge of the chisel. The heads should protrude about 5mm ($\frac{3}{16}$in).

9 Apply more putty to the front of the glass to fill the rebate. Smooth it off with a putty knife to form a neat triangular line of putty which covers the heads of the glazing sprigs and lines up with the putty on the inside of the glass. Use the flat edge of the knife, sprung slightly, to squeeze away the surplus putty. When you reach the corners, try to achieve neat mitre joins in the putty.

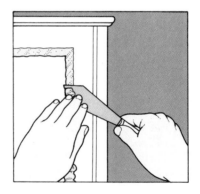

10 Leave the putty for about two weeks before painting it. When you do paint it, allow the paint to spread onto the glass by 3mm ($\frac{1}{8}$in) to keep out the rain.

Metal windows

A metal window can be reglazed in the same way as a wooden one, except that you will need metal casement putty, or a putty that the glazier recommends.

Instead of glazing sprigs, metal clips are used to hold the glass in place. They can be removed with pincers or pliers. You can often use them again, but buy new ones if they've rusted.

There is no need to paint the rebate of a metal window unless it is rusty.

Getting rid of broken glass

Disposing of broken glass can be difficult. One way is to take it to your local bottle bank. Otherwise, wrap it thickly in newspaper and put it either beside or in your dustbin, clearly labelled 'Broken glass'.

Replacing damaged putty

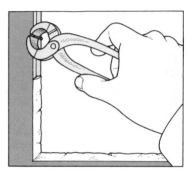

As putty hardens it tends to crack and eventually sections fall out. It is best to replace all the putty rather than re-putty the missing sections.

Remove the old putty with a chisel as shown on page 252. If the glazing sprigs have corroded pull them out, and then drive in new ones. Brush away dust, prime the rebate and apply the new putty.

Temporary cover for a window

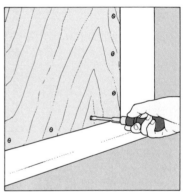

Polythene If the glass is smashed, cover the window with heavy-gauge polythene, secured with battens nailed around the frame.

Plywood If security is important, cut plywood to cover the window frame and fix it – preferably on the inside – with nails or screws.

Glazing tape A cracked pane can be temporarily sealed with waterproof glazing tape, which is transparent.

SCRAPER THAT SAVES THE SEAL

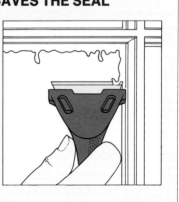

The simplest way to remove paint from the glass after painting windows is to use a window scraper. It is fitted with a blade that is inset slightly on the edges. This is to ensure that when you remove paint close to the frame, a thin strip of paint is left to retain a seal between the glass and the frame, or the putty. The seal stops rain from getting between the glass and the frame and causing rot.

Family transport

SAFETY IN AN EMERGENCY

Get off the road A breakdown can happen at any time, even with the best maintained of cars. If it happens, try to get the car off the road to a safe place where it won't cause an obstruction and be dangerous to you and other road users.

Alerting others If the breakdown has caused the car to come to a stop on the road itself or on the hard shoulder of a motorway, switch on the hazard warning lights and open the bonnet to indicate to other drivers that the car is stationary.

A motorway hazard Take extra care when getting out of the car on a motorway. The rush of air from a large vehicle moving at speed can cause the door to be flung open and drag you off your feet. Driver and passengers should wait well away from the motorway until help arrives.

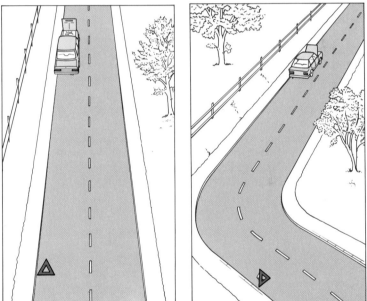

Use a warning triangle Where the breakdown has occurred near a bend in the road or brow of a hill, and your car carries a warning triangle, place the triangle at least 50m (55yds) behind the car to give advance warning to drivers. Allow more than 50m if the triangle will be obscured by the bend.

Keep clear of traffic Unless the car is stopped well away from passing traffic do not work at the side of the car next to the traffic flow, except when absolutely necessary – to change a wheel, for example.

Hair, loose clothing and jewellery When checking any part of the engine compartment, make sure you tuck away long hair inside your clothing, and remove any loose clothing or jewellery such as a tie or necklace which could get caught in the moving parts of the engine.

Getting help If the car breaks down, you'll have to walk to the nearest telephone or garage for help. On a motorway, marker posts show the direction of the nearest emergency phone. Remember that these phones

255

are one-way only so don't replace the receiver until instructed by the control officer – they cannot call you back.

Women alone If you are a woman on your own, tell the person on the phone who will give priority to your call. Return to your car and wait on the embankment, as there is a risk that a car on the hard shoulder will be rammed by another car. Get into the car and lock the doors if anyone approaches. Don't accept a lift from a stranger.

Fault-finder guide: car won't start

Starter turns engine slowly; lights go dim or don't work
Weak or flat battery. Push-start a manual gearbox car or start the engine with jump leads (check the car handbook to make sure this is possible). Follow the instructions on page 259. Recharge the battery or get a garage to check the battery and charging system.

Starter doesn't operate; no sound from engine; lights and windscreen wipers don't work
Completely dead battery or faulty battery connections. Check and clean the battery connectors at the terminals, also the earth lead from the battery to the car body. If the car still doesn't start, call a garage or motoring organisation.

Loud click noise when ignition key is turned to start position. Starter doesn't operate, but lights or windscreen wipers work
Starter motor problem, possibly a stuck gear in the starter. Try rocking the car back and forth in top gear with handbrake off to free the gear. Try starting again. If nothing happens, push-start a manual gearbox car or call for help if the car has automatic transmission.

Headlights and windscreen wipers work normally but starter motor doesn't work. No sound from engine
Faulty ignition switch, wiring, solenoid or starter motor. Try jiggling ignition key while turning it.

Check if there are any loose or disconnected wires at the solenoid. If you find any, tighten them.

If this doesn't work, push-start a car with a manual gearbox (page 259) or call a garage or breakdown organisation if the car has automatic transmission.

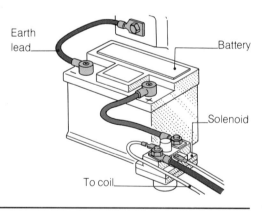

Earth lead — Battery — Solenoid — To coil

Starter motor turns engine strongly, but engine doesn't start
● No fuel in the tank – see *Checking for fuel*, facing page.
● Moisture in the ignition system. Clean ignition leads and components with a dry cloth – see *Dampness in the ignition system*, facing page.
● Disconnected or loose wires in the ignition system. Check leads from the ignition coil to the distributor and from the distributor to the spark plugs – see *Dampness in the ignition system*, facing page.
● Petrol hose broken or disconnected. Check all the petrol hoses.

Starter motor turns engine strongly, strong smell of petrol after repeated attempts at starting
Engine flooded with petrol. Wait for 15 minutes for excess petrol to evaporate, then try starting again without using manual choke. Follow the instructions in *Starting a flooded engine*, below.

BASIC CHECKS IF A CAR WON'T GO

Checking for fuel

If your engine won't start, or suddenly stops running, it could simply be that you've run out of fuel. Don't just rely on the fuel gauge, because it could be faulty.

To check if there is fuel in the tank, remove the filler cap and rock the car. You should be able to hear a sloshing sound from the filler pipe if there is fuel in the tank.

Dampness in the ignition system

A common cause of an engine failing to start in wet or foggy weather is dampness or condensation in the ignition system. Have a look at the distributor cap and the leads to the spark plugs to see if they have moisture on them – wiping the surface with a finger will leave a wet mark if any moisture is present.

● Disconnect the spark plug leads one at a time, to avoid confusing their positions, and wipe them dry with a clean dry cloth or paper tissue. Wipe the tops of the spark plugs themselves before refitting each of the leads securely.
● Wipe any moisture from the top of the ignition coil.
● Remove the distributor cap (fixed with either spring clips or screws) and wipe both the inside and outside of the cap.
● If possible, spray the whole ignition system with a moisture-repellent aerosol.

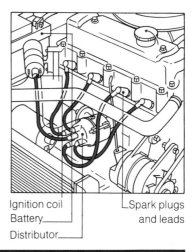

Ignition coil ⌐ ⌐Spark plugs
Battery⏌ and leads
Distributor⏌

Starting a flooded engine

If the engine has failed to start after several attempts, you may have flooded the engine with fuel, especially if the choke has been used. There will be a strong smell of petrol. Wait for about 15 minutes to allow some of the excess petrol to evaporate from the carburettor, especially if the engine is warm.
● When you try to start the engine again, depress the accelerator pedal slowly to the floor, and keep it there. Don't pump the pedal – you'll only flood the carburettor again.
● If you have a manual choke control, don't use it until the engine starts, and don't use it at all if the engine is warm.

Helping the battery to recover

Trying to start an engine is a big drain on the battery which, after several attempts, may turn the engine very slowly. If you have run the battery down in this way, switch everything off, including the hazard warning lights if it's safe to do so, and let the battery rest for 15 minutes. It may recover enough power to get the engine started if there is nothing else wrong with the electrical system.

● While allowing the battery to rest, check that the connections to the battery terminals are tight and free of corrosion (page 260).

● In an emergency, twisting the lead connectors on the battery terminals can sometimes cure a bad electrical connection.

● Check the fluid in the battery if you can (some batteries are sealed) and top up if necessary (see *Taking care of your battery,* page 260).

WHEN AN ENGINE OVERHEATS

Two signs that the engine is overheating are if the temperature gauge needle moves to 'hot' or the coolant warning light comes on when you are driving. Stop the engine as soon as possible, and allow it to cool down for at least 15 minutes before checking. If you remove the filler cap while the engine is hot, you could be scalded.

● After the engine has cooled down, check the coolant water level. Many cars have a translucent plastic expansion tank where the level can easily be seen.

● If your car doesn't have an expansion tank, slowly remove the filler cap from the top of the radiator, using a glove or cloth, and check the coolant level inside.

● In many cases of overheating, you can get going again by topping up the water level to the mark on the expansion tank or just below the filler cap on the radiator.

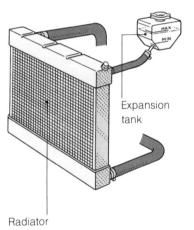

Expansion tank

Radiator

DO NOT top-up an overheated engine with cold water, which could damage it. Wait until the engine is cool enough to touch.

● In winter, one of the tell-tale signs of an engine running without enough cooling water is when the heater suddenly starts to blow cold air into the car instead of hot.

● While waiting for the engine to cool down, check for any obvious signs of a leak. A leaking coolant hose can be stopped temporarily by binding it with tape. A leaking radiator can be temporarily sealed with chewing gum stuck over the leak.

● Check the belt that drives the water pump and radiator fan on many cars – see *Checking and replacing drive belts,* page 261.

● As cooling systems are pressurised, a great deal of coolant can escape from the smallest leak. One way of reducing the loss is to drive with the filler cap removed from the radiator or expansion tank. But only leave the cap off for a short distance. Remember to keep an eye on the temperature gauge and check the coolant level frequently.

STARTING A CAR THAT HAS A FLAT BATTERY

If your battery is flat, you may be able to start your engine by getting someone to push the car so that it turns the engine (a push-start), or by using another car's battery (a jump-start).

Getting going with a push-start

Switch on the ignition and release the handbrake. Put the gear lever into third gear and hold the clutch pedal fully down while a couple of helpers push the car along at a brisk walking pace, then let in the clutch sharply. The momentum of the car will turn the engine which should then start, provided there is nothing else wrong.

Push-starting can normally only be done on cars with manual transmission.

Using another car's battery to give your car a jump-start

Check with your car's handbook that it is permissible to jump-start the engine. On some cars with electronic engine-management systems, serious damage can be done.

You will need a pair of jump leads – heavy-duty electric cables with large clips at both ends.

1 Park another car with a healthy battery next to your car so that the jump leads can reach both batteries, but don't let the two cars touch each other.

2 Jump leads normally consist of one red cable (for positive) and one black cable (for negative). Connect them between the terminals of the two batteries – first, run the black lead from Negative (−) to Negative (−), and then run the red lead from Positive (+) to Positive (+).

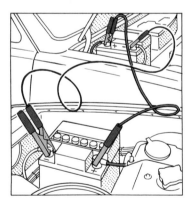

3 Get the engine of the donor car running at a fast idling speed, and make sure that all the lights and accessories on your own car are switched off.

4 If your battery is absolutely flat, wait for a few minutes for the other battery to boost the voltage in yours before starting the engine of your car.

5 Start your engine in the normal way. When it is running, disconnect the positive (red) lead from both batteries first, then disconnect the negative (black) lead.

TAKING CARE OF YOUR BATTERY

Checking the charge To check the state of your battery, switch on the headlights or the windscreen wipers and see if they operate normally without the engine running.

Tightening the connections If the headlights are dim or the wipers operate sluggishly, see if the leads on the battery terminals are tight to make good electrical contact. If they are loose, tighten the bolts or screws.

Removing corrosion White deposits on the terminals indicate corrosion which will prevent electrical contact. With the ignition switched off, disconnect the negative ($-$) lead from the terminal, then the positive ($+$) lead. Use a wire brush or sandpaper to clean both the connectors and the terminals to bright metal. Apply a smear of petroleum jelly.

Topping up the fluid Some car batteries are sealed and never need topping up. Most non-sealed batteries have a removable filler cap and a translucent casing with a maximum and minimum line near the top edge to measure the fluid level. If the level is low, top it up with distilled water or topping-up fluid (in an emergency, clean tap water will do). If there are no markings, add water until the plates inside the battery are covered.

HOW TO RECHARGE A BATTERY

If the battery power is low, especially in winter when there is a heavy demand on it, the battery may need to be recharged. You can buy an inexpensive battery charger which operates from the domestic mains. The battery can be charged either on or off the car.

1 Disconnect the battery leads from the terminals first. If the battery has a filler cap on top, check the fluid level. If necessary, top up the level with distilled water before charging.

2 Clamp the black lead from the charger to the negative ($-$) terminal on the battery, and the red lead to the positive ($+$) terminal. Then switch on the charger. Several hours of charging may be necessary.

3 A low amperage reading of 1 or 2 amps on the charger over a period of an hour will show that the battery is fully charged.

4 Unplug the charger from the mains supply before removing the clips. Then reconnect the battery leads.

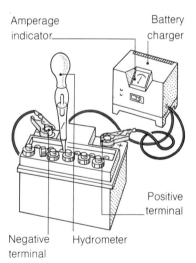

Amperage indicator

Battery charger

Positive terminal

Negative terminal

Hydrometer

Checking the charge An accurate way of checking the state of charge is to use an inexpensive battery hydrometer to measure the specific gravity of the fluid. A reading of at least 1.275 should be obtained if the battery is fully charged. Follow the instructions given with the hydrometer.

CHECKING THE IGNITION SYSTEM

If the battery is supplying current and turning the starter motor at normal speed, any starting or running problems could be due to a fault in the ignition system.

● Look for any obvious loose wires around the upper part of the engine, then check that the thicker leads going to the spark plugs, distributor cap and ignition coil are all clean and securely connected. Any traces of green corrosion on the terminals are signs of a possible bad connection causing the engine not to start or to misfire.

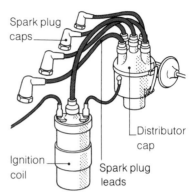

Spark plug caps
Distributor cap
Ignition coil
Spark plug leads

● Unless the cause of the ignition fault is obvious, call a garage or breakdown service. Further checks are best left to them.

CHECKING AND REPLACING DRIVE BELTS

● All car engines have at least one, and possibly more, belts to drive the generator and water pump, and perhaps a power steering pump as well.
● A slipping or broken generator drive belt will not allow the battery to be charged efficiently. On many cars the same belt also drives the engine water pump and fan, so the engine may overheat.
● If a belt is slipping when the engine is running, it will make a screaming noise. This means it needs adjustment and is wearing rapidly and will soon break. Drive belts also deteriorate with age and eventually break.
● Carry spare belts in the boot, plus spanners of the right size.

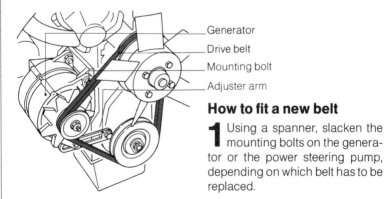

Generator
Drive belt
Mounting bolt
Adjuster arm

How to fit a new belt

1 Using a spanner, slacken the mounting bolts on the generator or the power steering pump, depending on which belt has to be replaced.

2 Push the generator or pump towards the engine. If the old belt is still in place, this will release the tension on it so that it can be detached from the pulleys and removed.

3 Fit the new belt to the pulleys, making sure it is correctly engaged in the grooves. It should not be necessary to stretch or lever the belt onto the pulleys. If the belt won't fit, you probably have the wrong size.

4 Pull the generator or pump away from the engine to tension the belt, and retighten the mounting bolts.

5 A correctly tensioned drive belt should feel reasonably tight. If you press it fairly hard with your thumb midway along the longest run between two pulleys, it should not move more than 12mm ($\frac{1}{2}$in).

6 Check the tension of the belt again after about 100 miles because new drive belts always stretch.

GETTING TO KNOW THE FUSE BOX

● If both headlights or both rear lights won't light up, the likely cause is a dirty or blown fuse (see also page 266).
● The fuse box is usually on the side or rear of the engine compartment, or inside the car under the fascia (look in your car handbook).

● Fuses are colour-coded to indicate the fuse rating. Details of the rating and circuits are usually printed on the fuse box cover.

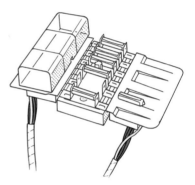

● Remove the fuse from the relevant circuit (headlights or rear lights, for example) by unclipping or pulling it from its terminals. Check if it has blown – the wire will be broken at the centre. If not, clean the metal ends on the fuse and refit it securely.
● Always fit a replacement fuse of the same rating, never a higher rating. If the new fuse blows again when the lights are switched on, there is a short circuit. Call a garage or breakdown service.
● Note which type of fuses are fitted in your car and always carry spares.

HOW TO UNFREEZE DOOR LOCKS

De-icer Squirt de-icer into the lock, using the extension nozzle to push aside the protective inner flap.

Warm cloth Soak a sponge or cloth in hot water and apply it to the outside of the lock.

Hot key In very low temperatures, heating the key with a flame will usually free the lock, although you may need to try more than once. Never try to force the key; it could break in the lock.

Last resort If you have absolutely nothing to help you, try placing a warm hand over the outside of the lock, and keeping it there for a couple of minutes – or change hands every minute. Then try the key.

Graphite lubricant Prevention is better than cure, and to avoid door locks freezing, they should be lubricated with a graphite-based lock lubricant. It will also prevent the lock from wearing.

GETTING OUT OF SNOW OR MUD

The natural reaction of most car drivers when they get stuck in snow or mud is to accelerate in the vain hope that the tyres will grip. All this will do is dig the tyres further into a trench, making it even harder to get the car free.

● The golden rule if the driving wheels cannot grip is to try and prevent them from spinning. Use 4th or 5th gear and partly disengage the clutch to start the car rolling.

● If this fails, try 3rd gear and reverse gear alternately to get the car rocking backwards and forwards until you can feel the tyres grip as the car is rolling.

● If the driving wheels have dug right into the snow or mud, put the floor mat from the boot or even an old coat under both driving wheels to form a grip for the tyres.

TIPS FOR JACKING UP THE CAR

Handbrake and gear If you have to jack up the car to change a wheel, pull the handbrake fully on and put the car in first gear – or Park on an automatic.

Support the jack Park the car on firm, level ground. If the ground is soft – grass, for example – place a board or the carpet from the boot under the jack to prevent it sinking under the car's weight.

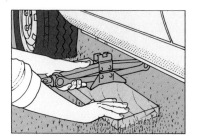

Chock the opposite wheel If possible, the car should also be chocked to prevent it from moving. Try to find a brick, large stone or wooden block, and put it in front of the wheel on the opposite side of the car to the one being changed.

Locating the jacking points Find the fitting point for the jack nearest to the wheel that you want to change. The four jacking points are usually fitted to the side sills under the car. There should be one point behind each front wheel arch, and one in front of each rear wheel arch. If you are in any doubt, look in your car's handbook.

Types of jack There are two main types of jack, depending on the model of car. The post type (above left) has a metal tongue that fits into a tube at the jacking point on the car. The scissor type (above right) has a pad that fits under the jacking point.

Clear the jacking tube Make absolutely sure that the jack head is firmly fitted to the jacking point before raising the car. Use a stick or a screwdriver to clear the jacking tube of any dirt that might prevent the jack from fitting properly.

Tilt the jack If your car has a post jack, tilt its base slightly towards the car when it first touches the ground. As the car is raised, it will lean slightly, allowing the jack to sit squarely on the ground.

WARNING: KEEP CLEAR

Remember that the jack which is supplied with the car is designed for wheel-changing only. Don't put your arms or feet under the car when it is raised. Never use the car jack to hold up the car while you carry out any repair work underneath.

How to change a flat tyre

Some wheel nuts are covered with plastic caps. Take them off first, or the wheel brace won't fit. The wheel brace may be incorporated in the jack handle on some cars.

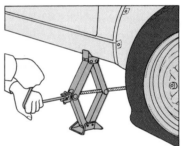

1 Before raising the car remove the hubcap, using the end of the wheelbrace or a screwdriver. Plastic ones just pull off. Then slacken the wheel nuts or bolts slightly. It's easier to turn them while the weight of the car is preventing the wheel from moving.

If the nuts are extremely hard to shift, put your foot on the wheelbrace. Stamp on it if necessary. And do remember that you should be undoing the nuts anti-clockwise.

2 Slowly operate the jack so that it raises the car until the tyre is well clear of the ground. It must be raised high enough for the inflated spare wheel to be fitted onto the hub.

If the jack or the car show any signs of sliding, lower the car and reposition either car or jack in a more secure place.

Now remove the wheel nuts completely and put them in a safe place where they won't get dirty – perhaps in the hub cap.

3 Take off the wheel. Fit the spare, and secure it with the nuts or bolts.

Wheel nuts Some cars have the bolts fitted to the hub. The nuts have one conical side which goes on towards the wheel.

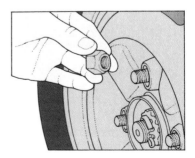

Wheel bolts Some cars have wheel bolts that fit into holes in the hub. It can be difficult to align the holes in the wheel with those in the hub. Support the wheel with the jack handle placed under the tyre so that one hole is aligned, and screw in the bolt by hand. It will then be easier to fit the remaining bolts.

4 Tighten the wheel nuts or bolts in a diagonal fashion so the wheel is correctly centred. Use only moderate pressure.

5 Lower the car, remove the jack and tighten the nuts or bolts with your full strength. Finally, replace the hubcap.

MIND YOUR BACK!

Changing the wheel of a car can put great strain on your back. If you have ever suffered a slipped disc, it would be wise to call an emergency service such as the AA or the RAC to do the job. If you must do it yourself, kneel close to the car when taking the wheel off and putting the new one on. And keep your back very straight. Beware when taking out the spare; it can be in an awkward position.

FIRST AID FOR THE EXHAUST

If the noise from the exhaust suddenly becomes very loud or if there is a sudden rattling sound, a pipe has probably broken or become detached. Look in the engine compartment or under the car – without jacking it up which could be dangerous. Remember that the exhaust system gets very hot when the engine is running, so use thick gloves if you have to touch the pipes.

Tying up with wire If the exhaust pipe is broken or dragging on the road, it can often be held together by binding with wire, provided you can reach it without jacking up the car. But this is only a very temporary get-you-going measure.

Warning: poisonous gas Exhaust fumes contain carbon monoxide – a tasteless, odourless gas that can kill. If you have to drive the car with a faulty exhaust, open all the windows and drive at a moderate speed to a garage or exhaust centre.

WHEN THE LIGHTS GO OUT . . .

A dud pair If both the front lights, both the rear lights, or one front and one rear light on the same side fail to work, the cause will usually be a blown fuse (page 262).

Side and rear lights If one light goes out, replace the bulb. Most sidelight and rear light bulbs can be removed in one of two ways:
● Remove the screws attaching the lens cover on the outside.
● Unclip the back of the lamp inside the engine compartment or boot.

Corrosion Rust or white corrosion inside the bulb holder could be causing a faulty electrical contact. With the lights switched off, use something abrasive, such as a nail file, to scrape off the corrosion.

Check the bulb If possible, check to see if the bulb filament is broken. If the bulb glass is black or dark brown, it has failed because of overheating. If the glass looks milky, it has cracked and air has got in. Fit a new bulb.

Emergency swap On some cars you can fit the number plate light bulb to replace a failed rear light bulb, as a temporary measure.

WINDSCREEN WIPER TROUBLE

Total failure When the windscreen wipers fail to work, the cause is usually a blown fuse. Check and replace it if necessary (page 262).

 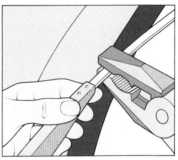

One blade fails If one of the wipers fails to work, the cause is usually a loose nut securing the arm. Switch off the wipers in the 'park' position and lift the cap at the base of the wiper arm, using a screwdriver. Then tighten the nut.

Juddering blades The problem is usually due to wear on the blade. For a temporary cure, switch off the ignition when the blades are vertical. Then twist the wiper arm so that the rubber blade is at a right angle to the windscreen glass.

A broken windscreen

If the windscreen is broken while you're moving, visibility will usually only be affected if it is made of toughened glass. Most of the windscreen will break up into a multitude of small pieces that remain in place. Signal what you are doing, and pull into the side of the road.

DO NOT smash the windscreen with your fist while driving. Your hands are likely to get cut, and glass may get into your eyes.

How to get going again If you need to get underway immediately, knock out the glass with something heavy or with your fist wrapped in cloth, and remove the rest with gloves or a rag. Place a cloth over the dashboard first to prevent the bits falling down the demister slots.

Close all the car windows, and – wearing glasses if you have any to protect your eyes from bits of glass – drive to a garage. Or call a windscreen replacement service.

TOUCHING-UP PAINT DAMAGE

However careful you are with a car, stone chips and minor scratches are bound to appear. Any paint damage must be repaired as soon as possible to prevent corrosion of the exposed metal underneath.

Light surface scratches

If the scratch hasn't penetrated through to the metal, polish carefully with a paintwork renovating compound (or paint restorer):
● Wash the car and let it dry.
● Apply the renovating compound using a clean damp cloth, preferably muslin. Rub lightly in a circular motion over a patch about the size of a dinner plate. Then move to the next patch.
● Don't rub too hard, particularly on outside corners where the paint may be thin; you can easily cut through to the undercoat.

Deeper scratch marks or chips from stones

The areas most vulnerable to stone chips are the front panel under the bumper, the leading edge of the bonnet, the edges of the wheel arches, and the lower part of the door panels and side sills.

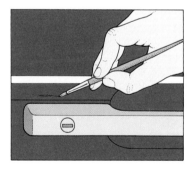

● Very small chips need no preparation; just apply a touch-up paint. Always shake the can thoroughly – you should hear it rattle. Build the paint up in thin layers, allowing each coat to dry.
● Larger chips with rust spots need treating with rust inhibitor (see *Dealing with Rust*, page 270).
● Deep scratches can sometimes be filled with paint alone.

Blending in new paint

Allow new paint to harden for at least a week before merging it into the surrounding paintwork with renovating compound. Then apply a polish.

Restoring the shine to non-metallic paint

For non-metallic paintwork that has lost its shine through age, polish carefully with a paintwork renovating compound.

Metallic paintwork

Leave anything other than slight surface scratches to a garage.

REPAIRING MINOR BODY DAMAGE

Most minor body dents can be repaired quite easily. First, restore the metal almost to its original shape, and then level the surface with a thin layer of body filler.

Dents away from a fold or edge of a panel Most dents can be pushed back into shape by pressing or knocking from behind. This may mean removing some interior trim panels first. If you can reach behind the panel, push it firmly outwards. In many cases, the panel will spring back into position.

If it doesn't, place a flat wood block over the dent on the outside and gently beat the dent out from behind the panel, using a hammer with a round head.

If the dent is inaccessible from behind Drill a small hole in the deepest part of the dent and screw in a self-tapping screw. Leave it protruding by about 15mm ($\frac{1}{2}$in).

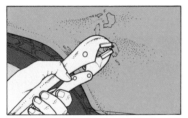

To remove a shallow dent, grip the screw head with a self-locking wrench (Mole wrench) and pull outwards.

Deeper dents may need more leverage. Use a claw hammer under the head of the screw, levering against a piece of wood.

Using levelling filler

1 Remove any rust or flaking paint and clean the surface back to bare metal with a power drill and sanding disc, or with a piece of coarse abrasive paper.

2 Mix small batches of body filler and hardener, following the maker's instructions. The filler usually hardens within a few minutes, which leaves little working time.

3 Apply the filler with a plastic spatula or a flexible wallpaper scraper. The filler surface should be fairly smooth and slightly higher than the surrounding paint. Add more layers of filler until the level is correct, then leave for about 30 minutes to harden. Don't try to sand the filler while it's still soft; it might come away from the metal.

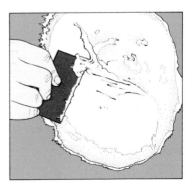

268

4 Once the filler is dry, shape it until it's level with the surrounding bodywork. Use a rasp or a wood sanding block wrapped with coarse (100 grit) abrasive paper. Then smooth it with fine (400 grit) paper.

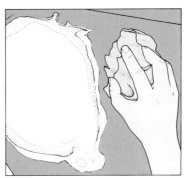

5 Fill any remaining imperfections with bodystopper, and then give a final rub down.

6 Clean the surrounding paintwork with a cloth moistened with white spirit.

Repainting minor dent repairs

A can of touch-up paint and a small brush are all you need for small dents, but repairs larger than a 2p piece need aerosol spray paint.

1 Mask off the bodywork all round the repair with pieces of newspaper stuck down with strips of masking tape. The paper will protect the rest of the car from drifting paint as you spray.

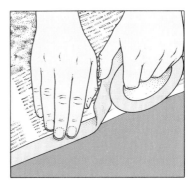

2 Choose the correct shade of primer – vital for a good colour match – and shake the aerosol can thoroughly before spraying. Spray on the primer coat, holding the can in a vertical position about 300mm (12in) from the panel.

Apply the paint spray in a horizontal motion starting at the top and working down to the bottom of the repair.

3 Follow the primer with as many as six top coats to find the right depth and colour match.

DEALING WITH RUST

Before it gets a hold Repair any damage to the paintwork, and spray on anti-chip compound to vulnerable areas on the underside of the car, before the rust gets started.

Slight surface rusting Applying a rust converter or inhibitor which contains acid in a liquid or jelly form will usually stop surface rusting.

Using rust inhibitors Brush on the rust inhibitor and work it in well. Follow the manufacturer's advice as to whether to wash it off or let it dry.

Beware Take care not to get rust inhibitor on the paint work – it will discolour it.

Larger rust patches Deal with well-established rust as explained under *Repairing minor body damage*, page 268.

Freeing rusted bolts One way to free rusted nuts and bolts, particularly on aluminium parts, is to pour on a small amount of fizzy cola drink. The acids and carbon dioxide in the drink will help to eat away the corrosion and release the hold on the threads. Wait until it is dry before trying again to move the nut.

TELLTALE SIGNS THAT RUST IS AT WORK

● Small bubbles or marks on the paint surface appear in the early stages.

● Later, the metal becomes weak. Press on the affected area with your fingers – any give in the metal, accompanied by a crunching sound, indicates advanced rust.

● As layers of corrosion expand the metal, the paint lifts and a rust spot is exposed.

CLEANING YOUR CAR

Ice scraper If you don't have a scraper, you can remove ice or frost from the windscreen with a phone card.

Windscreen Clean the windscreen with a cloth dipped in a bucket of warm water containing a couple of tablespoons of white vinegar. Polish with a clean, dry cloth. Smears can be removed with a cloth moistened with methylated spirit.

Washing the car Always use a proper car shampoo or wash-and-wax type cleaner dissolved in clean, warm water. Detergent washing-up liquids usually contain salt which corrodes metal.

Be methodical Start by washing the roof, followed by front and rear windscreens, then the bonnet and boot, and finally the sides. This way, some of the dirt and grit from lower down will be loosened as the water drains off the roof.

Under the wheel arches Use a hose to wash off dirt from the underside of the wheel arches.

Finishing off Wash the car again with clean warm water and use a chamois leather or a proprietary substitute to remove surplus water. Pay particular attention to the door sill panels and the undersides of doors. The drain holes of doors should be cleaned by poking a screwdriver through the slots.

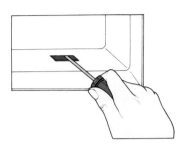

Regular vacuuming Keeping the interior clean will remove destructive grit from the carpets and will help to preserve the car's resale value.

Upholstery stains Keep a stain removal kit in your car for dealing with stains on the upholstery. The kit should include a dry cleaning solvent for grease stains, a spray bottle of all-purpose cleaner and paper tissues.

TYRE SAFETY

Keep a regular check on the tyres The condition and air pressure of the car's tyres, including the spare, should be checked once a week. Pay particular attention to the inside walls of the tyres which are not normally seen.

Watch the tread depth Take note of the tread depth on each tyre to see if it needs replacing. Preferably use a proper tread depth gauge which can be bought from car shops.

To be legal, a tyre must have a tread on the entire width and circumference, and the depth must be no less than 1.6mm. On a 10p coin, the top of the letters in the word PENCE are 2mm from the edge. So if the tread comes up to the letters the tyre is still legal – but only just.

Damage to the tyre Remove any stones or nails from the tread with a screwdriver and check for any large cuts. Examine the inner and outer sidewalls for cuts and bulges which may mean that the tyre should be repaired or replaced.

WHAT YOUR CAR TYRES CAN TELL YOU . . .

● More tread depth in the centre of the tyre than on the outside edges means the tyre is under-inflated.
● Excessive wear in the centre suggests it's over-inflated.
● Excessive wear on the outside or inside of the tread on both front tyres means incorrect front wheel alignment.
● Excessive wear on the tread of one front tyre could mean worn suspension or steering parts. Take the car to your garage.

DO'S AND DON'TS IN THE GARAGE

DO seal a concrete floor of a garage with concrete paint which is available from DIY stores. It prevents damp from rising and keeps the garage a bit warmer in cold weather.

DO keep the garage tidy, especially the floor – accidents will be avoided. Tools and tins of flammable substances, such as paint, should be stored in a safe place.

DO invest in a fire extinguisher. There is always a risk of fire in a garage, so make sure there are no piles of paper or other combustibles lying around.

DO make sure that cables and switches of electric power tools are sound. Fit a safety cut-out switch in the wall: it automatically cuts the power supply if there is a short circuit.

DO keep a bag of cat litter handy for absorbing oil spills. Dilute any spills with paint thinner or white spirit, sprinkle with cat litter and sweep up when the liquid has been absorbed.

DON'T work on a car in the garage with the engine running and the garage doors closed. Carbon monoxide from exhaust fumes can kill. If you need to run the engine, park the car with the exhaust pipe outside the garage, well clear of the doors.

DON'T ever wear a tie, loose clothing or jewellery while you work over a running engine. And keep long hair tied back. It could get caught in a moving part, such as the cooling fan.

DON'T leave power tools plugged in after use, and put away cables.

DON'T ever use a naked flame in a garage, particularly if the garage is used to store highly flammable liquids such as petrol, paraffin or even paint. Fumes from a battery that is being charged are also flammable and can cause an explosion if ignited.

DRIVING THE SAFE WAY

Clear vision Before driving off, make sure you have clear vision out of all the windows and in the mirrors. Clean off mist and condensation on the inside and frost on the outside. And have a clean, dry cloth inside the car to clear any misted-up windows during the journey.

Danger near home Many accidents occur within half a mile of the driver's home, so be aware of potential hazards as you set off – particularly pedestrians, schoolchildren and cyclists.

Rear vision Look in your rear-vision mirrors frequently so that you're constantly aware of traffic behind you and at the sides.

Long-distance check Before any long journey, check the engine oil, radiator coolant and the condition and pressures of the tyres, including the spare. It doesn't take long and might prevent a breakdown and hours of inconvenience. Also make sure that the windscreen, headlamps and rear lights are clean, and that the lights and flashing indicators at front and back are working.

272

Roof-rack safety If you're carrying a roof rack, make sure the load is securely lashed down and covered with a heavy-duty cover that won't be ripped to shreds at high speeds. Check the tightness of the roof-rack fittings after you have loaded. The weight can cause the fittings to settle and become loose.

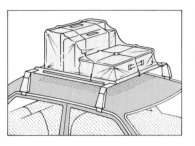

Avoiding drowsiness When driving long distances, make sure your car is well ventilated to avoid drowsiness. Every couple of hours, stop and stretch your legs. It won't add much to your journey time, and you'll be more alert when you get back on the road. Never carry on driving if you are feeling tired. Pull off the road – at the next exit or service area if you are on a motorway – and take a break. Have a short nap, if necessary.

Don't be a road-hog On motorways, keep to the left-hand lane if possible to allow other cars to overtake. Remember that heavy vehicles cannot use the right-hand lane of a three-lane motorway, so don't 'hog' the middle and right-hand lanes at a slower speed. It will cause traffic behind you to bunch up, or even cause other drivers to lose patience and possibly cause an accident.

Keep your distance Always keep the correct stopping distance behind the car in front by following the two-second rule. When the car in front passes a bridge or sign, start to say: 'Only a fool breaks the two-second rule'. If you pass the mark before completing the sentence, you are driving too close.

Beware of wind When driving fast in a high wind, be prepared for your car to veer unexpectedly because of turbulence caused by high-sided vehicles, such as coaches and lorries, or because of a lull in the wind caused by a bridge.

Watch your speed Keep an eye on the speedometer when driving. On motorways in particular you may find that your speed has crept up without your being aware of it.

Use your indicators Signal your intention to change lane or to turn off the road well in advance so that drivers behind you have a chance to slow down or overtake.

Driving in bad weather

Rain: poor visibility and slippery roads

● Rain makes it harder to see the road ahead and reduces the tyres' grip on the road surface. So always slow down when it rains and leave extra space between you and the vehicle in front so that you can stop safely if necessary.

● When driving in heavy rain, switch on dipped headlights and take care when overtaking large vehicles – the spray from their wheels can block your vision.

● A light shower after a long dry spell can create slippery roads when the water mixes with oil and rubber on the surface. Take extra care when cornering and braking.

● The distance it takes to stop increases greatly when the road is wet. The safe rule is to allow double the usual distance.

Fog: see and be seen

● Driving becomes dangerous when fog occurs in unexpected patches. Reduce speed and switch on your lights so other drivers can see you.
● To give you maximum visibility, switch on your windscreen wipers and use the demister to prevent the windscreen from misting up.
● Follow the direction of the road using the cat's-eyes or centre white line as a guide while concentrating on the road ahead.
● Don't follow a car too closely. It can give a false sense of security.
● Keep a constant check on your speed. In fog it's easy to drive faster than you think.

Snow and ice: keeping a firm grip on the road

● Leave a lot of space between you and the vehicle in front, and always brake and steer gently to avoid the wheels locking and the car skidding. Gentle pumping of the brake pedal on and off will reduce the risk.
● Descending a hill needs more care than climbing. Control the speed by driving in a low gear and occasionally using the brakes gently.
● Soft snow will give reasonable grip because the tyre treads can bite into it, but hard-packed snow gives very little grip. Remember that snow can pack into the treads and reduce the grip of the tyres still further. If in spite of everything the car starts to slide, pump the brake pedal on and off to slow the car and regain control.
● If the car is stuck in deep snow and you have no help, engage third and reverse gears alternately, letting the clutch out with minimum engine revs, to rock the car back and forth until the tyres can grip.

● If you get stuck in snow or on ice, don't let the wheels spin excessively. They will melt the frozen surface and make the problem worse. Place gravel, an old sack or twigs under the front of the driving wheels, then select second gear and let the clutch in slowly with minimum acceleration.

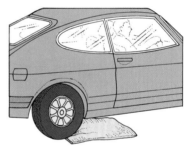

THE DANGERS OF BLACK ICE

In winter the road can become covered by an invisible layer of thin ice – known as 'black ice'. It is most likely to occur where an otherwise dry road surface is in shadow and the temperature is below freezing. The driver's first indications of black ice are a light feeling from the steering wheel and a lack of control. This can be immediately followed by a dangerous skid. Always reduce speed when black ice conditions are likely.

BUYING A USED CAR

Decide what you want Before you start looking for a secondhand car, decide what you need from it. How many passengers will you carry? Do you require a large boot – for holidays, perhaps? Do you sometimes carry heavy loads? Will you usually be driving in city traffic or will you do a lot of motorway driving? Do you usually travel with children?

Narrow the choice Read the car magazines to find a couple of models which meet your needs. You will also get an idea of price. Generally, used cars are more expensive in the south of Britain than in the north.

Garage or private seller? When deciding whether to buy from a private seller or a reputable garage, bear in mind that a garage must abide by the Trade Descriptions Act which controls statements made in advertisements. So you have more legal protection from a garage if the car develops a fault than from a private seller.

Take a friend When you start looking at cars take someone with you – preferably someone with a knowledge of cars. A friend may spot things you miss, and ask questions you forget. And you've got a witness to anything that is said.

What to look out for

MoT certificate Make sure that a car which is three years old or more has a current MoT certificate. This shows that it was safe when it was tested, but of course is no guarantee that it's still safe.

The mileage
● Most cars cover about 10,000 miles a year, so for a three-year-old car a mileage between 25,000 and 35,000 miles would be reasonable. If it's much higher, the car could have been used for business and driven hard.
● Remember that the reading on the car may not be correct – the mileage recorder could have been turned back. So try to judge if the mileage corresponds to the general condition of the car. A worn brake-pedal rubber and wear marks on the gear lever indicate a car that might have done more than 60,000 miles. A worn or sagging driver's seat is another sign of high mileage.
● Beware also of very low mileage which indicates that the car might have been left unused for long periods or used only for short journeys. Both can cause engine problems. A car that has been regularly used and serviced is a better bet.

Rusted bodywork Rust is probably the most damaging thing of all on cars over five years old.

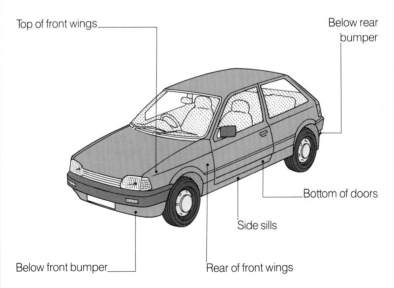

Top of front wings

Below rear bumper

Bottom of doors

Side sills

Below front bumper

Rear of front wings

● Look for rust at the top and rear of the front wings, along the side sills, below front and rear bumpers, and the bottoms of the doors.
● Sometimes a rust blemish on the paintwork can indicate more serious corrosion underneath. Press the panel gently with your thumb. If there is a cracking noise, it indicates advanced corrosion.

Engine compartment Have a look at the general state of the engine. A dirty engine and surrounding area suggests that the car hasn't been well looked after and that servicing may have been neglected.

Crash damage Walk round the car and look along the doors and wings from each of the four corners. Any crash repairs will show up if they haven't been well done. You will see ripples or a change in the texture of the paint if there is a lot of body filler underneath. Take a small magnet with you; it will be attracted to metal but not to plastic body filler. Look also for variations in the paint colour.

Shock absorbers At the corners, check the shock absorbers by pushing down hard on the body and letting go. The car should rebound once just past the level position, then go back. That's one-and-a-half swings. Any more means the shock absorbers need replacing.

The tyres Examine as much of the tread as possible, as well as the sidewalls, to see if the tyres will need replacing soon. There should be more than 2mm of tread all over the tyres and the sidewalls should not be cracked or damaged. Uneven wear on the tread suggests steering or suspension problems. Don't forget to look at the spare wheel, as well.

Making the final decision

If you are worried by any of the checks, look for another car. If you are pleased with what you have seen so far, arrange for an independent mechanical inspection. The AA or the RAC will send an engineer if you are a member. Or contact a firm that specialises in checking cars (see Yellow Pages under 'Car inspection').

The fee may sound expensive but an inspection by an expert could save you from buying a car that needs costly repairs, and it will certainly give you peace of mind.

SERVICING A BICYCLE

Mending a flat tyre

Flat tyres are usually caused by a faulty valve or a punctured inner tube. Inflate the tyre with the valve at the top of the wheel.

Check whether the valve is leaking by submerging the tip in a glass of water. If you can see any air bubbles, the valve is faulty and you must change it. If there are no bubbles, check the inner tube for a puncture.

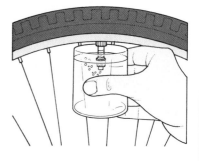

Replacing a valve

Unscrew and clean the valve. On older Woods valves, you only need to replace the rubber insert, available from bike shops. More modern Schrader valves should be completely replaced. You will need a special forked tool to unscrew them from the threaded valve tube.

Repairing a puncture

It is easier to repair a puncture if you take the wheel off first, but you don't have to. These instructions will work for either method.

1 Check the outer tyre for any nails, stones or glass that might have caused the puncture – or could cause another one. Then inflate it as far as you can and slowly turn the wheel in a bowl of water. The puncture will be indicated by air bubbles.

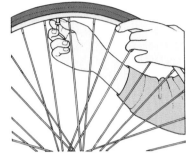

2 Unscrew the locking ring, which secures the valve to the rim, and push the valve inwards slightly to free the sides of the tyre. Insert tyre levers at 75mm (3in) intervals between the rim and tyre on one side only. Lever the tyre over the rim and when you can, run a lever all the way round the rim to free the rest.

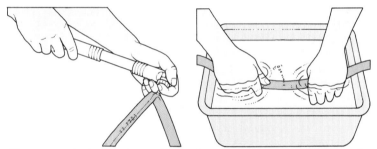

3 Pull out the inner tube and inflate it enough to give it shape. Pass the whole tube through a bowl of water – there may be more than one puncture. Note where the bubbles come from.

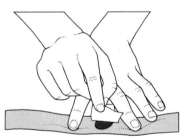

4 Dry the whole tube with a cloth and mark the punctured area with the chalk provided in the repair kit. Deflate the tyre fully and then rough up the surface around the puncture using abrasive paper. This gives the adhesive a grip. Spread adhesive thinly over the area around the puncture and leave to dry for several minutes.

5 Pick a patch of the right size from the repair kit and peel off the backing paper. Put it over the puncture and press down firmly on the carrying paper. Once the patch has stuck, remove the carrying paper and dust the repair with chalk. Before replacing the inner tube, check that there are no sharp objects inside the outer tyre.

277

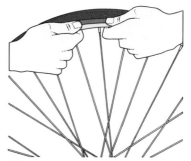

6 Clean any dirt from around the wheel rim, fit the valve into the rim hole, and feed the inner tube carefully into the tyre. Refit the tyre's free edge at the valve hole. To secure the tyre, hold it in the correct position as you pull the valve stem through and screw the nut firmly into place.

7 Lubricate the edge of the tyre with soapy water, and then roll the tyre's free edge over the rim with your fingers, starting from the valve. Take care not to pinch the inner tube between the tyre and the wheel. Lever the last part of tyre with your thumbs – anything harder could damage the tyre.

8 Check that the tyre is fitted evenly all the way round. Loosen the valve to ensure a correct fit, tighten it again and then inflate the tyre.

Adjusting the brakes

There are two main types of brakes – hand-operated rim brakes with the controls on the handlebars, and hub brakes, such as a back-pedal brake. Most bikes have rim brakes.

Whatever type your bike has, you should check regularly that the brakes are properly adjusted. To do this, push the bicycle along at walking speed and apply the brakes. Both wheels should stop dead.

● If the brake lever has to move more than halfway when you apply the brakes, an adjustment is needed.

● If your brakes grind, squeak, judder or seem slack, they also need adjusting. At the same time, check that the rim is clean and that the brake blocks are properly aligned with the rim. Tighten the mounting block if necessary, and change the brake blocks if they seem worn.

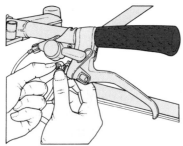

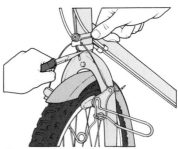

1 Find the adjusting barrel on your handlebar brakes and loosen the adjusting locknut. To loosen the brakes, screw the adjusting barrel in towards the locknut. To tighten them, screw it out. When you have found the right position, hold the adjusting barrel in its new position and tighten the locknut.

2 If the adjusting barrel has moved as far as it will go, loosen the brakes completely by screwing the adjusting barrel right in. Then adjust the brake cable at the caliper by undoing the anchor bolt. Tighten the cable as required and do up the anchor bolt. A tool called a third hand will grip the brake blocks as you work.

KEEP IT MOVING

● A bike in regular use needs to be lubricated once a month as grit causes damage and wear to all moving parts of a bicycle. Use bike oil or other suitable lubricant in a spray or can, and a special chain lubricant on the chain. Don't use vegetable oil – it will clog up the bike.

● Before oiling, clean the bike with a damp cloth, but avoid getting water in the bearings. Remove oily dirt with a cloth dipped in paraffin or white spirit. Finish by polishing any metal and painted surfaces with household wax to prevent rusting.

● Always keep a repair kit handy for punctures.

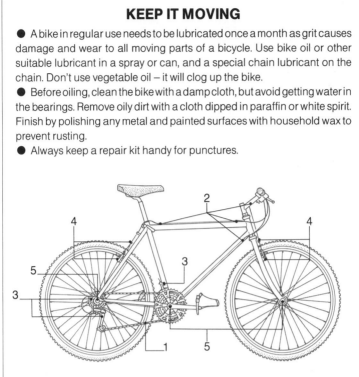

1 The chain Treat the chain monthly with a Teflon chain lubricant – avoid using gear oil as it attracts dirt and the chain will wear quicker.

2 Brake and gear cables Use a spray can monthly on all spots where the cables pass through guides, especially under the bottom bracket.

3 The gears and mechanisms Clean thoroughly and then oil every month. Wipe off excess oil afterwards.

4 Rim brakes Oil pivot points or pulleys lightly every month with a can (not a spray), concentrating on the controls. Avoid getting oil on the wheel rims and wipe off any excess oil afterwards.

5 The bearings Once a year, the bearings should be dismantled, cleaned and refilled with ball-bearing grease. Leave this job to an expert if your bike has sealed bearings. If there are any signs of wear, replace the bearings.

Buying a secondhand bicycle

● Check the frame carefully at the welded joints, particularly the crank spindle (bottom bracket) to see if the tubes are cracked.

● If the bike's wheels aren't aligned properly, it may be because the frame is distorted. To check the alignment, get someone to hold the bike upright and look at it carefully from both ends.

● Turn the bike upside-down and spin the wheels. Look carefully for the condition of the tyres and for buckled wheels. Spoked wheels can usually be straightened, but cast alloy ones can't.

● The condition of the brakes, paintwork and saddle will give you a good idea of how much use, or abuse, a bike has had.

● The manufacturer's number is stamped on the bike's frame, usually around the bottom bracket or seat tube. If you are worried, the police will have a list of stolen bike numbers.

Easy gardening

DESIGNING YOUR OWN GARDEN

Before you begin, decide what you want your garden to be: a pleasant place to sit out in, a children's playground, a pretty picture to view from the house, or a mix of all three.

Take your time Don't be in too much of a hurry to change things, or you may overlook some of your garden's best points. Look at the site in winter when the trees are bare and the borders empty; with only the bare bones there, good and bad features will be easy to pick out.

If you've taken over an established garden, live with it for a while – preferably a whole year – before beginning on alterations. New seasons can bring pleasant surprises as different flowers and foliage come into their own.

Angles and aspects Check the way your plot lies in relation to the sun. This determines what time of day different areas receive sunlight and for how long. Remember that in summer the sun rises much higher in the sky, so more of your garden will receive light, and the light will last longer.

Try it out on paper Before making any large-scale changes to a garden, take photographs of its different aspects – in winter, if possible – and then use a felt-tipped pen to sketch in additions such as paths, pergolas, trees, ponds, new beds or rockeries.

If you have a slide projector, project a slide of the garden onto a large sheet of white paper and do your landscaping on that.

Planning permission You may need to get permission for building work such as a new wall or conservatory. Ask the supplier or builder for advice, and check with the local council before you order the work to start.

Allowing for growth Make a list of the new plants and shrubs you plan to use and look up their fully grown dimensions in a good plant catalogue or gardening book. Check that they won't end up overshadowing a patio or favourite sunning spot, or drop leaves into gutters and ponds.

Stuck with a long, narrow garden? Consider turning it into a series of 'rooms' by creating screens across it with hedging or climbers on wires or a trellis framework.

Planning a patio? Remember that an average-sized garden table and four chairs occupies a space of about 2.5m x 2.5m (8ft x 8ft).

Be practical Plan garden paths wide enough to take a wheelbarrow or perhaps a pram, and don't forget a place for the washing line.

The next step Once you're happy with your plan, try it out in the garden using string, rope or a garden hose to mark out the beds and paths.

280

Year-round planning It's not necessary to think only of summer. You can have colour all year round with trees and shrubs such as Japanese maple (right), cornus or *Parrotia persica*, which have brilliant-coloured leaves and stems. If you have room for a large tree, try *Liquidambar styraciflua*. Its bright red and orange leaves will add a blaze of colour to your garden every autumn.

A sprinkling of winter flowers such as winter crocuses, hellebore or snowdrops will also help to cheer up beds and borders.

Temporary arrangements Use annual plants to give you a first-season display. If there are shrubs you can't resist buying but don't know where to put, plant them in tubs until you decide.

USING WALLS AND FENCES

Good companions Make the most of your wall space by planting climbers in colourful combinations that do well together:
● If you live in a mild area, use myrtle with its fine leaves to set off the deep green and orange of the Chilean glory vine (right).
● Many clematis varieties, such as *C. alpina* and large-leaved hybrids, will scramble happily over roses or grape vines.
● Ivy makes a good backdrop for gaily coloured nasturtiums.

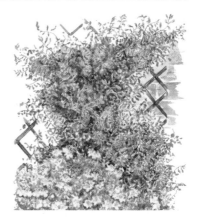

Putting up a new fence? Don't creosote the poles if you want to grow climbers against them. It will take many weeks for the poisonous fumes to dissipate. Use an alternative such as a copper naphthenate preservative instead, which will be kinder to plants. Read the instructions on the container before you buy the product, and follow them carefully.

Planting near a wall
● Be sure to make the planting hole large enough to accommodate the plant's roots comfortably, especially in the case of plants that have been bought without much soil around the roots.
● Don't site plants too close to a wall: 150-300mm (6-12in) is about right for a climber. Wall shrubs should be a little farther out, but no more than 1m (3ft) from the wall.
● Keep new plants well watered until they have established themselves.

Tying up a climber Use plastic or raffia ties, and check regularly to make sure they do not become too tight as the stem thickens. Old tights cut into strips also make good ties for soft-stemmed climbers which may be damaged by harder materials.

The right plants for your wall

North-facing walls Dampness and lack of sunshine are problems. Try clematis hybrids, climbing hydrangea (lower plant, above), ivies, winter jasmine or the roses 'Gloire de Dijon', 'Mme Alfred Carrière' and 'Mme Grégoire Staechelin' (upper plant, above).

South-facing walls Plenty of warmth, but dry soil could be a problem. Try honeysuckle and passion flower (above), or annual climbers such as nasturtium and morning glory. You can also try more tender plants such as ceanothus, Mexican orange or myrtle.

East-facing walls Lack of sunshine, sometimes with cold winds as well. Plant flowering quince (lower plant, above) or forsythia (upper plant, above). Most roses can also cope.

West-facing walls The most hospitable wall position of all. Plant decorative shrubs and climbers such as magnolias, camellias, wisteria, honeysuckle or *Clematis Montana* (above).

FOUR ANNUAL CLIMBERS

Climbers don't have to be permanent fixtures in a garden. Sow these four in early spring for quick growth and an extra splash of colour during summer. Sweet peas and nasturtiums can be sown outside, but morning glory and black-eyed Susan need to be germinated indoors.

Black-eyed Susan Grow this climber in milder regions for its light orange flowers with deep brown centres. For best results, grow it in a sunny, sheltered spot, or in a greenhouse. It will grow to about 1.8-3m (6-10ft) in a season.

Sweet pea This dainty climber comes in a huge range of colours and is easily grown from seed. It reaches a height of about 1.8m (6ft) and needs support.

Morning glory Most suitable for mild areas. Varieties in rich scarlets and purples are available as well as blues. It will grow to about 2.5-3m (8-10ft) high in a season.

Nasturtium Use an array of brightly coloured climbing nasturtiums in yellows, reds and oranges to cover a hedge, or just leave them to scramble over a bank. They will spread about 1.8m (6ft), but make sure you buy the climbing variety as bushy types are also available.

Fast growers for quick cover

Clematis montana The fastest-growing of all the clematis family and one of the easiest to grow. In good conditions it may grow as tall as 12m (40ft). To encourage vigorous growth, cut it back by about a third after the first flowering. Like all clematis, *montana* prefers alkaline soil and the roots and main stem need to be protected from direct sun – by growing shrubs to shield them, if necessary.

Akebia quinata This creeper with its fragrant, deep purple flowers will happily twine its way up any support on a warm or sheltered wall, quickly reaching a height of around 4.5m (15ft) with a spread of about 1.8m (6ft). In favoured spots it may eventually grow as big as 6-9m (20-30ft).

Honeysuckle Climbing varieties of honeysuckle are vigorous and hardy, with strongly scented flowers ranging from pale creamy-white to bright orange-red. Grow them in a lightly shaded spot with well-drained soil and dig in plenty of compost.

Russian vine Grow this vigorous climber for the fastest wall cover of all, but don't let it get out of hand – a Russian vine can easily grow 5m (16ft) in a single season.

Brandt grape vine Red-gold leaves give welcome autumn colour with this vine. Growth is rapid during summer, and the eventual size is about 8.5m (28ft) or even more.

Virginia creeper Choose this hardy climber for warm red foliage in autumn. For best effects, provide horizontal support.

Attaching climbers to a wall or fence

Choosing the right support
● Wooden or plastic trellis is quicker and easier to put up than the traditional wires threaded through vine eyes.
● For annual climbers, use plastic netting stretched on a wooden frame.

Protecting buildings Check the condition of bricks, roof tiles, pipes and gutters before growing a vigorous creeper against a building. Climbers seldom cause problems when buildings are in good condition – in fact, they may even help to protect the brickwork. If there are cracks or weak spots, however, the building could be damaged by the weight of the creeper, or by root or tendril growth.

If a wall cannot take a trellis Use self-supporting climbers such as ivy, climbing hydrangea or Virginia creeper, which will eventually adhere to the wall of their own accord. They may need staking at first, though.

Before you plant a climber Prepare the soil and fix any supports in place before you start planting, even if you are only going to tie the plant to a stake. Never leave a climbing plant without support or prevailing winds could rock the roots and cause it to die.

Setting up a trellis Always set a trellis slightly away from the wall – about 25-50mm (1-2in) is best. Nail it onto small wooden blocks or battens, or screw it onto the wall through old cotton reels spaced at regular intervals. That way, air will be able to circulate around the plants, and wooden trellises will be less likely to rot. For the same reason, a wooden trellis should stop short of soil level.

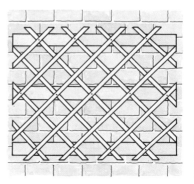

Planting climbers

Clearing the soil Remove any rubble or bricks from the earth around the base of the wall or fence before you begin planting. They may contain lime mortar which will make the soil too alkaline.

Protecting pipes and drains
● Avoid planting creepers which produce thick woody stems in spots where they could get behind downpipes and gutters and do damage.
● Plant climbers well away from drains and soakaways which the roots could penetrate.

Planting close to paving If you're planting in a narrow strip between a wall and a patio or pathway, choose a shallow-rooting climber such as ivy that won't disturb the paving.

Don't let them dry out Dry soil can be a problem near house walls, especially if projecting eaves and guttering shield plants from rain. Dig plenty of organic matter into the soil, or a mixture of moist peat and bone meal, to make the soil more water-retentive.

GETTING THE BEST FROM BULBS

Buy with care Always select bulbs carefully, especially if they are 'bargain' lots. Good bulbs are plump, firm and free from blemishes. They should also be of a good size for their type, or they may not flower the first year.

Where to plant them Bulbs look their best in clusters, rather than strung out in a flowerbed. Plant a group in a corner, under a tree or in a tub by the house, or plant them in window boxes.

Planting bulbs in grass A random scattering of flowers in spring can be very attractive, but be sure to choose low-growing varieties such as 'February Gold' and 'Jenny' daffodils, and *kaufmanniana* tulips. To get a natural look, toss the bulbs onto your lawn and plant them where they fall.

What depth? Many bulbs suffer from shallow planting. As a rule of thumb, make the hole three times the length of the bulb.

When the flowers are finished
● Cut off dead flowers before they turn to seed, or the plant will be weakened for the following year.
● Don't trim the leaves of bulbs or tie them into knots once the plants have flowered. Leave them to turn brown and die off naturally so that they can return nourishment to the bulb for the next year's flowers.
● If you want to replace flowering bulbs with bedding plants in early summer, carefully lift out the bulbs and replant them in a corner of your garden with wire netting beneath them. Lift and replant in autumn.

Four favourite bulbs

Daffodils Put daffodil bulbs in before the end of October. 'Species' bulbs (small varieties developed from wild daffodils) should be planted in holes 75mm (3in) deep, and other varieties at twice that depth.

Tulips Plant tulip bulbs from October until the end of November, in holes about 100mm (4in) deep.

Snowdrops If possible, plant snowdrops immediately after flowering, while still in leaf. If you do sow them as bare bulbs, make the holes about 75-100mm (3-4in) deep and plant them before the end of September.

Crocuses Crocus bulbs need to go into the ground before the end of September, and about 50-75mm (2-3in) deep.

Indoor flowers at Christmas time

For early flowering you'll need to buy 'prepared' bulbs which have been treated to speed up their development. September 15 is generally considered to be the best date for planting bulbs if you want Christmas flowers, but even then the exact timing can't be guaranteed.

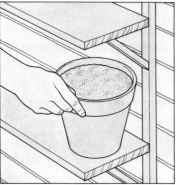

1 Place the bulbs close together, but not touching, in a bowl of potting compost or well-soaked bulb fibre. The tips of the bulbs should be just below the rim of the container. Cover with compost or bulb fibre and water well.

2 Place the container in a cool spot such as a shed or bury it in a shady corner of the garden. Darkness is not essential, but coolness is. Do not put the pot in a black plastic sack as some people do; this may encourage mould.

3 After 10-12 weeks, young green shoots should appear, or paler shoots if the bulbs are being kept in the dark. When the shoots are about 50mm (2in) long, bring the bulbs indoors into a cool room. They should come into flower around Christmas time.

GROWING A LAWN FROM SEED

Buying grass seed

Getting the right mix Sowing seed is the cheapest way to make a lawn, and it also enables you to choose a mix that suits your needs.
● Choose a mixture of lawn seed with a high percentage of rye or meadow grass if the lawn is going to have to stand up to wear and tear from children and pets.

● For a bowling green finish, it's advisable to go for a type with more of the grasses called bents and fescues.

Calculating the amount of seed Measure the length and width of your lawn to get the number of square metres or yards to be seeded. Allow 36-60g of seed per square metre ($1\frac{1}{4}$-$2\frac{1}{2}$oz per square yard). Use the higher figure if the weather is particularly wet or dry, or if you are using a heavy-duty mix containing rye grass. It may also be advisable to use more seed if birds are frequent visitors to your garden, although most grass seed now contains a bird-repellent.

Sowing the seed

The right time of year March and September are the best months of the year for sowing a new lawn. There is usually enough sunshine and enough rain to give the grass a good start.

Preparing the ground Before you scatter grass seed, dig the ground well over, rake it to a fine surface, and remove any sticks and stones. Then firm the soil by walking over it slowly with your weight on your heels to fill in any soft spots or hollows. Rake lightly again before sowing the seed.

Distributing the seed evenly Divide the area to be sown into metre or yard squares, and measure out the right amount of seed for each. Then scatter each square by hand, casting half the seed up and down, and half across. Lightly rake in the seeds. They will germinate in about three weeks, depending on the weather.

Looking after a new lawn

Watering Never let a newly sown lawn dry out. Water regularly with the finest spray possible, so that you don't disturb the seedlings or knock them out of the ground.

The first cutting Don't attempt to mow your new lawn until the grass has grown to at least 50-75mm (2-3in) high, and even then set your mower blades as high as possible. If the blades are too low, you may drag the seedlings out of the ground.

Weeds Avoid selective weedkillers for about six months after planting a lawn. You'll disturb the seedlings less if you just use a kitchen fork to take out weeds as they appear.

PUTTING DOWN TURF

Ask to see a sample Turf varies considerably, from strips of meadow treated with weedkiller, to specially grown new grass. If you buy without seeing it, you may end up with something completely unsuitable for your garden. Make sure your turf does not contain a higher proportion of coarse grasses than you are prepared to put up with, as they cannot be eradicated later with weedkillers or by mowing. Also check for weeds.

Thick or thin turves? There's no absolute rule about how thick or thin turves should be but, in general, the thinner the turves, the more quickly the grass will take root. Most professional greenkeepers use turves that are about 30-40mm (1¼-1½in) thick.

Small areas and tricky corners Consider buying turf in rolls, rather like stair carpeting, if you have only a small piece of ground to cover or if there are awkward spots that ordinary turves won't fit into. Some turf is grown on a fine backing and can be cut into any shape with kitchen scissors. Ask a garden centre to order it for you, or look in the Yellow Pages under 'Turf supplies' to find a local supplier.

Taking care of turf Try to get turf delivered as close to the day you want to lay it as possible. If you can't manage to lay it straight away, keep it stacked in rolls, preferably away from direct sunlight. If conditions are very dry, damp it down well using the finest spray on your hose. Small squares of turf should be stacked flat, or their soil backing is liable to crack.

Laying turves Make sure the pre-pared ground is smooth and level before you put down turves, or they may lift up over bumps and fail to 'take' properly. Lay the turves as you would bricks in a wall, stagger-ing the joins in alternate rows. If you need to kneel on new turf to put down the next row, place a plank over the turves to protect them.

Irregular lawns Edge oddly shaped lawns with a strip of whole turves so that any small odd-shaped pieces finish away from the edge.

Watering Keep new-laid turf well watered. If the turves dry out they will shrink and leave unsightly gaps which take a long time to fill in. Water every two to three days when the weather is warm and dry, less often when cool or wet.

CARING FOR YOUR LAWN

Feeding the grass For green grass all year round, apply a high-nitrate lawn fertiliser at the end of March. Sulphate of ammonia fertilisers are a popular choice and will turn your lawn green very quickly, but water the grass daily for the first few days or it may get 'burnt'. Choose a warm day after there has been a spell of rain and the soil is moist, but the grass is dry.

If necessary, use a fertiliser which contains a weedkiller as well, to tackle two jobs at once.

When to water To find out if a lawn needs watering, try walking heavily on it. If there is no 'give' or springiness in the grass, it is lacking moisture.

Drought conditions You don't have to stand back and watch your lawn die when rain is scarce and hosepipes are banned.
● Siphon used bath water into large containers and use it to water the grass, but avoid water that contains bath foam or oil.
● If lack of rain has made the ground hard and compacted, spike it with a garden fork before watering. This will help to ensure that the maximum amount of moisture can soak in.
● If your mower has a detachable grass box, leave it off when rain is scarce. The clippings will help to keep in moisture.

Frost Never walk on a frozen or frosty lawn. You will bruise and possibly kill the tender grass blades.

Freeing the young shoots A compacted mat of dead or dying material known as 'thatch' tends to collect around the base of grass plants, clogging the lawn and stopping light and air from reaching new shoots. To prevent this, drag a rake lightly over the lawn surface at the beginning of the year, in midsummer and again in autumn.

If your lawn is large, it may be worthwhile buying a purpose-made, wheeled scarifier to make the job easier.

Spiking Regular spiking three times a year lets air and water into the soil and helps to keep any lawn in good condition. Use a lawn spiker, a garden fork or spiked shoes (all available from garden centres), and do the job in January, early summer and late autumn.

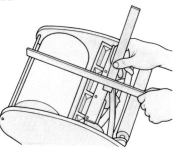

First cut of the season Set the mower blades at their highest level at the beginning of each season, and gradually lower them as the weeks go by. At the height of the season, most lawns should be cut at about 12-25mm ($\frac{1}{2}$-1in), depending on the amount of wear and tear they have to cope with.

DO NOT mow your lawn for three days before or after applying fertiliser or weedkiller, and don't scatter cuttings over flowerbeds if you have applied a weedkiller which acts on broad-bladed leaves – it may kill your plants.

Treating lawn troubles

Bald patches Reseeding is the answer. Break up the bald patch with a fork and work the soil to a fine surface. Scatter seed over the bald patch, and lightly rake it in. Keep the patch well watered, using the finest spray possible. Treat the new seedlings gently as they appear, especially when mowing or using weedkiller.

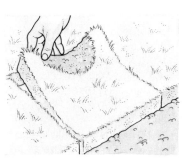

Broken lawn edge Repair the damage by cutting out a neat square of turf that includes the broken edge. Reverse the turf so that there is a straight edge facing outwards and the ragged edge is on the inside, where it will be much less noticeable. Fill in the damaged area with soil and sprinkle grass seed over it.

Bumps and hollows Neatly slice off the top layer of turf around the problem spot. Dig away or fill in the soil beneath to level it. Then replace the turf, firm it down and water well.

Moss You're more likely to get rid of lawn moss if you first find and treat the cause. This may be too much acidity in the soil (try adding lime), dampness (in serious cases it may be worth digging up the lawn and laying drains) or a spot that's too shaded (prune any overhanging shrubs or trees). If nothing else works, use a proprietary moss-killer/fertiliser to control the problem.

LAWNMOWER CARE

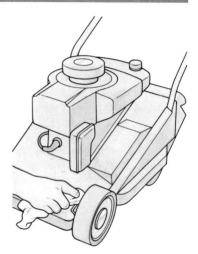

When summer's over Before you put your lawnmower away for the winter, give it a good all-over cleaning and check-up so that it will be ready for use at the beginning of next spring.

● Wipe all moving parts with a lightly oiled rag so that they don't rust even though not in use.

● Check that none of the blades or cutters has become nicked or distorted by stones.

● Check to see whether mower blades need sharpening or resetting. The blades of a cylinder mower should meet tightly so that they cut the grass cleanly.

● Examine electric mower cables for holes or cracks in the insulation, and have the cable replaced if necessary.

● If you have a motor mower, drain the petrol and oil tanks, and clean the spark plug. Fill the oil tank with clean oil but leave the petrol tank empty.

Getting repairs done If your annual inspection reveals that repairs or new parts are needed, or if the blades need sharpening, get the job done right away. If you leave it until spring you will find that other mower owners have done the same and you could have a long wait.

Storing a mower Never leave a motor mower standing for months on a damp surface or in a damp place, or it will almost certainly be hard to start in spring. Stand it on a piece of cardboard or a block of wood and keep the area well ventilated to avoid condensation.

GARDENING IN A SMALL SPACE

Roof gardens and balconies Get a surveyor to check that the roof or balcony can take the extra weight before embarking on an extensive planting project – pot plants can be surprisingly heavy. Reduce the load by using lightweight plastic containers filled with peat-based compost, rather than clay pots and soil. If necessary, cut down further by leaving the plants in their pots and filling the gaps in the containers with vermiculite.

Growing bags Heavy-duty, compost-filled plastic bags with slits for plants can be bought from nurseries and used as instant flower or vegetable beds on a balcony, roof garden or patio. Edge the bags with a line of bricks and, after planting, cover the top with a layer of shredded bark to disguise the plastic. Empty the contents onto your compost heap after each season – plants won't grow well in the same bag for a second year.

Make space with mirrors To make a small garden look bigger, mount a large mirror on marine plywood (bought from a timber merchant) and fix it to a wall to look like a doorway or a window. If you can manage two mirrors opposite each other you'll get the illusion of infinity. Train a climber around the mirror to hide the edges. Or hang a wrought-iron gate in front, or a trellis angled to suggest perspective.

Using perspective Clever land-scaping can make even a tiny garden seem bigger. Taper paths so that they are narrower at the far end than at the front to increase the appearance of receding into the distance, or plant dwarf versions of trees such as conifers against a back wall. If you have parallel side beds, slope the edges towards each other at the far end.

Watering a hanging basket In midsummer hanging baskets need watering twice a day. If you find this a chore, consider attaching them to pulley systems bought from a garden centre.

If dripping is a problem, water the baskets by tipping ice cubes onto the top, so that moisture is slowly released as they melt. But make sure that the ice does not actually touch the plants, or it could damage them.

Planting a strawberry barrel Before filling a strawberry barrel with compost, stand a piece of drainpipe upright in the centre. Fill it with pebbles as you put in the compost, drawing the pipe up through the soil as you go. The stones will act as a central drainage system and prevent the soil from becoming waterlogged.

Container plants for shady corners

Foliage plants Many decorative leaves grow well in places that receive little sunlight. Ivy, ferns, *Fatsia japonica* and hostas (above) are popular choices.

Begonias Buy trailing or upright varieties in reds, yellows and pur-plish tones to brighten up darker spots. All begonias will tolerate partial shade.

Busy Lizzies Colourful, easy-to-grow busy Lizzies are ideal for hanging baskets or boxes that don't get much sun. Look for double versions that give even more colour.

Lily of the valley These shade-lovers quickly form clumps. Waxy, white bell-like flowers appear in April or May, or a month sooner if brought indoors.

London pride The most popular of the large saxifrage family produces masses of small pink flowers in early summer.

Primulas and polyanthus Grow in partial shade for a bright display in winter and early spring. Keep the soil moist: they won't do well if allowed to dry out.

Violets and pansies All the *Viola* family prefer shade, from tiny heartsease to large-flowered hybrids such as 'Crystal Bowl' pansies.

Plant partners for hanging baskets and boxes

- Pale pink tulips with dark blue grape hyacinths.
- All-white mix of 'Snow Queen' geraniums, white busy Lizzies and white trailing lobelia.
- Pink ivy-leaved geraniums with pale and dark blue trailing lobelia.
- 'Falling Star' pink fuchsias with mixed *Begonia semperflorens* and trailing blue lobelia.
- Pink and mauve night-scented stocks with white *Chrysanthemum frutescens* and purple trailer *Maurandia*.
- Pink and white sweet williams with purple heartsease.
- Pink petunias with blue *Campanula isophylla* and ivy.
- Pink and yellow antirrhinums with blue and white trailing lobelia.
- Dark red geraniums with silvery cineraria.
- Pink antirrhinums with white alyssum and blue lobelia.
- Red salvias with white trailing lobelia and blue campanulas.
- Yellow and red gazanias with white marguerites.

WINDOW BOX TIPS

- Choose a box that is at least 200mm (8in) deep to give room for root growth and prevent the soil from drying out too rapidly.
- If you prefer, grow plants in pots inside a window box instead of filling the box with soil. It may make plant care easier if you can lift them out and change them around without disturbing the roots.
- Aim to keep the soil moist, but don't let your window box become waterlogged. In summer it may need watering every day.
- Choose low-growing plants if you want the maximum amount of light from your window, or consider climbers that you can train up against the wall alongside the window.
- If your box is in an exposed position – on a wall or a balcony, for example – make sure it's securely fixed in place with brackets or strong wire. A powerful gust of wind could turn the heavy box into a lethal hazard.

A decorative basket in six steps

1 Stand the empty basket frame in the top of a bucket to hold it in position while you work.

2 Line the frame with black plastic or a compressed cellulose liner bought from a garden centre.

3 Starting at the bottom, make holes in the lining to take trailing plants. Poke the plant roots into place, filling the basket with compost as you go.

4 Plant the tallest plants in the middle of the top of the basket. Make a depression in the soil around them to help retain moisture when you water.

5 Plant more trailers around the rim of the basket. If necessary, encourage stems to hang down by pegging them with hairpins.

6 Drench the basket well with water. Leave it in the bucket to allow excess water to drain away before you hang it up.

CHOOSING THE RIGHT CONTAINERS

Plastic pots Cheap, light and durable, and they keep the soil moist. Sunlight can turn some plastics brittle, however, and they may eventually crack.

Glass fibre containers If you want the appearance of stone without the weight, glass fibre containers may be the answer. They can be moulded and coloured in a variety of ways, and are light, strong, long-lasting and repairable. But they are also more expensive than other materials.

Reconstituted stone containers (crushed stone moulded into shape) Stone imitations of classical urns and vases are attractive, especially in a period setting, but they are extremely heavy. Use with care on balconies.

Terracotta pots Baked clay containers are attractive in almost any surroundings, but they break easily and are heavy.

Wooden holders Wood looks good and keeps plant roots warmest in winter. But unless you buy a hardwood such as teak, elm or oak, you'll need to treat it with wood preservative to prevent rotting. Look for containers that are guaranteed pestproof.

KEEPING HOUSE PLANTS HEALTHY

New to indoor gardening? Choose foliage plants rather than more temperamental flowering ones if you're not an experienced indoor gardener. Try aspidistra, *Cissus antarctica*, coleus, *Dracaena marginata* (right) or *Fatshedera*. The rubber plant and Swiss cheese plant are also decorative and easy for beginners to grow; so is mother-in-law's tongue.

Avoid garden soil Use only potting compost, or you may find that the heat of your house activates weed seeds and fungal diseases.

Give them a spell in the sun If you have a garden, put your house plants outside during July and August so that they can benefit from all-round light for a change.

House plants for free

Miniature fruit trees Grow decorative plants from orange, lemon or grapefruit pips. Soak the pips overnight, press into pots of compost and leave in a warm, dark spot such as an airing cupboard until they sprout.

Instant greenery Create attractive house plants at no cost from the green tops of fresh carrots or pineapples. Cut off the edible part of the carrot or pineapple just below the top, and push the cut end into a pot of compost. Cover new pineapple plants with a clear plastic bag secured with a rubber band until they start to grow.

Growing an avocado plant Press four cocktail sticks into a whole avocado stone. Fill a jam jar with water and, using the sticks to support it on the rim, place the stone over the jar with the base just resting in the water. A root should emerge from the stone within about a month. Let the root grow to at least 40mm (1½in), then transfer the stone to a pot of compost to grow further.

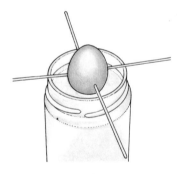

Common pot plant problems

Central heating A centrally heated room in winter has air as dry as that of a desert. To help house plants cope, group them together so that they can create a moist microclimate around themselves. Install a humidifier or mist the leaves about once a week with a fine spray. This has the added advantage of keeping the leaves clean and deterring red spider mite.

Dusty leaves Wash rubber plants and other leathery leaves that tend to get dusty with a mixture of milk and water to make them shine.

Unsuitable companions If you're putting more than one plant into a container, make sure they all have the same needs. Moisture-loving indoor azaleas, for example, won't put up with the same dry conditions as a cactus collection.

Watering house plants

How to tell if a house plant needs water Tear off a strip of newspaper and press it against the potting soil for a count of five. If the paper comes away damp the plant is still all right; if the paper is dry the plant needs water.

Moisture-lovers Ferns, African violets and other damp-zone plants must have moist air around them, but won't do well standing in a pool of water.

You can keep them damp but without the risk of waterlogging by placing their pots on saucers of pebbles and making sure that the pebbles are kept wet all the time. Or leave a bowl of water alongside the plants to increase humidity.

Watering when you're away

Group house plants together when you go away, and leave them out of direct sunlight. Choose a cool room in summer, and one at about 16-18°C (60-65°F) in winter. They should be fine for up to a week if you give them a good watering before you go, but if you're going to be away much longer, you'll need to use self-watering devices such as these:

● Buy water-conducting wicks from a garden centre and run them from buckets of water to the pot plants.

● Fill glass jars or plastic containers with water and place a strip cut from an old pair of tights into each. Make a hole in the lid of each container, thread one end of the tights strip through it, and screw it on. Poke the other end of the strip through the hole in the bottom of a plant pot with a pencil. Stand the pot on top of the container.

● Cover pot plants with large plastic bags supported on sticks so that they do not touch the leaves. Tie the bag around the pot rim.

● Line your bath with plastic sheeting and place a thick layer of newspaper on top. Put pot plants on the newspaper and spray until leaves, soil and newspaper are damp. Drape plastic sheeting over the shower curtain rail and tape it to the sides of the bath. Leave the bathroom light on. Not suitable for succulents, African violets or furry-leaved plants.

Fault-finder guide: house plants

Limp, wilted leaves; lower leaves turning yellow and dropping off Usually caused by under-watering. Check on moisture needs of plant (see next page) and test the soil regularly for dryness.

Leaves limp and showing signs of rot; leaves turn yellow and fall off
Too much water. Put pebbles in the bottom of the pot to improve drainage and allow the soil to dry out a little between waterings. Never leave the pot standing in water.

Brown, shrivelled leaf tips, or flower buds falling off
Dry air is the problem. Mist the plant frequently, move it to an unheated room, or install a humidifier.

Slow growth, few flowers, pale or spotted leaves
Poor soil. Dose regularly with pot plant fertiliser in spring and summer.

HOW TO CARE FOR YOUR HOUSEPLANTS

	Water requirement (growing period)	Water requirement (inactive period)	Suitable for centrally heated rooms	Suitable for cold rooms	Suitable for dark rooms
Aechmea	M	M	✓		
African violet	M	M			
Aspidistra	M	M		✓	✓
Asplenium	P	S			✓
Beloperone	M	S	✓		
Cacti	M	S	✓		
Cape primrose	M	S	✓		
Chlorophytum	P	M	✓		
Cineraria	P	M		✓	
Cyclamen	M	M	✓		
Ferns	P	M			✓
Helxine	M	S		✓	
Hydrangea	P	S		✓	
Ivy	M	M		✓	
Mother in law's tongue	M	S	✓		✓
Mother of thousands	P	S		✓	
Palms	M	S	✓		
Philodendron	M	S	✓		✓
Rubber plant	S	S	✓		
Scindapsus	M	S	✓		✓
Swiss cheese plant	M	S	✓		
Yucca plant	P	S	✓		

S = water sparingly; M = water moderately; P = water plentifully

GROWING PLANTS FROM SEED

Seed shaker Use a jam jar with holes punched in the top to shake out fine seeds such as grass and annuals. It distributes the seed more evenly and helps you see how much you are using.

Save money on seeds Share packets of seeds with other gardeners and swap cuttings. You'll cut down on waste and have more variety.

Sowing seeds that you have harvested yourself Seed bought in packets comes with sowing instructions, but if you harvest your own seed, follow the rule that the smaller the seed, the shallower it needs to be sown: tiny seeds such as begonia on the surface; medium-sized seeds such as lettuce, carrot and onion about 15-20mm ($\frac{1}{2}$-$\frac{3}{4}$in) down; and large seeds such as peas and beans about 25-40mm (1-1$\frac{1}{2}$in) deep.

● Do not buy F1 hybrid plants or seeds (check the packet) if you intend to collect your own seeds after flowering. The harvested seed will not produce plants that are reliably like the parents.

To avoid sowing fine seeds too thickly Mix the seed with sand and shake well to combine together before sowing. Alternatively, make a crease down the centre of a piece of paper, put the seeds into the crease and slowly tilt the paper, tapping the hand that holds the seeds gently with one finger of the other hand.

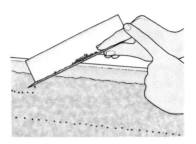

Seeds with special needs

Faster parsley Speed up germination time by pouring hand-hot water over the seed and leaving it to soak overnight before planting.

Lettuce and carrot These seeds need cool conditions to germinate. Summer sowing should be done in the early evening when the soil has cooled down. Water the ground well to lower the temperature, and keep it shaded from the sun until the first shoots appear.

Protecting beans and peas To keep field mice away, mix a little paraffin with some sand and stir bean and pea seeds into the sand to give them a light paraffin coating. Then sow as usual.

Planting out seedlings

A tool for transplanting If you don't have a proper dibber for making holes when transplanting seedlings, an old pencil or ballpoint pen will do the job just as well. Make evenly spaced rows of small holes for the seedling roots, and press the plants in firmly. Water well after planting and shield from strong sun if necessary.

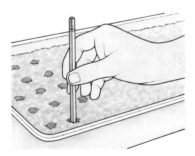

Thinning out If seedlings are too thickly sown, nip off some of them at the base with a pair of tweezers. If you try to pull them out, you will disturb the roots of the others.

Mini-greenhouse A clear plastic drinks bottle with the base cut off makes an instant miniature greenhouse for a new seedling. Just press it into the ground around the plant. It'll offer protection from pests, too.

Wilting Protect larger planted-out seedlings from wilting in hot weather by making cones of newspaper to keep off the sun. Turn up the base of the rim and weight it down with pebbles to stop the newspaper blowing away.

Storing seeds

Storage conditions Keep leftover seed in a cool, dry place, preferably in an airtight tin. To absorb moisture from the air in the tin, wrap a handful of milk powder in a double layer of tissues and seal it with a rubber band.

To check that stored seeds are still viable Dampen a small pad of kitchen paper, sprinkle a little seed on top and place in an airtight tin in a warm spot. If the seed has not sprouted after about ten days, it is unlikely to be viable and you will need to buy new ones.

NEW PLANTS FROM CUTTINGS

Temporary pots Start off cuttings in pots made from old yoghurt, cream or margarine containers. Use a hot metal skewer to make drainage holes in the bottom. If you use larger flower pots to raise cuttings, put several into each pot, spacing them out around the edge.

Instant greenhouse Use strong, clear plastic bags as greenhouses to bring on cuttings or young plants. Put several pots inside one large bag, or place smaller bags over individual plants and secure them with an elastic band around the pot. Support the bags with twigs stuck into the soil, if necessary. Never allow the plastic to touch young plants, or they may burn in the sunlight.

HOW LONG DO VEGETABLE SEEDS KEEP?

Two years from purchase date	Three years from purchase date	Five years from purchase date
● Cucumbers	● Beans	● Brussels sprouts
● Hybrid tomatoes	● Carrots	● Broccoli
● Leeks	● Peas	● Cabbage
● Marrows		● Cauliflower
● Melons	**Four years from**	● Celery
● Onions	**purchase date**	● Chinese cabbage
● Pumpkins	● Beetroot	● Kale
● Spinach	● Non-hybrid tomatoes	● Lettuce
● Squash	● Peppers	● Radish
● Sweetcorn	● Swedes	● Turnips

Note Parsnip seeds won't keep from one year to the next. Buy new ones every season.

HOW TO BUY PLANTS

Houseplants

If possible, buy indoor plants from a nursery or garden centre where they are grown in a greenhouse, and look for plants with labels that tell you how to care for them. Check carefully for any signs of pests or diseases: problems can spread rapidly when plants are kept indoors.

If you buy houseplants in winter, wrap them securely in newspaper to protect them from the cold air on the way home. Be sure to close the paper over any tender growing tips. If possible, give new houseplants a few days in a cool spot before exposing them to central heating.

Container-grown plants

Don't buy container-grown plants that have any wilted, yellow or diseased leaves, or that have weeds growing in the potting compost. Turn over the leaves to look for insect pests on the underside (right) and avoid any affected plants.

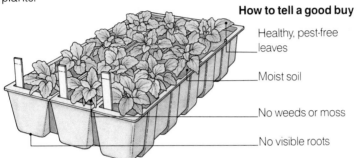

How to tell a good buy

Healthy, pest-free leaves

Moist soil

No weeds or moss

No visible roots

Bare-rooted shrubs and trees

Bare-rooted roses and other plants are often sold pre-packaged in supermarkets, but that doesn't mean they are always in good shape. Examine carefully before you buy and avoid any that are showing signs of growth with leaf buds opening or white hair roots appearing. Stems should be woody and not shrivelled. Plant during the winter months, between October and March.

TIPS FOR SUCCESSFUL PLANTING

Container-grown plants Disturb the roots as little as possible during planting, so that they continue to benefit from the compost they are grown in. Water as usual after planting.

Bare-rooted trees and shrubs Spread the roots out for planting like the spokes of an umbrella: if they get twisted it could stunt their growth. As you cover the roots with soil, shake the tree from time to time to make sure the soil firms down well between them. Water well after planting.

Support stakes Knock in supports before you plant a new tree, or you may damage its roots. A circle of twigs about 500mm (20in) high makes a better support for a border plant than a single stake, and it's less noticeable.

PRUNING TIPS

The tools for the job A pair of sharp secateurs and a pruning saw with a narrow blade will be enough to tackle most pruning jobs. If there's a lot of cutting to do, consider getting a pair of stronger hand pruners as well, and a tree saw if there are many heavy jobs.

● Always buy strong, good quality tools and keep them sharp, or crushing could leave plants open to infection.

Flowering shrubs Prune shrubs that bloom in spring straight after flowering, and summer-flowering ones between January and March before new growth starts.

Evergreens Prune conifers in late summer or early autumn, and evergreens that are not in flower in May. Prune others after flowering.

Hedges To keep the base leafy and green, cut hedges into pyramid shapes in spring so that the top is narrower than the base. A wider base will also prevent the hedge from being split under the weight of snow in winter.

Pruning climbers Winter pruning is best for buddleia, bignonia, *Clematis jackmanii* and other climbers that flower on new growth. However, prune straight after flowering for climbers that flower on the previous season's growth – early flowering clematis, jasmine, forsythia, honeysuckle and ornamental quince, for example.

HOW AND WHEN TO PRUNE ROSES

Hybrid tea and floribunda roses March is the best time to prune these roses.

First cut off any dead, diseased or thin wood, then trim back the main shoots. The length of the shoots is less important than the number of buds left on the stem, so count the buds from the base of each shoot and make the cut just above the second or third one.

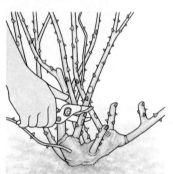

Shrub roses Both old roses and modern shrub roses produce most of their flowers on shoots pruduced from old wood, so light pruning is best. Do the pruning in winter, removing any dead, thin or decayed wood, and shorten the main stems by about one-third.

Rambling roses Cut untidy, flowered shoots right down to the base in autumn and tie new shoots to the trellis. If there are few new shoots, leave some of the flowered shoots in place, cutting them back just a little.

Climbing roses Remove any crossing shoots or thin shoots in autumn and reduce the height of the main stems by about one-third so that they do not blow about in the wind. Remove any side shoots that spoil the shape of the plant and cut others back by about two-thirds.

Miniature roses Cut off any dead, diseased or thin wood in March, and trim back the main stems to about one-third of their length.

FERTILISING YOUR GARDEN

Choosing the right fertiliser Buy fertiliser according to your garden's needs. A brand with a high proportion of nitrogen (N) will encourage leaf growth, one rich in phosphorus (P) will build stronger roots and one with plenty of potassium (K) will help to produce flowers and fruit.

If you just want to give your plants an all-round boost, use a general-purpose fertiliser such as Growmore or Phostrogen at regular intervals during the growing season.

Organic fertilisers Choose fertilisers made from plant or animal matter rather than chemicals if the idea of organic gardening appeals to you.

● Organic matter such as horse manure, cow dung and compost adds bulk to the soil as well as feeding it, and it can improve the quality of even poor soils such as heavy clay. Nutrients are released slowly, so you need only apply fertiliser from time to time.

● Some of the best buys for faster-acting organic fertilisers include dried blood, horn and hoof, bone meal and the cheaper extracts of seaweed. Look on the bag for the N, P and K content of the fertiliser, and choose according to your needs.

In need of nitrogen? Yellowing leaves and poor growth are a clear symptom. Dig in a high-nitrogen fertiliser such as dried blood. If the problem persists, the soil may be too alkaline. Buy a tester kit and if necessary dig in an acidifier such as peat or sequestered iron.

When to feed fruit trees Late February or early March, when the buds are beginning to swell, is the best time to fertilise fruit trees. The spring rains quickly wash the nutrients down into the soil to feed the roots.

Getting off to a good start Seedlings will do better if the soil around them is well fertilised and rich in nutrients. About ten days to two weeks before sowing seed, apply a general-purpose fertiliser such as Growmore to the soil or compost.

Look out for bulk bargains

The most economical way to build up a thick layer of topsoil in a new garden – or any garden with poor soil – is to hunt around the neighbourhood for a good source of cheap or free bulk fertiliser.

If you live near the sea, seaweed may be the answer. If there are farms around, ask about collecting horse manure or cow dung. If there is a local mushroom grower you will probably be able to obtain spent mushroom compost – an alkaline additive – very cheaply (some garden centres will also supply it, but they will be more expensive).

Three free fertilisers

Wood ash If you live in an area where it is permitted, burning garden debris can be a useful way of making fertiliser and getting rid of rubbish at the same time. The ash contains potash, a potassium and oxygen compound, and can be sprinkled around any garden plants. Wood ash will also repel cutworms, beetles and some other insects.

Comfrey leaves Try to find room for a patch of comfrey in a corner of your garden – it's an easy way to enrich the soil with potassium and trace elements. Soak the leaves in a tub of water or just let them rot down for a valuable fertiliser.

Autumn leaves If you don't mind tackling a rather messy job, you can turn autumn leaves into a valuable fertiliser for your garden. Rake up the leaves and run a power mower over them to chop them up (if the leaves fly about you may need to keep raking them together). Use as a nutritious mulch for flowerbeds.

301

Enrich your soil with compost

Different ways to make compost

Constructing a compost heap A compost heap should be at least 1m (3ft) square. The easiest way to make one is to buy four pieces of rigid plastic-coated wire mesh and tie them together with plastic-coated wire or twine to form a box. Line it with sacking or old blankets or sheets and make a lid from a piece of old carpet to keep out the worst of the rain.

Mini-compost heap If you have only a small garden, but still want to make compost, use a heavy-duty plastic rubbish sack to compost down kitchen refuse and lawn clippings. Make holes at intervals a few inches apart in the bag, and turn the contents from time to time. Dig the compost into your soil or use as required when well rotted.

No room for a mini-heap?

● If even a compost bag is too big for your garden, dig a trench about the width and depth of a spade at the back of a flower or vegetable bed. Every evening, add the day's collection of organic kitchen scraps (vegetable matter and eggshells only; no meat) and any lawn clippings to the trench. As each section of trench fills up, cover it with 50mm (2in) of earth and move on to the next section.

The organic matter in the trench will take a few months to decompose but you can plant shallow-rooting crops such as marrows within a few weeks. Wait about six months before planting any root crops, however.

● Another space-saving method is simply to bury small quantities of kitchen scraps, grass cuttings or torn-up newspaper in unused spots of the garden. Worms will slowly distribute the compost as it decays.

What to use for compost

● Any plant-based material – that won't take too long to decompose is suitable – for example, small garden clippings, raked-up leaves and grass cuttings.
● Vegetable waste from the kitchen also works well on a compost heap, as does shredded paper.
● Add a compost activator to speed up the process of decomposition.
● Never put hard pieces of wood on your compost heap. They will take too long to break down.

DO NOT add mouldy or diseased plants to a compost heap. You could spread the infection when you use the compost.

Winter compost Make a special effort to dig in as many kitchen peelings as possible during autumn. They will break down during the winter and you'll be rewarded with rich compost in spring.

A use for weeds Keep a black plastic bag in the corner of the garden for pulled-up weeds. Leave the bag in the sun, but keep it sealed so that rain can't get in, and don't add wet weeds – or if you do, leave the bag open so that the moisture can evaporate. In about six to eight weeks the weeds will bed down to a rich compost. Open the bag and turn the contents from time to time to aerate them.

NATURAL WEED CONTROL

A flower to fight weeds A member of the marigold family can help in the battle against weeds. *Tagetes minuta* produces root secretions which discourage perennial weeds such as couch grass and ground elder as well as some garden pests. The marigold is a half-hardy annual and needs to be started off under glass or indoors, before planting out in late May. You can buy the seed from the Henry Doubleday Research Association (page 324).

Mulching Spread a 75-100mm (3-4in) layer of well-rotted manure, compost or shredded bark under larger plants – not seedlings – in spring to smother weeds. It will help to fertilise the soil and keep in moisture at the same time.

Weeding Getting rid of weeds is less of a chore if you do it regularly. Use a Dutch hoe to cut through weed stems, but don't let the blade go too deep or you may slice into the roots of garden plants – the blade should just skim under the soil surface. For large-scale weeding in an open space, try a garden flame-thrower – bought from a garden centre or hired from a tool-hire shop – but avoid using it near other plants.

Easy weed digger An old-fashioned potato peeler makes an ideal tool for digging individual weeds out of a lawn.

Preparing overgrown ground If you're clearing a weedy patch for cultivation, remove as many weed roots as possible when you dig over the soil. This will weaken weeds by depriving them of stored food reserves.

Getting rid of uprooted weeds Check that the centre of a compost heap is hot before you add weeds to it, or the weeds will survive and you will get a new crop when you spread the compost. If it is cool, add grass clippings, which heat up quickly.

Burn or throw away perennial weeds such as bindweed, docks and ground elder. If you want to add them to a compost heap, dry them out thoroughly in the sun first.

Ground-cover plants to smother weeds Discourage weeds by planting low-growing plants under larger bushes and shrubs. They will eventually close up and strangle any weeds that sprout, but the ground must be clear when you put them in and kept weed-free until they start to spread.

Here are nine effective anti-weed covers:
- *Acaena buchananii*
- Aubrieta
- Snow in summer *(Cerastium tomentosum)* (right, above)
- Wild strawberry
- Ivy
- *Polygonum affine*
- *Sedum spurium*
- Creeping thyme
- Lesser periwinkle *(Vinca minor)* (right, below)

FIGHTING PESTS AND DISEASES WITHOUT POISONS

The first line of defence against garden enemies is to choose healthy plants: ask a garden centre for advice on what does well in your area and which varieties are most resistant to pests and diseases.

The next step is to boost your plants' natural immunity. Help them stay healthy by keeping the ground well-fertilised, weed-free and clear of decaying vegetation. Make sure compost is completely rotted down before using it as a mulch, or it could harbour weeds and diseases. If insects or infections do strike, tackle the problem right away.

Aphids Move into action as soon as you notice aphids in the garden – usually early spring. If left, they will suck the sap from young shoots and buds, distort plant growth, and bring mould and virus diseases. Hosing them off with water is often all that's needed, but if this fails, dowse the affected shoots in tepid soapy water (not detergent, which could harm the plant). Use the hardest jet that will not damage the plant.

Control aphids in a greenhouse or conservatory by introducing natural predators such as the Australian ladybird *Cryptolaemus* or the parasitic wasp *Encarsia formosa*. Contact the Henry Doubleday Research Association or British Organic Farmers (page 324) for information.

Slugs and snails Set jars of beer or milk into the ground to attract slugs and snails which will fall in and be drowned, and if your compost heap is harbouring the pests add some poisonous rhubarb leaves to the pile to drive them away.

It will also help to leave a pile of dry leaves under a hedge to encourage hedgehogs which will soon make a meal of any slugs or snails they find.

Moles To drive moles away without harming them, try burying empty bottles up to their necks in the garden – moles are said to dislike the sound of the wind as it blows across the open tops.

If you get desperate, try ultrasonic vibrators or mole traps (available from garden centres). Alternatively treat the runs with a harmless chemical called ammonium sulphate, which will also see off troublesome cats if you sprinkle it in your garden.

Violet ground beetle   Devil's coach horse   Lacewing   Hoverfly   Ladybird   Ichneumon fly

Insect friends Not all garden insects are pests; some actually do good by devouring the plant attackers. The ones that deserve your protection include ladybirds, hoverflies and lacewings which eat greenfly; the ichneumon fly which attacks caterpillars; devil's coach horses and violet ground beetles which prey on a variety of pests.

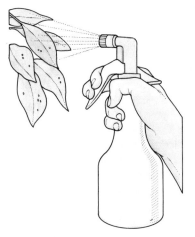

Earwigs If earwigs are a problem, stuff a flowerpot full of dry grass or straw and up-end it on a stick. Earwigs will crawl in at night, and you can burn the contents in the morning to kill them off.

General-purpose insect spray Before you resort to more powerful insecticides, try spraying with a weak solution of washing-up liquid. It's an effective remedy for many common pests.

Caterpillars Spray with the bacterium *Bacillus thuringiensis berliner*, which attacks caterpillars but won't harm other insects. Buy it from a good garden centre or through British Organic Farmers or the Henry Doubleday Research Association (page 324).

GARDEN SAFETY: CHEMICALS

● Mix only as much weedkiller or pesticide as you can use immediately.
● Always follow the instructions on the label exactly.

● Paint a skull and crossbones onto the labels of poisonous chemicals to remind users to be careful.

  Keep all weedkillers and pesticides locked away and out of the reach of children and animals. Don't keep garden chemicals in the kitchen or anywhere near food, and never decant liquid poisons into empty drinks bottles.

● Bring children and pets indoors before you start spraying, and keep them out of the garden for the time advised on the label. Do not let them eat or touch plants that have been sprayed.
● Don't spray the garden on a windy day. The spray will drift over plants you're not aiming at, and you'll be more likely to inhale it.
● Protect your hands with rubber gloves or gardening gloves when handling chemicals, and wear goggles or sunglasses when spraying to make sure that your eyes are shielded.
● Rinse spray containers thoroughly after use, or use them only for that purpose, not for misting or applying spray fertiliser.
● Do not pour leftover sprays into drains, streams, ponds or ditches. Dispose of them over as wide an area of soil as possible.
● Wash any sprayed fruit and vegetables before eating them.

CHEMICAL AND GREEN WAYS WITH PESTS

PROBLEM	CHEMICAL TREATMENT	GREEN ALTERNATIVE
Blackfly	Malathion; pirimi-carb; dimethoate; fenitrothion; permethrin	Apply derris or pyrethrum. Sow broad beans in autumn. Spray in late spring with garlic, stinging nettles or soap in water; or hose off the pests with water.
Black spot	Captan; benomyl; thiophanate-methyl	Remove seriously affected leaves from the plant and burn them. Also collect and burn any infected fallen leaves.
Botrytis	Benomyl; thiophanate-methyl	Remove affected parts; avoid crowding plants; keep ground free of weeds.
Cabbage root fly	Bromophos; trichlorphon	Cut cardboard or felt circles with a slit in the middle for the stem. Push down over plants to prevent grubs reaching the roots.
Cabbage white caterpillars	Resmethrin; mala-thion	Remove caterpillars by hand; dust with derris or pyrethrum.
Capsid bugs (holes in leaves)	Dimethoate; mala-thion; fenitrothion	Spray with pyrethrum or derris. Keep garden tidy and clear away garden debris and rubbish.
Carrot fly	Bromophos; chlorpyrifos	Sow carrots late in the season and destroy uprooted seedlings after thinning out. Sprinkle powdered garlic round plants.

CHEMICAL AND GREEN WAYS WITH PESTS (cont)

PROBLEM	CHEMICAL TREATMENT	GREEN ALTERNATIVE
Codling moth	Use fenitrothion or permethrin after flowering	Destroy affected fruit. Tie strips of corrugated cardboard or sacking round the trunks in July for caterpillars to pupate in. Remove and destroy before the next spring.
Cutworms (look for seedling stems eaten through at ground level)	Bromophos; chlorpyrifos	Keep weeds under control. Dig over soil regularly to expose caterpillars to birds and weather, especially during winter.
Eelworm	No safe chemical treatments available for home use	Try planting *Tagetes minuta* (see *A flower to fight weeds*, page 303) with affected crop.
Flea beetles (young brassica leaves pitted with small round holes)	Gamma-HCH	Spray with derris or pyrethrum.
Froghoppers (insects inside white froth)	Malathion; pirimiphos-methyl; permethrin	Hose off froth; pick off bugs; spray with derris or pyrethrum.
Greenfly	Dimethoate; formothion; pirimi-carb; pirimiphos-methyl; pyrethrins; fenitrothion; mala-thion	Hose off with water or soapy water. Spray with derris or pyrethrum.

307

CHEMICAL AND GREEN WAYS WITH PESTS (cont)

PROBLEM	CHEMICAL TREATMENT	GREEN ALTERNATIVE
Leatherjackets	Bromophos; chlorpyrifos	Hoe the ground often to expose grubs for birds.
Mildew	Benomyl; triforine	Remove and burn badly affected leaves. Select mildew-resistant varieties.
Onion fly	Dust the soil with bromophos or gamma-HCH before sowing	Hoe or dig over soil thoroughly during winter to disturb pupae.
Pea moth	Fenitrothion; permethrin	Plant early peas in November or February and avoid sowing them in March and April. Later sowings will be safe too.
Raspberry beetle	Fenitrothion; permethrin	Spray with soft soap solution or apply derris or pyrethrum as flowers open.
Red spider	Dicofol; dimethoate	Keep humidity level high in the greenhouse. Apply derris or release insect predator *Phytoseiulus persimilis* into greenhouse. Contact Royal Horticultural Society (page 324) for suppliers' names.
Scale insects	Malathion; pirimiphos-methyl; dimethoate	Wipe scales off leaves and stem with a soft rag or sponge dipped in soapy water.

CHEMICAL AND GREEN WAYS WITH PESTS (cont)

PROBLEM	CHEMICAL TREATMENT	GREEN ALTERNATIVE
Thrips	Fenitrothion; malathion; permethrin; pirimiphos-methyl; pyrethrins; dimethoate	Spray with soap solution, pyrethrum or derris.
Whitefly	Permethrin; dimethoate; malathion	Poke garlic cloves into ground around plants, or use natural predators (see *Aphids*, page 304). Apply pyrethrum or derris. Use a sticky insecticidal strip.

PLANT FOES OF COMMON PESTS

Some plants are said to be powerful pest-fighters – although there is no scientific evidence to prove that they do (or don't) work. Plant them in among the troubled crops, or make anti-insect sprays by chopping up about 450g (1lb) of leaves and stems and simmering them in 1 litre (2 pints) of water for 20 minutes. Strain the mixture when cool and add enough cold water to make 3 litres (5 pints) of spray.

PESTS	PLANT FOES
Ants	Tansy, spearmint, pennyroyal
Blackfly	Potatoes
Cabbage white caterpillar	Rosemary, marjoram, thyme, sage
Carrot fly	Rosemary, sage, wormwood
Cutworms	*Tagetes minuta*
Flea beetles	Mint, wormwood
Greenfly	Garlic
House flies	Tansy
Weevils	Garlic
Woolly aphids	Nasturtiums

WATERING YOUR GARDEN

The best time of day Water your garden in the evening, if possible, so that the moisture has time to soak well into the soil before it begins to evaporate in the sun's heat.

Winter watering Don't forget to water evergreen shrubs such as holly, laurel and rhododendrons during winter if there is a long dry spell. Container plants will also need occasional watering.

Give it a good soak Water garden plants heavily from time to time rather than giving them frequent light sprinklings. If only the top of the soil gets wet, the roots will grow towards the surface, where they will eventually shrivel and die. For best effects, water needs to penetrate at least 230mm (9in) into the ground. Don't worry about over-watering – it's almost impossible to flood plants growing in the ground if the weather's dry.

Mulching A layer of grass clippings makes a good summer mulch to keep the soil moist. It also discourages weeds, provided that you cut the grass before it runs to seed.

GARDEN COST-CUTTERS

Plant labels Save wooden ice cream spatulas and old plastic knives to use as garden labels. Write on them with ball-point pen or a waterproof marker.

Kneeling pad An old hot water bottle filled sparingly with foam rubber chips is a handy knee rest for low gardening jobs. A furry cover makes it even more comfortable.

PROTECTION FROM ICE AND SNOW

Growing tips If tender buds or shoots become frozen, thaw them out slowly by spraying with cold water before the sun shines on them. If you leave them, they may get scorched.

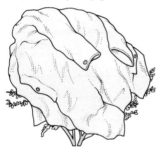

Tender plants Even quite late in spring, frost can do serious damage. Listen to weather forecasts and protect delicate plants with newspaper or old clothes on cold nights.

Conifers If snow is forecast, tie the branches of small conifers tightly to the trunk with string to prevent them breaking under the weight of snow. Do not leave them tied up for more than a day or two.

Seedlings Old car tyres make good temporary cold frames for new seedlings, if you don't mind the way they look. Sow the seeds inside the tyre and place a piece of glass or clear plastic on top. The rubber absorbs heat during the day and radiates it out again at night.

GARDEN TOOLS

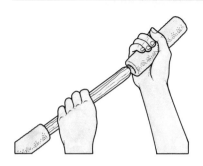

No more blisters If you find the handles of tools and machines such as mowers and shears uncomfortable to hold, consider buying foam bicycle handlebar grips from a cycle shop.

Slide the grips on over the tool handles. If they are difficult to push on, try smearing liquid soap over the handles first.

Choosing tools If you can afford it, buy stainless-steel tools. They will last a lifetime, and you'll find them easier to clean as soil doesn't stick to the shiny surface. Always pick up tools and try them out for balance before you buy. Many people find special 'lightweight' tools more comfortable to use – and easier on their backs.

Preventing rust Keep metal tools free from rust by greasing them with cooking or machine oil after you've cleaned them for winter storage.

HOW TO MAKE A GARDEN POOL

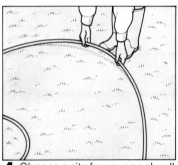

1 Choose a site for your pool well away from overhanging trees and shrubs which could make it difficult to keep the water clear of fallen leaves in autumn.

Once you have decided on the spot, mark out the perimeter on the ground. Use rope or a hose to mark out irregular shapes or curves (string won't stay in shape).

2 Dig out the pond hole, sloping the sides towards the centre at an angle of about 20 degrees from the vertical. This stops the sides from caving in, and allows ice to expand upwards if the surface freezes in winter. Make a ledge for marginal plants about 230mm (9in) down from the top and about 230mm wide.

3 Use a spirit level on a plank to check that opposite sides of the pond are level. Place the plank across the length and the width of the hole. If necessary, build up one side until the edges are level – if you don't, the pool lining will show on one side.

4 Line the hole with pieces of old carpeting, grass turves laid face down or a coating of damp sand to cover any sharp stones.

5 Line the pond with a flexible butyl liner. Plastic sheeting can also be used, but it will deteriorate and start to leak after a while – usually about 18 months to two years. Always use a double thickness if you do choose plastic. To calculate the size of lining you need, add double the depth of the pool to both the length and the width measurements. For example, a pool which is 0.5m (1½ft) deep, 2.7m (9ft) long and 1.8m (6ft) wide, needs a lining sheet 3.7m (12ft) long and 2.7m (9ft) wide.

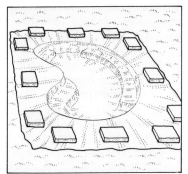 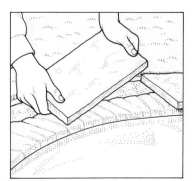

6 When you have fitted the flexible butyl lining into the hole, place heavy stones on the edges around the top to weight the lining down and keep it in place. Pleat surplus lining into neat folds at the corners of the pool.

7 Fill the pond with water and trim the sheeting around the edges so that it spreads only about 100mm (4in) from the water's edge. Fold it back along the ground and cover with a layer of soil. Lay paving stones around the edge.

8 Add water plants in containers. This keeps the water cleaner than having pockets of soil loose on the bottom, and you can move the plants around until you're happy with the effect. Use heavy clay soil in the containers rather than sandy soil or peat which may float away, and cover the soil in each container with pebbles.

Plants to grow in a pool

Iris kaempferi _____

_____ *Iris pseudacorus*

Water violet

Water soldier

Water lilies

Marsh marigold

For oxygen and clean water Canadian pondweed and water milfoil grow almost entirely underwater and help to keep down algae and aerate the water for fish.

Marginal plants Marsh marigolds, irises, ranunculus and water mint will grow in about 150mm (6in) of soil just under the water surface.

Surface growers Try to cover at least half the surface of your pool with greenery to shade the water and stop algae from forming.

Water lilies are easy to grow and decorative, but it's important to choose the right size for your pool. Try 'Gladstoniana' for a large pool, or 'Ellisiana' or 'Chromatella' for a medium pool. For tiny patio pools, choose a miniature variety – look for the word *pygmaea* in the name. These can grow in water as shallow as 100-250mm (4-10in), and will only spread to about 300mm x 300mm (1ft x 1ft).

● If a water lily is too short to reach the surface, cut off the leaves before placing the plant in position on the bottom of the pond. As new leaves grow they will soon find the right level.

Keeping a pool clean

Changing the water If you need to empty the pool for cleaning, or to repair a hole, fill a number of buckets or other containers with fresh water. If you have fish, allow the water to stand until it is the same temperature as the pond water. Transfer fish and plants from the pool to the containers, keeping deep-water and surface-growing plants separate. Clean the lining without using chemicals and rinse well. Patch up any holes with a butyl repair kit.

Removing fallen leaves Skim fallen leaves out of your pond with a child's shrimping net so that they don't rot and contaminate the water. If you're going away for any length of time, stretch fruit cage netting over the pond.

A GARDEN FULL OF FLOWERS

Buying seedlings in trays Unless you have a greenhouse or a conservatory which gets plenty of light, don't buy trays of half-hardy seedlings before the danger of frost is passed and you're ready to put them into the ground. If you leave the seedlings in their trays on an ordinary windowsill (unless it is south or west facing) they will become thin and spindly as they struggle to reach the light.

Plants for windy places Choose small plants – or dwarf versions of taller flowers such as golden rod – for windy beds. Even sunflowers come in the short 'Sunspots' variety.

A longer flowering season Sow flower seed at ten-day or two-week intervals rather than all at once, and plant out the seedlings at similar intervals to prolong the season. When the plants begin to flower, remove dead heads regularly to encourage new blooms.

Tall flowers for wall cover Climbing plants are an effective way of disguising an unattractive wall or fence but they seldom cover the whole surface. If yours have left exposed sections, plant a row of tall flowers in front of the climbers to act as a screen – delphiniums, foxtail lilies, sunflowers, *Crambe cordifolia* and coneflowers are some of the tallest.

Sowing annuals To make sure you don't mistake your annual seedlings for weeds when they germinate, sow them in blocks instead of rows and, if necessary, mark out the boundaries of the area with twigs and cotton twine to remind you where they are.

TEST YOUR SOIL-TYPE

To find out the composition of your garden soil, try this simple test. Fill a litre (2 pint) bottle two-thirds of the way to the top with water and add garden soil until the water level reaches the top of the bottle. Screw on the lid or hold your hand over the top and shake well. Put the bottle down and leave undisturbed for several hours.

The soil should settle at the bottom in three distinct layers: large sand grains on the bottom, smaller silt particles in the middle and tiny clay particles on top. Organic matter will float on top of the water.

● If the layers are about equal in depth, you have well-balanced, loamy soil ideal for garden plants.

● A thicker bottom layer of sand indicates light soil that needs more organic matter dug in.

● A thick top layer of clay means your soil is heavy and will benefit from digging in both sand and organic matter.

Cutting flowers for the house

How to pick flowers Flowers can be cut at any time of day, but foliage is best cut in the cool of the morning or evening rather than during the heat of the day when it will lose more moisture. Take a bucket of water with you, so that you can put cut flowers into water straight away.

Use secateurs rather than scissors, which may crush the stems and, if possible, leave the flowers standing in tepid water up to their necks for about 12 hours. Before arranging, strip off any leaves that will be below the water line, or they may rot and contaminate the water.

Flowers that can absorb water Begonias, violets, magnolias and gardenias can take in some moisture through their petals. Instead of giving them a long soak after they have been cut, immerse the flowers completely in cold water for a few minutes, then hang them upside-down to drain before arranging in a vase.

To revive wilting flowers Freshen up bought flowers by placing them neck deep in warm water (up to 43°C/110°F) when you get them home, and leave them for six to eight hours. If flowers are wilting in the vase, cut the ends off the stems and dip them in boiling water for a second or two. Plunge the stems all the way up to the flowers in cold water for a couple of hours or overnight to recover.

Delicate flowers Poppies and other fragile plants such as tobacco plants, hellebore and heliotrope will last longer after cutting if you singe the bottom of the stems with a match.

Keeping the stems straight Stop tulip and hyacinth stems from bending by wrapping them tightly in a bunch with wet newspaper after cutting. Leave the wrapped flowers to stand in a little water for about an hour before arranging them.

Hollow-stemmed flowers To prolong the life of dahlias, lupins, delphiniums and other hollow-stemmed blooms, turn the flowers upside-down after cutting and fill the stems with water. Plug the bottoms with cotton wool and arrange as usual.

Woody stems If cut flowers on woody stems, such as roses, begin to droop, crush or split the ends of the stems and dip them briefly into hot water.

If the arrangement is in a glass vase and crushed stalks would show, make a series of slits in the stems instead (right). Make the slits down to 50mm (2in) from the base of the stem and be sure to keep the water topped up in the vase.

Flowering twigs Cut budding twigs of hazel, willow, forsythia or other shrubs and trees at the beginning of spring. Bring them into a warm room and put them in water. They should soon open up and give you an early floral display.

Growing roses

Protection from winter winds If you have large shrub roses growing in exposed positions, cut back their main shoots by about one-third in early winter, before strong winds can rock them and disturb the roots. Do the rest of the pruning as for other shrub roses (page 300).

Miniature roses Don't let their size mislead you into thinking of dwarf roses as indoor plants. They must be grown on a patio or outdoor windowsill, although you can bring them inside when they're in bloom.

New plants from cuttings The easiest way to propagate species roses, rugosa varieties, old roses, ramblers and many floribundas is to take 230mm (9in) cuttings in August or September from the past season's growth. Some hybrid teas are now also propagated in this way.

Take the bottom of the cutting from just below a bud (above left), and the top from just above, and leave on only two leaves at the top of the stem. Dip the bottom of the cutting in hormone rooting powder and push it into the soil (above right) so that only one-third of the stem remains above ground. Leave the cuttings until the following autumn, watering regularly in dry weather. Any that are not going to take will soon look dead.

315

Roses for ground cover If your garden is big enough, try low-growing roses for an attractive ground cover among shrubs and trees. Choose varieties such as 'Pink Bells', 'Smarty' or 'Bonica' that grow no more than 1m (3ft) high, or look in a catalogue for a list of suitable types.

Dead-heading roses Remove spent blooms from your rose bushes regularly to encourage more flowers. Cut the stems back to the first five-leaf formation.

Long-stemmed roses For elegant, long stems remove all the buds but one on each main branch.

Planting tips for roses

● Plant roses only in well-drained soil.
● Dig in plenty of organic matter and fertiliser.
● Plant the rootstock so that the join with the graft is at soil level.
● Firm the ground well around newly planted roses.
● Get rid of weeds by hoeing rather than digging near roses – a spade could disturb the roots and encourage suckers from the rootstock.
● Feed roses well in spring, after pruning.
● Spray regularly against black spot, mildew and aphids.
● Cut off any shoots that begin to grow from the rootstock rather than above the graft. They are usually easy to recognise because they tend to have seven leaflets on each leaf rather than five.

What the names mean

Hybrid tea (or large-flowered) roses The flower arranger's favourite. Large blossoms appear on one or sometimes a few stems. Ideal for growing in rose beds.

Floribundas (or cluster-flowered roses) Flowers grow in clusters on the ends of branched stems. In bloom throughout summer, but frequent dead-heading is needed to keep clusters looking good, and to encourage new blossoms.

Species roses (wild roses) This group includes all naturally occurring varieties and their hybrids. Usually grown for scented blossoms, attractive foliage and bright red fruits.

Old roses Shrubby plants developed long before modern varieties and grown for their large, many-petalled flowers and strong scent. Old roses tend to have a shorter flowering season, and some types are vulnerable to black spot and mildew.

Modern shrub roses This is a very diverse group. Most varieties are hybrids between wild roses and old roses, and many have large, fragrant flowers. Plant shrub roses where they'll have plenty of room to grow in their own way.

Climbing roses These varieties flower on the current season's growth and need to be grown against a wall or a trellis where they can build up a framework of branches.

Ramblers The traditional cottage-garden rose, which produces sprays of small, many-petalled flowers on the previous season's growth. Every year, after flowering, remove most of the stems that have flowered and tie in the new long shoots that will blossom next summer. May be prone to mildew.

Miniature roses Small, bushy plants suitable for pots, raised beds or borders. Flowers are usually like small hybrid teas or floribundas.

CHOOSING ROSE VARIETIES

Roses for fragrance
- 'Ena Harkness': red hybrid tea.
- 'Fragrant Cloud': coral-red hybrid tea.
- 'Just Joey': copper-orange hybrid tea.
- 'Margaret Merril': pink-flushed white floribunda.
- 'Elizabeth of Glamis': salmon-pink floribunda.

Easy-to-grow varieties
- 'Peace': yellowish-pink hybrid tea.
- 'Silver Jubilee': silvery-pink hybrid tea.
- 'Wendy Cussons': cerise hybrid tea.
- 'Iceberg': white floribunda or climber.
- 'Queen Elizabeth': silvery-pink floribunda.
- 'Evelyn Fison': red floribunda.

Patio pot roses
- 'Marlena': crimson; grows 600-750mm (2-2½ft).
- 'Peek-a-Boo': apricot; grows 450-600mm (18in-2ft).
- 'Topsi': scarlet; grows 450-600mm (18in-2ft).
- 'Anna Ford': orange-red; grows 600-750mm (2-2½ft).
- 'Gentle Touch': salmon-pink; grows to 600mm (2ft).

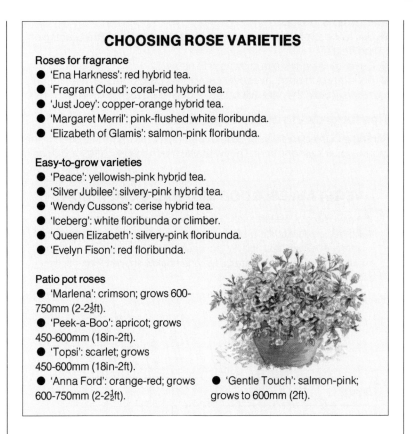

IN THE VEGETABLE PATCH

Feeding the soil Vegetables won't do well in poor soil, so dig in plenty of rotted manure or compost during the winter. Rich soil also holds more moisture and encourages worms which aerate the ground.

First crops If you're planting a new vegetable patch and the soil needs breaking up, start with a crop of potatoes or Jerusalem artichokes. Both plants will help to form a fine tilth for the next season.

Vegetable patch too small? Transfer more decorative, edible plants to a flowerbed. Herbs will not look out of place; nor will curly or red-leaved lettuces. Try chives and the feathery leaves of carrots for edging a floral display, or runner beans instead of sweet peas in a herbaceous border.

Watering All vegetables need plenty of water when they are in flower and while the first fruits are forming. Tomatoes, runner beans and celery get particularly thirsty.

Space saver Sow fast salad crops such as radishes, small lettuces and spring onions between rows of slow-growing root vegetables. The salads will be ready to harvest before the root vegetables take over.

Crop rotation For healthy crops and high yields, don't grow vegetables of the same type in the same place for two consecutive seasons. There are four main categories of vegetables – cabbages and root crops; peas and beans; the onion, leek and garlic family; potatoes and tomatoes – and all do better in a new spot each year. The ideal arrangement is to divide your vegetable plot into four and rotate your crops so that they don't grow in the same spot until four years later.

When frost is forecast
● Use a hoe to pile soil gently around potatoes to protect the plants from spring frosts.
● Cover globe artichoke crowns with straw.
● Bend surrounding leaves over cauliflower curds that are near maturity (don't do it while they are still small – it may stunt their growth).

Tips for growing better vegetables

Parsnips Don't harvest your crop of parsnips until they have been in the ground for at least one frost. They will taste much sweeter after a cold spell.

VEGETABLES: GOOD AND BAD COMPANIONS

Some people believe that certain vegetables do particularly well together, while others prefer to be kept apart. There is no hard-and-fast scientific evidence that this is the case, but if you want to conduct experiments in your own garden, the chart below shows which combinations to try and which to avoid.

	Beans	Beetroot	Cabbage	Carrots	Celery	Cucumbers	Leeks	Lettuce
BEANS			✕					
BEETROOT								
CABBAGE	✕							
CARROTS								✓
CELERY								
CUCUMBERS								
LEEKS								
LETTUCE			✓					
MARROWS	✓							
ONIONS		✓						
PEAS			✓					
POTATOES						✓		
RADISHES						✓		
SPINACH					✓			
STRAWBERRIES							✓	✓
SWEET CORN						✓		
TOMATOES			✕	✓			✓	

✓ Plants said to grow well together

✕ Plants said to dislike each other

Marrows and melons If cold, wet weather is keeping down insect numbers in spring, you will need to pollinate marrow and melon flowers by hand, or the fruit will drop off the stalk while small.

Pick the male flowers and insert them into the female ones – identified by a small swelling behind the petals. One male flower will fertilise about four female flowers.

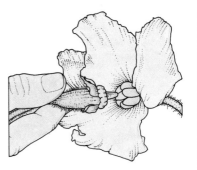

Broad beans Sow the seeds in autumn rather than spring. When they come up – late autumn or early winter – the growing tips will be harder and

VEGETABLES: GOOD AND BAD COMPANIONS (cont)

	Marrows	Onions	Peas	Potatoes	Radishes	Spinach	Strawberries	Sweet corn	Tomatoes
BEANS	✓								
BEETROOT		✓							
CABBAGE			✓						✗
CARROTS									✓
CELERY						✓			
CUCUMBERS				✓	✓		✓		
LEEKS							✓		✓
LETTUCE							✓		
MARROWS			✓				✓		
ONIONS			✗				✓		
PEAS	✓	✗							
POTATOES								✓	✗
RADISHES			✓						
SPINACH							✓		
STRAWBERRIES		✓				✓			
SWEET CORN	✓			✓					
TOMATOES				✗					

✓ Plants said to grow well together

✗ Plants said to dislike each other

stronger, and less attractive to blackfly. When the plants reach the height you want, pinch off the growing tips to discourage the pests. Cook the tips in boiling water for five minutes and serve as a vegetable – they taste rather like asparagus.

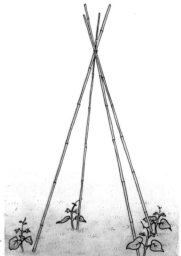

Vegetable beds Divide your vegetable patch into narrow beds about 1-1.5m (3-5ft) wide with pathways in between. You'll be able to reach the middle without treading on the soil and, if necessary, you can easily cover the rows with polythene tunnel cloches.

Runner beans Train runner bean plants up frames of three or four bamboo poles tied together at the top, tepee-fashion. The pods will hang down in the middle for easier picking. For bigger and better pods, spray the flowers with water to help them to set.

Potatoes above ground For easier harvesting, press potato tubers into the ground so that they are only just covered by soil, and place a thick layer of shredded bark or black plastic on top. The new potatoes will grow above the soil, making them much easier to collect.

Bushy varieties of peas can be grown in a similar way, with a mulch of water-soaked newspaper at least ten pages thick. This stops the pods becoming splashed with mud or rotting from contact with damp soil.

Ripening the last tomatoes Green, end-of-season tomatoes can be ripened by putting them in a box with a few ripe fruits. Gasses from the ripe tomatoes will speed up the ripening of the others.

Alternatively, leave the green tomatoes on the plant, pull out the supporting stakes, lay the plants down on a sheet of plastic and cover them with cloches. The last of the green tomatoes will be ripe within about three or four weeks.

Japanese-style tomatoes Tomatoes like a rich soil, especially when producing fruit. One trouble-free way of making sure they don't run out of nourishment is to adopt the Japanese method of planting them closely around a compost heap. They soon send their roots into the heap to feed on the rich nutrients inside.

A second crop of cabbages Don't pull out the stalks when you cut your cabbages. Leave them in the soil and cut a cross on the top. You should reap a harvest of mini-cabbages in the autumn.

Sweet corn Sow corn plants in pots and transfer them to your vegetable plot once they are a few inches tall. Put them in the ground in blocks rather than in rows: they will be better pollinated by the wind, and won't be blown over so easily in a gale.

320

French beans Most gardeners sow French beans straight in the open ground, but if the weather is very cold or wet they may not germinate outdoors, and will do better started off in pots indoors.

Winter greens If you have an unheated greenhouse, use it to grow Chinese leaves, endives and chicory for winter salads. Sow the seeds in August or September.

Thinning carrots Never leave uprooted seedlings lying around when you're thinning the carrot patch. Their smell may attract carrot fly. Destroy unwanted plants immediately by burning, throwing them away or burying deep in the compost heap.

Onions Mature onions will ripen faster if you bend over the tops.
  Growing onions is much quicker and easier if you buy onion sets (small, immature bulbs) ready for planting, rather than trying to grow them from seed.

FRUIT FROM YOUR GARDEN

Small gardens You can grow apples even if you haven't room for large trees. Cordon trees that grow against a wall (right) take up very little space, and they give a good yield as the angle at which the tree grows encourages fruit buds. 'Family trees' are another solution to the space problem: you get three different varieties of apples or pears grafted onto a single root-stock. Or buy the most compact

apple tree of all, 'Ballerina', which produces fruit on a single central stem.
  A few varieties can pollinate themselves, but for most apples you will need to have at least two trees of compatible varieties if you want to be sure of a good harvest.

Rhubarb Remove rhubarb flowers as soon as they appear, or they will weaken the plant. If you want to force an early crop of rhubarb, dig up the roots in autumn and allow them to become frosted. Place the roots in pots of peat or soil in early spring and leave in a dark place – if possible with a little warmth. Forced shoots will soon appear.

Shady spots The best fruit trees for deep shade are the 'Morello' cherry and the 'Victoria' plum. Both will fertilise themselves and they don't need to be planted in pairs.

Early strawberries If you have a strawberry bed and would like a few helpings of early fruit, dig up several plants in September and put them into pots. Let them spend the winter outdoors, but bring the pots into a greenhouse or conservatory in spring, and they will give you fruit a few weeks before the outdoor plants.

Weed-free strawberry bed To smother weeds, lay strips of plastic sheeting on the ground before planting a new strawberry bed. Cut slits or crosses in the plastic through which you can put in the plants. If your strawberry plants are already established, just spread plastic sheeting around them.

GARDEN SAFETY: POISONOUS PLANTS

Avoid these plants in gardens where children play or where pets are free to wander. All are poisonous, and many have tempting, brightly coloured berries or flowers.

- Box
- Columbine
- Daphne
- Foxglove
- Hellebore
- Honeysuckle
- Ivy
- Laburnum
- Monkshood
- Privet
- Spindle tree

NOTE Spring bulbs such as daffodil, narcissus, amaryllis and hyacinth look like onions but can be harmful if eaten. Make sure they're clearly labelled and kept out of reach of children.

Mixing fruit and flowers Rhubarb, artichokes and carrots make attractive foliage plants for growing in an ornamental bed and chives form a decorative edging.

Strawberries are an excellent ground cover for growing under shrubs – although picking is more difficult.

EIGHT EASY-TO-GROW HERBS

- Basil: grow basil in a warm, sunny spot with good drainage.
- Bay: needs plenty of sun and well-drained soil.
- Chives: edge flowerbeds with chives, or grow them in a clump.
- Marjoram: plant it in a sunny spot, or grow in a pot on a windowsill which receives plenty of light.
- Mint: grow peppermint or spearmint for the kitchen in a container to stop it taking over where it's not wanted. Bury the container in the ground so that it's not visible.
- Rosemary: grow rosemary in a pot until you decide on the best place for it – it won't do well if it has to be moved.
- Sage: grows into an attractive, shrubby bush, given time. Not fussy about growing conditions.
- Thyme: plant it on its own, or use as ground cover. Look for different flavours such as lemon thyme and caraway thyme.

GROWING A HEDGE

Shelter from wind Use a hedge rather than a wall or a fence to shelter an exposed garden from the wind. A solid barrier will create down-draughts on the sheltered side, but a hedge filters the wind. Most hedges will protect an area twice their height: for example, a 3m (10ft) hedge will shield plants up to 6m (20ft) in front of it.

Small gardens Consider a screen of climbing plants on a wire frame instead of a conventional hedge if you're short of space in the garden.

Most hedging plants grow to about 1m (3ft) thick, as compared with the 300mm (1ft) needed for a climber and wire frame.

Hedges are also greedy feeders, absorbing large quantities of water and nutrients, and they cast a dense shadow, which means that other plants won't grow closer than about 1m (3ft) away.

Growing a hedge from cuttings
The easiest and cheapest way to grow a hedge if you don't mind a wait is to take 230mm (9in) hardwood cuttings in October from shrubs such as berberis, privet or philadelphus. Make the bottom cut just below a bud and the top just above one. Trim off any leaves. Dig a trench and put in the cuttings to half their length. Fill in the trench and water well. After a year, replant the cuttings that have taken.

Pet-proof hedging If you want to keep out neighbourhood cats and dogs or keep your own pets in, try a hedge of rugosa roses which grow into a dense, thorny thicket. Hawthorn, holly and berberis also make good animal barriers.

Speedy screening Try Leyland cypress if you want a hedge in a hurry. Buy plants as young as possible, before the roots have grown into a tangled mass in the container. You can buy trees up to about 2.5m (8ft) tall, but the larger trees can be difficult to establish. Once the hedge begins to grow, clip the top regularly to maintain a bushy appearance.
● Leyland cypress is not suitable for exposed spots, as the roots don't grip the soil very firmly.

Rejuvenating an older hedge If a long-established hedge has become straggly and thin at the bottom, cut it back severely in spring to where the thick growth begins. Then trim the sides of the hedge to encourage new shoots at the base.

Hedge trimming Trim fast-growing conifer hedges such as Leyland cypress twice a year, in late July and in early October. Most other evergreen hedges should be trimmed in spring and again after flowering if necessary; however, privet usually needs to be clipped several times a year. Hedges such as beech, hornbeam and hazel that shed their leaves in winter need only one clipping in August.

GARDEN SAFETY: HEDGE TRIMMING

If you find yourself worrying about keeping the electric cord out of the way when using hedge trimmers, remove the socket on the end of your extension cord and slip a 1m (3ft) length of hosepiping over it. Replace the socket and fix the hosepiping to it with insulating tape. The stiff, thick piping will keep the cord well away from the teeth of the trimmer.

CHOOSING GARDEN FURNITURE

Wood

● Consider wood if you have a large garden and won't move the furniture often. The weight and bulkiness may be impractical for a smaller patch.
● Hardwoods such as teak and mahogany can stay outside all year round. Pine and other softwoods need to be brought in when it's wet.
● Avoid any wooden furniture which has been coated with polyurethane varnish. It will soon peel off.
● Check that joints are well made and do not 'give' when rocked.
● Make sure metal fittings are stainless steel or brass, which won't rust.
● Feed hardwood furniture with teak oil once a year in early spring. Protect metal fittings with regular oiling.

Metal

● Metal looks more delicate than wood, but good quality chairs and tables are heavy, so it's not suitable for frequent moving.
● Buy heavyweight cast iron or cast aluminium if you want it to stand outside all year round, and keep it well painted.
● If you go for lighter metals, look for furniture that is well made and strong enough to stay stable without twisting on an uneven surface.
● Try sitting in a metal chair for a while before making your decision. Some designs can become uncomfortable.

Synthetic materials

● Avoid cheaper plastics which may crack after a year or two.
● Both glass fibre and plastic are light enough to move easily, but glass fibre is heavier and won't blow over so easily.
● Be prepared to wash plastic furniture frequently, as it attracts dust.
● Check for hairline cracks or moulding faults that might break under a heavy weight.

Cane and rattan

● Cane and rattan are light and attractive, but need to be stored indoors for protection from sun and rain.
● Vacuum frequently when stored indoors, as dust rapidly builds up on cane and rattan furniture.

Useful addresses

British Organic Farmers
86 Colston Street
Bristol BS1 5BB.
Tel: 0272 299 6666.
Information and advice on organic gardening. Supplies of natural pest-control species.

Henry Doubleday Research Association
National Centre for Organic Gardening
Ryton Gardens
Ryton on Dunsmore
Coventry CV8 3LG.
Tel: 0203 303517.
Answers written queries to do with organic gardening. Supplies predator insects and bacteria, and seeds of *Tagetes minuta*.

Wye Bugs
Wye College
Ashford
Kent TN25 5AH.
Tel: 0233 812401.
Supplies parasites to control all greenhouse pests.

Royal Horticultural Society
RHS Garden
Wisley
Woking
Surrey GU23 6QB.
Tel: 0483 224234.
Wide range of advice, services and benefits for members.

You & yours

*R*earing young children (and their pets), enjoying holidays together and helping elderly relatives are all part of the pleasure and challenge of family life. Learn how to record the highlights on film – and how always to look your best.

Family life

A ROOM FOR YOUR BABY

Not too far away Keep your baby within earshot at all times, even during the night. In the early days you may prefer to have the cot next to your bed for easier feeding and changing.

Heating Draughtproof the room if necessary and make sure it's adequately heated. Thermostatically controlled electric heaters are best, since they keep up an even heat and are unlikely to get knocked over. Install a wall thermometer and don't let the temperature drop below about 13°C (55°F), or the baby may not be able to keep warm. High temperatures can be just as dangerous, so stay below 27°C (80°F).

Night-time lighting Ideally, nursery night lighting should cause as little disturbance as possible to you and your baby, while still giving you enough light to see what you're doing when you need to change a nappy. A dimmer switch is the best option, but it may be simpler – and cheaper – to install a low-wattage bulb.

Choosing toys The best toys are ones which are washable, safe and recommended for the child's age. Store them in brightly coloured plastic boxes bought from a hardware shop; the boxes are long-lasting and easy to sponge clean.

Doors and windows Fix a hook and eye at the top of the nursery door so that it stays slightly ajar for air to circulate, but keeps out other children and animals. Windows need safety locks as soon as children can get around on their own.

Changing table There's no need to buy a special changing table. Just store the baby's clothes in a small chest of drawers and use the top. For safety, place it up against a wall and build a smooth barrier about 100mm (4in) high onto the front to keep the baby from rolling off. Even with the barrier, never leave the baby unattended.

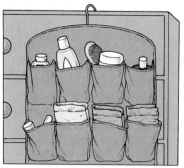

Stimulation Young babies notice more than you might think, so give them plenty to look at. Friezes on nursery walls are great favourites, as are hanging mobiles – but be sure to hang them out of reach. Avoid cot toys which could get tangled up with the baby.

Changing equipment Keep nappies, wipes and other changing items close to wherever you change the baby, but out of reach of other children. A hanging plastic shoe container makes a handy storage rack, and it's easy to attach to the wall.

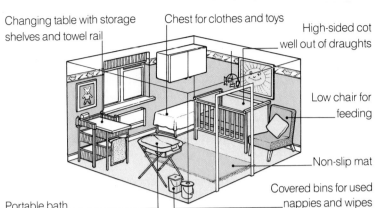

Changing table with storage shelves and towel rail

Chest for clothes and toys

High-sided cot well out of draughts

Low chair for feeding

Non-slip mat

Covered bins for used nappies and wipes

Portable bath

Planning a nursery Make room in your nursery for a changing table or improvised chest of drawers (see *Changing table*, opposite page), a portable bath, covered bins for used nappies and wipes, a low chair for comfortable feeding, and a high-sided cot.

COPING WITH BATH TIME

If it's a battle Cold may be adding to the baby's discomfort, so heat the bathroom first or, if it's easier to warm another room, buy a baby bath that you can move about.

Before you begin Lay out the baby's towel, a fresh nappy and clean clothes in a handy spot, along with any powders, creams or other equipment you'll be using. An effective after-bath routine should not give the baby time to become cold or uncomfortable.

Protecting the floor Bath time will be more fun for you and the baby if you don't have to worry about every splash, so spread something waterproof such as a child's plastic tablecloth over the floor. But be careful not to slip on it if it gets wet.

Meal time Feed the baby after the bath, not before. Newly fed babies may vomit if they get moved around too much.

How often to bath? Every day or every other day is best.

Staying clean between baths 'Topping and tailing' (cleaning face and bottom) is the time-honoured method. Do it at least twice a day, in addition to bathing.

BATHROOM SAFETY

● Burns and scalds from hot water happen in seconds and can be very serious. Always run cold water before hot for a baby or child's bath. Keep up the habit even when children are big enough to use the full-sized bath, and teach them to do this when running their own baths. Water for a baby's bath should feel tepid. Test by dipping your elbow in.
● Never leave a baby or small child alone in the bath, even for a few seconds. Rather ignore the doorbell or the telephone: your child's safety is more important.
● Remember: children can drown in very shallow water.

ALL ABOUT NAPPIES

How often to change? Every two to three hours is usually enough. Do it straight away if you notice that the baby is wet or has passed a motion, or you will have a sore bottom to cope with, too.

Nappy rash For a homemade remedy, try egg white whipped until medium-stiff and applied with cotton wool buds, or a paste made with water and fuller's earth.

At night Put out a clean set of baby clothes before you go to bed so that you won't have to fumble in the dark if a complete change is necessary in the middle of the night.

BATHING AND CHANGING EQUIPMENT

Baby bath Don't use a very big bath to start with, or a small baby may feel insecure and start to fret. Height is another important consideration: baths on stands may be more comfortable for you, but they also take up extra space and need to be very stable. Cheaper, space-saving designs include baths which can be secured to the bottom of an adult bath by means of suction feet, or which are supported on the side of the bigger bath by rods.

Alternatively, just buy a plastic baby bath (right) which can rest on top of the changing table, inside a full-size bath or on the floor.

Tiny babies (up to one month old) can even be washed in a hand basin. Hold the baby securely, making sure its head is supported at all times, and be very careful to avoid knocks. Always wrap a facecloth over the hot tap.

Changing box Save money by storing changing equipment such as wipes, creams, powders and nappies in plastic stacking boxes bought from a hardware shop, rather than paying extra for a specially designed kit.

Changing mat A mat is useful for changing nappies in public cloakrooms or where there isn't an easily accessible clean surface. Many also fold up into handy containers for nappy-changing items for day trips.

Bath-time kit Buy a large, soft towel with a hood to keep your baby warm and cosy after its bath. Other useful extras for the bathroom include blunt-edged scissors, cotton wool, cotton wool buds, a facecloth or sponge, a baby's hairbrush and nappy cream.

'Topping and tailing' equipment You'll need a bowl with two sections and either two different-coloured facecloths or a good supply of cotton wool. Always use the same facecloth and section of the bowl (label it to be sure) for face-washing and the others for bottom-washing.

FABRIC OR DISPOSABLE NAPPIES?

Both types of nappies have advantages and disadvantages. Here are some guidelines to help you decide which is best for your baby:

Disposable nappies

● The nappies themselves cost more to buy, but it often works out that there's not much difference overall once you've taken washing time and costs into consideration.

● You can save by buying disposables in bulk, and some high street shops will deliver free if getting them home is a problem. Local newspapers also sometimes carry advertisements for delivery services.

● Many makes come in both girls' and boys' styles for a better fit.

● If one brand leaks consistently, try another. Some manufacturers now make disposable nappies with elasticated legs to prevent leaks, and you should be able to find a style that suits your baby.

● Babies often need more absorbent nappies to cope with the extra urine when they start sleeping through the night.

● If you can't find one that's thick enough, try lining disposable nappies with special baby pad nappies available from chemists.

● Don't flush disposable nappies down the lavatory, whatever the instructions on the pack say. Blockages can be expensive to clear – and embarrassing if they're in someone else's house.

● Store packs of nappies out of reach of toddlers, in case they climb on them or suffocate on the plastic wrappers.

Fabric nappies

● Later children can use the same nappies if you care for them well, and this will cut the long-term cost considerably.

● You need at least 24 nappies (most packs contain 12), to allow time for washing, sterilising and drying.

● Buy nappy liners to go inside fabric nappies. They can be flushed down the lavatory, with their contents, and they reduce the amount of soiling on the nappy.

● Use special nappy pins and not ordinary safety pins, which may come undone and prick the baby.

● Be sure you have at least six pairs of plastic pants to fit over nappies and reduce leaking. Keep a check on the fit and buy new pants in larger sizes as your baby grows – tight leg elastic could be very uncomfortable for your baby.

● To clean soiled fabric nappies, first get rid of faeces into the lavatory, then soak the nappies in a large bucket containing a sterilising solution. Always keep a lid on the bucket, and place it out of reach of children. Wring out nappies after soaking, and wash in hot water.

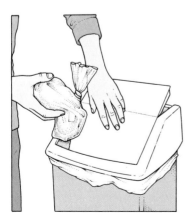

● If you use disposable nappies, get into the habit of saving small plastic bags for getting rid of nappies that have been soiled. Knot the bags tightly before placing them in the rubbish bin. More expensive versions of the same thing are the scented plastic nappy bags sold by chemists and some supermarkets. Make sure all plastic bags are kept away from children.

HOW TO PUT ON A KITE NAPPY

Kite nappies are quick and easy to fold, and they are suitable for babies of all ages, as you can adjust the length to fit any size. To secure the nappy, you will need two nappy pins. Prevent accidents by keeping the pins closed until you are ready to use them.

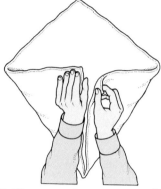

1 Place a clean nappy diagonally in front of you, so that it's in a diamond shape. Fold in the two sides to meet at the centre, making a kite.

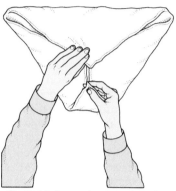

2 Fold down the top triangle of fabric and bring up the bottom point to meet it, adjusting the length to suit your baby. Place a disposable liner on top of the nappy.

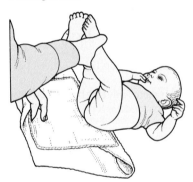

3 Slide the nappy under the baby so that the wide end is at waist level.

4 Bring the bottom flap up between the baby's legs, gathering the fabric around the legs so there are no large gaps. Adjust the front so that the folded edge comes up to waist level.

5 Bring the back right corner of the nappy round to the front and tuck it under the front flap on the right. The nappy should fit snugly without feeling tight.

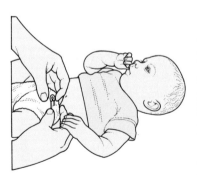

6 Pin the corners together through all the layers. Keep your hand under the nappy, and push the pin in horizontally to prevent pricks. Repeat on the left.

FEEDING YOUR BABY

Both breast and bottle feeding have advantages and drawbacks, and whichever you opt for – or if it turns out to be a compromise – the considerations in the box below may help you to decide.

BREAST OR BOTTLE: WHICH IS BEST?

Breast pros:
- Nature's intended baby food.
- Contains all nutrients in the right proportions.
- Easily digested.
- Contains antibodies which protect the baby from illness.
- Free.
- Requires no preparation.
- Helps mother regain figure.
- Cleaner nappies.

Breast cons:
- Only mother can feed.
- Limits mother's activities.
- Difficult in public.
- Can take time to get going.

Other points:
- Some women worry that they may not produce enough milk, but doctors say that this is actually a very rare problem.
- Not possible if mother is taking certain drugs.

Bottle pros:
- Father and other relatives can get involved.
- Frees mother from sole responsibility.
- Can do it anywhere.
- Can tell exactly how much milk baby is getting.

Bottle cons:
- Cost of equipment and feed.
- Takes time and effort to prepare.
- No natural antibodies.
- Easier to over-feed.

Other points
- Can take longer to digest.

Tips for better breastfeeding

Keeping up the supply The more you feed, the more milk you'll produce. If you can't fit in a feed every time, expressing your milk will have the same effect, and you can still use it in the baby's bottle. It will also help to take regular rests and eat a good, sustaining diet. Nursing mothers need between 2500 and 3000 Calories a day.

Baby not thriving? If you're worried that your baby is underweight or not doing well, ask the health visitor or midwife to weigh it and advise you.

Sore nipples To prevent discomfort, keep your nipples clean and dry and let air circulate freely around them as much as possible. Try sleeping topless at night, with a towel underneath in case you leak. Soothing creams are available from chemists and can also help, as can rubbing on a small amount of breast milk and letting it dry. Most importantly, make sure you're feeding the baby properly: inaccurate 'latching on' is responsible for a lot of discomfort.

Comfortable clothing Well-fitting bras that give good support are essential if you're breastfeeding, and front-fastening tops will make the job a lot easier, too. Buy only one or two bras before giving birth as your size may alter afterwards, and choose cotton fabrics to reduce perspiration. See page 449 for finding your bra size.

Warning signs See a doctor if you get sudden breast pains or flu-like symptoms. It could mean you have mastitis, an infection of the milk ducts.

How to burp a baby Make your baby more comfortable after a feed by helping it to burp up any air that's been swallowed along with the milk. Lay the baby flat on its back on your knee for a few seconds. Then sit it upright or support it against your chest and stroke gently up the back. Alternatively, sit the baby on your knee and support its chin with your right hand while stroking up its back with your left.

Regurgitation after a feed 'Possetting', or bringing up a little milk after feeding, is quite normal, but if you are worried about the amount or frequency, ask your doctor's advice.

Know the lie of the land Make a point of remembering where the mother and baby rooms are in the shops and centres that you use most.

Missing a feed If you're leaving the baby with someone else and won't be there for the next feed, express some breast milk before you go and put it into a bottle for the baby sitter to use. The bottle should be stored in the fridge and reheated by standing it in a pan of hot – not boiling – water until it reaches blood temperature. Don't stay away too long for the first time, though: some babies won't take a bottle if they're used to the breast.

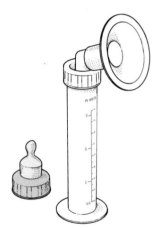 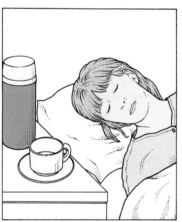

Expressing machine Buy an expressing machine so that you can store extra milk for future use (opposite page). Sterilise the pump after use in a sterilising unit (opposite page) or with sterilising tablets dissolved in water.

Last feed of the day Give your baby its last feed just before you go to bed. That way you'll have as much sleep as possible before it's time for the next feed. Prepare a vacuum flask so that you can have a warm drink at the same time.

Not enough milk? Many mothers worry about their milk supply, but in fact it is very unusual not to produce enough to feed your baby properly. However, breastfeeding can take time to get going, so don't be disheartened if your supply seems short in the beginning. Get help from your midwife, health visitor or doctor, or contact a local branch of the National Childbirth Trust (page 337), which has a network of breastfeeding counsellors. They may also be able to help if your milk seems to be drying up after the first few weeks – but even if you have to stop after that, don't worry: any period of breastfeeding, however short, will have done the baby a lot of good and boosted its natural immunity.

Storing extra milk Breast milk will keep for one day in a fridge, and up to three months in a freezer. Use sterilised ice cube trays for freezing, and unfreeze only as much as you need each time. Send for a leaflet on storing breast milk from the National Childbirth Trust.

DO NOT rely on breastfeeding as your only means of contraception. Many women are fertile again long before their babies are weaned.

WHAT YOU NEED TO BOTTLE FEED

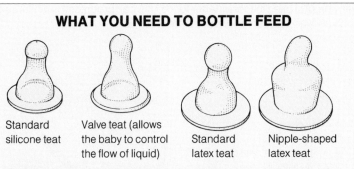

Standard silicone teat

Valve teat (allows the baby to control the flow of liquid)

Standard latex teat

Nipple-shaped latex teat

Bottles and teats Buy at least six of each so that you can get through a day without needing to stop and sterilise feeding equipment. Wide-necked bottles are best for easy cleaning, but experiment with different shapes of teats to find the one that's best for your baby.

Formula milk Not every formula is right for every baby, so be prepared to try out several if necessary. Cow's milk formulas, in particular, can cause problems, especially if there is a family history of allergies. Soya-based milks are usually a good alternative in this case, but ask your health visitor's advice before changing over.

Sterilising unit It isn't essential to have a sterilising unit, but it can save time and trouble. Buy a unit from a chemist and use it to sterilise bottles and teats after every feed. You can also sterilise plastic toys, and some types can take metal objects too, but check first. If you prefer, however, you can simply wash bottles and teats and then boil them, covered, for at least ten minutes in a large pan, or soak them in sterilising fluid – also available from chemists.

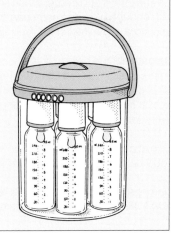

Starting on solids

How to tell when it's time Each baby is different, but most are ready to begin taking solid food some time between three and six months. Starting any earlier could make the baby overweight or encourage allergies by introducing foods its digestive system is not yet developed enough to cope with. Signs that it may be time to start include: still seeming hungry after a milk feed; wanting more feeds than before; starting to wake up during the night after having slept through for a few weeks.

Go slowly Begin by introducing solid food while still giving milk feeds. Start off with solids and then let the baby fill up on milk. If you do it the other way around, the baby will be too full of milk to want anything else. Give just one or two teaspoons of food a day to begin with, and gradually increase the amount according to the baby's appetite.

Starter foods Whatever you give at the beginning should be soft, smooth and easy to swallow. Homemade fruit and vegetable purées such as carrot, apple, banana and potato are ideal, or try a ready-made product such as baby rice. Wheat-based foods such as cereals and rusks used to be advised only after six months, but are now said to be safe for all ages, but go cautiously at first if there is a family history of allergies. Once the baby has got used to these starter foods, you can progress to meat purées such as liver, chicken and carefully filleted fish.

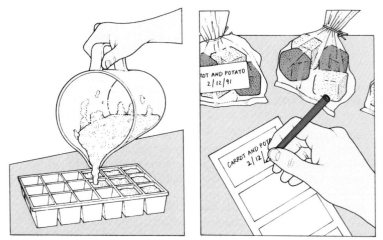

Make your own baby food It's quick, easy and economical to prepare baby food at home, even if you're busy. Simply purée the food, pour into ice cube trays and freeze. When solid, transfer the blocks to plastic bags, with enough blocks in each bag for one meal. Label and date each bag, and store in the freezer until required.

Be patient Don't worry if your baby rejects solid food at first: it's a very different texture to get used to after nothing but milk. And never make an issue of the matter, or you could end up with a fussy eater. Simply go back to milk feeds for a day or two and then try again. All babies learn to eat eventually, in their own way.

One at a time Introduce new foods gradually and one by one. That way, you'll be able to detect any allergies right from the start.

Dairy products Most babies are ready for milder dairy products such as cow's milk, yoghurt and cottage cheese at about six or eight months.

Firmer textures Between about six and eight months you can start giving slightly lumpier food by mashing rather than puréeing, or by buying prepared baby foods of a firmer consistency – check jars for grading.

Cook once – for everyone You don't have to prepare separate meals for your baby. Just cook your own food without seasonings, then remove a portion for the baby and purée it with some of the cooking liquid. Afterwards you can season the rest of the food.

If you're using the oven, you could wrap a few pieces of meat, fish or vegetables in aluminium foil and bake them alongside the family roast or main meal. When they are done, purée or chop finely for the baby.

Likes and dislikes Babies have their own tastes, just like adults. So make allowances if they prefer some foods and reject others.

Coming off milk As the baby takes in more solids, gradually decrease the amount of milk you give and, ideally, save it for the end of the meals. You can carry on with smaller breast or bottle feeds until you feel ready to stop – before 18 months for most mothers. Many babies still find this comforting even when they're well used to solids.

Learning to drink When the baby is about seven months old, buy it a training cup with a lid and spout. A good design should allow liquid to flow freely from the holes in the spout. Start off by giving the empty cup to the baby to play with at

mealtimes. Once it's become familiar, wrap the baby in a large overall and help it to take a small sip from the cup. Most babies splutter at first, but as they slowly get used to it, they relish the independence the cup gives.

DO NOT leave a baby on a table in a baby seat. The movements of the baby could bounce the chair over the edge of the table.

Foods that can cause problems
● Cow's milk and citrus fruits can cause allergies in the first six months.
● Eggs may be unsafe before six months. After that, try mashing or adding eggs to a purée, but always cook them first until both white and yolk are set solid.
● Nuts can choke small children. Give them only to over-fives.
● Sweet foods are best kept for special times. Also avoid putting sugary drinks in children's bottles.
● Salt is not good for children's kidneys, and if you don't add it youngsters won't acquire the taste.
● Honey has been linked with botulism food poisoning in babies, but is thought to be safe after nine months.

Teaching a baby to take solid food

1 Prepare a small amount of a suitable fruit or vegetable purée or a ready-made baby food. Add a little cool, boiled water if the consistency seems too thick to swallow easily.

2 Sterilise a plastic feeding bowl and two plastic spoons. Put a large bib with sleeves onto the baby, or a cut-off old shirt, to protect its clothes; then place plastic sheeting or a plastic tablecloth on the ground so that spills can easily be mopped up.

3 Seat the baby in a familiar highchair or partially reclining baby seat. Easy cleaning should be a priority, whatever arrangement you use – metal chairs are often better from this point of view than wooden ones.

4 Give one of the plastic spoons to the baby to play with, and make this a regular feature of mealtimes. Eating will seem more fun and you'll be encouraging independence for later on.

5 Using your finger or the other plastic spoon, scoop up a tiny portion of food and moisten the baby's lips with it. Then encourage the baby to take the food into its mouth. If you're successful, follow up with another morsel or two, and then finish with a normal breast or bottle feed.

COPING WITH CRYING

A screaming baby can be most upsetting. Keep calm and your attitude may rub off, but never leave a baby to cry for long or it could become insecure and hysterical.

Nine reasons a baby cries

Hunger or thirst Even if a baby has been fed recently, it may still want more. Or it may be thirsty. If the weather is hot or your house is warm, try cool, boiled water.

Heat or cold Are the baby's clothes right for the weather?

Wet nappy Check to see if it's time for a change.

Tiredness Put the baby to bed or rock it to sleep in your arms.

In need of comfort Try breastfeeding or talking with eye contact.

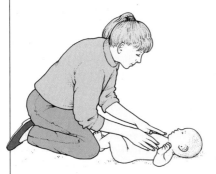

Irritable mood Sing to your baby and rock it gently in your arms. Take it for a ride in the car, or out for a walk in a pram or baby sling. If it's still fractious, try a gentle massage with baby lotion, or turn on a vacuum cleaner, radio or hairdryer: background noise often sends a baby to sleep within minutes. Swaddling the baby in a shawl may also help.

Colic Regular evening crying could be a sign of colic, which is sometimes caused by wind. Burp the baby by placing it stomach down on your knee while stroking up the back towards the head. Give warm, boiled water in a bottle to help bring up wind. Keep a record of your diet if you are breastfeeding, or of food given to the baby if not. It may be that a particular ingredient is causing the trouble. If problems persist, see your doctor or health visitor. Colic nearly always disappears by the time the baby is three months old.

Boredom Play with your baby and give it plenty of stimulation; even tiny babies love simple games such as peek-a-boo.

Teething Buy a water-filled teething ring and cool it down in the fridge before giving it to the baby to chew. Rubbing the baby's gums with a clean finger may also be soothing, or giving chewable foods such as rusks. If the baby is still in pain, try applying a teething gel such as Bonjela.

MOTHERS MATTER TOO

Motherhood doesn't mean one person giving up all her rights for the sake of others, even if it sometimes feels that way. Some simple tips could lighten the load and help you enjoy the experience more:

● It's natural for some mothers to feel a little low for a few weeks after giving birth, but if it is severe or goes on for more than two months you may have post-natal depression. Common symptoms include anxiety, tearfulness, feeling you can't cope or are losing touch with reality, rejecting the baby or feeling angry towards it, and losing track of time. If this sounds familiar, speak to your doctor, midwife or health visitor, or contact the Association for Post-Natal Illness or the National Childbirth Trust (see addresses below) for help.

● You'll feel better if you keep trim by exercising regularly. Ask your maternity ward sister or health visitor for a list of exercises for the first six weeks. After that, join an exercise class with a crèche or follow an exercise tape at home – most babies love to watch.

● Make time for yourself and build it into your daily routine, even if it's only ten minutes before you tackle the housework. Choose a time when the baby is usually asleep or when someone else can look after it, and do whatever you want to: relax, read, listen to music, lie in the bath, or just drink a cup of tea in peace. The only rule is, no chores.

Useful addresses

Association for Post-Natal Illness
25 Jerdan Place
London SW6 1BE.
Tel: 071 386 0868.
Helps mothers to identify and cope with the symptoms of post-natal depression.

National Childbirth Trust
Alexandra House
Oldham Terrace
London W3 6NH.
Tel: 081 992 8637.
Gives help and advice on all aspects of motherhood.

TAKING CARE OF YOUNG TEETH

Teething timetable Babies begin to cut their first teeth between about six months and one year, and usually have a full set by the age of three. You can help by gently rubbing their gums and providing teething rings and rusks to chew on. If necessary, give paracetamol in the dosage recommended on the pack. At six, the milk teeth start to fall out to make way for permanent teeth. If your child complains of pain, see a dentist.

The first toothbrush Buy your baby a toothbrush to play with before the first teeth appear, so that the shape becomes familiar early on. But don't let the baby hold the toothbrush when you're not there to watch or it could hurt itself.

Start a gentle brushing routine as soon as your baby has cut its first teeth. Brush regularly after meals and sweets.

Cutting down on sugar Offer your children raw carrot sticks and apples between meals, and keep biscuits and sweets for special occasions.

Getting to know the dentist Take children for regular dental check-ups from the age of about 18 months, so that they get used to it.

VACCINATION DO'S AND DON'TS

DO protect your child by making sure all vaccinations are given. Check with your local clinic, but usually they are given at two, three and four months for polio, diphtheria, tetanus and whooping cough (ask your doctor's advice about whooping cough if there is a family history of fits); and at 15 months for measles, mumps and rubella (German measles).

DO keep a record of all vaccinations and the dates they were given.

DO reassure a frightened child by drawing a picture of what will happen and by playing a game where a teddy bear or doll receives an injection.

DO help your child relax at the time by saying a nursery rhyme together as the needle goes in, and have a small comfort present ready for afterwards.

DON'T ever have an ill child vaccinated. Ask a doctor's advice if in doubt.

TOILET TRAINING TIPS

Teaching a small child to use the lavatory can be a daunting task, but all children get there eventually, so adopt a relaxed approach and be patient – turning it into an issue will only make things harder. Of course, you may be lucky: some children, often girls, succeed sooner than others.

Think ahead Buy a large, comfortable, easy-to-clean potty well before the baby is old enough to use it. When the time does come, it'll be a familiar part of life.

Making a start The right time to start potty training is when your child can understand basic instructions and is able to stay dry for a few hours at a time, which shows some bladder control. This is usually at the age of about two years, although parents who wait until a child is nearly three often find that training works faster.

Begin by putting the youngster on the potty after eating or drinking. Don't worry or nag your child if nothing happens, but give lots of praise and attention when it does.

No more nappies When a child is well used to using a potty, it's ready to stop wearing nappies. Choose a time when you don't have to go out much and, if possible, when the weather is warm enough to spend time in the garden, where accidents will be less messy. Dress the child in lined trainer pants without a nappy and put him on the potty every hour. Don't fuss if the pants get wet, but give lavish praise when the potty is used.

There's no rush Be prepared for toilet training to take time: getting upset will only make it worse. Be unstinting with encouragement, and make the child proud of his progress by putting up a calendar chart where you can stick a star each time he uses the potty successfully. Being allowed to watch

Monday ★ ★ ★
Tuesday ★ ★
Wednesday ★
Thursday ★ ★
Friday
Saturday
Sunday

parents or other children using the lavatory can also help, or hearing a running tap while sitting on the lavatory. You may even be able to find a book with pictures of children using the potty.

Still wet at night? If a child who is dry during the day still cannot get through the night, leave a potty next to the bed and suggest using it on waking during the night. Alternatively, gently wake the child and put it on the potty just before you go to bed yourself. Protect the mattress with a plastic covering under the sheet.

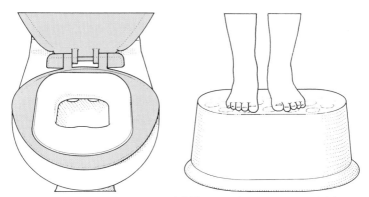

From potty to lavatory When your child is more than two years old, buy a trainer seat to fit your lavatory and a toddler step to help reach it. Teach children how to wipe themselves: it's particularly important for girls to wipe from front to back so that they don't spread bowel bacteria.

Bedwetting Toilet trained children may start to wet their beds again if something upsets them – the arrival of a new baby, or starting at a new school, for example. Go back to using a plastic sheet over the mattress and talk kindly to the child about the problem and what may be causing it, but don't fuss. Stick stars on a special calendar chart for every dry night. See the doctor if the problem persists: there may be a urinary infection.

TIME FOR BED

Get into a routine Children of all ages need a regular bedtime routine, so put a stop to active play after dinner and encourage quieter activities. After their baths, wind children down for bed by reading stories. If your partner comes home at this time, involve him in the reading but discourage starting up exciting new games.

Setting a bedtime There's no harm in letting children stay up at night, provided that they have opportunities to sleep during the day, and on the Continent this is quite usual. However, if you want time on your own in the evenings, it's best to establish and stick to a definite bedtime once youngsters are old enough to sleep through the night. Most under-fives should be in bed by 7pm, and school-age children under ten between 7pm and 8.30pm. Older children could have the same bedtime, but read in bed till around 9.30pm.

Small babies need a more flexible approach, however, and can't be expected to follow regular bedtimes. Most sleep through the night by five months, but not all.

Wide awake at midnight If your baby's still bright-eyed when you're ready for bed yourself, the problem could be too much rest too early in the evening. Try keeping the baby awake and active for around three hours before you go to bed.

Keep toddlers' daytime naps short and, if necessary, wake them by softly turning on the radio after about 1½-2 hours. Make naps early in the afternoon, so that the child will be sleepy again by bedtime.

Make it fun Help children look forward to bed by singing them to sleep and having favourite toys or comfort rags ready to cuddle.

Night lights Don't make bedrooms and passages so dark at night that your child can't find its way around if it needs to. Install a safety night light in the bedroom or a low wattage bulb on the landing, or give older children their own torches to use at night.

Bedtime stories Read non-frightening stories at bedtime to help your child relax. Children of about a year can also be left with cloth or board books to look at on their own if they don't fall asleep immediately.

BEDTIME SAFETY TIPS

● Keep the route to your room safe in case your child comes looking for you during the night. Erect a safety gate if there are stairs a wandering child could fall down, and move any furniture that could be tripped over or bumped into in the dark.

● Watch out for toddlers who suddenly learn to climb out of their cots. Either lower the mattress to prevent escape or let them sleep in a single bed. Some starter beds have raised sides for safety, or you can attach bed guards (right). Always check that guards do not have bars which could trap a small head, and attach them so that there is no room 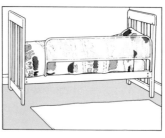 for your child to get its head caught between the headboard and the guard. Alternatively, let the child sleep in an ordinary bed and leave a pillow or padded quilt on the floor to soften landings.

When children can't sleep

Don't despair Many babies and children don't sleep through the night, despite what the textbooks say.

Be consistent If you decide to take a wandering child back to its bed rather than share your own, do so every night or you'll cause confusion. Stay with the child for a few minutes to help it feel more secure and put a spare bed in the room so that you can rest until it falls asleep.

Bed-sharing If you allow your child to get into bed with you, put pillows on the edge of the bed and along the floor for safety.

More than one sleepless child is likely to overcrowd the parental bed. Try letting non-sleepers share a room instead, so that they feel less lonely.

DO NOT take a young baby into your bed after drinking alcohol or taking medication that could make you sleep heavily – it is possible that you could crush the baby or suffocate it without noticing. Let the baby sleep in a cot next to your bed instead.

An end to sharing Once children have got used to sleeping with you, it takes time and patience to wean them away. A small present from the 'sleep fairy' for seven consecutive nights on their own might help. Or rewards such as staying up ten minutes later if they stop coming in to you.

Is something waking your child? Thin curtains in the bedroom may let light in, or bathroom noise may disturb a child's sleep. Even your own checking up could be a problem; if so, consider installing an intercom (right).

Make sure that bedding and pyjamas are not too heavy or too light – both heat and cold can cause night-time waking – and leave a small glass of water nearby in case of thirst.

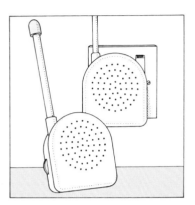

Don't ignore your child Never leave a child to scream in the night. Never lock its bedroom door or your own. You will make night-time fears worse and exacerbate the problem.

Nightmares Turn over the child's pillow and explain that this is turning the bad dreams away. The next morning, ask about any fears the child has and try to find out if something is wrong. Leave the room softly lit at night.

Early waking There is no reason why early risers shouldn't amuse themselves without disturbing the rest of the household. Set up safe toys on the bars of the cot for babies, and encourage school-age children to play in their rooms. Give them an alarm clock set for the time you wake and tell them that they must entertain themselves until the bell rings.

LEARNING TO TALK

Most babies start to say words such as 'mum' and 'dad' by their first birthday. By 18 months or two years they will have quite a large vocabulary of words such as 'ball' and 'more'.

New speakers often have trouble saying word endings clearly, so you may hear 'bor' for 'ball', for example, or 'da' for 'dad'. Repeat the word back to your child clearly so that it can hear the right ending. Smile while you speak to increase confidence. Don't reprimand fuzzy speech or you could make it worse.

Increase your child's vocabulary

See that the message gets across Talk slowly and clearly, and don't speak against background noise from a radio or television set, which may obscure what you're saying. Look directly at the child as you speak, and put emphasis and tone into your voice. Any child will be eager to copy if you sound interesting enough.

341

Keep up a commentary Let your child hear new words all the time by explaining what you're doing as you go about ordinary daily tasks. Use clear, simple sentences such as, 'Let's go to the shops now,' and, 'Here is your teddy bear.'

Buy books Even small babies of about six months or older can enjoy brightly coloured plastic books. Start off with books which have a single clear picture on each page, so that you can point to and name the object for the child.

Use gestures Body language will reinforce a verbal message in a child's mind, so make appropriate gestures whenever possible and encourage your child to copy them: waving when you say goodbye to visitors, for example.

Turn it into a game Point to your own nose, eyes, hair, mouth or other parts of your body and say each word clearly, getting the child to repeat it back to you. Or line up two or three favourite toys behind your back and bring them out one at a time, naming each – 'doll', 'car', 'book' or whatever.

Avoid baby talk It's no easier to learn, and it means nothing.

Build on your child's speech Expand on what your child says and use the opportunity to introduce new words. For example, if she points to her feet and says, 'shoes,' you could reply, 'Yes, they're brown/red/blue shoes.'

Help for poor speakers

When does a child need help? Ask a doctor or health visitor's advice if a child has not spoken, cannot put two words together or still speaks unclearly by the age of two. Problems such as poor hearing or fluid behind the eardrum may require treatment, and whatever the cause of the difficulty, the earlier help is given the better.

If your child passes the tests given by the doctor or health visitor, but you are still unhappy about its speech, ask to be referred to a speech therapist or audiologist for more detailed testing.

Giving new speakers a fair chance Are older children too talkative? Is the television constantly on? Does your toddler need more one-to-one attention from you? These are sometimes a poor speaker's only problems.

Stuttering Don't panic if your child's a stutterer: many children go through this phase and it may just be that there's so much to say it can't all come out clearly. Never interrupt or supply a difficult word; give the child the satisfaction of saying it, even if it takes time. Don't make an issue of stammering – nervousness could make it worse.

If the problem continues for more than two months, ask your doctor about referring the child to a speech therapist.

OLD WIVES' TALES ABOUT CHILD-REARING

'Breastfeeding prevents you regaining your figure'
Although you must eat sensibly, breastfeeding can actually help you slim because it uses up to 500-800 calories a day. It can also help your womb contract back into shape.

'Boys walk sooner than girls'
Every child develops at his or her own rate. Some children will walk by their first birthday and others not until 18 months. Second-born children tend to walk earlier because they copy their older brothers and sisters.

'Spare the rod and spoil the child'
Smacking a naughty child is not a magic cure for bad behaviour. In fact, it can encourage the child to become aggressive to others. It's better to say 'no' sharply and explain why. Punish, if necessary, by taking away a treat. Praising good behaviour can discourage bad behaviour.

CLEANLINESS AND HYGIENE

Keeping hands clean Most three-year-olds can learn to wash their own hands, but smaller children need help. Keep a cloth in the kitchen for wiping their hands before and after meals, and help them wash after using the lavatory or playing with pets. Make the experience more fun by letting children choose novelty soaps or turning hand washing into a question and answer game. Ask: 'What shall we do now?' after a meal. Correct answer: 'Wash our hands.'

In the bath Help toddlers to wash themselves, rather than doing it all for them. But don't leave them unsupervised, even for a moment.

Washing hair Swaddle a baby in a towel and hold it in the crook of one arm while using the other to wash its hair. Avoid tears for toddlers by buying a plastic hair shield from a chemist to keep soap out of their eyes (right). If your child is afraid of being dropped, let it kneel against the side of the bath instead of being held, so that it can feel the ground. Give the child a hand towel or swimming goggles to protect its eyes and try letting an older child apply the shampoo (while you watch): it may cheer up the victim.

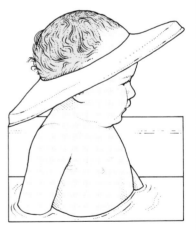

Nailbiting Discourage nailbiting by trimming nails regularly after baths, and by giving children other things to do with their hands, such as colouring in or playing with Plasticine or modelling dough. As a 'prize', stick stars on a calendar on days they don't bite.

Thumb-sucking Don't make too much of a fuss about thumb-sucking: it gives children comfort and almost never does any harm. If you want to stop the habit when the child's permanent teeth come through (usually at six), try the anti-nailbiting techniques above, or dip the child's thumb into a runny mixture of mustard and water, or paint the nail with clear

343

polish to change the taste. Do this only with your child's cooperation; try saying, 'Shall we do this to be grown-up?'

Alternatively, apply a small plaster (it won't taste so nice), or limit thumb-sucking to certain times of the day. Ask a dentist's advice if you are worried that thumb-sucking may affect the shape of a child's teeth.

WHEN A CHILD BEHAVES BADLY

Babies can't behave badly; they are too young to know better, so don't get angry, however exasperated you feel. Toddlers and older children need guidance, but make allowances for age and be consistent about what's acceptable and what's not.

Behaviour problems and cures

Temper tantrums Don't give in when children demand something you don't want them to have or do. Instead, distract them with toys, pets, games or interesting things to do. Use voice tones to get attention: 'Oh *look* at that bird in the garden.'

Older children sometimes stop a tantrum if ignored for a minute or two, but don't leave it any longer. Often a comforting cuddle – even if you don't think your child deserves one – is all that's needed.

Breath holding Blow on your child's face or gently tickle its ribs to encourage breathing out. Don't make an issue of breath holding or the child may use it as a habitual weapon to get its own way. A small number of children can actually make themselves pass out by holding their breath, but once unconscious they start breathing again immediately. See your doctor if it's a regular problem.

Self-induced vomiting Your child is doing this for effect, so show that it doesn't work. Remark calmly on the 'awful mess' and clear it up. Children of about four or older should be made to help. If a child vomits repeatedly, take it to see a doctor.

Biting Say 'no' sharply when you see a biter about to strike. Never bite a child back: it encourages further bad behaviour.

Bad language Don't overreact, or swearing could become another weapon. Say briskly: 'We don't use that word; let's say........instead,' and suggest a polite alternative. Over-fives could be diverted by a challenge such as spelling the new word. Avoid swearing in front of children.

Fights at the table If children quarrel at mealtimes, feed them in different rooms or seat them in opposite corners of the same room, but facing away from each other. Don't let children's squabbling ruin an adult meal either – send them to their bedrooms, and feed them afterwards.

Just being naughty Play a game where you pretend you have two children instead of one: a 'bad' William, say, and a 'good' one. When the child is naughty say, 'Oh dear, this must be the bad William. Let's shut our eyes and see if the good one appears instead.' Alternatively, try whispering a command such as, 'Don't do that.' The novelty of whispers instead of shouts can work wonders. If not, try singing the command or turning it into a rhyme such as, 'Eat that up now. Or there'll be a row.' The humour often defuses the situation.

A note about allergies Some parents have found that certain foods and food additives seem to precipitate bad behaviour in sensitive children. Ask your doctor's advice if you suspect the same.

Preventing jealousy over a new baby

A certain amount of jealousy is normal when a new baby arrives. Make allowances for how other children feel, and try to give them a fair share of attention. Don't leave a jealous older child alone with a new baby.

Explaining about pregnancy Don't tell children that there's a baby on the way until you're obviously pregnant, or they'll expect the baby to arrive immediately. Draw attention to books and television programmes that show animals or human babies being born. Point out other pregnant women and mothers with babies.

Make them feel part of it Let children stroke your tummy and feel the baby kicking. They will also enjoy being involved in preparations such as sticking up wall friezes in the nursery, and once the baby is born they can help with small tasks such as nappy changing and feeding.

Helping other children enjoy a new baby Arrange for someone your children like to look after them while you're having the baby, and when the baby is born give each child a small present 'from the new baby'. Praise them generously and often to make up for the attention you'll be giving the baby, and try saying things like, 'Look, the baby is smiling just like you. Soon it'll be as clever as you are, too.' Refer to the new arrival as 'our' baby.

Quarrels and fights

Be fair Don't decide who's in the wrong without hearing both sides.

Teach them to share When two children both want the same toy, let each have it for a short period. Time each one's turn with an alarm clock or kitchen timer to make it completely fair.

Time to be alone with you Older children need time and space to be with their parents without always having other children there too. Try to organise a short card game or a game of football in the park with one child while your partner cares for the other.

Getting them together Squabbling children can often be united in an activity they both enjoy and can do together. Try reading, sticking in pictures or playing a story tape.

If you could only hear yourselves... Tape children's squabbles on a cassette recorder with a microphone. Playing the recording back can make even little ones see the funny side of the situation.

Show them how to be reasonable Teach children to express themselves through words rather than physical violence. Try saying, 'Don't hit your brother. People are not for hitting. Tell him you're angry because he shouldn't have torn up your painting.'

Show sympathy Tell a wronged child that you know how it feels because you remember feeling the same when you were little. Being understood is often more important than exacting retribution.

Impartiality Don't constantly compare one child favourably or unfavourably with another.

Private territory Every child needs a place of its own and somewhere to keep toys, clothes and other personal possessions. If separate bedrooms are impossible, give each child a corner of the shared bedroom to use as its own personal space. Define the boundary clearly with shelving units, furniture or room dividers.

Should you punish?

Rewards work better Children who are constantly told off rarely improve, since there's little incentive. Giving praise when they behave well, even in very small ways, is more successful. Use punishment only as a last resort and make it as mild as possible.

'Time out' Children of four or older can understand the principle of time out. If they are consistently naughty send them out of the room for five minutes, or make them sit in an uninteresting place such as at the bottom of the stairs. Explain that they are not to move until the clock hands reach a certain place, or until the kitchen timer rings. If the child disobeys, make it return until the time is up.

Deprivation Doing away with small treats or reducing pocket money is an effective punishment. But don't be too hard, and save this for serious misdemeanours.

Smacking The dangers of smacking outweigh the benefits. It's easy to be carried away by anger and punish more severely than you meant to. It stops working if used often and it can incite children to smack others.

TEACHING GOOD MANNERS

Start early Even a two-year-old can say, 'Down, please,' after a meal.

Lead the way Children love imitating adults, so be sure to say 'please' and 'thank you' to your child when appropriate.

Meal-time manners Encourage older children to thank you after a meal, so that it will be a habit when they are out visiting. It may also drive home the point that you've worked hard to prepare their food.

Making way for others Teach children of five years or older to let others go first. Set an example by doing it yourself, and point it out when you see strangers being polite.

Foundations for the future When adults ask your children how they are, teach them to ask the same question in return after giving their reply. It's a habit they'll keep for life.

Handling interruptions If children who are old enough to know better interrupt a conversation, explain to them that you want to hear what they're saying but that it's polite for them to wait until you've finished your conversation. When you have finished, invite them in an interested tone of voice to say what they wanted.

Telephone technique Children over four are old enough to learn to say, 'Hello. Who's speaking please?' when they pick up the receiver – but make sure they tell you straight away. Teach children never to give their name or address on the telephone, in case of nuisance calls.

Thank-you letters Help children to write letters to say thank-you instead of making a telephone call to someone who has sent a present. Younger ones could paint or draw a picture while you write the words, and new writers could pencil in, 'Dear.......' or 'Love from.......' even if you have to help with the rest.

SIMPLE WAYS TO AMUSE CHILDREN

Start collecting Odds and ends of all sorts can come in handy for modelling and making things. Save bottle tops, cereal packets, used wrapping paper, wallpaper offcuts, toothbrushes, flour shakers, magazines, old office paper or computer print-out, big buttons (smaller ones could be swallowed), cotton reels, yoghurt pots and anything else that could be useful. Store supplies away in shoe boxes until needed.

Basic equipment Put together a simple activity kit so that everything is in one place when children want to use it. The kit could include:
● Children's safety scissors.
● Non-toxic crayons and felt-tipped pens (buy safety-topped pens with a hole in the lid to prevent suffocation if sucked into the windpipe).
● Non-toxic paint in squeezable plastic bottles (use yoghurt pots for individual containers).

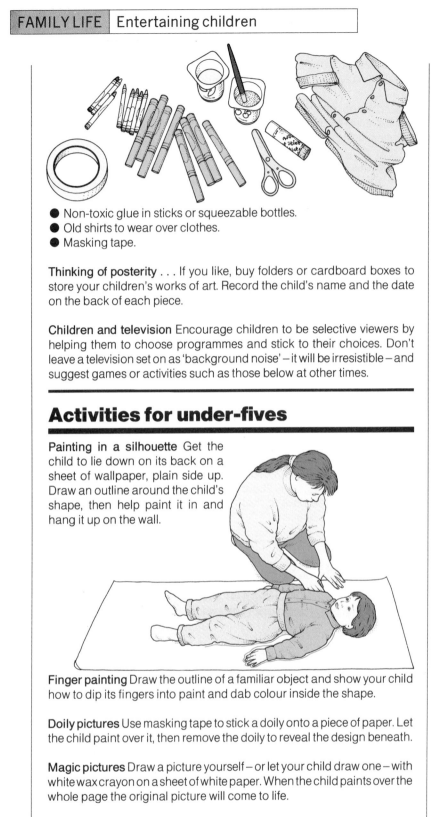

- Non-toxic glue in sticks or squeezable bottles.
- Old shirts to wear over clothes.
- Masking tape.

Thinking of posterity . . . If you like, buy folders or cardboard boxes to store your children's works of art. Record the child's name and the date on the back of each piece.

Children and television Encourage children to be selective viewers by helping them to choose programmes and stick to their choices. Don't leave a television set on as 'background noise' – it will be irresistible – and suggest games or activities such as those below at other times.

Activities for under-fives

Painting in a silhouette Get the child to lie down on its back on a sheet of wallpaper, plain side up. Draw an outline around the child's shape, then help paint it in and hang it up on the wall.

Finger painting Draw the outline of a familiar object and show your child how to dip its fingers into paint and dab colour inside the shape.

Doily pictures Use masking tape to stick a doily onto a piece of paper. Let the child paint over it, then remove the doily to reveal the design beneath.

Magic pictures Draw a picture yourself – or let your child draw one – with white wax crayon on a sheet of white paper. When the child paints over the whole page the original picture will come to life.

Home-made modelling dough Make modelling dough by mixing 750g (1¾lb) flour with 400ml (¾ pint) of water and add food colouring. It should keep for a week in an airtight container. Alternatively, use a roll of unfrozen pastry – the results can then be baked and eaten.

Keeping shop Help your child paint a cardboard box to look like a shop counter when turned upside-down. Wash out and save old food-containers to stock the shop.

Printing Teach children to print simple designs using small pieces of sponge, leaves or vegetables cut into shapes – a half potato with a star or a letter cut out of the middle, for example. Dip the objects in paint, then press them onto paper.

Making a house Fold a piece of paper in half and draw the shape of a house on one side. Cut out the windows and three sides of the door so that you can fold it back. Draw in scenes of what's going on inside on the page behind.

Mouse paperweight Find a rounded garden stone that's too big to swallow, and help your child to draw and stick on a nose and eyes made of paper and a piece of string for a tail.

Books and reading Encourage children to enjoy books by reading to them as soon as they can understand simple stories. Let them join the local library and help them choose suitable books – or ask teachers and librarians for recommendations. Give books as presents, or consider making a monthly book allowance for older children.

Cardboard daffodils Cut simple flower shapes from a piece of cardboard and cut out the cups from the bottom of a cardboard egg box. Glue the base of each cup to the centre of a flower shape. Use a straw for the stem.

Glove puppets Save old gloves and mittens to make into puppets. Cut out facial features from felt or paper, and stick or sew them into place. Older children will be able to make the faces themselves with a little help.

Entertainment for older children

Stained glass windows Draw a window divided into four sections on a piece of thin, white paper and paint each section with a different coloured pattern, or help your child to paint them. Attach a piece of tracing paper or greaseproof paper over the top with masking tape, and glue four thin black paper strips onto the tracing paper to give a paned effect. Tape the picture to a window so that light shines through.

Blow painting Help your child to dab a large blob of paint onto a piece of paper, using a paintbrush. Then show how to make a design by blowing gently (never sucking) through a straw.

Animal mosaics Draw the outline of an animal on a piece of stiff paper and cut coloured paper into small squares. Show your child how to stick them inside the outline to make a mosaic picture.

Table tennis If you have room, set up a table tennis table. To fix dented table tennis balls, put them into a saucepan of boiling water until the dent goes. It won't work if the ball is cracked, though.

Necklaces Thread a piece of ribbon or string with large buttons or painted cotton reels to make a colourful necklace in minutes.

Blowing bubbles It's simple to make bubble liquid at home: just mix one part of washing-up liquid with three parts of warm water. If you don't have a blower, twist one end of a piece of wire into a circle and form a handle with the other – or unbend a paperclip and twist it into a loop at one end. Dip into the liquid, and blow.

Jewellery box A pretty box is easy to make. Line a shoebox and lid with felt or coloured paper and let your child glue sequins, shells or cut-out fabric shapes on the outside.

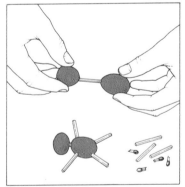

Potato people Show children how to join potato heads and bodies with matchsticks, and stick in matchsticks to make arms and legs. Use radishes for a variation, or acorns joined with pins (under supervision – and make sure the sharp ends are well pushed in). Alternatively, bend and twist pipe cleaners into human shapes.

Finger puppets Cut out finger-shaped outlines from felt or scraps of material and sew them together to make puppets that fit over the top of a finger. Paint, sew or stick on facial features. Then cut out one side of a cereal packet to look like a theatre and paint a backdrop on the inside behind. Use the puppets to put on a show.

Pressed flowers Place flowers and leaves between sheets of greaseproof or blotting paper and press inside a heavy book for about 48 hours.

Watch them grow Children love seeing the results of their work spring up in the garden. Show them how to sow bulbs such as hyacinths and daffodils in the autumn (page 285), and seeds such as tomatoes and sunflowers in the spring. Or try fast-growing mustard and cress in a container on a windowsill indoors.

FUN WITH CARDS

Snap The whole pack is dealt out among the players, who then turn over their cards together in quick succession until two cards of the same rank appear. When this happens the first to shout 'snap' collects the pair and puts it aside. When all the cards have been turned over, those that have not been collected into pairs are reshuffled and dealt out again. The game continues until there are no more cards left to reshuffle. The winner is the one with the most cards.

Pairs Even little ones stand a fair chance of winning at Pairs. Deal out all the cards face down on a table and let children take it in turns to turn over one card at a time. When two cards of the same rank are exposed, the one who has just turned over a card may collect the pair and have another turn. When all the cards have been used the winner is the one with the most pairs.

Learning to shuffle cards Teach children to shuffle a pack of cards by holding them in the left hand with the picture sides facing left. Using the right hand, the child lifts off some of the cards on the right of the pack and then shuffles them into the remaining pile in the left hand. Alternatively, get the child to divide the pack roughly in half, and hold both halves face down on the floor with their top inside corners touching. With practice, the child should be able to interleave the cards from the two halves by flicking through the piles with its thumbs.

CHILDREN'S PARTIES

Ideas for under-fives

Invitations If you can deliver them by hand, make your own invitations by drawing clown, animal or pirate faces on plain white, paper plates. Overleaf, write your address, party time, the child's name and an RSVP phone number.

Games Children under three are too young for organised games apart from the most simple – 'Ring a ring of roses', for example. Instead, arrange for them to play with toys in a safe room under supervision, with taped music in the background. Three-to-five-year-olds enjoy simple games: 'Pass the parcel' (using newspaper or paper bags for wrappings), 'Blind man's buff', and musical bumps or statues will all go down well.

Entertainment
● If you hire an entertainer, check he'll do a short show (half an hour maximum) of magic or puppets; under-fives can't concentrate for long.
● Save money by dressing up your partner or friend in clown, Father Christmas or fancy dress costumes.
● Hire a projector screen and cartoon from a local photographic shop or get a film from the video shop.

351

● Provide a singing break for everyone to sing their favourite songs. If possible, accompany the children on the piano or a guitar or buy backing tapes.

Supervision Under-fours need one-to-one attention, so invite parents or minders to stay. If this is impossible, obtain a contact number in case of an emergency. For four and five-year-olds, enlist enough adult volunteers to ensure one adult per five children. Limit numbers sensibly.

Presents Don't let your child unwrap presents as guests arrive. Place them in a box for later so you will know which guest to thank.

Tea
● Ask parents to bring highchairs for tiny tots.
● Don't over-cater: children are often too excited to eat much (see also page 602).
● Avoid too much chocolatey food (it's mucky and unhealthy) and dangerous snacks such as peanuts, which can easily get stuck in the windpipe.

Safety Each guest is your responsibility.
● Move all china and other breakable or dangerous items out of reach. Keep the front door firmly shut after each arrival and have a guest list so you know who's in your home.
● When the party ends, keep the children in one room until they're collected, so they can be found quickly.

Giving a party for children over five

● If possible, share a party with another parent whose child's birthday is near your child's. It reduces the cost.
● Consider hiring a hall if you're short of space. Older children can be very boisterous.
● Enlist adult volunteers – about one adult to eight guests.
● Start with an ice-breaking game such as Happy Families (each new arrival gets a badge bearing a character's name, such as Snow White. They then have to find the other members of the fairy story – all seven dwarfs.) Treasure hunts, dead lions (lying on the floor and keeping still), dance competitions and musical chairs (you can use cushions instead) will also be popular.
● If you want to hire an entertainer for the afternoon, ring round for quotes as prices vary. Find out what's included; some entertainers provide party bags and game prizes.
● Save time and energy by buying one present for each child instead of making a bag of small items. Examples might include a set of crayons, a puzzle book or a necklace.

Theme parties for the over-fives

Swimming parties Many pools can be hired for special occasions. It may also be possible to hire a room at the pool where you can lay out food for the children after their swim. Ensure you have adequate supervision (at least one adult per two children), and that all guests (even swimmers) wear armbands.

Leisure centres If your local centre runs gym classes for children, you may be able to hire an instructor to supervise a party. Alternatively, some centres will organise a choice of games and arrange catering.

Disco Look for advertisements in your local paper or shop window for discos to hire with or without an operator. Ask for references and previous customers.

Magic shows Find a magician through the Yellow Pages under 'Entertainers', your local paper or by word of mouth. Ring round for price quotations, and check references.

Cinema, pantomime or theatre Ensure you have adequate supervision (one adult to six or eight children) and transport; if necessary ask parents to drop guests off at the venue. Organise food afterwards at a local pizza/hamburger bar – some will provide a cake free of charge.

Dressing-up parties Cowboys and Indians, goodies and baddies, pirates, science fiction and cartoon characters can all be themes for fancy dress parties. Pick a theme which is easy to make a costume for or you will find the guests don't come in fancy dress.

KEEP YOUR CHILDREN SAFE

Never assume your child is too old or sensible to do something dangerous. If your children are out visiting, don't be afraid of warning their hostess that they might not be used to such things as pets, ponds, roads or unbolted windows.

Safety precautions round the house

Electrical sockets Where there are babies and toddlers, install plastic covers in all sockets to stop inquisitive fingers. Socket covers are available in packs from chemists, electrical retailers and specialist children's shops.

Wires Television and video wires should be tucked away so heavy equipment can't be pulled down.

Lightweight furniture Remove anything which could fall on top of a child who is learning to pull himself up. Avoid using tablecloths.

Sharp-edged furniture Cover corners with Perspex protectors so that knocks are less dangerous.

Medicines and household cleaners Never store medicines on a high shelf (children might reach them by standing on chairs). Lock them away. Avoid toilet cleaners which hang inside the lavatory bowl: children can remove and suck them.

Windows and doors Install window locks to prevent children falling out and add bolts to the top of front and back doors. Replace glass in patio doors with safety glass, or cover existing glass with an antishatter safety film; it holds the pieces in place if the pane gets broken.

Plastic cups Don't allow children to drink out of glass tumblers as they may drop and break them. Use plastic cups instead.

Cooker safety Fix a pan guard across the top of a cooker to prevent infants burning themselves. Always have saucepan handles turned inwards to prevent children grabbing them. Keep small children away from the oven when it is in use and teach them not to touch anything hot. As soon as possible, teach them not to play with the cooker controls either – especially with gas cookers.

Fireguards Never leave a child unattended near a fire or heater, and leave fireguards in place at all times.

Safety locks Kitchen cupboards and the fridge should be secured with safety catches to prevent children opening them.

Kettles, hot drinks and teapots Buy a curly kettle flex which is less likely to hang over the side of a work surface and switch off all appliances at the mains when you have finished using them. Never leave hot drinks or a teapot within a child's reach.

Stair gates Gates should be installed at the top and bottom of stairs for the under-threes.

SAFE TOYS FOR SMALL CHILDREN

Have a good look first at toys you are planning to buy for small children. Keep an eye out for safety marks such as the Lion mark (the manufacturer will be a member of the British Toy and Hobby Manufacturers Association); the British Standards number; and the CE mark, showing that the toy conforms to the European Toy Safety Directive.

● Make sure all moving parts, such as motors, are enclosed and that edges are smoothed off.

● Eyes in dolls and teddy bears should be firmly fixed.

● Kits should be kept away from small children – they may swallow one of the parts.

● Wooden toys should show no signs of splintering.

● There should be nowhere for a small child to trap his fingers.

Garden safety

Ponds and water butts Fence or fill in ponds (however shallow) and don't buy a house with a stream in the garden if your children are under ten. Secure water butts with a tightly fitting lid.

Swimming and paddling pools Never leave the children unattended by a pool and ensure that water containers of all types have a firm lid. Swimming pools should be fenced and/or covered with a weight-bearing safety cover.

Tools and chemicals Keep firmly locked away.

Garden play equipment Swings, climbing frames and slides should all be checked regularly for stability and damage.

Animal droppings Clean up the garden regularly.

Poisonous trees and plants Cut down or restrict the following to back borders, away from playing areas: yew trees, laburnum, foxgloves, rhubarb leaves and deadly nightshade. Teach children not to eat berries and which plants to avoid.

Car safety

The legal requirements

Babies under the age of one are not allowed to travel in the front seat of a car unless they are in an approved rearward-facing carrier or a properly restrained carry cot. Between one and 14, they must wear a proper restraining device (an adult seatbelt is not enough) and children over 14 and adults must wear seatbelts. Children of all ages must be strapped in at the back if there are appropriate restraints available, such as baby seats, child seats and adult seatbelts.

British Kitemark

Which car seat? Choose a car seat according to your child's age and weight. Look for the British Kitemark, a British Standards number or an E sign, indicating the European Approval Mark.

Safety seat extras Some safety seats have built-in backs and sides, which are good for protecting sleeping children, and other makes recline.

Fitting car seats

Fitting a car seat can be more complex than it looks. Restraints may have to be secured to a metal pole in the boot (this varies according to the car make) or under the seat, though some can be used with existing seatbelts. To be safe, ask a garage to fit it for you.

TIPS FOR SAFE TRAVEL

● Always insist that your child is strapped in if he or she is travelling in someone else's car.
● Never take another child passenger unless you can strap them in.
● Store shopping in the boot or tucked under the seat. Loose parcels can hit children in a collision.

Teaching safety to your children

● Drill children from toddler age upwards in road sense.

● Join a local Tufty Club group (see below), which runs preschool playgroups for the 0-4-year-olds to teach safety through play.

● Teach children never to cross a road without you or a carer. Point out the dangers of driveways across pavements.

● Discuss the 'stranger danger' as soon as your children can understand the idea, but don't alarm them. Teach them simple defence techniques such as kicking and screaming: Kidscape will give you more detailed guidance (see below).

● Teach children their home phone numbers and addresses. Write this information in indelible pen on coats and the *inside* of satchels – you don't want a stranger to be able to read it.

● Encourage older children to supervise younger ones but keep a watchful eye out.

● Discourage cycling on the roads until children have passed their cycling proficiency test. Get young children to stick to the garden or the park if possible.

● Teach school-age children to wait with the teacher until you or a friend collects them at the end of the day. If you ask someone else to pick up your child, tell the teacher and the child.

Useful addresses

Child Accident Prevention Trust
28 Portland Place
London W1N 4DE.
Tel: 071 636 2545.
Gives advice on all aspects of child safety.

Kidscape
World Trade Centre
Europe House
London E1 9AA.
Tel: 071 488 0488.
Advises on how to teach children simple self-defence techniques.

The Tufty Club
Royal Society for the Prevention of Accidents (ROSPA)
Cannon House
The Priory Queensway
Birmingham B4 6BS.
Tel: 021 200 2461.
Playgroups countrywide which teach safety to 0-4s through play.

UNDERSTANDING OLDER CHILDREN

Set weekly routine tasks Household jobs for the over-fives can include laying the table daily, wiping place mats, cleaning out any pet cages and tidying rooms.

Encourage reluctant helpers round the house by 'paying' for such jobs with pocket money, graded according to age and your pocket.

Teach money sense Open a savings account for the over-fives and encourage them to save. Regular pocket money, given out on the same day each week, will help them understand how to use money. The amount will depend on their age – what they need, or want to buy – but try to keep it in line with that of their friends. Adjust it as and when it seems necessary.

Bedtimes Allow older children to stay up for an extra hour one night a week. They'll stick to their bedtime more happily on the other days.

Going solo Be cautious about letting children out for the first time on their own. Wait until they're about eight to ten years old and always accompany them to their destination – a local shop or friend's house – before they do it alone. If possible, ring to check they've got there safely or quietly 'shadow' them. Never let the journey exceed more than about five minutes for under-12s.

Find a partner If your child regularly has to make a long journey, such as the walk to school, find another parent or older child to accompany him.

Keen cooks Allow them to make a meal for the family once a week, under your supervision, from six or seven onwards.

Budding gardeners Give them a space in the garden of their own to grow whatever they like.

Communicating with your adolescent

● Set aside special times for being alone with a teenager, such as a shopping trip or a meal in a restaurant.
● Be prepared to show your own feelings. Teenagers are more likely to see you as 'human' if you tell them what you're thinking and talk about your own teenage experiences.
● Keep abreast with your adolescent's school activities. Find out what his curriculum consists of at school and try reading the textbooks.
● Welcome your children's friends home: that way, they'll feel less like roaming the streets. If you don't like the company your teenager keeps, discuss the subject calmly.
● Draw up a list of informal house rules so everyone knows where they stand. Then they will know if they have to ring home after a certain time, or not to help themselves to alcohol around the house.
● Involve teenagers in adult activities and conversation.
● Put up a noticeboard for general messages, perhaps in the kitchen, to tell each other where you are or who has phoned. You can also leave a list of emergency phone numbers.
● If communication falters over a particular problem, ask a mutual family friend or relative to talk to your teenager instead.

Teenage finance

Monthly allowance Consider making a regular monthly allowance to your teenager to replace weekly pocket money. Pay it into a savings account and stipulate certain items which have to be bought out of it – non-essential clothing, money for outings. It fosters money sense.

Earning their way Encourage teenagers to do certain chores – cleaning the car or carrying your shopping, for example – to 'earn' this allowance.

Save it Get your teenager to save up for something he really wants. Don't be persuaded into buying expensive birthday or Christmas presents, but suggest he saves part of his allowance to go halves with you.

Telephone contributions Place a contributions box next to the telephone if your teenager is a regular caller, or consider installing a pay phone for their outgoing calls if your children are constantly on the phone.

ARRANGING A HOLIDAY

If you are thinking of going abroad, contact your doctor to see what inoculations may be necessary. And ensure that your passport is in order well in advance. Visas can be arranged through your travel agent, or contact the relevant consulates.

Holiday insurance checklist

Book it early Take out travel insurance when you book your holiday. That way, you'll be covered if you have to cancel.

Illness and cancellation Your travel insurance should cover you against cancellation through illness, death or other unforeseen circumstances, although generally will not cover natural disasters such as earthquakes. It should also cover you against medical treatment required abroad because of illness or accidents.

Accidents Check that the insurance company undertakes to fly you home for treatment within a certain time. You'll have to pay for medical treatment abroad and claim it back later, so make sure you have enough to pay in an emergency.

Theft or loss of money or possessions Estimate how much it would cost to replace your travel wardrobe and make sure your insurance covers the amount. Check too that the insurance covers missing luggage.

Holiday delays Some insurance policies cover passengers against delays at airports or seaports; some will also pay out for accommodation while waiting.

Making a claim Most insurance policies only cover part of the cost – you may have to pay the first £20 or £30 yourself. To reclaim any money spent, keep any medical receipts or relevant statements: from the hotel manager after a theft, for example.

Travelling with children

Childcare facilities

● If you are booking with a holiday firm which offers a children's club, check the following: the ratio of staff to children; staff qualifications, experience and age; activities provided; location of club; and age range of children admitted.

● Check if a babysitter service is available. Note that baby patrols are merely occasional checks on children and not one-to-one supervision. Baby listening services (using an in-room radio monitor checked by the switchboard) can't always detect children moving around.
● Request a highchair and cot in advance, if necessary, and check the age of the equipment.

Coping with flying

● Ask the tour operator or airline if children's meals are provided.
● Request a travel cot (sometimes called a bassinet) if necessary: not all airlines offer them.
● Ask for non-smoking seats, which are better for children.
● See if you can 'check in' and reserve your seats over the telephone just before departure if you live near the airport. Some airlines do this, and it saves hanging around the departure lounge with toddlers.
● Check travelling times before booking: early or late flights can be unsettling for infants.
● Most airlines count baby buggies as hand luggage.

Packing for children

Food Pack baby food, cans or packets for fussy eaters (plus a can opener) and snacks.

Nappies Packs of disposable nappies can be carried as hand luggage. Most foreign countries do sell disposables although they're usually more expensive than in Britain.

First aid To prevent medicine bottles breaking, store them in old plastic ice-cream containers or wrap them in towels.

Include insect repellent; antihistamine lotion for stings and sunburn; suntan lotion with high protection factor; water purifying tablets; scissors; plasters and bandages; a thermometer; and medicines (junior paracetamol in liquid form or soluble tablets; and rehydration packs for diarrhoea).

Clothes If travelling to somewhere hot, include sun hats and cotton clothing. Buy suitable swimming aids (a rubber ring, arm bands or costumes with built-in floats) and brightly coloured swimming hats for easy recognition of children by the pool.

Practical items Just in case, pack a torch, a sewing kit, money belts and a cord to serve as a clothes line.

Games for children Take board games, cassette players and cassettes, cards, pencils and paper – and allow one cuddly toy per child.

Luggage Spread children's possessions among the rest of the family luggage in case one case goes astray. That way, you should have some of the things you need.

Label luggage clearly and securely; if you identify it by sticking on a magazine or cartoon picture, the children will enjoy spotting the cases at the other end of a plane journey.

Taking the stress out of holidays

● Ease journey boredom by packing small individual bags of surprise amusements: colouring books, puzzles, notebooks or cartoons. Keep a travelling bag to hand with essentials: a change of children's clothes, sick bags, toys, drinks and snacks, tissues.

● Think up journey games: 'I spy'; sing-along songs; counting the number of passengers, traffic lights or red lorries passed on the road. Make up sentences from the car number plates in front, or spot car registration letters in order from A to Z.

● If flying, ask the stewardess if your children can visit the flight deck. On their return, get them to draw it.

● To prevent jet lag, give the children fruit juice and water rather than tea or coffee, and try to book a flight that arrives in the local evening – that way, they can adjust to the country's sleeping hours.

● Dress children in layers which can be easily altered to suit the temperature.

● Avoid travel sickness by keeping the car well ventilated, and not allowing smoking; sucking or chewing sweets (especially when landing or taking-off in an aeroplane); not talking about sickness; and by asking your doctor for medication to take with you.

KEEPING HOLIDAYS HAPPY

● Watch your children at all times – it's easy to let down your guard when you're relaxed – and supervise them carefully near water and heights.

● Cope quickly with upset tummies by giving plenty of cooled, boiled water and rehydration salts, available from chemists. Progress to plain foods and bottled/boiled water.

● Store medicines out of reach of children.

● Keep children out of hot sun between 12 noon and 2pm.

Holidays at home

Holiday playschemes Telephone your local council's recreation and leisure department for details of holiday playschemes. Check supervision levels (there should be at least one adult to eight over-fives) and the activity programme to ensure it suits your child.

Arrange outings Contact the local tourist board for details of interesting places to take the children – farms, museums or castles, for example. The *Let's Go with the Children* books cover different areas in Britain and are available from most book shops, published by Cube Publications.

Sports centres Many leisure centres run sport holiday programmes for the over-fives, including cricket, multisport, swimming and others.

Picnics Pick an open place (not too secluded) and take a party of friends for company and security.

Bus and train rides If your children are used to cars, rides on public transport are a great novelty. Alternatively, go roller skating or bowling.

360

TIPS FOR WORKING MOTHERS

● Have an alternative childcare plan in case your regular minder is not available. Check in advance among your neighbours to see if one might take over in an emergency.

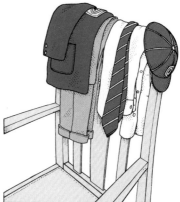

● List house rules and basic information for carers and older children, including what to do in an emergency. Leave contact numbers for yourself and partner, and a spare key with a neighbour. Make sure your carer knows.

● Put out children's clothes and uniforms the night before, pre-cook meals for the freezer when you have some time at the weekends, and remember to put all school dates in your diary and on a family wall calendar.

● Make time for your family on returning from work, however tired you are. Be flexible about bedtimes so you have time to hear about their day, and tell them about yours too.
● Use your days off to keep in touch with your children's activities – visit playgroups, pick the children up from school or invite their friends round.
● Contact useful organisations such as the Working Mothers' Association (page 363) for emotional and practical support.

DO'S AND DON'TS: BABY SITTERS

DO find someone through word of mouth and check references.

DO leave contact numbers where you and a neighbour can be reached.

DO discourage your sitter from bringing a companion. It might distract her.

DO consider forming a baby-sitting circle with other mothers. It's cheaper, and you'll be sure that your sitter is experienced with children.

DON'T employ anyone under 16 as she probably won't have the maturity or experience to deal with problems.

DON'T go out without introducing your child to the sitter beforehand. Invite her round first to check they get on.

DON'T go out without telling your sitter where everything is – the kitchen, child's bedroom, telephone, clean nappies and a change of child's clothing. Write vital instructions down.

DON'T forget: it can be illegal to leave a child without adequate supervision.

Arranging childcare

By the time you're about seven months pregnant, you should have explored the options. The golden rule about childcare is finding someone your child gets on with: experts say a child can cope perfectly well without his mother as long as there is a regular carer whom he knows.

Au pairs

● Not suitable for babies under six months.
● Help with older infants as well as housework.
● Work for not more than five hours a day, five or six days a week, depending on your arrangement.
● Receive a nominal wage, a room of their own and free bed and board.
● Are treated as part of the family – share the sitting room and meals.
● Au pair agencies are listed in the Yellow Pages under 'Employment agencies and consultants', in your local paper and by The Federation of Recruitment and Employment Services (see facing page).
● Agencies provide a brief outline of experience and background and should, if necessary, provide a replacement.
● Points to check include: does she speak English? Is she used to children and pets? Is she used to the town or country? Does she smoke?
● Agree the terms of employment in writing before she starts.

Mothers' helps

● Are not usually qualified in childcare, so look for someone with experience and maturity.
● Duties involve housework and caring for the children.
● Agencies are listed in the Yellow Pages under 'Employment agencies and consultants' or local papers – always check references.
● Watch how she gets on with the children while you're interviewing her.
● Questions to ask include: What would she give your toddler for lunch? How would she tell him off? What would she do to amuse him?
● You are responsible for tax (if applicable) and National Insurance.

Nannies

● Can live in or out.
● Look for the NNEB (Nursery Nurse Examination Board) certificate.
● No general housework except chores relating to children – cleaning children's rooms or doing their washing.
● Be sure to outline house rules clearly – no smoking, visitors only with your permission or payment for using the telephone.
● Nannies charge according to experience. You are expected to deduct tax and National Insurance.

Sharing a nanny

● Advertise for a partner or organise it through an agency.
● Decide if the nanny should be based at one house or both.
● Be sure you are all clear about holiday arrangements.

Childminders

● Childminders look after your children in their own home.
● Obtain a list of registered minders through the social services department of your local authority – they have been checked for basic safety.
● Choose a minder from The National Childminding Association (see facing page) – they lay down a code of practice for members.
● Points to check: How safe is the minder's home? Is the side gate secure? What activities are provided for the children?
● Childminders charge an hourly or daily rate. You may also be expected

to pay the childminder for three or four weeks' holiday a year and if your child is absent or ill.

● Check she's insured in case your child has an accident. If you pay a friend regularly to look after your children, she should register as a childminder with social services for the same reason.

● Ask how many children she cares for and what ages they are.

Useful addresses

The Federation of Recruitment and Employment Services
36-38 Mortimer Street
London W1N 7RB.
Tel: 071 323 4300.
Holds a list of au pair agencies.

The National Childminding Association
8 Masons Hill
Bromley
Kent BR2 9EY.
Tel: 081 464 6164.
Has a code of practice for child-minders and runs local groups.

The Working Mothers' Association
77 Holloway Road
London N7 8JZ.
Tel: 071 700 5771.
Emotional and practical support for working mothers.

GROWING OLDER

For those living at home

If elderly people want to remain in their own home but could do with some assistance, there are many ways of getting help.

Grants and allowances Your local social services department or Citizens Advice Bureau can advise on what's available and whether you qualify. Or contact Age Concern or Help the Aged (pages 368-9).

Nursing care District nurses can be contacted through the local social services department or your doctor. They are part of the NHS and make home visits to help with bathing, changing dressings or giving injections, for example.

For full-time nursing care, you will probably have to find somebody privately. Private nurses are expensive, though, and will not do ordinary household work such as ironing or cooking. To find a nurse either full-time or part-time – look in the Yellow Pages under 'Employment agencies and consultants', or ask Age Concern for advice. Always check references.

Home helps Your local social services department will tell you if an elderly person is entitled to a home help to assist with shopping, cleaning, laundry and so on. Some local authorities charge an hourly rate for their home helps. Your doctor can tell you how to find one.

Alternatively, find a private home help through the local newspaper, library noticeboards or by word of mouth. They charge by the hour.

Live-in companion To find some-one to live with you, do some light housework and keep you company, look in the Yellow Pages for domestic agencies, listed under 'Employment agencies and consultants'. Alternatively, advertise in a church journal, local paper or *The Lady*. Write a detailed job description so both parties know where they stand, and always check references.

Temporary carers For those who work as full-time carers, a break can be invaluable. Write to Age Concern for its fact sheet 4, *Holidays for Older People*, or contact the Crossroads Care Attendant Scheme (page 368). They have a network of local volunteers available for short periods free of charge (although contributions are welcomed), but there is usually a waiting list. Your doctor or local social services may be able to arrange respite care. Local old people's homes sometimes take in temporary residents for a week or two for a fee.

Dental care and chiropody For those on low incomes, dental care is often subsidised. Ask your dentist for details and see if he will do home visits.

Many social service departments and voluntary groups run their own chiropody practices, available on the NHS and usually free of charge for pensioners. Charges vary according to the area, but most are heavily subsidised.

Meals on wheels Meals on wheels are organised through the local social services department and voluntary groups such as Age Concern. The number of meals provided and the charge for them varies.

Laundry For those who can no longer manage their own washing or who are incontinent, some social services departments offer a collect-and-deliver laundry service.

Telephones You may be able to obtain help with the cost of installing and renting a phone, but you'll have to pay for the calls. Help the Aged will advise. British Telecom will suggest suitable equipment for the disabled.

Adaptations around the home There are plenty of gadgets that can greatly improve someone's ability to stay in their own home (see facing page). Contact voluntary groups such as the Carers National Association and the Disabled Living Foundation (page 369) for advice.

Alarm systems Invaluable in case of a fall, they can sometimes double as a telephone. Your social services department may provide some systems, or contact private companies listed in the Yellow Pages under 'Burglar alarms & security systems'. Help the Aged has a Community Alarms Department which gives personal advice free of charge.

Transport For help in getting to and from the hospital or day centre, contact your doctor, hospital, social services department or local voluntary organisations. Age Concern runs its own transport networks which are usually free, although contributions are welcomed. Be prepared for long waits though – pick-up times can't always be guaranteed.

Someone to talk to If an elderly person is feeling isolated and would like to have a volunteer visit them at home, contact the local branch of Age Concern – they will be able to put you in touch with someone. In some areas, it is also possible to go into primary and secondary schools and get involved with school activities. If you are in London, contact Pensioners Link (page 369) for school involvement; outside London, Age Concern or the local social services department will probably help.

KITCHEN AIDS FOR ELDERLY PEOPLE

There are hundreds of small, inexpensive gadgets that can make a radical difference to life around the house and garden. These gadgets for the kitchen will help with weak wrists, shaky hands or poor eyesight. You can get a fuller list of gadgets available from the Disabled Living Foundation (page 369).

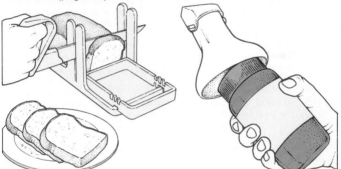

Cutting guide and carving knife The board has a frame that holds bread or meat steady while you are cutting it. The guide for the knife means you get even slices.

Screw jar and bottle opener Adjustable screw-top openers fitted to the underside of a table can help to open jars of jams, sauces, pickles and so on.

Egg topper Scissor-action boiled egg cutters take the top off a boiled egg one-handed.

Personal drink maker A table-top water heater which heats just one mugful at a time. The boiled water is dispensed straight into the mug, so there is no lifting and pouring involved.

Extra-long oven mitts Made of a material that is resistant to heat, liquid and grease, the mitts come in different lengths. The longest covers the arm up to the elbow.

Kitchen timer Some kitchen timers come with small raised markings at one-minute and five-minute intervals. If you have an egg on the stove for instance, you can set the timer to ring after three or four minutes.

Upright dustpan and brush As both the dustpan and brush have long handles, there is no need to bend down.

Reachers Lightweight tongs which can be used to pull objects towards you or to grip an object are invaluable for those who are bed or chair-ridden.

Alternatives to living on your own

Warden-supervised homes

A group of homes under one roof supervised by a warden. There is usually a communal sitting room and activities are organised – bridge clubs or outings, for example. Local housing associations and local authorities both run homes such as these, charging subsidised rents. Most are furnished, although not all, and there is usually a waiting list.

Contact the local authority's social services department, Age Concern, Help the Aged and Citizens Advice Bureau for lists of homes in your area. They are best suited for those who can still look after themselves but would prefer help to be close at hand.

Privately built retirement homes

Built by developers for private sale, many of the homes have built-in features such as bath rails, ramps, panic buttons and few stairs. Service charges can rise steeply, however, and you may have to move away from your district to find a suitable home.

In some cases, builders offer a 'buy back' scheme where they agree to repurchase the house from you should you need to move on to more specialised care. Consult a lawyer or the Citizens Advice Bureau before you sign anything.

Moving in with relatives

Living with relatives can work well but needs a lot of thought beforehand. It is easiest if both generations can have their own space (a special granny flat is ideal, or at least a separate kitchen), and the Centre for Accessible Environment (page 369) can advise on adapting the space that is available.

If you do decide to move in with a relative, check that you are all compatible; that everyone in the family is happy about the proposed move; whether bills would be shared or paid by one or other of you; and whether some adjustments may need to be made to the house – aids in the bathroom, for example, or handrails on the stairs perhaps.

GETTING OUT OF THE HOUSE

For details of day centres in your area where you might find activities and company, contact your local social services, Age Concern or Help the Aged. If possible, visit several and choose the one you like best.

● Is the atmosphere pleasant?
● What facilities are on offer?
● Are your contemporaries good company?
● Is a meal provided, and what sort?
● What are the opening hours, and is transport available to and from?
● Who is running the day centre? Are they friendly, and could they cope in an emergency?

An old people's home

There are two main types of old people's home, residential homes (which provide general help with dressing and day-to-day activities), and nursing homes (which offer skilled nursing care and have to be run by a qualified doctor or nurse).

Residential homes run by the local authority Each authority provides a certain number of homes and places, and the social services department will tell you what's available in your area. Ask your social worker, if you have one. Places are allocated according to need, and you may have to go on a waiting list.

Private residential homes The local social services can provide you with a list of private homes in your area. The standards and cost of private homes vary enormously.

Voluntarily-run residential homes Age Concern, Help the Aged and Counsel and Care for the Elderly (pages 368-9) can all help you find a suitable residential or nursing home for no charge. GRACE, an organisation which matches a person's needs to a particular home, charges a small fee.

Nursing homes Nursing homes have to be registered with local authorities, and your local social services department or hospital will probably provide a list. If not, look in the Yellow Pages under 'Nursing homes'. There are very few NHS nursing homes, most are private or run by charities. Word of mouth is one way to find a good one.

DEALING WITH DIFFICULT RELATIVES

● Ask yourself *why* you have a problem with them – are you trying to make them do what *you* want?
● Put yourself in their shoes – perhaps they're lonely, or bored, or depressed. Organise things for both of you to do; evening classes or trips to the cinema.
● Don't respond to rudeness with rudeness – try and ease the situation with kindness and humour.
● If there's a big argument, ask a family friend to mediate; they have a better chance of seeing everyone's point of view.

What to look for in a home

Draw up a short list of homes that you would like to visit, and check with the local social services department and health authority that they have all been registered and recently inspected.

Staff Do you like them and the person in charge? Are they friendly to other residents? What is the staff ratio to residents – for people needing full care, this should be about one staff member to three to five residents.

Brochure Ask if they have a brochure explaining the number and size of rooms; facilities; fees; extras; services provided, and so on. If there isn't one, ask about all of these things when you visit.

Bedrooms Are there double rooms for couples? Do they have their own bathrooms? If not, how many share? Are there aids for the disabled, such as alarms and bath rails? Is there a good heating system?

Visitors and outings Can visitors stay overnight? Is there a communal sitting room with television? Is the home near friends and family, and can residents stay overnight elsewhere if they want to?

Atmosphere Do residents seem happy, and are they able to pursue their own hobbies in their own time? Does the home arrange social events and outings for the residents?

Meals Ask to see a typical week's menu and try and sample a meal. Are snacks and cups of tea available between meals? What times are meals served?

Health Do residents keep their own doctor or is everyone registered with one practice? How is medication administered – do residents look after their own, or do staff give it? If residents become ill or frail, will they be encouraged to move elsewhere?

Finance How much are the basic fees, and how much will extras cost – laundry, a single room, chiropody or a special diet, for instance? Are statements of charges sent out regularly to relatives where applicable? Can residents keep their own pension books? Are they covered by personal insurance for accidents or theft of personal belongings? What notice will be given of increased charges?

Trial stays In many cases it is possible to arrange a trial stay of a week or fortnight in a home to check that it is suitable. Age Concern produce three leaflets (numbers 10, 11 and 12) on choosing accommodation. They are available on request.

Dealing with any problems

Speak to the person in charge of the home first if you have any complaints. If this does not prove satisfactory, you can contact the social services department (for a residential home) or the district health authority (for a nursing home).

Paying the bills

Local authority homes The local authority subsidises most residents in its own homes, depending on their ability to pay; this is assessed according to both income and capital.

Private and voluntary homes Charges vary greatly, although nursing homes are usually more expensive than residential homes. You may be entitled to Income Support towards the cost of living in a home – contact social services for advice. If you own your home, you will be expected to sell it to pay for home care unless an elderly or incapacitated relative still lives there.

Useful addresses

Age Concern
1268 London Road
London SW16 4ER.
Tel: 081 679 8000.
Provides help on all aspects of old age, from choosing residential homes to care in your own house.

Alzheimer's Disease Society
158-160 Balham High Road
London SW12 9BN.
Tel: 081 675 6557.
Will advise on coping with Alzheimer's disease, runs a support network and advises on other illnesses.

Association of Crossroads Care Attendant Schemes Ltd
10 Regent Place
Rugby
Warwickshire CV21 2PN.
Tel: 0788 573 653.
Has a network of temporary carers available free of charge.

British Red Cross Society
9 Grosvenor Crescent
London SW1X 7EJ.
Tel: 071 235 5454.
Will advise on help in the home for elderly people.

Carers National Association
29 Chilworth Mews
London W2 3RG.
Tel: 071 724 7776.
Provides advice and information for carers.

The Centre for Accessible Environment
35 Great Smith Street
London SW1P 3BJ.
Tel: 071 222 7980.
Will advise on adapting accommodation to an elderly person.

Counsel and Care for the Elderly
Twyman House
16 Bonny Street
London NW1 9PG.
Tel: 071 485 1550.
Gives free general advice on choosing an old people's home and obtaining grants.

Disabled Living Foundation
380-384 Harrow Road
London W9 2HU.
Tel: 071 289 6111.
Has information on adapted equipment for the disabled elderly.

GRACE
35 Walnut Tree Close
Guildford
Surrey GU1 4UL.
Tel: 0483 304 354.
Will match the requirements of an old person with a suitable home for a fee.

Help the Aged
16-18 St James Walk
London EC1R 0BE.
Tel: 071 253 0253.
Has a wide range of leaflets available offering advice on finance, mobility and so on.

Pensioners Link
405-407 Holloway Road
London N7 6HJ.
Tel: 071 700 4070.
Organises volunteers to visit isolated people and arranges contacts with local schools.

WHAT TO DO IF SOMEONE DIES

Death at home

● Inform the doctor. If it is an expected death, he may not come straight away.
● The funeral director will normally take the body away. Most run a 24 hour service, but may charge you extra for collecting the body outside normal office hours.
● Every death must be registered within five days (see next page). To register the death you must be either a relative of the person, someone who was present at the death or someone who lives in the same house.

In hospital

● The hospital administrative staff will contact relatives and assist with arrangements.
● If you want the body transferred directly to the funeral directors from the mortuary, you will have to take home with you any personal belongings of the dead person.
● A relative or friend must provide written authorisation for the body to be removed from the hospital.

Overseas deaths

● If a British person dies abroad, whether a visitor or a resident, the death must be registered according to local requirements.
● Get the British Consul or his representative to register the death as well;

if this is not done, there will be no official record of the death in Britain, which could cause problems with the will.

● If you decide to bring a body back home, it will be expensive and the paperwork will be complicated. Larger firms of funeral directors usually have agents abroad who can arrange transport and deal with the paperwork.

● The doctor who registers the death overseas must be specific about the cause of death – 'natural causes' is not regarded as sufficient explanation under British law.

Registering a death

● The name, address and telephone number of your local registrar will be on noticeboards in post offices, doctors' surgeries and Citizens Advice Bureaux, or look in the phone book under 'Registration of births, deaths and marriages'.

● You will need a doctor's certificate confirming the death; the dead person's National Health Service Card, which may be at home or with the doctor; and a marriage certificate where applicable. You may need several copies of the death certificate.

● The registrar will give you two forms: the green one, a certificate of disposal, is for you to give to the funeral directors; the white one is for dealing with social services and claiming benefit.

● If there is a delay in obtaining the death certificate, you must inform the local registrar in writing that a medical certificate of the cause of death has been signed by a doctor. The death certificate must be presented within a further nine days.

Finding the will

When someone dies the responsibility for sorting out his or her affairs (known as the 'estate') is taken on by the 'executor' named in the will. This is generally the widow or widower, a friend or a relative. Where the dead person's estate is large or complicated, a second professional executor, such as a solicitor, may also have been appointed.

● The executor needs to find the will – if it is not at home, check with the solicitor or bank – as it gives the executor(s) legal authority to act. It may also contain instructions about the funeral and burial or cremation.

● The executor will also need to apply for probate at the Probate Registry (address from the local Citizens Advice Bureau or listed in the phone book under 'Probate Registry' if you live in England; in Scotland, executors need to be 'confirmed' by the sheriff's office. Ask for 'letters of administration' – they give the power to act as executor.

● If there is no will or named executor, the closest relative should apply for probate.

● The costs involved in sorting out the estate – including that of the funeral – are also the responsibility of the executor. Any expenses incurred can be claimed back from the estate later.

THE BENEFIT OF THINKING AHEAD

Arranging a funeral is an unhappy experience, and those with the courage to face facts beforehand can make things easier for everyone. By sorting out your funeral details in advance, you will save your family and friends additional stress at the time of your death. It will also work out cheaper – you can sometimes get a better deal with a prepaid funeral plan, and you have the time to compare costs.

If you are holding onto your savings to pay for a funeral and this is preventing you from claiming benefits, think about paying for it in advance. That way, you'll have peace of mind and may also be entitled to help.

THE DUTIES OF AN EXECUTOR

When you are naming an executor for your estate, don't choose anyone much older than yourself – they may die first. If one person, such as your husband or wife, is going to be the beneficiary, then they are probably the best person to wind up your affairs. Otherwise choose a close relative or friend.

Winding up an estate can take a long time, and can also be complicated. If you retain a solicitor to do it for you, his fees will come out of the estate when it is finally sorted out. The executor is responsible for:

- Finding the will.
- Arranging the funeral.
- Finding out what has been left.
- Finding out what debts are owed.
- Applying for probate.
- Possibly raising a loan to pay off any capital transfer tax and to cover probate fees.
- Distributing as much as possible before probate is granted.
- Accumulating all the assets in one place.
- Clearing outstanding debts.
- Distributing legacies.
- Transferring property, such as a house, from one name to another.
- Preparing a final account and dividing up what is left.

Organising a funeral

Most people are buried or cremated in the rites of their religion, whether active believers or not. For non-believers, a secular funeral conducted by a member of the family or a friend can be arranged – for information and suggested wording of such a service, contact the British Humanist Association (page 373).

To arrange a burial

The funeral director will advise on what documents you need to bury a body. Burial charges vary, but include gravedigging, a service at the graveside, church or chapel, and maybe a choir or organist. Charges are generally paid by the funeral director and then included on the bill under the heading 'Disbursements'.

Churchyard burials This is at the discretion of the parish priest – in theory, anyone who lives in the parish, whether Christian or not, can be buried in the church grounds. But in practice, most are very overcrowded. In any case, unless you have a family connection with a piece of ground, the vicar or rector will decide where the grave is to go.

Cemeteries of a certain denomination Some graveyards are reserved for particular religions – contact your local social services department for information or ask the funeral director.

Private burials If you want to be buried on your own land, you must obtain permission from the local authority planning department and inform the local authority environmental health department.

To arrange a cremation

Cremation usually is cheaper than burial but involves more paperwork.

Doctors' certificates You will need two certificates, so ask your doctor to arrange for a colleague to see the body.

Cremation application forms Four copies need to be filled in, one by a member of the family, two by the doctors who saw the body, and one by the medical referee at the crematorium. You can get the forms from undertakers or crematoriums.

Chapel service at the crematorium You can provide your own clergyman or use one of a rota at the crematorium. The service will be brief, so if you want a longer religious service, organise one in your local church; the body can be taken for cremation before or afterwards.

Ashes You must decide what is to be done with the ashes. They can be buried or scattered in a churchyard, buried behind a memorial plaque in the crematorium or scattered by the family wherever they wish. They are usually available 24 hours after the cremation.

Cremation following an overseas death To cremate a body brought from abroad, send all the documentation from overseas plus the cremation application form to the Home Office, E4 Division (see facing page). Telephone them to explain the urgency, and mark your application 'Cremation – urgent'.

Choosing a funeral director
Which firm to use? Most firms belong to the National Association of Funeral Directors (see facing page). Their code of practice includes providing a brochure about services and charges, a written estimate and a high standard of conduct. Also ask your doctor or friends for recommendations, or look in the Yellow Pages under 'Funeral directors'.

Compare costs Funeral costs vary enormously, so get a friend to ring around two or three firms for quotes to avoid unnecessary expense.

Budgeting Be quite clear about how much you can afford to spend and stick to it. Even a basic funeral – involving undertakers' services, a coffin, a hearse, one following car and bearers – will cost you hundreds of pounds. Extras – such as linings, brass handles, more cars – are available if wanted, but don't let yourself be persuaded. Remember, it is a business transaction for the funeral director.

ANNOUNCING A DEATH

After you have rung around close relatives and friends, the best way to inform people of a death is to place an announcement in the local paper or national papers. You can do this in writing or by phone (papers generally ring back to check that phone messages aren't hoaxes), or the funeral director will do it for you as part of the service.

Include information about the funeral if appropriate – date, time and place – or let it be known that a memorial service will be held at a later date. If you don't want flowers, say so, or state 'family flowers only'. If you specify 'cut flowers only' you will be able to send them to a hospital or old people's home afterwards. Or suggest that a donation is made to some charity instead.

Getting on with life

Inform relevant people
Employers, insurance companies, pension operators, banks, building societies and credit card companies will all need to be told urgently of a

death. Make sure you have several copies of the death certificate for this – photocopies will not do.

Remember to cancel membership of organisations such as the AA and libraries, and inform hire purchase companies. You may be able to claim back any unused subscriptions, but don't count on it. Professional advisers – solicitor, dentist, accountant and so on – need to be told.

Claiming benefits

Any benefits available will depend on your individual circumstances. Your local social services department can advise you. Ask for their free leaflets NP45, *A Guide to Widow's Benefits*, FB29, *Help when Someone Dies*, and IR23, *Income Tax and Widows*.

Sorting out your housing

If it is your husband or wife who has died, and the family home is in their name, ask a solicitor about altering it to your own. This will depend on the terms of the will, however.

If you live in rented accommodation, get advice from a solicitor or the Citizens Advice Bureau about your rights as a tenant.

Personal possessions

Some of the dead person's possessions may have been allocated in the will, but you must decide what to do with the rest. Personal effects – such as clothes and shoes – are best dealt with quickly as they can be very distressing. Good-quality clothes can be taken to local charity shops.

COPING WITH BEREAVEMENT

● Take your time – expect to feel dazed and shocked.

● Don't rush into changes in your lifestyle – selling your house or changing jobs – until you have adjusted to your new situation.

● Try and see your friends as much as possible, and talk about the death as freely as you want.

● If there are new responsibilities that you are not confident in – such as finance – ask friends for help.

● Find company and support in groups of other bereaved people – your doctor or the Citizens Advice Bureau will be able to put you in touch.

Useful addresses

British Humanist Association
14 Lambs Conduit Passage
London WC1R 4RH.
Tel: 071 430 0908.
Will advise on non-religious burial services.

Cruse
126 Sheen Road
Richmond
Surrey TW9 1UR.
Tel: 081 940 4818.
Offers a counselling service to the bereaved.

Home Office, E4 Division
50 Queen Anne's Gate
London SW1H 9AT.
Tel: 071 273 3776.

Gives approval for the cremation of bodies brought from abroad.

National Association of Master Masons
Crown Buildings
High Street
Aylesbury
Bucks HP20 1SL.
Tel: 0296 434 750.
Supplies names of local masons.

National Association of Funeral Directors
618 Warwick Road
Solihull
West Midlands B91 1AA.
Tel: 021 711 1343.
Supplies names of local firms.

Your rights as a consumer

TAKE CARE WHEN SHOPPING

What the law says

When you buy something in a shop, you are protected by the Sale of Goods Act which insists that the goods the shopkeeper sells you must measure up to the following three tests.

They must be of merchantable quality They must be fit for sale and also reasonably suitable for the purpose for which they are intended: a vacuum cleaner must pick up dust; a can opener must open cans.

They must be fit for purpose In addition, they must be fit for any *specific* purpose for which you say you want them. If you ask for fabric to cover a chair seat, they can't sell you dress fabric; if you ask for an adhesive to stick wood and get one that sticks ceramics, it's not 'fit for purpose'.

They must be as described If you want a pink electric underblanket, and the packet says it's a pink one but when you get it home it's blue, it's not as described.

If the goods don't measure up in any of these ways, don't use them: you are entitled to a suitable replacement or your money back. You do *not* have to accept a credit note, so don't. Why should the shop be earning interest on your money while you decide what you want to buy?

But you can't get a replacement or refund simply because you don't like something, or it doesn't fit, unless you bought it at a store with an exchange/money-back policy.

Is the price correctly marked?

Even if goods are priced wrongly, you do not have the right to buy them at the marked price. The shopkeeper can change it to the correct price, but you are entitled to report him to the Trading Standards Officer.

Buying privately

You are not as well covered by law when you buy from a private person, so take extra care when buying privately:

● Before going to see an item, make a checklist of the points that are important to you in any given purchase. If you want to buy a rabbit hutch, for example, a water-tight roof and a secure door are going to be essential.

● Take a friend along with you as a witness to the sale.

Note: some dealers pose as private individuals selling from home so as to evade the requirements of the Sale of Goods and Trade Description Acts. If you suspect this, report the person to your local Trading Standards Officer, found by contacting your local county or borough council.

Buying secondhand

All three basic requirements of the Sale of Goods Act apply. You can't expect goods to be in perfect condition, but they should work unless you were told otherwise. If you buy a secondhand dishwasher and find it doesn't function, you're entitled to your money back. Before you buy anything:

● Know the approximate secondhand value of what you're buying. Look in local papers, *Exchange & Mart*, and on noticeboards.

● Take a really good look at the item in daylight, and if possible have a demonstration.

● Take along an expert if you're buying something expensive, such as a piano, car or mountain bike.

Paying for things

Using a credit card If the goods turn out to be faulty, you have rights against the credit card company provided the goods cost more than £100 and less than £30,000.

Buying on hire purchase You don't actually own the goods until all the instalments have been paid. So if you get behind with repayments, the company may repossess the goods.

Buying on credit With credit, the goods become your property immediately. If you fall behind with repayments, the finance company can take legal action to recover the loan but not the goods.

Guaranteed satisfaction

● Many goods carry a guarantee: if they go wrong within a specified period, the manufacturer will mend them free of charge. You usually have to sign the guarantee at the time of purchase, or shortly after, and return it to the maker. Keep a copy of the terms.

● The law requires that goods should be repaired under the manufacturer's guarantee within a reasonable period of time, but does not specify how long. But many trade associations do specify a time limit in their codes of conduct for members. If a member firm fails to honour the guarantee period, you can contact the trade body and ask for the case to be referred to arbitration. But note: this usually removes your right to go to court if the judgment goes against you, so it's better to go straight to the Small Claims Court.

● Guarantees are also sometimes called warranties, especially in the motor trade.

Shopping by post

Your legal rights are the same as when buying in a shop (see facing page). There is an added advantage that you can usually return items merely because you don't like or want them, provided you deal with a firm that belongs to a trade association with a code of practice, such as the Association of Mail Order Publishers. But make sure you fulfil the requirements of the mail order firm, such as 'return within seven days of receipt', since it is not legally obliged to take goods back if you change your mind about wanting them.

Tips for postal shopping

● Keep details of your orders, ideally as a photocopy.

● When ordering from an advertisement, keep a copy of the ad and the title and date of the publication you saw it in.

● On your copy of the transaction, make a note of how you paid: cheque number, credit card or postal order. Never send cash.

375

● Get a certificate of posting or use recorded delivery when returning unwanted goods.

● Keep copies of any correspondence with a mail order firm.

Unsolicited goods

If you get a parcel you haven't ordered, together with a demand for money, remember that you don't have to pay for unsolicited goods.

● Write to the company that sent them pointing out that you didn't order any goods and ask them to collect them.

● If you keep the goods unused and in their original packaging, and no-one calls for them within six months, you can keep them.

Club selling

Clubs usually specialise in things like books and records. Your initial order is likely to be a bargain, after which you agree to buy a certain number of items within a specified period of time. These items are usually sold at less than shop prices.

Club shopping is a good way of building up a book or music library, but be sure that you really want a long-term supply of the goods and you are well organised. Most clubs offer an 'item of the month' which you will be sent unless you say you don't want it. The club should:

● Spell out the special offers and the conditions of joining.

● Indicate any extras, such as postage and packing.

● Say how long it is before you can cancel your membership.

Buying in sales

Be quite clear – your rights when buying in sales are the same as when buying at full price, no matter what the shop signs say. Goods must be of merchantable quality, fit for purpose and meet their description. But if you want to take goods back, act quickly. Check sale goods the minute you get them home. Don't leave them in their packaging for a couple of months and *then* hope to make a successful claim.

Watch out for these attempts to confuse you:

'**Sale goods not exchanged**' Not true. If something is faulty, take it back and demand a replacement or refund *unless* you could have seen the fault in the shop (the pattern is crooked on the fabric, for example), or if it was pointed out to you by the sales staff at the time. ('There is a slight chip in the rim, madam.')

'**No cash refund on sale goods**' Not true. If goods are faulty you can ask for a replacement or a refund. You are *not* obliged to accept a credit note to be spent in the shop at a later date.

'**Recommended retail price £50, our price £30**' This kind of notice is illegal.

'**Reduced from £50 to £30**' For this claim to be made, the goods should normally have been sold at the higher price in either the shop itself or a named branch of the same chain for at least 28 consecutive days in the last six months. But even so, it is up to *you* to decide whether you think the goods are worth £30.

'**Worth £50, our price £30**' A possibly illegal claim – again it is up to you to decide.

'**Elsewhere £50, our price £30**' This sign is illegal unless the shop specifies the name and location of 'elsewhere'.

Golden rules for sale shopping

● Don't buy anything you don't really want or need.
● Carry measurements of family sizes with you. Likewise, take details of fabric or wallpaper requirements. If you buy too little, it can be difficult to match batches; and some items truly are the end of the line.
● Check dimensions for kitchen appliances and furniture: you'll want to know if you can get items like a large sofa through your doors.
● Have a thorough look at shop-soiled or imperfect items. These are sometimes bought in specially by the shop and may be so stained that you will never get them clean.
● Watch out for offers of credit. Check how much interest you will be paying. If a store urges you to take out its store card, check the APR (annual percentage rate of interest, page 40) which may be higher than on your normal credit card.

Putting down a deposit

When you put down a deposit on something you want to buy, you enter into a binding contract with the trader: he will supply the goods and you will pay the balance. If you change your mind, you lose your deposit, and the trader can sue you for any money lost as a result of the failed transaction. But if the trader goes bust, you are also likely to lose your deposit, so:
● Try to avoid paying a deposit at all. Only pay up if it's something that creates a risk for the trader – booking a package holiday or ordering hand-blocked wallpaper that's not normally stocked, for example.
● Only put down deposits at reputable outlets, rather than stores that have been open for just a short time.
● Don't be lured into parting with a large deposit because a discount is offered. Home improvement firms often offer the one against the other.
● Pay your deposit by credit card if the item costs over £100. If the trader goes bust the credit card company is equally liable and you should be able to claim from them.
● Check if the company has a special account for customers' deposits. If it does, your money will be safe even if the firm goes broke.

Defective goods and services

A product is considered defective if it is not as safe as people are entitled to expect. If you (or someone else) are injured by something because of its design rather than incorrect use, you can claim compensation.
● If you bought the goods, you will have to sue the supplier (usually the retailer) under the law of contract.
● If someone else bought the goods, but you were injured and can prove they are defective, you can claim unlimited compensation for personal injury, death or damage to property over £275. You will have to sue the producer, importer or organisation (if it's an 'own brand' label). Retailers are liable only if they will not disclose their supplier.
● Under the Sale of Goods Act, it is the retailer's responsibility to provide a remedy for any defective goods he supplied. Don't let him pass the buck to the manufacturer.

Labelling and instructions

● Check the label *before* you buy an item: a radio set may not receive the wave length you require; a saucepan may not be suitable for your type of hob.
● If the information you need isn't on the label, ask. Then you'll be able to

claim your rights under the Sale of Goods Act (page 374) if you have a problem with the goods later.

● Read the instructions before you use new equipment. If you don't understand them, ring the manufacturer (the address should be on the packaging or any literature supplied) and ask. Don't just take the item back to the shop.

Defective services

● If you've received a service which isn't up to scratch, ask for it to be remedied. This applies as much to smeary window cleaning as to a poor decorating job. If the person concerned refuses, take the matter up with a more senior member of staff, the appropriate trade association, the Citizens Advice Bureau or your local Trading Standards Officer (found through your county or borough council). If a considerable sum of money is involved, go to the Small Claims Court (page 382).

● Before anyone undertakes a service for you, be quite sure what you are expecting to get and what they are expecting to deliver. If you assume that a quotation for decorating your sitting room includes lining the walls, make sure it does − before the work is done.

Buying at auction

Conditions of sale These are printed in the catalogue or displayed on the auction room wall, and they normally exclude the three major rules of the Sale of Goods Act (goods must be of merchantable quality, fit for purpose and as described). It's up to you to decide if the goods are what you want before you bid.

The catalogue Since it is covered by the Trade Descriptions Act, the facts in it are required by law to be correct. A sideboard labelled 'Georgian' should be of that period and not a reproduction. Items with something wrong are marked WAF ('with all faults') and AF ('as found'). Take a good look at pieces marked like this.

Tips for bidders Bidding at auction may be unnerving at first, but you'll get used to it. Remember to:
● Study the catalogue carefully.
● Have a good look at the items you are interested in.
● Fix an upper price limit and don't go above it.
● Be ready to remove goods quickly, possibly immediately after the auction (the catalogue will state when). You may need to borrow or hire suitable transport.

OLD WIVES' TALE: BIDDING AT AUCTION

If you blow your nose or scratch your head you will have made a bid. No. You will only have bid if you raise your hand and the auctioneer indicates that he accepts it. If you can't face bidding yourself, ask a member of the auction room staff to bid on your behalf; make sure they know the maximum amount you're prepared to pay.

Car auctions Many cars sold at auctions are in fairly poor condition, so it's not advisable to buy a car in this way unless you are a good mechanic yourself, or know someone who can look at the car. Even so, you won't have much chance to inspect a vehicle, and if you find something wrong after buying, there's little chance of a refund. However, if the vehicle was sold with a warranty, or a description stating 'no mechanical faults', you might be able to get your money back.

Doorstep selling

● Always answer the door with the chain on when you are not expecting anyone to call.
● Check proof of identity, particularly if they claim to be selling for the disabled or unemployed.
● Never let anyone into the house while you are there on your own. Make an appointment for when someone else is at home.

Your rights

● If a product is faulty, you have the same rights as if you bought it in a shop (page 374).
● You have the right to cancel most arrangements within seven days as long as the trader didn't have an appointment.
● For life assurance, you have ten days to think about it.

How to say no

● Most reputable firms will accept a 'no' once they've delivered their sales pitch.
● If a salesman does refuse to leave your home, call the police. Report them to their head office the next day.

If you are interested

● Don't say yes on the spot – take a day or two to check you can't get a better price elsewhere.
● Ignore phrases like 'I can do a special discount if you sign tonight' or 'Prices are going up next week'.
● Check what you are actually getting. Ask to see pictures, and where possible, samples. With big projects, like loft extensions, insist on visiting one of their finished jobs.
● Check what the total cost will be – are there hidden charges? Does it include labour where relevant?
● If you pay a deposit, make sure you get a proper receipt on paper printed with the firm's name, address and telephone number.

DO YOU WANT TO LIVE IN A SHOWROOM?

With some products, like double glazing or special exterior paint, you may be offered a discount if you agree to let your home be used as a showhouse. It may be a bargain (check the prices quoted to be sure it is), but the company will be showing people around your home. Be quite sure that you and the company are agreed on how long the arrangement will last, or how many visits it involves.

Renting and hiring goods

● Check the total hire charge.
● Check on penalties if you over-run the hire period. You might need a piece of equipment for longer or be unable to return it.
● Check if you have to pay a deposit, how much it is and under what conditions the hire firm might keep it.
● Check on insurance. You are not responsible for damage caused by fair wear and tear (blunting of a chainsaw blade, for example) but you

will have to compensate the hirer if you lose or damage the goods.
● On long-term arrangements, such as renting a video, check when you can end the hire agreement. The Consumer Credit Act 1974 says you can terminate an agreement after 18 months, whatever the contract states, as long as payments are less than £300 a year. But if the payments are more, you can only terminate an agreement if the contract says so.

EATING IN RESTAURANTS

Making a complaint

If the food is not up to standard Complain as soon as possible. Don't wait until you've finished eating. You can ask for another dish or simply refuse to pay the bill. Restaurants generally prefer to deal with complaints rather than upsetting other customers.

If the wine is corked or poor Complain to the wine waiter and either get it replaced or refuse to pay for it. Don't drink it all first.

If the service is poor Refuse to pay the service charge but explain why to the manager.

Tips for restaurant-goers

● Pay separately for pre-dinner drinks or you will find that VAT and service charge apply to them as well on the final bill.
● Turn up when you've booked a table or the restaurateur may sue you for lost profit – that's why they take your phone number when you book.
● The proprietor has a right to refuse to serve you if you are incorrectly dressed or don't behave appropriately.
● Restaurants must display their prices, including VAT, so that you can read them before you take a table. You are obliged to pay these amounts, plus any indicated service charge. Some restaurants ask for a percentage service charge; others leave it up to you.
● When you get your bill, check whether the service charge is already included. Some restaurants include it in the total bill but leave the bottom line of a credit card slip blank. This gives the impression that service charge should be added in – and you end up paying it twice.
● Always check your bill against the prices on the menu and make sure there are no additions.

HOLIDAY PROBLEMS

When you book

Use a reputable travel agent Those belonging to ABTA (Association of British Travel Agents), page 383, have agreed to abide by a code of conduct that states:
● Holiday brochures should be truthful.
● If an operator has to cancel or alter a holiday, you must be told as soon as possible and offered a full refund or another holiday of the same or better standard.
● There must be no major alterations to the holiday later than 14 days before departure.
● There must be no surcharges because of currency fluctuations later than 30 days before departure. Any others, such as fuel costs, must be proved to be necessary.

● If you get to your resort and there is no accommodation available, you must be offered alternative accommodation of the same standard. If it is lower, you must be paid compensation.

● If the company goes bankrupt before you take your holiday, you must be compensated; if it is during your holiday, ABTA undertakes to get you home once it's finished as booked.

Check the small print If there are features which are important to you, ask about them before you book, and confirm any agreement in writing.

Keep your correspondence Keep any letters written to you and copies of your replies. You may need them later.

Making a complaint

Talk to the tour operator's representative Many travel firms have representatives on site. They are there to make sure you enjoy yourself, and also to sort out problems. Take a copy of the brochure and booking form with you when you talk to the representative.

Collect evidence of your complaint If other guests are equally dissatisfied with the arrangements, get them to write a signed statement saying so. Take photographs of the nearby motorway that wasn't mentioned in the brochure, the tiny swimming pool or the substandard rooms.

When you get home Write to the managing director of the travel firm detailing your complaints and including:
● Copies of any statements and photographs you have as evidence.
● Travel dates, including the time and place of your arrival and departure.
● Your hotel and resort address.
● Your booking reference number and the name which the holiday was booked in.
● What you want as compensation for breach of contract and any extra unexpected expenses on the holiday – taxis to a beach that was supposed to be within walking distance, for example.

Do not be threatening, though. The whole matter may be resolved easily at this stage.

Get advice from ABTA The association will give advice on how to seek redress, and possibly on realistic levels of compensation.

What can go wrong on the journey

Long delays You will not get compensation for delays from the transport company but your travel insurance may well cover it (page 358). Most airlines or coach companies will provide meals and accommodation after a set period of delay, however. Complain to a representative of the transport company, preferably with other passengers to support you, if these services aren't offered.

Overbooking Airlines frequently overbook their flights. If you are seriously delayed you might be able to get compensation. Ask the airline for a form to apply for 'denied-boarding compensation'.

Lost luggage Report lost baggage immediately to the airline. Also ask for the Lost and Found office and report the details. Get a receipt stating that you have reported it for insurance purposes.
● The airline may pay for you to buy basic necessities while they try and trace your luggage.
● If the amount of airline compensation looks low, claim under your own insurance policy.

HOW TO COMPLAIN

When you make the complaint

● Be clear what you're complaining about and what compensation you want. Under consumer law (page 374), you have a right to a replacement, a complete repair or your money back if goods are faulty. You don't have to accept a credit note.

If a service is unsatisfactory you can ask to have it repeated (a poor respray job on your car, for example) or for money to compensate for the problem – a dry cleaner might have ruined an irreplaceable garment.

● Don't be rude, be reasonable. You're much more likely to get results.

● Establish who you should talk to. If you are phoning, ask the operator who you should speak to and check with that person that they can help you before telling your story. You don't need to talk to a very senior person at this stage; you may be able to resolve your problem at a lower level.

● State your case clearly and concisely. Don't confuse the issue by adding statements like 'and the sales girl was very rude when I bought it'. You're complaining about a specific problem. Stick to that.

● Take your receipt with you but don't hand it over. If you are complaining by letter, enclose a photocopy of it.

If you get no satisfaction

1 Take the matter to a higher authority, such as the firm's Managing Director. Send any correspondence by recorded delivery, stating your complaint and the compensation you require.

2 Take up the matter with the appropriate trade association. Many of these operate a code of conduct which their members should follow and they may be able to arbitrate in your complaint. You can get a full list of trade associations and their codes of practice from the Office of Fair Trading (see facing page).

3 If you feel strongly aggrieved, take the matter to court (see below). If you incur heavy costs in postage, photocopying or phone calls, include these in your request for compensation.

The Small Claims Court

You can often sort out unresolved complaints about goods or services by taking your case to a Small Claims Court. These informal, but still official, hearings deal with claims of £1000 or less in England and Wales, £500 or less in Northern Ireland and £750 or less in Scotland. All that's required to take a claim to this court is some of your time and a certain amount of paperwork. If your case is complicated, get advice either from a solicitor or a Citizens Advice Bureau before proceeding with your claim.

Is it worth the trouble? Before going to law over a complaint, check that who or whatever you are complaining about is *worth* taking to court. If they can't pay up you're wasting your time. If they can, it may be worth starting proceedings.

Issue a summons in the county court Ask county court officials to help with this procedure. They are not allowed to give legal advice but can assist with form filling. There is a small fee for issuing this summons.

At the hearing held in front of an arbitrator
● Be sure you have all the facts and any supporting documentation with you.
● Take a friend if you feel daunted.
● Be sure what you are claiming. As well as the actual cost of an item or

correcting poor workmanship, you can claim for inconvenience, expenses (which may include court fees, witnesses' expenses or photocopies or documents) and a sum for distress.
● Any decision made in this court is final – generally, there is no appeal.

Free legal advice

● The Citizens Advice Bureau (see below) gives advice and has professional lawyers working with their volunteers. They can also tell you which solicitors in your area have experience of your type of case.
● Neighbourhood Law Centres are run by professional lawyers and will both advise you and act in court. If they take your case, their services are generally free (including court work) although you may be asked to pay a contribution.
● Legal Advice Centres give advice but don't carry out court work.
● Trade unions provide a legal service for their members.
● Motoring organisations, such as the AA and RAC, provide legal advice on motoring matters – and representation in certain cases.
● Consumer Advice Centres, run by some local authorities, will advise on court action and may write to the shop or firm you are in dispute with on your behalf.

Legal Aid Board

The Legal Aid Board (see below) runs two schemes to help with payment of legal costs – legal aid, and the green form scheme. The Legal Aid Board or your local Citizens Advice Bureau will tell you if you are eligible for help and how to apply.

Solicitors

● Most solicitors offer an initial half-hour consultation for a small flat fee. It is well worth it as they will advise you on the strength of your case and your chances of getting legal aid.
● Any later interviews will be expensive – bills can run into hundreds of pounds – so shop around before you instruct a solicitor.
● If you want to apply for the Legal Aid Board's green form scheme, tell the solicitor at the first meeting. If he doesn't operate the scheme, he will be able to tell you who does.
● The Solicitors' Directory, found in public libraries, will tell you which solicitors in your area deal with which sorts of cases.

Useful addresses

Advertising Standards Authority
Brook House
2-16 Torrington Place
London WC1E 7HN.
Tel: 071 580 5555.
Acts as advertising watchdog.

Association of British Travel
Agents (ABTA)
55-57 Newman Street
London W1P 4AH.
Tel: 071 637 2444.
Members follow code of practice.

Office of Fair Trading
Field House
Breams Buildings
London EC4A 1PR.
Tel: 071 242 2858.
Has full list of trade associations.

Legal Aid Board
Newspaper House
8-16 Great New Street
London EC4A 3BN.
Tel: 071 353 7411.
Helps people on low incomes to meet the cost of legal action.

National Association of Citizens
Advice Bureaux
115 Pentonville Road
London N1 9LZ.
Tel: 071 833 2181.
Will provide the address and phone of your local office.

Pets and their care

CHOOSING A PET

Pets can be a great source of education, friendship, protection and happiness, but they are entirely dependent on their owners for every aspect of their well-being. Consider getting one only if you're prepared to take responsibility for feeding, companionship, exercise and health for the whole of an animal's life.

What sort of animal is best?

Dogs and cats are long-standing favourites, but many other species also make good pets. Consider a range of options, not just the obvious ones, and base your decision on practical considerations such as:

How much time do you have?

Dogs (page 386) A dog requires full-time commitment and should not be left alone for long periods during the day.

Cats (page 401) They'll enjoy your company when it's available, but are also quite happy to spend long stretches alone.

Rabbits (page 405) Twice-daily feeding and general attention is essential, and the more you handle them the better they will respond.

Guinea pigs, rats, hamsters, gerbils, mice (pages 407-10) They need feeding and attention at least twice a day, and preferably more often.

Fish (page 410) You'll need to find time for daily feeding and checks on conditions in the tank.

Birds (page 413) They need to be fed every day and have their cages cleaned out at least twice a week. Many can amuse themselves but parrots won't be happy for long without human company.

Tortoises (page 415) Be prepared to spend time supervising their feeding and getting housing conditions just right.

How much house room can you offer?

Dogs Don't choose a dog until you've worked out where you're going to exercise it and how often, and how you'll get rid of its waste. Also consider how boisterous a pet your home and family can put up with. Dogs come in all shapes and sizes, so you should be able to find a suitable one once you've made these decisions. A garden will make dog-keeping easier, but isn't absolutely essential, provided that you make other arrangements for outdoor exercise.

Cats A cat is a good choice for city or flat dwellers, and you don't need to have a garden.

Rabbits A sheltered outdoor area is the best place to keep rabbits; they tend to be too messy for indoor living.

Guinea pigs, rats, hamsters, gerbils, mice Easy to keep indoors.

Fish Indoor aquariums and outdoor ponds are equally suitable, but fish won't thrive in just a bowl.

Birds You'll need a draught-free spot for the cage, and heating during winter unless the bird is acclimatised.

Tortoises You can use an outdoor pen in summer but tortoises will need constant heating indoors in winter unless they are hibernated.

Suitable for children?

Dogs Very young children may not be strong enough to stand up to an energetic puppy, so it could be best to wait until the youngest is about three. Attention lavished on a new baby can also make a dog extremely jealous; make sure it knows it's still loved.

Cats Children of all ages will enjoy a cat, but they'll need to be watched when they are very small in case they hurt it. Although the risks (page 419) are small, it is best not to buy a cat or kitten while you are pregnant. Take special precautions when handling cats in pregnancy.

Rabbits Ideal pets for school-age children who are responsible enough to care for them under supervision.

Guinea pigs, rats, hamsters, gerbils, mice Suitable for responsible children over the age of about six, with some help from parents.

Fish Suitable for all ages, under supervision.

Birds Suitable for all ages, under supervision.

Tortoises Responsible children from the age of about 12 onwards will be able to care for a tortoise on their own; younger ones will usually need some help from their parents.

The cost

Dogs Bigger breeds cost much more to keep in all respects than smaller ones. Basic expenses for all dogs usually include: purchase price; initial visit to the vet; first vaccinations and annual boosters; desexing; pet insurance; holiday kennel fees; food.

Cats They're generally less expensive than dogs, but you'll probably still have to pay to buy the animal, feed it, inoculate it, have it neutered and cared for by a vet, and to put it into a cattery if you go away. Cats kept indoors will have fewer injuries and lower vet's bills than those which are free to roam.

Rabbits The expenses are relatively low: commercial rabbit food (table scraps are not enough), housing, vet's fees, holiday care.

Guinea pigs, rats, hamsters, gerbils, mice Purchase price, food, housing and vet's bills are all comparatively inexpensive.

Fish Tanks and ponds can be quite costly to set up, but running costs and food are generally inexpensive. Purchase price of fish varies according to the species.

Birds Cost depends on the type of bird and the cage it needs. A budgie won't set you back much, but an imported parrot or rarer species could be costly. Small cages are inexpensive, but flight cages and aviaries can be a big investment.

Tortoises Costs vary depending on the type, but tortoises are usually quite expensive to buy, and specialist care and advice can also be costly. Tortoises are no longer imported into Britain so you are unlikely to obtain one from a reputable dealer and a secondhand pet could be difficult to find. A legitimately sold tortoise should come with a licence from the Ministry of Agriculture, Fisheries and Food.

How mobile are you?

Dogs For housebound people, a dog can be a rewarding companion, and fosters a valuable feeling of being needed. However, you will need help from someone who is prepared to exercise the dog. Consider getting an adult dog so that you can tell in advance how much exercise it's going to need.

Cats One of the best pets if you're infirm or cannot get about easily. Their independent nature and natural cleanliness mean that they are less trouble than a dog and won't need to be exercised.

Rabbits Owner's mobility not important except for cage cleaning.

Guinea pigs, rats, hamsters, gerbils, mice Mobility less important.

Fish Owner's mobility less important.

Birds Owner's mobility less important.

Tortoises Owner's mobility less important.

IF YOU'VE DECIDED ON A DOG

How to choose

A dog to suit your circumstances Consider how a dog will affect every aspect of your way of life before you buy one, since incompatibility is likely to make both owner and dog unhappy. Ask yourself, for example, if you are prepared to go for a regular daily walk. If not, don't buy a large or energetic dog. Have you time for daily grooming? No? Then don't think of an Old English Sheepdog.

If you're finding it hard to decide, it may help to consult a book of popular dog breeds and characteristics; your local library should have one, or any good bookshop or pet shop.

Pedigree or crossbreed? Pure-bred dogs have the advantage of more predictable traits and characteristics. On the other hand, mongrels are often hardier and healthier and although they frequently join the family as an unplanned act of kindness, they could be the most loyal and loving pet you'll ever have.

Breeder or animal shelter? The decision will probably depend on whether you want a pure-bred or a cross, and whether you are prepared to consider a grown dog or only a puppy. Breeders will, of course, be able to sell you a pedigree puppy of the sort you want – though you may have to wait if a litter is not available immediately – and there is no question that a puppy of six to eight weeks brought up in a secure environment with consistent care will make the most well-adjusted family pet. If you do buy from a breeder, ask a vet to recommend a reputable one or contact the

Dog Breeders' Associates (page 400). Avoid 'puppy farms' which deal in large numbers of dogs and are not registered with the Association, and anyone who claims to have puppies always available.

Animal shelters can sometimes offer puppies, but older dogs are more common. Some adult dogs already have bad habits, but most can be overcome with good training. And by giving the animal a home you will almost certainly have saved its life. Before you decide on a dog, obtain as much information about its background as you can from the shelter.

Male or female? Neutered dogs of both sexes make home-loving and affectionate pets. By contrast, uncastrated male dogs tend to roam, mark out territory with their urine, dominate their owners and other dogs, and try to ride small children. Females are less difficult, but need to be kept away from other dogs when on heat (about three weeks every six months). Unless you have a pedigree dog you plan to breed from, neutering should be done within the first 18 months of life.

Dachshund

Beagle

Afghan Hound

Collie

Poodle

Long or short hair? Long-haired breeds need daily grooming so they're not suitable if you're pressed for time, and dogs such as Corgis and German Shepherds which have soft undercoats will need special attention at certain times of the year when they moult whole handfuls of hair. All dogs, however, regularly shed small amounts of hair, and long hairs can be easier to remove from carpets than short hairs, which become embedded in the pile. Poodles and woolly coated dogs such as Bedlingtons need to have their coats clipped every two months at a professional grooming parlour. This can be costly, but people with asthma or allergies may tolerate these breeds best and find that their coats cause less irritation.

A puppy with a pedigree Before you buy one, ask if the litter has been recorded at the Kennel Club. This means you'll be able to show or breed from the dog later on. Also ask for a signed copy of the pedigree, but remember that however impressive a dog's credentials, they don't guarantee a friendly temperament or good health, and the points below and in the box on the opposite page still apply.

Selective breeding means that some dogs are prone to particular health problems – breathing difficulties in the case of Bulldogs, for example. Find out from a vet what you're letting yourself in for before you buy a pedigree puppy.

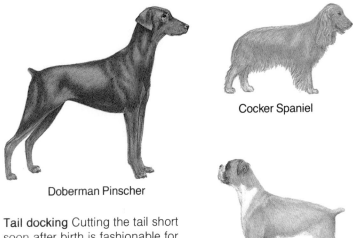

Cocker Spaniel

Doberman Pinscher

Boxer

Tail docking Cutting the tail short soon after birth is fashionable for certain breeds such as Boxers, but it is unnecessary. If you would like your pup to keep the tail it was born with, let the breeder know before the litter is born.

Breeds that bite All dogs are potential biters, and it's important for children to know this and keep their faces away from a dog's mouth. Breeds with bad reputations are Pomeranians, Yorkshire Terriers, Chow-Chows, West Highland Whites, Miniature Schnauzers, Pit Bull Terriers, Fox Terriers, Maltese Poodles, Cocker Spaniels, Collies, Afghans, Dalmatians, Dobermans, Rottweilers and German Shepherds.

Picking a puppy

A friendly, affectionate nature is essential for a family pet, especially if there are young children around. Here's how to find a puppy that's confident and playful, and neither aggressive nor insecure:
● Call the puppy to you; it should approach in a friendly, inquisitive and confident manner.
● Make a sudden loud noise. The puppy should react, but not with obvious fear.
● Pick the animal up and see if it will settle into your hands without struggling or biting. A well-adjusted puppy won't object even if you turn it onto its back.
● Put the pup down and watch to see if it runs happily back to the rest of the litter. Slinking off into a corner on its own is a bad sign.
● Observe the litter together to see how dominant or submissive your puppy is. Dominant dogs require much firmer owners, and all owners should feel confident that they will be able to dominate their dogs.
● Make a growling noise. Does the puppy growl back? Is it afraid? It's better just to be interested.

Dominant dog growls and clasps another from above to assert authority.

Submissive dog lowers its belly to the ground and offers its neck to another for biting.

● Gently pull its tail. Whimpering can show a submissive dog, but a dog that bites or appears resentful is likely to be dominant and will need a strong owner to control and train it properly.
● Observe your puppy's mother and any other relatives at the breeder's establishment. Their behaviour should give a good idea of what to expect from your dog.

HEALTH CHECKLIST

The ideal is to buy a puppy only subject to your vet's approving its state of health, but a quick preliminary check of your own can still save time, expense and disappointment:
● Ask the seller if the puppy you are interested in has had any health problems. Check that it has been wormed and, if old enough, inoculated.
● Pick up several pups and don't choose the runt of the litter, which will weigh a good deal less than the others. It could develop health problems as soon as you get it home.
● Look for fleas in the puppy's coat: a large number could indicate neglect on the part of the breeder or a puppy with low immunity.
● Examine inside the ears for black wax, which often means ear mites. This is another sign of neglect.
● Open the dog's mouth. The gums should be pink and the teeth straight. The front teeth should meet when the mouth is closed; if they don't the animal has an undershot or overshot jaw. In breeds such as Boxers and Collies this is normal, but in most it means you won't be able to show.
● Look at the eyes. They should be clear, of the same size and shape, and free of any discharge. Eyelids should fit snugly around the eyeballs.
● Feel the dog's tummy around its navel. A soft lump is likely to be a hernia which can be corrected only by surgery.
● Lift up the tail of your pup and its litter-mates. None should show any traces of diarrhoea.
● Count the toes on all four feet. There should be four, usually with a small fifth claw higher up on the inside of each leg (the dew claw). Don't worry if the dew claws are missing: not all breeds have them and others have them removed at birth. In any case, dew claws can be a nuisance if they catch on clothes or furnishings, and sometimes they have to be removed later anyway.

Dew claw

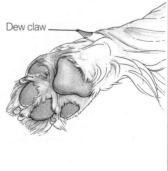

JOINING THE FAMILY

Bringing a puppy home You don't want a mishap on the first day, so make sure your home is ready before you set off to collect a new puppy:

● Check all fences, walls and hedges. Losing your inquisitive puppy is not the best way of discovering a small gap.

● Remove all sharp sticks and any other dangerous garden debris.

● Get everyone into the habit of picking up small swallowable items from around the house.

● Decide in advance where the puppy is to sleep and prepare its bedding (see *The first night*, below). It will need a rest after the upheaval and excitement of the move.

● Come straight home with your new pet. Arriving in time for the midday feed usually works well.

● Make sure that the puppy always wears a collar and identity tag when it is outdoors. See page 418 for pet identification schemes.

Adult dogs Treat grown dogs as puppies at first, particularly if they still need to be house trained.

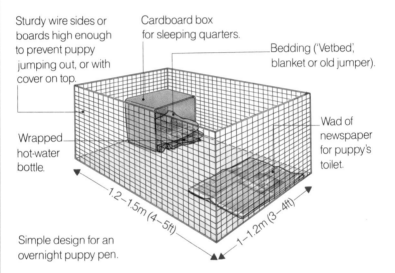

Sturdy wire sides or boards high enough to prevent puppy jumping out, or with cover on top.

Cardboard box for sleeping quarters.

Bedding ('Vetbed', blanket or old jumper).

Wrapped hot-water bottle.

Wad of newspaper for puppy's toilet.

1.2–1.5m (4–5ft)

1–1.2m (3–4ft)

Simple design for an overnight puppy pen.

The first night Help your puppy get over the loss of its mother and litter-mates by putting it in a small, escape-proof pen at night: it will feel more secure than if left to roam through the house. Place the pen in a warm, quiet spot and put a cardboard box on its side in one corner for a cosy sleeping nook. Line the bottom with an old jumper or a small blanket, or buy 'Vetbed' bedding from a pet shop. Give the pup a well-wrapped hot-water bottle as well, for comfort and warmth.

Introducing children Teach children from the start that animals are not toys and that they need to be treated gently or they may get hurt. Show them the right way to pick up a puppy, by grasping it under its chest with both hands and then holding it against your chest with one hand while supporting its weight with the other.

Explain that the puppy needs plenty of sleep, so that it will have energy for playtime later on.

When there are already other pets
Don't lavish all your attention on a new pet if there are already other animals in the house. Established pets need plenty of attention and reassurance at this time to help them feel that their place in the family 'pack' is secure. Introduce them to the new animal through a screen or baby gate at first and don't hold either pet; it's better if they're free to get to know each other in their own way.

Teaching good habits Place a thick layer of newspaper within easy reach of the puppy's sleeping quarters (see opposite page) and it will be unlikely to soil the rest of the pen at night. Laying good foundations at this stage will help with house training later on.

CARING FOR YOUR PUPPY

If you buy from a breeder, you will almost certainly be given a diet sheet. These are usually quite involved, with four different meals a day. Life will be much simpler if the puppy is weaned onto a good commercial diet before it gets the taste for gourmet meals. There are some excellent dry foods available – ask your vet.
Basic rules to follow are:
● Choose a dry food that is specially formulated for puppies. Adult dog foods may be too hard for new teeth to cope with and they sometimes cause stomach upsets.
● Make the diet change gradually over a period of three or four days so that the puppy's digestion can get used to it.
● Feed the pup four times a day – it can be the same food at every meal if it is designed for puppies.
● Make sure it is a 'complete' food. Read the labels carefully, as some bought foods require added mixers.
● Commercial puppy food needs no added supplements such as calcium or vitamins.
● Cows' milk may cause diarrhoea. Water is all that is needed and it should be available at all times.
● Follow manufacturers' recommendations for quantity, which can be according to the needs of the individual puppy. Puppies need plenty of food to help them grow and unless you have an exceptionally greedy pup it is difficult to overfeed a very young one.

Your first visit to the vet

Take your pet to a vet for a general examination within a few days of buying it. Before you go, write down questions you might like to ask. The vet will be able to advise you on vaccination, worming, feeding, de-sexing and probably also pet insurance.

Vaccinations Dogs in Britain are vaccinated against canine distemper, infectious canine hepatitis, leptospirosis, canine parvovirus and sometimes kennel cough. You can expect two or three visits in the first four months. After that, the dog will require an annual booster.

Patience pays in housetraining

The more time you spend with your puppy, the faster it will learn. But different breeds learn at different speeds, so be patient. Pen training (see *The first night*, page 390) is the soundest method for housetraining because it provides the puppy with a toilet area when you're not there.

DO'S AND DON'TS OF HOUSETRAINING

DO decide in advance where the puppy's toilet area will be.

DO take the puppy there as frequently as possible during the day.

DO learn to recognise when your puppy may want to go: after every meal; first thing in the morning and last thing at night; when it whines and circles with head down, sniffing.

DO reward lavishly with praise when the puppy uses the right area. Ignore accidents – clean them up using an odour eliminator.

DON'T leave the puppy alone in a place that you don't want it to use.

DON'T rub a puppy's nose in its mess. It won't understand.

DON'T punish your puppy if you discover it in the act. Unless you want a mess trailed through the house, it's best to let it finish and ignore the crime.

Outside toilet If you want the puppy to use an outside toilet area, paper training just adds an extra step. Instead, from day one, try to take the dog as often as possible to the toilet area you want it to use.

A key phrase If, every time the puppy uses its toilet, you say a phrase such as 'Be quick!', eventually you will be able to make it go at your request – useful on walks or last thing at night.

Training your dog to behave properly

Training can begin as soon as your puppy is established in its new home. The basic commands are: 'sit', 'down', 'stay', 'come' and 'heel':

'Sit' In a quiet room, with the dog on a leash, say 'sit' and press on its hindquarters until it sits. Give praise if it does what it's told.

'Down' Get the dog to sit, then press gently but firmly down on the shoulders and pull its forelegs forwards, saying 'down'.

'**Stay**' Make the dog sit, still on a leash, then move backwards away from it, saying 'stay'. Keep up the training until it will stay without being on a leash.

'**Come**' Get the dog to stay and then call 'come'. Use the dog's name, and give plenty of praise – and an occasional food reward – when it obeys.

'**Heel**' Teaching a dog to obey the 'heel' command is intended to get it used to walking by your side – 'at heel' – instead of excitedly rushing ahead and pulling on the leash.

With the leash hanging slack from your right hand, keep the dog on your left. Walk along and say 'heel', correcting with your right hand each time the dog strains ahead, then patting it with your left hand and giving praise when it behaves well.

If your dog misbehaves

Whatever a naughty puppy has been doing, always praise it if it comes on your command. By the time your calling has diverted its attention it is too late to punish the dog. If you *must* give punishment, remember:

● Dogs learn by associating one event with another, such as a stern tone of voice with an undesirable act, or praise with having carried out a command obediently. So be clear and consistent about misdemeanours.

● If a dog is to be punished it must be actually caught in the act – a few seconds late is too late.

● Punishment is best delivered by a loud noise or a thrown object, so that it is not associated with you. Try banging saucepan lids together, or throwing a cushion or magazine that will give the dog a fright but not hurt.

● A dog should obey you because you dominate it, *not* because it is afraid of you. If you do use punishment, make it mild enough not to cause harm or instil fear.

● Never call a dog to you to punish it – go over to the dog yourself. If it associates answering your call with punishment it will stop coming.

● Be consistent, and use an appropriate tone of voice: lavish and warm to reward, flat and calm to give commands, low and firm for 'No'.

Tips for training sessions

● Above all, be patient. Make it fun.
● When the puppy is very young, don't train it for any longer than ten minutes at a time.
● Many owners find that dog obedience classes are helpful. Classes can begin when the puppy is fully vaccinated. Early training is the best way of preventing bad behaviour later.

Facing the outside world

Between eight and 12 weeks of age, puppies pass through a very sensitive period in their development. At this stage they need to be introduced to people, new sounds, street noise – and particularly other puppies and vaccinated older dogs. A puppy well 'socialised' at this stage will grow into a well-adjusted dog. Remember that the puppy has not been vaccinated, so take precautions such as not allowing it to sniff other dogs' faeces.

DO NOT hit a dog under any circumstances during this time – a loud 'no' will be sufficient to get your point across.

On the streets Dog faeces on the streets are a health hazard (see *Internal parasites*, page 419) and unpleasant for everyone. Commercial 'poop scoops' are available to clean up the mess, but it is just as easy to carry a sturdy plastic bag with you when you go walking. Put it over your hand as a glove, pick up the droppings, then turn the bag inside out, and dispose of it in a bin.

Growing up As the dog approaches maturity – usually around the age of about six months – the commercial puppy diet can be changed to an adult formula. At this stage, the amount of food will be determined by the dog's weight. Run your fingers over his ribs. There should be 6mm ($\frac{1}{4}$in) of fat over the ribs. But you should be able to count them. Increase or decrease food accordingly. Meals should be twice daily.

De-sexing Both dogs and bitches can be de-sexed from six months.

Identification Make sure your dog wears a collar with an address tag at all times. Consider enrolling it on the National Pet Register (page 418).

OLD WIVES' TALES ABOUT DOGS

'Bitches should be allowed to have one litter before being spayed.'
It makes no difference – and there are many medical advantages in spaying while the animal is young.

'Spaying makes bitches fat.'
Not true – *overeating* makes bitches fat.

'Castrating will damage a dog's personality.'
Any changes will be for the better – most dogs become more home-loving, less aggressive, and less likely to chase bitches.

Exercising your dog

A well-exercised dog will be more content at home. A longish walk once a day is enough. Make sure your dog is trained to come back on command if you intend letting it off the leash outdoors. By rewarding with lavish praise every time it comes to you, you will teach the dog to like coming back. Call the dog often, without necessarily putting on the leash. This way he won't associate coming back with always going home, signalling the end of fun.

To increase your dog's activity:
● Take a tennis racquet with you on walks. You can hit a ball much farther than you can throw it.
● Throw a ball down a slope. The dog will soon get tired running back up – and the ball will go much farther.
● Throw the ball behind you as you walk – as you continue walking, the dog has to run that little bit farther.

Bath time for your dog

Dogs with a healthy coat do not need bathing. However, since they are around the house, owners like them to smell fragrant, rather than 'doggy'.
● Start bathing your dog while it is still young. Talk all the time in a soothing voice and give it plenty of praise.
● Put a nonslip mat on the bottom of the bath to stop the dog's nails scratching the surface.
● Use baby shampoo for washing your dog's coat.

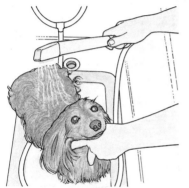

● Don't stand the dog in a pool of water – a shower hose in a bath without a plug is best.

● Wrap your dog in a towel as soon as the bath is over, to stop it shaking water everywhere.

Dealing with bad habits

Jumping up Deal with this problem when your dog is a puppy. Push the dog down with a firm command: 'Get down'. Ignore the dog until it has calmed down, then stoop to its level to pat it. Give praise and attention only when the dog has all four feet on the ground.

Pulling on the leash Leash training is best conducted at times other than on walks in parks or other open places.

● Check-chains or choker leads, which are loops that tighten under tension, are a useful aid if used correctly. As soon as a dog surges ahead, a quick jerk coupled with the command 'heel' should bring the dog back to your side. Fasten the chain as shown in the illustration, and make sure that it will loosen immediately when you slacken the tension on the leash.

● Keep the dog on your left. The secret is always to have the dog's attention, so praise it constantly while it's at your side.

● Another method is to say 'heel' and change direction immediately the dog starts to pull. Keep doing this until the dog walks obediently.

Excessive barking If your dog barks when left alone, give it strenuous exercise before you leave – take it for a run around the block or throw a ball for it in the garden, for example. If barking is triggered by the doorbell or other sounds, get the dog to lie down or send it to its bed. The more passive posture discourages barking and makes it more difficult. Don't prohibit all barking, however – it is the best deterrent against burglars.

Aggression outdoors If dogs are allowed to greet each other without restriction often and early in life, natural dominance and submission soon sort out their differences. However, if a fight breaks out:

● Don't yell and scream at the dog – you'll only encourage it to fight.

● Walk away, encouraging your dog to follow in the normal way. Pull it away if it is on a lead.

● Praise your dog if it comes. Under no circumstances try to discipline the dog physically – it will only inflame the situation.

● If you can, shower both dogs with copious quantities of cold water (a bucketful is not enough). If both owners are present, each could attempt to pull his dog away by the back legs. But this is only in emergencies – it is highly likely that you'll get bitten.

● Prevent the problem in future by avoiding confrontations when you can, and carry a strong stick to hit any dog that attacks your pet.

HOW TO STOP DESTRUCTIVE BEHAVIOUR

Like barking, destructiveness is a habit of bored or anxious dogs. While it is a puppy, give it only a few things to chew and praise it when it does.

● If you see a puppy chewing the furniture, a thrown object or a loud noise should discourage it. It may also help to paint a bitter substance such as oil of cloves or anti-nailbiting fluid on furniture legs.

● Buy rawhide chews for your puppy rather than giving it old shoes or cushions, which it won't be able to distinguish from new ones.

● Accustom your dog to being left alone for short periods at first, then lengthen them. Leave a radio on so that the dog feels less alone.

● Try to be unpredictable. Come back soon after you leave, then leave again. Vary the door you leave by and hang your coat in different places.

● Don't make a fuss when you go out, and avoid lengthy goodbyes.

● Give attention when your dog has calmed down, rather than when you first come home, and don't get angry if you find a favourite object has been destroyed – it will increase the dog's anxiety (and destructiveness).

● Sprinkle pepper round rubbish bins if your dog is a rummager.

● Deter a dog from running after cars and bicycles with a loud, firm 'no' before it gives chase. Once it's in hot pursuit, nothing is likely to work.

ENSURING YOUR DOG'S HEALTH

General demeanour and appetite If you sense that your dog is 'not itself', but it does not appear to be actually ill, watch it closely for 24 hours. Note whether or not it passes a motion or vomits. Let the dog sleep or rest undisturbed in a warm, quiet place if it wishes.

Watch the dog to see if it eats selectively, or not at all, in which case remove its food. Also note how much water it drinks. If there is no improvement in appetite and demeanour within 24 hours, see a vet.

DO NOT take a listless dog for a walk with the idea of perking it up – sometimes a lie down for a day is all it needs. If symptoms persist, see a vet.

Vomiting and diarrhoea Eating grass is a dog's deliberate attempt to rid itself of something unsavoury it has eaten. If vomiting is accompanied by diarrhoea, do not feed it for 24 hours – but provide water. If the dog vomits up the water, see your vet. Reintroduce food only if the vomiting stops. Vomiting for longer than a day or so can result in dehydration, particularly in puppies. See your vet if it persists.

Fleas See page 417 for ways to deal with fleas.

The dog's weight Obesity is common in dogs. But you can prevent it by following these guidelines:
● From the puppy stage, don't feed your dog titbits and sweet treats.
● Food rewards should be counted as part of a dog's daily ration – and meals should be reduced accordingly.
● Give vitamin tablets or raw vegetables as treats for good behaviour.
● All feeding should be from a bowl – not at the table.
● Praise and a pat are nearly as effective as food during training.
● Ask the vet to check your dog's weight – it is sometimes difficult for an owner to be objective about a pet.

Weight loss and undue thirst Weight loss over a period, despite adequate feeding, is a cause for concern. Discuss it with your vet – tests may be needed. Significant increase in thirst is also something to report to the vet.

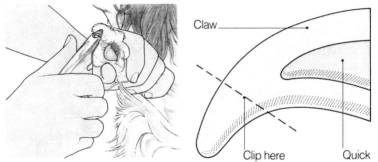

Claw

Clip here   Quick

Trimming a dog's claws Check your dog's claws regularly. Walking daily on pavements should keep them short, but if they seem too long for comfort, ask your vet to show you how to trim them. Be very careful to take off only the tip of the claw, and never risk cutting into the 'quick', which contains the nerve and blood supply. This can be very difficult to see, particularly if the claw is black, in which case it may be best to ask the vet to do the trimming.

Dew claws – on the inside of each leg a few inches above the other claws – sometimes tend to grow into the leg. The dog will lick at the paw and show discomfort. Get a vet to cut the claw – it may be infected.

DO NOT use scissors to trim a dog's claws. Buy guillotine-style clippers from a pet shop.

GOING TO THE VET

If your dog hates being taken to the vet, it may have picked up a sense of 'fear' from you. Try to make visits happy occasions with lots of praise and maybe a titbit or two, and act as normally as possible yourself. If you can, take the dog on regular walks past the vet's surgery.

First aid for a dog

Coping with fits

Most fits will be over by the time you've phoned the vet, so the best you can do is prevent the dog from hurting itself.
● Remove nearby furniture and place cushions and blankets to protect the dog's head.
● Clear up any vomit or faeces, or move the dog away from the mess.
● Darken the room and allow the dog to recover quietly.
● Don't try to pat or soothe your pet – you may get bitten, and it will be unaware of what you are doing in any case.

Causes of fits Fits have many causes, including epilepsy, poisoning, internal problems and, rarely, brain tumours. Call your vet, who will want to give the dog a check-up.

Heatstroke

English bulldogs and other shortnose breeds are particularly susceptible to heatstroke, although on a very hot day, or if left in a closed car, any dog may succumb.
Signs of heatstroke are:
● Rapid panting.
● Rapid pulse.
● Bright red gums.
● Hot legs and head.
● Eventual collapse.

What to do Cool the dog down as quickly as possible. Sit it under a shower of water, rather than submerging it in a bath – the water will soon warm up. Then wrap the dog in wet towels and direct a fan at it. If the attack is severe, take the dog to a vet.

Prevention Always open car windows if you are going to leave your dog inside, and never confine a dog in a car parked in direct sunlight. On hot days, walk your dog in the cool of the evening or early morning, and make sure the house is well ventilated. Keep the coats of long-haired dogs short in hot weather.

Poisoning

Common signs that a dog may have been poisoned are anxiety, trembling, weakness in the legs and salivating. If you suspect poisoning, get your dog to a vet as quickly as possible. If it is still conscious, you may be able to induce vomiting by feeding the dog a teaspoon of salt dissolved in a cup of warm water, or a cup of soapy water.

Caution Do not attempt to force-feed an unconscious or semiconscious animal under any circumstances – the food or water may go down its windpipe and cause suffocation.

Eye injuries

Prompt attention is essential for all eye problems. If a dog develops a half-closed or watery eye take it to a vet immediately. If the eye is swollen so that it cannot close properly, keep it wet by dripping water onto it, using a soaked cotton-wool ball. If a blow on the head has caused an eye to pop out – common in breeds such as Pekingese and Shih-tzus – keep the eye wet and take the dog to a vet. It may sometimes be possible to restore the eyeball to the socket by taking the hairs of both eyelids and pulling forward to try to cover the eye. If you try to do this yourself, be very careful never to push on the eye itself.

How to muzzle an injured dog

However docile normally, an injured dog may bite, so muzzle it before attempting first aid. (This does not, however, apply to dogs with breathing or chest problems. They should immediately be taken to a vet.) Any length of bandage or cord, such as a dressing-gown cord, will do for a muzzle.

 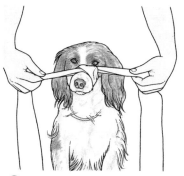

1 Make a large, open knot in the bandage or cord and – keeping your hands well away – loop it over the dog's muzzle.

2 Pull the cord tight to fasten the knot. The knot should be positioned over the top of the animal's muzzle.

3 Cross the ends of the cord or bandage underneath the dog's muzzle, then take them under and behind the ears to the back of the head. Tie the ends securely in a bow at the nape of the dog's neck.

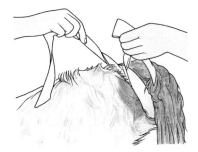

FOUR WAYS TO GIVE YOUR DOG MEDICINE

Getting a dog to take a tablet requires practice. Here are four methods to try next time your pet needs medication:

● Grasp the dog's upper jaw with your left hand to prevent biting (use your right hand if left-handed). Hold the tablet between the thumb and forefinger of your free hand and gently introduce the tablet into the dog's mouth. Push the tablet as far as it will go over the hump at the back of the tongue. Hold the dog's mouth closed and tap the throat lightly to encourage swallowing.

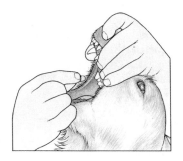

● Hide the tablet in a piece of cheese.
● Cut a pocket in a small piece of meat and insert the tablet.
● Some tablets can be crushed into your dog's food, but others have a special coating to control the rate of digestion and must be swallowed whole. Ask your vet's advice.

THE FINAL YEARS

Dogs of ten years or more can be helped in many ways to enjoy their last years.

● A check-up and blood tests may detect early failure of vital organs – and much can be done to make life easier for the dog.

● Teeth can be cleaned to help dogs appreciate their food more – and there are special diets for elderly dogs. Ask your vet.

● Painkillers can be used to ease arthritis, and supplements can be given to curb weight loss and anaemia.

Four vital questions

The decision whether to end a dog's life painlessly rests with the owner. A vet will give an opinion, but will not make the decision for you unless the animal is suffering. (In some cases, a vet is legally obliged to destroy an animal.) Before making a decision, however, consider the following questions. If the answer to any of them is 'yes', the time might have come to bring the dog's life to a close. Try to think only of the dog – it is, after all, entirely dependent on you:

● Does the dog no longer enjoy anything?

● Has its dignity diminished because it is no longer able to control all its bodily functions?

● Is there severe pain with no way of sufficient relief?

● Has the dog's quality of life worsened much over the past year?

Reassurance from your vet

Grieving for a departed pet is a largely ignored emotion. If you are distressed after having your pet put down, do not hesitate to talk to the vet. He or she may be able to put you in touch with someone else who has shared the same experience – and mutual support can be beneficial.

Allow yourself to grieve – it is far healthier than putting on a brave front. Because the circumstances of euthanasia are often upsetting, you may be left with the feeling that it happened too quickly. Once again, talk to your vet – he will assure you that you made the right decision.

Useful addresses

Royal Society for the Prevention of Cruelty to Animals
Causeway, Horsham
West Sussex RH12 1HG.
Tel: 0403 64181.

Wood Green Animal Shelters
Chishill Road
Heydon, Royston
Herts SG8 8PN.
Tel: 0763 838 329.

National Canine Defence League
1-2 Pratt Mews
London NW1 0AD.
Tel: 071 388 0137.

The Dogs' Home, Battersea
4 Battersea Park Road
London SW8 4AA.
Tel: 071 622 3626.

All the above organisations care for abandoned dogs, and have dogs available to good homes. Subsidised veterinary care if owner cannot pay.

The Kennel Club
1 Clarges Street
London W1Y 8AB.
Tel: 071 493 6651.
Registers pedigree dogs.

Dog Breeders' Associates
1 Abbey Road, Bourne End
Bucks SL8 5NZ.
Tel: 06285 20943.
Supplies information on breeders.

CHOOSING A CAT

Pedigree or crossbreed? A pedigree will be more expensive not only to buy but also to keep than a cross-bred cat. Pedigrees tend to be less hardy and will probably need frequent trips to the vet.

● Always consider breed differences and behaviour if you are buying a pedigree. For instance, Abyssinians and Somalis are active and climbing cats, so if you have valuable or treasured ornaments, they may not be a wise choice. Burmese and Siamese are very 'talkative' cats and are quite dog-like in their need for companionship. Persians and other 'ornamental breeds' are serene and slothful.

Abyssinian

Burmese

Siamese

Persian

Where to get a cat Specialist cat magazines and various organisations give detailed advice on breeds and breeders (see *Useful addresses*, p.405). Veterinary practices may have lists of litters of kittens born in the area, and newsagents' windows may also have advertisements.

Points to look for Get your kitten when it's about six to eight weeks old. Unusually small kittens may be malnourished or susceptible to disease.
● Avoid kittens with weepy eyes and noses – they may have flu, which can be fatal.
● Flaky bald areas with a greyish appearance may indicate ringworm, which can infect humans.
● Bloated stomachs may mean roundworms, which can be fatal in young kittens.
● Check the coat for fleas and black specks; fleas could mean anaemia.
● Black wax in the ears is a sign of mites.

Male or female? Male cats are more territorial than females. They fight more and have a tendency to spray urine around the house and to roam if allowed out. Neutering at six months will curb most undesirable habits.

Females can come into season from five months of age, so beware of a 'kitten' being pregnant. Have it spayed at five or six months, which prevents it having kittens and eliminates the problem of courting 'toms'.

Long or short haired? If you decide on a long-haired cat, you must brush and comb it every day. Long-haired cats generally have long undercoats which tend to get matted. Maine coon cats – so-named for their raccoon-like colouring – are an exception because they have a long outer coat or 'guard hair', which remains silky and is less trouble.

CARING FOR YOUR CAT

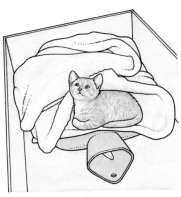
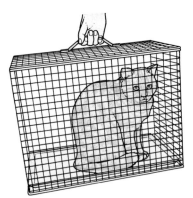

The first night A kitten loves to be in an enclosed place where it feels safe and secure. Make a den out of a cardboard box or buy a cat bed from a pet shop. Provide a hot-water bottle, wrapped in an old woolly. The kitten will be attracted by the heat. Old jumpers make good bedding.

Caging and transport You will need to visit the vet soon after getting your cat, so buy a cage to carry it in. Coated wire-mesh cages are best; wicker is less durable and less hygienic. Leave the cage around the house and feed the cat in it from time to time so that it gets used to being in the cage.

The myth of milk Kittens do not tolerate cows' milk well – it usually gives them diarrhoea. But older cats can tolerate it better. Try a little milk diluted with water first to avoid accidents.

Choosing the right food Find out what your cat was being fed before you got it, and feed it the same for at least a few days. If you want to vary the diet after that, make any changes gradually, to prevent diarrhoea.

Commercial kitten food should make up two-thirds of the cat's diet. Introduce your kitten to a variety of foods for the other third so that it does not become too fussy.

Essential vaccinations Have your kitten immunised against feline enteritis and cat flu. The first injection should take place at eight or nine weeks. This will be followed up four weeks later, and annual booster shots will maintain immunity. The vet will advise you about worming (page 416).

Litter trays and toilet training Kittens are naturally clean, so toilet training is rarely a problem.
● You can use an old baking dish as a litter tray. But a plastic tray is easier to clean.
● If you want your cat eventually to use the garden as a toilet, use soil instead of shop-bought litter in the tray. Cats are naturally attracted to fungi in the soil.
● If your kitten messes on the floor, transfer the puddle or deposit to the tray, which should attract the kitten to it next time.
● Clean the tray once or twice daily – some cats will not use a soiled tray.
● If you have two cats, give them a tray each.
● If you have an adult cat which has developed an aversion to its litter tray, substitute soil for the litter.

Deterring bad habits Training a cat by reward is not always effective. It is a good idea to teach kittens and cats from day one that unpleasant things will happen if they misbehave. But punishment should never be painful or excessive – merely unpleasant.

Cats hate loud noises and surprises. To discourage unwanted behaviour you need to be there or to set a booby-trap. For example, if you have a piece of furniture you don't want the cat to jump on, put something unstable on it, like a tin tray that will clatter to the floor when the cat jumps on it. Use a water pistol to squirt the cat if it scratches furniture. If you fire from a distance, the cat won't associate the water pistol with you.

Keeping tabs on your cat Give your cat a collar (with elastic to prevent strangling) and an address tag for identification. If you use a screw-on tag (above), secure the capsule with a blob of nail polish so that it can't come undone. Alternatively, get a microchip implant for permanent identification (page 418).

Be a friend to birds Don't wait for your cat to start catching birds: attach a bell to its collar right from the start. The tinkling will warn birds when the cat's about. Two bells are even better, because cats can quickly learn to move silently with one – some have learned to carry a bell in their mouths.

Keeping cats amused Play with your cat. A cat kept indoors enjoys human companionship and needs to be entertained.

● Buy your kitten a scratching post from a pet shop. A rope-covered one, impregnated with catnip or catmint, works well.

● Provide lightweight, durable toys for the cat to play with. They're easy to make out of cotton, corduroy or fake fur fabric.

Giving medicine You can give a cat medicine on your own if you use the right technique. Mix medication with food if you can be sure the cat gets the prescribed dose. But sick cats often go off their food, so it's worth learning to give them tablets.
● Practise on a healthy cat with vitamin tablets and worming pills.
● Accustom your cat at an early age to having its mouth opened by you. It's a useful skill (see next page) and will enable you to examine the condition of the cat's teeth regularly.

Teeth From the age of about three, you may notice a build-up of tartar – a brownish cement-like substance – on your cat's teeth. Allowing cats to gnaw meat off a bone once a week will help to slow down the build-up. But do not feed a cat on chicken, rabbit or fish bones, because they splinter easily and can cause injury. If training starts young, a cat will allow you to brush its teeth weekly. Once formed, tartar sets hard, harbours bacteria and eventually causes gum disease and tooth loss. Tartar can only be removed by your vet.

Vomiting and diarrhoea Cats often induce vomiting by eating grass. The most likely reason is a fur ball in the stomach. Vomiting and diarrhoea are often the result of a diet change, or of feeding milk to young kittens. Give the cat water only for 24 hours, but see the vet immediately if it passes blood. If vomiting is accompanied by constipation, give the cat two teaspoons of medicinal liquid paraffin every day for three days.

Weight loss Cats that lose weight despite normal feeding should be taken to the vet. If the coat is a bit lacklustre, the cat may be suffering from one of many viral diseases. Blood tests will be necessary for a diagnosis.

Cat bites and fights A soft swelling around the head or tail-base of your cat may be an abscess from another cat's bite or scratch. An abscess may make the cat very sick and it will need antibiotics, so see the vet. Some abscesses may need lancing under general anaesthetic.

Bladder infection Symptoms are spending an unusually long time at the litter tray and returning to it frequently. See a vet.

Skin problems These are usually revealed by tiny scabs that make the coat rough to run your fingers through. The scabs are usually the result of the cat grooming itself excessively. The most common reason cats do this is because they itch and the most likely cause is an allergy to fleas. See the vet for advice (see also page 417).

Clipping a cat's claws Usually only cats that spend most of their time indoors need their claws trimmed. Elderly cats sometimes cannot retract their claws and need regular trims.
● To make the claws unsheath, push gently on the paw from both sides.
● Look for the quick and clip about 2mm ($\frac{1}{16}$in) below it.
● Don't use scissors – buy guillotine clippers from a pet shop.

GETTING A CAT TO SWALLOW A TABLET

Sit or kneel on the floor, legs apart, with the cat between them facing away from you. Then, if you are right-handed, gently grasp the cat's head with your left hand, your fingers on its cheekbones.

● Tip back the cat's head until its chin is almost pointing at the ceiling. The lower jaw should slacken as a result.
● Keep the tablet held securely between the thumb and forefinger of your right hand.
● Use your middle finger to pull the cat's lower jaw down.

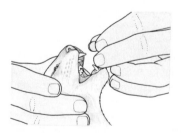

● Place the tablet just beyond or on the small lump on the cat's tongue at the back of its mouth. Return its head to normal to allow it to swallow.
● After a cat has swallowed, it usually licks its nose. If your cat doesn't, the chances are it will spit out the tablet. There's little you can do but keep trying – or ask a vet to help.

IF YOU ARE MOVING HOUSE

Moving can be quite traumatic for cats – and they tend to sense a move days before it occurs.

● Putting the cat in a cattery while you move can give you peace of mind. You can then give it your full attention after the move.

● Alternatively, lock the cat in a room with water and familiar surroundings during the move. The cat should be the last thing to go. At the new house, put it in a room with bedding, litter tray and food.

● Let it explore the inside of the house thoroughly – and feed it indoors for two or three days before you allow it out.

● Go with the cat on the first few outside visits – and don't leave it outdoors until you are sure it will come back.

Useful addresses

The Cats Protection League
17 Kings Road
Horsham
West Sussex RH13 5PP.
Tel: 0403 65566.
Cares for and shelters unwanted cats and has a re-homing service.

Feline Advisory Bureau
350 Upper Richmond Road
Putney
London SW15 6TL.
Tel: 081 789 9553.
Advises on boarding catteries, availability of kittens and buying from pedigree breeders.

Specialist magazines
The Cat
5 James Leigh Street
Manchester M1 6EX.

Cat World
10 Western Road
Shoreham-by-Sea
West Sussex BN4 5WD.

Both magazines provide general information for cat lovers.

RABBITS AS PETS

Obtaining a rabbit

If you buy a rabbit from a pet shop, it is likely to be a crossbreed – hardy and inexpensive. Baby rabbits are usually weaned at around eight weeks, so from about ten weeks onward is the time to buy. If you want a specific breed, the best way to choose is to visit an exhibition or show.

Housing a rabbit

Adult rabbits like their own territory and should be housed in separate hutches. You can let them share a common run, but be careful at first – male rabbits may fight or males and females may mate. Rabbits can be housed with guinea pigs.

● A rabbit hutch should be a rectangular shape and made of wood. Use 13mm ($\frac{1}{2}$in) heavy gauge wire mesh over the front of the enclosure.
● Paint the hutch with exterior-grade paint if it's going to be kept outdoors, and place it in a sheltered corner of the garden.

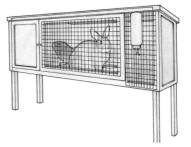

● Use sawdust as a floor covering, rather than wood shavings or straw which are not soft enough.
● Place an outdoor hutch in the lee of a wall or other draughtproof spot.
● Inspect and thoroughly clean the hutch once a week. But remove dirty sawdust, damp hay and droppings daily.

Times and types of feed

Twice-daily feeding is best: early morning and early evening. Give enough food for a small portion to be left after each meal. Make sure food is fresh-smelling and that hay is clean.

Foods traditionally fed to rabbits fall into four groups:
● Mixed cereals: oats, bran, wheat, barley and maize. You can buy premixed cereals from pet shops.
● Green food: young grass, cabbage leaves, cauliflower, greens and lettuce, apple peelings, celery, pea-pods and carrot and radish tops.
● Root vegetables: carrots, potatoes, swedes, turnips, parsnips, beetroot (beetroot may turn the urine red).
● Hay: provides bulk, which is essential to diet.

Water All caged animals need to have fresh, clean drinking water always available. The easiest arrangement for rabbits is a drinking bottle designed to clip to the cage – buy one from any good pet shop. Alternatively, use a heavy bowl that can't be tipped over.

Buck or doe?

You can tell the sex of a rabbit from about six weeks of age. By applying gentle pressure on either side of the genital opening, the penis of a male rabbit will protrude. By 16-24 weeks the male testes will have descended. Females have a slit-like opening.

DO'S AND DON'TS OF HANDLING RABBITS

DO handle your rabbit gently and frequently – it will help to ensure a calmer, more responsive pet.

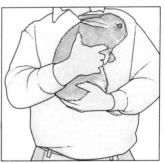

DO pick up your rabbit with both hands, one on either side of its body, just behind the front paws.

DO support the rabbit on one hand when you pick it up. If you're sitting down, support it on your lap.

DON'T pick up a rabbit by the ears or by the scruff of the neck.

DON'T try to restrain a struggling rabbit – you may get scratched by the claws on its powerful hind legs. Place it on the ground if it panics.

Health care for rabbits

Signs of ill health in rabbits are a listless appearance, unkempt coat, closed eyes and reluctance to eat. Common complaints include:

Fleas See page 417 for information on preventing fleas on all pets.

Diarrhoea Check recent foodstuffs. Mouldy hay, greens that have yellowed and dirty food may be the cause.

Sore hocks (The hock is the hind leg joint corresponding to the human ankle.) Mostly due to wet bedding and rough flooring. Good, clean housing is the solution – but wounds should be treated by a vet.

Tapeworm cysts Soft swellings on the shoulders and back. Don't allow your rabbit to graze in areas frequented by dogs and don't feed it grass picked from these areas – it may pick up worms. Ask your vet for advice on preventing parasites (see also page 416).

Abscesses Have any swellings round the mouth checked by a vet.

Respiratory disease Symptoms are pus in the eyes and a stuffy nose. Take the rabbit to a vet immediately.

Malformed teeth If a rabbit's upper front teeth do not meet properly with the lower ones, they can grow out of the mouth like tusks. Take a rabbit with this problem to a vet for regular trimming of the teeth.

HAMSTERS AND GERBILS

Buying: what to look for

You can buy hamsters or gerbils from pet stores or breeders, who may advertise in specialist magazines. Points to look for are:
● A good sheen on the coat and bright eyes.
● There should be no bald spots, scabs or sores.
● Staining under the tail could mean diarrhoea, which can be fatal in small creatures.
● Choose a juvenile hamster – three to four weeks old – which has a mass of fine silky grey hair in its ears. In a pet shop, another way to identify a juvenile is to pick it up. It will allow you to lift it and will be placid, while a mature one – older than about eight weeks – will resist and try to bite.
● Hamsters are nocturnal, so some sleepiness is acceptable if you go to look at one during the daytime. At temperatures around 22-25°C (75-80°F), hamsters become immobile.
● Gerbils should stand upright and be inquisitive. Drowsiness may be a sign of ill health.

Feeding hamsters and gerbils

● Feed both hamsters and gerbils with a commercial grain and seed mix, and supplement it with small amounts of fresh greens such as lettuce and dandelion leaves and carrot tops. Use a heavy feeding dish that cannot be tipped over.
● Make sure fresh water is available all the time, preferably from a feeding bottle that clips to the side of the cage.

Providing a home

● The minimum area for hamsters and gerbils is 510mm x 250mm x 200mm (20in x 10in x 8in).
● Avoid wooden cages: they are difficult to keep clean and dry, and tend to get chewed.
● Use sawdust or a mixture of dried peat and sand for the floor covering.
● Gerbils like to vary their nest site, so provide little pieces of tubing, a small hollow branch or a small jar to give your pet a choice.
● For a hamster, fix a separate nest box above floor level to save space.

● Provide playthings, such as small branches, jars, cotton reels – anything that has no sharp edges and is non-toxic.

● Provide a hamster with an exercise wheel to run on, but not a gerbil – it could injure its tail in the wheel slits.

● Provide plenty of clean dry hay for nesting material.
● Gerbils like to leap – so fix platforms at varying heights in the cage.
● Clean the cage scrupulously with warm water and disinfectant weekly and allow to dry. Use two cages in rotation if possible.
● Hamsters prefer to be solitary, but you can keep gerbils in pairs – of the same sex unless you plan to breed them.

Handle with care

● Talk to and handle your pet from the beginning. But go gently – if grabbed by the middle, the creature's instinctive reaction will be to inflict a painful bite. It may also bite if fingers are poked through the cage.

● The correct way to hold a hamster or gerbil is to cup it gently but securely in both hands. Handle your pet regularly from the start to tame it.

● A gerbil can be restrained on your hand by holding the base of the tail. But don't hold it any farther up the tail. It could cause injury.
● Practise early handling close to the floor. Hamsters and gerbils seem unable to flip over in midair to land on their feet if dropped.

GUINEA PIGS

Guinea pigs bought from pet shops are usually hardy crossbreeds of various colours and types. If you want a pure-bred guinea pig, it's best to visit exhibitions and agricultural shows where specialist breeders come to sell and display their animals.

Providing a hutch

Housing for guinea pigs can be the same as for rabbits (page 405). Rabbits and guinea pigs seem to enjoy each other's company – but don't overcrowd them. A guinea pig will enjoy a run in the sun if it is provided with some shade and an escape-proof pen. Move the pen frequently to prevent overgrazing and stop waste accumulating.

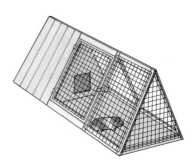

Feeding your guinea pig

Guinea pigs will eat the same range of food as rabbits (page 406), but serve cereals as a mash – two parts crushed oats to one part bran, dampened with water. Discard any uneaten portion as it will quickly sour.

Handling a guinea pig

The more you handle your guinea pig, the tamer it will become and the more you will get out of your relationship with it. When you lift a guinea pig, support its whole body with one hand and hold it with the other so that it can't jump out of your arms.

Common health problems

● Male guinea pigs sometimes develop impacted faecal material around the anus. Soften any matted lumps with Vaseline. Once it is cleared, smear more Vaseline around the anus to prevent build-up, and check daily.

● Guinea pigs' nails sometimes grow too long and curl into the foot. Keep the nails trimmed, but be careful to avoid the 'quick', which will bleed if cut. If this happens, dip the foot in talcum powder.

● Bald, red, itchy patches on the skin can be caused by mite infestation. Take your pet to the vet quickly: the complaint can cause great discomfort.

TAME RATS AND MICE

Mouse varieties There are four main categories of pet mice:
● 'Selfs' have a single body colour such as black, white, cream or tan.
● Two-toned mice are a combination of tan and another colour.
● 'Marked' mice are white with coloured patches.
● AOV (any other variety) mice include unusual types such as longhairs and chinchillas.

Rat colourings Rats come in many different colours, including hooded varieties which have heads of a different colour from the rest of the body.

Providing a home

● Commercially manufactured cages are often too small, but if you make your own, remember that rats and mice will chew through wood and plastic, so glass and metal cages are best. A cage 450mm × 300mm × 250mm (18in x 12in x 10in) can house two mice or one rat.
● For bedding, provide wood shavings, tissue paper or sawdust.
● Clean the cage at least twice a week to prevent smells and disease.
● Provide exercise wheels, ladders, hollow tubes and climbing frames – they will prevent boredom and encourage animals to exercise themselves.
● Don't keep male adult mice together – they may fight. However, rats fight less frequently than mice.

What to feed pet rats and mice

● Commercially produced foods are best, but rats also like to be given titbits, which helps in the taming process. They will readily accept biscuits, chopped apples (leave the peel on), tomatoes and dog biscuits. But don't give them too much; it could result in an unbalanced diet.
● Provide fresh water each day in small non-tipping bowls or dispensers that clip to the cage wire.

How to handle rats and mice

● You can pick up mice by the scruff of the neck, but never lift rats this way – they'll bite.

● Pick up rats by the shoulders, with your thumb pushed up under the chin to prevent biting.

A common rodent ailment

Respiratory problems caused by a virus are common in rats and mice. Stress caused by overcrowding, dirty cages and lack of attention can be a contributory factor. See a vet if you notice your rat or mouse wheezing.

AQUARIUM FISH

Setting up an aquarium

A large aquarium is easier to start than a small one because it is less likely to become overcrowded and the water is less likely to deteriorate. A reasonable size is 600mm × 400mm × 450mm (24in x 16in x 18in). When full, this weighs 68kg (150lb), so you'll need a strong stand.

● Place polystyrene tiles under the tank to absorb uneven stresses.

● You'll need about 75mm (3in) of gravel to make an under-gravel filter run efficiently.

● Use inert plants and rocks – ones that will not deposit particles, decompose or change in water, as limestone does. Before putting them in, soak them in a two-parts-per-million solution of potassium permanganate – available at chemists – for two to three days, to sterilise them.

● Allow the tank to settle for a week before introducing two or three cheap fish, such as common goldfish. That way, if your new aquarium is not successful and the fish die, you won't have wasted too much money.

● Always allow the temperature of the water in which the fish have been transported to equalise with that of the tank water before putting them into the aquarium. The best way to do this is by floating the transport bag in the tank for an hour or two and then netting the fish into the aquarium. Don't tip the transport water into the tank.

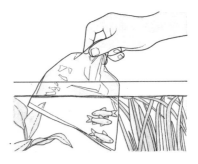

● You can keep about three fish for every nine litres (two gallons) of water. Install an air pump if you plan to stock your tank more densely.

Quarantining new fish

Don't introduce new fish into an established tank without quarantining them for at least two weeks. If your fish are valuable, increase the quarantine period to two to three months.

● Buy a simple quarantine tank for separating new fish. The only equipment it needs are a few rocks and a foam box filter.

● Valuable pond fish, such as koi, can be quarantined in a polythene paddling pool in a cool garage. Net the top of the pool to stop them jumping out, and don't run the car engine inside the garage.

Common fish ailments

White spot Tiny white spots appear initially on the fins. Left untreated they spread over the entire body and the fish dies. This is a contagious disease that can affect all the fish in the aquarium within a few days.

Slime disease The whole fish seems coated with an excess of slime, giving it a washed out appearance. It can be accompanied by fin erosion.

Fluke infestation The body takes on a greyish colour and the gills go red. Caused by a parasite which attacks the gills and fins.

Velvet A golden, dust-like coating covers almost the whole fish. It's normally a problem in tropical freshwater or marine fish.

Fin rot Tatty-looking fins can be caused by various illnesses, or they may be the result of damage from other fish or parasites.

Fungus Looks like cotton wool, and is brought on by skin damage.

Ulcers If the flesh appears 'pitted' or eaten away, your fish may have an ulcer. Paint the spot with Friar's Balsam (available from chemists).

Popeye and dropsy These are serious bacterial infections with similar symptoms. Afflicted fish take on a bloated appearance and their eyes look as if they are protruding.

Treating a sick fish

● Chemists and pet shops supply various treatments. Consult a vet if these don't work or if you're not sure what's wrong.

● Your quarantine tank can double as a 'hospital' tank if you clean it out thoroughly afterwards.

● Most fish problems are caused by poor conditions in the tank. Consider basic points of fish care: Is the tank clean? Do you have the right number of fish for the tank size? Is the water acidity correct? Are all rocks and plants inert?

Keeping your tank or pond clean

● The best way to keep a tank clean is to change part of the water at regular intervals: remove one-third of the water every fortnight or one-tenth every week, and replace it with clean water. At the same time, siphon waste matter from the tank bottom. Use a piece of rubber tubing or buy a sediment remover (right) from a pet shop.

If you can't always manage regular water changes, install a filter to help keep the water clean.

● Dechlorinate tap water for the tank by leaving it to stand for 24 hours. Or use a proprietary chemical such as sodium thiosulphate. One granule per 4.5 litres (1 gallon) will remove any chlorine.

411

Water quality

Kits are available for testing water hardness, acidity or alkaline content (pH), ammonia and nitrate levels.

Values to aim at are:
- pH 6-8 for fresh water and 8-8.3 for marine tanks.
- Distilled water should be used to top up evaporation losses to keep water hardness constant.
- Ammonia levels should not exceed 0.02mg per litre.
- Nitrates should not exceed 0.1mg per litre.

Feed the fish – not the tank

Feed tank fish twice a day, never giving more food than they can eat in two minutes: uneaten food will pollute the water. Buy commercial fish food from a pet shop or aquarium supplier.

KEEPING FISH IN PONDS

Fish that thrive in ponds include the common goldfish, harlequin or speckled goldfish, fantail, comet, veiltail, black Moor, lionhead, celestial, koi, golden orfe and minnow.

Maintaining a pond

The effort needed to keep a pond healthy varies greatly, depending on the siting and design of the pond. Points to consider include:

Shape A complicated shape may cause parts of the pond to stagnate; a simpler design will allow water to circulate freely. Avoid shallow shelves which tend to encourage the growth of algae.

Location If you site a pond near trees, leaves will fall in and rot, endangering the fish.

pH balance If the water is too acidic (see *Water quality*, above) place a piece of limestone or chalk in the pond. It will correct the balance.

Feeding pond fish Fish in ponds need feeding only in autumn and spring, to help them prepare for and recover from their winter fast. Never give food between November and March: they won't be able to digest it.

Coping with the weather

Frozen pond Ice can seal off the surface of a pond, preventing adequate oxygenation of the water. This is not a problem for periods of up to about a week, because the fish slow down and require less oxygen. But if freezing temperatures are predicted for long periods, it may be worth buying a pond heater.

Avoiding damage to a pond Another problem with freezing is that concrete ponds may crack. Ponds with sloping sides will force ice upwards and are less likely to be damaged than straight-sided designs.

Using a fountain Fountains are attractive and can help to prevent small pools becoming short of oxygen in hot weather.

Topping up the pond Watch out for excessive evaporation in hot weather. Top up your pond frequently with small amounts so that the water temperature does not drop suddenly.

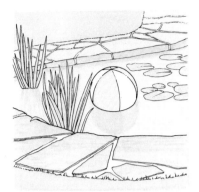

Making an air hole Float a rubber ball on your pond in winter. If ice forms, remove the ball to make a hole through which air can reach the fish. Draw off 30mm (1¼in) of water under the ice so that oxygen can reach the surface. Replace the ball at night to keep the hole open.

It a pond has iced over completely during cold weather, heat a flat-bottomed kettle or a pan of water and place it on the pond surface to melt a hole in the ice.
Warning Never break ice on a fish pond with a sharp blow; shock waves may harm the fish.

CARING FOR CAGE BIRDS

Most birds can be kept indoors or outdoors – although a single bird, such as a budgerigar, canary or parrot, will enjoy human company and attention and will probably prefer to be indoors. If birds are kept outdoors, either in large cages or purpose-built aviaries, they should be provided with a nesting box to sleep or take refuge in during cold or wet weather. The size will depend on the type of bird.

What kind of cage?

By law, cages have to be wider than the wingspan of the bird, but no cage for any bird can be too large. Those bought in pet shops for small birds such as budgies and canaries are often the wrong shape; and tall, narrow parrot cages are hopelessly inadequate. Good proportions are as important as the total volume.

● A parrot or cockatoo cage should be, at an absolute minimum, 560mm (22in) square at the base and 915mm (36in) high.

● If you are keeping a budgie or a canary, the cage should be at least 300mm × 600mm × 600mm (12in × 24in × 24in).

● A cage for a mynah bird should be not less than 1.5m (5ft) long.

413

Perches and toys

Furnish your bird's cage with a good perch and a few well-chosen toys, but avoid cluttering it with unnecessary 'ornaments'.

● Hardwood dowel perches are bad for birds' feet because they are uniform in diameter. Replace them with sticks of varying diameter, such as bamboo, ash or willow.

Do not cover the perch with sandpaper, as is sometimes suggested to prevent the claws growing too long; sharp grains of sand can become embedded in the bird's foot and may cause disease. Have the nails clipped by a vet instead, if necessary.

● Solitary birds will welcome a mirror. But don't be surprised if a male budgie regurgitates his food at it – it's a courting ritual.
● Provide parrots with branches of hardwoods such as ash, elder or beech for climbing and chewing. Scrub with soap and rinse well first.
● Lovebirds like to strip pieces of willow bark to line their nesting boxes.

Letting your bird fly free

All cage birds love the chance to fly free whenever possible. For larger varieties this is essential.
● If you intend to let your bird out, hand feed it occasionally from the start to tame it. Most young birds can also be handled, which will make it easier to catch them when you let them out – ask your vet's advice.
● Choose an uncluttered room for the bird to fly in, and hang a sheet over any windows that may deceive it.

A balanced diet

● Most pet birds are seed eaters. You can buy commercial mixtures which will give your pet a balanced diet.
● Parrots enjoy an additional treat of green leaf vegetables, pieces of fruit, and some carrot.
● Most birds like a spray of millet – but provide it only occasionally, because they tend to eat it to the exclusion of other foods.
● Always have grit available to help the bird digest its seeds.
● Make sure there is fresh drinking water daily or on alternate days. Use a proper bird's water-dispenser bought from a pet shop.

Common complaints in birds

Self plucking Many solitary birds develop this vice – it appears to be the result of boredom. Male parrots and budgerigars are the worst offenders.
● Introduce a mate – it can help. If fighting occurs, cage the newcomer separately. Sometimes the company is enough. However, peach-faced lovebirds usually resent a new mate if their partner dies.
● Provide a mirror for extra entertainment, or have a radio playing softly.
● Antipeck sprays seldom work and can damage plumage.
● Set up a cage which is big enough for the bird to fly in or, if you can't do this, consider finding a new home for the bird where it will be possible.

Scaly face This is a common, contagious mite infection of budgies, canaries and finches. The beak takes on a 'honeycomb' appearance.
● Paint the area with a ten per cent solution of benzyl benzoate emulsion at weekly intervals for three weeks. Buy it from a vet, chemist or pet shop.
● You may have to ask a vet to trim the beak.

Egg binding Female birds showing abdominal distension, straining, exhaustion, depression, and a tendency to squat on the cage floor may be egg bound. Raise the temperature to 30-32°C (86-90°F) for a couple of hours. If this doesn't work see a vet.

Catching an escaped bird

● Try luring the bird back into its cage with a favourite food, such as a spray of millet.

● If food can't entice the bird, try darkening the room as much as possible. Birds become subdued in dim light.

● Approach an escaped bird slowly and deliberately. Frantic chasing may result in sudden death. Canaries are particularly susceptible.

● Grasp the bird gently but securely when you do catch it. Some birds may be easier to catch if you throw a cloth over them before attempting to pick them up. Even small birds such as budgerigars can inflict a painful nip, but avoid tightening your grip if you do get pecked: you may strangle the bird.

● Approach a larger bird from above, when the wings are folded. If it flaps its wings during capture it may be injured.

KEEPING A TORTOISE

Although tortoises may no longer be legally imported into Britain, their long life span means that there are still many of them around – and they are being bred here. Mediterranean types are most common, but there are also some tropical tortoises in the country. If you're unsure of the breed of your tortoise, consult a vet.

Housing a tortoise

● Adult Mediterranean and tropical tortoises can be kept outdoors in summer. Make a pen by driving wooden posts into the ground and stretching 50mm (2in) chicken wire around them. Lay planks of wood flat on the ground and staple the base of the wire to the wood.

● Provide a sheltered area – a wooden box will do – and a shallow trough of clean drinking water.

Feeding tortoises

A good diet can go a long way towards keeping your tortoise healthy. Food-related complaints such as 'soft shell' and general malnourishment are usually the only health problems they suffer from.

● Feed your tortoise a wide variety of foods. It needs a source of animal protein as well as fresh fruit and vegetables. A balanced diet could include a mixture of chopped fruit and vegetables, cold hard-boiled eggs and whole sprats or tinned dog or cat food.

● Tortoises must also have extra vitamins and minerals. Sprinkle a powdered supplement (available from vets and pet shops) on each meal.

● Some tortoises like avocados.

● During summer, tortoises will eat grass, clover, weeds – and your bedding plants.

Tortoise hibernation

Tropical tortoises must not be hibernated, but owners usually choose to hibernate Mediterranean tortoises during winter, to avoid the expense of constant heating. Take the tortoise to a vet when the weather begins to grow colder, usually in mid-autumn, to assess whether it is the correct weight. An overweight or underweight tortoise must not be hibernated. Instead, keep it warm indoors.

● Use a rodent-proof box with a lid. Line the bottom with straw, hay, dry leaves or even chips of expanded polystyrene.

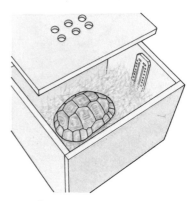

● Keep the box in a cool place such as a garage or shed where the temperature is fairly constant at about 4°C (39°F). Keep a thermometer in the box to check. A maximum and minimum thermometer is best, so that you can make sure there are no great temperature variations.

● Don't allow tropical tortoises to hibernate – house them indoors through winter in a 1.2m × 1.2m (4ft × 4ft) enclosure, with an infrared lamp in one corner. Temperature in the corner should be 30°C (86°F) during the day, 21°C (70°F) at night. Use newspaper as a floor covering.
● If your tortoise won't eat after coming out of hibernation, a vet can show you how to feed it by stomach tube to ensure adequate nutrition. The tortoise will begin to eat again when it is stronger.

ADVICE FOR PET OWNERS

Worms in pets – what to do

● Opinion about worming regimes varies widely. Ask your vet's advice when you take your pet for its first visit.
● As a rule, you should worm puppies and kittens fortnightly until 12 weeks of age. Worm them again at four months, then every six months.
● Some of the most effective worming preparations are available only from vets. You will not need to take the animal for a consultation, but you should know your pet's weight, so that the vet can prescribe the correct preparation and dosage.
● Remember that a puppy will gain weight rapidly – so dosage should be adjusted accordingly from fortnight to fortnight.
● Other young domestic pets, such as rabbits, tortoises, birds and hamsters, can be wormed if they don't seem to be growing rapidly. Ask your vet to recommend a good worming preparation and advise you on its use.
● Look out for little white worms, like rice grains, in your dog's or cat's motions during the summer. These are known as flea tapeworms and they can be passed on to children. Flea tapeworms cause irritation, rather than a dangerous disease. To get rid of them you need a worming preparation specifically for tapeworm – and you must get rid of fleas as they are prime carriers. The worms will return within three weeks if you don't.

Getting rid of fleas

Treating your house

For every flea on a pet, there will be thousands of immature fleas in carpets. Fleas like dark, dusty areas – under couches is a favourite spot. To get rid of them take the following steps:

1 Buy a flea spray from the vet to treat the house. The safest and most effective contains a flea hormone that interrupts the life cycle of the flea. The active ingredient is called methoprene.

2 Spray the inside of your vacuum cleaner bag, so that any fleas or larvae will be killed when you vacuum them up. Remember to respray whenever you change the vacuum-cleaner bag.

3 Spray every room to which your pets have access. You only need to do this twice a year. Concentrate spraying on skirting boards and under low furniture; then zigzag from one end of the room to the other to treat the carpets. Home flea sprays are fairly non-toxic, but don't allow children into the treated rooms for half a day.

Treating your pets

Ask your vet to recommend a good general insecticide. Used in large quantities these sprays are toxic, so follow the instructions carefully. They usually suggest you spray your pet at ten-day intervals during summer, but once a month is enough in winter. Spray the pet outdoors to reduce the amount of spray that you inhale.

Spraying a cat Cats tend to bring in fleas and pass them on to dogs, who often get blamed. Many dog-only households don't suffer from fleas.

Cats can become frightened and angry when sprayed, so start when the cat is young and try these tips to make it easier:

● Place the cat on a firm surface, such as a garden table, and lift it up gently by the scruff of the neck so that the front legs are raised. Because the cat's hind legs are still on the table, it should feel secure.

As you lift the cat up, have the can ready in the other hand, and be prepared to work fast – most cats won't stay still for long once you start spraying.

● Make one spray underneath, one on each side and a quick spray along the back. Don't spray the cat's head. The process should take only a few seconds and the cat is usually so surprised that it does not retaliate.

● Don't hesitate: the cat will react violently and the opportunity will be lost.

Spraying dogs Hold the dog by the collar and follow the same spraying sequence as with a cat. Dogs are usually no problem.

Flea collars Often used because they are so convenient, flea collars reduce the number of fleas a pet brings into the house. But they tend to repel fleas rather than kill them. Once a flea colony is established indoors, collars don't help. They may be an adequate form of control if your pet rarely goes outdoors and has little contact with other animals.

417

OBESITY IN PETS

Being overweight is one of the most common and least recognised problems in pets. It can take years off a pet's life and can certainly diminish its enjoyment of living.

Most cases of heart disease, leg and joint injuries, diabetes, arthritis and internal problems in dogs can be prevented by giving them a little less food and a little more exercise. However, if you honestly think you don't overfeed your pet, see a vet – the problem may be metabolic.

Obesity does occur in cats, but rarely.

Pet insurance

There are many insurance plans to cover your pet against accident or disease or against any injury that it might cause to other animals, people or property.
● Read through the various brochures at your vet's surgery.
● It is wise to take some precautions from the moment you get a pet.
● Pet insurance will almost certainly save you money in the years ahead.

Identifying your pet

Identichipping

A microchip with an identity number is painlessly implanted under your pet's skin. The number is put on a national register, along with the owner's details so that the pet can be identified and returned if it strays.

Police stations, dogs' homes and many veterinary surgeries have identichip scanners, so there is a good chance that if your pet is found collarless, the chip will be read. Ask your vet for details.

National Pet Register

Another way of having cats and dogs identified is to enrol them on the National Pet Register. For a small fee your pet is given an identity disc with a coded number and a 24-hour Pet Register telephone number.

Information about the owner is recorded on computer at the Register offices and can be called up if anyone finds the animal. Arrangements are then made to take it home or to look after it if the owner cannot be traced immediately. Ask your vet for details or telephone 0800 581553.

Holiday arrangements for pets

Animal accommodation Boarding kennels and catteries are the commonest form of arrangement, but they are suitable only for fully vaccinated animals. Ask your vet to recommend good establishments, and ask to be shown around before you leave your pet there. If you are refused, the operators may have something to hide.

Cat and dog minders Agencies can provide minders who will stay in your home, look after the house, and feed and exercise your pets. Cat minders can be arranged who only visit twice daily to feed and care for your cat. Your vet should have information on agencies and may also have heard reports from clients who have used them. Always ask for references if you plan to use an agency.

Vets as minders Many vets will board small pets for short periods.

Tranquillisers You can get tranquillisers from the vet to sedate your pet before setting out on a journey if it is a nervous traveller or gets car sick. But your animal's health should be checked by the vet before any drugs are prescribed.

Cages for cats In cars or on trains, cats feel more secure travelling in a cage. Wire mesh cages are the best – although enclosed, the cat can see out. A cat allowed to travel loose in a car can be dangerous.

Diseases you can catch from pets

Internal parasites Roundworms, hookworms and tapeworms are all transmittable from pets to their owners. Young children are particularly at risk from soil-borne roundworm infection which can give rise to the disease toxocariasis. Often the infection is harmless, but in a few cases there may be serious eye damage.
● Try not to let your pet foul public places and clean up scrupulously after it if it does, particularly in areas where children play.
● Regular worming (page 416) will treat all parasites.

Ringworm A scaly lesion may indicate ringworm, which is actually a fungal disease, not a worm. Take the animal to a vet.

Stomach upsets A few species of bacteria, such as salmonella and campylobacter, can cause gastroenteritis in people and animals. If you and your pet suffer a severe stomach upset simultaneously, both a doctor and a vet should be seen to carry out the necessary tests. Cases like this are rare, however.

Disease from cats A vague flu-like illness called toxoplasmosis that is harmful only to pregnant women can be caught from contact with cat faeces or raw meat. Few cats carry the disease, but pregnant women should avoid litter trays and wash their hands after touching a cat. Feed pets only cooked or canned meat, and wash your hands after preparing meat in the kitchen.

CLEANING UP AFTER YOUR DOG

You can buy a commercial poop-scoop from a pet shop or, alternatively, take a strong plastic bag with you on walks.
● Put the bag over your hand, pick up the dog's droppings, then turn the bag inside out over your hand with the droppings inside.
● Dispose of it in the nearest litter bin, or in the dustbin at home.

Quarantine and export of pets

Each country has its own regulations about taking in animals. Prepare early so you won't be delayed by red tape.
● Contact the embassy of the country you are going to at least two months before leaving so that they can send the relevant forms and information in good time.
● Contact the Ministry of Agriculture, Food and Fisheries, who will send information about Britain's export requirements.
● You'll need health certificates in all cases, and possibly extra vaccinations – against rabies, for example.
● If you take a pet out of Britain it will have to spend six months in quarantine before being allowed back in.

Using the family camera

GETTING TO GRIPS WITH HOW A COMPACT CAMERA WORKS

Most family photographs are taken with a compact camera which does most of the technical thinking for you, leaving you free to concentrate on composing the most attractive picture.

Don't be beaten by the weather

A compact camera, despite all its computerised components, is designed to work best on a fine day in summer.

A camera takes a picture by opening and closing its shutter at a speed which depends on the strength of the light. On a dull day, using average film, the shutter may work at 1/50th of a second or even slower – too slow to give you a sharp image of, say, a wedding guest throwing confetti over a bride and groom. To 'freeze the action' the speed needs to be at least 1/125th second. So what can you do to capture the action? You put a fast film, such as ISO 400, in your camera. This speeds up the shutter and gives you sharp pictures.

Choosing the right film

Most people with compact cameras use 35mm colour print film, from which they can get reprints and enlargements.

Films are made with varying degrees of sensitivity to light. They are referred to as 'slow', 'medium' or 'fast', and are rated by ISO numbers from 64 (slow) to 1000 and higher. The most widely used film is ISO 100 (medium).

Films are DX-rated, which means that their speed is automatically recorded by most cameras when they are loaded. In cameras without a DX-rating, you have to set the film speed manually.

A typical film box carries the following information:

Format The size of the film. Look for 35mm (or the numbers 135).

Type Colour, slide or black and white. Look for the words 'colour print film'. Number of pictures per cassette: 12, 24 or 36 exposures. The more exposures, the higher the price.

Speed Choose ISO 100 or 200 (usually marked boldly on the box as 100 or 200) for most of your photography. Buy faster film such as 400 or 800, or the superfast Ektar 1000, for action pictures in dull weather or for shots where light is weak but you don't want to use flash.

DX coding This tells you that the cassette carries magnetic information, like a cashcard. The information is transferred to the camera during loading, and enables the camera to make the correct exposure calculations.

Film expiry date Colour print film has a fairly long shelf life, and dealers usually sell out-of-date film at reduced prices. Even film over a year past its 'sell-by date' will give perfectly good pictures.

The right way to load a film

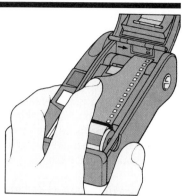

1 Open the camera and place the cassette in the film chamber over the rewind shaft.

2 Make sure that the film leader is correctly positioned alongside the film leader end mark.

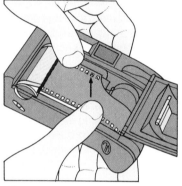

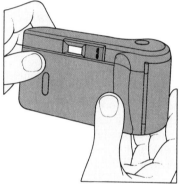

3 Check that the holes have engaged with the sprocket teeth. Then firmly close the back.

4 Check that the frame counter shows '1' – the first exposure. If not, see below.

Film stuck? If the film hasn't wound on automatically, check that:
● The film is inserted correctly.
● The batteries are correctly fitted.
● The battery indicator shows that the battery is still charged.

DO NOT load film in direct sunlight. If you are outside on a sunny day, turn your back to the sun and keep film and camera in the shade.

Holding the camera

Vertical When using the camera vertically for, say, a portrait shot, swivel it clockwise from the horizontal so that the shutter button is at the bottom.

In the wrong position, your fingers will cover the autofocus and flash windows.

Horizontal Hold the camera securely with both hands, keeping it as steady as possible.

Lightweight supports A compact, lightweight tripod is useful for long exposures, as for interior shots or night photography.

Alternatively, use a beanbag. You can buy them, but it's easy to make your own – sew 50g (2oz) of dried kidney beans into a cotton bag. A beanbag is portable and allows you to support your camera on irregular surfaces for long exposures and when you want to include yourself in the picture.

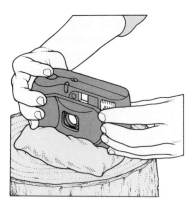

Don't stab! When you take a picture, press the shutter button gently. Don't stab at it. If you do, you'll shake the camera and get a blurred picture.

Getting the best out of flash

Many cameras have a flash unit which fires automatically when light is dull. They may also allow you to cancel the flash unit when flashlight might spoil the atmosphere of the scene or in places where flash is not permitted.

Know the range Flash has a limited range. Best results are from 1.5m to 3m (5ft-10ft), but check your handbook. If the subject is too close, the skin tones will be white and 'burned-out'. At 5m (16ft) and beyond, faces become darker. But you can increase the range by using faster film.

It is pointless using flash in a sports stadium or a large building like a cathedral – the athletes or the stained-glass window will be much too far away for the flash to have any effect.

Avoiding 'red-eye' The most common problem with flash is 'red-eye' caused by the flash bouncing back from the subject's eyes. In dimly lit rooms a person's pupils widen to let in more light. You can reduce red-eye by increasing where possible the light in the room. Some cameras have a pre-flash burst of light which causes the pupils in the subject's eyes to partially close before the flash itself fires.

Fill-in flash When harsh sunlight casts strong shadows, you can use fill-in flash to lighten the dark areas – especially when taking portraits. If the subject is in the shade, but there are also sunlit areas in the viewfinder, the camera will register the sunlight and the subject will be underexposed. Fill-in flash solves the problem.

Flash or natural light? Flash for an indoor picture can result in a washed-out, blue effect (left). By cancelling the flash, you can get a warmer picture from the natural light, using a fast film (below). Film: ISO 100 for flash; ISO 400 for natural light.

● If your camera has no fill-in flash mode, or any other form of exposure compensation, try putting your finger over the exposure window. This will cause the camera to register dark conditions, and the flash will then fire.

Using flash to 'stop' action Try using flash – even on a bright day – to take action pictures. Provided you're close enough to the subject for the flash to be effective, you are more likely to freeze the action of, say, a child on a swing than if you used the camera normally.

Stopping a swing The swing is moving too quickly to 'stop the action' with natural light using ISO 100 film (right). But if you use flash (above), you can stop the motion.

Avoiding badly composed pictures

A satisfying arrangement of the elements in a picture, whether people, buildings, trees or other objects, is called 'composition'. A well-composed picture is more pleasing than a confused jumble of shapes.

When composing your picture ask yourself a few questions:
● Are there too many dark shadows – particularly a shadow of yourself?
● Are there any background objects – TV aerials, street lamps, chimneys – to spoil the picture?
● Should you move to a higher viewpoint?
● Should you move in closer to the main point of interest?
● Should you use a vertical frame instead of a horizontal one?

Look before you shoot As you compose the picture, ask yourself: are there any background objects that might spoil the result? Film: ISO 100.

FAMILY AND FRIENDS

Outdoor pictures

● The best time for photographing people is on a bright, hazy day. Too little light will cause your pictures to come out dark, with possible camera shake as well. Too much light will make the prints appear washed out.
● Harsh sunlight makes people squint, and casts strong, unflattering shadows. Remember that shaded parts of a scene on a sunny day can be softened with fill-in flash – especially when you are close to the subject.

● Try placing your subject so the sun is behind her, and use the camera's fill-in flash, or backlight button, to get light on her face.

Fill-in flash The sunlight shining from behind the girl creates a halo effect on her hair. Fill-in flash prevents her face from being thrown into shadow. Film: ISO 100.

Indoor pictures

● Soft light coming through a window is an excellent source of illumination. Try to avoid using flash, and instead prop a sheet of white card, or hang a white towel near your sitter's face – just out of the picture on the opposite side from the window – to 'bounce' light into the shadows.

● Most people feel self-conscious when a camera is pointing at them, so try to create a relaxed atmosphere between yourself and your subject.

● Get the subject into a casual pose, leaning against a wall or sitting in a chair. Experiment with various poses; it may not be ideal always to have the subject right in the middle of the picture.

● Take more pictures than you might do outdoors. People increase their rate of blinking when being photographed, especially with flash, and you'll end up with several shots with the sitter's eyes closed.

● If your sitter is wearing glasses, look carefully in the viewfinder for unwanted reflections.

● Use your zoom if you have one. The 80mm setting is ideal for portraits, and it will encourage you to fill the frame and eliminate any unwanted surroundings. Although vertical framing is usually best for portraits, experiment with horizontal framing as well.

● If your camera has no zoom, move in close – but not closer than about 1m (3ft), otherwise the sitter's features may appear distorted.

Relaxed subject For a portrait, try to create a friendly atmosphere and put your subject in a relaxed pose (left). Film: ISO 100.

Natural light A nearby window gave enough light for this family portrait (above). Film: ISO 400.

Shooting a group

● A little time spent arranging the group will give rewarding results. Shots of everyone standing in a row may prove dull – try getting the front row to sit or kneel, the back row to stand. Keep the group tightly composed.

● Take at least half a dozen pictures – inevitably someone will turn their head, fidget or blink.

● This is the time when a few well-rehearsed jokes can relax the atmosphere and put everyone in a cooperative mood.

● Use the self-timer to include yourself in the group. Mount the camera on a stand so the group fits in the viewfinder, and leave a gap for yourself. You will have about ten seconds before the shutter fires.

● With a large group, it is often better to take the photograph from an elevated position so the people at the back aren't hidden. Try standing on a chair or a step-ladder, or even in the upstairs window of your house.

A smiling group Friendly backchat between the photographer and his subjects can result in a happy group shot. Film: ISO 100.

CHILDREN AND BABIES

Children quickly become bored with being photographed, so try to take them by surprise. Never tell children in advance that you intend to take pictures, they'll probably refuse to cooperate.

Shoot first, and worry about composition if there's time to spare and you are maintaining interest. With children, the spontaneous shot is usually preferable to an arranged pose.

Get down to their level Shoot from the children's eye level. Shooting from above may give you a background of floor, and the subjects will look too small in the frame.

Use a decoy With a very young child, choose the background and camera position, then place a favourite toy in range. Take pictures while the child remains absorbed.

Mother too Mother-and-child pictures are often the most successful because the child feels more secure and responsive.

Recording family 'scenes' Tears and tantrums are part of family life too, and can make excellent pictures for your album..

Building confidence Mother's presence helps to make a child more confident when facing the camera. Film: ISO 400.

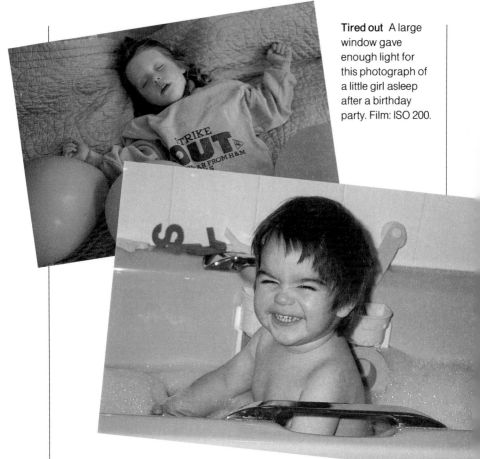

Tired out A large window gave enough light for this photograph of a little girl asleep after a birthday party. Film: ISO 200.

Bathtime A few colourful toys provide highlights in a bathroom scene taken with flash. Film: ISO 100.

Bathroom problems Bathtime is usually a good opportunity for picture taking, and you'll probably need flash, so watch out for spots of reflected light from wall tiles and mirrors. It helps to shoot down into the bath from a standing position.

Soft light for babies Babies may find flash distressing, so use the light from a window or a table lamp. Indoor lighting from normal lamps will give your pictures a yellow cast that can be quite effective.

Groups of children

● Try to arrange children in a tight group, especially when using flash. In a loosely arranged group, those farthest away from the light source will appear darker than those near to it. Flash has a pronounced fall-off after about 3m (10ft).

Flash for a group When using flash, keep a group close together (right), otherwise the flash won't light up the children at the back as well as those at the front (below). Film: ISO 100.

● Attracting everyone's attention can be tricky, especially at parties. You can be sure that in almost every shot you take, at least one child will be looking away from the camera. This can give the picture a nicely informal look, but if you want everyone to be looking at the camera, try blowing a referee's whistle – and then immediately take the picture.

FLOWERS AND GARDENS

Time of day The atmosphere of flower or garden photographs is affected by the time of day. The noon sunshine adds richness to the colour. Early morning or late afternoon sunlight softens the contrast between light and shadow, creating a more romantic mood.

Bright light for colour Massed crocuses show up best when photographed under the midday sun (right). Film: ISO 400.

Close-ups of flowers If you have a close-up or macro setting, use it to shoot individual flowers in dramatic close-up. The macro and close-up settings can only focus on a very limited zone, making the background blurred. This throws emphasis onto the main subject.

Getting in close A close-up picture focuses sharply on the flowers in the centre. Film: ISO 400.

Focusing with a macro lens Run the lens out to maximum length, including the macro setting. Check your handbook for the correct distance between camera and subject. This will typically be from 0.8m (2ft 8in) to 1.3m (4ft 3in). If the subject is too close or too far, most cameras have a symbol that blinks, and the shutter cannot be released.

Using the light in the garden

● Move around so that your subject is backlit – that is, the flower you are shooting is between you and the sunlight. This can intensify colour, rather like light coming through a stained-glass window.
● Watch for the long shadows of early morning sunlight which can make effective patterns. And try to capture the effects of ground mist and dew.
● For contrast, take pictures of your garden in the winter. On misty days use fast film (ISO 400), but keep to ISO 100 for snow.

WIDE OPEN SPACES

In the countryside the opportunities seem endless. But grand panoramic scenes can produce unremarkable pictures, often because there is no particular feature, such as foreground interest or a strong accent of colour.

427

Experiment Move yourself around to find the most pleasing effect. If you have one, use a brown filter to bring out the earthiness of the scene.

Weather effects Changing weather and the time of day give you the chance of more atmospheric results.

Low horizon Keeping the horizon low in the picture gets in the early morning sun partially hidden by mist (right). Film: ISO 100.

High horizon With the horizon high, a harbour is captured during a placid sunset (left). Film: ISO 100.

Winter trees To capture the delicate tracery of winter trees, the camera has to be kept perfectly still. Film: ISO 100.

Placing the horizon Take care where you place the horizon in the picture. A low horizon will give a wide expanse of sky; a horizon near the top of the picture will include a lot of foreground.

Creating depth Use a feature in the landscape to create perspective. Roads, winding paths and old stone walls can 'lead' you into the picture and add depth.

428

Framing the picture Use the overhanging branches of trees to frame your photographs.

Coping with bright patches Beware of exposure problems with snow or reflections from lakes or wet roads. Automatic cameras compensate for bright highlights, and tend to underexpose the rest of the picture. Use your backlight button. Alternatively, point your camera at a dark area, press the shutter button halfway down to hold the exposure reading, then reposition to take the picture (see below).

HOW TO LOCK THE EXPOSURE

With many compact cameras you can 'lock' the exposure. Try pointing the camera at a dark area of the scene, pressing the shutter button halfway, then repositioning the camera. You will get a photograph with a pale sky and detail in the shadows – because the camera has overexposed the film. If you point the camera at the sky, lock the exposure, then reposition for the final shot, you will get black shadow areas, and detail in the sky – because the camera has underexposed the picture.

BUILDINGS AND CITYSCAPES

Lighting a building When photographing buildings, try for an angle where the sun is behind you, and the building well lit. If the building is between you and the sun, it will appear dark in the picture. If the sun is immediately behind the building, it will appear as a silhouette. This may be attractive, but if you want detail in a backlit building, use your backlight control, or exposure compensation control. Flash will be useless because the building will be too far away.

'Falling' buildings Photographing a tall building from ground level may make it appear to be falling backwards. Try to find a higher position – for example, shooting from a nearby tall building. Another technique is to get back as far as you can and shoot from the middle distance.

Alternatively, emphasise the effect by moving in close, and make a feature of the perspective.

Including a friend When you pose someone in front of a famous building, first fill the viewfinder with the building, then get your friend to move in for a head-to-waist shot. Don't arrange the shot so that your friend is a tiny figure many yards from the camera. The figure may seem near enough in the view-finder, but compact lenses tend to reduce image size.

The building first Arrange the building in the viewfinder first, and only then get your friend to come into the picture close to the camera. Film: ISO 400.

Fine detail When photographing buildings, look out for the rich details that the eye often passes over (above). Film: ISO 100.

Street scene A photograph of a street musician (right) captures the mood of Covent Garden. Film: ISO 400.

Picking out details Don't overlook details of buildings, especially richly embellished architectural features.

City people Often, the most interesting shots in a city are of the city dwellers themselves as they go about their daily routine.

Cities at night Some cities are so brightly lit that you can shoot pictures by night, holding the camera in your hands. With a tripod, there is limitless scope for panoramic night shots of a city or individual buildings – historical ones are often attractively floodlit.

Cityscape The lights of buildings are enough to capture a night view of London. Film: ISO 400.

INSIDE LARGE BUILDINGS

A steady camera Mount your camera onto a beanbag, placed on a plinth or other firm surface.

Interior shots To photograph the inside of a large building, put the camera on a bean bag on a firm surface, use the self-timer to avoid shake, and shoot by natural light. Flash is useless in a big area. Film: ISO 400.

Avoiding camera shake Use your self-timer, so you don't have to fire the shutter manually and cause camera shake. The exposure will be about half a second to a second, so choose a moment when passers-by are not likely to step in front of the camera.

Fast film Hand-held shots may be possible with fast film. In a large, well-lit interior you can achieve pictures with film of ISO 400 or faster, but hold the camera steady – perhaps by leaning against a wall or pillar.

Using flash Fast film records reflected flashlight from farther away than slow film. ISO 400 film will register flash at a distance of 10m (33ft). Beyond that, flash is useless in a large interior, like a cathedral.

Avoiding flares Try to avoid flare spots from reflective surfaces by not pointing your camera at large areas of glass or mirrors.

SPORTS AND GAMES

Good light, fast film It's possible to get good photographs at sporting events with a compact camera if you have a combination of good light and fast film – ISO 400 or 800.

'Panning' Move your camera with the subject – a technique called 'panning'. With your feet firmly planted, keep the subject in the viewfinder and swing your body and camera in pace with the action.

Scene of the action Try to predict where and when the action will reach its peak. At a school sports day, for example, stand near the fences at a hurdling event, or back from the finishing line at a sprint with the competitors coming towards you – but don't get in the way!

Indoor events In a well-lit indoor stadium, you should be able to get action shots by using ISO 400 film without flash. Don't get closer than 4.5m (15ft). The closer you are, the more chance of blurred pictures.

Tough camera Photographing a
sport such as canoeing requires a camera that is
waterproof and able to take knocks. Film: ISO 400.

Sport compact If you enjoy taking pictures of sports and outdoor activities
such as climbing, you may find it worth buying a sport compact camera. It
will have a strong, waterproof cover and will be designed for rough-and-
tumble photography.

SPORTS PHOTOGRAPHY – A CHECKLIST

● Take at least two cassettes of fast film.
● Take a folding stool so that you can shoot above the heads of the crowd,
but check first with the people in charge of security to see if permission is
required.
● Try and arrive early to get the best view.
● When shooting, keep the camera level and steady, and don't stab at the
shutter button.

Fault-finder guide: poor pictures

Whole picture blurred
Caused by camera shake due to a too-slow shutter. For example, if you
use slow film (ISO 100) on a dull day the shutter will stay open long enough
for any slight movement of your hands to register on the film. Use ISO 400
film on a dull day. Or use flash if the subject is close enough.

Subject blurred, background sharp
Caused by the shutter moving too slowly to 'freeze' the action of a person
moving near the camera. For action and sports pictures, use ISO 800 film
or flash, or both.

Picture has a yellow cast
The pictures were probably shot indoors with domestic (tungsten)
lighting. Normal daylight-type film records domestic lighting as yellow. If
you want film for shooting indoors without flash, ask for tungsten or Type
B film.

Subject slightly out of frame
When you are shooting close-up in the macro mode, the viewfinder will
see the subject at a slightly different angle from the camera lens. This
'parallax error' can be corrected by moving the camera fractionally to one

side. Look in your camera's handbook for advice on parallax adjustment. Some cameras make the adjustment automatically when they are set in the macro mode.

Dark patch on the picture
This could be the camera strap, or even a stray finger! Next time, check to see that the lens is not obscured before shooting.

Bright patch on the picture
The patch is due to flare from a very bright reflection, or the sun shining directly into the lens. When using the backlight button against a strong light, fix a lens hood to the camera if it will take one, or shade the lens with your hand.

Sloping horizon
Camera not level, or you may have pushed down too hard on the shutter-release button.

Picture too light, with washed-out colours
Overexposure. Have you used very fast film in bright light, such as ISO 800 on sand or snow? Overexposure may also be due to a faulty shutter mechanism.

Picture too dark
Underexposure. Picture taken in conditions of extreme light and shade, where the camera was reading for the highlights while the lens was pointing mainly at the shadows. Could also be caused by using a dark filter, or by a faulty shutter mechanism.

Shutter won't fire
Battery failure or batteries wrongly inserted. Is the power switch set to ON? Film incorrectly inserted. Camera hasn't focused – check in the viewfinder for a flashing light.

Bright yellow patches and streaks
The film has probably been 'fogged' – light has leaked into it. Has the back been opened by mistake, or not properly closed?

Mechanical failure
Most mechanical faults in cameras are due to sand in the mechanism. Do not try any camera repairs yourself. They may invalidate the guarantee. Take the camera back to the shop where you bought it.

Cleaning your camera

● Keep the camera free of dust, dirt and sand. When putting in a film, avoid touching interior mechanisms, such as the film pressure plate. You might make them greasy.
● Use a soft, lint-free cloth to wipe the body and windows.
● Remove dust from the interior with a blower brush, an inexpensive device which combines a rubber bulb and a brush.
● Clean the lens with a blower brush, never with a cloth.

Long-term storage

● Before putting away the camera for more than a few weeks, clean it thoroughly.
● Remove the batteries.

● Make sure the lens cap is closed and put the camera in its case. If possible, include a small sachet of silica crystals in the case. They prevent damp by absorbing moisture. Most new cameras come with a silica pouch in the carton.

● Store the camera in a dry, warm place. Avoid excess heat, cold, damp and vibration. Don't leave your camera on a windowsill where the sun will shine on it, or near a source of heat.

Checklist for holidays

● Take plenty of spare film – ISO 100 for general use, ISO 400 for dull days and night shots.

● Don't forget spare batteries.

● A blower brush is essential after a day on the beach. And take a plastic bag to wrap up the camera when it is not being used. That will help to keep the sand out.

● Take a blue graduated filter to improve pictures when you want to intensify large areas of blue sky and perhaps sea and lakes. And a lens hood to shade the lens from the sun.

The final result

Enlargements

● Negatives of ISO 100 film will give substantial enlargements, although 180 × 125mm (7 × 5in) and 250 × 200mm (10 × 8in) are the most usual sizes. You can even order poster prints about 1.2m (4ft) high, which make a good present – and they are not particularly expensive.

● Fast photo labs with customer-operated enlarging machines enable you to do your own prints up to 360 × 280mm (14 x 11in). While using the machine you can enlarge areas of the negative, crop out unwanted parts, alter density and colour, and include or exclude borders.

● Out-of-focus and wrongly exposed pictures will never enlarge well. Choose only the sharpest images for enlarging.

● Fast and ultra-fast film, such as ISO 1000, will show a grainy print. This is characteristic of fast films, but can be an attractive feature.

● Always keep your negatives in their protective sleeves and carefully filed, free of dust and damp.

● If you lose a negative, you will not succeed in making good enlargements from the print alone. Although a print can be copied, it will lose clarity and definition.

Framing A wide range of easy-to-use frames can be bought at reasonable cost, together with card mounts of standard sizes such as 250 × 200mm (10 x 8in) and 300 × 250mm (12 x 10in).

Albums Choose an album with clear plastic sheets to hold down the pictures. Vary the layout from page to page, and include souvenirs of trips and holidays – airline labels, tickets, beer mats, event programmes and so on. Captions can be written on adhesive labels and stuck on the plastic sheet.

Greetings cards Some photo labs offer special prices for bulk prints, or for printing on card.

Extra set of prints If it's likely that friends or relatives may ask for copies of your holiday pictures, get an extra set printed when the film is developed. It's much more convenient – and probably cheaper – than ordering individual prints later.

Personal grooming & clothes

LOOKING AFTER YOUR FACE

No matter what your age, sex, skin colour or skin type, the basic requirements for healthy skin remain the same – a good diet, regular exercise, enough sleep and plenty of fresh air. Skin naturally looks after itself, shedding old layers and replacing them with new ones. If it is protected from the extremes of weather and too many chemicals, all that most people need to do is to wash their face regularly with mild soap and water. Women who use make-up need a more thorough cleaning routine, however, to make sure that all traces are removed at the end of every day.

Washing with soap

● Soap emulsifies the grease on your skin, allowing it to be washed off with water. The skin will generally replace the grease within hours, though.
● Too much washing, or using strong soaps, can strip the skin of protective oils. If your skin feels tight and dry after washing, try milder products – those which lather less – used less often. Apply moisturisers to help prevent dryness.

Medicated soap Helpful for some skin conditions, such as acne, but with no advantage over normal soap for most skins.

Chemical colourings, perfume or antiseptic in soap The more chemicals or additives in the soap, the greater the chance of irritating the skin. Use the simplest sort possible, with no additives, for the gentlest wash.

A routine for removing make-up

Cleansing Although most cleansers you can buy are creams and lotions, get a special cleansing bar if you like the feel of water on your face. This is solid cleansing cream in soap form. Otherwise, use a cream or lotion which is washed off with water or removed with tissue or cotton wool.

Toning Toners remove any remaining dirt, make-up or oily residues of cleanser. There are different varieties for different skin types – oily, dry or normal. Choose an alcohol-based astringent if your skin is oily, and an alcohol-free toner which won't remove so much oil if your skin is dry.

Moisturising Use moisturising creams or lotions on your face and neck to compensate for the skin's water loss. They keep the skin soft and supple by replacing lost moisture and forming a fine film that cuts down the amount that escapes. Use a light moisturiser during the day, since you'll be putting make-up on top, and a thicker one at night. Apply a special eye cream around your eyes – the skin here is paper thin and very sensitive.

Removing eye make-up Use a special eye make-up remover, gently swabbing it onto your eyelids and lashes with cotton wool or tissue.

Treating spots and blemishes

Spots If you are prone to spots, always clean your face thoroughly to remove excess oil which could clog the pores and make the problem worse. Apply an anti-acne lotion every night and don't squeeze the spots – it will inflame the skin and you may introduce bacteria from your fingers. Most spots will soon go away by themselves – they are often aggravated by stress, illness or menstruation. (See also *Acne*, page 472.)

435

Blackheads To extract a black-head, steam your face gently for a couple of minutes to open the pores. Then use clean fingertips, tissues or a special blackhead remover to squeeze out the blackhead. Use gentle pressure and never force out a stubborn blackhead – just try again in a few days. Afterwards, dab the area with antiseptic cream or witch hazel.

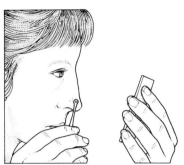

Whiteheads These small, white bumps cannot be squeezed out like blackheads but do eventually go away on their own. To speed up the process, rub occasionally with an exfoliating scrub (see below).

NINE THINGS THAT ARE BAD FOR YOUR SKIN

● Too much sun: whether you burn or not, sun can speed up the ageing and wrinkling process, and increase the risk of skin cancer.

● Too little sleep: this often makes the skin look dull and lifeless.

● Stress: difficult times may provoke the skin's sebaceous glands (which produce oil) to work overtime, leading to spots and pimples.

● Smoking: smoking reduces the amount of oxygen reaching the skin and leads to premature ageing. The muscle movements associated with drawing on a cigarette also encourage lines around the mouth.

● Alcohol: dehydration, a side effect of drinking, is bad for the skin.

● Sudden, extreme weight loss: losing a large amount of weight very rapidly may cause skin to sag. Avoid crash diets.

● The contraceptive pill: side effects of the pill vary, and some women find that it actually improves the state of their skin. In other cases, though, it may lead to spots.

● Pregnancy: being pregnant greatly alters the skin (although it too can have both good and bad effects). Once the baby is born, however, the skin returns to its original condition.

● Pollution: airborne pollution in cities and towns affects some skins. Be scrupulous about your cleansing routine.

Special facial treatments

Exfoliation The skin will look and feel softer, fresher and cleaner with occasional use of special exfoliating grains and scrubs. These remove dead skin cells, speeding up new cell growth and opening up blocked pores. Apply them to clean, damp skin, avoiding the eyes, and rub in gently with the fingertips (right). Wash off with fresh warm water.

Facial scrubs are widely available from chemists, or you can make your own with 75ml (5tbsp) cornmeal, 30ml (2tbsp) honey and 15ml (1tbsp) ground almonds or walnuts. Mix all the ingredients together in a small bowl, adding a little water if required, and then apply to your face. Leave the scrub on for five minutes before washing off with warm water and a flannel. Use a sink strainer over the plughole, or you could end up with a blocked bathroom drain.

Steaming A steam bath opens the pores and encourages the skin to sweat out impurities. Fill a bowl with hot water and lean over the bowl with your head covered by a towel. Steam for five minutes if you have oily skin, two minutes if it's normal or dry. Don't steam your face if you get broken veins – heat can make them worse.

Face masks Packaged in a variety of forms, masks are available for moisturising, deep cleansing and exfoliating. Choose a mask to suit your skin type and apply it onto clean dry skin, avoiding lips and sometimes also the eye area – check the instructions. After the recommended time – usually about 15 minutes – wash or peel the mask away, apply moisturiser and wait for at least two hours before putting on make-up.

FACE MASKS TO MAKE AT HOME

Cucumber and yoghurt mask for all skin types Cucumber is well known for its cooling and toning properties, and yoghurt is said to revive dull or tired-looking skin.

● To make the mask, wash a chunk of cucumber about 50mm (2in) long, but do not peel it.

● Liquidise the cucumber with five teaspoons of natural yoghurt until well blended.

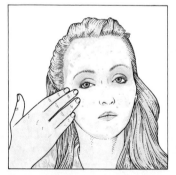

● Apply this mixture to your face, avoiding the lips and the eye area, and leave for 15 minutes.

● Rinse well with warm water, and then splash your face with cool water to close the pores.

Egg yolk and oil mask for dry skin Mix together the yolk of an egg, a few drops of olive oil and a few drops of lemon juice. Cleanse your face and spread on the mixture. Rinse off with cold water after ten minutes.

Egg white and cornflour mask for oily skin Beat the white of an egg until stiff; then fold in 30ml (2tbsp) cornflour. Cleanse your face and apply the mask. When tight and dry, rub off with a dry cloth and rinse with cold water.

Dealing with facial hair

Everyone has some facial hair. Women with sparse hair that is fine and fair are usually happy to leave it alone, but if it is darker or thicker you may prefer to bleach or remove it.

Bleaching

Unless facial hair is very thick, bleaching may be all that's needed to disguise it. Always use a bleach intended for the face, and follow the instructions on the pack. Do a patch test first, in case of allergies.

Plucking

Use tweezers to remove odd, stray hairs and neaten eyebrows. Clean the skin thoroughly before you tweeze, and pluck out one hair at a time, pulling in the direction of hair growth. Shape your eyebrows by removing hairs between and underneath the brows – never from above. Check your progress constantly by brushing the brows back into shape.

Depilatory creams

Use only creams which say they are suitable for the face and test on a small area first, to check for allergic reactions. Follow the maker's instructions, and never leave the cream on for longer than the stated time. Don't use depilatory cream on your eyebrows or anywhere near your eyes.

Waxing

Facial strip wax is suitable for chin, lip and eyebrow hairs. Smooth it on in the direction of hair growth, leave for the recommended time, then quickly whisk it off in the opposite direction. Don't wax for two hours after a hot bath or shower, or over inflamed skin, moles, rashes, warts or scars.

Electrolysis

The only way to remove unwanted hair for good is to destroy the root with a small electric current. Consult a professional electrolysist.

MAKE THE MOST OF MAKE-UP

A good foundation A properly applied foundation cream should not be noticeable, but that doesn't mean it's not important. Foundation hides blemishes, gives an even tone to your skin and provides a smooth base for other make-up. Choose a shade close to your natural colouring – to check the colour, dab a spot onto your jaw-line, not your wrist or hand where the skin is often a different tone.

THREE TIPS FOR CHOOSING YOUR FOUNDATION

- The most natural look is a foundation that matches your skin tone.
- A subtle rose-beige tint adds warmth to a sallow skin.
- To counteract redness, choose foundation with a slight tinge of green.

Concealing blemishes Use a concealer stick or wand to camouflage dark shadows and cover up blemishes. Apply it under or over your foundation, blending in the edges so that they are not noticeable. Dust lightly with powder.

Disguising lines A light dusting of translucent powder will help to hide any facial lines, but too much will have the opposite effect, so always use powder sparingly. After you've applied foundation, dip the powder pad into the loose powder and knock off the excess against your hand. Apply lightly over the whole face. Dust off loose powder with a large, soft brush, paying special attention to any fine lines around your eyes or nose.

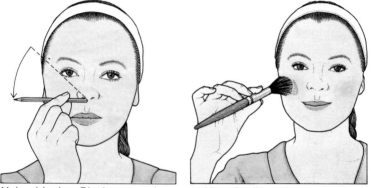

Using blusher Blusher can give your skin a healthy glow and help to accent bone structure, but it needs to be applied in the right place. Use the pencil test to guide you: hold a pencil so that it runs from the side of one nostril to the corner of your eye. Hold the nostril end steady and swing down the top of the pencil from your eye until it is level with your ear lobe. The area covered by the pencil shows where to apply blusher.

Before you begin, smile at yourself in the mirror; the roundest part of your cheek shows the best place to start. Use a brush to apply the blusher in a teardrop shape here. Then soften the edges and blend outwards towards the hairline, filling in the area indicated by the pencil.

Putting on mascara With your chin down and your eyes looking up, brush the lower lashes of each eye with mascara. Then, looking down, coat the upper lashes, top and bottom. Try to separate the lashes as you work, so that they don't stick together. Several thin coats look better than one thick covering, but let each coat dry out before you apply the next. When the final coat is dry, separate the lashes with a lash comb (right) or an old, clean mascara brush.

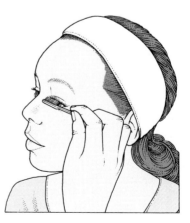

A finer point on eye pencils To get a finer point on your eye pencils, put them in the fridge for a few hours before sharpening.

Choosing eye shadow colours To find out which colours will suit you, look closely at the flecks of colour in your irises (the coloured part of your eye around the pupil). The variety can be surprising, but any of these colours should look good on you.

Keeping make-up fresh If possible, avoid dipping your fingers into make-up or skin-care products so that you don't transfer bacteria to them. Use clean cotton buds, applicators or cotton wool instead.

Dyeing your eyelashes If applying mascara every day seems too time-consuming, or if you're going on holiday and don't want to wear make-up on the beach, consider having your eyelashes professionally dyed or dyeing them at home with a kit. The colour lasts for about six weeks and never runs or smudges. For special occasions you can apply mascara as well. Never dye your eyelashes if you are suffering from an eye infection.

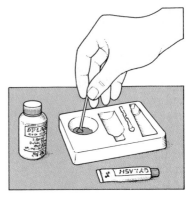

Longer-lasting lipstick Always include your lips when you apply foundation and powder. This gives a good base for lip colours. Outline your lips with a lip pencil, then fill in the line with lipstick that matches the pencil colour. For a smoother finish, apply lipstick with a lip brush instead of just using the stick. Blend the colour well into the outline, blot with a tissue, and dust lightly with translucent powder. Apply a second coat of lipstick on top.

Applying eye shadow

There is no single right way to put on eye make-up, but this technique is easy to master and gives a look that will suit most people.

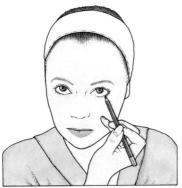

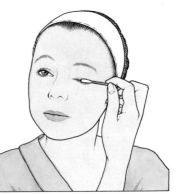

1 Use an eye pencil to draw a thin line just above the upper lashes. Then draw a similar line just below the lower lashes on the outer half of the bottom lid.

2 Gently blend and soften the eye-pencil lines with a cotton bud, taking care not to pull or stretch the skin around the eyes, which is very delicate.

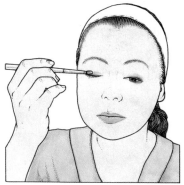

3 With a fine, soft brush, apply powder shadow over the top and bottom pencil lines, and over the top lid. Blend the powder smoothly towards the outer corner.

4 Apply a little darker eye shadow in and around the crease line on the outer edge of the top lid. Blend the darker colour carefully into the lighter.

Ten tips to improve your looks

Down-turned lips Take the bottom lip line slightly upwards at the corners and extend the upper line to meet it on either side.

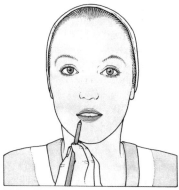

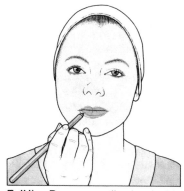

Thin lips Draw an outline just outside the natural line of your lips, in a shade slightly lighter than your lipstick. Fill in the line with lipstick. Apply frosty highlighter if you wish.

Full lips Draw an outline just inside your lips, in a slightly darker shade than your lipstick. Paint lipstick inside the line. Avoid frosted or glossy lipsticks.

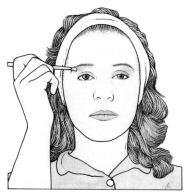

Prominent eyes Apply matt eye shadow in muted colours such as grey or dusty brown over the top lid, and blend up to the brow bone. Avoid very pale or frosted make-up.

Deep-set eyes Use a pale colour on the lid and a slightly darker shade in and above the crease. Avoid very dark colours – they will make your eyes seem even deeper.

441

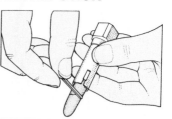

MENDING A BROKEN LIPSTICK

Slightly melt the broken edges of the lipstick with a lighted match and press them together. Smooth the edges of the break with a clean matchstick or a toothpick, and place the lipstick in the fridge until completely cool.

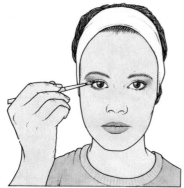

Eyes close together Line top and bottom lids from the centre out. Apply pale shadow to the top lid and the inner corner, and darker shadow on the outer corner.

Eyes far apart Use a darker shade on the inner half of the eye to emphasise it, and a lighter shade on the outer half. Do not apply shadow beyond the outer corner.

Heavy jaw Blend in a slightly darker shade of foundation or contouring stick down the sides of the jaw below the ears and along the jawline.

Wide nose Run slightly darker foundation or contouring stick down both sides of your nose. Apply lighter foundation in the centre and blend in well.

Crooked nose To make it look straight, use darker foundation or contouring stick on the side that sticks out, and paler colour on the other.

HEALTHY AND BEAUTIFUL HAIR

Washing and drying your hair

Which shampoo? Try out shampoos suitable for your hair type until you find the one that suits you best. If it seems to work less well after a time, switch to another brand – your hair may benefit from a change.

How often to wash your hair Wash your hair whenever it starts to look dull or greasy. Even a daily wash won't do any harm if you use a mild shampoo – ones that lather less are generally milder.

No time to shampoo? To clean your hair in a hurry without getting it wet, sprinkle it with cornflour or baby powder and then brush out thoroughly. Alternatively, swab your scalp with cotton wool soaked in eau de cologne.

Conditioning your hair If your hair feels brittle or tangles easily, it may help to use an after-shampoo conditioner. Conditioners make hair more manageable, reduce static and smooth the cuticle surface, which produces shine. Avoid conditioners, however, if your hair is oily, or condition only the ends.

Home-made conditioner To revive dull or limp hair, apply a mashed avocado or a beaten egg all over your hair and scalp. Leave it on for 15-20 minutes, then rinse out and shampoo.

Deep conditioning Ordinary after-shampoo conditioning may not be enough if your hair is very dry, permanently waved, coloured, or in poor condition. To make it look its best, give it an occasional treatment with a richer conditioner or a hot oil pack which is massaged in before washing and left on for several hours.

Home oil treatment For an economical oil treatment, heat about 30ml (2tbsp) – more for long hair, less for short – almond, coconut, sesame or olive oil in a jug or cup in a pan of boiling water until just warm. Rub well into hair and scalp and cover with foil or plastic wrap. Wrap a warm towel around your head and leave for at least half an hour, preferably overnight. Shampoo out and rinse well.

Blow-drying

Always begin with a cool setting and blow-dry all over to remove excess water. Lift the hair away from the scalp to give volume.

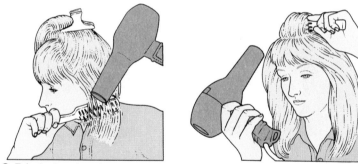

● For sleek styles, dry on a cool setting until nearly dry, then divide your hair into small sections and finish off on a warmer setting – but not hotter than feels comfortable on your hand. Begin with underneath sections of hair (above left), then move on to the sides, and finish with top and front layers (above right). Make sure the roots are dry before starting on the next section, or your hair will lie flat. If hair feels cold to the touch it is still damp.

● For a fluffier effect, once you have removed most excess water by drying on low heat, turn the hair dryer to a higher setting and dry small sections of hair while scrunching them up in the palm of your hand. A hair dryer with a diffuser attachment – a funnel that fits over the blower nozzle (right) – may make the job easier if your hair is permed or naturally curly.

Cutting, setting and styling

How often do you need a haircut? Have your hair trimmed every six to eight weeks to keep it in good condition, remove split ends and maintain the style. If you want your hair to grow longer, ask the hairdresser to remove the minimum amount, but don't stop having it trimmed.

Brushes and combs Use a comb with widely spaced teeth to disentangle knots or style wet hair. If you prefer to brush your hair at other times, choose a vent brush (a brush with holes in the top) or one with widely spaced prongs. Avoid brushes with densely packed bristles which can pull or stretch your hair or use them for occasional styling only.

CHOOSE A STYLE TO SUIT YOUR FACE

Round face Go for longer styles with volume at the neck or short styles that are full at the crown.

Square face Styles with curls or waves will give a softer overall effect. So will a wispy fringe.

Long, thin face Choose styles that are fuller at the sides, to give the impression of width.

Oval face Any simple, unfussy style that forms a frame around your face will look good.

Heart-shaped face Bouncy, shoulder-length waves or shorter cuts with fullness at the crown will help to balance a heart-shaped face. Avoid hairstyles that are very full at the cheeks.

TREATING HARDWORKING HANDS

Caring for your skin

The skin on the back of your hands, like that on your face, seems to age more quickly than other parts of the body because of exposure to ultraviolet light. Housework can also cause dryness and irritation, but with these simple precautions, you will have hands to be proud of:

Wear gloves

Plastic gloves Wear good-quality plastic gloves for washing up and other household chores. You may find cotton-lined gloves more comfortable than unlined ones, and less liable to cause irritation.

Cotton gloves Gardening gloves protect the hands from contact with soil, fertilisers and pesticides, and brambles and rose thorns.

Wool or leather gloves Since cold has a drying effect on skin and can lead to painful chapping, protect your hands in winter by wearing warm gloves.

Use barrier creams and sun screens

Apply a barrier cream if your hands are prone to dryness and before starting on mechanical or other work using grease. Protect your hands from ultraviolet light with a sun screen whenever you're in harsh sunlight.

Wash in warm water

Washing your hands in very hot water removes natural skin oils and has a drying effect on your skin. Always use warm water and a gentle soap, and then dry thoroughly.

Apply moisturisers

Get into the habit of applying hand cream each time you get your hands wet. Keep some cream in the kitchen, the bathroom and at work. A good weekly treatment for dry hands is to soak them thoroughly in warm olive oil, which conditions the skin, cuticles and nails.

TO REMOVE STAINS

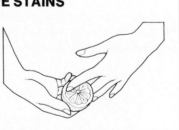

Where skin is stained or dis-coloured, rub it with half a lemon to clean and bleach it. Lemon juice tends to have a drying effect, though, so rinse it off after treating your skin. Dry well and massage with hand cream.

Taking care of your nails

The hard enamel-like part of our nails is called keratin, and is in fact dead nail. The only living part of our nail is the matrix, which lies at the base of the nail bed and is sometimes visible as a pale half-moon shape.

Cuticle treatment

To keep cuticles in good condition, push them back gently after a bath or shower and massage in cuticle cream every day. If you push and poke them too much, though, you can damage your nails – ridges, spots or lines will start to appear. Never cut or force back your cuticles.

How to manicure your nails

You don't need to manicure your nails every week – once they are in good shape, all they may need is regular trimming or filing to keep them neat, and occasional polishing if you use nail varnish.

You will need:

Cotton wool
Nail-polish remover
Cotton buds
Emery boards
Cuticle-conditioning cream
Cuticle remover

Rubber-tipped hoof stick
    or an orange stick
Hand cream
Nail buffer
Small bowl of water
Towel

1 Soak the cotton wool in nail-polish remover and hold it against each nail for a few moments. The old polish should then wipe off in a single stroke without smearing.

2 Hold the fine side of an emery board at a 45° angle to the nail and file from the side towards the centre in one direction only to give a neatly rounded tip. Do not file your nails to a point or they will split.

3 Round off the edges of your nails so that they feel smooth and won't catch on threads. Hold the emery board upright and brush the top layer of nail downwards with light strokes. Then brush the bottom layer lightly upwards for a neat finish.

4 Soften your cuticles with conditioning cream before you try to push them back. Apply a small blob of cream to the base of each nail and massage it gently into the skin.

5 Using a rubber-tipped hoof stick or an orange stick wrapped in cotton wool, gently loosen the skin around each of your nails and then soak your fingers for a few minutes in a bowl of warm water. Rinse your hands well in clean water and dry thoroughly.

6 Nudge the cuticle back with the hoof or orange stick, working from the middle of the cuticle out to the sides. Do not push too hard if the cuticles are built up: apply cuticle remover to the base of each nail or try soaking your fingertips in warm olive oil.

7 Massage a generous amount of hand cream into your hands, and make your nails shine using a chamois leather buffer. Always buff in the same direction, from the nail bed to the tip.

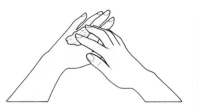

HOW TO POLISH YOUR NAILS

Before polishing your nails, wash and dry them thoroughly to remove any oily traces, or the polish will not stick. If necessary, wipe with cotton wool dampened with nail-varnish remover. You will need a nail hardener, a base coat, nail polish and a top coat.

● Apply nail hardener according to the instructions on the bottle.

● Cover the whole nail with the base coat, to prevent staining.

● Apply two coats of polish, but be careful not to overload the brush. Let the polish dry properly between coats.

● Paint the varnish on in three strokes, brushing from the cuticle to the tip. The first stroke should be down the middle, followed by the sides.

● End with top coat.

● Your nails will be touch-dry in about ten minutes, but won't be really solid for about an hour. If you want them to dry faster, use a spray dryer.

Special nail problems

Mending broken nails

Cracked or split nails can only be mended if you are applying polish, as the polish will hide the patch. Mending kits provide self-adhesive nail coverings and additional fixative.

1 Use an oil-free polish remover to clean your nail thoroughly, and then smooth it into shape with an emery board.

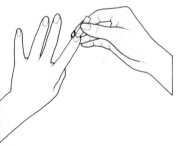

2 Cover the nail with a pre-shaped patch, and trim it carefully to size. Remove the paper backing and press down the patch.

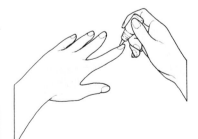

3 Spread a single drop of glue over the entire nail. Repeat with another drop, then dry.

4 Use the emery board to smooth off the edges, and then buff your nail to a shine.

False nails and extensions

Some false-nail adhesives can cause problems with your own nails. To avoid this, don't wear false nails for more than 24 hours. Stick-on false nails are the easiest to apply at home. Several kits are available which contain a set of nails and adhesive. Choose nails that match your own as closely as possible and trim them before applying, following the manufacturer's instructions.

Nail extensions should be left to a professional.

Hangnails

A hangnail is a split in the skin around the nail. Keep your hands and nails well moisturised, and trim any skin flaps carefully.

Nail biting

An unpleasant-tasting nail-biting deterrent helps some people to break this compulsive habit. In general, nail biters neglect their hands, and a regular hand-care regime should make you more aware of them.

PERHAPS YOUR POLISH DOESN'T LAST BECAUSE . . .

- You don't remove all oil traces from your nails before applying polish.
- Your nail polish is too thick – you are putting too much on.
- You don't apply a top coat.
- You don't renew the top coat daily.
- You don't wear gloves when you wash up.
- You don't leave your polish to dry for long enough.

KEEPING BREASTS IN SHAPE

- The best way to improve your bust line is with good posture. Pull your shoulders back and down – your bust will look bigger and higher.

- There is no way to change the shape and size of your breasts, but exercise will help to firm your pectoral muscles. Swimming is excellent, but the following exercise will also help:

Stand up straight with your feet slightly apart. Put your palms together, with your elbows up and out, and push them together as hard as you can for a count of ten. Inhale as you push, exhale as you relax. Repeat 10-20 times.

- Wash your breasts in cool, not hot, water. Hot water will stretch the skin, but cold water is said to stimulate circulation and firm up fatty tissue.

Bust creams Creams won't firm your breasts, but they will help to keep the skin soft and supple.

Single hairs around the nipple Nipple hairs are more common than women realise. You can deal with them by plucking, using a hair removal cream or electrolysis.

448

Buying a bra

● Make sure you get the right size. If possible, try the bra on when you buy it; if it leaves a mark on your skin when you take it off, it's too small.
● Don't buy a bra just before your period – your breasts are usually bigger then.
● Most women have one breast that is larger than the other – pick a bra that fits the larger one.
● Bras made of natural fibres, such as cotton or silk, let the skin breathe better than synthetic fibres, and you will sweat less.

ARE YOU WEARING THE RIGHT SIZE BRA?

To find your correct size, measure around your ribcage just under your bust with a dressmaker's tape. Add an extra five inches to this measurement and you will have your bra size – 34, 36, 38, and so on. Then measure around your full bustline. If this measurement is the same as your ribcage plus five inches you will take an A cup, if it is an inch more, a B cup; two inches more, a C cup; and three inches more, a D cup.

TAKING CARE OF YOUR FEET

Keeping them clean

Wash your feet every day and scrub the nails with a soft nail brush. Dry your feet thoroughly after each washing and whenever they get wet – after swimming, for example. Pay particular attention to the skin between the toes when drying your feet: moisture often gets trapped here. You should also change your socks or tights daily.

Common foot problems

Aching feet If you have been walking or standing for any length of time and your feet are aching, dissolve a cup of Epsom salts or baking soda in warm water, and give yourself a foot bath. Soak your feet for about 15 minutes and then dry them thoroughly. If your feet are often sore, badly fitting shoes may be the problem.

Athlete's foot A fungal infection which develops in the warm, damp area between the toes and causes itchy, peeling skin. To treat it, apply an antifungal cream or powder, and always dry your feet thoroughly after washing them. Use only your own towel, as athlete's foot is contagious.

Bunions A bunion is a deformity of the big toe joint which is usually caused by wearing shoes that are too tight. If it becomes very painful, see a chiropodist who can treat it with padding and strapping.

Calluses Calluses are caused by friction or pressure from shoes that are new or don't fit properly. To remove the hard skin which builds up, use a

449

pumice stone or callus remover, available from chemists. If you cannot get rid of all the dead skin yourself, see a chiropodist for treatment.

Corns Cones of dead skin with the pointed end (the nucleus) facing inwards are called corns. They can be very painful if they press on a nerve. Ease the pressure with corn pads, and see a chiropodist for treatment.

Chilblains Areas of swelling and discoloration caused by cold, damp weather and poor circulation. Wear thick woollen socks or tights to keep feet warm and dry, and improve your circulation by exercise, foot massage and wearing long johns or warm trousers. If chilblains become really painful, see a doctor.

Ingrowing toenails A toenail – usually on the big toe – can start growing inwards on the sides, causing swelling, redness and pain. To prevent this, avoid tight shoes, don't cut your toenails too short, and always leave them straight across the top. In cases of extreme pain, your nail may be infected – consult a chiropodist or doctor.

Verrucas This type of ingrowing wart on the sole of the foot is caused by a virus which is often picked up at swimming pools. If walking becomes painful, try one of the verruca remedies sold by chemists, or see a doctor.

Smelly feet

Foot odour is usually a sign that your footwear is preventing sweat from evaporating and stopping a free flow of air around your feet. Try these tips to solve the problem.
● Wash your feet several times a day, or as often as necessary, and dry them well each time.
● Dust your feet with foot powder or talc before putting on footwear.
● Wear socks and tights made of natural fibres and avoid synthetic shoes or shoes with synthetic linings.
● Allow shoes to air thoroughly after wearing, and try not to wear the same pair two days running.
● Go barefoot whenever possible, especially when it's warm.
● Try dabbing your feet twice a day with surgical spirit.
● Buy deodorising inner soles for your shoes.
● Use an antiperspirant spray on your feet.

Steps to take for healthy feet

Foot exercises for high heels

Keep your feet and ankles supple with these exercises.

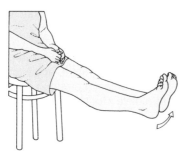

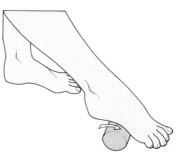

● Sit on a chair and stretch your legs out in front of you. Move your feet up and down at the ankles. Repeat ten times.

● Roll each foot backwards and forwards over a bottle or a wooden exercise roller. This exercise is particularly good for tired feet.

● Stand barefoot with your feet together. Slowly rise onto the balls of the feet, and then slowly lower yourself. Repeat ten times.

● To improve foot flexibility, practise using your toes to pick up a pencil and hold it for a count of five; then drop the pencil. Repeat ten times with each foot.

Well-fitting shoes

Most foot problems are caused by ill-fitting shoes, so take your time when buying a new pair.
● Buy shoes that don't cause any pressure or friction.
● Try on both shoes – many people have one foot larger than the other.
● Try shoes on at the end of the day when your feet will be at their largest. Shoes bought in the morning may become uncomfortable later in the day.
● If they aren't comfortable in the shop, don't buy them – you shouldn't have to 'break-in' new shoes.

A properly fitting shoe should:

● Not be too tight, especially around the toes which should lie naturally.
● Have a gap of at least 12mm ($\frac{1}{2}$in) between the end of your big toes and the end of the shoe.
● Fit snugly at the sides and have a heel that doesn't slip off easily when you stand on tiptoe.

A relaxation massage

Try this foot massage to improve circulation, relax tense muscles and soothe tired feet. Rub your foot with hand cream or body lotion. Massage the ball of the foot with both hands, using firm, circular strokes, then massage the instep and heel. Finish by pinching between the first and second toes with your thumb and forefinger. Continue pinching between the bones, working all the way up the foot and then down again. Repeat with other toes.

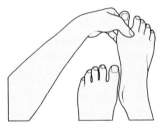

Go barefoot

Give your feet a break from shoes every now and again. Walking on sea sand or soft grass is particularly beneficial.

A home pedicure

A weekly pedicure takes only a few minutes and keeps your feet in good condition. It also helps to prevent foot problems such as ingrowing toenails and patches of hard skin from developing. The best time to do it is after a bath, when the skin is soft.

You will need:

Cream for removing rough skin
Nail brush
Pumice stone
Towel
Nail clippers or scissors
Emery board
Hand cream or body lotion
Cuticle remover

Cotton buds
Cotton wool
Nail-polish remover
Toe spacers
Base coat
Nail polish
Top coat

1 Massage your feet with exfoliating cream for removing rough skin. Use firm, circular movements to rub away dead skin.

2 Remove any nail varnish. Soak your feet for three to five minutes in warm water with a little added bubble bath or liquid soap.

3 Scrub the nails with a soft nail brush and use a pumice stone to rub away hard skin from the heels and balls of the feet.

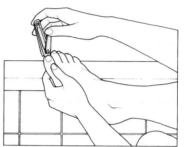

4 Dry your feet thoroughly. Trim nails straight across with nail clippers or scissors.

5 Use the rough side of an emery board to smooth over the ends of your toenails so that they won't catch on socks or tights. Make sure that the nails keep their square shape, however, and don't file down the sides or try to round off the corners.

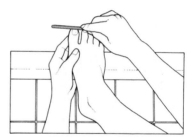

6 Clean under nail tips with an orange stick wrapped in cotton wool. Then apply cuticle remover to the cuticles and push them gently back with a cotton bud. Never cut or force overgrown cuticles back – all they require is regular treatment. Wash off any excess cuticle remover. Dry well.

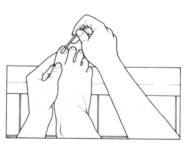

7 Massage cream or lotion into your feet.

8 If you want to polish your nails, first wipe with varnish remover to take away any traces of cream or lotion. Separate your toes with toe spacers or pieces of cotton wool. Paint on a layer of base coat and two coats of nail polish. Use one stroke down the centre of the nail and one down each side.

452

BATH-TIME TIPS

Equipment for the bathroom

Flannel or sponge Use a pure cotton flannel or natural sponge that feels good against your skin for all-over washing. Launder flannels frequently and rinse sponges out after every use to keep them fresh and soft. If a sponge does get clogged with soap, leave it to soak overnight in a vinegar solution. Then rinse in clean water and shake out to dry.

Soap Choose a mild soap that won't dry out your skin. In general, the more a soap lathers, the harsher it is. Avoid antibacterial or deodorising soaps; they can cause irritations.

Pumice stone Use a pumice to rub away hard skin on feet and elbows.

Loofah A loofah is invaluable for removing dead skin all over your body. Choose a long one that can reach difficult areas such as between your shoulder blades.

Body brush Buy a long-handled brush to scrub your arms and legs, remove dead skin and give a healthy glow to your skin. If the brush is scratchy, soak it in water for a few hours and then leave it to dry overnight in an airing cupboard.

Bath additives: what do they do?

Bath salts They soften the water as well as scenting it. But they tend to dry out the skin and are best avoided if you have very dry skin.

Bath gels Also water softeners as well as gentle body cleansers. They are meant to be used in place of soap. They are usually detergent based and are not really suitable for dry skins.

Bubble baths Fun and indulgently luxurious. But they are usually detergent-based and not advisable for dry skins unless they also contain moisturising ingredients.

Bath milks Contain no harsh ingredients, such as detergents and alkalis, so are good for dry skins. But not good for oily skins.

Bath oils Coat the skin with a fine film of oil and protect against the dehydrating effects of water. Particularly good for dry skins. Be careful when getting in and out of the bath, as oil can make the edges slippery.

Herbal baths Can be chosen for their soothing, relaxing or invigorating effects, depending on how you feel and how you want to feel. See below.

Seaweed baths Said to contain all the minerals of sea water and to help to cleanse the body. Enthusiasts say they are particularly good if you have rheumatism or aching joints and muscles.

Making your own additives

A homemade infusion of herbs can have a stimulating or soothing effect, depending on the herbs used. Advocates of herbal baths advise stimulating herbs in a morning bath and soothing herbs if you bath at night. They also recommend that a herbal bath should include flowers as well as leaves.

Put your choice of dried herbs in a muslin bag, tie it firmly to the

453

hot-water tap, and let the hot water run through the bag. You can also use fresh herbs from your garden, but they are less concentrated than dried herbs, so you will need a larger quantity. When the bath has finished running, put the bag into the water and leave it there to float. Use it as a flannel if you like.

DO NOT add loose herbs to your bath. Bits of leaf will stick to your skin and may clog the drain.

How different herbs affect you According to herbalists, different herbs can have quite different effects.

- Camomile is calming.
- Elderflower is soothing.
- Fennel tones the skin.
- Lavender is relaxing.
- Marjoram is tranquillising.
- Mint is stimulating.
- Nettles stimulate the circulation.

- Oregano is antiseptic.
- Parsley relieves itchy skin.
- Pine is refreshing.
- Rosemary is astringent.
- Sage counters stress.
- Thyme is stimulating.
- Lemon balm relieves tension.

A milk bath Cleopatra was reputed to bathe in asses' milk. Milk is indeed excellent for softening dry skin, leaving it feeling silky smooth. Add a pint of milk to the bath water, or a cupful of powdered milk, then shower it off.

A honey bath Add a few drops of clear honey to the bath water to scent it.

An oatmeal bath Put a handful of oatmeal in a muslin bag and use it to scrub your skin. It's an excellent alternative to soap and helps to remove dead skin as well as to clean. A handful of oatmeal added to the bath water is good if your skin feels dry and itchy – a condition known as 'winter itch'. Shower afterwards to remove any excess.

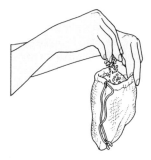

A salt bath Add a cup of salt to your bath to help heal wounds and keep them clean. You can also use dry salt before a bath to help rub off dead skin cells – the American dancer Isadora Duncan claimed that she kept her skin soft in this way.

WHAT YOUR BEST FRIEND WON'T TELL YOU

Sweat itself does not smell unpleasant, and a lot of people actually find the smell of fresh sweat rather attractive. But when it has been on the skin for several hours, the body's natural bacteria make it decompose, which is what causes body odour. Most body smells would evaporate if allowed free access to fresh air, but convention – and the weather – demand that we wear clothes. And the body's bacteria thrive in those warm damp areas where sweat clings to clothes – particularly to synthetic fabrics which prevent air circulating.

Deodorants and antiperspirants

Regular washing is the best way of removing sweat before it starts to smell unpleasant. In addition, change your clothes and clean them regularly. If you want extra protection, use a deodorant or antiperspirant.

What do they do? Antiperspirants dehydrate sweat glands so that they produce less sweat. Deodorants don't prevent sweating – they just stop it from smelling. Unless you sweat heavily, a deodorant is probably all you need. But don't worry if you prefer to use an antiperspirant – sweat is lost all over the skin and a little less under the arms won't do any harm.

What type of applicator? Both deodorants and antiperspirants come in a choice of applicators, including sprays, roll-ons, creams and sticks. Roll-ons, creams and sticks are more accurate in their application than sprays, but sprays dry faster. If you prefer a spray, be sure to choose an environmentally friendly one that won't damage the world's ozone layer.

DO NOT use a deodorant or antiperspirant on inflamed or broken skin. Most products should not be used immediately after shaving your underarms, though a few brands claim that they have no ill-effects. If you get any adverse reaction, wash the product off with clean water, discontinue use straightaway and change to another brand.

Feminine hygiene There is no reason to use a 'feminine' vaginal deodorant, as the vagina itself secretes a moist fluid that keeps it clean and free from infection. Daily washing with soap and water should be sufficient, and artificial deodorants and douches may cause irritations. If the vagina smells unpleasant there may be an infection. See your doctor so that the cause can be identified.

THE PERFECT PERFUME

If you are planning to splash out on an expensive perfume, take your time and find one that suits your personal taste. When you try one out, leave it to dry on your skin before you make your final decision – smell it again about 20 minutes after you first applied it. Don't try more than three fragrances in one day, though, or they will get muddled up, and don't try all three at the same time.

Where to apply it
Perfume rises, so it's best to put it lower down on your body to get the full effect. Put it on the body's pulse points – behind the knees, the ankles, the nape of the neck, behind the ears, inside the wrists, the temples and the crook of the elbow. These points are where the blood runs close to your skin, warming up the perfume and allowing it to develop fully.

Choosing the right concentration
Buy a higher concentration of perfume if you want scent to last longer and smell stronger, and a lower concentration if you want a lighter fragrance that evaporates more quickly. But remember that the time a perfume lasts depends on your skin and the particular scent as well, so try out different strengths before you buy.

The strongest perfume concentrations are called *extrait* or *perfume* (15-30 per cent pure perfume essence), and *parfum de toilette* or *eau de parfum* (8-15 per cent). Then come *eau de toilette* (4-8 per cent), *eau de cologne* (3-5 per cent), and *splash cologne* (1-3 per cent).

BUYING NEW CLOTHES

Before you spend any money Look at your wardrobe objectively. Most of your clothes probably fall into one or two basic styles: dresses, suits, casual wear, mix-and-match jackets and skirts and so on. Make a list of any extra items or accessories you need to dress these styles up or down and to get more wear out of what you already have. Stick to this list when you go shopping and you'll be very unlikely to make a mistake.

The right colours for you Skin tone is the most important factor in finding colours to suit you. To determine your tone, hold a piece of white fabric next to your chin and around your face, then repeat with a piece of cream cloth. One shade will flatter your colouring; the other will make your skin look dull and washed out.
● If white looks good, you have a cool skin tone and should choose colours based on blues and pinks such as fuchsia, lavender, dusty rose, raspberry, wine and electric blue. Grey and black will also flatter your skin tone.
● If cream suits you better, your skin tone is warm and you'll look your best in shades such as salmon-pink, peach, coral, gold, terracotta, honey, brown and rust.

Going shopping? Wear clothes that are easy to take off and put on again, and a minimum of jewellery. Put on the shoes, underwear and make-up you intend to wear with the new item.

Read the labels Don't just buy by looks. Check the fibre content label to get an idea of a garment's comfort and durability, and the care label (page 103) to make sure that cleaning will not be more time-consuming or expensive than you are prepared for.

Buy the best Value for money with clothes means buying the best quality you can afford. These clothes will never be cheap, but they won't necessarily be the most expensive designer items either. Look for the following signs of quality.
● Clean, odour-free fabric than doesn't hold creases when crumpled by hand (except for linen, which creases easily).
● Linings that are smooth and invisible from the right side.
● Checks, stripes and cross seams that match up neatly.
● Flat, smooth seams with well-finished edges.
● Straight, regular and unbroken stitching.
● Zips that lie flat and work smoothly.
● Securely attached trims, pockets, buttons and fasteners.

Styles to suit your figure

Are you tall?

Go for Gathers and full or pleated skirts; trousers pleated at the waist; large prints; multicoloured outfits; bulky fabrics; contrasting belts.
Avoid Vertical stripes; long, straight skirts; small patterns; single colours.

Are you short?

Go for Long, straight skirts; small prints; neat, vertical stripes; cropped sweaters; short jackets or jackets with fitted waists; outfits in one colour; a simple, uncluttered look.
Avoid Horizontal stripes; contrasting belts; wide skirts; large, bold prints; chunky fabrics.

Are you plump?

Go for Single colours; V-necks; matching belts or beltless styles.
Avoid Patch pockets and gathers; horizontal stripes; large prints; contrasting belts.

Are you thin?

Go for Round or crew necks; horizontal stripes; plaids and patterns; patch pockets, pleats, yokes, frills and other details.
Avoid Clinging fabrics; V-necks; vertical stripes.

Are you pear-shaped?

Go for Tops with neck, bust or shoulder details; padded shoulders.
Avoid Horizontal stripes; wide belts; short skirts.

Are you top-heavy?

Go for V-necks; long, narrow sweaters; cross-over style tops.
Avoid Full or fancy tops; high waistlines; puffed sleeves and ruffles; padded shoulders; large collars.

How to give your clothes a longer life

A stitch in time You'll save yourself time and trouble if you attend to small repairs straight away.
● Reinforce loose buttons, hooks and eyes or poppers as soon as you notice them.
● Take stray threads through to the wrong side of the garment and darn them neatly into the back of the fabric so that they can't come undone.

Stronger seams Check the seams of new clothes before you wear them. Repair any broken or missed stitches, and sew zigzag stitching along any edges where the fabric could fray. If you don't have a machine that can do zigzag stitching, reinforce the edges with small hand stitches.

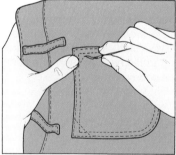

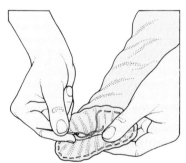

No more torn pockets Prevent patch pockets from coming adrift by sewing a small triangle of stitching in each top corner.

Sweater cuffs Sew a few rounds of shirring elastic on the inside of sweater wrists to stop them from stretching with wear.

Keeping pleats in place Strengthen the stitching at the top of kick pleats in narrow skirts. If the pleat runs the full length of the skirt, turn the skirt inside-out and stitch from the top of the pleat opening to the folded pleat edge. This shifts the strain at the point where the skirt often rips.

Clothes with slits Slits at the bottom of tight-fitting trousers and at the wrists and side seams of blouses and shirts can be awkward to mend, so reinforce them in advance. Turn the garment inside-out and sew a straight stitch across the seam allowance at the top of the slit.

Knees and elbows Apply iron-on patches inside the knees of jeans, and inside the elbows of jackets and shirts that get a lot of rough use.

Strengthen sweater elbows invisibly by weaving in yarn of the same colour at right angles to the knit of the sweater. Use a darning needle and work on the wrong side, splitting the original fibres as you go.

Perspiration protection Use cotton underarm shields to guard delicate fabrics from perspiration if stains are a problem. Stitch them in or attach with poppers for easy washing.

Cleaner collars and cuffs Wipe around your neck and wrists with a ball of cotton wool soaked in witch hazel before you get dressed. You'll save on cleaning bills and get better wear from delicate clothes. Always wear a scarf with a suede or leather jacket, to protect the collar.

When you get home Change into a casual outfit. You'll feel more relaxed and your work wear will last longer.

CARING FOR YOUR CLOTHES

Everyday care

Spot problems early When you take off your clothes, check them for stains, tears, undone hems or seams, and loose buttons. Clean or repair any damage before wearing again, or the damage will get worse.

Loose threads Never cut or pull a snagged thread. Use a needle or a fine crochet hook to pull it to the inside, then darn it into the back.

Clean enough to wear again? Hang up clean clothes as soon as you take them off, and let them air before putting them away. Allow 24 hours for moisture to evaporate before you wear them again. To freshen up a suit, hang it inside-out on an outdoor washing line for an hour or two.

Hangers The cost of good quality hangers is minimal compared to the value of your clothes. Buy strong plastic or wooden hangers and avoid wire, which may leave rust stains or pull your clothes out of shape. Hang shirts, jackets and coats on shaped or padded hangers, and skirts and trousers on hangers with suitable hooks or crossbars.

Tips for special situations

Rolled collars To keep a soft roll on the collar of a special blouse, slip a twist of tissue paper under the collar.

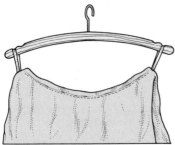

Long dresses Sew loops inside the waist of a long dress so that you can hang it up without the end trailing on the floor.

Preventing creases in pleats A pleated skirt won't crease if you pack it rolled up lengthways and threaded into a pair of tights.

Straps slipping off a hanger? Put a rubber band around each end of the hanger to keep the straps in place.

Storing clothes flat Flat storage is best for knitwear and loose, fine or soft fabrics. Very thin garments should be stuffed loosely with tissue paper before being folded and put away. To reduce creasing clothes stored in a pile, put heavier items at the bottom and lighter ones on top.

Sticky zips To get them to slide smoothly, rub the teeth with soap or graphite from a pencil lead. Remove any excess carefully with a tissue so that it doesn't come off on the fabric.

Caring for jumpers

Removing fluff from a jumper Wrap a strip of adhesive tape around your hand, sticky side out, and brush it or dab gently over the garment.

To stop a new fluffy jumper from felting The wool may be less likely to mat together if you freeze the jumper in a plastic bag before wearing it.

Storing woollens in summer Wrapping woollen items in newspaper is said to deter moths, but check in advance that the ink won't come off and mark the clothes, or wrap them in tissue paper first. Further antimoth measures (page 101) may still be necessary, however.

A new life for an old garment

If bra straps fall off your shoulders Sew a thin piece of elastic between the straps at the back to keep them up.

Sweater too tight? It could still make a comfortable cardigan. Mark the exact centre of the front and machine stitch down each side about 5-10mm ($\frac{1}{4}$-$\frac{1}{2}$in) from the centre line. Cut between the lines and finish the edges with binding ribbon or decorative tape.

Out-of-date dress If the style of a dress is dated but the fabric is still good, cut off the top and turn it into a blouse, or make the bottom into a skirt.

The end of the line When you no longer have any use for a garment, donate it to a charity shop if it is in good condition. It is not necessary to wash the clothes first, although clean garments are greatly appreciated.

If clothes are too worn to donate, remove any buttons, poppers or zips that could come in handy for repairing other clothes. Use the fabric for dusters or throw it away if unusable.

ANTICREASE TREATMENTS

● Hang creased clothes in the bathroom while you take a bath or shower. Close the door and windows to keep in the steam, and the creases should fall out. Air-dry the clothes before wearing them.

● If a creased item can be tumble-dried (see chart, page 104), place it in the dryer with a damp towel, and tumble for about ten minutes.

● If you can't get rid of a hemline crease when shortening or lengthening a skirt, try ironing the crease under a damp cloth, or sponge with soapy water along the line and press with a steam iron.

● Remove a white crease line from blue jeans by mixing permanent blue ink with water until you get the right shade. Apply the mixture to the crease with a small brush and allow it to dry.

Keeping stored clothes fresh

● Clean all clothes before storing them away for a season but do not use starch or fabric conditioner – some moulds can feed off them.
● Leave doors and drawers slightly open to allow air to circulate.
● Hang pomander balls (opposite page) in cupboards, and place sachets of dried herbs or potpourri in drawers.

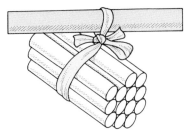

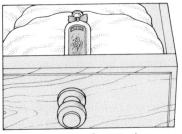

● To reduce dampness in cupboards, tie about 12 sticks of chalk together and hang them up to absorb moisture.

● Unwrap bars of scented soap or open empty perfume bottles and place them in drawers to keep clothes smelling fragrant.

● Line drawers with good quality, ungummed lining paper or quilted fabric. Gummed paper attracts insects and is difficult to remove.
● An open box of bicarbonate of soda will absorb odours.
● Discourage moths by hanging bunches of fresh or dried bay leaves in your cupboard, or strips of dried orange peel in a stocking. Sprinkle allspice berries or cedar chips into drawers.

HOME SAFETY: CUPBOARDS

If there are children in the house, make sure that all cupboard doors can be opened from the inside. Place mothballs, moth crystals and insecticidal strips out of reach of children and pets.

Storing special fabrics

Fur Store small fur items at home in a cold, dry place, covered with soft fabric or muslin. But consider professional storage if you have a fur coat or other large piece that you won't be wearing for several months. Shops that sell furs may offer the service or be able to advise you.

Leather and suede Keep leather and suede clothing in a cool, well-ventilated cupboard, covered with soft cloth or muslin. Stuff soft leather items with white tissue paper and store them flat.

Linen Store linen rolled up rather than folded, to prevent creases. Cover with white tissue paper, soft cloth or muslin.

Silk Pad clothes made of silk with white tissue paper, and store them flat. Cover with white tissue paper, soft cloth or muslin.

Velvet Pad the inside with white tissue paper and hang the garment on a padded hanger. Cover with white tissue paper, soft cloth or muslin.

Wool Use white tissue paper to pad particularly delicate woollens, fold, and store flat.

HOW TO MAKE A POMANDER BALL

Completely cover an orange or lemon by sticking whole cloves into the skin. Mix together in a plastic bag 5ml (1tsp) ground cinnamon and 15ml (1tbsp) orris root powder (buy it at a health food shop) for a small fruit, or double the quantity for a larger one.

Place the clove-studded fruit in the plastic bag with the spices and shake until well coated. Store it in tissue paper for about two weeks, then attach a piece of ribbon and tie the pomander up in your wardrobe.

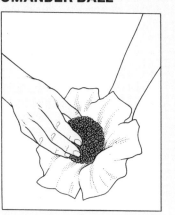

SIMPLE SEWING TIPS

Stop your thread snarling up You can prevent tangles while sewing if you rub the thread on a dry bar of soap or a fabric softener sheet.

All-purpose thread Keep a spool of clear, monofilament thread in your sewing box for hard-to-match fabrics and emergency repairs when you don't have the right colour.

If synthetic thread clings to the fabric Place the thread in the fridge for a few hours before you begin sewing. The humidity should reduce clinging.

Difficult fabrics

Heavy cloth If you have difficulty pushing a needle into thick, heavy fabric, rub a bar of soap over the cloth on the wrong side before you stitch.

Plastic-covered fabric Stop your needle from sticking by rubbing it occasionally in talcum powder.

Buttons

Replacing lost buttons To make sure you buy the right size, measure the buttonhole and buy replacement buttons that are slightly smaller in diameter than the length of the hole. If the button is chunky, the thickness and the diameter added together should be 3mm ($\frac{1}{8}$in) less than the length of the hole.

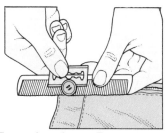

Removing a button To protect your clothes, slide a comb under the button and cut the thread between the button and the comb with nail scissors or a razor blade.

If buttons keep coming off Dab a little clear nail varnish over the top of the thread from time to time. This should strengthen the fibres and reduce the chances of breaking.

Heavy-duty thread for hard wear To sew buttons securely onto coats or other heavy clothing, use a double strand of your strongest thread, a length of 2.5-4.5kg (6-10lb) fishing line, or a piece of dental floss.

TIPS FOR THREADING A NEEDLE

- Cut the thread at an angle.
- Hold the thread against a background of contrasting colour.
- Lick the end of the thread or apply clear nail varnish or hair spray.
- Loop thick darning thread around a piece of thin cotton. Thread both ends of cotton through the eye of the darning needle and pull the thicker thread through.
- Buy an old-fashioned wire needle threader.
- Solve the problem for ever with a threader intended for the disabled but equally useful for anyone who's tired of fiddling. Contact the Disabled Living Foundation (see *Useful addresses*, page 369) for a copy of the *Keep able* catalogue.

TAKING CARE OF ACCESSORIES

How to shop for shoes

A good time to shop Buy shoes towards the end of the day, when your feet are a little bigger than in the morning. But don't go shopping for shoes when your feet are very hot or when you've been standing or walking all day. Your feet will probably be too swollen to get an accurate fit.

Take your socks along Always try on new shoes with the kind of tights or socks you intend to wear with them.

Finding the best fit Don't buy shoes strictly by size. Walk around in them in the shop before deciding, and try on both shoes of each pair – most people have one foot slightly larger than the other. (See also page 451.)

Make sure they're wide enough Be particularly careful to check the fit across the broadest part of your foot. Shoes that are too narrow can become very painful.

Tips for finding a flattering style
- Choose neutral or darker colours if you take a large size. White and brightly coloured shoes will draw attention to your feet.
- Thicker ankles look more shapely in medium heels. Avoid completely flat shoes and very high heels.
- Round toes flatter narrow feet and larger sizes.

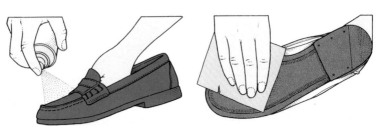

Before you wear your new shoes Apply a protective stain-repellent polish or a spray such as Scotchguard to keep shoes looking new. If the sole feels slippery, rub it on a rough pavement or a piece of coarse sandpaper to give it some grip. Alternatively, glue a strip of sandpaper to the sole.

Looking after your shoes

Shoes too tight? Saturate a ball of cotton wool in surgical spirit and rub it inside the shoes on the problem area. Put on the shoes and walk around in them for a few hours. To solve the problem permanently, rub alcohol inside the shoes and put them on shoe stretchers – available from good shoe shops – for at least two days.

Make your own boot trees A couple of kitchen-towel cylinders tied together, or rolled-up newspapers, will keep boots in shape.

Stop laces coming undone If you dampen your laces slightly before tying them up, the knot will be much tighter and should stay tied.

Give your shoes a break Don't wear the same pair of shoes two days running. Give shoes at least a day to recover their shape and allow any odour or moisture to evaporate.

For a waterproof finish Protect your shoes from rain with a waterproofing shoe spray, or apply a light coat of floor wax after polishing.

Help in a hurry

No shoe horn to hand? Use an expired telephone card or a large serving spoon to slip on tight-fitting shoes.

To stop shoelace ends unravelling If your laces have lost their metal tips, try turning the ends briefly in a match flame. Roll the melted fibres into a neat tip while still soft. Alternatively, wrap the end in clear adhesive tape or dip it in glue or clear nail varnish.

If leather shoes get wet Stuff the shoes with newspaper and leave them to dry out naturally, away from heat and sunlight. When completely dry, rub with a leather conditioner such as saddle soap; then polish.

Cleaning and shining your shoes

For a brighter shine Polish your shoes in the evening and buff them up the next morning, instead of polishing and buffing at the same time.

Alternatives to shoe polish You can shine your shoes effectively even if your polish runs out. Try floor wax sparingly applied, spray furniture polish or window-cleaning spray. You can even rub your shoes with the inside of a banana skin, but leave them to dry without buffing if you do.

463

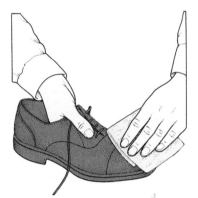

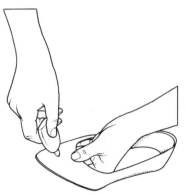

Steam-cleaning for suede To make suede shoes look like new, hold them over a pan of boiling water, turning them so that the steam reaches all parts of the suede. When the steam has raised the nap, stroke the suede with a soft brush in one direction only. Allow the shoes to dry before wearing.

Scuffs on suede shoes Raise the nap on small suede scuff marks by rubbing with a dry sponge or a stiff upholstery brush after each wearing. If marks remain, rub carefully with fine sandpaper.

White shoes Oily marks from tar and grease often come off with nail-polish remover, white spirit or metal cleaner such as Duraglit. For more stubborn scuffs and stains, disguise them with a little Tipp-Ex.

Putting a shine on patent leather To renew their gloss, rub with a tiny amount of petroleum jelly or vegetable oil, or spray with window cleaner. Buff with a paper towel.

Canvas and cloth Spray fabric protector or starch over new canvas shoes to keep them looking clean for longer. If you do need to wash cloth shoes, stuff them with paper towels while still damp to retain the shape, and cover them with liquid starch for better wear. Leave to dry before wearing.

Salt stains in winter Wipe the salt marks off with a solution of 1 tablespoon of vinegar in a cup of water.

Wooden heels Give wooden shoe heels a special shine with an application of furniture polish.

Disguise the damage Scuff marks that can't be cleaned off can often be disguised with a felt-tipped pen of the same colour as the shoe. Try the same technique where leather has come away from a high heel.

Washing trainers Some trainers can be washed by machine (page 132).

Socks, tights and stockings

Making tights last longer
● For longer wear, it may help to store new tights and stockings in the freezer. First wet them thoroughly and wring them out; then freeze in a plastic bag. Thaw out and allow to dry before wearing.
● Snags and ladders may be less of a problem if you starch your tights very lightly when you wash them.

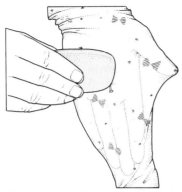

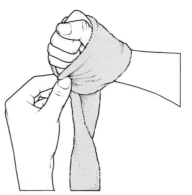

Stopping ladders A very light starching will make your tights and stockings more ladder resistant. If ladders do develop, rub them with wet soap, spray with hair spray or dab on a little clear nail varnish at the ends of the ladder.

Sizing up socks Did you know that you can use your hand to gauge your foot size when buying socks? To check the fit, wrap the foot of the sock around your clenched fist. For a good fit, the heel should just meet the toe.

Caring for purses and handbags

Storing them away Maintain the shape of leather bags and purses when they're not in use by stuffing them with tissue paper. Place each one in a separate flannel bag or pillowcase to stop the leather sticking together.

Cleaning and conditioning Keep leather looking good by wiping it with a cloth dampened in a mild soapy solution from time to time, or apply a colourless leather conditioner with a dry cloth.

To brighten up patent leather Spray it with a little glass cleaner or rub on a small amount of petroleum jelly. Wipe clean with an absorbent paper towel.

Stop metal trims from tarnishing While a bag is still new, paint a coat of clear nail varnish over any metal clasps, catches or decorative trims to keep them looking bright.

Hints about hats

Choose a shape to suit your face
● A wide-brimmed hat looks good on a square face.
● A curved brim with detailed decoration suits a long face.
● A deep-crowned hat worn low on the head, or another style tilted at an angle, is best if your face is round.
● A medium brim worn at an angle is attractive over a heart-shaped face.

Caring for felt hats Run a soft brush over your felt hat after each use, and store it in a plastic bag to keep it clean. If your felt hat gets wet in the rain, blot the drops with a tissue and then run over the spots with a wad of tissue paper, using a smooth circular motion.

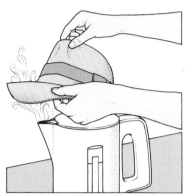 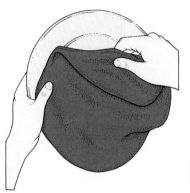

Droopy felt hat Steam the hat for a few seconds, then brush gently in the direction of the nap.

Wet beret? Slip the beret over a dinner plate of the same size to stop it shrinking as it dries.

LOOKING AFTER JEWELLERY

Getting dressed Put on jewellery after you've finished dressing and applying your make-up. Pearls and some stones and metals can be damaged by cosmetics, hair spray and scent, and sharp pieces of jewellery may snag on your clothes.

Watches and water Rusted parts are expensive to replace, so wash your hands carefully and don't trickle water over a watch that's not waterproof.

Storage tips Keep individual pieces of jewellery separate to prevent tangles and scratches. A plastic ice-cube tray makes a handy organiser that fits neatly into most drawers.

Earrings for pierced ears are particularly easy to lose, so fasten them through the holes of large buttons, or line part of your jewellery box with foam rubber and stick the posts into it.

Pamper your pearls Wear pearls as often as possible, even if you keep them out of sight under a shirt or a sweater. The natural oils in your skin help to prevent drying out and cracking.

Don't let chains rub together Wear only one chain at a time and have pendants fixed so that they don't run on the chain. Friction between two pieces of metal will rub off minute particles, and could cause marks on skin or clothes.

Jewellery dip cleaners Keep your metal cleaning dips just for jewellery. If you use them to clean other objects as well, such as cutlery, metal from these may be deposited onto your jewellery, including the stones.

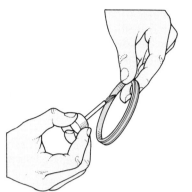

Chain in a knot? A light dusting of talcum powder may help to undo the tangle. If that doesn't work, lay the chain on a sheet of waxed paper and place a drop of baby oil on the knot. Work the chain free with two pins, and wash out the oil with warm, soapy water.

If jewellery marks your skin Marks from jewellery may be caused by tiny particles of metal or tarnish coming off, or by an allergy to the metal. In either case, clean the piece thoroughly; then apply a coat of clear nail varnish to the part that touches your skin.

Just to be sure Inspect stone settings, clasps and necklace threads regularly to make sure that they are secure. Have all valuable pieces checked and cleaned once a year by a jeweller, and revalued for insurance every two years.

Cleaning stones and settings

Clean frequently worn items every four to six weeks. Treat one item at a time, and keep hard stones such as diamonds, rubies and sapphires separate from metal jewellery and pearls, opals and other softer gems that could get scratched. Use bowls for washing and rinsing; if you do it in the sink, small pieces could disappear down the drain.

Cleaning kit

● General-purpose cleaner: weak solution of washing-up liquid in warm water, with a drop of household ammonia added.
● Diamond-cleaning solution: mix one part of cold water with one part of household ammonia.
● Jewellery dips such as Goddard's Gold and Platinum Jewellery Care or Goddard's Silver Dip for pieces with tarnished or intricate settings that are difficult to polish.
● Warm water for rinsing.
● Old, soft toothbrush or clean mascara brush.
● Chamois leather or soft, lint-free polishing cloth.

How to clean different types of jewellery

Amber Swish pieces of amber around in the general-purpose cleaning solution. Rinse in warm water and dry immediately on the chamois leather or polishing cloth.

Amethyst, aquamarine, garnet, peridot, ruby, sapphire, topaz If safe for the setting (see *Gold, silver, platinum*, next page), soak the stones for a few

467

minutes in the general-purpose cleaner. Brush the setting, rinse, and dry with a chamois leather or soft cloth. If the setting cannot be soaked, hold it over the bowl for brushing, then clean the stones with chamois leather or lint-free cloths wrung out in the cleaning and rinsing water.

Cameo Don't immerse cameos in water. Use a soft brush dipped in the general-purpose cleaner. To rinse, clean the brush, dip it in fresh water, and apply to the cameo. Blot with a towel and rub up with chamois leather.

Coral, jade, jet, lapis lazuli These substances are porous and shouldn't be soaked. All they need is gentle polishing with a soft, dry chamois leather or lint-free cloth.

Diamond Depending on the setting (see *Gold, silver, platinum*), either soak the piece in the diamond-cleaning solution for about 30 minutes, or clean with a brush dipped in the solution.

Tap the back and sides of the mountings of soaked pieces gently with a brush when you remove them from the cleaning solution; then swish again in the cleaner and drain dry on a paper towel. Alternatively, use a jewellery dip for pieces with settings that are tarnished or hard to polish.

Emerald Emeralds are soft and easily chipped. Limit home-cleaning to polishing with a dry chamois or soft, lint-free cloth.

Marcasite Clean carefully with a soft, dry bristle brush.

Opal, turquoise These stones are fragile and porous. Polish with a dry chamois leather or soft cloth to clean them, and avoid soaking.

Pearl (natural and cultured) Wipe pearls with a damp chamois to remove any skin acids or dirt that may have accumulated. Alternatively, if they are not in a brooch or other metal setting that could stain them when wet, wash your pearls briefly in a weak solution of washing-up liquid and warm water. Rinse and leave to drain dry on a white towel for at least an hour – dye from a coloured towel could be absorbed by the pearls.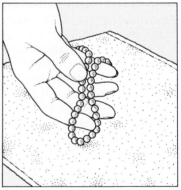
To avoid straining the stringing when treating a pearl necklace, lay it on a white cloth-covered surface while you wipe with the damp chamois and keep it cupped in your hand for support when you wash it in the cleaning solution. Have the stringing replaced regularly to prevent accidents.

Costume jewellery Most pieces of costume jewellery can be quickly washed in the cleaning solution, rinsed in clean water, and lightly brushed. Drain dry on a towel, away from heat.

Gold, silver, platinum

● Most – but not all – jewellery and settings made of precious metals can be immersed briefly in a jewellery dip. Brush to remove embedded dirt, rinse well in clean water and dry with a soft cloth.
● Hollow, open-ended bracelets and older, closed-back settings should not be immersed. Polish them with chamois leather or a silver cloth impregnated with tarnish inhibitor.
● Use a long-term foaming silver polish to maintain the appearance of silver necklaces and bracelets.

Family health

*H*ow to deal with a multitude of ailments – from merely inconvenient to downright embarrassing or possibly serious – that crop up from time to time in every household.

TAKING MEDICINE

Expiry dates Check the expiry dates of medicines and get rid of any that have passed it.

Where to keep them Medicines do not belong in the bathroom or kitchen – dampness and heat can speed their deterioration. The best place is another room in a separate small cabinet or closet that can be securely locked away from children. Some medicines should be kept in a refrigerator. The label will tell you.

DO NOT tell children that medicine tastes nice or that tablets and capsules are sweets. They may seek them out when you are not looking and poison themselves. Be honest about the taste. Give the child a fruit drink or a biscuit before and after taking unpleasant medicine.

Swallowing a tablet The best way to swallow a tablet or capsule: place it in your mouth with a small amount of water, tilt your head backwards, and you can swallow readily. Follow with more water.

Time for your medicine If medicine must be taken at certain times, and you're afraid you'll forget, set your alarm watch or clock for the correct interval between dosages.

Label-side up When you're pour-ing medicine out of a bottle, keep the label-side up. Then any drips or spills won't stain the label and make the directions hard to read. When you've finished, wipe the mouth of the bottle with a clean cloth so the cap doesn't stick.

Catching the drips When giving a liquid medicine to a child, hold a small paper cup under her chin. Whatever dribbles into the cup can be mixed with a little water, and she can drink the rest down.

BEFORE YOU TAKE ANY MEDICATION

To get the most out of your medicine – whether over-the-counter or prescription – you should ask your doctor or chemist the following questions:
- What is the medicine supposed to do?
- What side effects may occur?
- How many times a day should you take it; before or after meals?
- Should you continue to take it after you're feeling better but while there's some still left?
- Should you avoid alcohol while taking the medicine?
- Can prescription be refilled without an appointment?

TIPS FOR THE SICKROOM

Plastic sick bag If your patient feels as though he may be sick, put a dustbin liner in a wastepaper basket or bucket and keep it near him at all times. When the bag has served its purpose, tie a knot in the neck and drop it in the dustbin.

Handy holder To prevent bed-side-table crowding, hang a multi-pocketed shoe bag by the bed. It makes a handy holder for tissues, spectacles, combs, and all the other little things that a bedridden patient may need.

Covers too heavy on your feet? Get a large cardboard box and cut out two sides. Put the box at the foot of the bed under the covers with your feet inside.

Taking someone's temperature

Don't take someone's temperature immediately after they have been very active, had a bath, a full meal, a hot or cold drink, or a cigarette, because you may get a false reading. Wait for about half an hour.

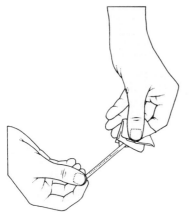

1 Take the thermometer out of the holder in which it is kept. Rinse it under cold water and dry it with a tissue.

2 Hold the thermometer at the unshaped end and shake it down sharply two or three times to return the mercury to the bulb.

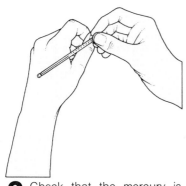

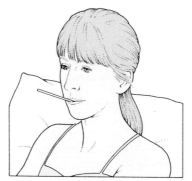

3 Check that the mercury is below 35°C (94°F). To see the line of the mercury, hold the thermometer over the back of your hand with the magnifying section towards you, then rotate it slightly with your fingers.

4 Place the bulb under the patient's tongue and tell her to close her lips but not her teeth. Wait two minutes. Remove the thermometer and take the reading. Normal temperature for most people is about 37°C (98.6°F).

Taking someone's temperature under the arm

If the patient is severely ill, has difficulty breathing or is very young, it may be safer to take the temperature under the arm. There is less risk of the thermometer breaking.
● Rinse, dry and check the thermometer (see previous page).
● Place the bulb in the patient's armpit and gently fold the arm across the patient's chest so that the bulb is in contact with the skin all round.
● Wait five minutes and then read the temperature.
● Temperature taken under the arm is lower than when it is taken under the tongue.

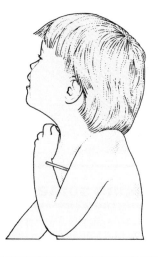

ACNE

The most common of all skin complaints, acne is the scourge of teenagers. In its mildest form there may be only pimples and blackheads, though these can be distressing at an age when appearance is important. In severe cases, pimples may fill with pus or turn into cysts.

The best home treatment is regular washing with medicated soap or detergent lotion and hot water. Keep a check on your diet to see if chocolate, nuts, sweets or fats make the spots worse.

See your doctor if the condition does not improve, or the spots turn to cysts – painless lumps about 25mm (1in) across. He may prescribe a lotion, antibiotics, or a vitamin A or hormone preparation.

DO'S AND DON'TS FOR ACNE SUFFERERS

DO get as much sunlight as possible. Sunbathing will often help.

DO try proprietary antiseptic and keratolytic creams. A chemist will be able to advise you.

DO consult your doctor if there are cysts. Left untreated they may leave scars. Also see the doctor if the acne doesn't improve with home treatment or if the lotions cause a skin reaction.

DO wash your hair regularly and keep it short. Hair falling on your face can increase the number of spots.

DON'T use oily or greasy cosmetics. Ask your chemist to recommend a non-greasy cosmetic.

DON'T squeeze or pick the spots. They will get worse and may leave scars.

DON'T despair if spots do not respond to treatment immediately. It may take weeks or months, but acne is unlikely to go on getting worse indefinitely – sooner or later it will improve.

ANKLE INJURIES

The ankle is the joint that most often suffers from sprains. The injury can be caused by twisting the foot as you walk or run, or by jumping from a high place. It causes pain and swelling in the joint. For treatment, see *Sprains and strains*, page 674.

A serious sprain can be very difficult to distinguish from a broken bone. So if there is any doubt, and the injured person cannot support himself on the ankle, assume that a bone has been broken and take him in a car to the Accident and Emergency Department of your local hospital or call an ambulance.

APPENDICITIS

Pain in the abdomen may be the first sign of appendicitis. If the problem is not treated, it may subside, only to recur – a condition known as chronic appendicitis.

However, the pain may increase and move to the lower right abdomen – which is a surgical emergency. So a doctor should be seen as early as possible.

The symptoms can take between four and 48 hours to develop. Because they are extremely variable, the condition can be difficult to diagnose. Call the doctor immediately if the pain gets worse, becomes continuous, or keeps the sufferer awake – and call him in any case if the pain lasts longer than four hours.

ASTHMA

Asthma tends to run in families, and may be associated with eczema, an inflammation of the skin.

Asthma may appear for the first time in childhood, or in adolescence, often as an extension of hay fever. It can also appear completely out of the blue later in life – the so-called late-onset asthma, which can be much more disabling than other forms and is often associated with recurring chest infections.

The symptoms

● Coughing, wheezing and difficulty in breathing. The main difficulty is in breathing out, rather than in.
● In children, persistent coughing at night may be the only symptom of the asthma.
● Drawing in of the lower ribs on breathing in. This is especially obvious in babies and young children.

What causes asthma?

● Respiratory infection may trigger off inflammation of the air tubes in the lungs.
● Allergy to certain substances, including house-dust mites, animal fur, feathers, pollen or some foods.
● Night-time attacks in children are often associated with house-dust mites, down pillows or pets sleeping in the bedroom.
● Anxiety, perhaps before an exam, or excitement before a big event seems to bring on attacks in some people.

Treating asthma

● Wheezy breathing occurring for the first time in a child should be reported to the doctor.

● A child must be encouraged to lead as full and normal a life as possible, yet at the same time be helped and supported to do this by parents and doctors who understand how modern drugs can be used to prevent and control attacks.

DO'S AND DON'TS OF ASTHMA

DO keep a diary about your asthma. Jot down when you get attacks and what seems to bring them on. This can help you and your doctor understand the value of different types of treatment.

DO get to know your limitations and do not be afraid to admit them. If something bothers you, such as cigarette smoke, say so.

DO keep regular hours and get as much sleep as you need.

DO avoid emotional stress.

DO carry prescribed medication with you always. You will feel more confident and be less likely to get an attack if you know you have an inhaler or tablets in your pocket or handbag.

DON'T smoke, or go into dusty, smoky surroundings.

DON'T allow yourself to become an invalid. Take as much exercise as you can cope with physically. Swimming is particularly helpful as it teaches breathing control – and usually pools are free from dust and pollen.

DON'T have carpets, heavy curtains or furniture that harbours dust in the bedroom. Avoid woollen blankets, feather pillows or eiderdowns, and keep the mattress covered. Vacuum the room and mattress daily.

DON'T over-protect an asthmatic child. Preventing him from doing things he enjoys can make the asthma worse. But do not try to pretend his condition does not exist, as you may overlook a build-up to severe illness.

DON'T acquire furry or feathered pets if you have an asthmatic child. But if you already have one, it is best not to get rid of it as that may worsen the child's asthma. Fish are fine.

BAD BREATH

The most common cause of bad breath is failure to take care of your teeth and gums. Clean your teeth after every meal, and use dental floss or dental sticks to clean between them. If your gums bleed, it's a good indication they're infected and are the cause of the bad breath. If the bleeding doesn't stop after a few days of flossing, see your dentist.

Other causes

Bad breath can also be caused by bronchitis and infections of the nose and throat. The problem should clear up when the particular ailment has been cured.

Constipation does not usually cause bad breath.

BANDAGES: HOW TO PUT THEM ON IN DIFFERENT SITUATIONS

The easiest way to dress a wound

The simplest type of bandage has a dressing attached to it, and is sold in chemists' shops under the name of sterile dressing, field dressing or lint dressing.

You just take the dressing from its sealed wrapper, put it on the wound and bind it in place with the bandage.

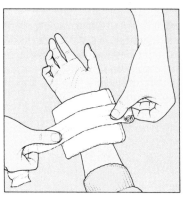

DO NOT use a sterile dressing if the seal has already been broken. It might cause infection.

Binding an elbow or knee with a crepe bandage

If you're trying to bandage a knee or elbow, a sterile dressing is difficult to keep in place, so you might have to use the type of bandage sold in rolls. Gauze bandage is hard to use, so buy a stretch type. It may be called a crepe, elasticated or conforming bandage. It's easier to put on, and because it follows the contours of the body the pressure on the wound is evenly distributed. The bandages are sold in different widths: 25mm (1in) for fingers and toes, 65mm (2½in) for arms and 90mm (3½in) for legs.

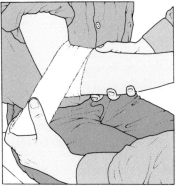

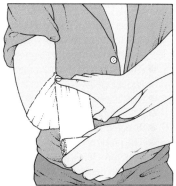

1 Start by putting the end of the bandage on the inside of the elbow, and make a firm turn to hold it in place. Make the next turn below the first, and then make alternate turns above and below the elbow, covering two-thirds of the previous one. Apply the outer surface to the skin so that you can unroll it easily.

2 Bandage outwards from the person's trunk, maintaining even pressure all the time. Finish with a full turn over the previous one then fold in the end, and fix it with a safety pin or adhesive plaster.

The arm or leg should be bandaged in the position that it will remain in.

Finishing off with a knot

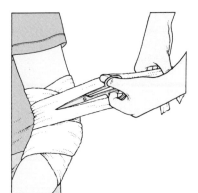

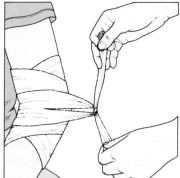

1 If you don't have a safety pin or any adhesive plaster to finish off the bandage, leave a piece of bandage free when you finish binding the injury. Cut the end of the strip in half lengthways.

2 Tie the two strips together with a single knot, pulling fairly tight at the bottom of the cut. This will stop the cut tearing further. Make sure that the knot does not press on the wound.

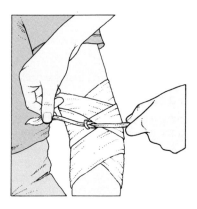

3 Take the two ends around the limb again and tie them off, preferably with a reef knot (right over left, then left over right). Once again, make sure that the knot does not press on the wound. Finally, tuck in the ends of the bandage to keep it neat.

IS THE BANDAGE TOO TIGHT?

It is easy to bind a bandage so tightly that it interferes with the nerves or the blood circulation. After applying a bandage, and again ten minutes later, check for these warning signals:

● The injured person has a tingling feeling in the fingers or toes, or loses feeling altogether.
● The fingers or toes are very cold.
● The injured person is unable to move the fingers or toes.
● The beds of the fingernails or toenails are unusually pale or blue.
● The pulse of an injured arm is weak compared to the other arm, or the pulse is completely absent.

If any of these danger signs occur take off the bandage and apply it again more carefully.

Putting a tubular bandage on a finger

Seamless tubular bandages are easier to put on a wound than conventional bandages because they do not need to be tied in place. They resemble stockings without feet, and they are available from chemists in various sizes to fit different parts of the body, including a finger. They are all supplied with applicator tongs which allow you to slip them on over a dressing.

1 Cut a piece of tubular bandage at least $2\frac{1}{2}$ times as long as the finger and push it loosely onto the applicator. Put the applicator and bandage over the finger and hold the bandage at the base of the finger.

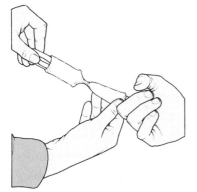

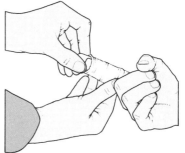

2 Draw the applicator off the finger, together with half the bandage. Then turn the applicator completely around so that the bandage is twisted.

3 Push the tongs gently back down the finger, sliding the bandage off them as you go and leaving the finger covered with two layers of material.

How to make an emergency dressing

If you have to treat a wound without a first aid kit, you can improvise dressings and bandages.

● To make a dressing, take a clean handkerchief and turn it inside-out so that the side that was protected from dirt can be placed on the wound. If you need a larger dressing, use a clean pillowcase or towel in the same way.

● Or wind toilet paper around your fingers to make a fairly thick pad. Slide it off the fingers and put the untouched side – which was at the back of your hand – onto the wound. It will be quite sterile.

● Or strip the wrapping off a packet of paper handkerchiefs and put the whole pad on the wound.
● Do not put fluffy material such as cotton wool directly on a wound, because the fibres will stick.
● Don't touch the surface that will be in contact with the wound. Dirt on your fingers could cause infection.
● Bandage the dressing onto the wound with any piece of reasonably clean material, such as a scarf, tie or old linen.

Making up your own first-aid kit

A first-aid kit should be kept in a sealed plastic box, such as an old ice-cream container. Put the box on the top shelf of the hall cupboard or some other place out of the reach of children.

DO NOT keep first-aid materials in unsealed containers in the bathroom or kitchen; they may deteriorate in the damp air.

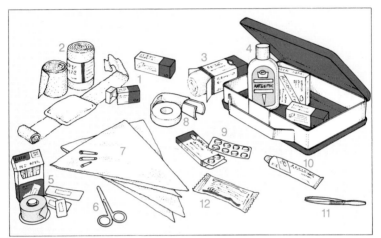

1 **Sterile dressings (also called field dressings)** Come in various sizes for covering wounds.

2 **Crepe or conforming bandages** For binding sprains, and for bandaging wounds in awkward places such as elbows and ankles.

3 **Cotton wool** For cleaning cuts and grazes.

4 **Antiseptic lotion** To use with the cotton wool when cleaning wounds. Also antiseptic wipes.

5 **Plasters** Different sizes to cover small wounds. Also sticking plaster.

6 **Blunt-ended scissors** For cutting bandages and plaster.

7 **Triangular bandages** For sling or emergency bandage. And safety pins.

8 **Tubular gauze bandages** For finger injuries. Also applicator tongs.

9 **Aspirin or paracetamol** Preferably sealed in foil to give longer life.

10 **Antihistamine cream** For insect bites and stings.

11 **Tweezers** For removing splinters.

12 **Sterile eye dressing** Comes with bandage attached.

● Write the address and phone number of your doctor and the address of your local hospital on a piece of paper and fix it to the inside of the lid.
● Do not keep old medicines left over from a previous illness. Flush them down the lavatory or return them to the chemist.
● First-aid kits can be bought ready-made from chemists, but you can make up your own from the items shown here.
● When you go on family holidays, take the kit with you.

BLACK EYE

A blow to the eye socket causes internal bleeding which turns the skin dark blue or black and produces a swelling.

● Put a cold compress (see *Bruise*, page 482) over the eye to limit the swelling and relieve the pain.

● Cool the eye for at least 30 minutes, replacing the compress if it becomes warm.

● Go to a doctor as soon as possible to check that there is no serious damage to the eye or a fracture of the skull. A blow which is violent enough to blacken the eye may cause either.

DO NOT put raw steak on a black eye; it is ineffective and just wastes expensive meat.

BLISTERS

D o not burst a blister deliberately unless the taut skin is causing acute discomfort. Opening the skin increases the risk of infection, and the blister will usually heal within a week, burst or not.

If you decide to burst it, follow these steps.

1 Wash the blistered area thoroughly with soap and water, and also wash your hands so you don't introduce germs into the wound when you pierce the blister.

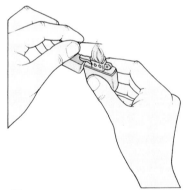

2 Pass a fine needle through a flame and let it cool for a moment. Do not wipe off any soot and do not touch the point.

3 Hold the needle flat on the skin and press the point gently but firmly into the blister – just enough to burst it.

4 Remove the needle and make a second puncture on the opposite side of the blister.

5 Remove the needle and press gently on the blister with a clean piece of cotton wool.

6 Wipe away the moisture with the cotton wool, and cover the blister with a plaster (adhesive dressing).

A burst blister If a blister bursts by itself, expose it to the air as much as possible in hygienic conditions, but keep it covered with a bandage if there is a risk of dirt getting in.

Doctor's advice See a doctor if a blister becomes infected, with a swollen, tender or inflamed area around it. Also see a doctor if blisters occur without any obvious cause. Multiple blisters are a symptom of several diseases, including shingles, chickenpox and impetigo.

HOW TO AVOID BLISTERS

● Take care when cooking or ironing. Cooks often receive burns on the arm when the oven door swings closed as they remove food.
● Wear protective gloves for any heavy manual work.
● Only buy shoes that fit well, and break them in with short periods of wear before wearing them all day.
● For country walks, wear comfortable boots or shoes, with two pairs of socks to reduce friction on the feet. They can be a thin cotton pair next to the skin, with a thicker pair of woollen oversocks.

BODY ODOUR

Perspiration is the main cause of body odour. Bacteria multiply in places where perspiration cannot evaporate quickly – armpits, feet and groin. The best remedy is bathing or showering daily – or more frequently if necessary.

Wash or dry-clean outer garments regularly. Keep underclothes fresh, changing them at least daily. Choose clothes made of natural fibres – air circulates better through natural fibres than artificial ones, keeping down bacterial growth.

If these measures are not enough, use a deodorant, which contains agents to kill bacteria, or an antiperspirant to deal with sweating. Stop using any product that causes irritation.

BOILS

Most boils burst within a week of starting, but if the infection goes very deep it may take two weeks for the boil to 'come to a head'. It can be speeded up by applying hot cloths or magnesium-sulphate poultices to the boil. Take paracetamol or aspirin to relieve the pain.

DO NOT apply creams or antiseptics to the skin; they will not penetrate and so will not help to cure the boil.

When the boil bursts, cover it with a clean, dry dressing to prevent infection entering the wound.

See your doctor if the boil hasn't burst after two weeks.

WHY DO YOU GET BOILS?

Boils occur in hairy parts of the body and where friction takes place, such as the nostrils, armpits, back of the neck and between the legs.

They are caused by infection from bacteria, particularly in people with low resistance due to exhaustion, poor nutrition, diabetes mellitus or a blood disorder. The bacteria create infection in the skin, often around a hair follicle. A severe boil, deep under the skin, is called a carbuncle.

480

BREAST CANCER: DETECTING THE WARNING SIGNS

To check for possible signs of breast cancer you should look for any changes in the appearance of your breasts. You can do this when you are bathing or dressing. Or, if you prefer a routine, examine the breasts at the same time each month, immediately after your period, or – after the menopause – on the first day of each month.

Your self-examination may reveal an irregularity – from a difference in the size or shape of the breasts to over-prominent veins. Most irregularities are unlikely to mean that cancer is present, but to make absolutely sure, you should show any findings to your doctor. It may also reveal a lump.

Looking for irregularities

1 Undress to the waist and stand in front of a good-sized mirror. Note the size and shape of each breast and also look out for any existing irregularities. If you have not already done so, report these to your doctor.

In future examinations look for any unusual changes or differences – such as a swelling or discoloration of either breast.

2 Place your hands lightly behind your head. This will emphasise any difference in size or shape between your breasts. Turn sideways and look again.

Then concentrate on the nipples, looking for any excessive upward or outward thrust of either nipple. Also look out for any sign of bleeding or weeping from either of the nipples.

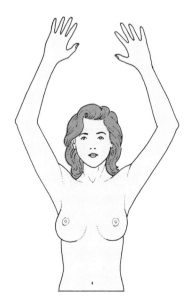

3 Briefly stretch your arms above your head. Again, this will emphasise any difference between your breasts that has occurred during the past month. You should also look for any unusual rash on the breasts or nipples and any unusually prominent veins over either breast.

4 Place your hands firmly on your hips and push inwards. Look at your breasts carefully while you continue pressing. This action will emphasise any puckering of the skin – or any turning in on itself of either nipple. Make sure to look at the undersides of your breasts for puckering, lifting up each breast to do so.

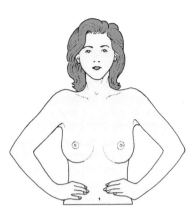

Feeling for lumps

During the examination, you should also feel the breasts for lumps. Lie on a firm surface with your head on a pillow. Feel with the flat of the pads of the middle three fingers, keeping the fingers straight. Each time you feel, press the breast tissue gently but firmly towards the chest wall.

1 Start to feel near the nipple, keeping your other arm by your side. Move your fingers out over the breast, with a spiral motion.

2 Feel the bottom of the breast, then feel the outside of the breast.

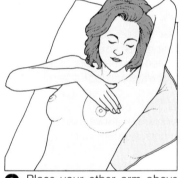

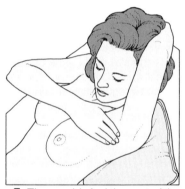

3 Place your other arm above your head and then go through the same examination of the entire breast.

4 Thoroughly feel the part of the breast that extends towards the armpit. Repeat the examination on the other breast.

BRUISE

Put a cold compress on the bruise to help limit the swelling (see the facing page).

Apply it as soon as possible and keep it on for at least 30 minutes. Alternatively, hold the bruised area under a running cold tap. If a leg is bruised, lay the casualty down and prop up the leg on a pillow. For bruises on the trunk, lay him down with pillows below head and shoulders.

See a doctor:

● If the pain is severe, or if there is difficulty in moving the bruised part 24 hours later.

● If bruises occur without any apparent reason.

HOW TO MAKE A COLD COMPRESS

Put some ice cubes into a plastic bag, tie the neck of the bag and crush the ice with a heavy saucepan or a hammer. Wrap the bag in a cloth before using it. If you don't have any ice, use a bag of frozen peas instead.

Alternatively, soak a small towel in cold water, preferably water from the fridge, and wring it out.

How to treat a bruised arm

1 Put the person with the bruise in a comfortable position and get him to raise and support the injured part before and during the treatment. This helps to reduce bleeding in the tissues.

2 Apply a cold compress at once. If necessary, fix it in place with a stretch bandage.

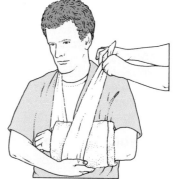

3 Support the arm in a raised position for 30 minutes to help reduce the swelling.

CHEST PAIN

A pain in the chest may be clearly related to breathing, or it may be quite unrelated to it.

Pain related to breathing

Painful breathing can indicate a disorder of the lungs or their lining (the pleura), or of the bones, muscles or skin of the chest.

The pain forces the sufferer to take short and often rapid breaths. There is often a cough as well.

See a doctor as soon as possible if there is:
● Severe pain.
● Breathlessness.
● High temperature.
● Blood-stained spit.

Pain not related to breathing

Chest pain that is not associated with breathing may have a connection with exertion or with eating.

Pain brought on by physical exertion usually feels 'crushing', and may radiate to the neck, the shoulders or the arms. This sort of pain passes off with rest. It is usually a symptom of a heart disorder, and is known as cardiac or anginal pain.

If the pain is associated with eating it may be caused by indigestion or a duodenal ulcer.

See a doctor immediately if:
● There is paleness of the skin and sweating.
● You suspect a heart condition (page 675).
● The pain is not improved after an hour's rest.

Treat indigestion by resting in a chair and taking an antacid. Alternatively, mix half a teaspoon of bicarbonate of soda in a glass of water and drink it.

CHICKENPOX

An attack of chickenpox is heralded by a highly irritating rash which starts on the body and spreads to the arms, legs, face and head.

The rash begins as raised pink spots which change to watery blisters. These then burst or shrivel up, and form scabs. The spots appear in crops over about four days.

The patient has a slightly raised temperature and may feel quite ill for three or four days.

Chickenpox patients are infectious from about four days before the rash appears until all the blisters have formed scabs. The scabs disappear about a fortnight after they begin to form. An attack of chickenpox usually means you can't get it again.

What you should do

Most cases of chickenpox do not need medical attention, and can be treated at home.
● Keep the rash clean and dry by having a quick shower every day and patting the skin dry.
● Apply calamine lotion to the rash with cotton wool twice daily to ease the itching.
● Do not pick the spots, or they will leave little pockmarks.
● Drink plenty of liquid. It does not matter if the patient refuses food during the illness.
● Rest, and take paracetamol in the doses recommended on the container to reduce fever and discomfort.
● There is no need to isolate a child infected with chickenpox from your other children, because it is better to have the infection in childhood than in adult life. But keep the patient away from children who are being treated for serious diseases.
● Try to avoid spreading the infection to babies under six months and to women in late pregnancy.
● Avoid spreading the infection to elderly people. They may develop shingles, a painful and sometimes long-lasting disease.

484

When to call the doctor

See your doctor if:
● The patient has a high temperature, is vomiting or is coughing excessively.
● The patient becomes drowsy, or develops a severe headache or becomes confused.
● The eyes themselves (not simply the eyelids) are affected.
● The spots become infected.

COLD SORES

Cold sores can be brought on by illness (usually a cold), stress, exposure to extreme cold, sunburn or menstruation.
Severe outbreaks of cold sores, or cold sores on babies or infants, or those where blisters are near the eye, should be treated by a doctor. And frequently recurring attacks can be a sign of another, underlying, medical disorder.
Do not touch the blisters and then other parts of your body – particularly your eyes. The virus that causes the blisters is easily spread around the body.

What you can do

Ease the pain of cold sores in the mouth by rinsing your mouth frequently with diluted proprietary mouthwashes and sips of iced water. A cold sore cream or spirit of camphor may dry up blisters on the lips or around the mouth.
If you are prone to cold sores, use a sun-screening lip salve when you are out of doors.

COLDS

Colds are caused by viruses, not by getting wet or physically cold, but infection is more likely if the body's resistance is reduced by illness, tiredness, stress or depression.
The following suggestions will help to reduce the miseries of the symptoms:
● Keep the patient's temperature down by giving paracetamol in the doses recommended on the container. Although the patient may feel cold his temperature may actually be raised.
● Do not wrap up in extra clothes or blankets, and do not heat up the room excessively. Rather, allow the body to lose some of the excess heat being generated. Babies are particularly vulnerable to overheating. They should be kept in a comfortably warm room wearing as little clothing as possible.
● Take extra drinks, especially cool drinks, to replace fluids being lost and to cool the body. Lack of food is not important, but fluid loss makes the patient feel worse, and in babies can be dangerous. Babies should, if possible, be given additional water or diluted fruit juice between their milk feeds in amounts to produce at least three wet nappies every 24 hours.
● A linctus or cough mixture may ease cough symptoms, but if you are taking drugs for another condition, check with your doctor or chemist that it is safe to take both. Some medicines can add to the effect of alcohol and make it dangerous to drive.

485

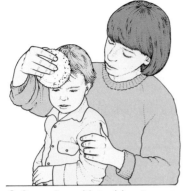 

● Sponging with tepid water may cool and soothe children. Sponge the face and hands, or give an all-over sponge in the bath.

● Steam inhalation may help. But be careful not to expose children to the danger of scalding if boiling water is used.

● Do not smoke, and avoid tobacco fumes.
● Do not use nose drops. They may appear to give immediate relief but can cause the nose to become more blocked.
● A walk in the fresh air may ease symptoms.
● Extra sleep or rest in bed will help you to recover.

CONCUSSION

A blow to the head or a heavy fall onto the feet can shake and disturb the brain enough to cause concussion. The person usually suffers a brief period of unconsciousness, but it may be so short that it goes unnoticed.

After the spell of unconsciousness, he may suffer from nausea and vomiting and may remember nothing about the incident.

Anyone suffering these symptoms, or who has been unconscious, should see a doctor. Don't let him drive or take alcohol.

CONSTIPATION

It is quite common and normal for a baby to go for a week without emptying its bowels, but with adults, when waste material stays in the rectum for several days, it becomes difficult to pass – and this is constipation. Lack of exercise, dietary fibre and fluid intake – or too much nervous tension – can all cause constipation, which in turn can lead to piles (haemorrhoids).

● Walking, jogging or swimming are good exercises for stimulating the bowel muscles.
● Eat plenty of dietary fibre, such as bran, wholemeal bread, leafy vegetables and fresh or dried fruits.
● Drink plenty of fluids, preferably water, fruit juice and milk.
● Laxatives that stimulate the bowel can be taken to get over an immediate problem, though you should stop as soon as normal habits are restored. Suitable short-term laxatives include castor oil, cascara, syrup of figs, senna and Epsom salts.
● If you think the cause is nervous tension, or if constipation persists for more than two weeks, see your doctor.

CRAMP

The painful muscle spasm called cramp has various causes:
● Becoming cold during or after exercise such as swimming.
● Poor muscular coordination during exercise.
● Loss of salt from the body through severe sweating, vomiting or diarrhoea.
● It also occurs for no apparent reason when people are asleep.

Relieving the pain Cramp can be relieved by stretching the affected muscles. You can do this yourself, but it is often easier if another person gently forces the limbs straight.

CUTS

Minor cuts only need medical help if infection has set in or if the wound was caused by a dirty or rusty object.

The amount of blood lost and the extent of the injury usually show whether the wound is serious, but puncture or stab wounds can be deceptive (page 657). If the bleeding is severe, see page 655.

1 When treating a minor cut, first stop the bleeding by pressing on the wound with a clean cloth such as the inside of a clean handkerchief or a wad of paper tissues.

2 Clean the skin around it with cotton wool and lukewarm water with soap or a mild antiseptic. Wipe outwards and away from the cut and make sure the water you are using does not run into it. Use each swab once and then change to a fresh one.

3 Dry around the cut with a new piece of cotton wool, and put on a plaster or a sterile dressing.

DANDRUFF

Dandruff can occur at any age, but is especially common among young adults. Although it is often associated with excessively greasy skin, it can affect any scalp – dry or oily.

The cause of dandruff is unknown, and so it cannot be cured, only controlled. In mild cases, twice-weekly use of a normal shampoo may be enough. Treat severe dandruff with a shampoo containing salicylic acid, tar or selenium. Follow the maker's instructions for frequency of use. (Pregnant women and nursing mothers should avoid selenium.)

If the condition persists after several weeks, see a doctor who can decide if the cause is eczema or dermatitis and recommend other treatment.

EARACHE

Severe earache is usually a sign of ear infection, particularly in children. Infections of the middle ear (behind the eardrum) are very common among children under ten, especially during winter, and may be associated with a cold. A baby may keep crying and rubbing its ear.

Let the sufferer rest, and to ease pain, give painkillers in the recommended dosage. Cool drinks will help reduce temperature, and replace body fluids lost through fever. Do not probe the ear, and do not use eardrops unless they are prescribed by a doctor.

When to get medical help

See your doctor if:
● Earache persists despite painkillers, such as paracetamol.
● If a child is feverish and crying inconsolably.
● If there is any discharge.

EYE INJURIES

The most common injury to the eye is getting a piece of grit or an eyelash lodged in it.

Contact lenses can also get displaced or stuck to the eyeball. If you have any trouble removing a contact lens, get medical help rather than risk hurting the eye.

Removing grit from the eye

1 Tell the person not to rub the eye. Turn the face up to the light and gently draw the eyelids away from the eyeball – first the top, then the bottom. Ask the person to look up, down, left and right while you look for the grit.

2 If you can see it, try to wash it out. Tilt the head to the injured side and run cold or lukewarm water over the eye from a tap or jug. Or get the person to blink her eyes underwater.

3 If this doesn't work, try to lift off the grit with a moistened corner of a clean handkerchief.

If you're still unsuccessful, see a doctor.

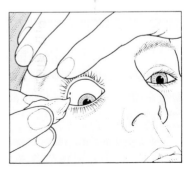

DO NOT try to remove anything that is on the black or the coloured parts of the eye, or that is sticking firmly to the eye. Cover the eye with a clean, folded handkerchief and bandage it loosely in place. Then take the person to their doctor, or to the Accident and Emergency Department of the local hospital.

Getting to the underside of the upper eyelid

 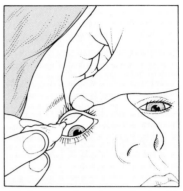

1 If the piece of grit is lodged on the underside of the eyelid, press a matchstick gently on top of the lid and then draw the lid up over the match by pulling up the eyelashes.

2 Remove the piece of grit with the moistened corner of a clean handkerchief. Replace the lid by pulling down gently on the lashes. You can treat the bottom lid in the same way.

Chemical burns to the eye

If chemicals – either liquid or solid – get into the eye, flood it with water immediately. Chemicals can cause serious damage.

You may need to force the eyelids open if they are shut tight in a spasm of pain.

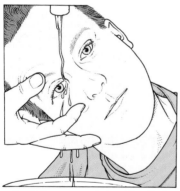 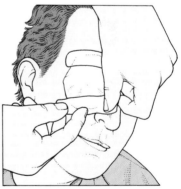

1 Tilt the person's head, with the injured eye down. Flood the open eye with gently running water from a tap or jug for at least ten minutes.

2 Dry the eye and put a clean dressing lightly over it. Get the person to the Accident and Emergency Department of your local hospital immediately.

Sharp object in the eye

Do not try to remove anything, such as a sliver of flying glass, which has become embedded in the eye. You could cause severe damage.

Telephone 999 and ask for an ambulance.

While you are waiting, protect the eye by covering it with a paper or plastic cup and taping or bandaging it on. Put a bandage over both eyes so that the injured person is not tempted to move them. Reassure the person while you wait for the ambulance to arrive.

FAINTING

If someone says they feel faint, tell them to lie down or sit with the head down beneath the knees. Loosen any tight clothing at the neck and the waist.

A person who actually faints should have the feet raised above the level of the head to increase the blood circulation to the brain. Make sure that the breathing passage is clear by turning the head to the side and tilting it back. If the fainting attack lasts for more than a few seconds place the person in the recovery position (page 676).

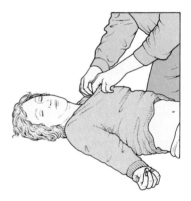

1 Lay the person on her back with her legs above the level of her head. Hold the legs up, or prop them up on a chair or a pile of cushions.

2 Loosen tight clothing at the neck, chest and waist, and ensure that she gets plenty of fresh air. If she is indoors, open the windows; outside, protect her from the sun with an umbrella or other source of shade.

3 She should recover from the attack very quickly, but when she does tell her to lie down or stay seated for a few minutes more until she feels completely better.

4 Check for any injury that may have happened during a fall. If a blow to the head was hard enough to cause a wound, the injured person should see a doctor, because there is always a risk of a fractured skull or concussion.

If you are in any doubt about the person's condition, get medical advice from your doctor or the local hospital.

DO NOT give someone who has fainted anything to eat or drink until they have returned to full consciousness. Then only give them sips of cold water.

DO NOT give any alcohol, such as brandy. It lowers the rate of the body's vital activities, and may make the condition worse.

Spotting the warning signs

● A person who is about to faint becomes pale or greenish-white, and may yawn frequently, showing that he is lacking oxygen.
● The skin is cold and clammy.
● Beads of sweat appear on the face, neck and hands.

490

CAUSES OF FAINTING

● The blood supply to the brain is suddenly reduced, perhaps by an emotional shock which causes the heartbeat to slow down.

● Being in a hot, stuffy atmosphere.

● A drop of blood sugar due to missed meals. This can be a cause of fainting among people who are on diets.

● Standing still for long periods of time, as soldiers sometimes do when on parade. This can be relieved by rocking gently from the heels to the balls of the feet.

● Sometimes there may be a more serious cause such as illness or injury, in which case a doctor should be consulted.

FLU

Flu isn't the same as a cold. It brings on high temperatures, and can be dangerous if it strikes someone with heart disease, chronic lung disease or diabetes, or who is over 65.

Consult the doctor if the flu attacks anyone in your family who is in one of these categories.

The warning signs

● Headache.

● Aching muscles and back.

● High temperature with a feeling of cold.

● Sweating.

● General weakness.

● Coughing, and pain behind the breastbone which is made worse by coughing.

● Nasal catarrh and sneezing.

What you can do

● Put the patient to bed.

● Give extra drinks to replace fluid loss caused by fever.

● Give paracetamol in the doses recommended on the packet.

● To help ease coughing and chest pain, give hot lemon-and-honey drinks or a cough mixture.

● Do not allow the patient to return to work or school until the main symptoms are over – usually in about three to seven days. Unnecessary effort will prolong illness and increase the risk of pneumonia. It will also spread the disease.

How long will it last?

The worst will be over in two or three days, but aching muscles, headache and fever may go on for a week.

General weakness may continue for a few weeks more, and the patient may suffer from depression.

PREVENTING AN ATTACK OF FLU

Flu epidemics occur most winters. Anyone who is over 65, or suffers from heart disease, lung disease or diabetes, should be immunised in September or October. But if an epidemic is caused by a new strain of virus, immunisation may not be effective, as vaccines can only be produced against known viruses.

491

FOOD POISONING

Vomiting, diarrhoea and stomachache can begin at any time between two and 36 hours after eating infected food. Various bacteria, including salmonella, and many types of virus can bring on the typical symptoms of food poisoning.

The listeria bacterium causes a flu-like illness, with fever, sore throat, headache, swollen glands and skin rash. Children, old people and the sick are most vulnerable. Listeria in pregnancy may cause a miscarriage or death of the baby.

What you can do for a patient

● If vomiting and diarrhoea occur, just give the patient sips of water. Don't give any food or milk. The stomach is trying to get rid of an irritant; don't irritate it any more.

● An antidiarrhoeal medicine, such as kaolin mixture, can help to reduce the stomach pains. But don't give it to babies.

● When the stomach begins to settle – probably after 24 hours – start feeding the patient with bland food, such as soup, biscuits, bread or potatoes. Avoid milk and milk products which may prolong diarrhoea. Also avoid tea or coffee, and acid drinks like lemon and orange juice. They might make the vomiting start again.

● The patient can gradually go back onto a more normal diet as the symptoms die down.

AVOIDING FOOD POISONING AT HOME

Don't leave creamy foods, processed meat or fish at room temperature for a long time. Keep it in the fridge.

● Cook poultry and pork thoroughly, so that there is no pink meat on the inside.

● Don't allow any other food to come into contact with raw poultry. And thoroughly clean a chopping board and plates after they have been used for raw poultry.

● Throw away any food that has passed its use-by date.

● Clean out your fridge regularly.

● When you heat up cold meat, make sure it is thoroughly recooked. Do not repeatedly reheat food.

● Throw away any canned food that looks or smells as though it's 'going off' – and, of course, any that has developed mould.

● Avoid restaurant food which you suspect has been unhygienically prepared. This is particularly important when you are on holiday in warm climates.

● Don't refreeze any frozen food once it has thawed. If you want to preserve it, cook it as part of a dish and then refreeze.

● Don't eat the green parts of potatoes.

● Remember that microwave cookers may heat food without cooking it. Heating in a microwave may not destroy germs.

● Keep flies off food. During a warm summer it may be wise to buy a mesh fly guard. Alternatively, cover food with a clean tea towel or a large bowl if it's not in the refrigerator.

GERMAN MEASLES

German measles is a normally harmless disease which has one terrible side-effect – if a pregnant woman catches it her baby may be born seriously handicapped.

About 25 per cent of babies whose mothers get German measles in the first 16 weeks of pregnancy are born deaf or blind – sometimes with heart disease – or are stillborn.

Several other viral illnesses mimic German measles. A blood test is the only reliable way to confirm that the illness and rash are due to German measles.

The warning signs of German measles

● A general feeling of being off-colour for a few days, with no obvious symptoms.
● A rash of tiny pink, slightly raised spots appears behind the ears or on the face. They then spread downwards to the rest of the body (see also *Measles*).
● Glands become swollen, particularly behind the ears.
● The joints may swell and become painful. This is most likely to occur with young women.

What you should do

● Keep the patient indoors and away from pregnant women for four days after the rash appears.
● Give paracetamol to relieve any pain.
● Consult your doctor if the joint pains become severe or if the patient develops a high temperature, a severe and persistent headache or becomes drowsy.
● A woman who is in contact with German measles in early pregnancy, and doesn't know if she is immune, should ask her doctor for a blood test. If the test shows she is infected the doctor may ask if she wants an abortion.

IMMUNITY FROM GERMAN MEASLES

● Children become immune from German measles for life by catching the disease – you can't get it twice. So let your child visit a friend or relative who has it.
● All children should be immunised with MMR (measles, mumps, rubella) vaccine in their second year.
● Women of child-bearing age who do not know if they are immune can get a blood test from their doctor. They can then be immunised from the disease if necessary.

GRAZES

Minor grazes of the sort usually suffered by children rarely need medical attention. You can treat the graze as explained below. But if dirt or grit is embedded in the wound, there is a risk of infection, and you should see a doctor.

What you should do

● Wash your hands before treating the wound.
● Clean the area around the graze with clean cotton wool which has been dipped in lukewarm soapy water.

● When you're cleaning the arm or leg around the graze, wipe outwards, away from the wound.

● Carefully remove any loose dirt or gravel, either by washing or with tweezers.

● Dry the area with clean cotton wool.

● Cover a small graze with a plaster. Cover a large graze with a sterile dressing (page 475). If you do not have a sterile dressing, dress the wound with a clean, folded handkerchief turned inside-out so that the untouched side is on the wound. Fix the dressing in place with a bandage or sticking plaster.

● Do not cough on the injury or on the dressing. You could introduce infection.

● Do not dress the wound with cotton wool, because the fibres will stick to it and will be difficult to remove.

● See a doctor straight away if the wound is very dirty or if it was caused by a rusty object. The casualty may need a tetanus injection or a course of antibiotics.

● If pus starts to ooze from the wound later, or the wound becomes sore and inflamed, see a doctor.

HANGOVER

The aftereffects of heavy drinking are caused not only by alcohol but also by preservatives and chemical byproducts from fermentation, called congeners, in the drinks. There are usually more congeners in dark-coloured drinks than in light-coloured.

Alcohol also dries out the body by increasing the amount of urine that the body discharges.

Brandy, blended whisky and red wines have high alcohol and congener contents and so tend to produce the worst hangovers. Gin, vodka, white wine and malt whisky contain fewer congeners and are less likely to cause a bad hangover.

These are only general rules, however, as the amount of congener can vary from one brand to another, and their effect varies from person to person.

Ways to avoid hangovers

● Drink less.

● Discover which drinks affect you most, and keep off them.

● Alternate alcoholic drinks with soft drinks such as mineral water.

● Never drink on an empty stomach. Even a glass of milk can be a great help.

● Dilute spirits with water or soft drinks to reduce the dehydration and stomach irritation they cause.

● Reduce the rate at which alcohol enters your bloodstream by drinking slowly.

● After a drinking spree, drink as much water as you can before going to bed to compensate for the loss of body fluid.

● In the morning, drink more fluids.

● If you have a headache, take paracetamol rather than aspirin, which will irritate an already irritated stomach.

OLD WIVES' TALES: HANGOVERS

Plenty of black coffee sobers you up quickly There is no stimulant or drug that will speed the rate at which alcohol is removed from the bloodstream.

A 'hair of the dog' cures a hangover An alcoholic drink on the 'morning after' will not help. And reliance on an early morning drink can lead to alcoholism.

HAY FEVER

The term hay fever covers allergic reactions to a host of substances – including plant pollen, animal hairs, dust, perfumes or cosmetics, tobacco fumes, food additives and alcohol.

Symptoms include sneezing, coughing, wheezing, blocked or runny nose, headache, swollen, streaming eyes and loss of the sense of smell. Hay fever is usually most widespread in spring or summer when pollen is in the air, but can occur all year round if sufferers are allergic to house dust or mattress dust.

What you can do

● Avoid being exposed to the substance that causes the hay fever (if you can identify it).

● Remove old, dust-collecting furniture from your home.

● Vacuum carpets, furniture and your mattress frequently.

● Keep pets out of the house.

● Avoid fields and gardens during the pollen season (spring and early summer).

● Don't have fresh flowers in the house during the pollen season.

● Throw out toys that collect dust and can't be washed.

● Avoid tobacco fumes.

● In the bedroom, use foam pillows and possibly a foam mattress. Dust the room with a damp cloth every two days, and have a minimum amount of furniture.

● Try antihistamine medicine that can be bought from a chemist.

When to see your doctor

See your doctor if the symptoms become troublesome. A wide range of treatment is available.

HEAD INJURIES

Any head injury which is severe enough to cause bleeding or a bruise could also fracture the skull or cause concussion (page 486). Head injuries can be caused by falls – off a ladder or down a flight of stairs, for example.

What to look for

If you think that someone may have suffered a blow to the head, look for any or all of the following symptoms. If you find any, take the person to the doctor or to the Accident and Emergency Department of your local hospital.
● Drowsiness, confusion or unconsciousness.
● Loss of memory. Inability to remember the accident.
● Vomiting.
● Severe headache.
● Bruising or a deep cut on the scalp.
● Also get medical help if the person is drunk, suffers from epilepsy or is a small child.

HICCUPS

Most attacks of hiccups are over in ten to 20 minutes, but occasionally attacks can last for days, causing distress and interfering with sleep.

Hiccups are usually caused by irritation of the diaphragm – a muscular partition which separates the chest cavity from the abdomen. Hiccups occur when the sufferer overfills the stomach with food or drink, and the diaphragm goes into spasms.

Cures are based on the fact that carbon dioxide gas, a product of breathing, inhibits the spasms.

What can be done?

● Breathe in and out of a paper bag to build up carbon dioxide in the body. Don't use a plastic bag; it may cause suffocation.
● Simply holding the breath works in the same way, and the hiccups may stop.
● Folk remedies, including drinking water slowly (perhaps while standing on your head), sucking ice, pulling on the tongue or being given a fright, may also be successful.

When to see the doctor

If the hiccups last more than a day, you should see a doctor, who may examine you for some abdominal disorder which could be causing the hiccups.

HYSTERIA

A fit of hysterics is usually caused by an emotional upset or mental stress. The attack may resemble an epileptic fit, but is more dramatised and is 'staged' to gain sympathy and attention. It will continue as long as there is an audience.

In an adult, hysteria may vary from temporary loss of control – when the person shouts or screams – to a noisy display or arm waving, tearing at clothes and hair, and rolling on the ground in an apparent frenzy.

Although genuinely distressed, sufferers take care not to hurt themselves. They may, for example, 'collapse' into a fairly safe position. They may also move weakly to suggest illness.

What you should do

● Be gentle but firm. Reassure and try to calm the person.
● Ask relatives and onlookers to leave the area.
● When the attack has subsided, suggest diplomatically that the person sees a doctor.

DO NOT slap a hysterical person on the face as it may cause psychological harm.

INDIGESTION

Indigestion is usually caused by eating too much rich, fried or fatty foods, or by drinking too much alcohol. Symptoms include burping, hiccups, discomfort in the stomach, a hot sensation behind the breastbone, flatulence and nausea.

What you can do

● Take half a teaspoon of bicarbonate of soda in a glass of water, or antacid tablets or mixtures which can be bought from a chemist.
● Rest in an easy chair.
● Drink small amounts of non-alcoholic fluids.
● For more lasting relief stop smoking (which increases stomach acid) and eat smaller amounts more often and more slowly. Cut down on alcohol, spicy and fatty foods, dairy products, beans, onions and seasonings such as black pepper, vinegar and garlic.

INSOMNIA

By far the most common cause of poor sleeping is worry – which can prevent you from going to sleep or from getting back to sleep after waking during the night. Depression often disturbs sleep, especially through early waking.

You may also be disturbed by your environment – by noise, but also by someone else in the room, by light, heat or cold, or by the unfamiliarity of new surroundings (especially when travelling).

Irregular hours can set off sleep problems – shift-work, travelling, or feeding a baby at night. Some illnesses may make sleep difficult, usually because of pain.

On the other hand you may already be getting as much sleep as your body needs. If you need only five or six hours' sleep each night, it is fruitless to search for ways of getting eight hours. And remember that sleep tends to become more broken over the age of 55.

The pros and cons of sleeping pills

Doctors have no certain cures for insomnia. But they may be able to help by treating an illness which is keeping you awake, or by prescribing sleeping pills to get you through a bad period of stress.

But before you start taking sleeping pills on a regular basis, consider the possible consequences:
● Their effect can last for several hours after you wake up – which can be dangerous if you operate machinery or drive a car.

● Your body may get used to the drug so that you have to take more for the same result.

● It may be hard to give up the pills because it can take days or even weeks for normal sleep to return. And during that time you may sleep badly and have nightmares.

● Sleeping pills can react badly with some other drugs, and must never be taken with alcohol. The combination can kill you.

DO'S AND DON'TS FOR POOR SLEEPERS

DO ask your doctor for treatment to relieve pain or depression.

DO try to go to bed at the same time as your partner.

DO wear ear-plugs or install double glazing to deal with noise. Hang thick curtains to keep out light.

DO take steps to be comfortable in bed. This may mean buying a new bed because old ones eventually sag.

DO develop a night-time routine. For example, taking the dog for a walk, locking up the house, cleaning your teeth, reading in bed.

DO try a relaxation technique after turning the light out. For example, think of something pleasant, such as sunbathing on a deserted beach.

DO try relaxation exercises such as yoga or deep breathing.

DO try taking exercise in the afternoon.

DO take a hot bath before going to bed.

DO read in bed if this helps you to relax.

DO try a malted-milk drink (or just warm milk) or chamomile tea when you go to bed.

DO give up shift-work and frequent travel (if possible) and hectic socialising – you may be trying to sleep when your body feels it is the wrong time of the day.

DON'T eat anything that you find indigestible before going to bed.

DON'T take stimulants – coffee, tea, chocolate drinks, cigarettes – in the evening.

DON'T get into an excited state – by watching a horror film, for example, or by tackling work problems – just before going to bed.

DON'T take naps during the day.

MEASLES

Once a common disease of childhood, measles is becoming quite unusual in Britain. The most obvious symptom is the rash of brownish-pink, slightly raised spots which starts behind the ears and spreads in blotches over the whole body.

But before the rash breaks out, a dry, irritating cough generally occurs and the patient develops a high temperature. The cough can occur up to four days before the rash starts. The eyes are usually sore and red, or 'heavy', before the rash.

The disease is likely to last five to seven days after the rash starts.

Once you've had measles, you can't catch it a second time. To prevent the disease, all children should be immunised with MMR (measles, mumps, rubella) vaccine in their second year.

What you should do

● Put the patient – usually a child – to bed and give cool drinks to bring the temperature down. It does not matter if the child does not want to eat, as long as plenty of fluids are taken.

● Notify your doctor.

● Keep the child quiet and resting while there is a high temperature and illness. Many children prefer the room darkened because their eyes feel sore.

● If necessary, give temperature-reducing drugs such as paracetamol in the doses recommended on the packet.

MENOPAUSE

What does it mean?

The menopause (or change of life) is when a woman's fertility cycle winds down and finally stops. The ovaries gradually stop producing the sex hormones oestrogen and progesterone, while periods become erratic before finally ceasing. The process can take months or even years so it's important to continue contraception until your doctor thinks it's no longer necessary.

Signs that the menopause is starting

● Change in periods. Timing will be haphazard and they may be lighter or heavier than usual.

● Hot flushes, which can happen several times a day. They are often accompanied by sweating, particularly at night.

● Uncomfortable sexual intercourse. The lack of oestrogen can dry the lining of the vagina. Apply a cream or jelly (such as KY Jelly) which can be bought from a chemist.

● Palpitations (as though the heart is beating faster and louder).

● Emotional upset or depression.

● Hair thinning. Ask your hairdresser for advice. A new style might disguise the problem. If hair thinning is severe, disuss Minoxidil treatment with your doctor. It's expensive and must be applied to the scalp every day, but it may restore hair growth.

● Thin and fragile bones (a condition known as osteoporosis). You could be more at risk of breaking bones if you fall. Some women also 'shrink' in size slightly.

How to cope

See your doctor who might recommend a course of Hormone Replacement Therapy. HRT controls hot flushes and reduces the risk of osteoporosis, heart attack and cancer of the ovary. You will continue to have regular monthly bleeding similar to periods and the risk of breast cancer may be increased. Your doctor should be able to advise you without referral to a specialist.

● Talk to your partner about any sexual problems you may have. Lack of communication is one of the main reasons for marital trouble.

● Take more exercise. Swimming, unlike tennis, shouldn't endanger any brittle bones. And exercise strengthens your bones and may help to cure depression.

● Confide in similarly aged friends who may be going through the same experience.

MISCARRIAGE

At the first sign of a miscarriage the woman should go to bed and rest, and the doctor or midwife should be consulted. However, resting may not prevent a miscarriage if it is inevitable.

Three warning signs occur in succession if the miscarriage takes its full course.

● The commonest symptom is loss of blood from the vagina. If the embryo has not been dislodged, the pregnancy may continue.

● If the condition becomes worse, pains like small labour pains may come and go at regular intervals. This is a sign that the threatened miscarriage may have become inevitable.

● The bleeding may also increase at this stage.

Avoiding sex If you have a threatened miscarriage, avoid intercourse until the bleeding has stopped.

Effect on the baby Because the bleeding of a threatened miscarriage comes from the placenta (afterbirth) and not from the baby itself, a threatened miscarriage does not increase the risk of abnormality for the baby.

MUMPS

A large swelling on one side of the face is the most obvious sign of mumps. It is caused by a saliva-producing gland swelling up in front of the ear and over the angle of the jaw.

A day or two later the gland on the opposite side of the face may also swell. Other saliva-producing glands under the tongue and under the jaw may also be affected.

A person with mumps may also suffer earache and pain in the jaw when eating.

Who gets it?

Mumps is a common infection, mostly affecting children over the age of two, and occurs in epidemics every three or four years. But it can also attack older people, and may cause inflammation of the testicles in men, inflammation of the ovaries in women, and inflammation of the pancreas in both sexes, producing pain in the abdomen. It can also cause viral meningitis.

The illness is usually over within a week. Someone who has had mumps is unlikely to catch it again.

What you should do

● Keep the patient at rest for a few days.
● If chewing is painful, offer soups and drinks.
● If a testicle is swollen or sore, support the scrotum with close-fitting

underpants or an athletic support. Take a painkiller such as paracetamol in recommended doses.

● All children should be immunised with MMR (measles, mumps, rubella) vaccine in their second year.

When you should call the doctor

● If the testicles are swollen or sore.
● If there is severe or persistent earache.
● If there is severe or persistent pain in the abdomen – the lower part of the trunk.
● If there is severe headache, with a stiff neck.
● If the patient finds light uncomfortable.

HOW LONG IS IT INFECTIOUS?

Sufferers from mumps are infectious for about six days before the glands begin to swell, and remain infectious for a further two weeks. As it is impossible to prevent spread of the disease in the symptomless period, there is usually no point in isolating the patient once the disease has started to show itself.

NOSEBLEEDS

Bleeding from one or both nostrils can have a number of different causes – blowing too hard, sneezing, picking the nose, air-pressure changes, sinus infections or high blood pressure. Occasionally some type of blood disorder may be the cause, and sometimes there may be no apparent cause for a nosebleed at all.

Nosebleeds are a common complaint which are very unlikely to lead to complications. Most attacks stop within an hour.

1 Loosen any tight clothing around the neck.

2 Sit in a chair with your head slightly forward and pinch the nostrils together. Stay like that for at least ten minutes.

3 Breathe through the mouth. Do not swallow, spit, cough or talk. Have a bowl close by to catch any dripping blood.

4 After ten minutes, release the nostrils gradually. If the bleeding has stopped, sit quietly for a while, and do not blow your nose again for at least three hours.

5 If the bleeding starts up again, squeeze the nostrils together for a further ten minutes.

6 If the bleeding still continues after about an hour, see a doctor or go to the Accident and Emergency Department of your local hospital. You should also see a doctor if you lose so much blood that you become pale or dizzy.

PILES

Piles, or haemorrhoids, are swollen veins inside or outside the anus. They may itch or they may be painful and bleeding.

Piles are often caused by constipation and straining to empty the bowel. They can also be caused by obesity, pregnancy or even a chronic cough.

What you can do

● Relieve the pain with hot baths or a hot compress (a sponge or flannel squeezed out in hot water and pressed onto the anus). Or get a haemorrhoid ointment or suppositories from a chemist.
● Push internal piles back with the hot sponge.
● Relieve constipation by eating wholemeal bread or cereals, fruit and vegetables and drinking plenty of water.

When to see the doctor

● If you have severe pain or bleeding, or if internal piles cannot be pushed back in.

PREMENSTRUAL TENSION

The symptoms of premenstrual tension usually appear between two and seven days before the period is due, and clear up soon after it starts. They may include moodiness and fatigue, as well as discomfort in the breasts, back and abdomen. Often, there is also a slight increase in the woman's weight.

What you can do

● Avoid stress during the week before a period.
● Cut down on salt, which makes the body retain fluid.
● Cut down on caffeine (tea, coffee and cocoa) and alcohol, which can make you more irritable.
● Extra vitamin B6 (page 513) taken on the days when PMT occurs may reduce symptoms.

If the symptoms are severe, see your doctor, who may prescribe hormone treatment.

RASH

A rash over the whole body, accompanied by a raised temperature or a cough, is usually a sign of one of the childhood illnesses.

German measles A rash of tiny pink, slightly raised spots begins behind the ears or on the face, and then spreads down to the rest of the body. Glands become swollen, particularly behind the ears. The patient may have felt generally off-colour for a few days before the rash started. (See also page 493.)

Measles A rash of brownish-pink, slightly raised spots starts behind the ears and spreads in blotches over the whole body on about the fourth day. A dry, irritating cough and sore eyes start one to four days before the rash. (See also page 498.)

Chickenpox Highly irritating rash that starts on the body and spreads to the arms, legs, face and head. The rash begins as raised spots which quickly change to watery blisters. Slightly raised temperature. (See also page 484.)

Scarlet fever A rash of tiny spots. It feels rather like sandpaper and turns white when pressed. It begins on the neck and chest and then spreads over the whole body. Sore throat, high temperature and vomiting. (See also below.)

SCARLET FEVER

A sore throat, a rash of tiny spots beginning at the neck and spreading over the whole body, a high temperature and vomiting are the main symptoms of scarlet fever.

The disease is highly contagious and lasts for one or two weeks. The rash goes away after four or five days.

What you should do

● Encourage the patient to rest, and remember that he may be infectious for seven days and pass the illness on to others.
● Give plenty of cool drinks.
● Give temperature-reducing drugs such as paracetamol in the doses recommended on the container.
● Notify the doctor that you suspect scarlet fever.

SLINGS

Once an injury to a hand, arm or chest has been treated, use a sling to give the damaged area support.

Slings are normally made from a triangular bandage – a piece of calico that can be bought ready-made from a chemist. But you can make your own with a piece of material about 1m (3ft) square, either cut or folded diagonally.

Alternatively, there are a number of ways to improvise a sling.

Making an arm sling

1 Get the casualty to support the injured arm with his hand. Place an open triangular bandage between the chest and forearm, its point stretching well beyond the elbow. Take the upper end of the sling over the shoulder on the uninjured side, around the back of the neck to the front of the injured side.

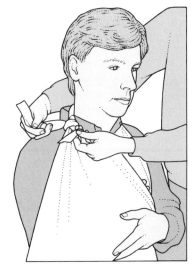

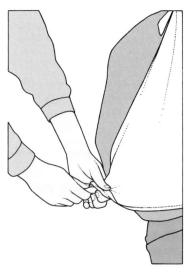

2 Take the lower end of the bandage up over the hand and forearm and tie just above the collarbone. The hand should be slightly higher than the elbow, and the fingers should just protrude from the sling.

3 Pin the point of the sling near the elbow, or twist and tuck it in. If the arm was bandaged before the sling went on, check that the beds of the fingernails are not turning blue. If they are, loosen the bandage.

Improvising a sling

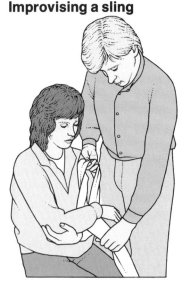

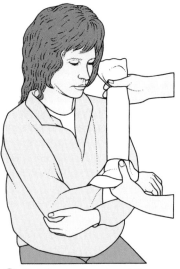

1 If you don't have a triangular bandage or a large piece of material, take a scarf, tie or belt and make a loop round the wrist.

2 Put the ends around the person's neck and tie them in the hollow above the collarbone on the uninjured side.

USING CLOTHING TO SUPPORT AN ARM

● Turn up the bottom edge of the injured person's jacket and pin it firmly to the front of the jacket at chest level. The arm will be snugly supported inside the fold.

● Or pin the sleeve of the injured arm to the front of the jacket.

● Or push the hand inside the fastened jacket at chest level, so that it's supported by a button or zip.

504

SLIPPED DISC

A disc is a shock-absorbing layer between each of the vertebrae in the spine. A slipped disc is caused by the gradual degeneration and softening of these discs.

When a disc 'slips', its soft core protrudes from its fibrous casing and presses on one of the nerves leading from the spinal cord to other parts of the body. This causes pain in the back, which can be extremely severe. If the disc presses on the sciatic nerve, the pain is felt in the leg, and is known as sciatica.

The warning signs

Most slipped discs occur in the lower back which is where the pain is mostly felt. The pain may also spread down around the buttocks and hips and along one or both legs.

The pain often starts suddenly just after you have lifted something heavy or have straightened up after bending. It might come after repetitive bending, as when you are washing a car with a bucket and sponge. Sometimes it comes on gradually.

The pain may be made worse by bending, getting up after sitting, coughing or straining. It is easier when lying flat, standing or walking.

The lower leg and the outer foot may also become numb.

What you should do

● Lie down on a firm flat bed which does not sag. If necessary, get somebody to put a wide board the full length of the bed under the mattress. On no account try to move anything heavy yourself.

● Take painkillers, such as aspirin or paracetamol, in the doses recommended on the container.

● A hot-water bottle or heat lamp applied to the painful area may give you relief.

● If the pain is not relieved after a day or two of rest, consult the doctor who may arrange physiotherapy. Some cases may require immobilisation in a plaster jacket or corset, or traction.

Manipulation may help but can be dangerous, and should be considered only after discussion with the doctor.

Many mild attacks of back pain get better after a few days of rest and then never recur. About 75 per cent of more severe attacks recur within five years, but may then get better. However, in severe cases, your doctor may recommend a CT scan to discover if an operation is necessary to remove the slipped disc.

How to avoid a slipped disc

The best way to avoid back trouble is to keep your spine straight, particularly when lifting things.

Here are some examples of the wrong and the right ways of holding your spine.

Sleeping

Wrong A soft bed does not support the spine and can cause back pain. Even so, many people unwisely use a 'comfortable' mattress that sags in the middle.

Right It is essential to have a firm bed to support the spine. If you do have a soft bed, place a rigid board under the mattress. Get a timber merchant or DIY supermarket to cut a piece of blockboard to the right size for your bed, or half the width of a double bed.

Moving furniture

Wrong Do not try to lift a heavy, household object – such as a table or chest of drawers – by yourself.

Right Find someone to help you. Bend your knees slightly and keep your back naturally straight.

Working in the garden

Wrong Do not bend from the hips with straight legs to pull out weeds. This movement, not digging itself, is the most common cause of backache in the garden.

Right Go down on one or both knees as close to the weeds as possible to save stretching. This applies to picking up any object, not just weeding the garden.

Lifting an awkward object

Wrong Don't bend and lean forward. When lifting anything out of a car boot, ease it onto the sill and then get close to it.

Right Squat by the object, with your feet about 300mm (12in) apart. Keep close to the load and pull it into your body while carrying.

Carrying shopping

Wrong When you are doing the shopping, don't try to carry everything in one hand. The uneven weight will make you lopsided and put a strain on your spinal cord.

Right Put the shopping into two evenly weighted bags, and carry one in each hand so that you are properly balanced. If you have a long way to walk, take a rest occasionally. When you put the bags down, don't bend forward; bend your knees until the bags rest on the ground.

PREVENTING AN ATTACK OF BACK PAIN

When you're doing any work in a bent position, there is a simple exercise that can help to prevent back pain. Every now and again, stand up with your hands in the middle of your back. Bend back as far as you can, keeping the knees straight (right). Hold for a couple of seconds, and repeat several times.

Try to keep your back and abdomen muscles strong with regular exercise such as walking and swimming. Specific exercises include:
● Lie on your back and lift your head.
● Lie on your back and pull one knee toward the opposite shoulder with both hands.
● Lie face down and lift head and shoulders.
● Lie face down and lift one leg at a time.
Repeat each exercise several times.

SNORING

Snoring is brought on by loss of muscle tension in the tongue and jaw. That's why people tend to snore when lying on their backs – the jaw drops down and the tongue slides back. If the snorer's partner pushes him onto his side the snoring will often stop.

Causes of snoring

Snoring has been blamed on:
● Smoking.
● Drinking alcohol.
● Heavy meals.
● Obesity.
● Colds.
● Enlarged adenoids or tonsils.

● After middle age, when muscles and tissues in the respiratory area loosen, there is often an increase in snoring.

Remedies worth trying

● Sleep on your side or front.
● Sew a small rubber ball, or something uncomfortable, into the back of the snorer's pyjamas to prevent him lying on his back.
● Increase the humidity of the air in the bedroom by installing a humidifier.
● Avoid alcohol for several hours before going to bed.
● Diet to lose weight if you are too heavy.
● Give up smoking.
● Avoid heavy meals late in the evening.

STYES

A stye is an infection of the glands at the eyelash roots. It begins as a painful swelling and later fills with pus and bursts. Untreated, a stye may last for a week.

To speed it up, dip a small pad of cotton wool into boiling water and when it has cooled off a little, apply it to the eyelid, keeping it in place for ten to 15 minutes. Repeat every two or three hours. Wash your hands thoroughly before and after each treatment.

When the stye bursts, wash the area well. If it has not burst after three days, and is painful or unsightly, see your doctor.

SUNBURN

If sunburn is very severe and distressing, take the patient to a doctor who may prescribe a cream or medicine to give relief.

See a doctor if the patient has a headache, nausea or a high temperature because he may be suffering from heat stroke as well as from sunburn.

If the sunburn is out of all proportion to the time the skin was exposed to the sun, the patient may be suffering from a condition called photosensitivity, which can be brought on by some medicines. A person who is taking medicine should see his doctor, who may prescribe a different one.

Treating mild sunburn

The symptoms of sunburn can range from skin that turns pink and feels rather hot to skin that becomes red, swollen, blistered and extremely painful.

Reasonably mild sunburn can be treated at home without seeing your doctor.

● Keep the skin cool with calamine lotion or cold compresses. Make the compress by soaking a towel or other cloth in cold water and squeezing out the excess. Or put ice cubes in a plastic bag, knot the opening of the bag and crush the ice with a hammer, brick or heavy saucepan. Wrap the bag in a towel or other cloth before putting it on the patient's skin.
● Antihistamine creams are rarely worth using; they have little effect and may cause allergies.
● Leave blistered skin exposed to the air.
● Take aspirin or paracetamol to relieve the pain.
● Avoid clothes that rub the sore area.

● Do not allow further exposure to the sun until the symptoms have disappeared.

HOW TO AVOID SUNBURN

Sunburn is caused by the ultraviolet rays of the sun. Fair-skinned people, who have little pigment in the skin, burn more easily than people with dark skin.

● To prevent sunburn, avoid overexposure to the sun on the first day of a holiday, particularly if you are fair skinned. Expose the skin for only 30 minutes the first day, increasing by 30 minutes each day until you have developed a suntan which will give protection.

● Remember that light cloud does not stop the sun from burning.

● Use a suntan lotion or cream, and choose one which gives protection from ultraviolet A (UVA) as well as ultraviolet B (UVB). Put more on after swimming. Even if you do not swim they need to be renewed every two hours. Filter-type sun-screens may contain substances that cause skin reactions, so follow the instructions on the container.

● Remember you can be burnt even while feeling cool in the water.

● Do not expect artificial skin-tanning creams to give protection.

● Keep small children covered with a shirt for most of the time during the first days of a holiday. Increase their exposure gradually. And try to keep them out of the sun in the middle of the day. Give them lunch – perhaps followed by a rest – in the shade.

TOOTHACHE

If you develop toothache at night or during a weekend when you cannot contact your dentist, look in the Yellow Pages for a dentist who operates an emergency service (though fees for such services can be high). Alternatively, ask the Accident and Emergency Department of a hospital if they know a dentist who can help, or ask the nearest police station or chemist.

● While you are waiting for a chemist, relieve the pain by dabbing a little oil of cloves (available from chemists) on the sore area, and by taking painkillers such as aspirin in recommended doses.

VERTIGO

An unpleasant feeling of giddiness, called vertigo, usually has a cause related to the ear.

The giddiness may be accompanied by nausea and deafness, and also by fiickering of the eyes – a condition called nystagmus.

Vertigo can arise from several medical conditions:

● An injury to the head.

509

● Ménière's disease and labyrinthitis, two ailments that disturb the hearing and also the balance of the inner ear.
● High blood pressure.
● A blockage of the blood vessels leading to the brain.
● Travel sickness.
● Overbreathing – when the patient breathes harder and faster than normal, usually brought on by pain, anxiety or sudden mood changes.

What you should do

The patient should lie down quietly and rest until the attack ends. The length of an attack can range from seconds to hours.

Consult a doctor if:
● The attacks recur.
● There is severe vomiting.
● Deafness develops.

The doctor may prescribe drugs to relieve the symptoms, but even without treatment a person may recover spontaneously.

WHOOPING COUGH

A child who has a cold with a runny nose and bouts of excessive coughing may be in the early stages of whooping cough.

As the disease develops the cough will become worse, mainly at night. A few days after the cold begins, the 'whoop' will start – a sudden noisy intake of breath at the end of a coughing spasm. Vomiting may also occur after the coughing.

Whooping cough may last any time from three weeks to as long as four months.

What you should do

● Whooping cough is a serious disease that can lead to pneumonia and to severe dehydration of the body if fluid loss from the vomiting is not controlled. So notify your doctor as soon as you suspect that a child has it.
● The doctor may prescribe antibiotics for the patient and also for other children in the family. The antibiotics do not cure whooping cough, but may prevent it from spreading to other people. In severe cases the patient will be sent to hospital for treatment.
● While nursing the patient at home, provide extra drinks to make up for fluid loss by vomiting.
● Cough medicines from the chemist may help the cough.
● Don't expose the child to cigarette smoke – it makes the cough worse.

THE RISKS OF IMMUNISATION

Because whooping cough is more dangerous than the risks of immunisation, all children should have a course of three injections (usually with diphtheria and tetanus vaccine) in their first year.

Because of a rare chance of complications, consult your doctor:
● If the child has fits or epilepsy.
● If there is a history of epilepsy in brothers, sisters or parents.
● If the child has a disorder of the nervous system or is known to have suffered brain damage at birth.
● If there is a feverish illness at the time of the proposed injection.
● If there has been a severe reaction to a previous dose of the whooping cough vaccine.

Food & nutrition

*H*undreds of tips for making mealtimes even more enjoyable. Whether you want to find quick recipes for busy days or plan a feast for friends, bake a perfect cake or rescue a disaster, cater for children or master your microwave, you'll find a kitchen hint to help.

Healthy eating

GETTING THE NUTRIENTS

Balancing your diet A good daily diet should include a variety of foods from each of four groups: fruit and vegetables (five portions); cereals, breads and grain products (four portions); milk and dairy products (two portions); and poultry, meat, fish, pulses and eggs (two portions).

How much protein? Seventy-five grammes ($2\frac{1}{2}$oz) a day is plenty for most people's needs, and any normal, balanced diet will provide this, even a vegetarian one. Meat, poultry, fish, eggs, milk and cheese are the most concentrated sources, but you can also get valuable amounts from bread, cereals and other grain products, and from pulses and nuts. Many fruits and vegetables contain protein too – for example, apricots, cherries, plums, asparagus, potatoes, brussels sprouts and spinach.

A small amount of protein can go a long way – a 100g ($3\frac{1}{2}$oz) pork chop, 150g (5oz) of cottage cheese and 100g ($3\frac{1}{2}$oz) of tuna will supply a 75kg (12st) man's daily needs. A child weighing about 30kg ($4\frac{1}{2}$st) could get his or her allowance from just two cups of milk, 25g (1oz) of cheese, two slices of bread and a baked potato.

Grain products If four portions a day sounds like a lot, try cereal for breakfast, a slice of bread with lunch, rice with dinner and three rye crackers for a snack. Eat them with cheese to get a serving of dairy products as well.

Fruit and vegetables To get your four portions, choose fresh fruit, raw vegetables or home-pressed juice for snacks between meals.

Choosing dairy foods Milk, yoghurt, cheese and other dairy products are a rich source of vitamins and minerals, and add protein to the diet. Eat them as snacks, or incorporate them into main courses or desserts. Choose low-fat products if you are watching your weight, but give children full-cream milk for extra energy.

GUIDE TO VITAMINS IN FOOD

All vitamins are important for good health. They come from many different sources, so as long as you eat a balanced diet of fresh, unrefined foods, you should be getting plenty. Vitamins A, D, E and K can be stored in the body, but B and C need to be eaten daily.

VITAMIN	FUNCTION	SOURCES
A (retinol)	For healthy skin, eyes, teeth, gums and hair.	Liver, eggs, cheese, butter, margarine, milk, green and yellow vegetables.
B1 (thiamin)	Helps convert sugars and starches into energy, and helps the heart and nervous system to function.	Bread, flour, pork, offal, milk, breakfast cereals, pasta, yeast extract.

GUIDE TO VITAMINS IN FOOD (cont)

VITAMIN	FUNCTION	SOURCES
B2 (riboflavin)	Keeps the skin healthy and helps to release energy from food.	Liver, kidneys, eggs, grain products, milk, cheese, yoghurt, potatoes.
B3 (niacin)	For healthy skin, digestion, circulation and nervous system.	Liver, meat, poultry, fish, bread, grain products, nuts, pulses.
B6 (pyridoxine)	Helps functioning of nervous system, and enables body to use protein and build red blood cells.	Many foods, especially meat, fish, eggs, unrefined grains, green vegetables, root vegetables and pulses.
B9 (folic acid)	Used in forming new tissue and red blood cells; prevents some types of anaemia.	Liver, kidneys, meat, green vegetables, fresh fruit, yeast, wheat germ, pulses.
B12	As B9.	Meat, liver, kidneys, eggs, fish, cheese, fortified breakfast cereals, yeast extracts.
Pantothenic acid	Helps digestion of fats and carbohydrates.	Many foods, especially animal products, cereals and pulses.
Biotin	Enables body to obtain energy from fats.	Offal, egg yolk, dairy products, grains, fish, fruit and vegetables.
C (ascorbic acid)	For healthy bones, gums, blood vessels and other body tissue.	Citrus fruit, tomatoes, peppers, green vegetables, potatoes, blackcurrants and rosehips.
D (calciferol)	Maintains calcium supply to build strong bones and teeth.	Milk, egg yolks, margarine, liver, oily fish, fish-liver oils, sprouted seeds; also manufactured by skin when exposed to sunlight.
E (tocopherol)	Helps body tissue, muscles and red blood cells to function properly; promotes resistance to infection.	Most foods, including vegetable oils, grain products, eggs, meat, animal fats.
K (menadione)	Vital for normal clotting of blood.	Green vegetables, liver, potatoes and eggs.

513

THE MOST IMPORTANT MINERALS

This table shows the main minerals needed for good health and the foods you can obtain them from. Others, the so-called trace elements such as cobalt, copper, iodine and zinc, are needed in much smaller quantities and any normal, balanced diet should supply enough.

MINERAL	FUNCTION	SOURCES
Iron	Used in building red blood cells which carry oxygen round the body.	Red meat, pulses, eggs, grain products, fortified breakfast cereals and nuts.
Calcium	Builds muscle tissue and strong bones and teeth; helps blood to clot.	Dairy products, nuts, leafy green vegetables and sardines.
Phosphorus	Helps body get energy from food and build healthy bones and teeth.	Milk, cheese, meat, fish, poultry, grains, pulses and nuts.
Magnesium	Necessary for growth of all body cells; helps body to digest food.	Milk, grain products, vegetables, meat, eggs, nuts and pulses.
Sodium and chlorine	Needed for muscle and nerve functioning, and to regulate water balance.	Most foods. Excessive amounts in some processed foods.
Potassium	As for sodium and chlorine.	Fruit, vegetables, meat, milk and grains.

Ensuring a good supply of vitamins

Make room for raw food Crisp salads, fresh fruit and crunchy raw vegetables should be part of everyone's daily diet. They are rich in vitamins that soon get lost in cooking and processing.

Cut down on cooking Steam vegetables whenever possible, rather than boiling, to conserve vitamins. If you do boil them, use the least amount of water you can and keep it boiling briskly so that the cooking time is as short as possible – the longer vegetables are in water, the more nutrients they lose. Add the cooking water to soups, stews or sauces afterwards.

Potatoes Boil or bake potatoes whole in their skins to retain vitamins.

Serve food right away Take hot fruit or vegetable dishes to the table as soon as they are ready – keeping them warm will destroy vitamins.

Special needs Smokers and people under stress need extra vitamin C, so fresh fruit and vegetables are specially important in their diets.

Orange juice Squeeze your own juice – the fresh product contains about twice as much vitamin C as prepared juice.

DO NOT add bicarbonate of soda to the water when cooking vegetables or you'll destroy the B and C vitamins.

Root vegetables Remove soil by scrubbing with a stiff brush rather than peeling. It saves vitamins – and time.

Garnishes Watercress and parsley are tasty garnishes that add a touch of colour to any dish – and they're full of vitamin C.

Who needs more minerals?

Women Periods and pregnancy can deplete iron supplies, causing tiredness and lack of energy, so eat more of the source foods at these times. Vitamin C aids the absorption of iron, so try to combine the two in meals – a single bowl of bran cereal with a glass of orange juice provides the full daily requirement for a healthy adult.

A good supply of calcium is also important for all women to help prevent brittle bones (osteoporosis) in later life, and pregnant and breastfeeding women need even more.

Babies and children Growing bones and teeth need plenty of calcium. Many fun foods are good sources: milk shakes and homemade ice cream (flavour them with real fruit and don't sweeten too much), cheese and nut snacks, and fish cakes made from sardines or other tinned fish with the bones well mashed in.

Vegetarians and vegans If meat and animal products aren't part of your diet you could be going short of iron, which can be hard to absorb from plant foods. You can increase absorption by eating fruit and vegetables that are rich in vitamin C with every meal.

DO'S AND DON'TS: FIBRE

DO eat a variety of fibre-containing foods as there are different sorts of fibre and your body needs some of each. All of it comes from plant foods, so choose from fruit, vegetables, salads, pulses and grains.

DO eat fruit and vegetables raw whenever possible, and use every part when you cook. Peeling, puréeing and processing can remove a lot of fibre.

DO drink plenty of liquid when eating fibre-rich foods, or they could make you constipated.

DON'T just add bran to a diet overloaded with refined food that's high in fat and sugar. To stay healthy you'll still need to include more whole grain products, fresh fruit and vegetables and less processed food.

DON'T become a fibre fanatic – more than the recommended daily amount (see table next page) could prevent iron absorption.

FACTS ABOUT FAT

How much do you need? Believe it or not, fat is good for you – *in moderation*. It's a concentrated form of energy, and a storehouse of vitamins A, D, E and K. But two tablespoons a day is all the average adult needs, and more soon turns into unwanted pounds.

Saturated and unsaturated 'Saturated' fats are the ones associated with high cholesterol levels and heart disease, while 'unsaturates' are believed to be much healthier. A quick rule of thumb is that in general the harder the fat at room temperature the more saturated it is likely to be. Meat fat, lard, suet, butter, harder margarines, coconut oil and palm oil are heavily saturated; soft margarines, other vegetable oils and fish oils much less so.

Blended oils Avoid products labelled simply 'vegetable oil' or 'blended oil': they tend to be of low quality and often contain saturates. Go for pure oils such as sunflower, soya, corn or olive instead.

FOODS RICH IN FIBRE

Make high-fibre foods, such as those listed below, part of every meal – they're filling and help to keep your digestion in trim. 25g (1oz) is the recommended daily allowance for an adult.

FOOD	GRAMMES OF FIBRE PER 100g (3½oz)
All-Bran	26.0
Apples	2.0
Baked beans	7.3
Bananas	3.4
Beans, dried haricot	25.4
runner	2.9
Biscuits, digestive	5.1
Bread, white	4.1
brown	6.4
wholemeal	8.5
Cabbage	3.4
Carrots	2.9
Flour, white	4.0
wholemeal	8.1
Nuts, hazel	6.1
Pasta, white	5.5
wholemeal	6.0
Peanuts	8.1
Porridge oats	7.7
Potatoes	1.8
Raisins	6.8
Rice Krispies	4.5
Rice, white	3.0
brown	4.2
Shredded Wheat	12.3

Oily fish Darker-fleshed fish such as mackerel, salmon and herrings (kippers) are not only delicious and low in saturated fats, they also contain a fatty acid (one of the building blocks of more complex fats) called Omega-3, which actually reduces the risk of heart attacks and blood clots.

Fat you can't see Stay away from processed foods such as liver paste, pâté, sausages, salami, meat pies, fried foods and chocolates – they're all full of hidden fat. Look for low-fat alternatives, or eat unprocessed foods instead.

Once in a while Homemade biscuits and cakes are healthier than the bought variety if you cook with unsaturated fat such as sunflower margarine. Keep them for occasional treats, though, and if you do buy biscuits or cakes read the label to see how much saturated fat you're getting.

Low-fat alternatives
● Instead of whole milk, use skimmed milk in sauces and baking, and semi-skimmed for drinking if you find skimmed too thin.
● Buy tinned fish in brine rather than oil.
● Choose less fatty Edam, Camembert or cottage cheese and avoid hard or cream cheeses.
● Use yoghurt to replace cream in desserts and mayonnaise and oily dressings on salads.

CUTTING DOWN ON FAT

● Eat red meat only once or twice a week, and less fatty alternatives such as fish, chicken, turkey or vegetable dishes the rest of the time.

● Oily fish twice a week should keep your heart healthy and help to counteract the effects of saturated fats in other foods.

● Choose lean cuts of meat and trim all visible fat before cooking.

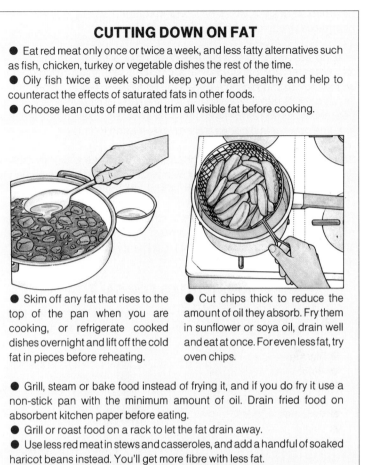

● Skim off any fat that rises to the top of the pan when you are cooking, or refrigerate cooked dishes overnight and lift off the cold fat in pieces before reheating.

● Cut chips thick to reduce the amount of oil they absorb. Fry them in sunflower or soya oil, drain well and eat at once. For even less fat, try oven chips.

● Grill, steam or bake food instead of frying it, and if you do fry it use a non-stick pan with the minimum amount of oil. Drain fried food on absorbent kitchen paper before eating.

● Grill or roast food on a rack to let the fat drain away.

● Use less red meat in stews and casseroles, and add a handful of soaked haricot beans instead. You'll get more fibre with less fat.

● Don't eat more than three or four eggs a week.

● Brown meat in the least amount of oil, or avoid browning altogether.

● Spread butter or margarine thinly onto your bread and toast, or cut them out altogether. You may not even notice the difference.

● Make your own salad dressings with sunflower or olive oil, and avoid bottled dressings which often contain saturated oils.

● Chicken has little fat and if you remove the skin before cooking, you'll get rid of most of it.

PASS THE SALT?

Salting food 'Think before you sprinkle' is the rule. An adult needs only 3g (⅛oz) of salt a day and we get easily that much from the natural salt in food. Adding extra can push the figure up to 20g (¾oz) or more, straining the kidneys and contributing to high blood pressure.

Cutting down Don't suddenly stop adding salt altogether if you're used to the taste. Reduce the amount gradually so that your taste buds have time to adapt. Always taste food before adding any extra salt.

Low-salt diets Cutting out all added salt will reduce intake to about 6g (¼oz) a day, which is low enough to help most people with high blood pressure, although some low-sodium diets may recommend even less. Your doctor will be able to advise you.

Avoid salty flavourings such as stock cubes, Marmite, Bovril and soya sauce if you're on a low-salt diet, and also baking powder and bicarbonate of soda, which have a high sodium content. Buy low-sodium alternatives from a health food shop.

Making salt go farther The Japanese have a clever way to use less salt – they mix it with sesame seeds to make a seasoning called *gomasio*, which they use in place of pure salt. To make it, put ten teaspoons of sesame seeds into a heavy frying pan with one teaspoon of sea salt and heat gently, stirring all the time, until golden-brown. Then grind the mixture to a fine powder in a coffee mill and use sparingly.

Sea salt It's less purified than ordinary salt and has a slightly different flavour (some types may also contain a little more iodine), but otherwise it's no better for you, so be just as careful with the amount you use.

Eating out If you're worried about salt, Chinese and Japanese restaurants may be a bad choice. Some of their meals could contain as much as 12g ($\frac{3}{8}$oz) compared with about 3g ($\frac{1}{8}$oz) in a French or Italian meal.

SUBSTITUTES FOR SALT

An addiction to salt makes it easy to overlook other flavourings. Next time something needs seasoning during cooking, try one of these:

- Mustard
- Herbs
- Tomato purée
- Lemon rind and juice
- Wine, beer or cider
- Garlic
- Chilli
- Toasted almonds
- Black pepper
- Paprika
- Finely chopped onion
- Horseradish
- Plain yoghurt
- Buttermilk

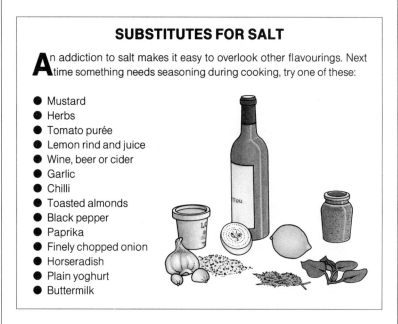

A TOUCH OF SWEETNESS

When you need a lift Try a piece of fruit next time you feel peckish. It'll satisfy a sweet tooth, make you feel fuller, and give you valuable vitamins, minerals and fibre instead of the nutritionally 'empty' calories of snacks such as sweets, chocolates or biscuits.

Brown is better....or is it? In fact white and brown sugar are virtually the same from a nutritional point of view – they give you energy, but not much else. Even honey has only tiny amounts of other substances the body can use such as vitamins and enzymes – the rest is sugar and water.

Hidden sugar Avoid it as much as you can by checking the labels of processed foods. Sucrose, dextrose, glucose, lactose, maltose and fructose all mean sugar.

Nervous, overactive, can't concentrate? If this sounds like your child, the problem could be too much sugar. Cut down on cakes, biscuits, sweets and sugary drinks, and see what happens.

EASY WAYS TO EAT LESS SUGAR

● Slowly reduce the amount of sugar you take with tea and coffee until you give it up altogether.

● Drink pure fruit or vegetable juices instead of sugared squashes or fizzy drinks, or dilute sweetened drinks with mineral water.

● Buy breakfast cereals with little or no added sugar and sweeten them with dried fruit rather than sugar.

● Use dried fruit in cakes and desserts. Their natural sweetness means you'll need less sugar, or none at all.

● Serve fresh fruit rather than puddings after meals.

● Buy fruit tinned in pure fruit juice rather than sugar syrup.

● Go for low-sugar or sugar-free preserves instead of jam.

SENSIBLE DRINKING

Know what you're getting

● A normal glass of wine or sherry, a single measure of spirits and half a pint of beer each contain about one unit, or 8g ($\frac{1}{4}$oz) of alcohol.

● A large glass of red or white wine or half a pint of cider contains about 12g ($\frac{3}{8}$oz), or one and a half units.

● Strong lager may contain as much as two units per half pint.

What's the limit? Twenty-one units a week is considered a safe limit for men. Women tend to weigh less and have a smaller proportion of water in their bodies, so a drink raises their level of blood alcohol more. For them, the limit is 14 units a week. Pregnant women are advised not to drink at all as even small amounts of alcohol may harm an unborn baby.

Tips for safer drinking

● If you're very thirsty, have a non-alcoholic drink first.

● Avoid alcohol during the working day.

● Eat something before you take a drink, or have your drink with a meal.

● Choose low-alcohol or non-alcoholic drinks sometimes.

● Add a splash of mineral water to your glass of wine.

● Drink slowly – put the glass down after each sip.

● Don't be persuaded to 'have one for the road'.

TRUE OR FALSE?

WHITE WINE IS LESS FATTENING THAN RED WINE.
False. Only dry white wine has fewer calories than red wine, but the difference is not enough to have any effect on your weight (94 Calories compared with 97). Other whites all have more: medium has 107, sweet has 133 and sparkling whites 108 Calories.

CLEAR SPIRITS ARE LESS LIKELY TO GIVE YOU A HANGOVER.
True. Gin, vodka and other clear drinks contain fewer of the additives used to give taste and colour (called 'congeners'), which are thought to be the cause of many hangover symptoms. For the same reason, white wine tends to cause fewer problems than red.

MIXING DRINKS MAKES YOU DRUNKER
False. It's the number of alcohol units you consume that makes you drunk, not how you get them. Mixing often gets blamed because it tends to happen when people are drinking more in any case.

PLANNING MEALS

What is a balanced meal? Any meal that gives you carbohydrate, protein, fibre, vitamins and minerals in the right amounts without too much salt, fat or sugar will be well-balanced. Here's how to plan such a meal quickly:
● Choose a high-fibre carbohydrate food such as potatoes or bread.
● Select a variety of vegetables or salads that will go well with the carbohydrate food you've chosen.
● Add a protein-rich food such as fish, chicken or dried beans or lentils. Red meat is fine occasionally and in small quantities, but don't make it the centrepiece of every meal, or it will push up your fat intake considerably.

The weekly schedule For minimum effort and to avoid last-minute crises, draw up a rough outline of menus at the beginning of each week. Vary the meals to make the best use of available time and ingredients, and to keep them interesting; and take into account any special meals you need to prepare. Take the list along with you and you'll find it makes shopping much easier, too.

Everyone can help Deciding what's for dinner is one job the whole family can share. Ask every member to write down his or her favourite meals, and use the list to help you plan your week's menus – or for inspiration when your own ideas run out.

Fussy eaters Watch what hard-to-please family members order next time you're in a restaurant with them. The results could be surprising and may give you some good ideas to use at home.

Cutting costs Food is one area where lower bills need not mean lower quality if you shop with care. Cheaper cuts of meat have virtually the same nutritional value as more expensive ones and can be just as tasty. Less expensive oily fish such as mackerel and herring are a bargain too: nutritionally they're about the same as salmon.

Starches Ring the changes on the old rice-or-potato regime with some new ideas: just for a start you could try meals based on pasta, couscous, corn tortillas, pitta bread, dumplings, pastry, cracked wheat, noodles, bread rolls, oatcakes, chapattis or pancakes instead. Use wholegrain products whenever possible for extra fibre.

Convenience meals Many prepared meals bought in supermarkets are nourishing and tasty – and a real help on occasions when you run out of energy or time. Check the ingredients lists and choose meals which do not contain large amounts of saturated fat, sugar or salt. Serve with a salad, or round off with fresh fruit to increase their vitamin content.

Working cooks If you don't have time in the evenings to prepare elaborate family dinners, invest in a slow cooker and go for curries, casseroles and pot roasts that can be left to cook during the day. Prepare the ingredients the night before, keep them in the fridge overnight, and put them on to cook before you go to work the next morning. Alternatively, choose food which will cook in minutes when you get home – grilled, microwaved and stir-fried dishes are the fastest.

New ideas Look out for unusual combinations and flavours in cookery books and magazines, and try to include one new dish in your schedule each week.

Leftovers Food is more likely to be appreciated the second time around if you don't just reheat it in the same form. Turn last night's casserole into a pie or savoury crumble, for example, or put thin slices of cooked meat into a stir-fry, or dice it into cubes for a curry.

CHECKLIST FOR A HEALTHY MEAL

● Include a protein-rich food such as eggs, chicken, fish, meat, cheese, dried beans or lentils.

● Allow plenty of fresh fruit and either cooked or raw vegetables.

● Vary quantities of high-energy foods such as bread, cheese, rich sauces and sweet things according to individual needs and tastes. Children and teenagers need a high energy intake, as do sports players and anyone who does hard physical work. Office workers, the elderly and those who lead relatively inactive lives, need far less of these foods.

● Remember that appearance and variety stimulate appetite, so try to include a number of different colours and shapes, and foods with contrasting textures, in every meal.

● Serve at least one crisp, crunchy dish. The extra chewing will make you feel more satisfied and discourage overeating.

FEEDING CHILDREN

Because they are growing fast and keeping active, children need more nutrients in relation to body size than adults. Their diets should contain plenty of nourishing protein foods such as meat, fish and cheese, and fresh fruit and vegetables for vitamins and minerals.

The value of milk Calcium and vitamin D are important for strong bones and teeth, and milk is one of the best sources. It also contains other minerals, protein and B vitamins. Children under five, however, need the high energy value of full-fat milk and should not be given skimmed milk.

Save their teeth Few children are able or willing to brush their teeth after every meal, so make it a habit to finish with a piece of cheese or a few nuts to counteract the effects of acid-forming bacteria on their teeth. Apples won't work as well, since they contain sugar and acids that may contribute to decay.

Children should always brush their teeth after eating sweets, however, or after sweet drinks.

Packed lunches Save time and money by planning weekday meals so that you can make up lunches with items from the previous night's meal.

● Cook a little more chicken or roast meat so that there will be some left for sandwiches.

● Prepare extra pasta, rice or potatoes for a salad.

● Heat up a leftover casserole and pack it in a vacuum jar for a hot meal on a chilly day.

521

TIPS FOR HEALTHY PACKED LUNCHES

- Use wholegrain or mixed-grain breads for sandwiches.
- Mix scrambled or hard-boiled egg with cress, chopped cucumber or alfalfa sprouts for a tasty sandwich filling.
- Blend a small ripe banana with a glass of low-fat milk and a little honey for a thick milk shake.
- For a creamier taste and added food value, mix 30ml (2tbs) of skimmed milk powder into 225g (8oz) cottage cheese. Add crushed bacon bits or chopped dried fruit for flavour.
- Make jelly with fresh fruit juice and gelatine, and add chunks of whole fruit. Use 600ml (1 pint) of juice to one sachet of gelatine.
- Prepare coleslaw with grated carrot, shredded cabbage, chopped apple and raisins bound together with low-fat plain yoghurt.

- Pack salads made with pasta, rice, cooked dried beans and combinations of finely chopped vegetables in plastic containers. Include a small fork for the child to eat with.

- Include unusual fruits for a change. Kiwi fruit are convenient and can be eaten with a teaspoon. One kiwi fruit contains more than the daily requirement of vitamin C.

- Spread thin slices of ham or other lean cooked meats with favourite pickles or mustards, then roll up and pack in boxes.
- Make sandwich pastes by blending in a mixer any leftover cooked meat or fish with low-fat yoghurt or mayonnaise and seasonings. Use the pulse button if your machine has one, to avoid over-fine puréeing.
- Pitta bread makes an easy container for cheese, salad, meat or just about any filling, and it's quicker to prepare than sandwiches. Buy the smaller size so that you can include several with different fillings.

FOOD FOR THE ELDERLY

Eat less fat Most people become less active as they grow older, and their energy requirements from food drop as a result. So cut down on fats if you're worried about putting on weight.

You don't have to cook every day Stock up on some handy convenience meals for days when you don't feel like cooking. Longlife ones are particularly useful as you can store them without a fridge or freezer, and they are quick to heat up in a saucepan or a microwave oven. Serve with a salad for extra vitamins, or have a piece of fruit for dessert.

Calcium Your bones aren't growing any more, but they still need calcium to stay strong. Drink plenty of skimmed or semi-skimmed milk, and keep eggs and cheese in stock for quick, high-calcium meals.

Finding the fibre High-fibre foods are important to help beat constipation, which can plague some older people. If chewing vegetables and other fibre foods is difficult, try softer fruits such as berries instead. Raspberries are rich in fibre, and so are bananas and dried fruits such as apricots and prunes. Cereals will be easier to chew if you eat them with hot milk.

Loss of appetite Elderly people who live alone sometimes lose interest in food because the social side is missing. If this is a problem, consider regular arrangements to share meals with friends or family members who live close by. Keep the food simple – sandwiches, salads and pasta, for example, which are healthy and quick to prepare.

Vitamin D You may not be getting enough if you don't go out much, since it's manufactured by the body from sunlight. You can increase your intake by eating more margarine, eggs and oily fish such as sardines, kippers and mackerel. Cod liver oil supplements will also help.

Two meals for the effort of one When you cook mince, do enough to provide meals for two days, but use it in different ways. For example, you could have shepherd's pie one day and spaghetti bolognese the next.

DIABETIC DIETS

Avoiding sugar Diabetics need to avoid sugar, both by itself and in sugary foods, although some diabetics can take very small amounts.
● Fresh or dried fruit and fruit sugar (fructose) can be useful substitutes for sugar in cooking, but they are still high in calories, so it's best not to use them in very large quantities.
● Sorbitol (a product made from sugar but more slowly absorbed) can take the place of ordinary sugar in baking. Buy it from a chemist or a health food store.

Special diabetic products Most chemists and food shops now keep a good range of diabetic products but they can be expensive and are mostly no lower in calories than non-diabetic foods. A better idea may be to look for ordinary low-fat, low-sugar options such as jam without added sugar, diet drinks or tinned fruit in natural juice. Read the labels thoroughly, though – many surprising foods such as tomato sauce and peanut butter may contain sugar.

Soft drinks If you don't like diet drinks, try fizzy mineral water mixed with unsweetened fruit juice instead.

Diabetics can teach the rest of the family A diabetic diet is a healthy diet, low in fat and sugar and high in fibre. So if the whole family adopts a diabetic or nearly diabetic eating plan with regular meals everyone will benefit, and there will be no need to cook separately.

Diabetic children It's hard to be left out when your friends pass round cakes and sweets, so make a special effort to bake sugar-free biscuits and cakes for a diabetic child's lunchbox, and to pack alternative treats such as nuts or diabetic chocolate now and again.
● Explain the child's condition to teachers and mothers of friends so that they know what is safe to offer when you're not there.

DO NOT make changes to a diabetic person's diet without first consulting their doctor or dietician.

523

WHEN YOU CAN'T DRINK MILK

Milk substitutes If you're allergic to cow's milk or you find it hard to digest, try soya milk or goat's milk, which rarely cause problems. Most supermarkets and health food shops keep both, as well as products such as goat's-milk yoghurt and cheese. Buy the milks in liquid or powder form, and use them in exactly the same way as ordinary milk.

Margarine Go for a brand that does not contain whey, as this can cause the same problems as milk. Kosher margarine is always whey-free, but check the labels of other types to be sure.

Sauces and soups If they call for milk, use stock instead.

Puddings, cereals and cakes Try fruit juice where you'd normally use milk, or use soya or goat's milk.

Let the buyer beware Read the labels of prepared and processed foods before handing over your money. Milk and milk products are used in a surprising variety of foods, particularly biscuits and cakes.

GLUTEN-FREE DIETS

Who needs them? The answer is: anyone who has difficulty digesting a protein called gluten, found in some grains. The problem is known medically as coeliac disease, and symptoms may start before the age of three, with diarrhoea, wind, and occasionally even weakness or malnutrition if the victim can't absorb enough protein.

Luckily, a gluten-free diet is all that's needed to control the condition. This means avoiding wheat, barley, rye and their products, and in some cases oats, which contain a gluten-like substance.

Substitutes Rice, maize (corn) and buckwheat are the most useful alternatives to wheat. Use them as flours for thickening sauces and in batters, coatings and doughs. Flakes of millet can also be stirred in to thicken sauces and stews, or you can use puréed vegetables.

Keeping up the fibre You lose valuable fibre when you cut out gluten-containing foods, so make sure to replace it with other sources of roughage such as gluten-free bread and biscuits, brown rice, peas, beans and fresh fruit and vegetables.

Buckwheat flour To make your own, grind raw buckwheat grains in a coffee grinder. If the flavour's too strong for your taste, mix it with equal quantities of rice flour.

Prepared foods These can be a serious problem as so many contain hidden gluten, often in the form of thickening agents. Read all labels carefully, particularly on sauces, salad dressings and baking powders, and take care with beer since it is sometimes made with wheat. Buy Japanese Tamari rather than ordinary soya sauce, which is often thickened with wheat flour.

Eating out Always ask about ingredients when eating in a restaurant. Sauces are a common problem, and one that's easy to overlook. Even mayonnaise, mustard and vinaigrette could be thickened with flour.

Porridge Just because you can't eat oats doesn't mean you have to forgo a warming, nutritious breakfast. Millet flakes, buckwheat flakes and rice bran work just as well and can be cooked in exactly the same way, but you will have to vary the cooking time according to the grain you use.

TIPS FOR VEGETARIANS

Be prepared If not all the family is vegetarian, keep a supply of bought – or homemade if you prefer – vegetable burgers and sausages to serve when others have hamburgers or meat dishes. Put them in a bun, or dish up with salads or vegetables.

Ensuring a good supply of vitamin B12 You'll need to take vitamin B12 as a supplement if you're a vegetarian who doesn't eat much dairy produce or if you follow a vegan diet which excludes animal products completely. Buy the tablets from a chemist or health food shop.

Balancing proteins Combine two or more protein foods in each meal and you'll get a better balance of amino acids (the building blocks of body proteins) than if you eat only one at a time. Lentil soup and wholemeal bread is a good mix; or cooked, dried beans and rice; or a jacket potato with cheese.

Using seeds To pep up a vegetarian meal and add crunchiness and flavour, you can't beat seeds. Sprinkle sunflower, sesame, pumpkin or other favourites on almost anything, sweet or savoury. Salads, breads, soups, casseroles and even cakes taste particularly good this way, and you'll be giving yourself an extra source of protein.

Go nutty Walnuts, cashews and other nuts are a high-protein replacement for meat in dishes such as lasagne.

Seventy grammes (2½oz) of nuts provides the same protein as 100g (3½oz) of beef. Combine the nuts with colourful vegetables such as green and red peppers, tomatoes and courgettes, to make a nutritious main dish.

Full of beans Dried beans and other pulses such as peas and lentils are economical, versatile and rich in protein. Use them fresh or dried (soak them for a few hours first), or even tinned when you don't have time to cook. If other members of the family are meat-eaters you can save time by preparing the vegetables and seasonings first for dishes such as soups, stews and curries, then dividing them into two parts and adding meat to one and beans to the other.
CAUTION Kidney beans can be poisonous if not properly prepared. To cook them safely, boil hard for ten minutes, pour off the water and simmer until soft in fresh water.

Snacks and sandwiches Marmite and cheese aren't the only options for vegetarians. Try experimenting with new combinations; for example: mashed avocado with lemon juice; peanut butter and banana; grated carrot, raisins and mayonnaise; soft cheese and walnuts; scrambled egg with mushrooms and tomatoes; cottage cheese with chopped dates.

SIMPLE WAYS TO SLIM

Work with your body Treat it well, and your body will be an ally in the fight against fat.
● Regular exercise can increase metabolic rate (the rate at which you burn up energy) and help you to stay slim.
● Crash diets have the opposite effect: the body protects itself from starvation by conserving as much energy (and hence fat) as possible, and your metabolic rate could actually fall, making you fatter in the long run.
● Don't go for any diet that gives fewer than 1000 Calories a day for women, or 1200 a day for men.

Cutting calories The best way to do it is to reduce the fat in your diet (page 516), since fat is the most concentrated form of food energy. A mere 50g (2oz) of cheddar cheese, which is high in fat, gives you 200 Calories, but you'd have to eat a pound of apples to get the same effect.

DO YOU NEED TO LOSE WEIGHT?

Use these tables to check the ideal weight range for your height and build, and to give you a target figure to aim at if you want to lose (or gain) weight.

Ideal weight ranges for women

Height (ft in)	(m)	Slight build (st lb)	(kg)	Medium build (st lb)	(kg)
5 0	1.52	7 5 - 8 3	46.7 - 52.2	8 0 - 9 0	50.8 - 57.1
5 2	1.57	7 10 - 8 9	49.0 - 54.9	8 6 - 9 6	53.5 - 60.0
5 4	1.63	8 2 - 9 1	51.7 - 57.6	8 12 - 9 12	56.2 - 62.6
5 5	1.65	8 5 - 9 4	53.1 - 59.0	9 1 - 10 1	57.6 - 64.0
5 6	1.68	8 8 - 9 7	54.4 - 60.3	9 4 - 10 4	59.0 - 65.3
5 7	1.70	8 11 - 9 10	55.8 - 61.7	9 7 - 10 7	60.3 - 66.7
5 8	1.73	9 0 - 9 13	57.1 - 63.0	9 10 - 10 10	61.7 - 68.0
5 10	1.78	9 6 - 10 5	60.0 - 65.8	10 2 - 11 2	64.4 - 70.8
6 0	1.83	9 12 - 10 11	62.6 - 68.5	10 8 - 11 8	67.2 - 73.5

Ideal weight ranges for men

Height (ft in)	(m)	Slight build (st lb)	(kg)	Medium build (st lb)	(kg)
5 2	1.57	8 13 - 9 5	56.7 - 59.4	9 2 - 9 12	58.1 - 62.6
5 4	1.63	9 3 - 9 9	58.5 - 61.2	9 6 - 10 3	60.0 - 64.9
5 6	1.68	9 7 - 10 0	60.3 - 63.5	9 11 - 10 9	62.1 - 67.6
5 7	1.70	9 9 - 10 3	61.2 - 64.9	10 0 - 10 12	63.5 - 68.9
5 8	1.73	9 11 - 10 6	62.1 - 66.2	10 3 - 11 1	64.9 - 70.3
5 9	1.75	9 13 - 10 9	63.0 - 67.6	10 6 - 11 4	66.2 - 71.7
5 10	1.78	10 1 - 10 12	64.0 - 68.9	10 9 - 11 7	67.6 - 73.0
6 0	1.83	10 7 - 11 5	66.7 - 72.1	11 1 - 12 1	70.3 - 76.7
6 2	1.88	10 13 - 11 13	69.4 - 75.7	11 8 - 12 9	73.5 - 80.3

Substitutes for cream Yoghurt and low-fat fromage frais are less fattening than cream. Use them in place of sour cream on jacket potatoes, and in dips and spreads. Season with garlic, chopped fresh herbs, spices, mustard, lemon juice or tomato purée.

Yoghurt also makes a low-fat dessert topping, or it can be frozen with chopped fruit and honey as an alternative to ice cream.

Sauces and gravies Don't use fat and flour to thicken sauces if you want to lose weight. Instead, purée vegetables such as carrots, spinach and peppers for a tasty low-fat sauce. Or make gravy by skimming off any fat and reducing the juices from a roast until concentrated.

Can't say no to pudding? Go for fresh fruit rather than a sugary dessert. It's less fattening, and your sweet tooth will still be satisfied.

Yoghurt Buy natural, low-fat yoghurt, rather than the flavoured variety, which contains added sugar. If you find the taste of plain yoghurt too sharp, mix in a little sugar-free jam or chopped fruit.

Drink plenty of liquids Your body can lose a lot of water when you go on a diet, so drink plenty of low-calorie liquids such as water and herbal teas. Pure vegetable juices such as carrot and tomato are also non-fattening, and you can cut down the calorie content of fruit juices by diluting them with water. Avoid alcohol, which is high in calories and low in vitamins.

Slimming snacks If you're a nibbler make sure you always have a good supply of fresh vegetables available for snacks. Try carrots, celery, radishes, green peppers, tomatoes or even fresh beans or peas.

Large build (st lb)	(kg)
8 10 - 9 11	55.3 - 62.1
9 2 - 10 4	58.1 - 65.3
9 8 - 10 12	60.8 - 68.9
9 11 - 11 2	62.1 - 70.8
10 0 - 11 6	63.5 - 72.6
10 3 - 11 10	64.9 - 74.4
10 6 - 11 13	66.2 - 75.7
10 12 - 12 5	69.0 - 78.5
11 4 - 12 11	71.7 - 81.2

Large build (st lb)	(kg)
9 9 - 10 8	61.2 - 67.1
9 13 - 11 1	63.0 - 70.3
10 4 - 11 9	65.3 - 73.9
10 7 - 11 13	66.7 - 75.7
10 10 - 12 3	68.0 - 77.6
10 13 - 12 7	69.4 - 79.4
11 2 - 12 11	70.8 - 81.2
11 9 - 13 5	73.9 - 84.8
12 3 - 14 1	77.6 - 89.4

527

KEEP TRACK OF CALORIES

This table gives the calorie content per 100g (3½oz) of different foods. In some cases this is about the weight of an average serving, but in others it's far more than anyone is likely to eat at one time. To arrive at an accurate count, weigh each portion and calculate its calorie content from the chart – unless you're very experienced, guessing won't be reliable.

Nutritionists recommend a daily allowance of about 1000-1500 Calories for women who wish to slim, and 1200-1700 Calories for men. Once you're happy with your weight, 2150-2500 Cal a day is recommended for women and 2400-3400 Cal a day for men, the exact figure depending on your age, activity level, metabolic rate and individual needs.

FOOD	CALORIES PER 100g	FOOD	CALORIES PER 100g
Breads, cereals and grains		**Dairy products, fats and oils**	
Bread, wholemeal	215	Egg, raw	147
white	230	Cheese, Camembert	300
Cornflakes (without milk		Cheddar	406
and sugar)	368	cottage	96
Muesli (without milk		Stilton	462
and sugar)	368	Milk, skimmed	33
Porridge, cooked		semi-skimmed	46
(no milk or sugar)	44	whole	65
Pasta, cooked	117	Cream, single	212
Rice, cooked white	123	double	447
cooked brown	118	Yoghurt, flavoured	81
Flour, wholemeal	318	low-fat, plain	52
white	350	Butter	740
Biscuits, water	440	Margarine	730
digestive	471	Low-fat spread	366
Cake, fruit	322	Vegetable oils	899
sponge (with fat)	464	Animal fats	891
Meat, poultry and fish		**Vegetables, fruit and nuts**	
Beef, raw mince	221	Most vegetables	10-30
roast sirloin	284	Broad beans, boiled	48
rump steak (grilled)	218	Lentils, boiled	99
Lamb, roast leg	266	Onions, fried	345
chop (grilled)	255	Mushrooms, fried	210
Pork, roast	286	Peas, boiled	52
chop (grilled)	332	Parsnips	56
sausage (grilled)	318	Potatoes, boiled	80
Bacon (grilled back)	405	chipped	253
Ham	120	roast	157
Chicken, roast		Sweetcorn	123
no skin	148	Most fruit	40-60
meat and skin	216	Avocado	223
Cod, baked or grilled	95	Bananas	79
fried in batter	199	Raisins	246
Mackerel, grilled	188	Prunes, stewed	82
Sardines, in oil	217	Dates	248
in tomato sauce	117	Almonds	565
Tuna, in brine	133	Hazelnuts	380
in oil	289	Walnuts	525
Mussels, boiled	87	Peanuts	570
Prawns	107	Peanut butter	623

Stocking the larder

OUT AT THE SHOPS

Try to do as much shopping as you can on a single weekly expedition and make a comprehensive shopping list. Keep a basic list of items you need regularly every week and add to it as you notice stocks getting low. Also add any ingredients called for in your weekly meal list (page 520).

Don't shop when you're hungry You'll buy too much and go for things you feel like at the time, rather than ones that will be useful days later.

Bright and early The earlier you go, the wider the choice and the fresher the produce you'll find.

Which shops are best? It depends on what's handy, of course. But always choose reputable businesses with high standards of cleanliness, a regular turnover, and friendly, helpful staff.
Buy from specialist shops when you can. You may get fresher and cheaper spices, for example, from an Indian or Middle-Eastern delicatessen which sells large quantities of them.

Make friends with shopkeepers You'll find most are only too happy to offer advice and point out good buys. Butchers often do special cuts of meat for customers they know, and many delicatessens, cheese shops and even wine merchants will let you taste before you buy.

Ask for what you want There could still be stocks at the back of the shop, even if not on the shelves. And if they don't keep the item, ask the shopkeeper or the buyer if he can order it for you. Even staff in large supermarkets are usually willing to help.

Special offers or a waste of money?

Coupons Cut out coupons for items you already use and keep them in your purse for the next shopping trip. If they're for products you wouldn't otherwise buy, think hard about whether you really need them before you bother to save the coupons, or you may be wasting your money.

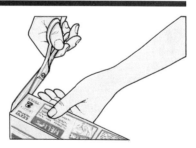

Discounted brands Compare prices carefully: supermarkets' own brands may be better value than special offers on other makes.

Damaged tins and packets Don't buy rusty or leaking tins, however small the puncture, or food in packages with a broken seal. Bacteria may have got in and caused the contents to spoil.

Food that's close to its use-by date Cheese, meat, vegetables, prepared meals and other perishables are often reduced as they approach their use-by dates. Make the most of these offers, but always check that the date hasn't actually expired, and only buy items you'll use up quickly.

529

To buy or not to buy in bulk

Whether it's stocking up on 24-tin packs of baked beans at a cash-and-carry, or simply choosing the biggest bottle of oil at your local supermarket, buying in large quantities has disadvantages as well as benefits to consider:

Staleness Even dry goods such as flour and breakfast cereals can go stale, so buy large quantities only if you're sure you can use them up before the expiry date.

Storage space Don't buy in bulk unless you've plenty of storage space. Dry goods and tins need to be in a cool but dry place, or they may spoil.

Inferior quality Don't be tempted by cheap bulk packs of unknown brands: they may be poor quality goods that you end up throwing away. If possible, buy a single pack to try first.

Cash flow Bulk buying ties up your money, so think carefully if you're on a tight budget.

Wastage Although it seems very cheap at first, a whole or half carcass of meat will contain some fatty or tougher pieces as well as leaner, more tender ones. If your family aren't used to cuts such as belly of pork, beef shin and neck of lamb, buy one or two from a butcher and try them out before committing yourself. Also remember that there'll be more waste from bone and fat than on ready-butchered cuts.

Trays of ripe fruit can be a wonderful bargain when there's a glut, but they don't last long. So make sure you've got the time to turn them into jams or preserves, or freeze them.

Not always cheaper Don't assume that you're getting a better price because you're buying more. Take a calculator to compare unit prices.

BUYING WITH SAFETY IN MIND

You can't protect your family from every passing germ, but if you follow these tips you'll certainly cut down on any risks they're taking:
● Shop at clean, tidy shops with good standards of hygiene. Dirt and disorder could spell danger.
● Don't take food from any freezer filled above its load line.
● Never buy or eat food that's past its 'use-by' date.
● Avoid anything with damaged packaging.
● Inspect eggs before you buy, and don't take any that are dirty or cracked.
● Take a coolbag (right) with you to the shops, and pack chilled foods into it to keep them cold until you get home.
● Don't pack raw and cooked meat in the same bag. Juices from raw meat contain bacteria that could be harmful if they leak onto cold meats such as ham and salami that won't be cooked before being eaten.

TEN TIPS TO CUT COSTS

● Try supermarket brands: they may be just as good and much cheaper.
● Buy fruit and vegetables that are in season, and keep an eye on how the prices fluctuate through the year.
● Experiment with cheaper cuts of meat and poultry, particularly in casseroles and for use in slow cookers or pressure cookers.
● Use chicken thighs or drumsticks instead of breasts.
● If you like the taste of butter, use it where flavour is important – on toast or in sponge cakes, for example – and go for cheaper margarines when you won't notice the difference.
● Do as much preparation as possible at home. Marinated meat, kebabs on skewers, peeled vegetables and other ready-to-cook foods are certainly time-savers, but will add to the cost of a meal.
● Buy a whole chicken at a time or a large joint of meat, rather than several small, individually wrapped packs. Cut it up into pieces at home and use it over a couple of days in different dishes. Alternatively, roast the whole piece, and serve the leftovers with salads or in a curry or risotto.
● Spend your money on nourishing, unprocessed foods such as fresh fruit and vegetables, whole grains, meat and fish. The more a food is processed the more nutrients it loses and the more expensive it gets.
● Don't hesitate to substitute a cheaper fish of the same type for a more expensive one – plaice for Dover sole, for example. Always check fish prices – they can fluctuate rapidly.

● Buy dried pulses such as haricot beans, lentils and chickpeas instead of canned ones. They are much cheaper, but you'll need to plan ahead to allow time for soaking (usually six to eight hours) and cooking (half to one hour for lentils, one to two hours for beans, two to three hours for chickpeas).

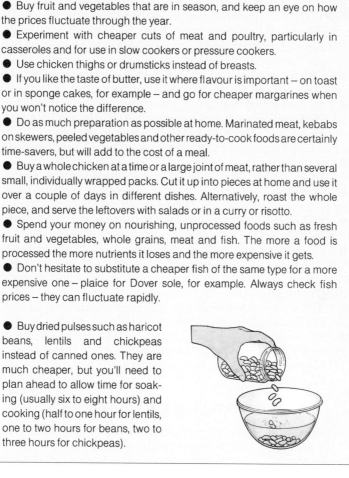

What the label tells you

Ingredients lists Did you know that by law nearly every manufactured or processed food must carry a list of ingredients? The main exceptions are dairy products, drinks with over 1.2 per cent alcohol, and chocolate and cocoa products. Ingredients have to be listed in descending order of weight, so if you check the first few items you'll have a fairly good idea of where your money's going.

Additives Manufacturers don't have to disclose the flavourings they use, but other additives such as colourings or preservatives must be listed either by E number or by their name and purpose. If you want to keep tabs on them, you may find it worthwhile to buy a book which lists all the E numbers and tells you what they are. Some supermarkets also provide pamphlets explaining the most common additives.

Decoding the message Subtle changes of wording on product labels can mean a lot. A product called 'strawberry yoghurt' or 'strawberry flavoured yoghurt', for example, must by law contain at least some real strawberries (although it may have artificial flavourings as well). One labelled 'strawberry flavour', however, need not contain any real fruit.
   A drink called 'orange squash' must be at least 25 per cent real orange juice, but one labelled 'orange flavour' may be completely artificial.

Additives aren't all artificial

Do you automatically return a product to the shelves when you see E numbers on the label? If so, you could be missing out on some good buys. Not all additives are synthetic; in fact many are natural substances, and a product which is free of artificial extras could still list E numbers on its label. The trick is to know whether you're looking at friend or foe:

● E100 Friend – curcumin, an orange-yellow colouring extracted from turmeric root. Used in biscuits, cheese and margarine.

● E102 Possible foe – tartrazine, an extract from coal tar. Used as yellow dye in foods such as soft drinks and smoked fish. May cause headaches and hyperactivity in children, or allergic symptoms such as migraine and skin rashes. Also affects some asthmatics and people sensitive to aspirin.

● E220 Possible foe – sulphur dioxide. Preserves fruit and fruit products. Can cause nausea, headaches or asthma in some sensitive people.

● E300 Friend – vitamin C by another name. Used to stop fruit turning brown and fatty foods going rancid.

● E306 Friend – better known as vitamin E. Added to a range of foods to preserve fats and oils.

● E320 Possible foe – a chemical preservative known as butylated hydroxyanisole. Added to a range of processed foods, drinks and snacks. Can affect some asthmatics, hyperactive children and people with allergies. Should not be given to babies.

● E322 Friend – a soya extract known as lecithin. Used in low-fat spreads and as an emulsifier in chocolate.

● E621 Possible foe – monosodium glutamate. Used as a flavour enhancer, but it can cause headaches, nausea, palpitations and dizziness for some. Banned from baby foods.

HOW TO TELL WHEN FRUIT IS RIPE

Melons Sniff the stalk end: a sweet, heady scent means a melon is ready to eat. Alternatively, press the end and see if it gives slightly.

Kiwi fruit Feel for slight softness.

Pineapples The centre leaves will pull out easily when the fruit is ripe.

Bananas Ripe bananas have yellow skins evenly speckled with small brown spots, and no trace of greenness. Don't store them in the fridge, or they'll start to blacken.

Avocado pears The flesh of a ripe avocado pear should feel firm, but give very slightly when gently squeezed. Never push hard, or you will bruise the flesh of the fruit.

● If you don't need to use avocado pears straight away, buy firmer ones and keep them wrapped in newspaper for a few days in a warm place, such as an airing cupboard, before using.

● You can use a microwave oven to soften an avocado pear that's still a little hard. See page 573.

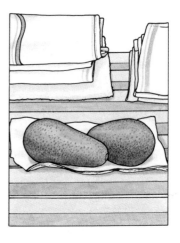

BONING UP ON MEAT

Don't rely on colour A bright red cut of beef or lamb may look more appealing than a dry, browner piece, but in fact there's little difference. Red flesh has simply been more recently cut from the carcass. After cutting, the pigment in the meat will slowly turn it from red to brown. The variations will disappear during cooking, in any case.

Choosing pork Never take a chance on pork that may be past its best. Fresh meat will be pink in colour, with a smooth texture, little or no gristle, and firm, white fat. The bones should be a pinkish-blue colour.

Hanging Red meat needs to be hung to improve its tenderness and flavour. A good butcher should be able to tell you how long his meat has been hung. For beef, this should be at least ten days; for lamb, four.

Going by the fat Choose cuts with an even marbling of visible fat throughout the meat and a minimum of surrounding fat – especially if you are going to trim it off. The colour of meat fat varies according to the age and breed of an animal, but in general it should be firm, dry and cream-coloured.

Breast of lamb Breast may not look like much when you buy it – a long, thin cut streaked with fat – but in fact it's one of the most versatile and economical cuts of lamb. Roast or pot-roast it on the bone, cut it up for a casserole (above), or remove the bone and stuff and roll the joint before roasting.

Poultry pointers
● Look for a plump breast, undamaged skin, pliable legs, and a supple breastbone. Fat should be creamy-white to yellow in colour.
● If you find ordinary chicken bland and flavourless, you may prefer the taste of a corn-fed fowl – look for yellowish skin and flesh and a label that says the chicken has been fed on corn.
● Some people choose to buy 'free-range' poultry for humanitarian reasons or because they prefer the taste or find that there is less fat on these birds. Before you spend the extra money, however, look on the pack for information, or ask your supermarket manager or butcher to explain what the 'free-range' label means. Different producers may adhere to different standards.

Coarser cuts Slower cooking methods such as braising or stewing will bring out the best in cuts such as beef brisket and chuck steak; scrag, breast or middle neck of lamb; and neck end or collar of pork.

Special occasions A crown roast makes a festive centrepiece for any celebration dinner. It consists of two best ends of lamb joined together in a ring, with a savoury stuffing in the centre. You'll have to give your butcher a day's notice to prepare it, though.

Lean beef Expensive topside, rump and fillet are not the only lean cuts of beef.

● Shin (right) – meat from the foreleg or hindleg – is economical and has little fat, but you'll need to cook it slowly in a casserole or stew to soften the connective tissue.

● Silverside is also lean. Buy it unsalted for roasting, or salted for boiling. If buying the salted sort, ask the butcher whether it needs to be soaked before cooking.

HOW TO BUY SEAFOOD

Finding out if a fish is fresh

● If a fish has bright eyes, a glistening skin and firm flesh it will be fresh.

● A bright red colour under the gills is also a good sign, and so is a fresh, salty smell.

● Avoid any fish that is dull or limp, or that has red, sunken eyes or smells strongly of ammonia.

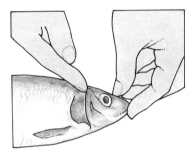

Ready-cooked shellfish Shells should be intact and the shellfish should feel heavy for their size. Poorer quality shellfish may contain liquid if the shells are cracked before cooking, so check by shaking them gently. Cooked prawns and shrimps should always be firm and pink in colour.

WHEN TO FIND THE FISH YOU WANT

Fish seasons vary from year to year and region to region, so there are no fixed dates, but the table below gives an idea of when you can expect to find various types of fresh fish at a reasonable price. Imported and frozen fish are generally available at other times as well.

FISH	SEASON
Cod	June – February
Coley	August – February
Dover sole	May – February
Haddock	May – February
Hake	June – March
Halibut	June – March
Herring	May – December
Lemon sole	May – March
Mackerel	All year, but best April – June
Monkfish	All year
Mullet, grey	September – February
red	May – November
Plaice	May – February
Salmon	May – August

WHEN TO FIND THE FISH YOU WANT (cont)

FISH	SEASON
Sardine/pilchard	March – September
Sea bream	June – February
Skate	May – February
Snapper	All year
Sprats	October – March
Trout	All year
Tuna	All year
Turbot	April – February, but best in summer
Whitebait	February – July
Whiting	June – February

Be flexible Catches of fish vary with the tides, the weather and the time of year, so buy what's plentiful and don't stick too rigidly to your shopping list. You'll get better value and fresher fish.

Choosing crabs Male crabs have larger claws than females, so there is more white meat in them. On the other hand, female crabs have more and better quality dark meat inside the shell. So make your choice according to preference.

Oysters, mussels, scallops and clams When live, the shells should be closed or should shut rapidly when tapped; after cooking they should open up. Discard any that don't behave like this. (See also page 550.)

AT THE DAIRY COUNTER

Sizing up eggs Eggs are graded according to weight, and most recipes assume size three unless otherwise stated. Children sometimes prefer smaller eggs and those with heartier appetites larger ones, so buy what suits your family best. Here's what you'll be getting:

Grade 1: 70g or more.
Grade 2: 65g – 70g.
Grade 3: 60g – 65g.
Grade 4: 55g – 60g.
Grade 5: 50g – 55g.
Grade 6: 45g – 50g.
Grade 7: Below 45g.

Butter basics All types of butter have to contain at least 78 per cent natural milk fat but flavours do vary, so experiment until you find a favourite.
● Most British butter is of the 'sweetcream' type, which is mild and delicate in flavour.
● Continental or 'lactic' butters (usually wrapped in silver foil and labelled 'salted' or 'unsalted') have a full flavour and fine texture.

Margarine The fat content must be no less than 80 per cent, and no more than 10 per cent of it can come from milk. Margarines also have to have vitamins A and D added to bring them up to the same level as butter.

Polyunsaturated margarine The fat content is the same as other margarines, but at least 45 per cent of the fats must be polyunsaturated.

Low-fat spreads They're made from the same ingredients as margarine – vegetable oils and fats, water and vitamins A and D – but the proportion of fat is lower (sometimes as low as 25 per cent) and the amount of water much greater. This makes them fine for spreading on bread, but not usually for cooking. The water can make toast soggy.

Which milk to buy?

Pasteurised whole milk (silver top) Whole milk is rich and creamy at the top and thinner lower down. Suitable for babies and small children, but not for anyone trying to cut down on fat.

Homogenised milk (red top) Whole milk that has the cream evenly distributed is sold as homogenised milk. The fat content is the same as for silver top, so it's suitable for children but not for those who want less fat.

Channel Islands milk (gold top) The richest milk of all, with a minimum of 4 per cent fat and a delicious, creamy taste. Use it for special occasions or where taste is important – in filter coffee, hot chocolate or creamy desserts and custards, for example.

Sterilised milk (blue top or crown cap) Particularly useful if you're not a regular milk drinker, since it keeps unopened for several months without refrigeration. Also handy for taking on trips or going camping.

Ultra-heat-treated milk (UHT or longlife) UHT milk comes in cartons that are easy to store, and unopened packs will last up to six months. Use it as a standby or for egg custards or homemade yoghurt, where it works particularly well.

Semiskimmed milk (red and silver striped top) The lower fat content makes semiskimmed milk unsuitable for small children, but it's a good compromise for adults who want the taste of whole milk without the fat.

Skimmed milk (blue and silver checked top) Don't give it to children, because of the very low fat content, but use it if you want to cut right down on fat for slimming or health reasons.

DO NOT leave milk sitting on the doorstep longer than necessary if you have it delivered to your home, especially on a warm, sunny day. Exposure to sunlight will rob it of vitamins and rapidly turn it sour.

CALCULATING HOW MUCH TO BUY

Meat The quantity you need depends largely on the cut you're using and the way you cook it. You'll need less, for example, for a dish with a rich sauce, and more for a plain roast. As a rough guide, estimate about 100-175g (4-6oz) per portion for boneless cuts, and 175-350g (6-12oz) for meat on the bone.

Poultry Allow about 225-350g (8-12oz) of chicken or turkey per person and you won't go far wrong. Duck and goose have much more fat, so make it about 700-900g (1½-2lb) when you're serving these. As a quick guide to how many a whole bird will feed, calculate:

Chicken	2-2.5kg (4½-5½lb)	6 portions
Turkey	2.5-4kg (5½-9lb)	8-10 portions
	4.5-6kg (10-13lb)	12-16 portions
	6.5-9kg (14-20lb)	18-30 portions
Duck	1.5-2kg (3½-4½lb)	2 portions
	2-3kg (4½-6½lb)	3 portions
	3-3.5kg (6½-7½lb)	4 portions
Goose	5kg (11lb)	6 portions

Fish and shellfish Allow about 175g (6oz) fish on the bone per serving; and for filleted fish, about 100g (4oz). Whole fish weighed with head and bones will feed two to three per 450g (1lb). Shellfish is richer so allow slightly less: for easy calculating, assume that crabs and lobsters will yield about half their weight in meat.

Pasta and rice Calculate about 50g (2oz) per person for an accompaniment or side dish; but double the quantity if pasta or rice is the main part of a dish – a risotto or pasta main course, for example.

KEEPING THINGS COLD

Using your fridge effectively

How cold? A temperature between 0°C (32°F) and 5°C (41°F) is best. Check with a fridge thermometer bought from a kitchen shop or supermarket. Warmer than this and food poisoning bacteria will start to multiply; colder, and your food will freeze.

Keep the door closed It wastes energy to leave a fridge door open, and the temperature inside will rise quickly.

No hot food Let cooked food cool to room temperature before you put it in the fridge; the motor will have to work much harder to keep the inside cold if something's heating it up.

What goes where?
● Raw food at the bottom and cooked at the top is the general rule. This way, drips are less likely to spread bacteria to food that may not be heated up again.
● Meat, chicken and fish should be unwrapped for the fridge, placed on a plate and covered with a large bowl. If they are left in their wrapping, or tightly covered with plastic film, air will not be able to circulate around the food.

Trouble-free freezing

Setting the level Set the dial on your freezer so that the inside temperature is between −18°C (0°F) and −23°C (−10°F). Check the temperature with a freezer thermometer bought from a kitchen shop – freezer gauges are not always accurate.

Star markings A one-star freezer (top right) is safe for storing ready-frozen food for up to a week; a two-star freezer (second from top, right) for up to a month; and a three-star freezer (second from bottom, right) for up to three months. Only a freezer marked with four stars (bottom right) is suitable for freezing fresh food.

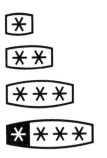

Getting it all wrapped up Make sure that all food bound for the freezer is wrapped and sealed in an airtight container.
● Use plastic containers with press-on lids for liquids and brittle items and freezer-weight bags sealed with twist ties or freezer tape for others.
● Freezer foil and foil dishes are also suitable, but don't use them for acid foods, or holes may eventually appear. Place foil-wrapped foods inside a sealed freezer bag or cover with plastic freezer wrap before storing.
● Avoid glass jars – they may crack as the contents expand.

Label everything Even the best memory is fallible, so label and date all food before it goes into the freezer. Make sure it's thoroughly wrapped and sealed so that it's airtight, too.

Don't take chances Never freeze anything that's not completely fresh. Low temperatures can't kill bacteria: they'll just lie dormant and begin to multiply again when the food is thawed.

Plastic containers Try freezing empty margarine tubs, yoghurt cartons or other plastic containers before you use them for freezing food. Some plastics turn brittle and split at low temperatures and may not be suitable.

Meals for one If you have a microwave oven, keep a few portioned-out meals on microwave-proof plates in the freezer. Simply thaw and reheat when one of the family has to eat alone.

Dishes all end up in the freezer?
They don't have to: line dishes with foil before using them to freeze casseroles, pies or puddings. Lift out the foil and food when solid, cover with another piece of foil if necessary, and store without the dish. To thaw and reheat, unwrap the food and place it back in the original dish.

Freezing liquids Don't freeze liquids in containers filled right to the top. Leave at least 25mm (1in) of space to allow for expansion.

Unfreezable foods The following foods don't freeze well, so store them above 0°C (32°F):
● Whole eggs: uncooked eggs will crack their shells and hard-boiled ones become rubbery if frozen.
● Cooked potatoes: they may turn leathery if you freeze them whole, but if you mash them first they should be fine.
● Cooked custards: they tend to separate out on thawing.
● Single cream: separates out on thawing. Richer creams with over 40 per cent butterfat can be frozen.

● Salad vegetables: lettuce, watercress, celery and other salads will just turn limp and mushy.

● Avocado pears and aubergines: the flesh will discolour and lose its texture if frozen.

● Mayonnaise: can curdle when unfrozen.

● Garlic: dishes flavoured with garlic can develop a musty taste after even a short spell in the freezer. Cook without it if you're going to freeze food, and add it after thawing.

● Jelly: goes watery when thawed out. However, mousses and cream mixtures with added gelatine usually freeze well.

● Fizzy drinks in bottles or tins: the containers may explode as freezing makes the contents expand.

DO'S AND DON'TS ABOUT THAWING

DO let frozen meat thaw out slowly in a fridge or cool place. Bacteria could multiply if you put it somewhere warm.

DO thaw out frozen poultry in its wrapping, and puncture the seal so that it can 'breathe'. Stand it in a container in the fridge to make sure no liquid drips onto other food.

DO cook food as soon as possible after thawing, and quickly use up anything that's accidentally allowed to defrost.

DON'T refreeze food after thawing unless you cook it first.

DON'T run warm or hot water over poultry to unfreeze it more quickly, or bacteria may multiply. Letting it thaw out in a fridge is best, but if you're in a hurry place the wrapped bird in a bowl of cold water and change the water frequently. Don't cook it until it has thawed out completely.

FRESH PRODUCE AT ITS BEST

Tips for storing fruit

 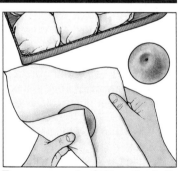

Soft fruit Leave currants on the stem and berries – strawberries, raspberries and loganberries, for example – unhulled. Store the fruit in a colander in the fridge, then remove the hulls or stems just before serving.

Too many apples? Wrap the fruits individually in paper or foil, pack into boxes and keep them in a cool, dark, well-ventilated place. Kept like this they should last for several months. Don't store bruised fruit or it will rot and contaminate the rest.

Left with half a lemon? Cover the cut surface with plastic wrap or waxed paper and it should last for several days in the fridge.

539

Freezing fruit If possible, remove stones or pips before freezing; they could taint the fruit. Don't freeze any fruit that's not in perfect condition, except for slightly overripe fruit, which can be frozen if puréed first.

To stop frozen fruit going brown Soft fruits such as apricots and cherries are prone to this problem, but it can often be prevented by sprinkling a little citric acid or lemon juice over raw fruit, or adding it when cooking.

Stocking up on vegetables

Avoid plastic bags Remove vegetables from plastic wrappings before you store them. They will sweat and go soggy if they can't breathe.

Onions A vegetable basket or wire rack is the best place to store onions. Place it in a cool, well-ventilated spot.

Lettuce This is one exception to the 'no plastic bags' rule. Lettuces do best in a plastic bag in the fridge, with the stem end left on. This treatment often works to revive a limp, tired lettuce if you sprinkle it with water before sealing the bag. ● To refresh loose lettuce leaves, rinse them in cold water, then shake off any excess water and place them in a plastic bag in the fridge for half an hour.

Carrots, beetroot and turnips Don't store these vegetables with the leafy green tops still on, or nutrients will be drawn up into the leaves.

Root ginger It's easier to peel a large piece in one go than to fiddle with small bits each time a recipe calls for ginger. Grate off what you need and store the rest in the fridge, wrapped in clingfilm. It should keep for weeks.

Potatoes and root vegetables They will last longest in a cool, dark place with good ventilation.

Waste not Purée leftover vegetables and freeze them in small containers. Defrost, and add to sauces or soups for extra flavour and fibre.

Fresh herbs Grow your own fresh herbs or buy them from a supermarket or greengrocer. Most herbs on the stalk will last for several days if washed and placed upright in a glass with enough water to reach the stalk. Cover the glass loosely with a plastic bag so that they don't dry out.

More parsley than you need? Remove the stalks, chop the leaves finely and pack into ice-cube trays with a little water to moisten them; then freeze. When solid, transfer the blocks to a freezer bag, and use straight from frozen in soups, sauces and casseroles.

Cheaper vegetables You'll save money and get better quality produce if you choose loose vegetables rather than prewrapped packs.

STORING MEAT AND FISH

When to rewrap Meat and poultry that are stored in a fridge need to have air circulating around them to keep them fresh. Remove the original wrapping and place the food on a plate, covered loosely with a piece of foil or a large glass bowl.

Meat and poultry for the freezer, on the other hand, need airtight packaging. Rewrap red meat in tightly sealed foil packages or in freezer bags. Poultry just needs an extra layer of wrapping on top of the original in case there's a puncture that could cause freezer burn.

Avoid the 'what can it be?' problem When rewrapping meat for the freezer, remove the label from the original packaging and tape it to the new wrapper so that you'll have a record of the contents, the weight and the date it was frozen.

Well stocked Don't throw bones and scraps away: boil them up into a concentrated stock, allow it to cool and then freeze in ice-cube trays. Add straight to stews and sauces; there's no need to defrost first. A good stock can also be turned into soup with very little effort.

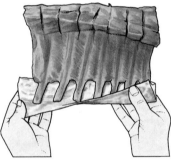

Protecting freezer wrappings Pad any sharp, protruding bones with a double layer of foil or kitchen paper before wrapping meat for the freezer. You'll be less likely to puncture the wrapping.

All stuck together? Burger patties, chops and slices of meat will separate easily if you interleave them with a double layer of non-stick paper when preparing them for the freezer.

Meatballs freezing out of shape? Freeze meatballs first on an open baking tray. When they are firm you can transfer them to a freezer bag and store them without fear of squashing.

Fish in the fridge It's safest to keep fish on the bottom shelf and well wrapped up to reduce the chance of a spill affecting other food. Fish is best bought and used on the same day, but if that's impossible it will last for 24 hours in the fridge.

Freezing fish at home

To freeze fish safely, use only fish that you know is fresh out of the water, and don't risk refreezing a fish that may have been frozen and thawed before sale. Ask your fishmonger if in doubt.

1 To freeze a whole fish, lay it, uncovered, on a dish or tray in the freezer. When the fish is frozen solid, take it out and dip it briefly into cold water, which will form a thin layer of ice over the fish.

2 Return the fish to the freezer, and repeat the process until the ice is about 5mm (¼in) thick. Then wrap, seal and store in the freezer.

THE CLINGFILM CONTROVERSY

Over the past few years there has been much disagreement about the safety of clinging plastic food wraps such as clingfilm. Most food scientists now agree that harmful chemicals from these wraps can be absorbed by the fat molecules in food, although it is not known if the quantities are large enough to pose a real risk to health.

For the sake of safety, clingfilm manufacturers and the Ministry of Agriculture, Fisheries and Food now recommend that self-clinging wraps be used only in situations where they can't come into contact with fatty food – to wrap onions or lemons (neither of which contains fat) for the fridge, for example, or to cover a container. They are also not suitable for use in conventional ovens, and food should not be microwaved when in direct contact with clingfilm.

CAUTION Many shops still use clingy plastic films on foods such as cheese and cold meat, which should be packaged in thicker non-clinging plastic or in foil or paper instead. Point this out if you notice it, and buy products from the counter where you can have them wrapped as you wish.

FRESHER BREAD AND CAKES

Let them breathe Bread and cakes need to have a little air circulating around them, so don't store them in completely airtight containers. Condensation and mould will quickly develop if air is unable to circulate.

Biscuits, on the other hand, will stay crisp longer if stored in an airtight tin or jar.

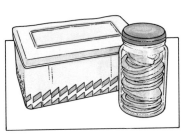

Mouldy bread Throw bread away as soon as you notice signs of mould. Scald the inside of the bread bin with boiling water to destroy any mould spores that could contaminate the next loaf.

Cakes and biscuits Store cakes and biscuits in separate containers: a moist cake makes for soggy biscuits.

Storing a rich fruit cake Don't let your special cake dry out while its flavour is maturing: turn it over before you store it away, pierce the base several times with a skewer and then pour over a few tablespoons of sherry, brandy or whisky. Wrap it in greaseproof paper, and cover with a double thickness of foil. It should stay moist for several months.

Bread's gone stale? Freshen up stale bread by splashing it with a little cold water, wrapping it in foil and giving it about five minutes in a hot oven to crisp the crust.

Pastry
● Dry pastry mixes, such as crumble toppings without added water, store well for one or two weeks in a fridge or up to two months in a freezer, simply wrapped in a plastic bag.
● Most biscuit pastry will also freeze well. Shape the mixture into a roll and slice it into rounds or place cut out or piped biscuits on a baking tray. Freeze the uncooked biscuits on the baking tray until solid, remove from the tray and store in a rigid container.

Bread dough Unrisen dough can be stored in a home freezer for up to a month. For best results, use one and a half times as much yeast as the recipe recommends. Thaw the dough for five or six hours at room temperature, or overnight in the fridge, allow to rise, and bake.

Leftover bread Use a food processor to turn leftover bread into breadcrumbs, or grate it into crumbs by hand. Store the crumbs in a sealed plastic bag in the freezer.

Tired of soggy sandwiches? Try putting mayonnaise, mustard, pickles, tomato, cucumber or other moist ingredients on the inside, and meat or cheese next to the bread.

KEEPING DAIRY PRODUCTS

Iced-up ice cream? Next time you put an opened carton of ice cream back into the freezer, press a sheet of waxed paper on top of the ice cream to exclude air and prevent ice crystals from forming.

Cheese is choosy Cheese needs protection from moisture and temperature extremes, so wrap it tightly in foil or greaseproof paper (not clingfilm – see opposite page) and store it in a cool place or in the fridge. The ideal temperature is about 10-12°C (50-54°F). Bring it up to room temperature for about an hour before serving.

Instant decorations Don't leave leftover whipped cream in the fridge to go sour. Pipe it into rosettes on a baking tray lined with non-stick paper. Freeze the rosettes until firm, then lift them off the paper and store them frozen in a box. Use straight from the freezer for an instant dessert topping.

Herb butters Small cubes of butter flavoured with fresh herbs or spices are a handy way to liven up food in seconds. Soften the butter – don't melt it – mix in flavourings to taste, shape into small pats and freeze. Use thawed or frozen to top grilled steaks or chicken joints.

Testing an egg for freshness Dissolve 15ml (1 tbsp) of salt in 570ml (1 pint) of water, and lower the egg into it. A fresh egg will lie on the bottom on its side and a stale egg will float to the top (left). If the egg turns upright but does not float to the top it is still safe to eat, though it's not at its freshest.

Storing eggs
- Store eggs, pointed end down, in a fridge or a cool place.
- Leave them in the box, since the porous shells quickly pick up tastes and smells from other foods.
- Buy eggs in small quantities and use them up within a week or two, when they're at their freshest.
- Eggs usually work best in cooking if they're at room temperature, so take them out of the fridge about 30 minutes before you need them.

Leftover egg white or yolk Both whites and yolks will last for about three months if frozen. With whites, pour them into a small container and cover the surface with a circle of greaseproof paper. Yolks freeze better if you mix them with 2.5ml ($\frac{1}{2}$ tsp) of salt or sugar for every three yolks (make sure to label them so that you know what you've added).

Freezing yoghurt Bought yoghurt usually contains a stabilising ingredient and freezes well, but the homemade variety tends to separate on thawing. It's worth experimenting, however. Homemade yoghurt with added fruit or honey often freezes more successfully than plain, and it makes a good low-fat alternative to ice cream.

A supply of fresh milk If you find it hard to predict how much milk you're going to use, buy several extra cartons to keep in the freezer. Thaw them out as you need them.

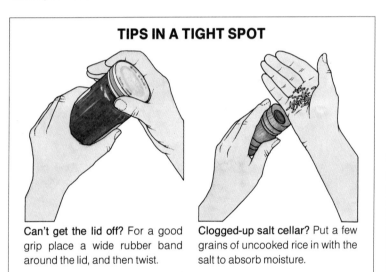

TIPS IN A TIGHT SPOT

Can't get the lid off? For a good grip place a wide rubber band around the lid, and then twist.

Clogged-up salt cellar? Put a few grains of uncooked rice in with the salt to absorb moisture.

Salt runs too fast? Unscrew the shaker top, wash it and leave to dry. Then use clear nail polish to block up some of the holes. When the polish is dry, replace the lid. If the salt still runs out too fast, block up a few more holes.

Short of an egg? If you need an extra egg for a cake recipe that uses either a raising agent or selfraising flour, you can replace the egg with 15ml (1 tbsp) of vinegar without affecting the result.

Cake stuck to the tin? Loosen the sides with a knife, place the tin on a wet cloth while still hot, and try again after a few minutes. If the cake is still stuck, try to loosen the base with a flipper or fish slice. Disguise any damage with cream or icing, or use the pieces for a trifle if it breaks.

Hard-boiled eggs crumble when you cut them? Try wetting the knife first for cleaner slices.

WHERE'S BEST FOR WINE?

Chilling white wine White wines and sparkling wines need only about an hour in the fridge to chill them. Don't keep any wine in the fridge for much longer, or it will lose its flavour.

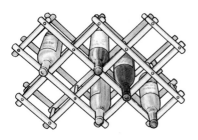

Storing wine If you're planning to keep wine for longer than just a few days, lay it horizontally so that the cork stays moist. A dry cork could let air into the bottle.

Wines vary in the length of time that they can be kept, but any wine you buy from a shop should be ready to drink, though many will still improve with time.

Unfinished bottle? If this is a common problem in your household, it may be worth buying a gadget such as 'Vacu-Vin' (right) to pump out the air and reseal the bottle. This should keep most wines drinkable for several days. Alternatively, freeze leftover wine in an ice-cube tray, and use it to flavour casseroles, gravies or sauces.

Laying down wine The older a wine is, the more expensive it tends to be, so you can save money by buying younger wines that age well and letting them mature at home. Read the label for guidance, or ask for advice from staff at a specialist wine shop.

To age wine successfully, a suitable storage place is essential. Ideally, wine should be stored in a dark, clean place with a constant temperature of about 10-15°C (50-59°F), away from any vibration. If you can't provide these conditions, don't invest a lot of money in laying down wine.

Sherry, port and other fortified wine Store these drinks on their side to keep the corks moist. A few days before opening, gently stand the bottle upright to allow the sediment to settle at the bottom.

MAKE A HANDY HOLDER FOR STRING

Don't keep kitchen string at the back of a drawer where it's hard to reach when you need it. Buy a small plastic funnel and attach it to the wall so that it stays upright. Put the ball of string in the top of the funnel, with the loose end trailing out of the spout.

Tips for easy cooking

GETTING THE MEASURES RIGHT

Measuring spoons To be sure of getting exact quantities, buy a set of British Standard measuring spoons and use level measures. Ordinary spoons vary in size and aren't reliable. For quick metric conversion, a standard tablespoon is roughly equivalent to about 15ml ($\frac{1}{2}$fl oz) and a teaspoon to about 5ml.

American recipes American measures are different, so convert to metric or Imperial before you start following a recipe. An American pint is 475ml (16fl oz) and a cup measure is 225ml (8fl oz). The standard American tablespoon is similar to the British: about 15ml ($\frac{1}{2}$fl oz). For quick converting:

1 cup butter = 225g (8oz)
1 cup flour = 150g (5oz)
1 cup grated cheese = 115g (4oz)
1 cup breadcrumbs = 50g (2oz)

Sticky situations Ingredients such as honey, syrup and treacle are easily measured out if you place the whole tin or jar on the scales and note its weight. Subtract the weight you want from the weight of the tin and spoon out the contents until the scales show the correct weight. You'll find measuring by spoon easier if you slightly warm the tin and the spoon beforehand.

Liquid measures Use measuring spoons for small quantities of milk, water, oil and other liquids:
1 tablespoon = 15ml ($\frac{1}{2}$fl oz)
2 tablespoons = 35ml ($1\frac{1}{4}$fl oz)
8 tablespoons = 140ml (5fl oz)
    For larger amounts, use a measuring jug, or improvise:
1 average-sized teacup or small yoghurt pot = 150ml ($5\frac{1}{4}$fl oz)
1 milk bottle = 1 pint (570ml)

Weights missing from scales? Small weights are easily mislaid and expensive to replace, but did you know that the change in your pocket could be a handy alternative? For metric scales, a 20p coin weighs exactly 5g and a £1 coin a little under 10g. If your scale is Imperial, you can use a 2p piece for a $\frac{1}{4}$oz weight and a 1p piece for a $\frac{1}{8}$oz weight.

WEIGHING WITHOUT SCALES

Smaller amounts of some ingredients are best measured in tablespoons. The quantities below are all equal to about 25g (1oz) in weight.

INGREDIENTS	LEVEL TABLESPOONS
Almonds,	
flaked	3
ground	$3\frac{1}{2}$
Breadcrumbs,	
fresh	7
dried	3
Butter and	
margarine	2
Cheddar,	
grated	3
Chocolate,	
grated	$3\frac{1}{2}$
Cocoa	$2\frac{1}{2}$
Coconut	
desiccated	4
Cornflour	$2\frac{1}{2}$
Currants and	
raisins	2
Curry powder	5
Flour	3
Porridge oats	4
Rice, uncooked	2
Sugar,	
granulated	2
caster	2
icing	$2\frac{1}{2}$
Syrup	1
Yeast granules	$1\frac{1}{2}$

CONVERTING INTO METRIC

Most cookbooks give both metric and Imperial measures, but older books and passed-on recipes often rely on ounces and pints.

OUNCES	GRAMMES (APPROX)
1	25
2	50
3	75
4 ($\frac{1}{4}$lb)	115
5	150
6	175
7	200
8 ($\frac{1}{2}$lb)	225
9	250
10	275
11	300
12 ($\frac{3}{4}$lb)	350
13	375
14	400
15	425
16 (1lb)	450

FLUID OUNCES	MILLILITRES (APPROX)
$\frac{1}{2}$	15
1	25
2	50
3	90
4	115
5 ($\frac{1}{4}$ pint)	140
6	175
7	200
8	225
9	250
10 ($\frac{1}{2}$ pint)	285
11	315
12	345
13	375
14	400
15 ($\frac{3}{4}$ pint)	450
16	475
17	490
18	520
19	550
20 (1 pint)	570

MAKING THE MOST OF MEAT

How to cut meat Cut steaks or strips of meat across the grain so that you avoid pieces with long fibres. You'll preserve the shape, and the meat will be more tender when cooked.

Better browning Before you fry or sauté meat, pat it dry with absorbent kitchen paper. Moisture could cause spitting and prevent browning.

Meat curls up during cooking? Steaks, chops and bacon rashers will lie flat if you slash the fatty edges with a sharp knife before cooking.

Tying up a joint Use strong, thin cotton string to tie up meat for the oven. Many synthetic strings will melt.

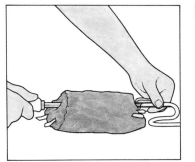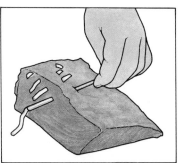

Larding Very lean fillets of beef or veal benefit from larding with pork fat to make the meat less dry. Buy larding fat from a butcher, trim it into strips about 5mm ($\frac{1}{4}$in) thick and thread it through the meat at 50mm (2in) intervals using a larding needle.

Skewers Metal skewers are best for grilling, as wooden ones tend to char, but both sorts are suitable for using in the oven. If you want to use wooden skewers on a barbecue, soak them in water for a few minutes first to prevent charring.

Guard of honour or crown roast of lamb The exposed bone ends won't burn if you cover each one with foil before cooking. When the roast is done, remove the pieces of foil and replace them with cutlet frills to make the chops easier to pick up, or with cherries or baby onions to decorate the joint for a special occasion.

Marinating

There's nothing like a marinade to tenderise meat and add flavour. Here are two basic mixtures which will provide enough marinade for four to six servings of meat or fish.

● Marinade for red meat: mix together in a bowl 570ml (1 pint) red wine, 50ml (2fl oz) olive or sunflower oil, 50ml (2fl oz) red wine vinegar, 1 peeled and thinly sliced onion and 12 whole black peppercorns. Pour it over the meat and leave for at least two hours, or preferably overnight, turning once or twice.

● Marinade for poultry and fish: combine 150-285ml ($\frac{1}{4}$-$\frac{1}{2}$ pint) olive oil with the juice of half a lemon, two bay leaves crumbled into pieces and 5ml (1 teaspoon) of dried thyme, oregano or mixed herbs. Pour over the meat or fish and leave for two hours or longer, turning occasionally.

Marinade spilling? Try putting both marinade and meat into a clean plastic food bag inside a bowl, rather than just loose in the bowl. That way, you should be able to turn over the pieces without slopping the liquid.

Carefree carving A shoulder of lamb is easily carved if you loosen the blade bone before roasting. Cut around the blade as closely as possible on both sides without removing it. The meat will shrink away from the bone during cooking, leaving the carver with a much simpler task.

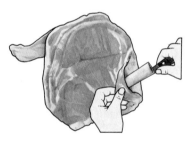

Flattening escalopes If you haven't got a meat hammer, place the escalopes between sheets of plastic wrap or non-stick kitchen paper and pound them with a wooden rolling pin or the bottom of a small, heavy frying pan or saucepan.

Skimming off fat Don't waste time trying to siphon off liquid fat from a stock, soup or stew. Cool the food, then refrigerate it until the fat sets solid, when you can lift it off.

Fresh herbs for flavour Flavour a joint by rubbing it with crushed fresh herbs such as rosemary, thyme, oregano, basil or garlic before cooking. You can also make slits in the flesh and poke in small cloves of garlic or sprigs of herbs.

Mince without mess When making mince at home, attach a plastic food bag to the mincer outlet with a rubber band. You'll catch the meat neatly as it comes out and prevent spills.

Making mince go farther Add a handful of oatmeal or porridge oats to a Bolognese sauce or shepherd's pie to make more of the meat. It's economical, rich in fibre and thickens the juices a little.

PREPARING POULTRY

Jointing a chicken

It is cheaper to buy a whole chicken and joint it yourself than to buy prepared joints, and you end up with pieces such as the back which can be turned into stock.

Jointing takes only a few minutes with a knife, and even less if you have poultry shears.

1 First remove the legs. Pull each leg in turn away from the chicken body and cut down to the thigh joint (the top joint where the leg joins the body). Twist the thigh to break the joint, and cut through it to detach the leg.

Cut each leg in half through the 'knee' joint to separate the thigh from the drumstick, cutting along the thin strip of fat that you will see on the underneath of the joint.

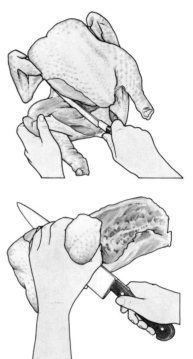

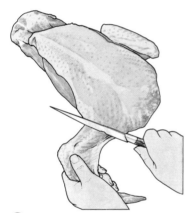

2 Pull the wing on one side away from the body. Slice through the top joint where the wing joins the body, to separate the wing. Repeat on the other side. If you wish to remove the wing tips, use a heavy-bladed knife.

3 Hold the top of the chicken firmly with one hand, and cut horizontally across the body from the tail end towards the neck to separate the breast from the back. Use a larger knife or poultry shears to cut through the rib bones.

4 Place the breast piece, skin side up, on a chopping board and cut down on one side of the breast bone to divide the two breasts. If necessary, tap the back of the knife with a heavy weight to break through the bone.

The chicken is now jointed into six good eating pieces: two drumsticks, two thighs and two breasts. The rest of the carcass will make good stock, although the wings are also very good roasted in the oven until crispy.

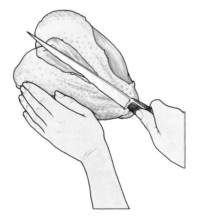

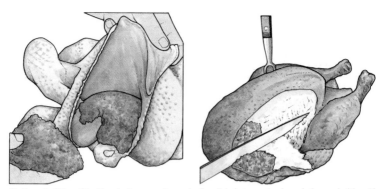

Safer stuffing Stuff only the neck end of a chicken or turkey (above left) – if you fill the whole cavity the stuffing may not cook all the way through. You'll be able to slice the stuffing together with the breast meat (above right) when the bird is cooked.

Fillers for flavour Before roasting a chicken or turkey, place an unpeeled whole apple or peeled whole onion in the cavity, together with a few sprigs of fresh herbs. The flesh will be moist and the juices full of flavour.

Quick fix Next time you want a tasty coating for chicken joints and you're in a hurry, try a packet of stuffing mix. It's ready seasoned, so just dip the pieces of chicken in beaten egg, then toss them in the stuffing mix until well coated, and bake or fry as usual.

Finishing touches To pep up a plain roast chicken, slide lemon slices, fresh herbs, seasoned butter or sliced mushrooms under the skin before cooking. Slide your fingers in under the skin at the neck end and loosen the skin all the way down the breast. Roast the bird as usual (page 574), and you'll have a dish that not only looks good, but one with a delicious flavour as well.

● Alternatively, make small cuts in the flesh with the point of a knife and push in slices of garlic to flavour the meat.

SIMPLE WAYS WITH SEAFOOD

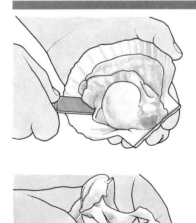

Scallops To open scallops, place them with the rounded side down in an oven at about 150°C (300°F/ Gas Mark 2). After a few moments they should open up enough to allow you to insert a sharp knife and run it along to cut free the flat shell.

Hold the scallop under running water and slide the knife under the membrane that attaches the scallop to the shell (above left). Cut the scallop free, and discard the brownish, frilled membranes and black intestinal thread (left), leaving only the white flesh and the orange 'coral'.

Scallops should always be cooked very gently to prevent them becoming tough.

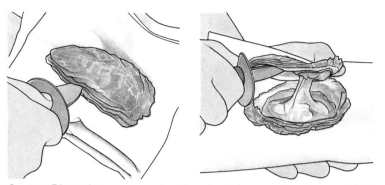

Oysters Discard any open oysters that don't close up when tapped. Hold each closed oyster firmly with a cloth, flat side up, and with the hinged end towards you. Insert the tip of an oyster knife, or any short, strong knife, into the small gap in the hinge and twist the blade to separate the two halves of the shell. Slide the knife along to sever the muscle holding the shell together. Discard the upper shell and loosen the oyster.

● If oysters are hard to open, soak them in soda water for five minutes – it seems to relax the muscle that holds them closed.

Mussels Before cooking pull away the wiry 'beard' which sprouts from the shell of the mussel. Discard any mussels which are already open, or are floating on the top of the water, or which do not close up when tapped. They are probably dead and unsuitable for eating. Scrub the shells of the live, closed mussels with a stiff brush under cold running water, and scrape off any barnacles.

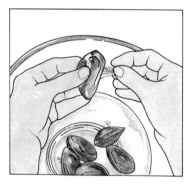

CLEANING FISH

Wherever you buy your fish, cleaning, gutting and filleting are almost always best left to the experts. Most fish in supermarkets are sold as ready-to-cook fillets, and if you buy a whole fish, staff at the fish counter should offer to clean it for you. The same applies to any good fishmonger. Tell them if you want the fish's head left on or taken off.

Serving a cooked lobster

1 Lay the lobster on a board and twist off the large claws and all the legs. Hold it the right way up, with the tail extended.

With a large, heavy, sharp knife pierce the shell where the head meets the body and cut the lobster completely in half down its entire length. If necessary, hit the back of the knife with a heavy weight, such as a wooden rolling pin, to help crack the shell. Split the head in two in the same way.

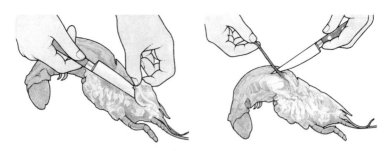

2 Pull the two halves of the lobster apart. Remove the transparent stomach sac and gills from the head sections, and the grey-black intestine which runs down the body.

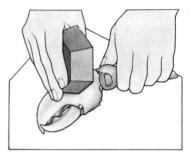

3 Crack the claws carefully with a hammer, a heavy scale weight, a rolling pin or a nut-cracker, and extract the meat with a thin-bladed knife or skewer. Remove the firm, white tail meat and scoop out the remaining soft, creamy meat from the body. Season to taste and arrange all the meat back in the shell for serving.

HOW TO PREPARE VEGETABLES

Skinning green and red peppers Place them directly on the shelf of an oven preheated to 180°C (350°F/Gas Mark 4) for about 20-25 minutes, when the skin should be blistered and cracked. Or scorch the peppers under a hot grill, turning frequently, until the skin is blistered all over – about ten minutes. Remove the peppers from the oven or grill and place them in a loosely tied plastic bag for about five minutes. Rub them together in the bag to loosen the skin; then peel it off.

Skinning tomatoes If you have a gas hob, spear the tomato on a fork and hold it in a gas flame until the skin blisters and splits. It will then be easy to peel. If you don't have gas, plunge the tomatoes into a pot of boiling water for a few seconds until the skin splits. Rinse in cold water, and then carefully peel off the skin.

Globe artichokes Hold the artichoke firmly on the edge of a table and push down hard on the stem to break it off. This will pull out the tougher fibres at the same time. Trim the spiky tops off lower leaves with a pair of scissors and then cut off about 12mm ($\frac{1}{2}$in) of the leafy top with a knife.

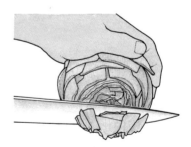

Slicing a tomato Use a bread knife or other serrated knife, and you'll cut through the skin without squashing the tomato.

Faster garlic There's no need to peel a single clove of garlic before you crush it. But if you're using several, peel them first or you'll block the crusher with the skins.

Peeling shallots and small onions Blanch the vegetables in boiling water for a minute. Drain them and trim off any stalks and roots you can see. Then pull away the skins.

Getting grit out of leeks It's easier to remove grit from leeks if you slice them into rings before rinsing. If you want to keep the leeks whole, soak for a few minutes in cold water, then slit them lengthways down the centre, stopping short of the base. Wash well under running water.

Bitter aubergines? Cut the flesh into cubes or slices, place in a colander and sprinkle with salt. Leave it to stand over a bowl for about 30 minutes, then rinse and dry with absorbent kitchen paper. Use as directed in the recipe. The bitter juices will have been drawn out, and you'll find the aubergine absorbs less oil during cooking.

Pumpkin without the strings Use an electric mixer to mash cooked pumpkin. The fibres will stick to the beaters as they turn, leaving you with a smooth pumpkin paste.

Don't battle to peel raw pumpkin The skin comes off easily once it's cooked. Cut the pumpkin into chunks and steam, skin and all, for about seven minutes; then peel. Alternatively, bake the pumpkin whole: one and a half hours at 180°C (350°F/Gas Mark 4) is about right for a pumpkin 300mm (12in) across. When ready, cut off the top, scoop out the seeds, cut into slices and remove the skin.

Corn on the cob Remove the silks from fresh corn by pulling away the outer husk with as many of the strands as possible, and then scrubbing with a vegetable brush under cold running water. To revive a wilted cob, cut a slice from the stalk end and stand it upright in cold water for about an hour.

If onions disagree with you Before you give up on this tasty vegetable try pouring boiling water over peeled and chopped onions and leaving them to soak for about a minute. Drain off the water and use the onions as the recipe directs. Many people find that the problem disappears.

Onions too strong for a salad? For a milder flavour, soak the rings in cold water for about an hour, then drain before using.

Cutting onions without tears Cut off the top end of the onion only, leaving the root end intact. Peel back the skin over the roots and use it as a handle while you slice. It's thought the milky juice at the root end causes tears.

Getting rid of celery strings Use a potato peeler to remove the strings from each stalk of celery, whether you are planning to cook it or eat it raw. For crudité, to serve with dips, cut the celery into similar-sized sticks once the strings are removed.

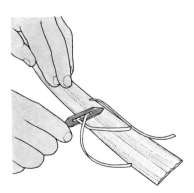

Jerusalem artichokes If possible, peel Jerusalem artichokes after cooking – it saves nutrients and makes the job easier. If you do need to peel them first, use a stainless-steel peeler or knife, and put the peeled artichokes straight into water with a squeeze of lemon juice added to stop them turning pinky-grey.

Too late to soak dried beans overnight? Speed up the soaking process by placing the beans in a pan with enough water to cover. Bring to the boil for two minutes. Remove from the heat and leave to soak for an hour. Drain and cook as usual.

If beans cause wind It may help to throw away the soaking water rather than adding it to the recipe. In addition, try bringing the beans to the boil and simmering them for ten minutes before draining off the water and cooking them as usual.

Serving an avocado pear

Believe it or not, there *is* an easy way to get an avocado neatly out of its skin. Follow these steps and you won't end up with a shapeless mess:

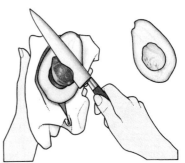

1 Use a stainless-steel knife to cut the avocado in half lengthways. Cut through as far as the stone all the way around the fruit. Twist the two halves gently in opposite directions in order to separate them.

2 Remove the stone from the halved avocado by striking it sharply with a sharp knife so that the blade lodges in the stone. Give the knife a quick twist and the stone should come free of the soft flesh without damage or mess.

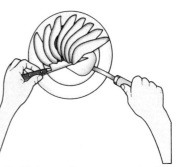

3 Carefully peel the skin off one half, or remove it with a paring knife if it does not come away easily. Place the skinned half, cut side down, on a chopping board and cut it into thin slices with a small knife. Do not separate the slices as you cut them.

4 Slide a cake server under the sliced avocado half and transfer it carefully to a serving plate. Gently fan out the slices as you push them onto the plate. Sprinkle with lemon juice to prevent browning. Then peel, slice and serve the other half.

MAKING THE BEST USE OF FRUIT

More juice from citrus fruit Oranges, lemons and other citrus fruit will yield more juice if you warm them first. Before squeezing, either pour boiling water over the fruit and leave it to stand for five minutes or if you have a microwave oven, give it 30 seconds on High (100 per cent power).

Removing currant stems You don't have to pick redcurrants or blackcurrants from their stems individually. Simply hold each bunch of fruit over a bowl and draw the prongs of a fork through it to pull off the currants. Or freeze the fruit on the stem, place it in a plastic bag and break off the stalks by rubbing the currants together.

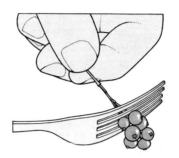

To stop cut apple turning brown Sprinkle the cut pieces with lemon juice or if you're cooking the apple add a little lemon juice to the pan.

Not sure how many lemons to buy? Calculate the number of lemons you need according to how much juice your recipe calls for. An average lemon produces about 70ml (4tbsp).

Dried-out lemon Cover the lemon with boiling water and leave it to stand for five minutes, then squeeze. You may still get a surprising amount of juice out of it.

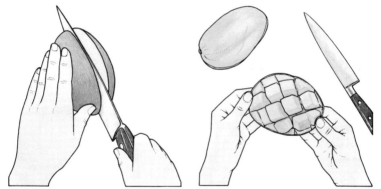

How to serve a mango First find out which way the stone lies by placing the mango on a flat surface and watching how it falls – the stone will always be parallel to the surface. With a sharp knife, cut through the mango on one side of the stone, to remove a thick slice. Score the flesh into squares, cutting down to but not breaking the skin. Push the slice inside out so that the cubes come off the skin. Repeat on the other side.

If oranges are difficult to peel Pour boiling water over the oranges and leave them to stand for five minutes. Drain, and allow to cool. The peel should come away easily and the fruit should readily divide into segments.

Segmenting an orange With a knife, remove the rind and all the white pith from the orange. Then, holding it over a bowl to catch the juice, cut out each segment by slicing down between the flesh of the segment and the membranes separating it from the adjoining segments on either side. Work round the orange until all the segments are removed and only a soft core of membranes remains. Squeeze out the core to extract the remaining juice.

KNOWING ABOUT NUTS

Removing hazelnut skins Bake the shelled nuts on a tray in a hot oven or in a microwave until the skins split, or toast them under a hot grill, shaking occasionally. Rub the nuts in a dry cloth to remove the skins.

Chestnut skins To get rid of the skins, slit the chestnuts with a sharp knife down one side. Place them in boiling water and bring slowly back to the boil. Drain and peel the chestnuts while they are still hot, and scrape away the inner skins at the same time.

If you have a microwave oven, slit the skins, place the chestnuts in an open container and microwave them on High (100 per cent power) for one or two minutes, stirring once. Return any which do not peel easily for a further 30 seconds.

Brazil nuts The shells will crack more easily and you will be less likely to break the nuts inside if you give them several hours in the freezer before cracking.

Cracking a coconut The easiest way to crack a coconut is to find its natural fault line. First pierce the eyes with a skewer or a corkscrew and pour out the liquid. Hold the coconut with one hand and turn it round while you tap along the 'equator' with a kitchen steel or a hammer. Eventually a crack will appear. Keep tapping until the coconut breaks.

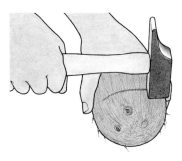

Blanching almonds Place the nuts in boiling water for 30 seconds, drain and pinch off the skins.

Ground almonds Freshly crushed almonds have a much better flavour than the ready-ground nuts sold in packets. Grind your own blanched almonds whenever you need them in a food processor.

Cooking with whole almonds If you want the nuts to stay crisp in a cake or cooked dish, toast or roast them until light golden-brown first.

USING DAIRY PRODUCTS

Butter curls Elegant curls are easy to make if you first dip the curler into warm water. Pull it lightly across a block of firm butter; then drop the curls into a bowl of iced water and store them in the fridge.

Milk in a vacuum flask Keeping milk hot for any length of time subtly alters its taste, which is why drinks from a vacuum flask can taste different. Most people don't mind the change in coffee or cocoa, but find it unpleasant in tea. To avoid the problem, put black tea into the flask and take a separate container of milk to add when you're ready to drink it – or use a non-dairy milk substitute.

Easier whipped cream You'll save time and effort if you chill the whipping bowl and beaters or whisk in the freezer before you begin.

556

EGGS WITHOUT EFFORT

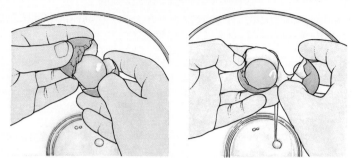

Separating yolk and white Tap the egg sharply against the edge of a mixing bowl, or rap it with the back of a knife to crack the shell. Hold the egg upright over a bowl and carefully pull the shell apart. The white should run out into the bowl, leaving the yolk in the bottom half. Gently tip the yolk back and forth between the two halves of the shell until all the white has run out.

If a small piece of shell or a speck of yolk gets into the white, use an empty half shell to remove it.

Coating food with egg An egg will go further but still work as well for coating if you beat in 15ml (1tbsp) of oil.

Boiling eggs To prevent cracking, take eggs from the fridge about half an hour before boiling, so that they warm up. It also helps to pierce the rounded end of the shell with a pin to let air escape during cooking.

If an egg does crack, quickly add two tablespoons of vinegar or salt to the water to set the white.

Whipping egg whites Use a clean, dry bowl without any trace of grease. Whip eggs at room temperature for a greater volume of whipped white. And don't whisk the whites before you need them – the structure breaks down when they're left to stand, and they won't whip up as well again.

Make double cream go further Add one egg white for every 285ml ($\frac{1}{2}$ pint) of cream before whipping. It also whips more easily and gives a greater volume if you add 15ml (1tbsp) of milk to every 150ml ($\frac{1}{4}$ pint) of cream.

For a fluffier cream Whip in a little sifted icing sugar with the cream for a fluffier result and cream that's less likely to separate. Use 5ml (1tsp) to 150ml ($\frac{1}{4}$ pint) of cream.

Piped cream Whip the cream until it just holds its shape. The heat of your hand and the effort of forcing it through the piping bag will cause it to stiffen further.

Cream gone sour? Don't throw it away: add it to shortcrust pastry for a light, crumbly texture and a delicious flavour. Rub the fat into the flour as usual; then stir in 70ml (4tbsp) of soured cream to every 225g (8oz) of pastry and add water to bind.

No-mess grating Place grater and cheese inside a plastic bag and grate, holding the cheese and grater from the outside. To avoid the cheese crumbling on the grater, chill it thoroughly before attempting to grate it.

Ripening soft cheeses Slightly underripe soft cheeses such as Brie and Camembert can be ripened by placing them in a microwave oven set to Defrost. Fifteen to 30 seconds is long enough for a 75g (3oz) piece.

Substitutes for dairy products

Buttermilk Mix together 175ml (6fl oz) of natural yoghurt and 50ml (2fl oz) of milk for a substitute of similar consistency.

Crème fraiche Make your own by mixing 285ml ($\frac{1}{2}$ pint) soured cream with 450ml (15fl oz) double cream. Cover and leave to stand at room temperature for several hours, or until it thickens; then refrigerate. Don't use UHT cream; it won't work.

Sour cream Add 15ml (1tbsp) lemon juice to 285ml ($\frac{1}{2}$ pint) single cream.

Single cream You can make cream at home by melting together 125g ($4\frac{1}{2}$oz) unsalted butter with 150ml ($\frac{1}{4}$ pint) milk. Heat gently but do not boil. Then blend it in a liquidiser or food processor for ten seconds. Leave to cool, stirring occasionally.

Whipping cream Heat together 125g ($4\frac{1}{2}$oz) unsalted butter with 285ml ($\frac{1}{2}$pint) creamy milk until the butter is melted, but do not allow the mixture to boil. Sprinkle 2.5ml ($\frac{1}{2}$tsp) of gelatine powder over the top, and stir until dissolved. Blend in a food processor for ten seconds. Chill until firm.

HAVING TROUBLE WITH MAYONNAISE?

Curdling Add 15ml (1tbsp) of boiling water to the mixture and beat hard. If it remains curdled, start again with a clean bowl and a fresh egg yolk. Very gradually beat the curdled mayonnaise into the new egg until you obtain a smooth consistency.

Mixture's too thick Thin it down with a little warm water or single cream.

Allergic to eggs, or just want a low-fat alternative? Try tofu (soya bean curd) mayonnaise: place 175g (6oz) tofu, 35ml (2tbsp) milk, 35ml (2tbsp) lemon juice and 15ml (1tbsp) sunflower or olive oil in a food processor or blender and mix until smooth. Season to taste with salt and pepper.

THE KNIVES IN YOUR KITCHEN

The basic four A few high quality, well-chosen knives are an essential part of every cook's equipment. These four should be able to tackle most tasks in the ordinary kitchen, but you can always supplement them with more specialised tools for filleting, boning or carving, if necessary:
● Small paring knife with 75-90mm (3-3$\frac{1}{2}$in) blade: for paring and cutting small fruits and vegetables.
● Cook's knife with 125-180mm (5-7in) blade: for general peeling, paring and chopping.
● Cook's knife with 200-230mm (8-9in) blade: for chopping, slicing and dicing.
● Serrated bread knife with 255mm (10in) blade.

How to choose a knife The best knives are made from a solid piece of steel ground down to give a blade and tang (the part of the blade that is embedded in the handle). Look for knives with a tang that extends all or almost all of the way down the handle, and that is firmly riveted into place. Avoid knives which have only a short piece of blade glued into the handle.
  Choose a blade cast from high quality carbon steel or stainless steel.

Carbon steel knives hold a fine cutting edge for longer, but easily rust and stain. They can also discolour fruits such as apples, pears and lemons, and may taint the flavour. Stainless steel needs more frequent sharpening, but resists most stains and won't affect the taste of fruit.

Sharpening kitchen knives

To keep a sharp knife in tiptop condition, run it through a manual or electric sharpener before every use, or give it three or four light strokes on each side on a steel. If the knife has been neglected for a long time and the blade is very dull, run it through the sharpener several times, or use a steel and apply a heavier pressure for up to 15 or 20 strokes.

Have your knives professionally sharpened about once every two years or when home sharpening no longer gives a good cutting edge. Look in your local Yellow Pages under 'Hardware retailers', or ask at kitchen shops, key-cutters, tool and lawnmower repair services.

Sharpening on a steel

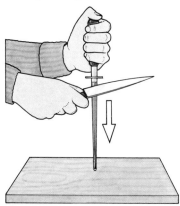

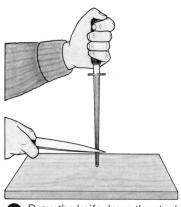

1 Hold the steel, point down, on a non-slip board. Place the widest part of the blade edge at the top of the steel and hold it at an angle of about 45°.

2 Draw the knife down the steel, keeping the same angle but sliding across the blade, so that when it reaches the bottom, the tip is against the steel.

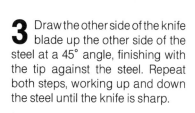

3 Draw the other side of the knife blade up the other side of the steel at a 45° angle, finishing with the tip against the steel. Repeat both steps, working up and down the steel until the knife is sharp.

Looking after your knives

● Use a wood or polypropylene chopping board, which will not blunt the blade.
● Never use a good kitchen knife for cutting paper or string, or for prising off lids.

● Store knives in a knife block or in a magnetic knife rack.
● Don't hold a knife blade over an open flame – you will ruin the temper of the steel.
● Hand-wash carbon steel knives immediately after use to prevent staining. Remove small marks with a nylon scouring pad, and more serious stains with the flat end of a wet cork dipped in a powder cleaner.
● Rub carbon steel blades with a drop of cooking oil after washing and drying, to protect them from water vapour and steam in the kitchen.

KITCHEN HYGIENE CHECKLIST

● Get everyone into the habit of washing their hands in hot, soapy water before touching food and after using the lavatory, stroking pets or handling raw meat.
● Keep knives and food preparation surfaces clean and dry at all times.
● Don't use the same utensils or chopping boards for cooked and raw foods without washing them in between.
● Don't handle cooked meat after raw, without first washing your hands in hot, soapy water.
● Make sure that all meat, fish and poultry dishes are thoroughly cooked or heated up before eating.
● Use non-porous polypropylene chopping boards rather than wooden ones, which may harbour bacteria.
● Keep tea towels clean and use disposable paper towels for mopping up messes.
● Defrost frozen foods thoroughly, or they may not cook properly.
● Don't leave cooked food in a warm place. The bacteria will multiply much faster than if it's somewhere cool.
● Make sure rubbish bins are covered and don't allow pets into the kitchen. Keep pet feeding bowls separate from the other washing up.
● Throw away any chipped china. Bacteria can breed in the cracks.
● Never leave any food standing around uncovered. Hot food should be covered with a net to keep flies off, and bowls and jugs should have a plate or a piece of plastic wrap over them.
● Use a clean spoon each time you taste food.
● Wash cans before opening. They are often dusty, and many supermarkets spray the shelves with insecticide. Wash can openers whenever you use them to remove any food particles from the mechanism. Keep a separate opener for pet food.

TRUE OR FALSE?

Carrots help you see in the dark.
Partly true. The orange pigment in carrots – carotene – is vital for healthy eyesight. They body converts it into vitamin A, which is essential for some eye functions, and helps to prevent infections of the eyes, nose and throat.

Fish is good for the brain.
False. Fish is a highly nutritious food, but it doesn't have any special effects on the brain.

Honey is a 'miracle' food.
False. Honey is a combination of glucose and fructose (both types of sugar) and water, with vitamins and enzymes in very small quantities. It gives you energy, but not much else.

TIPS FOR BETTER BAKING

Baking 'blind' Bake pastry bases separately before filling them, to prevent sogginess or undercooking. Line a dish with pastry, then place a piece of foil or crumpled greaseproof paper gently on top of the pastry. The paper or foil should be large enough to cover all the pastry. Sprinkle a layer of beans or rice on top to weigh down the paper, or use ceramic baking 'beans' bought from a kitchen shop. Bake for 10-15 minutes at  200°C (400°F/Gas Mark 6), then remove the rice or beans and the paper. Return to the oven and cook for a further five minutes.

Oven temperature Always bake pastry in a hot oven – about 200-230°C (400-450°F/Gas Mark 6-8). The richer the mixture, the hotter the oven should be, but very sweet pastry needs a slightly lower temperature – about 180-200°C (350-400°F/Gas Mark 4-6).

Choosing pastry dishes Metal dishes are best for pastry. They conduct heat much more efficiently than glass or ceramic, so you'll be less likely to end up with a soggy base. Place a preheated metal baking tray under the tin for even better results.

How much pastry do you need? Pastry is usually measured by the weight of flour the recipe uses, so 200g (7oz) of pastry means pastry made from 200g (7oz) of flour. Amounts needed depend on recipes, but here is a basic guide for open pie bases:
150-180mm (6-7in) base: 115g (4oz)
200-230mm (8-9in) base: 175g (6oz)
● 250g (9oz) of shortcrust pastry is enough for one medium double-crust pie, or 12 small double-crust tartlets.

Pepping up a pie If you want to give an extra touch of interest to a sweet or savoury pastry crust, try adding one of the ingredients below. All quantities are suitable for 200g (7oz) of rubbed-in shortcrust pastry:
● 40g (1½oz) grated Cheddar cheese.
● 25g (1oz) finely chopped nuts.
● 35ml (2tbsp) desiccated coconut.
● 5-10ml (1-2tsp) curry powder.
● 7.5-10ml (1½-2tsp) dried herbs.
● 5ml (1tsp) dry mustard powder.
● 35ml (2tbsp) toasted sesame seeds.
● Grated rind of an orange or lemon.
● 5ml (1tsp) mixed spice or cinnamon.
● 15ml (1tbsp) finely chopped stem ginger (fresh or preserved in syrup).

Apple pie Add cheese for an extra tang. Cut small cubes of Cheddar, Cheshire, Lancashire or Wensleydale, or grate it coarsely, and mix with the apples before you fill the pie. An average 450g (1lb) pie will need about 75g (3oz) of cheese.

Sticky dough Biscuit pastry and other sticky high-fat mixes will be easier to handle if you wet your hands first. Roll the pastry out between sheets of non-stick or waxed paper to avoid adding too much flour.

DO'S AND DON'TS FOR PERFECT PASTRY

DO choose a cool day for pastry-making. Or open windows to keep the kitchen cool.

DO keep all equipment and ingredients as cool as possible.

DO use only the tips of your fingers when rubbing in or handling pastry; they're the coolest part of your hand.

DO handle pastry as lightly as possible, and roll it out in one direction only. Be careful not to stretch the dough when turning it.

DO allow the pastry to 'rest' in the fridge for at least 15 minutes before rolling out, to prevent it shrinking in the oven.

DON'T guess quantities. Weigh all ingredients accurately.

DON'T add more than just enough water to bind the dough. Too much water makes pastry hard and tough.

DON'T flour the rolling-out surface and the rolling pin too heavily, or you will upset the balance of the recipe.

Cooking up a cake?

Keep the kitchen warm Most cakes do better if they are prepared at a temperature of 20°C (68°F) or more. If your equipment and ingredients have been stored in a cool place, take them out about two hours before you are ready to begin, so that they have time to warm up.

Using butter Unsalted butter will give your cake a better flavour.

Stop your mixing bowl from slipping Place a damp cloth underneath to hold it steady.

One-stage cakes All-in-one recipes for cakes are very quick to make, but they are suitable only for soft tub margarines, or softened butter or margarine. Don't beat the mixture too hard, or the texture will be heavy.

Out of chocolate? Don't panic: 50ml (3tbsp) of cocoa powder mixed with 15ml (1tbsp) of butter or margarine will do just as well.

Save time Next time you need a round of greaseproof paper to fit a favourite baking tin, cut out several of the right size so they're ready when you need them.

Caught short? If you suddenly find that your self-raising flour is coming to an end in the middle of a recipe, you can make up the difference with plain flour. Just add 12.5ml (2½tsp) of baking powder to each 225g (8oz) of plain flour and you'll get the same effect.

Candied peel gone dry and hard? Revive it with a one-to-two-minute soak in boiling water. Dry well and chop into the cake.

Keeping the fruit afloat Toss dried fruit in a little flour before adding it to a cake mix. The pieces will stay separate and be less likely to sink. Glacé fruit should be rinsed first and then floured.

Make your own baking powder For a mix that's just as good as the bought product and a good deal less expensive, sieve together: 25g (1oz) bicarbonate of soda, 25g (1oz) rice flour and 50g (2oz) cream of tartar. Stir well to mix and store in a screw-topped jar. Use in the same way as commercial baking powder.

Capacity of cake tins If you don't have the shape of tin called for in a recipe, just change to another tin of a similar capacity.

Capacity	Round tins	Square tins
1.1 litres (2 pints)	180mm (7in)	125mm (5in)
1.7 litres (3 pints)	200mm (8in)	180mm (7in)
2.3 litres (4 pints)	230mm (9in)	200mm (8in)
3.4 litres (6 pints)	250mm (10in)	230mm (9in)
4.5 litres (8 pints)	280mm (11in)	250mm (10in)
5.7 litres (10 pints)	300mm (12in)	280mm (11in)

Valentine cake You can make a heart-shaped cake without buying a special tin. Just bake two cakes, one round and one square, with the diameter of the round cake the same length as the side of the square one. When the cakes are cool, cut the round cake in half and place the halves against adjacent sides of the square cake to make a heart. Decorate with icing or fresh cream to disguise the joins.

How to fill a piping bag If you're having trouble, place the bag inside a measuring jug, turn the top of the bag over the rim of the jug, and fill with the piping mixture.

Easy greasing Save old butter and margarine wrappers to wipe round the inside of cake tins for handy, no-mess greasing. Store the wrappers in a plastic bag in the fridge if you don't need them immediately.

Don't get stuck The richer a cake mixture, the more you need to line the tin before baking. For a light sponge cake, simply grease the tin, then dust the inside lightly with flour. Victoria sandwich cakes need to be lined with a round of paper on the base. Richer fruit cakes should be baked in a fully lined tin. If you use non-stick silicone-coated paper you won't need to grease the tin or the lining.

Caster sugar substitute If you run out of caster sugar while cooking, use granulated sugar ground up in small batches in a food processor or blender. Process at high speed for a few seconds only.

HOW TO TELL WHEN A CAKE IS COOKED

Use one or more of the following tests:
● Press the top lightly with your fingertips. The surface should feel firm and springy when the cake is cooked.
● Examine the edges of the cake. If they're starting to shrink away from the tin, the cake is done.
● Listen to the cake. If you hear any bubbling or sizzling, it still needs a little more time in the oven.
● Pierce the centre of the cake with a skewer or an uncooked piece of spaghetti. Pull it out again slowly. If it comes out clean, you can take out the cake. If it doesn't, wait a little longer.

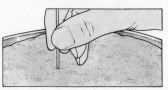

Easy ways to decorate a cake

Butter cream icing To make a rich icing suitable for almost any cake, beat together one part (by weight) butter to two parts icing sugar. Flavour with vanilla essence, orange or lemon juice and zest, instant coffee powder or cocoa dissolved in a little boiling water, or brandy or liqueur.

Glacé icing For a quick sponge cake topping, mix icing sugar with just enough fruit juice or liqueur to give a smooth but not runny consistency.

When you don't want icing Decorate a plain sponge cake without icing it by placing a lacy doily on top and sieving icing sugar over it. Remove the doily to leave a design on the cake.

Sugared flowers and fruit Use edible flowers, such as nasturtiums, violets or roses, or small fruits such as grapes and berries. Gently wash and dry them. When dry, brush with a little lightly beaten egg white and then dip them into caster sugar. Place on non-stick paper and allow to dry before using on the cake.

Chocolate leaves Pick a few well-shaped leaves such as rose or bay, wash them gently and allow to dry. Melt the chocolate and paint a thin, even layer on the underside of each leaf, spreading it right to the edges. When completely set, carefully lift off the chocolate, using the tip of a knife if necessary. The leaf vein will be marked on the chocolate. Store in a cool place until needed.

Fondant icing Ready-to-roll fondant icing can be bought from many supermarkets, or you can easily make your own. For enough icing to cover a 200mm (8in) cake, sieve 450g (1lb) icing sugar into a bowl. Make a well in the middle and pour in one egg white and 50ml (2fl oz) liquid glucose. Beat with a wooden spoon, gradually incorporating more and more icing sugar from the well edges. When well mixed and stiff, knead in a few drops of food colour if required, roll out, and lay over the cake.

MAKING YOUR OWN BREAD

If the kitchen's cold Put a little flour in the mixing bowl and warm it up in a very low oven before you begin – or microwave it on full power for ten seconds. You'll find the dough rises more easily.

Flowerpot loaves Terracotta flowerpots make good containers for baking bread, but they need to be seasoned first. Clean a 100-125mm (4-5in) pot thoroughly, oil the inside well with vegetable oil and place in a 190°C (375°F/Gas Mark 5) oven for 30 minutes. Allow to cool; then repeat and cool again before using. Grease the inside of the pot and sprinkle it with crushed wheat or wholemeal flour before putting in the dough.

Savoury special Add a teaspoon of garlic powder to the flour next time you're making bread. It gives a delicious flavour, especially when the bread's served warm or toasted.

Stop your crusts from cracking Use a sharp knife to cut shallow slashes in the top. Make the slashes at regular intervals, and bake as usual.

Bread without the effort A food processor or food mixer with a dough hook can do the kneading for you – and it's faster too. Follow the manufacturer's instructions and don't overload the machine.

How to tell when bread is cooked Correctly cooked bread should be golden-brown, well-risen and firm. If it looks ready, turn the loaf over and tap the base of the loaf with your knuckles – it should sound hollow. To crisp the sides and base, take the loaf out of its tin for the last five minutes of baking.

Instant pizza Use leftover French bread to make a quick pizza snack. Slice it horizontally, then sprinkle the bread with a little olive oil and cover with toppings such as sliced tomato, salami, ham, Mozzarella cheese, tuna, anchovies, olives and a sprinkling of chopped or dried herbs. Bake in a hot oven until crisp and golden.

WHEN YOU DON'T HAVE A . . .

Proper space to work Make extra space by laying large baking trays across pulled out kitchen drawers. Or place a big chopping board over the sink.

Baking tray Turn a roasting pan upside-down and use the bottom for baking biscuits or other pastry goods.

Steamer Use a metal colander placed inside a large pot with about 25mm (1in) of water in the bottom. Cover with a well-fitting lid, and check regularly to make sure the water hasn't boiled away. Or fit a large metal sieve across the top of a pot of boiling water and cover with the lid.

Piping bag Cut a small hole in one corner of a strong plastic food bag. Fill the bag with cream or icing, and pipe it out of the cut corner.

Biscuit cutter Use the rim of an inverted wine glass, or a jam-jar lid. Or roll out the dough and cut it into squares with a knife. This method has the advantage that you don't have to keep rolling out the scraps.

Corkscrew Drive a large screw well into the cork with a screwdriver. Tie a piece of string around the top of the screw and pull to remove the cork, or pull it out with a pair of pliers. Alternatively, screw a large hook or eye into the cork, then place the handle of a wooden spoon through the hook or eye and use it to pull out the cork.

Rolling pin Use a milk or wine bottle instead.

Lid for a pot Cover the top with aluminium foil crinkled down on the sides to keep in the steam, or cover with a plate.

Nutcracker Try cracking nuts with a wrench or pair of pliers, or place them on a chopping board and tap sharply with a heavy kitchen weight.

565

WHEN YOU DON'T HAVE A . . . (cont)

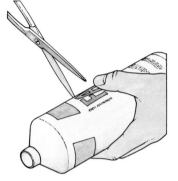 

Funnel Cut the top from an empty washing-up liquid bottle with a pair of kitchen scissors or a sharp knife. Wash it well, invert, and use as a funnel. Or use an empty tin to funnel liquids: wash the tin and punch a hole in the bottom at the rim.

Flour dredger A kitchen sieve will work just as well as a dredger to dust flour evenly onto your work surface or rolling pin. Alternatively, sprinkle the flour lightly through your fingertips to achieve the same result.

Kitchen apron Use a large plastic rubbish bag as a disposable apron. Cut holes for your head and arms, and throw out the bag when you're finished.

Knife sharpener The unglazed bottom of a mug makes a good stand-in sharpener. Hold the blade at a low angle to the unglazed surface and draw it slowly back and forth across the surface so that you sharpen down the whole length of the blade.

Fault-finder guide: baking

Baking problems usually have a cause that's easy to track down and put right. This chart shows the most likely reasons why things go wrong.

Fault	Causes
Cakes	
Cracked or peaked top	Too much raising agent. Cake tin too small. Mixture too wet or too dry. Oven too hot.
Sunken middle	Under-cooking or oven too cool. Too much raising agent. Mixture too wet. Over-creamed fat and sugar. Heavy beating after adding egg. Slamming oven door.
Hard, brown crust	Over-cooking or excessively hot oven. Too much sugar. Tin too large.
Crusty sides	Over-greased tin.
Dry, crumbly texture	Too much raising agent. Fat not well rubbed in or creamed. Mixture too dry. Baked too slowly.

Fault	Causes
Cakes (cont)	
Large holes, uneven texture	Over-mixing or uneven mixing. Raising agent and flour poorly blended.
Uneven rising	Oven not preheated. Oven or shelf not level. Cake not in centre of oven.
Fruit sunk to bottom	Mixture or fruit too wet. Glacé fruit too sticky. (Rinse and flour fruit before adding.) Fruit pieces too large and heavy. Too much raising agent. Oven too cool.
Shortcrust pastry	
Cooked: hard, tough texture	Not enough fat. Too much liquid. Over-handling. Cooking too slowly.
Raw: crumbly and difficult to handle; doesn't stick together	Too much fat. Wrong type of fat – usually too soft. Not enough liquid. Selfraising flour used.
Shrinkage during baking	Pastry stretched during rolling out. Not enough resting time. Pastry too wet.
Suet pastry	
Hard and tough	Too much liquid. Not enough raising agent. Oven too hot.
Puff/flaky pastry	
Hard and tough	Too much liquid. Oven too cool. Pastry not kept cool before baking. Fat heavily rolled in.
Poor rising, not flaky	Fat too warm. Not enough resting time. Oven too cool.
Soggy middle	Under-baking. Oven too hot.
Choux pastry	
Thin and shapeless	Ingredients wrongly measured. Water not boiling when flour mixed in. Inadequate beating. Egg added too quickly.
Too thick and heavy	Ingredients wrongly measured. Inadequate beating. Oven too cool.
Cracking	Oven too hot.

Fault-finder guide: baking (cont)

Fault	Causes
Batters, pancakes, puddings	
Heavy or soggy	Batter too thick. Fat or oven too cool. Too much batter. Under-cooked.
Puddings don't rise	Batter too thin. Too little egg. Oven too cool.
Pancakes tear	Batter too thin. Not enough egg.
Scones	
Dense, heavy texture	Over-handling of dough. Too much raising agent. Too much or not enough liquid. Oven too cool.
Uneven, rough surface	Too little kneading or mixing. Too little liquid or too much flour.
Scones spread out and lose shape	Too much liquid. Over-greased baking tray. Uneven kneading. Twisting cutter when cutting out.
Speckled surface	Flour and raising agent not well sieved. Too much sugar. Granulated sugar used instead of caster sugar.
Bread	
Top crust breaks away	Yeast not left to prove long enough. Surface dried out during proving. Oven too hot.
Pale crust and flat top	Cake flour used instead of bread (or 'strong') flour. Too little salt or yeast. Dough too wet. Not enough kneading.
Dough collapses in oven	Over-rising of yeast.
Coarse, uneven texture with large holes	Too much liquid. Over-rising. Not enough kneading after rising. Oven too cool.
Crumbly texture, and bread soon goes stale	Too much yeast. Cake flour used. Rapid rising in too warm a place. Under-rising or over-rising.
Sour, yeasty flavour and bread smells of alcohol	Over-rising. Too much yeast. Stale yeast or fresh yeast creamed with sugar instead of dissolved in tepid water.

RESCUING DISASTERS: CAKES AND BISCUITS

Dry fruit cake Pierce the cake with a skewer and pour about 35-70ml (2-4tbsp) brandy or fruit juice over it. Leave it to soak for 24 hours. Or crumble up the cake, mix with a little melted butter or cream, and a dash of brandy or rum. Pack the mixture tightly into a pudding basin and steam for about an hour. Serve as a rich pudding, with cream or custard.

Soft biscuits Biscuits or crackers that have lost their crunch can be revived by placing them on a baking tray in a hot oven for about five minutes. They will crisp up on cooling.

Burnt sponge cake If it's not too badly charred, cut off the burnt parts and sprinkle the cake lightly with sherry or fruit juice. Mask the damage with butter cream icing or fresh whipped cream, and decorate with nuts or toasted coconut. Alternatively, cut it up into cubes and use it in a trifle.

Cake undercooked or sunken in the middle Turn your disaster into a ring cake. Cut out the soggy centre with a sharp knife, using the rim of a small bowl or other round shape as a guide. Cover with almond paste or icing as usual. During the summer months, fill the centre with seasonal fruits such as strawberries, raspberries or redcurrants.

COOKING IN A MICROWAVE OVEN

Standard power ratings Almost all microwave ovens sold after September 1990 have been tested to standard specifications for power output. Check it has been tested to standards laid down by the International Electronic Technical Commission. Methods of rating older ovens vary. If in doubt, contact the manufacturer and ask for the new rating for your model.

Adjusting cooking times for different power ratings Cooking times given in recipes and on packs of prepared food usually assume a 600W or 650W oven. If your microwave has a higher or lower rating you will need to shorten or lengthen the time accordingly. There's no foolproof way of converting, as time also depends on oven capacity, but as a rough guide, lengthen the time by one-quarter for ovens of 500W or less, and reduce it by one-tenth for ovens of over 700W.

Find the hot spots Here's a simple test to reveal variations in oven temperature. Cover the floor of the oven with slices of white bread with the crusts removed. Set the oven to High (100 per cent power) and watch through the door to see where the bread browns fastest.

Microwave cookware

What's safe to use? Non-metallic containers such as glass, china, earthenware, some plastics and polystyrene are best – as well as anything manufactured for microwave use or labelled 'microwave-safe'.

Avoid metal containers. The microwaves will bounce off them, creating a flashing effect known as 'arcing' which can damage the oven.

WHAT DOES A MICROWAVE DO WELL
– AND NOT SO WELL?

GOOD	POOR
Reheating food	Pastry
Defrosting	Batters such as Yorkshire pudding
Melting chocolate	Cheaper cuts of meat which need long,
Dissolving gelatine	slow cooking
Smooth sauces	Large joints of meat
Vegetables	Rich fruit cakes
Softening butter	Meringues
Cooking fish	Frying (temperature cannot be safely con-
Scrambling eggs	trolled)
Making porridge	Foods which require browning
Shelling nuts	Soufflés
Peeling tomatoes and	
onions	
Baking potatoes	
Stewing fruit	

Note Some microwave ovens have a browning element which increases their versatility. Combined microwave/conventional ovens will be able to cook all foods well.

Plastic precautions Don't cook foods rich in fat or sugar in plastic. The high temperatures they reach could melt the container.

Wood and wicker Microwaving dries out the natural oils in wood and wicker, and wicker has been known to catch alight, so avoid using them in a microwave.

Not sure if a dish is suitable? Before you risk a favourite dish or a special piece of china, try this simple test: place the empty container in the oven with a small glass of water standing in the centre. Heat for a minute on High (100 per cent power). If the water heats up but the dish stays cold, you can safely use it in your oven. If the container is hot and the water cool, don't use it.

Cook-in bags Use boiling, roasting or special microwave cooking bags to keep food juicy and your oven clean. Always pierce the top of the bag first, to allow steam to escape.

Bigger is better Choose a slightly larger container for microwave cooking than you would otherwise use. This gives liquids room to boil without spilling, and makes stirring or turning easier.

Round or square? Round dishes are much better for microwaving than square or rectangular dishes, which have a tendency to overcook food in the corners.

How deep? Choose a shallow, open dish for faster cooking. It exposes a greater surface area of food to the microwaves.

FOOD SAFETY FOR MICROWAVE USERS

● Cook food taken straight from the fridge for a little longer than food at room temperature.

● Read and follow the instructions on the pack when microwaving frozen or chilled products. Check that the instructions apply to your oven's power rating. If they do not, adjust the cooking time – see page 569.

● Stir runny foods such as casseroles and sauces occasionally to ensure even heating. Bubbling doesn't necessarily mean the food is heated all the way through.

● Don't be tempted to try to cook a lot of dishes at one time in a microwave oven. They will cook faster and more evenly one at a time.

● Allow for standing times where they are given in recipes. This will ensure that the food is evenly heated right through.

● Follow closely all recipe instructions for turning food by hand, stirring, or using an oven's automatic turntable. Food may not cook properly if you ignore these directions.

● Test food with your finger or a microwave thermometer to make sure it is hot all the way through before serving. If parts are only cool or warm, return the food to the oven for a little longer.

● When recipes give a range of cooking times, cook the food for the shorter time, then check to see if it is done. If not, return it to the oven for the remainder of the time, checking frequently.

● See page 127 for more information on using a microwave oven safely.

Making the most of your microwave

Ring cakes Ring-shaped moulds are ideal for making cakes in a microwave oven, as mixtures cook quickly and evenly. If you don't have a mould, use an ordinary microwave-safe mould or dish and place a jam jar in the centre, half-filled with water.

Perfect bacon Rashers of bacon cook quickly and cleanly by microwave. Place the rashers side by side on a piece of kitchen paper and fold over or place another piece of kitchen paper on top. The timing depends on the thickness and size of the slices, but 30 seconds on High (100 per cent power) is usually enough for one rasher, or 45 seconds for two.

Easy hollandaise sauce Place 25g (1oz) butter in a 570ml (1 pint) heatproof jug. Cook on High (100 per cent power) for 30 seconds or until melted. Beat in 2 egg yolks. Microwave for a further 15 seconds, then beat hard until it becomes smooth. Gradually add a further 25g (1oz) butter in small pieces, beating hard until thick and smooth. Season to taste with lemon juice, salt and pepper and it's ready to serve.

Getting dough to rise For faster rising, place bread dough in a bowl covered with a piece of oiled plastic wrap and cook for three or four 15-second bursts on High (100 per cent power) until doubled in size – alter the length of the bursts if necessary, depending on the dough. Allow five to ten minutes standing time between bursts.

Converting recipes Adapting conventional recipes for a microwave oven is largely a matter of trial and error, but there are some rough guidelines you can follow. For quickly cooked dishes, use High (100 per cent power) for about a quarter of the conventional time. For slower dishes such as casseroles, cook on Medium (50 per cent power) for about half the conventional time. Always use microwave-proof containers instead of conventional pots and pans.

MICROWAVE QUESTIONS AND ANSWERS

Q *What is the point of the standing times given in some microwave recipes?*
A Standing time applies only to certain foods, particularly meat, eggs and cakes. The temperature of the food remains high and it carries on cooking during this time, even though you've taken it out of the oven. Standing time depends on the size and density of the dish, so it's safest to follow the instructions in your recipe.

Q *I've noticed that some microwave ovens have a temperature probe. What is this used for?*
A The probe is useful for cooking joints of meat, casseroles, jams, and any foods which need to be cooked at a fairly precise temperature. The probe is pushed into the food so that when it reaches a set temperature the power switches off automatically.

Q *Can I cook my Christmas turkey in the microwave oven?*
A This depends on the size of the bird and the capacity of your oven. A 650-watt model should take a bird weighing up to 5.4kg (12lb), but check the manufacturer's instruction book for details. For a brown, crispy skin, transfer the turkey to a conventional oven for the final 15 minutes, or sprinkle it with sweet paprika before microwaving.

Q *How can I make cakes look more appetising if they don't brown in the microwave?*
A Use soft, dark brown sugar or golden caster sugar instead of white, or substitute wholemeal flour for white, if possible. Look for recipes that allow the addition of chocolate, cocoa, treacle or spices; or add a little yellow food colour to a sponge cake mix. Or just sprinkle the top with toasted nuts or brown sugar after cooking.

To soften hard butter Unwrap the butter and microwave it on the Defrost setting. A 250g (9oz) block straight from the fridge usually needs about one minute.

Plumping up dried fruit With a microwave, there's no need to soak dried fruit for hours before using it in a recipe. Instead, put it in a bowl, cover with water, fruit juice or cold tea, and microwave on High (100 per cent power) for three minutes. Leave the fruit to stand until cool, pour off the excess liquid, and use as required.

Brown sugar gone hard? Sprinkle it lightly with a little water and place it in a strong plastic bag. Tie the bag loosely and microwave on High (100 per cent power) for 20-60 seconds.

Spreading jam on a cake Warm jam in the microwave for a few seconds before attempting to spread it, and you won't pull up crumbs or tear the top of the cake.

Marzipan or almond paste You'll find the paste easier to handle if you microwave it on High (100 per cent power) for a few 20-second bursts before rolling it out.

Shelling nuts You can use your microwave oven to make nuts that are hard to crack, open more easily. Place about 150g (5oz) of whole nuts in a medium-sized microwave-safe bowl together with about 70ml (4tbsp) of water. Heat, covered, on High (100 per cent power) for two to three minutes, when the water should be boiling. Allow to stand for a minute, drain, and crack with a nutcracker.

Peeling onions To prevent tears and make peeling easier, trim off the ends of the onions, but do not peel. Place on kitchen paper on the floor of the oven and microwave on High (100 per cent power) for a minute. Remove the skin and chop or slice.

Ripening an avocado Avocados that are still a little unripe can quickly be softened in a microwave oven. Place whole, unpeeled fruit on the bottom of the oven, and heat on High (100 per cent power) for a minute, or until slightly soft. Allow to cool completely, then peel and slice.

KITCHEN COST CUTTERS

● Make full use of a conventional oven to economise on fuel. If you're baking a cake, prepare a casserole to cook on another shelf at the same time. Or when you're doing a roast, wrap the vegetables to go with it in foil and bake them alongside the meat for the last 30-45 minutes.

● Freeze leftover vegetables and gravy to add to soups later on.

● Don't cook vegetables in separate pots if you're already boiling potatoes. Just put them in a colander and steam them over the potato pan.

● Buy Parmesan cheese in blocks, rather than ready-grated, and grate off what you need each time. It's cheaper, tastes better and lasts longer.

● Mix expensive olive or nut oils with mild vegetable oils such as sunflower to make them go further.

● Buy herbs growing in small pots rather than tiny bunches of picked leaves. With a little care, the plants will last for months.

● Save any leftover pieces of bread, biscuit and cake. Dry the bread in the oven and then grind it up to make breadcrumbs; and crumble up the biscuits and stale cake to make crumbs for a sweet dish.

● If you're cooking on an electric stove with sealed hotplates, turn off the heat about two minutes before cooking is finished – or five minutes if you're using a heavy stainless-steel pan. The plate will stay hot enough to finish cooking the food without using up any more electricity.

● Freshen up dry bread by sprinkling it with water or passing it quickly under a running cold tap and then placing it in an oven preheated to 150°C (300°F/Gas Mark 2) for 15-20 minutes.

BASIC COOKING METHODS

Getting a roast just right

Using a rack Roast your meat or poultry on a rack in the roasting tin. This ensures that the surface crisps and browns all round, as the meat does not sit simmering in its own juices.

Roasting bags Cook meat in a roasting bag to eliminate the need for basting – and keep your oven clean. The outside will still brown, but it may not be quite as crisp as with conventional roasting as the bag has the effect of partially steaming the food.

Cooking in foil Roast in foil to reduce shrinkage and do away with the need for basting. Uncover the meat for the final 15-20 minutes, to allow it to brown on the outside.

Add fruit for flavour Instead of stuffing a roast chicken or turkey, try packing the neck end (see *Safer stuffing*, page 550) with chunks of apple, diced mango or soaked dried apricots. The fruit will flavour the bird and keep it moist, and it can be served as an accompaniment.

573

For the crispest pork crackling Loin of pork and hand of pork are the joints that give the best crackling. Prepare the skin by slashing it at intervals with a very sharp knife, or ask your butcher to do it. Just before you are ready to put the joint in the oven to roast, rub the skin lightly all over with oil and sprinkle with salt. Place the pork on a rack in a shallow roasting tin – deeper tins will trap evaporating liquid and make the crackling soggy.

Alternatively, cut off the skin with a thin layer of fat, sprinkle it with salt and roast it separately, as the French do.

ROASTING TIMES FOR MEAT AND POULTRY

The roasting times below are recommended times only, and may be varied according to different ovens, or to your taste. Meat on the bone usually takes slightly longer to cook than boned and rolled cuts.

TYPE OF MEAT	ROASTING TIMES
Pork ● Well cooked	● 35 minutes per 450g (1lb) + 35 minutes. Roast at 220°C (425°F/Gas Mark 7) for 15 minutes, then reduce to 180°C (350°F/Gas Mark 4) and continue cooking until the juices run clear when you pierce the joint.
Lamb ● Medium rare ● Medium ● Well done	● 10 minutes per 450g (1lb) + 10 minutes. ● 20 minutes per 450g (1lb) + 20 minutes. ● 30 minutes per 450g (1lb) + 30 minutes. Roast lamb at 220°C (425°F/Gas Mark 7) for 15 minutes, then reduce to 180°C (350°F/Gas Mark 4) for the rest of the time.
Beef on the bone ● Rare ● Medium ● Well done	● 15 minutes per 450g (1lb) + 15 minutes. ● 20 minutes per 450g (1lb) + 20 minutes. ● 25 minutes per 450g (1lb) + 25 minutes. Roast beef at 220°C (425°F/Gas Mark 7) for 15 minutes, then reduce to 180°C (350°F/Gas Mark 4).
Beef off the bone ● Rare ● Medium ● Well done	● 12 minutes per 450g (1lb) + 12 minutes. ● 15 minutes per 450g (1lb) + 15 minutes. ● 20 minutes per 450g (1lb) + 20 minutes. Roast at 220°C (425°F/Gas Mark 7) for 15 minutes, then reduce temperature to 180°C (350°F/Gas Mark 4).
● Chicken	● 20 minutes per 450g (1lb) + 20 minutes. Roast at 200°C (400°F/Gas Mark 6) until juices run clear when bird is pierced.
● Duck	● 30-35 minutes per 450g (1lb). Roast on a rack at 180°C (350°F/Gas Mark 4), then increase the heat to 200°C (400°F/Gas Mark 6) for the final 20 minutes. Baste occasionally.
● Goose	● 15-20 minutes per 450g (1lb) + 15 minutes. Roast on a rack at 200°C (400°F/Gas Mark 6), basting frequently.

ROASTING TIMES (cont)

Timing a turkey

Roast a turkey at 180°C (350°F/Gas Mark 4). Unless the bird is self-basting, brush it with oil, spread with softened butter or lay strips of streaky bacon over the breast to keep it moist during cooking.

Wrapping turkey in foil reduces the need for basting and keeps in the natural juices; but the bird will take longer to cook and you will need to uncover it at the end for 30-45 minutes to allow for browning.

OVEN-READY WEIGHT	SERVINGS	COOKING TIME	
		(without foil)	(with foil)
2.3-3.6kg (5-8lb)	6-10	2-2½ hours	3-3½ hours
3.6-5kg (8-11lb)	10-15	2½-3 hours	3½-4 hours
5-6.8kg (11-15lb	15-20	3¼-3¾ hours	4-5 hours
6.8-9kg (15-20lb)	20-30	3¾-4¼ hours	5-5½ hours
9-11.3kg (20-25lb)	30-40	4¼-4¾ hours	Not advised

Making stews and casseroles

What's the difference? Technically, a stew is cooked on top of the stove and a casserole is cooked in the oven. Both dishes are easy and economical, and will cook without attention if you're busy. And if you're entertaining and guests are late, they will keep hot without spoiling.

Browning the meat Meat is usually sautéed before being added to a casserole or stew. This starts the cooking and adds flavour and colour. But if you're short of time, omit this and add the meat straight to the pot.

When browning meat in fat, fry only a few pieces at a time. If you try to cook too much at once, it will steam and not brown.

Thickening a stew Thicken dishes cooked on top of the stove after cooking, or they may stick to the bottom of the pot. Mix 25g (1oz) each of softened butter and flour and stir in gradually until the consistency is right.

Tougher cuts of meat Use wine, beer or tea in a stew or casserole to tenderise coarser cuts.

Stews cooked on top of the stove should only just be hot enough to cause the surface to ripple gently. If they bubble or boil, even tender meat will become tough. On a gas cooker you may need to place a heat-reducing mat under the pan to get the temperature low enough.

ITALIAN-STYLE LIVER

The secret of the delicious liver served in Italian restaurants lies in the thinness of the slices. To reproduce the taste at home, buy only the freshest, firmest calf's liver (other livers taste too strong) and keep it well chilled until you are ready to use it. Slice the liver as finely as you can – the pieces should be about 6mm (¼in) thick. Season with salt and pepper, and fry very quickly over high heat in a little butter or oil. Serve with chopped parsley and lemon slices.

RESCUING DISASTERS: CASSEROLES, STEWS, SOUPS AND CURRIES

Too much salt Add a peeled, cut-up potato and simmer until soft; then lift out the pieces. You can also counteract saltiness by adding a little plain yoghurt, a dash of sweet sherry, a pinch of sugar or a small can of tomatoes, depending on the recipe. Simmer for at least five minutes afterwards to allow the flavours to blend.

Bottom burnt onto the pan Don't stir the food, but quickly fill the sink with cold water and plunge the base of the pan into it to cool it down. Carefully lift out as much of the food as you can without removing any burnt bits, and transfer it to a clean pot with a little extra liquid. If a burnt taste remains, add spices or herbs, tomato paste, wine or Worcestershire sauce to mask it.

Thin consistency Thicken by reducing the liquid: remove the lid and boil rapidly, stirring occasionally, until the excess liquid has evaporated.

Alternatively, make a *beurre manié* thickener. Take a little more butter than flour and work the two together to form a smooth paste. Stir small pieces of the mixture into the simmering liquid until it reaches the correct consistency. Extra *beurre manié* can be kept in a closed container in the fridge for several weeks.

Curry too hot Stir in a little plain yoghurt, cream or coconut milk to tone down a fiery curry or spice dish.

Curry sauce too thin Stir in a spoonful of desiccated coconut, or simmer the curry, uncovered, to reduce.

Cooking under a grill

Getting the temperature right Always preheat the grill until it's hot (usually five to ten minutes) before cooking under it. Most foods should be placed about 75-100mm (3-4in) from the heat for even, thorough cooking. Reduce the temperature if the food seems to be cooking too quickly.

Turning meat under the grill Use tongs to turn grilling meat. If you pierce it with a fork, some of the juices may be lost.

Grilling fish Place fish fillets or cutlets under the grill on a lightly oiled metal dish. The heat will be conducted to the underside and you won't need to turn delicate fish, which could break up.

Tomato garnish For a quick and easy vegetable to serve with grilled meat or fish, cut a tomato in half and sprinkle with grated Parmesan cheese. Cook under a hot grill for four to five minutes, until bubbling.

Tips for faultless frying

How to tell when the oil's hot Use a cooking thermometer to gauge when oil is at the right temperature for frying – about 180°-190°C (350°-375°F) for most foods. If you don't have a thermometer, drop a 25mm (1 in) cube of bread into the hot oil; it should turn golden-brown in 60 seconds.

Choosing oils For most types of frying, mild flavoured oils such as sunflower, corn or soya are best, and won't dominate the flavour of the food. Use stronger oils such as olive, sesame or walnut if the flavour is needed – for example, in sauces, stir-fries, stews and salad dressings.

Frying in butter If a recipe calls for butter, use half butter and half oil instead. It will be less likely to burn.

Better coatings Dry food thoroughly on absorbent kitchen paper before coating it in batter for frying. The batter will cling much better.

How to get a lighter, crisper batter
Use beer for the liquid in the batter mix, or add a tablespoon of sherry or brandy to the batter for a lighter, crisper effect. This works particularly well for coating fish or seafood.

Spitting If frying food spits, cover the pan with a wire-mesh pan-guard or an upturned colander. The holes will allow the steam to escape and the food will still turn brown, but you won't get spattered with grease.

DO NOT heat oil until it is smoking, as this spoils the flavour. What's more, fat can burst into flames if heated above smoking point.

DO NOT throw water over fat that catches fire. Turn off the heat and cover the pan with a lid, chopping board or large plate to kill the flames.

Using a steamer

Seasoning Steamed food should be well seasoned with flavourings such as herbs, spices, lemon juice or black pepper, or it may taste rather bland. Avoid adding salt before cooking, however, as it will draw out moisture and flavour.

Consistent cooking Cut foods into evenly sized pieces so that they cook at the same rate.

Keep a check on the liquid Keep the steaming liquid at boiling point all the time, and top it up with boiling water whenever necessary. This is especially important if you're steaming a pudding for hours – the pan may boil dry if not filled up occasionally.

Steaming fish

This old-fashioned method is the best way to steam fish: place fillets of fish between two Pyrex plates with a knob of butter or a sprinkling of herbs for flavour. Balance the plates on top of a pan of boiling water. The fish will cook in the steam produced by its own moisture. Cooking time is usually between five and 20 minutes, depending on the thickness of the fillets and the type of fish.
● If you're boiling carrots, potatoes or other vegetables at the same time as steaming the fish, do the fish over the vegetable pan to save energy.
● Check fish frequently during steaming to prevent overcooking.

Barbecues and open fires

Getting the equipment together Long-handled tongs make handling barbecue food safer and easier, as shorter tools quickly get hot. Oven mittens are also essential, and a cloth and bowl of water for dealing with any sudden flare-ups.

How to tell when the fire's hot enough When your coals are hot enough to cook over they will be ash-grey or white rather than bright red.

Cooking all the way through To make sure larger pieces of meat or chicken cook right through, partially cook them in a microwave or conventional oven first, then put them on the barbecue to finish off.

Corn on the cob Fresh corn can be cooked over a fire in its husk. Remove the large outer husk; then pull back the inner husks and remove the silky threads inside. Rinse the corn in cold water and spread it generously with butter. Replace the husks and tie them over the corn with fine wire. Cook on the barbecue for 15-20 minutes, turning occasionally. Remove the husks before serving, using gloves if necessary.

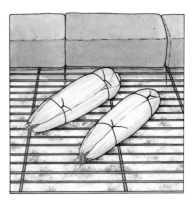

Barbecued bananas For an unusual barbecue dessert, cook bananas in their skins over a low fire for about eight minutes.

Sausages To cook sausages evenly and make turning easier, skewer them from end to end with metal skewers.

Catering for vegetarians

● Vegetable kebabs work well on a barbecue. Try chunks of vegetables such as courgettes, green and red peppers, baby corn, onions and carrots, or use whole cherry tomatoes or button mushrooms. A few pieces of soaked, dried fruit such as apple or apricot will add a tangy taste. Brush the kebabs with a glaze made from honey and soya sauce seasoned with cayenne pepper, mustard, garlic, salt and pepper. Or use oil flavoured with chilli or Worcestershire sauce, chopped herbs and lemon juice.
● Make or buy lentil or nut burgers to serve in buns.
● Wrap up foil parcels of vegetables with herbs and butter to cook on the barbecue.
● Make small parcels of Brie or goat's cheese wrapped in vine leaves. Cook over the fire until the cheese is melted.

Carving a roast

'Resting' time Any joint of meat or poultry will be easier to carve if you leave it to stand for about 15 minutes after cooking. This allows the flesh to reabsorb some of the juices and firm up. Cover the joint with foil, or leave it in a turned-off oven.

Non-slip dish Rest your carving board or meat dish on a mat or tea towel to prevent slipping. A carving board with spikes will also help to hold the meat firm while you carve.

Rib of beef

Before you buy a rib of beef, ask your butcher to cut through the chine bone (the thick bone at right angles to the ribs), which is too thick to deal with at home. When it is cooked, carve as follows:

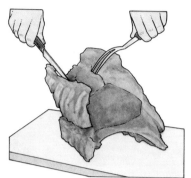

1 Stand the joint with the ribs pointing downwards and cut down between the chine bone and the meat to separate the ribs.

2 Hold the knife horizontally and cut between the meat and the end rib to separate the meat from the bone.

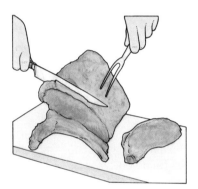

3 Carve the separated section of meat downwards into slices of the required thickness. Then repeat Step Two, separating the next section of meat from its rib bone and carving it into slices. Repeat until you have enough slices.

Leg of lamb or pork

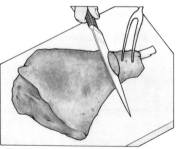

1 Place the rounded side on top. Make a vertical cut across the width of the leg near the knuckle.

2 Make a second cut a little farther away from the knuckle at about 45 degrees to the first.

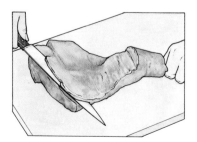

3 Continue carving in this way along the length of the joint. Near the end of the leg it may be necessary to pivot the knife around the central bone to carve slices.

Chicken and turkey

Carving poultry is easier if you remove the wishbone before roasting. Pull back the neck skin to expose the breast flesh and with a small, sharp knife remove the V-shaped wishbone just under the flesh. Wrap the skin back over the breast and roast as usual, with or without stuffing.

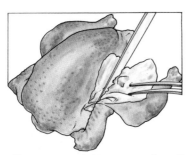

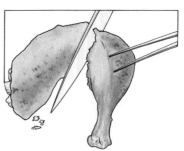

1 Place the bird breast up. Cut off one leg, slicing through the joint where the thigh joins the body.

2 Cut through the leg at the 'knee' joint to separate the thigh from the drumstick.

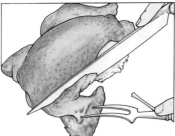

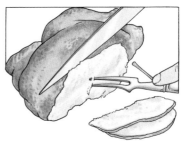

3 Separate the wing on the same side. Slice downwards close to the corner of the breast, near where the wing joins the body.

4 Carve the breast meat into neat slices, starting at the wing end and working back towards the leg end.

5 Start again with Step One on the other side of the chicken or turkey and work through Steps Two, Three and Four in the same way.

Duck and goose

Carve a duck or goose in the same way as chicken or turkey, but do not halve the leg joint unless it is unusually large. Smaller ducks and geese can simply be cut into quarters.

VEGETABLES WITH VARIETY

Beetroot Baked fresh beetroots taste just even better than boiled ones, and lose less of their colour and nutrients. Wash the beetroots thoroughly, leaving on the ends. Then wrap several together in a large piece of foil. Bake at 200°C (400°F/Gas Mark 6) for one and a half to two hours, or until tender. Vary the cooking time according to the size of the beetroots.

Cabbage Try braising cabbage to bring out its flavour. Shred the leaves finely and sauté with a knob of butter for two minutes. Add black pepper and a few tablespoons of stock, cover, and cook until tender (about four to six minutes), shaking the pan occasionally.

Baked potatoes in half the time Boil jacket potatoes for five minutes before baking, and they should be ready in about half the usual time. To speed up cooking even further, push a metal skewer through each potato to conduct heat to the centre.

Need a new idea? You can pep up almost any cooked vegetable by arranging it in a flameproof dish and covering it with a layer of grated hard cheese such as Cheddar or Parmesan. Sprinkle with pepper and place under a hot grill until the cheese melts.

Steaming versus boiling Steaming takes a little longer than boiling, but preserves more nutrients. If you do boil vegetables, make sure the water is boiling rapidly before you add them. The faster vegetables are cooked the fewer vitamins will be lost. Add the cooking water to a soup or stew afterwards so that no nutrients are wasted.

Cooking spinach You don't have to add water to spinach. The water which clings to the leaves after washing will be enough.

Minty peas and potatoes Cook peas or new potatoes with a sprig of fresh mint in the water. Or mix a little chopped mint into butter to add just before serving.

Boiling old potatoes Old potatoes should be peeled, cut into pieces if large, and simmered gently to prevent breaking up. Add a little lemon juice to keep them white.

TWO METHODS FOR FLUFFY RICE

Absorption method

Most professional cooks believe that using just enough water for the rice to absorb it all during cooking is the best way to ensure light grains that don't stick together. Some also insist that rice should be washed before cooking to remove excess starch, or allowed to soak for thirty minutes.

The instructions below are suitable for white, long-grain rice, but for brown rice you will need to extend the cooking time to about 25-30 minutes, and for Basmati rice reduce it to about eight to ten minutes.

1 Measure the rice by volume in a measuring jug, allowing 50-90ml (2-3fl oz) of rice per person. Put the rice aside and measure out twice as much water or chicken stock as rice.

2 Place the liquid in a pan and bring it to the boil. Add the rice and 2.5ml (½tsp) salt per 285ml (½ pint) of liquid. Bring the liquid back to the boil immediately after adding the rice and salt. Stir once.

3 Cover the pan with a tightly fitting lid and turn the heat right down. Leave the rice to cook gently without lifting the lid.

4 Open the pan after about 15 minutes. The water should all have been absorbed, and the rice should be tender but still firm. If some water remains, cook the rice uncovered for two to three minutes until the pan is dry. Stir the rice with a fork to separate the grains; then serve.

Rice in the oven You can save on fuel bills by cooking rice in the oven alongside other dishes. Use the same measures as above, but put the rice and salt into a casserole dish and pour in the boiling liquid. Stir well and cover the dish tightly. Cook at 180°C (350°F/Gas Mark 4) for about 35-40 minutes for white rice or one hour for brown.

Fast-boiling method

Allow 570ml (1 pint) of water or chicken stock for each 50-90ml (2-3fl oz) portion of rice. Bring the liquid to the boil in a large pan. Add the rice and half a teaspoon of salt per serving. Boil fast for 12-15 minutes for white rice, 25-30 minutes for brown, or eight to ten minutes for Basmati.

Taste a few grains. They should be soft but not soggy. If the rice is not quite done, continue boiling, testing frequently. When ready, drain the rice into a sieve and rinse it with boiling water.

If you prefer, you can let the rice dry in the oven. Spread it out evenly in a shallow, warmed dish and give it ten minutes, uncovered, in the centre of an oven preheated to 160°C (325°F/Gas Mark 3).

RESCUING DISASTERS: RICE AND VEGETABLES

Soggy or sticky rice Pack rice that has stuck together into a lightly oiled ring mould, then bake it in a fairly hot oven for about ten minutes. Turn the rice ring out onto a serving plate, fill the centre with cooked vegetables, decorate with a few sprigs of fresh herbs, and serve.

Over-cooked brussels sprouts Serve them as a purée and no one will know. Drain the sprouts and purée in a food processor until just smooth, or rub them through a sieve. Stir in a little butter or egg yolk and sprinkle with nutmeg before serving. You can do the same thing with other vegetables such as carrots or parsnips.

Limp lettuce Crisp up a lettuce that has gone limp and floppy by placing it in a bowl of ice-cold water with the juice of half a lemon. Leave for 30 minutes, dry the leaves and use.

COOKING WITH FRESH FRUIT

Rhubarb too acid? Add the juice of an orange when cooking to improve the taste. Or try a pinch of bicarbonate of soda or a cube of jelly.

Thickening fruit juices for a pie Toss fruit lightly in flour or cornflour before adding it to a pie. Any juices which come from the fruit will thicken evenly.

Fruit pies boiling over? Try adding a few dabs of butter to the filling before topping with pastry. Add very little liquid if the fruit is juicy.

Baked apples To prevent apple skins from bursting while they bake, cut through the skin in a circle around the middle before cooking.

Party piece in minutes If you're too short of time to prepare a dinner party dessert there's nothing easier or more impressive than an arrangement of exotic fruits such as mangoes, papaws, passionfruit, kumquats, lychees, guavas, kiwi fruit and star fruit. Pile them up unpeeled in an elegant bowl or on a wide platter and decorate with sprigs of orange or bay leaves.

TIPS FOR SEASONING FOOD

Fresh herbs or dried? Fresh herbs taste better than dried, but if they are not available substitute dried herbs. Use only one-third of the amount, as dried herbs are more concentrated.

If you want to use dried herbs in a dish which will not be cooked, such as a salad, pour a little boiling water over them and leave to soak for a minute before draining and adding. They will have a better flavour and more colour.

Spicy dishes Prepare curries and other spiced dishes by frying the spices in fat or oil first, rather than adding them straight to the dish. Frying takes away the 'raw' flavour and makes spices more digestible. Always fry spices quickly over medium heat, and watch them constantly, as they quickly burn.

Nutmeg Buy nutmegs whole rather than ready ground. The flavour keeps better, and you can grate just what you need onto sweet or savoury dishes such as spinach, mashed potatoes, egg custards and rice puddings.

Paprika for browning Sprinkle sweet paprika over food – especially cheese-topped dishes – to help with browning.

HOMEMADE YOGHURT

1 Heat 570ml (1 pint) of sterilised or UHT milk to 43°C (110°F). If you don't have a thermometer, test the temperature with your fingertip: the milk should feel very slightly warmer than your finger.

2 Stir in 50g (2oz) skimmed milk powder and 15ml (1tbsp) plain yoghurt.

3 Pour the mixture into a prewarmed vacuum flask. Seal the flask and leave it in a warm place for about seven hours.

4 Pour the yoghurt into a bowl to cool, and then refrigerate it for about four hours before serving. Homemade yoghurt will keep for four or five days in the fridge.

Variations Flavour homemade yoghurt by stirring in fruit purée, chopped fruit, nuts, muesli or spices.

Cooking with yoghurt To prevent yoghurt separating out when heated, mix 5ml (1tsp) cornflour with a little cold water for every 275g (10oz) of yoghurt. Add it to the yoghurt and stir over a moderate heat until boiling. Cook for a minute, stirring all the time, then add to the recipe.

No UHT or sterilised milk? You can still make yoghurt from ordinary pasteurised milk. Bring it up to the boil, remove from the heat and cool to blood temperature; then follow the method on the previous page.

COOKING WITH CHEESE

● Take care not to overcook dishes containing cheese; it may become stringy and tough.

● Add cheese to sauces at the end of cooking, and don't boil the sauce after adding the cheese. Just warm it gently until all the cheese is melted.

EASY WAYS TO COOK EGGS

No poaching pan? To poach eggs without a special pan, boil up a wide saucepan of water, add a tablespoon of vinegar and swirl a spoon around in it to create a 'whirlpool' effect. Crack the eggs and quickly tip them into the pan (it's easier if you break them into a cup first). Simmer gently, covered, for about three minutes or until the eggs are set. Lift them out with a draining spoon. Fresh eggs will poach best and spread least.

Fat-free fried eggs If you like fried eggs but want to cut down on fat in your diet, try this method:

Place a Pyrex or other heatproof plate on top of a pan of boiling water. When the plate is very hot, break an egg onto it and leave it to cook for about six to eight minutes, until set.

Hard-boiled eggs

● You can ensure that the yolks of hard-boiled eggs end up in the centre by placing them in a pan of cold water and stirring over heat until the water boils, to keep the eggs moving. Once the water's boiling, stop stirring.

● To prevent a black ring forming around the yolks of hard-boiled eggs, drain them as soon as they are cooked, tap and crack the shells, then run the eggs under cold water for a few minutes.

● Before peeling, roll hard-boiled eggs over a firm surface with the palm of your hand. The shell will crack all over and come away more easily.

● If you don't have time to boil and mash eggs for a sandwich filling, scramble them until very dry, season, and mix in mayonnaise when cool.

Scrambled eggs and omelettes For a fluffier result, add a little carbonated water when you beat up the eggs. A tablespoon of dry sherry will pep up the flavour too.

Looking after your pans Don't use omelette or pancake pans for other purposes, or you may damage the surface and cause your omelettes or pancakes to stick.

Making soufflés

Advance preparation A mixture for a hot soufflé can be completely prepared for baking, then covered with plastic wrap and refrigerated for one to two hours before cooking. Take it out of the fridge about 20 minutes before baking, to allow it to return to room temperature.

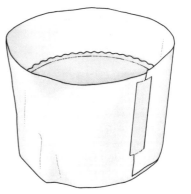

Soufflé tomatoes For an unusual way to serve soufflé, scoop out the centres of several large 'beef' tomatoes and fill them about three-quarters full with soufflé mixture. Place on a baking tray and bake in a hot oven.

● You could also experiment with other vegetables such as scooped-out green or red peppers, or large mushrooms. Alternatively, make individual soufflés in small dishes.

Cold soufflés To prepare a dish for a cold, set soufflé, secure a band of greaseproof or non-stick paper around the outside of the tin with sticking tape. The paper should come up about 50mm (2in) above the rim. Pour in the soufflé mix so that it rises above the rim. When the souffle is set, remove the paper, using a knife dipped in hot water to separate it from the soufflé if it doesn't come away cleanly.

Basic soufflé recipe Melt 25g (1oz) butter, stir in 25g (1oz) flour and cook gently for a minute or two. Gradually add 150ml ($\frac{1}{4}$ pint) milk and bring to the boil while stirring.

Let the mixture cool slightly, then add 75g (3oz) grated cheese, chopped ham or mushrooms, or other filling. Beat in three egg yolks and season with salt, pepper or herbs.

Whisk the whites of the three eggs until they stand in soft peaks and fold them into the mix. Pour the soufflé mixture into a greased 180mm (7in) soufflé dish and bake in the centre of the oven at 200°C (400°F/Gas Mark 6) for about 35 minutes. Serves four.

Don't open the oven Leave your soufflés to bake in peace – a quick rush of cold air could make them collapse.

Quick mix A can of condensed soup makes a quick and tasty soufflé. Beat up three egg yolks with the soup in a 1 litre (1$\frac{3}{4}$ pint) soufflé dish. Whisk the whites and fold them into the yolk and soup mix. Bake for 40 minutes at 190°C (375°F/Gas Mark 5).

RESCUING DISASTERS: SOUFFLÉS

Collapsed baked soufflé Spoon savoury soufflé into a lightly buttered, shallow, flameproof dish and sprinkle with grated cheese. Grill until bubbling and scatter with fresh, chopped herbs before serving.

Scoop out a collapsed sweet soufflé into a wide, shallow dish and mask the top with whipped cream or Greek yoghurt. Scatter flaked, toasted almonds over the top and serve.

Unset cold soufflé Always check a cold soufflé before removing the collar from the dish. If it has not set, place the soufflé in the freezer until just frozen. Serve it iced, and call it soufflé glacé. If there's no time for freezing, fold in a little whipped cream and serve in elegant stemmed glasses.

MAKING JAMS AND PRESERVES

Getting the pectin right A well set jam needs a good balance of pectin and acid. For the best results, combine fruits with differing pectin contents, such as apples and blackberries or strawberries and redcurrants.
● Fruits rich in pectin which will give a good set are apples, gooseberries, blackcurrants, redcurrants and damsons.
● Those with a moderate amount include plums, greengages, raspberries, apricots and loganberries.
● Fruits with very little pectin are strawberries, cherries, blackberries, pears and rhubarb. Vegetables are also low in pectin.

How to keep soft fruit whole Sugar has a hardening effect, so sprinkle it over soft ingredients, such as strawberries or marrow chunks, before using them in a preserve. Let the sugared fruit stand overnight; then cook as the recipe directs.

Setting tests for jam

For best results, combine the temperature test with either the drop or the cold plate test. Start testing the jam when it reaches 105°C (220°F).

Temperature test

You will need a cooking thermometer for this method. Let the thermometer warm up and cool down gradually by placing it in hot water before and after use. To heat the jam, stir it thoroughly, then place the thermometer in the pan so that the bulb is completely immersed but not touching the base.

Drop test

Dip a wooden spoon into the jam, hold it horizontally and let the jam cool slightly. Tilt the spoon and allow the jam to drop from the edge. When it has been sufficiently boiled, small droplets of jam will run together on the edge of the spoon forming large drops. These larger drops should fall cleanly from the rim of the spoon.

Cold plate test

Drop a small spoonful of jam onto a cold plate. If it has reached setting point the surface will set as it cools, and should crinkle when pushed with a fingertip. Take the jam off the heat while you are doing the test, or it may boil beyond the setting point while you are waiting for the sample to cool.

RESCUING DISASTERS: JAM

Runny, unset consistency If you reboil the jam the flavour may be spoiled, so set it with gelatine instead. Dissolve the gelatine in a little water, then warm the jam and stir evenly into the gelatine solution. Repot and use within a few weeks, or the gelatine may attract mould.

Crystallised jam Heat the jam very gently until melted, then repot. Use up fairly soon, as the crystals may eventually reappear.

LIVENING UP YOUR LEFTOVERS

Pâtés and pastes Leftover meat, poultry or fish of almost any kind can be made into a tasty spread. Put the meat through a mincer, or flake the fish with a fork, mix in a little melted butter or cream, some finely chopped fresh herbs, salt, freshly ground black pepper, and a tablespoon or two of brandy or sherry if you wish. Spoon into small jars or pots and serve with thin toast.

If you aren't going to eat home-made pâté right away, pour a thin layer of melted, clarified butter (butter that has been heated till foaming and then strained through muslin) into the jar before putting on the lid. Sealed like this, pastes and pâtés should last about three or four days in the fridge. Write a label for each jar with the contents and date so you don't lose track.

Instant gazpacho Make your own version of this cold Spanish soup by whizzing up leftover salads with vinaigrette dressing in a blender or food processor. Refrigerate, and serve when cold. Add extra tomatoes, tomato juice or other salad ingredients if necessary. Use chilled chicken stock to thin the soup if it is too thick.

Rice the second time around You can easily revive boiled rice to make a second meal: sauté a finely chopped onion in a little oil until soft, stir in the rice and heat it up thoroughly. Alternatively, make a rice salad: toss the rice in a tasty French dressing and add a handful of fresh chopped herbs and a red pepper, diced finely. Serve cold.

Extra vegetables Purée vegetable leftovers with a little stock to make tasty sauces or soups. Add a dash of cream for richness, if you like.

Flat beer Leftover beer can be used to plump up dried fruit for a rich cake mixture or added to casseroles for extra flavour.

No need to waste wine Even if it's no longer any good for drinking, you can add leftover wine to wine vinegar to extend it, or freeze it in ice cube trays to add to casseroles or sauces.

Pasta pie Grease a pie dish and press leftover unfilled pasta such as spaghetti or macaroni over the base and sides. Fill with a mixture of chopped cooked meat, mince or fish. Add a layer of cooked vegetables and top with a white sauce or grated cheese. Bake in a moderate oven until thoroughly heated.

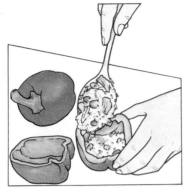 

Stuffed vegetables Use hollowed-out red and green peppers, aubergines or tomatoes for this recipe, or boil onions until soft and remove the middle. Fill with a mix of leftovers such as cooked rice and chopped meat or chicken, with some minced onion, seasoning and a little cream, melted butter or olive oil. Bake in a medium-hot oven for 20-30 minutes, or until soft.

Two uses for stale cake If sponge cake has dried out, sprinkle it well with sherry, top with fresh or canned fruit chunks, and cover with custard and cream to make a quick trifle. Revive fruit cakes or sponges by soaking individual portions in fruit juice, liqueur or sherry, and warming them up in the oven. Serve as a hot dessert, with egg custard, cream or ice cream.

Fish cakes Flake leftover fish with a fork and mix well into about twice as much mashed potato, add a small knob of butter and a little cream or milk. Season with salt and pepper, shape into flat 'cakes' about 12mm ($\frac{1}{2}$in) deep, dip in beaten egg, coat with breadcrumbs and fry till golden brown – about six minutes – on either side. To use up mashed potato, add tinned tuna fish, mix well and finish as above.

Reheating meat Leftover meat and poultry needs to be reheated very thoroughly, always making sure that the heat goes right through to the centre. It's easier to reheat meat without drying it out if it's in gravy or a sauce – it can then be simmered for several minutes without harm. Never reheat meat more than once.

Sausages to spare? Cut cooked sausages into thick slices to add to stews, soups or casseroles about 15 minutes before serving. Alternatively, wrap 25mm (1in) pieces in thin puff pastry, brush with milk or beaten egg and bake until golden-brown. Serve as cocktail snacks or accompaniments to other dishes. Always make sure sausages are heated all the way through before serving.

EASY MIXES FOR QUICK MEALS

Savoury mince mix

Make up a large batch when you have time and freeze the extra, so you have a quick main course on hand for busy days.

70ml (4tbsp) oil	1.8kg (4lb) lean minced beef
4 medium onions, chopped	700g (1$\frac{1}{2}$lb) can tomatoes
4 sticks celery, chopped	70ml (4tbsp) Worcestershire sauce
225g (8oz) carrots, peeled and chopped	2 beef stock cubes
	Ground black pepper

You'll need two large wide pans to deal with the quantity. Divide the oil between them and sauté the vegetables until lightly coloured. Add the mince and stir until evenly browned. Add the remaining ingredients, then cover and simmer for 20-25 minutes. Allow to cool, remove any solid fat that forms on top, and pack into four 570ml (1 pint) freezer containers. Freeze for up to three months. Each container will give about four portions.

Meals based on savoury mince

Chilli con carne To a thawed container of mince, add 10-15ml (2-3tsp) chilli powder or Tabasco sauce and two 425g (15oz) cans of kidney beans, drained. Cook for ten minutes, stirring occasionally.

Shepherd's pie Place a thawed container of the savoury mince in an ovenproof dish and top with a layer of mashed potato. Bake at 190°C (375°F/Gas Mark 5) for 20-30 minutes, until heated right through.

Spaghetti Bolognese Thaw and heat one container of the savoury mince in a pan with 50ml (3tbsp) tomato purée, a clove of garlic and 10ml (2tsp) of dried oregano or mixed herbs. Spoon it over freshly cooked spaghetti or other pasta shapes and sprinkle with Parmesan cheese.

Speedy pizza Thaw and heat one container of the savoury mince. Cut six muffins in half and toast them. Spread the meat on top of the muffins, sprinkle with cheese and oregano, and add olives, salami or other ingredients if you wish. Grill for three to four minutes, until cheese is bubbling. Makes 12 small pizzas.

Beef and tomato stew

This simple stand-by keeps for up to two months in a deep-freezer, so make double or triple the quantity and freeze the extra.

50ml (3 tbsp) olive oil	25g (1oz) plain flour
900g (2lb) lean chuck steak, cut into 25mm (1in) cubes	400g (14oz) canned tomatoes
350g (12oz) onions, skinned, halved and thinly sliced	2 beef stock cubes
	15ml (1tbsp) mixed dried herbs
225g (8oz) carrots, peeled and sliced	285ml ($\frac{1}{2}$ pint) cold water
	Salt and freshly ground black pepper

Heat 35ml (2tbsp) of the oil in a heavy-bottomed saucepan or a flameproof casserole dish. Add half of the chuck steak and cook over a high heat until lightly browned all over. Remove the meat from the pan and set aside. Brown the remaining meat and set it aside with the rest.

Add the rest of the oil, the onions and the carrots to the pan, and cook over a moderate heat for three to four minutes. Return the meat to the pan, stir in the flour and add the remaining ingredients. Bring to the boil while stirring, then reduce the heat to low. Cover with a tightly fitting lid and simmer for two to two and a half hours, until the meat is very tender, stirring occasionally. Serves four to six.

Variations

Beef pie Allow the stew to cool completely after cooking (keeping it overnight will actually improve the flavour). Spoon it into a deep pie dish, adding just enough of the sauce to barely cover the meat and reserving the rest. Place a pie funnel in the centre, then cover the dish with shortcrust or puff pastry. Bake in a hot oven for 30-40 minutes, until the pastry is golden-brown. Heat the remaining sauce and serve with the pie.

Beef curry Omit the carrots and mixed herbs, and add 15-35ml (1-2tbsp) curry powder after cooking the onions. Fry the curry mix quickly, taking care not to burn the spices. Then add the meat and follow the main recipe. Serve with hot rice, poppadoms and chutney.

Goulash Omit the carrots and herbs from the main recipe, and add a sliced green pepper and two cloves of crushed garlic with the onions. Stir in 35ml (2tbsp) sweet paprika when you add the flour. Top with soured cream and parsley to serve.

Extra vegetables You can add up to 450g (1lb) celery, turnip, swede, green pepper or other vegetables to the basic stew, but you'll need a little extra beef stock – just enough to barely cover the ingredients.

Pork, turkey or chicken stew Substitute diced pork or turkey if you want a change from beef, or use chicken portions. Turkey and chicken will need 1-1½ hours' cooking; pork takes about the same time as beef.

Basic batter

115g (4oz) plain flour
Pinch of salt
2 eggs (size 3)
285ml (½ pint) milk or milk with water

Sieve the flour and salt into a bowl, make a well in the centre, and beat in the eggs and half of the liquid until smooth. Stir in the remaining milk and beat throughly. If you do not need the batter immediately beat it again before using. It will last for about a day in the fridge.

Dishes to make with batter

Toad-in-the-hole Preheat the oven to 220°C (425°F/Gas Mark 7). Place 450g (1lb) of pork sausages in a greased baking tin about 180mm x 280mm (7in x 11in). Bake in the oven for ten minutes, pour off any surplus fat, then pour the batter over the sausages and bake for 40-50 minutes. Serves four.

Fruit batter pudding Follow the recipe for Yorkshire pudding, using the large baking tin. Toss 225g (8oz) of apple slices or other fresh fruit in 25g (1oz) sugar and add to the hot fat in the tin before pouring in the batter. Serve as a dessert, with plain yoghurt, cream or custard. Serves four.

Pancakes Lightly oil a small frying pan and heat until fairly hot – test by dropping in a tiny amount of batter: it should sizzle immediately if the oil is ready. Pour in a little batter, tipping the pan to coat it thinly and evenly. Cook until the underside is golden and the top is set. Toss or turn over and cook on the other side until golden. Roll up the pancake and place in a warm dish. Continue until all the batter is used up, then serve the pancakes with sugar and lemon juice, or a filling of your choice. Makes about eight pancakes.

Yorkshire pudding Preheat the oven to 220°C (425°F/Gas Mark 7). Add 25g (1oz) fat or oil to a baking tin about 180mm x 280mm (7in x 11in), or 18 individual tins, and bake for 40-50 minutes for one large pudding, or 20-25 minutes for small, individual puddings. Serves six.

One-step white sauce

25g (1oz) butter or margarine
25g (1oz) plain flour
285ml ($\frac{1}{2}$ pint) milk, stock or combination

Whisk together all ingredients in a saucepan and stir over moderate heat until boiling. Cook, stirring all the time, for two to three minutes, until thickened and smooth. Season to taste.

Cheese sauce Add 75g (3oz) grated cheese and 5ml (1tsp) of made-up mustard to the basic mix. Heat gently, without boiling.

Parsley sauce Stir 35ml (2tbsp) finely chopped parsley into the basic mix.

Anchovy sauce Add 10ml (2tsp) anchovy essence to the basic mix.

RESCUING DISASTERS: SAUCES

Curdled hollandaise sauce Stir an ice cube into the warm sauce.

Lumpy sauce or gravy Smooth out the sauce by whisking hard in the pan. If still lumpy, rub the sauce through a sieve or purée it in a blender.

Curdled egg custard Quickly plunge the base of the pan into cold water, then whisk in 10ml (2tsp) cornflour for every 570ml (1 pint) of custard. Or pour the custard immediately through a sieve into a clean bowl to remove the curdled parts and cool the sauce quickly.

Dessert sauce too sweet Tone it down with a little lemon juice.

Scone mix

225g (8oz) self-raising flour
5ml (1tsp) baking powder
A pinch of salt
50g (2oz) butter or margarine

Sift flour, baking powder and salt together into a mixing bowl and rub in the fat evenly. Store in a plastic bag in the fridge for up to a month or in a freezer for up to three months. Makes 8-12 scones, depending on size.

Scones to make with the mix

Plain scones Add 115-150ml (4-5fl oz) milk to the basic recipe and mix to a soft dough. Roll out to a thickness of 12mm ($\frac{1}{2}$in) and cut into rounds with a 60mm (2$\frac{1}{2}$in) cutter. Bake on a lightly floured baking tray at 220°C (425°F/Gas Mark 7) for 12-15 minutes.

Cheese scones To the basic mix add 115g (4oz) grated cheese, 5ml (1tsp) dry mustard and a pinch of salt. Combine to a soft dough with 115ml (4fl oz) milk, and cook as for plain scones.

Fruit scones Mix basic ingredients to a dough with 115-150ml (4-5fl oz) milk. Add 75g (3oz) currants, sultanas, chopped glacé cherries or dates, and 25g (1oz) caster sugar. Mix and cook as for plain scones.

Savoury cobbler topping Mix with the dry ingredients, 115-150ml (4-5fl oz) milk, 15ml (1tbsp) of chopped fresh herbs or 5ml (1tsp) of dried herbs, and a little salt and pepper. Cut into rounds, and arrange on top of a cooked, hot casserole. Bake for 15-20 minutes at 220°C (425°F/Gas Mark 7).

Sweet dessert sauce

15ml (1tbsp) cornflour
285ml ($\frac{1}{2}$ pint) milk
35ml (2tbsp) sugar
15g ($\frac{1}{2}$oz) butter or margarine

Blend the cornflour in a pan with a little of the milk and the sugar. Stir in the remaining milk. Place on moderate heat and stir until boiling. Cook gently, stirring all the time, for two to three minutes, until thick and smooth. Remove from the heat and add the butter. Use on stewed fruit or puddings in place of custard. Serves four.

Flavourings

Brandy or rum Add 35ml (2tbsp) brandy or rum after cooking.

Chocolate Stir in 35ml (2tbsp) drinking chocolate powder after cooking.

Coffee Add 10ml (2tsp) instant coffee dissolved in 35ml (2tbsp) hot water to the finished sauce.

Ginger Add 5ml (1tsp) ground ginger and 50g (2oz) finely chopped stem ginger in syrup after cooking.

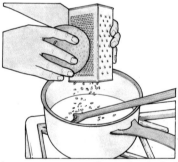

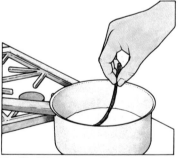

Lemon or orange Grate the rind of an orange or lemon on the finest side of the grater and stir it into the cooked sauce.

Vanilla Warm the milk and steep a vanilla pod in it before making the sauce, or add 2.5ml ($\frac{1}{2}$tsp) vanilla essence after cooking.

Quick tips for easy toppings

● For chocolate-butterscotch ice cream topping, roughly chop a Mars bar into a pan with 15ml (1tbsp) milk and heat very gently, stirring until melted. Pour over the ice cream and serve.
● Chocolate cream sauce for desserts and ice cream can be made by melting an equal weight of plain chocolate and evaporated milk in a pan over a low heat. Beat until smooth, and serve.
● Shave curls of chocolate from a block with a potato peeler.

Entertaining guests

PLANNING A PARTY

Room for everyone If you're catering for large numbers at home or in a hall, you will need to allow a space 1.2m x 1.2m (4ft x 4ft) per person. When placing guests around a large table, leave elbow room of about 760mm (2½ft) between settings.

Choosing guests The smaller the party, the more careful you need to be in choosing your guests. Two visitors with strong – and differing – opinions could ruin a small dinner party, for example. Guests need not know each other, but should have something in common. Try to shake the mixture up a bit, however, or the evening could be dull – if everyone is from the same profession or background, shop talk may take over and spoil the party atmosphere.

Balancing men and women Don't feel you have to invite the same number of men and women, even if it's a small dinner party. Single guests often appreciate thoughtful introductions, but obvious matchmaking can be embarrassing.

Preparing in advance

Draw up a list Always make a detailed checklist before you start planning a party, or you may forget something vital. Divide the tasks up so that you spread the load over weeks or days, and use the list as a countdown schedule, ticking off every task as it's completed. Your list could include: arranging to borrow or hire equipment, ordering food and wine, guest list, menu planner, shopping list.

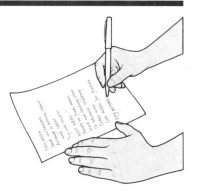

Deciding on a menu Flip through recipe books to get new ideas, then test them out on the family well before the party day, so that you're familiar with the recipes. Don't be too ambitious; cook dishes you know you can do well even if they are plain, rather than experimenting with fancy new recipes that may go wrong.

Avoid last-minute cooking For any type of entertaining, it's best to avoid dishes which need attention just before serving, or you'll have to disappear into the kitchen and abandon your guests. If you choose a hot dish, make sure it's one that won't spoil if left to keep warm. Cold starters, cold puddings and cheese make entertaining easier, as they're ready whenever you need them.

Shopping for a party Once you've decided what to cook, you can make a detailed shopping list. Buy any non-perishable items ahead of time to spread the cost and the workload.

Be realistic Consider the amount of time and work involved in what you're

593

planning to do. If necessary, ask a few friends to help, or consider hiring caterers. With careful planning, an experienced party-giver with plenty of time and a well-equipped kitchen may be able to cater for as many as 25-30 people – but others might find 10-12 guests more reasonable.

Kitchen equipment Once you've decided on the guest list and the menu, check on the equipment you'll need. Few ordinary kitchens are equipped to cater for large numbers, so you may need to borrow or hire cooking pots and serving dishes.

Cooking in advance Catering is much less trouble if you cook as many dishes as possible before the day, and then store them in the fridge or the freezer until needed. If you're short of fridge or freezer space, ask neighbours if they can help.

A map for guests Make sure all guests have directions to your house, or to the party venue. Send a simple map with the invitation if the place is unfamiliar, and hang balloons on the door or a lantern at the gate to illuminate the house number.

What if it's wet? Always check the weather forecast the day before a party, and see that there's a place to leave coats, umbrellas and boots, if necessary. If you're planning a barbecue, make sure there are covered cooking and eating areas in case it rains.

Sending invitations

Allow plenty of time For a large, formal occasion such as a wedding, it's usual to send out written or printed invitations at least four weeks in advance. For smaller, informal parties, write or telephone to invite guests about two weeks in advance.

Check the invitations Before you send them, check all invitations to make sure you haven't left off any vital information: your name, the address of the party, date and time, purpose, theme if there is one, type of dress, and an address or telephone number for replies.

All written invitations should say 'R.S.V.P.', indicating that you need a firm response. If you prefer, put 'Regrets Only', but you may find that some people will not reply at all.

Printed invitations If you need formal invitations printed or engraved, approach a local stationery store or printer several weeks in advance. They can usually offer patterns and examples for you to choose from.

Wording an invitation A formal invitation should be written in the third person, for example, 'Mr and Mrs John Smith request the pleasure of your company . . .' If it's informal, there are no rules.

HIRING, BUYING AND BORROWING

Large parties Unless you frequently entertain large numbers of guests, it's cheaper to hire equipment such as cutlery, plates, dishes, trays and bowls rather than buy. Look for specialist catering hire companies in your local newspaper or Yellow Pages under 'Catering equipment hire'. If you ask around you may even find friends or a local church group or school who can lend you what you need.

Borrowing glasses Most off licences and wine merchants will hire out glasses, or they may lend them free if you buy your drink there, although you'll be expected to pay for breakages and losses. Real glasses are preferable to plastic, but make sure you can cope with the washing up.

Tables and chairs If you need only a few extra tables and chairs, it's easiest to borrow from friends, but otherwise they can be hired, complete with tablecloths. If your dining table is small but you have space around it, set up card tables with firm plywood covers on top. Alternatively, if you have a smooth-surfaced door, take it off its hinges, unscrew the handle and place the door on top of a smaller table – it should seat about ten. If you're short of tablecloths, use sheets instead.

Cutlery Plastic cutlery is not strong enough for cutting most food, and is not suitable for a smart occasion. Borrow or hire the real thing.

Paper plates and napkins Disposable paper plates save on washing up, but if you're serving hot food, make sure you buy the kind what won't buckle or go soggy. Also be careful of brightly coloured paper napkins which may run when wet – the colour could end up on someone's party dress or on your tablecloth.

Returning equipment after the party Keep a list of everything you hire or borrow and where it comes from, to make returning things simpler. Cross off each item when you've returned it.

SERVING DRINKS

Non-drinkers Don't forget to order soft drinks for non-drinkers. Fresh fruit juices and cordials mixed with mineral water will go much further than fizzy drinks as they tend to be more refreshing.

Don't be caught short To be on the safe side, over-cater rather than under-cater on drink for your party. Buy from a wine shop that sells on a sale-or-return basis, so that you can return any unopened bottles.

When guests arrive It's traditional to serve sherry or spirits to your guests when they arrive, but by no means essential. A glass of wine, still or sparkling, is usually appreciated just as much.

Can't afford champagne? If the budget won't run to champagne for wedding toasts or other celebrations, buy sparkling wine instead. It is much less expensive and has the same effect – many people won't even notice the difference, particularly if you choose a wine made in the same way as champagne. Look for labels which say the wine was made by the 'classic' or 'traditional' method.

Bulk buying Ask for a discount if you buy a case of 12 bottles or more. Most wine shops will also give a refund for unopened bottles.

Party punch For informal occasions such as buffets or barbecues, a punch (page 606) can work out much cheaper than wine or spirits. Serve in a large punch bowl with a ladle, or in jugs for easy pouring.

A good supply of ice Order or make twice the amount of ice you think you'll need. Keep ice for drinks separate from ice for chilling, which will not stay clean.

HOW MUCH DO YOU NEED?

The smaller the party, the more people tend to drink. For over 50 guests, calculate at least three drinks per head, but for 10-15 people you may need to double that amount. The chart below gives the number of drinks you'll get per bottle.

	BOTTLE SIZE	NUMBER OF GLASSES
Wine	75cl	6
Sherry, port	70cl	12
Vermouth	75cl	16
Spirits	70cl	32
Liqueurs	70cl	30
Mixers (with spirits)	500ml (50cl)	5
Mixers (as long soft drinks)	500ml (50cl)	3
Minerals/mineral water	1 litre	4

Fridge too full to chill the wine? Buy ice in quantity and chill wine bottles in large plastic bins filled with ice – or fill the bath with ice.

If guests go over the limit Never allow anyone who has had too much to drink to drive home after a party. Offer to arrange a taxi or a lift home, or even a bed for the night. If necessary, consider taking away the car keys.

Good ways with wine

White wine Chill all white wines to about 10°C (50°F) before serving. Don't over-chill or the flavour will be lost; an hour in the fridge is usually enough. Serve sweet wines at a slightly lower temperature (6-8°C/43-46°F) than dry whites. In emergencies, you can chill a white wine in the freezer, but only for five minutes, and set a timer so that you don't forget about it.

Red wine Most red wines are ideally served at room temperature – about 18°C (65°F). Beaujolais, Burgundy and some light Italian red wines are best served slightly colder – about 16°C (61°F). Uncork or decant red wine about an hour before serving to allow it to develop its flavour.

Broken cork If the cork breaks when you are opening a bottle of wine, push the part that remains in the neck into the bottle.

After pushing in the cork, you will usually need to strain the wine to remove any small bits of cork that may have crumbled off. Use a fine tea strainer, a piece of muslin or a coffee filter, and decant the strained wine into a carafe or a clean bottle.

Pouring wine Before pouring any wine, wipe the mouth of the bottle with a clean cloth to remove any cork or dirt particles which may contaminate the contents.

What goes with what? There's no strict rule about serving white wines with fish and red wines with meat, but generally it's a good guide. If you're not sure which wine to choose, consult an expert. Many off-licences have knowledgeable, well-trained staff who can help you choose wines to match your menu and budget.

Decanting wine Old red wines and ports may also need decanting to separate the wine from any sediment that has formed. To decant a wine, leave the bottle standing upright for a few hours so that the sediment settles at the bottom. Then, holding the bottle up to the light, pour the wine carefully and smoothly into another container, leaving behind the dregs. Never decant champagne, sparkling wines or white wine of any sort.

Opening champagne The trick to opening bottles of champagne or sparkling wine safely is first to chill them – warm champagne will always explode on opening as it's under greater pressure. To remove the cork, twist the bottle, not the cork. Use a napkin to hold the cork, point it out of harm's way, and don't let it go – flying corks go with great force and can cause injury or damage. Have the glasses lined up ready for pouring.

Keep your champagne bubbly A trace of detergent on a glass can kill champagne bubbles, so always make sure champagne glasses have been rinsed in clear water after washing.

How far to fill a wine glass Apart from champagne, wine should be poured only halfway to the top of the glass, so that the drinker can savour the bouquet as well as the taste. Fill champagne glasses almost to the rim, so that the bubbles last as long as possible.

A PERFECT DINNER PARTY

Spread the workload Plan your menu so that as many dishes as possible can be prepared a day or two in advance, or more if you have a freezer.

Special diets Check any special needs such as vegetarian or diabetic food with your guests before planning your menu.

Timing the meal Don't plan to serve the meal the minute guests arrive. Allow extra time in case they are a little late, and time to have a drink beforehand. If you invite guests for 8pm, for example, aim to start the meal between 8.30 and 8.45pm.

What you can do in advance

Salads Prepare salad ingredients on the day, preferably only one or two hours in advance, as cut salads soon start to lose their nutrients. Make the dressing and keep it in a screw-topped jar in the fridge, ready to shake and add only at the last moment. Ensure that the lid is firmly on before shaking, or you could end up with vinaigrette all over your party clothes.

Vegetables Get vegetables ready for cooking early in the day and keep them in polythene bags in the fridge. Par-boil potatoes for faster roasting or, if vegetables are to be boiled, prepare pans of boiling water while the main dish is cooking. Peeled potatoes won't discolour if you put them in a bowl and cover them with cold water.

Desserts and puddings Cold desserts should be made in advance and, if possible, decorated and stored in the fridge – but cover them well so they don't pick up flavours from other foods. Hot puddings such as baked sponges can often be baked in advance and warmed up before serving. Otherwise, prepare them for the oven before the meal starts, and preheat the oven to the right temperature so that it's ready when you need it.

Garnishes Arrange fresh decorations such as slices of lemon or sprigs of herbs on a serving platter an hour or two before they will be needed. Cover the garnishes with plastic wrap or an inverted bowl and leave them in a cool part of the kitchen until you're ready to decorate the food.

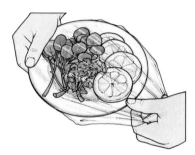

Dinner plates Put plates to warm in the bottom oven or warming drawer, or warm them in a dishwasher, using the final cycle.

Coffee tray Measure out coffee for after the meal, so that you need only add the water. Set a tray with coffee cups, milk or cream jug, sugar bowl and any after-dinner chocolates.

Setting the table Lay the dinner table well in advance, and make sure you've included condiments and serving spoons as well as the settings and decorations.

Wine Chill white wine or open bottles of red about an hour in advance. Make sure you have plenty of ice ready for pre-dinner drinks.

Snacks Lay out any nuts, olives or other pre-dinner nibbles.

Bathroom check-up Make sure there's a clean handtowel and soap.

Time to relax Build some time before the guests arrive into your schedule to allow you to change and rest for a few minutes. You will feel more relaxed and eager to greet them if you haven't been rushing non-stop.

HOW TO PLAN A DINNER MENU

● Choose a variety of different types of food. Don't opt for a fish starter followed by a fish main course, for example, and make sure that there is a good balance between richer and lighter dishes.

● Provide contrasting colours to stimulate the appetite. If the dishes themselves are plain, add variety with colourful garnishes.

● Use different textures to give contrast. For example combine crunchy salads with a creamy main course, or sprinkle nuts over a soft mousse.

● Choose a good balance of flavours, and don't have too many spicy dishes in one meal.

● A variety of shapes adds interest, so use different serving dishes.

Setting a dinner table

Polished tabletops If you're worried about spills damaging a polished tabletop, lay a piece of plastic sheeting or clingfilm under the tablecloth. If hot dishes will be placed on the table, place a blanket under the cloth. Don't put mats under the tablecloth; they will create an uneven surface that may cause spills. Put them on top where they can be seen.

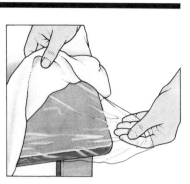

Patterned or plain? Food generally looks best on plain white china or china that contrasts with the colour of the food. Strong colours and intricate patterns may be attractive on their own, but they often clash with food and look less effective when filled.

Candle power Candles give atmosphere to a room, even when there's other lighting as well. An electric light with dimmer switch turned down low and supplemented by candlelight is ideal for most dinner parties. Keep candles below eye level so that guests can see across them. Small candles floating in a bowl of water make an unusual decoration, and they're safer than taller candles, too.

Positioning a buffet table If you have the space, place your buffet table in the centre of the room to allow guests to walk around it. If the table has to be against a wall, leave a gap so that you can slip in and replenish empty dishes.

A seating plan for your guests For larger dinners with more than about eight guests, a seating plan pinned to the dining-room door and a typed or handwritten name card at each setting will help them find their places without a lot of milling about.

Place settings at a dining table

Lay the cutlery in the order in which it is to be used, working in from the outside. Knife blades should face the plate, and no more than three forks and three knives should be laid at any one time. Place a folded napkin on the plate or to the left of it. Set a water glass above and slightly to the right of the plate. Wine glasses go to the right of the water glass.

The dessert spoon and fork can either be lined up with the rest of the cutlery, with the spoon on the right and the fork on the left, or laid at the top with the spoon above the fork. Lay the spoon handle to the right and the fork handle to the left.

599

Arranging a buffet table

Arrange a buffet table in logical order to avoid congestion: dinner plates first, then rice or pasta, the hot main course, vegetables, salad, bread, butter, relishes and condiments, and lastly cutlery and napkins. Drinks should go on a separate table nearby. If you have a large number of guests, try to have more than one table of food, with a similar arrangement on each one.

Try to allow space at a buffet for guests to put their plates down while they help themselves. This is essential if they have to serve themselves and there's a dish which needs two hands for serving. If guests will be eating standing up, serve food which can be eaten with only a fork and provide plenty of surfaces where they can put down their glasses. It will also help if you pre-butter the bread for your guests.

DINNER TABLE DECORATIONS

● Keep table decorations and candles below eye level, or they'll get in the way of conversation.

● Fresh flowers always look good on a dinner table, but keep them small and avoid strongly scented varieties. Don't use a vase which could be knocked over; if necessary, weight it down with stones to keep it stable. Or float flower heads in a crystal bowl filled with water.

● For an unusual centrepiece, use a display of seasonal fruits and vegetables. In autumn you could fill a basket with shiny red apples and nuts in their shells, or in summer you could line a basket with fresh herbs and fill it with tomatoes, peaches or strawberries.

HOW TO FEED AN EXTRA GUEST

Soups Add stock, wine or cream to extend soup without spoiling the flavour.

Casseroles Depending on the type of casserole, add a tin of sweetcorn, kidney beans, tomatoes or other suitable ingredients. A dash of wine will make the juices go farther without watering them down.

Rice If there's no time to cook an extra portion, heat and stir in a tin of drained kidney beans or chick peas, or mix toasted almonds, cashews or peanuts.

Desserts If you are not sure a dessert will stretch to an extra portion, offer a bowl of fresh fruit as an alternative.

Bread Most supermarkets now sell part-baked bread and rolls which can be kept in a freezer until you need them. They will bake within minutes in an emergency.

Making a roast go farther A roast will usually stretch to another portion if necessary, and extra vegetables will help to eke out a small joint. You could also open a packet of stuffing, add a few nuts or chopped dried fruit, and bake it in the oven to accompany the meat.

SAVOURY SNACKS AND NIBBLES

Guacamole Blend together an avocado, lemon juice, garlic and a dash of chilli sauce. Purée until smooth, add a roughly chopped tomato, blend again and season.

Stuffed cherry tomatoes Cut off the tops of the tomatoes, scoop out the insides with a teaspoon and fill with seasoned and mashed avocado or a cream-cheese mix.

Savoury sticks Small pieces of contrasting foods speared on a cocktail stick make a delicious mouthful. Try thinly sliced smoked ham wrapped around cubes of melon, whole unpeeled prawns with a stuffed green olive, or peppered salami wrapped around Feta or Mozzarella cheese.

Dips For easy entertaining, try these dips, served with crunchy vegetable slices or pitta bread.
- Plain yoghurt, wholegrain mustard and salt and pepper to taste.
- Fresh chopped herbs such as basil, chives or parsley mixed into fromage frais and seasoned with black pepper.
- Cream cheese with a handful of chopped walnuts and a little mayonnaise and Worcestershire sauce.
- Equal quantities of peanut butter and Cheddar cheese gently melted with a little curry paste and served hot.
- Stilton or other blue cheese crumbled into cream or mayonnaise and seasoned with black pepper.

CATERING FOR CHILDREN

Choosing the food Party food for children of any age should be colourful, fun and easy to eat, preferably with fingers.

Sweet or savoury? Children are often drawn to sweet foods because they are more colourful, so make some novelty savoury foods to tempt them – the mini-kebabs or spiral sandwiches on the next page, for example.

Party cakes Avoid rich, creamy cakes and sticky icings at children's parties. A simple sponge birthday cake (see recipe, page 603) with easy-to-roll fondant icing will be as effective and a lot less messy.

Strong flavours Avoid spicy foods, and strong tastes such as garlic. Most children prefer milder food.

Serving sizes Keep portions small enough for youngsters to manage. If very small children will be there, lay on some bite-sized foods.

Don't forget the mothers If mums are also invited, make sure there's some adult food and drink for them too.

Party treats for children

Pizza squares Top a thin layer of bread or scone dough with slices of tomato, grated cheese, and a little diced bacon, ham or tuna. Bake on large trays and cut up into small squares when cooked.

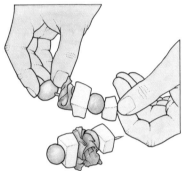

Animal biscuits Make a savoury cheese-flavoured biscuit dough and cut it into small animal shapes before baking. Most kitchen shops sell novelty biscuit cutters, including animal shapes.

Mini-kebabs Older children will enjoy tiny kebabs of ham, cheese, pineapple cubes and seedless grapes threaded onto cocktail sticks. Never serve cocktail sticks to small children.

Novelty sausages Thaw out frozen shortcrust or puff pastry, cut it into strips, and wrap it in spirals around cocktail sausages. Bake in a hot oven for 15-20 minutes.

Chequerboard sandwiches Make brown and white sandwiches with different fillings, cut into squares, and arrange on a serving plate to make a chequerboard. Or cut them into novelty shapes with biscuit cutters.

Sandwich spirals Cut bread into thin slices and spread with a variety of toppings. Roll up each slice like a small swiss roll and cut into rounds to give a spiral effect. Alternatively, cut a loaf of bread lengthways into slices, layer with different fillings and cut into fingers.

Decorating a children's cake Use coloured fondant icing to decorate a simple birthday cake for a child's party. A clock face is a popular choice, with the hands pointing to four o'clock, for example, for a fourth birthday; or make a clown's face with coconut for hair.

Healthy dips Simple dips of cream cheese, yoghurt or peanut butter are popular with children of all ages. If your children like them, add mild flavourings such as chopped chives or tomato sauce to the yoghurt or cream cheese. Serve with carrot, celery or other vegetable sticks for dipping. For a sweet dip, mix yoghurt and honey, and prepare pieces of fruit for dipping.

Baby burgers Make mini-sized burgers to serve in small party pittas. They're much easier for small hands to grasp than full-sized buns.

Traffic light jellies Set layers of red, orange and green jelly in tumblers, to make a traffic light pattern.

Chocolate crispies Melt 175g (6oz) chocolate and stir in 50-75g (2-3oz) breakfast cereal and a few pieces of dried chopped fruit. Spoon into paper cases and allow to set.

Party drinks Serve colourful pure fruit juices topped up with fizzy mineral water, rather than sugary, artificial drinks. Add ice cubes with pieces of fruit frozen inside for fun.

Personalised goodies For an individual touch, pipe children's names onto savoury or sweet biscuits with cream cheese or icing.

Chocolate-coated fruit Dip pieces of fruit into melted chocolate. Leave the stalk end uncoated for easy holding.

One-stage birthday cake

115g (4oz) soft margarine
115g (4oz) caster sugar
2 eggs (size 3)
115g (4oz) selfraising flour
5ml (1tsp) baking powder

Place the ingredients in a bowl and beat for two to three minutes with a wooden spoon, or one minute with an electric hand mixer. Turn into two greased, base-lined 180mm (7in) tins and bake at 190°C (375°F/Gas Mark 5) for 20-25 minutes. Fill with jam or butter cream (page 564) when cool.

Variations

Flavourings For an orange or lemon cake, mix in the grated rind and juice of one fruit; and for a chocolate cake, add 30ml (2tbsp) of cocoa powder blended with 30ml (2tbsp) hot water.

Small cakes Add an extra 25g (1oz) of selfraising flour to the basic ingredients. Spoon the mixture into 18-20 paper cases. Bake at 190°C (375°F/Gas Mark 5) for 15-20 minutes.

603

Walnut or almond cake Mix in with the other ingredients 25g (1oz) finely chopped walnuts or ground almonds.

Baked fruit pudding Arrange 225g (8oz) fresh or drained canned fruit such as pears, apples or pineapple in the base of a deep, buttered 200mm (8in) tin or dish. Mix an extra 25g (1oz) of self-raising flour into the cake ingredients, and spoon the mixture over the fruit. Bake at 190°C (375°F/Gas Mark 5) for 50-60 minutes. Turn out and serve with custard.

RELIABLE PARTY RECIPES

Simple starters

Salmon mousse

212g (7$\frac{1}{2}$oz) tin of pink or red salmon
200g (7oz) plain creamy fromage frais
1 spring onion or a few chives, chopped
1 sachet gelatine
150ml ($\frac{1}{4}$ pint) dry white wine
Salt and black pepper

Remove the skin and bones from the salmon and purée the flesh with the fromage frais and spring onion or chives. Sprinkle the gelatine over the wine and heat gently until dissolved; then stir into the salmon and season. Pour into a mould and chill until set. Turn out and serve with toast. Serves six.

Avocado, orange and mint salad

3 sweet oranges
3 ripe avocados
15ml (1tbsp) lemon juice
35ml (2tbsp) olive oil
35ml (2tbsp) chopped fresh mint
Freshly ground pepper
Mint leaves to garnish

Peel the oranges, removing all the white pith (page 555) and dividing them into segments. Catch any juice in a bowl. Peel, stone and slice the avocados (page 554). Arrange orange and avocado slices in circles on serving plates. Combine any orange juice with the lemon juice, oil and mint, season with pepper, and pour over the salad. Garnish with sprigs of mint. Serves six.

Main course party pieces

Devilled chicken

50ml (3tbsp) Worcestershire sauce
50ml (3tbsp) tomato purée or ketchup
12 chicken pieces such as wings or drumsticks

Combine the Worcestershire sauce and tomato purée or ketchup. Toss the chicken in the mixture until evenly coated. Place under a moderately hot grill or over a barbecue and turn frequently until cooked right through. Serve hot or cold. Serves four.

Beef with mustard and walnuts

900g (2lb) fillet steak
35ml (2tbsp) sunflower oil
50ml (3tbsp) ready-mixed coarse grain mustard
150ml ($\frac{1}{4}$ pint) red wine
150ml ($\frac{1}{4}$ pint) double cream
50g (2oz) walnut halves
Salt and black pepper

Cut the steak into thin strips and sauté it in the oil. Stir in the mustard and add the wine. Simmer, uncovered, for three to four minutes. Add the cream, walnuts and seasoning, stir, and just bring to the boil. Serve immediately with rice or pasta. Serves six.

Ginger and orange mackerel

4 medium mackerel, herrings or other small, whole fish, cleaned and with heads removed
25mm (1in) piece of fresh ginger root, peeled and grated
Freshly ground black pepper
15ml (1tbsp) soy sauce
35ml (2tbsp) olive oil
Juice of an orange
Orange slices to garnish

Slash the thickest parts of the fish with a sharp knife and place them in a shallow dish with the ginger, pepper, soy sauce, oil and orange juice. Leave for at least an hour.

Remove the fish from the marinade and cook under a hot grill for about ten minutes, turning once and basting with the juices. Serve hot, garnished with orange slices. Serves four.

Greek fish plaki

700g (1$\frac{1}{2}$lb) cod, haddock or other white fish fillets
50ml (3tbsp) lemon juice
15ml (1tbsp) olive oil
1 medium onion, thinly sliced
398g (14oz) tin chopped tomatoes
115ml (4fl oz) dry white wine
Salt and freshly ground black pepper
Chopped parsley

Cut the fish into serving-sized pieces and sprinkle with lemon juice. Heat the oil in a large pan and fry the onion until soft. Add the fish, tomatoes, wine, salt and pepper. Cover and simmer for ten minutes. Garnish with chopped parsley. Serves four.

Quick and easy puddings

Chocolate pots

200g (7oz) plain or bitter chocolate
115g (4oz) unsalted butter
Large tot of brandy or rum

Melt the chocolate and butter together in a bowl over a pan of hot water. Add the brandy, beat until smooth and spoon into small individual pots. Decorate with a whirl of whipped cream or yoghurt. Serves four.

Lemon and honey syllabub

285ml ($\frac{1}{2}$ pint) double cream
150ml ($\frac{1}{4}$ pint) white wine
Grated rind and juice of half lemon
35ml (2tbsp) clear honey

Place all the ingredients in a bowl and whisk until the mixture will just hold a trail. Spoon into stemmed glasses and chill. Serve decorated with lemon slices or toasted almonds. Serves four.

Pear and ginger upside-down pudding

Topping
50g (2oz) butter
50g (2oz) soft brown sugar
25g (1oz) walnut halves
496g (15oz) tin pear halves, drained
Base
115g (4oz) wholemeal or plain flour
2.5ml ($\frac{1}{2}$tsp) bicarbonate of soda
10ml (2tsp) ground ginger
115g (4oz) soft brown sugar
1 egg (size 2)
75g (3oz) black treacle
115ml (4fl oz) milk
50ml (2fl oz) sunflower oil

Preheat the oven to 180°C (350°F/ Gas Mark 4). Melt together the butter and sugar for the topping and pour the mixture into a greased or lined 230mm (9in) cake tin. Arrange the walnuts and pears on top.

Sift together the flour, bicarbonate of soda and ginger for the base; then stir in the sugar. Beat together the egg, treacle, milk and oil, and mix into the dry ingredients to make a smooth batter. Pour over the pears and bake for 40 minutes, until firm. Turn out onto a serving plate and serve with yoghurt, custard or cream. Serves six.

COCKTAILS AND PARTY PUNCHES

Hot ginger cup Put in a pan a bottle of ginger wine, 285ml ($\frac{1}{2}$ pint) orange juice and a stick of cinnamon. Stud an orange and a lemon with whole cloves, then cut into thick slices and add to the pan. Warm over a gentle heat for about ten minutes, without boiling. Serve hot.

Lamb's wool punch (or wassail bowl) Bake or poach four large Bramley apples until soft. Discard the skins and cores, and mash the pulp in a large bowl. Heat 1 litre (2 pints) light ale and 570ml (1 pint) sweet white wine or cider with a stick of cinnamon, a small piece of bruised root ginger and 5ml (1tsp) grated nutmeg, until almost boiling. Pour the hot liquid onto the apple pulp and sweeten with brown sugar. Reheat, strain and serve.

Strawberry gin cream Place 200g (7oz) fresh or frozen strawberries in a blender with a large measure of gin, 150ml ($\frac{1}{4}$ pint) single cream and a dash of lemon juice. Blend until smooth, sweeten to taste with sugar, and serve with crushed ice.

Sparkling wine cup Mix equal quantities of peach, mango or passion fruit juice with sparkling white wine. Serve with sliced fruit and sprigs of mint.

Non-alcoholic tropical punch Dissolve 200g (7oz) creamed coconut in 285ml ($\frac{1}{2}$ pint) water. Purée four ripe bananas with the juice of two lemons, add to the coconut mixture, and top up with lemonade.

Frosting glasses for special drinks

Dip the rim of the glass into egg white and then lightly into caster or granulated sugar. For coloured frosting, mix a little food colour evenly into the sugar.

A more beautiful home

*I*deas for designing a successful room. Advice on how to achieve the right lighting and flooring. Tips for dealing with windows and renovating furniture. Guidance on putting up paper and paint. And, finally, hints on how to move house with smooth efficiency.

Getting the right look

DESIGNING SUCCESSFUL ROOMS

Careful planning

● Before you alter or buy anything, make sure you know what you want to do in each room.

● Make a floor plan to scale. It will help you achieve what you want and will save you time and money when buying paint, flooring, curtains and furniture.

● Keep cuttings from magazines with good ideas for fabrics, wall colours and floor-coverings. Consult friends about their decor, if you like it, and read any decorating books you can find.

Make the most of your space

● Visualising each of the rooms empty of furniture will give you a better idea of its shape, size and potential.

● Don't be bound by convention – imaginative use of space, using screens on sliding track, for example, can be both practical and appealing.

● Multipurpose rooms and hallways can provide far more room in small flats and houses. Put a dining table in a wide hall, or convert an understairs cupboard into a shower.

Use colour skilfully

● A colour scheme that repeats or echoes throughout the house will give an impression of space and unity. Different shades of the same colour can be used on the walls in one room, in the curtains in another, and on the floor in yet another.

● Pick out colours from a favourite rug, picture or vase and use it in the decoration of the room. Consult a colour wheel (page 611) or manufacturers' colour cards for suitable colour harmonies.

Don't overdecorate

● Take your time. Decide on the paint or paper for walls and woodwork, and the colour of the flooring, and then pick your other furnishings. If money is tight, you can do it bit by bit.

● Simple and uncluttered spaces tend to look more restful and tidier than rooms stuffed full of treasured items.

● Too many different colours or fabric patterns will create a feeling of confusion. Stick to plain colours with single bright-coloured objects of focus for a calmer effect.

Checklist for DIY decorators

How much can you afford? List each room and what is needed. Decide what you can do yourself and when to call in a professional.

Are immediate repairs needed? List all the good and bad points of the house, including all structural work and repairs that need dealing with urgently – leaking roof or wall cracks, for example.

Do central heating, plumbing and new wiring have to be done? If so, get them over with before starting to decorate. Are there enough electrical sockets around the house, particularly in the kitchen and workrooms?

How long are you staying? If you think you might move soon, don't plan built-in cupboards. They will have to stay with the house.

What are your household needs? Do you have children and pets, or hobbies demanding space? If you work at home, where are you going to put your office?

Is the house secure? You may want to replace doors or windows if they have rotted and seem easy to open from the outside.

What are the focal points? Fireplaces, pictures, rugs, beautiful light fittings or collections – decide what you want to accentuate and choose your colours accordingly.

Personal design preferences? Decide which sort of style you want in the house – traditional farmhouse, country, modern, oriental and so on – and which range of colours you want to see.

DECORATING COST CUTTERS

● Style and colour change with fashion. If you like to keep up to date, pick neutral colour schemes with lasting appeal (whites, greys or beiges) and add bright, contemporary accessories to give the room a modern feel.

● Modern reproductions of Victorian cast-iron baths and fireplaces often work out better value than originals. Old baths may need re-enamelling, and are very heavy. Some floors can't support the weight of cast-iron fittings, and plumbing-in old baths can be expensive.

● Use small or non-directional pattern wallpapers, fabrics and floor coverings – large pattern repeats mean buying more to match the pattern.

● Cut-price fabric shops, theatrical suppliers and mail order outlets often provide excellent bargains for lavish fabric decor schemes.

● Rework your old furniture to fit a new scheme rather than buying all new pieces. Sofas can be re-upholstered in matching fabrics, and old wooden cupboards can be painted.

● Collect good quality secondhand sheets for dyeing and fabric painting. They can make unique bedspreads, screens, curtains and cushion covers.

● Try to avoid fittings and fixtures that need matching accessories – bathroom taps, for example. You'll save yourself unnecessary expense.

Kitchen and bathroom planning

Kitchens and bathrooms need particular attention, especially if they lack space. You will generally need to call in experts, and the rooms will usually cost more to refurbish than others in the house.

Creating a kitchen

● Ideally, the three sides of the 'work triangle' (fridge, sink and cooker) should total around 4-7m (13-23ft). Greater distances mean unnecessary walking, and anything smaller is restricting.

● Plan to work from left to right, and have the fridge/worktop/sink/worktop/hob/worktop in an unbroken sequence.

● Investigate kitchen appliances and space-saving fittings: a dishwasher means less cluttered worktops; a combined washing machine and tumble dryer takes up less room than separate machines.

● Worktop corner space is often wasted. Try fitting a special corner sink or hob unit, a slim-line dishwasher or an ironing board that folds away.

● Some fitted units incorporate a pull-out table for eating – useful for very small or galley kitchens.

Creating a bathroom

● Check that continental taps, showers and toilets are suitable for local water pressure.
● Get the plumber to look at the site beforehand – some sanitary ware designs cannot be fitted without considerable extra cost.
● Sunken baths need floors at least 1m (3ft) deep and corner baths can waste space.
● Cisterns set into the wall and wall-hung toilets and bidets look neat but require trap-door access to the plumbing.
● If you want to put in an extra bathroom in older homes and attic conversions, make sure that your boiler and water tank are large enough to provide adequate hot water.
● Remember, it is more expensive to plumb into walls or rooms where there is no existing pipework.

Whole house planning tips

Double glazing It takes about 25 years to recoup the cost of double glazing although it does prevent heat loss, especially in homes with large windows. Period home owners should ensure double glazing is in keeping with the rest of the house style, or it may devalue the property.

Fitted floor coverings, wallpapers and murals If specially installed at the start, these can sometimes be taken with you when you move, but it is doubtful they will fit anywhere else without major alteration.

Dividing and linking areas Rooms that give privacy when you want it and open out for entertaining are very useful. Consider installing partitions, sliding doors or folding screen panels.

FREE – AND ALMOST FREE – IDEAS

● Several paint and wallpaper manufacturers offer free advice about colour schemes.
● Some specialist furniture shops have an in-store interior design service for a modest fee, refundable if you then order an agreed amount of goods through them. Bring a floor plan, any photographs or sketches of furniture, and samples of existing fabrics and floor coverings. If you list the problems in advance and include magazine cuttings of schemes you admire, it will give them an idea of your taste.
● A few fitted kitchen, bathroom and bedroom specialists will do on-the-spot computer-aided perspective drawings free of charge if you provide a floor plan. However, you are restricted to using the ranges which they sell.
● Some paint shops offer a special paint mixing service for matching the colours of tiles, carpet, towels or plain fabrics. You may end up paying about ten per cent more than for ready-mixed paints, but it will save you time and worry.
● With accurate scale elevation drawings of a room, most furnishing shops can give rough on-the-spot estimates for blinds, curtains and wallpapers. To get an estimate for carpet and other floorings, take a floor plan with you.
● Home furnishing magazines often provide a colour-scheme service for a small fee. Cost is usually on a room-by-room basis. Send in any information, floor plans, samples and so on and list the problems clearly. Allow around four to six weeks for replies.

CHOOSING A COLOUR SCHEME

What will colour do for your home?

● Painting everything white is safe, and gives a sense of space, but using colour helps you to create an individual atmosphere in each room.

● Colours divide up into advancing (warm), receding (cool) and neutral groupings. Oranges and reds give a warm feel; blues and greens are cooler; and whites, greys and browns provide a neutral background.

● Different colours affect emotions. Everyone responds differently to colour depending on personal taste, but in general bright colours create a cheerful atmosphere whereas a neutral colour scheme is more soothing.

● You can accentuate or diminish your home's good and bad points. If a room is full of sunlight during the day, the colour you paint it will either emphasise or counter this. Red might be too strong, for example.

USING A COLOUR WHEEL

This wheel of 12 colours can provide you with many different combinations of colour to use in your home, some of which are more unusual or dramatic than others.

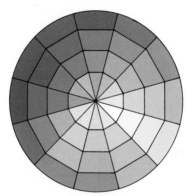

Monochromatic schemes Pick a single colour on the wheel and use it with a variety of its different tints. Adding white will make pastel colours; adding black dulls colour.

Complementary schemes Pick two colours opposite each other on the wheel – or three colours at equal distances. Watch the tonal balance, though – only one colour should be dominant. Use the others as accessories or on minor surfaces.

Related schemes Using two or more colours next to each other on the wheel will give a room a restful and harmonious effect.

How to pick the right colour range

Think of your favourite colour Pick a colour and visualise all its different shades. Thinking of an example in nature might work – if it's green, imagine all the shades seen on trees throughout the year, ranging from light spring greens to autumn reds.

Consult a colour wheel A colour wheel will show you a series of different colour combinations that you can use – some striking, others more muted (see above).

Observe the natural light Some designers advise covering furnishings with sheets and waiting for a few weeks before deciding on whether the room needs to be painted with warm or cool shades.

Start with a multicoloured fabric If you are buying new curtains, for example, make them the starting point for your colour scheme. Choose a soft colour in the fabric and buy a matching paint for the walls.

Artificial light affects colour If you are repainting a room that is mainly used at night, or has artificial lighting only, remember that the type of bulb and the texture and colour of lampshades also affect the final colour. Try to see a sample of paint and fabric in both artificial light and daylight to get an idea what they will look like at all times of the day.

Altering proportions with colour

Shorten a dark hallway Paint a door or wall at the end of a long, dark hallway in white, red or sunny yellow to bring it 'forward'.

Widen a hallway Lay floor tiles in wide horizontal stripes of colour.

Widen a staircase Don't have strips of painted wood either side of the floor covering – lay the covering across the full width.

Make a floor seem larger Paint the skirting boards the same colour as the floor to give the room a larger feel.

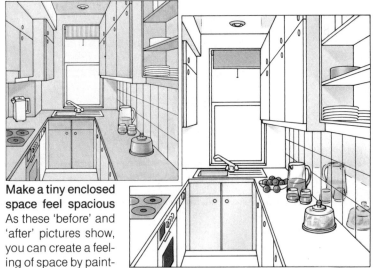

Make a tiny enclosed space feel spacious As these 'before' and 'after' pictures show, you can create a feeling of space by painting walls, woodwork, shelving and all details in white, blue or green. Use mirrors where possible. Painting low ceilings with gloss paint gives a shimmering reflection and an impression of space. Make sure there are no cracks, though, as they will show up.

Colour tips to bear in mind

● Use neutral colours for large expanses (such as walls and floors) and highlight accessories or upholstery with accent colours in strong, contrasting hues.
● All shiny surfaces intensify colour, so are generally best reserved for smaller areas.

● Never give two or more colours equal weight. One, preferably the lighter one, should dominate. Make a colour board to help get the colour proportions right. Stick samples of paint or fabric onto a piece of grey or white card. Use larger samples for walls and floors, smaller ones for curtains or cushions.

● Texture affects colour. Different painting techniques, such as stippling, rag rolling or sponging, will produce a different impression of the same colour. And on fabrics, a satin pillow of the same colour as a velvet sofa will seem lighter and brighter. Transparent materials add space.

● Colours change depending on what they are placed next to: red next to blue seems yellower than the same red next to black, for example. Next to white, red seems brighter.

● Where a dark and light colour are next to each other, they will accentuate each other.
● The eye tends to mix colours at a distance. You may find small-print wallpapers or fabrics on walls or in curtains merge into one colour.
● Lining curtains in warm cream or buttery yellow (rather than traditional beige) will give the room a warmer feel.
● Paintwork, skirting boards and dado rails can be a neutral link or an integral part of a colour scheme.

Fault-finder guide: colour schemes

The room seems too cold
Check which direction the room is facing. Painting north-facing rooms red or yellow will not necessarily make them warmer, as the northern light can cast a bluish tinge. Try a textured stippled effect in two shades.

The overall effect is dull
Perhaps it needs some colour accents. Try adding brilliant colour in your accessories – a vase, rug, curtains, cushions, lamps, picture or furniture.

The room seems restless and bitty
There are probably too many contrasting colours. Add accessories in similar tones to link the different colours together.

The room looks too warm
To lighten and cool down a room, add neutral grey, beige or white accessories and white-painted woodwork.

LIGHTING YOUR HOME

Correct lighting will dramatically improve a room. Before you buy any fittings, make yourself a rough lighting plan that shows what you want to use and where.

● What will the room be used for, and what sort of atmosphere do you want to create? Will it need soft, relaxing light or practical task lighting?

● Is the area large or small? More light makes smaller rooms seem bigger, and large rooms need several light sources to look inviting.

● Who is going to use the room? Is it for children (freestanding lamps might not be a good idea) or for someone elderly who would benefit from switches by their bed, for example.

INVEST IN ENERGY SAVERS

A number of energy-saving bulbs are available in a variety of shapes. They may be fluorescent or tungsten-halogen. They are all more expensive than a standard tungsten bulb, but work out cheaper in the end.

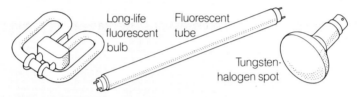

Long-life fluorescent bulb

Fluorescent tube

Tungsten-halogen spot

● Compact long-life fluorescent bulbs are small and square and need an adaptor for regular fittings. Many bulbs are sold with a free adaptor, and the adaptor will last for up to four changes of bulb. The bulbs last around 8000 hours each (a regular bulb lasts for 1000 hours) and use a quarter of the electricity. Savings are high once you calculate the difference to your electricity bill and the fewer changes of bulb.

● Standard fluorescent tubes give out up to five times as much light as a filament bulb of the same wattage.

● Tungsten-halogen light bulbs give a cool, white light and last twice as long as a regular filament bulb.

● Standard tungsten bulbs that last two or three times longer than normal (up to 3000 hours) can also be found. But they use the same amount of electricity as normal bulbs.

Lighting plan tips

Rearrange the room to fit the wiring If you want to create a new effect in a room, it is always a good idea to see if you can make do with the existing wiring. Rewiring is expensive and may not be necessary if you buy the right fittings for a new room arrangement.

Redecorating If you are planning to do any decorating, make sure that the electrician has finished any wiring before you start. See that any switches or wall lights are correctly positioned from the start, because once the wires are chased into the walls, it is a major decorating job to change them.

Home plans Some specialist lighting firms can plan your lighting for you free or for a small fee if you order your light fittings from them.

Recess sizes Check that there is sufficient room for the fittings you choose. Ceiling recessed downlighters, for example, often require a depth of at least 300mm (12in) which is more than the ceiling cavity of many homes. Mini downlighters, however, can be fitted into a 150mm (6in) recess, and some can be surface mounted.

Get advice Consult an electrician about your needs before you buy anything. Too often, electricians are presented with light fittings totally at odds with a home's current wiring system.

Know your light fittings

Downlighters Cylindrical fittings usually recessed into the ceiling. Small versions are called mini downlighters.

Uplighters Fittings which throw light upwards from wall or floor. May be fitted to the wall or freestanding.

Spotlights Fixed or adjustable beams of light used for accenting or highlighting a feature. They are often fixed to a track for flexible use but are always surface mounted.

Task lighting Light sources for close work – usually a spot or freestanding table lamp with flexible arm.

Pendant fittings Suspended ceiling lights, available with adjustable rise-and-fall fitting.

Bulkhead lights Enclosed wall fittings originally designed for ships and outdoor use; special insulated fittings available for shower areas.

Track Base for spotlights that allows them to be moved; may be surface-mounted, recessed or suspended from ceilings.

Tracks are not suitable for bathrooms as they may react to water vapour and corrode.

Which light goes where? The pendant dining lamp (1) hangs low over the table to avoid glare. The living area has recessed downlighters (2), wall-fixed uplighters (3), a freestanding lamp (4) and two table lamps (5). Practical task lighting (6) is available on the desk and behind the armchair (7), and the pictures are lit by an adjustable ceiling spotlight (8).

STOP THE WASTAGE 🍃

● Install door-activated cupboard lights which switch off automatically when the door is closed.

● Use low-energy bulbs in places where lights are left on for long periods – in hallways or on exterior walls, for example.

● Dimmer switches save hours of bulb life. They can be fitted instead of ordinary wall switches and used with any sort of tungsten bulb. Tungsten-halogen and fluorescent bulbs need special switches.

Room-by-room lighting: a checklist

Kitchens and dining rooms

● Worktops and sinks should be well lit with small fluorescent strips under cupboards and shelves, but make sure you don't store perishable food above them.

● Install ceiling-fixed spotlights or recessed downlighters for general light.

● Provide table light by using an adjustable pendant lamp with a wide shade and a silvered bulb – but make sure the light falls on the food, not in the diners' eyes, by hanging it low over the table. The silver coating on the bulb will prevent glare.

● Highlight a dresser, sideboard or serving counter with small adjustable spotlights or downlighters.

● Wall lights controlled by a dimmer switch work well with candles for atmospheric dining.

Bathrooms

● All light fittings must be approved for use in a bathroom, and operated by a pull cord or from outside the room.

● Recessed downlighters provide a bright general light.

● Use enclosed bulkhead fittings for small bathrooms and shower areas so there is no exposed light fitting.

● Mirrors or mirror-cupboards with built-in lighting are practical for putting on make-up and shaving.

Home offices and hobby rooms

● Strip lights on ceiling and walls give a bright working light.

● Use adjustable table lamps for task lighting – typing, drawing or sewing, for example.

● For craft work, a magnifying lamp fitted with a daylight simulation bulb won't distort the colour of paint, silk or yarn as much as the light given off from an ordinary light bulb.

● Clip-on builders' inspection lamps provide inexpensive accent and background lighting.

● Lengths of track can be made into 'L', 'U' or square-shaped arrangements and can also be fitted around a mirror or worktop.

Landings and halls

● Dimmer-operated downlighters in the ceiling provide a good general light which can be left on a low setting through the night for children.

● Compact fluorescent fittings are fairly economical if left on all night.

● Install lighting in any cupboards under the stairs.
● Wall-fixed uplighters wash a wall with light. Placed diagonally at different heights, they can make a narrow hall look wider. Take care to position them so as to avoid glare when people go up or down the stairs.

Bedrooms

● Bedside and dressing-table lights can all be fixed to the walls.
● Make-up mirrors fitted with tungsten bulbs at 150mm (6in) intervals can be made from ready-wired lengths of frame. The frame can be fitted either side of the mirror or all the way round.
● Fit wardrobe interiors with a light activated by the door.
● Dimmer switches in children's rooms are a good alternative to night lights.

Living rooms

● Keep the lighting low – it's more restful – and use lamps on side tables.
● Dimmer-operated mini downlighters provide an overall light that's not too bright.
● Accent lighting – for highlighting collections or paintings – can be provided by spots fitted with antiglare diffusers, or better still, use recessed low voltage downlighters.
● Use uplighters to highlight period mouldings or ceiling roses.
● Standard lamps stand at the ideal height for piano playing or reading.
● By fixing small spots under shelves or in alcoves, you can create pools of light and shadow.
● Choose shades for table lamps that are lined with white – they won't distort the colour of the light. Try and see shades both lit and unlit when buying them to check that they will fit in at all times of the day.

RENEWING A CENTRAL LIGHT FITTING

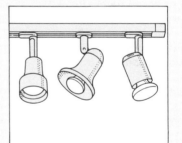

● Replace an old pendant lamp in the middle of the ceiling with an adjustable rise-and-fall fitting.

● Fix a length of track across the existing outlet and fit it with tungsten spotlights.

● Put in a centre-fixed three-way spot to brighten up the room – it will provide enough light for a small kitchen.

Outside the house

● Light up patios or beautiful shrubs and trees with waterproof outdoor floodlights. Light leafy trees from their bases to get the full effect of their height.
● Beam an outdoor spotlight onto a garden pathway, steps or pond – it deters intruders and welcomes guests. Or install special heat sensitive security lighting which will light up at anyone's approach.
● Insulated candle lights will add a festive feel to outdoor activities, such as barbecues.

USING MIRRORS CREATIVELY

● A wall of mirror running from skirting board to ceiling makes small, dark halls, bathrooms and basements feel much lighter, brighter and wider. Or panel the side of the bath with mirror.

● Replace wooden wardrobe doors with mirrored ones to give a feeling of space in bedrooms, but check the hinges and frames to see that they can take the extra weight. Or build in a wall of storage space with sliding mirrored doors.

● Fixing panels of arched mirrors or mirror tiles at regular intervals on a wall gives an illusion of space beyond the arches.

● Panels of mirror in alcoves either side of a chimney breast increase the feeling of space. Install glass shelves for displaying a collection and combine with display lighting.

● Double a room's available light by placing a mirror opposite or adjacent to a window. Or line a window recess with mirror panels.

● A mirror at right angles to a work surface where it meets a cupboard or wall gives the impression of a larger worktop.

Tips on making the most of mirrors

Watch reflections No one wants to look at themselves eating, so avoid putting a mirror behind a dining table.

Disguise black spot on mirrors Stick small pieces of foil onto the silvered backing. Damaged antique mirror glass will need costly resilvering.

Large mirrors on staircases It is disconcerting – and possibly dangerous – to face a mirror reflecting the stairs you are walking down, so avoid mirrors at the bottom of a staircase.

Posters and books Printed words will reflect back-to-front so pick a plant or table arrangement to reflect in a mirror instead.

Prevent steaming Fit panels of antimist acrylic mirror on bathroom walls and cabinets.

Bathroom mirror In bathrooms where the basin is beneath the window, fix a mirror on a flexible arm to the window frame. Or remove a window pane and fit a pane of mirror glass instead.

Mirror tiles Sold in DIY shops and mostly self-adhesive, mirror tiles need absolutely flat walls to prevent a distorted image. Most mirror tiles come with self-adhesive pads in each corner for fixing them to the wall. If the wall isn't flat, stick the tiles to a sheet of plywood and screw the plywood to the wall. Put the corner tiles on last, to cover the fixings.

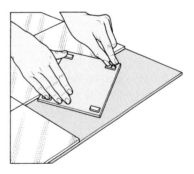

BEWARE OF MIRRORS OVER FIREPLACES

If you plan to have a mirror over a working fireplace, make sure that the fender projects at least 450mm (18in) from the grate. It will prevent anyone standing too close when they are looking in the mirror.

CARPETS AND HARD FLOORINGS

Picking your colour scheme

Colour underfoot is very dominant in any room (a floor takes up roughly one-sixth of a room's total surface area), so when you're choosing new floor coverings, always take along any samples of fabrics, wallpaper and paint colours. If possible, look at large flooring samples under home lighting conditions, because domestic tungsten lighting distorts colour. What was a subtle grey daytime carpet can become a drab beige at night, and reds and blues alter too.

Light-coloured carpets make small rooms feel larger, but may show stains. Dark, rich colours make large rooms feel more intimate and camouflage dirt and stains better, but lint and dust will show up.

Metal carpet plates at doorways interrupt the flowing look of a carpet, so order wooden carpet plates instead and paint or stain them.

What goes under the flooring?

Whether tiled, carpeted or laid with cushioned vinyl, floor surfaces must be level and damp-free. Different underlays suit different areas and carpet:
● Floors need to be covered with flooring hardboard if tiles, linoleum or vinyl are to be laid.
● Thick underfelt is good for levelling surfaces with minor irregularities but may stain light carpets if it gets wet.
● Rubber underlay is generally best for even floors. Don't use it if you have underfloor heating, though – it can give off an unpleasant smell.

Whatever your flooring choice, never skimp on floor preparations or carpet underlays, and it is worth having your floor coverings fitted professionally – they will look better and last longer.

What will a carpet fitter do?

Before buying a carpet, find out exactly what the fitter will and will not do.
● Most fitters will not trim the bottom of a door, but will take it off its hinges and leave it for you to deal with. You will have to call in a carpenter (some carpet shops will recommend one), or trim it yourself (see below).

TRIMMING A DOOR BOTTOM

The amount you have to trim from the bottom of a door so that it opens snugly over a carpet is usually quite small, so it can be tricky. Working so close to the edge can cause the saw blade to slip off the cutting line. And if the door is veneered, the veneer on the underside is likely to be splintered by the action of the saw.

Clamp a piece of scrap softwood to the underside and saw through it, too, when you're trimming the door. The saw will stay in the line of cut and there should be no splintering.

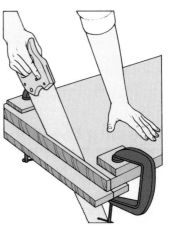

● Many will not lay hardboard over floorboards before they put the carpet down. The carpet supplier might know someone who could do it.

● Check beforehand whether they will repair – at their own expense – any damage they cause to skirting boards and decoration.

● Good fitters will generally take away any offcuts to make into threshold mats for you. This is done with an overlocking stitch called a 'whipping stitch'. Most carpet suppliers will also do it.

● Most carpet and flooring fitters will do advanced installations – cutting out shapes, inlaying patterns and borders, and patching worn or damaged areas invisibly.

Carpet-buying tips

Shop around Numerous floor-covering bargains exist, but you must be sure exactly what you need. Pricey, top-quality carpets are made to last – so if you're just doing up your house to sell it, they probably won't be appropriate.

Measure your room(s) beforehand Draw a plan of the room to scale on graph paper, making allowances for alcoves, hearths and wardrobes. Any fitter will do his own measuring as well, but it will give an accurate idea of price and avoid wastage.

Check with the carpet supplier about aftercare services Discount shops and DIY stores may sell cheaper flooring but may not provide the aftercare service of specialist shops, which include stretching, easing, adjusting stair carpets to even wear (page 71) and cleaning. Ask about fitting charges too; some shops charge, others don't.

Inform sales staff of relevant facts Tell them if you have large numbers of children or pets, because this will affect your carpet choice.

Thicker doesn't always mean better Manufacturers can crimp and bulk carpet fibres so that they appear thicker than they really are. Avoid these, and 'open' carpets too. Bend carpet samples backwards until the backing shows through – the denser the pile, the more hardwearing the carpet should be.

LOOK AT THE CARPET'S LABEL

When you are buying a new carpet, take a look at the carpet's label. It should classify the carpet as:

A = **contract** for shops and hotels
B = **very heavy wear** on halls and stairs
C = **heavy wear** for bedsits and children's playrooms
D = **general wear** for living rooms
E = **medium wear** for dining rooms and rooms not in constant use
F = **light wear** for bedrooms

Choosing the right carpet

Carpets come in two main types (tufted and woven) but there are others. Be sure to choose according to your needs in each room, taking into account the amount of wear the carpet is going to get.

Carpet strength, durability and wearability are determined by the fibre content (or blend of fibres); the density of pile (the number of tufts in a given area); the type of pile; and its height.

620

Tufted carpets

Most carpets are made by stitching tufts into a woven primary backing and then securing them with a Latex adhesive and another secondary backing. The carpet pile (or surface) is then finished in one of these ways.

Cut pile
There are several types of cut pile carpet.

● Saxony long pile – a luxurious carpet for light wear, suitable for use in bedrooms.

● Saxony short pile – less soft but harder wearing; suitable for living rooms and halls.

● Twist pile – sturdy and hard wearing, with twisted, thicker tufts in a dense pile.

● Velour (or velvet) pile – a smooth, hard-wearing surface, but it can shade with use.

Loop pile A hard-wearing carpet with small, tight loops of uncut tufts.

● Berber – a loop pile with a nobbly, tweed look. Generally suitable for light traffic areas as it doesn't wear well.

Cut and loop pile
A medium carpet with a textured effect, suitable for living areas but not hallways or stairs.

CARPET FIBRES

Carpets can be made of natural or man-made fibres – or a mixture of the two. The most popular natural fibre is wool, although cotton, silk, sisal and others can be used.

Nylon, the strongest man-made fibre, comes under various brand names such as Antron, Bri-nylon, Celon, Enkalon, Perlon, Timbrelle and Tactesse. It was considerably developed in the 1980s, leading to the production of new fibres which are durable, fire-resistant and easy to clean. It is frequently combined with wool in an 80/20 mix (80 per cent wool, 20 per cent nylon) in carpet manufacture.

Acrylics (Acrilan, Courtelle, Dralon) are the synthetics which most closely resemble wool, and are used for medium and cheaper-priced carpets.

Polypropylene (Meraklon), polyesters (Dacron, Terylene, Trevira) and viscose rayon (Evlan) are also used in carpet construction.

Woven carpets

Two different weaving methods are used, one called Axminster, the other Wilton. Both types of carpet can have the pile finished as above.
● In Axminster carpets, the pile is woven in rows of 'U'-shaped tufts and then attached to a base backing material. It is mainly used for multicoloured carpets.

621

● Wilton carpets have a pile and backing that are closely interwoven to give a thick carpet with a velvety surface. It is generally used for plain carpets or carpets of up to five colours.

Bonded carpets

The pile of the carpet is bonded to a backing with adhesive before it is rebacked with cloth or foam. It is also known as 'needlefelting'.

Natural coverings

Woven sisal, coir, coconut, seagrass and various types of rush can be loose-laid or fitted. Available in different finishes and colours, many are latex-backed so underlay is needed only on uneven floors.

Taking care of your carpet

● Dirt and grit are a carpet's greatest enemies. Grit can work down to a carpet base and eventually cut off fibres, so vacuum regularly – daily if necessary.

● Although new manufacturing methods or treatments mean that removing stains from new carpets is easier, there are some stains – hot black coffee, tea or curry, for example – that no fibre can repel. In these cases, clear up what you can (page 72) and call in the experts. Plain carpets will always show stains more than patterned ones.

● For areas of very heavy wear or bedsitters, trim the edges of the carpet to leave a border around the room. This can be decorated with tiles, or simply by painting the floorboards. If you buy a carpet 'square' with finished edges which is about 250-300mm (10-12in) smaller than the room, it is far easier to clean than fitted carpet, and you can turn it regularly to ensure even wear.

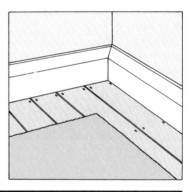

Hard-flooring cost cutters

Renovation Before covering over old floorboards and parquet, consider renovating or sanding them instead. Floor-sanding machines are easy to hire, but wear ear protectors and a mask and seal off the room – the job is very noisy and dusty. If you want to do more than one room at a time, it's probably best to call in the experts.

Recycled floors Some architectural salvage companies sell reclaimed floorboards and ceramic tiles at less than half their price new.

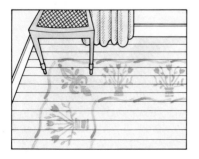

Decorating floorboards Floorboards can be painted or stained a new colour. There are many specialist products available, but yacht paints and varnishes (available from ships' chandlers) are usually more durable. Or you could stencil a border pattern on them. Linoleum and some vinyls can also be painted, but test them first.

622

WHICH HARD FLOOR COVERING?

MATERIAL	ADVANTAGES/ DISADVANTAGES	LAYING AND CLEANING
Ceramic floor tiles Come in a wide range of shapes, sizes, colours and grades. Choose heavy duty tiles (grades 3-4) for floors.	Hygienic and cool but can be noisy and slippery – and crockery won't survive being dropped.	Level floors: DIY laying possible but difficult. Uneven floors: leave to an expert.
Quarry tiles Pre-sealed tiles are hard and frost-proof. Welsh handmade tiles come in varied terracotta reds; machine-made tiles more uniform but include cream and black. Never use wall tiles on the floor – they may not be strong enough.	Unsealed tiles mark badly from grease and stains unless properly sealed before use. Can be textured to prevent slipping.	Leave tile laying to an expert. Before use, seal untreated tiles sparingly with equal quantities of boiled linseed oil and white spirit. Otherwise use recommended sealants.
Wooden floors Wood strip comes in various woods – oak, beech and mahogany are expensive. Veneered chipboard is cheaper. Also parquet (wood block) and wood mosaic tiles.	Suitable for kitchens and bathrooms but can be noisy. Shows marks easily unless treated with hard-wearing finishes.	All floors must be lined with hardboard sheeting. Leave woodstrip and wood block to an expert, but you can lay tiles. Seal with a tough finish or coating such as two-part flooring lacquer.
Linoleum Made from natural fibres and available in tiles or sheet form in varied thicknesses.	Durable and self-healing as small scratches close up again through use.	Leave laying to an expert.
Vinyl A huge range of patterns and colours; can be flexible (looselay), cushioned or rigid. Comes as both sheet and tiles.	Waterproof and quiet, but does mark fairly easily.	Leave large areas for an expert but small areas possible. DIY tiles easy to lay.
Cork tiles Made from cork mixed with resins and then compressed and bonded. Can be bought unsealed, sealed with polyurethane, or coated with clear vinyl.	Warm, quiet and tough, especially when coated with vinyl. Tiles may chip with time, and 'lift' if saturated with water.	Seal both the sides and edges of untreated cork to stop water penetrating. Use matt varnish rather than gloss. It looks more natural.

623

'Floating systems' Some floorboard manufacturers stock boards that can be nailed over a existing thin foam underlay or vinyl floors – not deep-pile carpet, though. A floor like this can be taken up when you move home and be refitted.

Hardboard Sealed and painted sheets of hardboard make good-looking, tough, temporary flooring and also provide sub-floors for future carpets and tiles. Make sure you use the flooring grade of hardboard for this. Plastic-veneered floorboards can also look good, costing only a third of the price of a new wooden floor.

Laying costs Remember to include the cost of professional laying for tiles and other hard flooring materials. Beware of tiling cowboys – there are plenty of them about. Obtain several estimates and get recommendations from friends.

Room-by-room flooring

Kitchen and utility rooms

Vinyl, ceramic, rubber, linoleum and cork floorings are all practical. Pick a material that goes with the rest of the decor – high-tech kitchens suit white ceramics, for instance, or a granite-patterned vinyl. Quarry tiles and slate are traditional favourites on farmhouse-style kitchen floors, but they are cold and hard – anything that drops on them will break.

Open plan living/ dining areas

For toughness, comfort and glamour, carpet is the most obvious choice. A top quality 80/20 per cent wool/nylon twist pile carpet treated against staining should last a family at least four years. A 50/50 per cent wool/polypropylene carpet with a three-coloured, textured pattern is an alternative if you want a change from a plain carpet but can't afford anything too expensive.

If you're worried about carpet stains in the dining area, consider laying vinyl, linoleum, cork or carpet tiles, matching them to the carpet in the living area.

Halls and landings

First impressions count for everything in these heavy-wear areas. Halls are generally 'short stay' places so you can afford to carpet them in a bright colour or a small pattern.

Decide on a colour for halls and landings, open all the doors and place your flooring samples on the floor. See whether the colour leads the eye through smoothly into the other rooms: abrupt colour changes will make areas feel smaller.

Home offices

Static build-up from carpets can cause problems with computers. Most modern carpets have been de-staticised but older or inexpensive carpets

---

RUGS TO THE RESCUE

Inheriting a previous owner's fitted carpets, complete with bald patches and stains makes a depressing start to a new home. Rather than going to the expense of replacing all the carpets, hunt out some good rugs to cover the blemishes. Buy one-off rugs or oriental kelims, numdahs or dhurries. You can find a range of styles and colours.

may still be untreated. Vinyl, rubber, linoleum, sisal and cork floors are good alternatives, or you can have your carpet treated with an antistatic treatment (page 71).

Bathrooms and cloakrooms

Hygiene and comfort are the top priorities here. Vinyl, linoleum, cork and ceramic tiles are all easy-to-clean, sensible choices. If you want carpet, pick one in a man-made fibre, such as foam-backed polypropylene. It repels water and is less likely to smell and distort when wet. Other carpets should be avoided in the bathroom.

Bedrooms

Fitted carpets are warm, comfortable and quiet. Since most bedrooms have light use, you should be able to get away with white, cream and all the pastel colours in light-duty carpets. Or you could use wooden floorboards or vinyl tiles with deep pile rugs and dhurries. Children's and teenagers' bedrooms will need tougher carpets.

Useful addresses

British Carpet Manufacturers
Association Ltd
72 Dean Street
London W1V 5HB.
Tel: 071 734 9853.
Publishes a helpful booklet on all aspects of buying carpets and taking care of them.

English Heritage,
Colour Research Unit
Keysign House
429 Oxford Street
London W1R 2HD.
Tel: 071 973 3657.
Can advise on historical colour schemes and materials.

DECORATING YOUR WINDOWS

● Do you want your windows to be the focal point of a room?
● Are the proportions of the windows right, or would you like them to appear taller or wider?
● What is the view like? Are you overlooked?
● Is heat or sound insulation needed?

The answers to these questions should give you some idea of whether to go for curtains, blinds or the bare look.

Curtains

Fabrics Choose fabrics which are both decorative and practical. Different fabric types will give a room a different feel – lace will make it seem light and airy, whereas velvet gives an enclosed sense of warmth. Choosing a dramatic patterned fabric will draw the eye to the window area, particularly when the curtains are closed.

Headings or pelmets? The tops of curtains themselves need to have heading tape attached – this pulls the fabric into pleats or gathers, depending on the style required. You can also fit tall headings, which will hide the track when the curtains are closed. Alternatively, protect the curtain tops with a pelmet made from wood, hardboard or fabric.

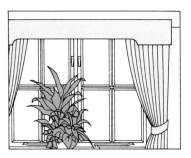

Tracks or poles? Curtains are usually hung from either a track or a pole. Both must be wider than the window frame so curtains can be drawn well back. Pick a track that matches the weight of the material: the shop assistant will be able to help. Track is cheaper, but poles are generally more elegant and sturdier. Both can be fitted with cording sets or draw rods for opening and closing curtains from the side.

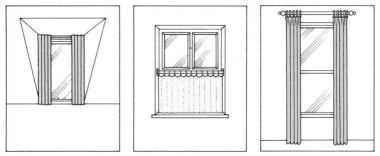

Length of curtains Short, sill-length curtains are best on small dormer windows; half-window café curtains can look good where privacy is needed but you want maximum daylight; and floor-length curtains will give an impression of larger, more spacious windows.

Linings Pick the lining colour with care as it will affect the overall colour of both the curtains and the room. Beige is traditional, but custard yellow will give a warmer feel. Blackout lining is good where there is strong street lighting or bright evening sun.

Blinds

Roller or pleated? Pull-up roller blinds tend to be more practical for use in kitchens, bathrooms or conservatories. Pleated blinds come in a variety of designs, most of which are more decorative than roller blinds.

Blind materials Paper, canvas, fabrics, wood or metal slats – take your choice. Use a washable fabric in the kitchen or wooden slats in a room that needs shade.

Make your own Most DIY shops have blind kits to which you add your own choice of fabric. You will need to stiffen the material you've chosen first, either with a commerical fabric stiffener or by using Unibond glue – just follow the instructions on the tin.

DON'T WASTE ENERGY 🍃

● On average, most British homes will lose 10 per cent of their heat through their windows.

● Heavy, lined curtains are the most efficient way of keeping in heat and keeping out draughts and cold. Best of all are floor-to-ceiling curtains with a centre overlap, but don't hang them in front of a central heating radiator or you will lose your heating.

● If your radiators are beneath the windows, either build the windowsill out slightly and hang your curtains to that length (so hot air is not lost behind them), or use 'false' full length curtains (which never close) with a blind to cover the window glass.

● Use special insulated cloth as curtain lining to help keep in the heat.

● Mount curtains and blinds outside the window recess for the best insulation – but don't cover radiators.

● Wooden-slatted blinds give more protection against heat loss than metal ones, but all slatted blinds allow cold air in around the edges.

Leaving the window bare

Feature the frame Any window with an interesting shape or moulding could be left uncovered. If you don't want to be overlooked, consider using stained, tinted or etched glass.

Keep the view Paint the walls in plain colours so as not to detract from the view. If the window is deeply recessed, line the recess with mirror to give extra light and reflect the scenery.

Make your own recess Surround the window with bookshelves to create an illusion of depth, and a 'frame' for an attractive view.

An indoor greenhouse Block out unsightly views by covering a double-glazed window with glass shelves (page 48), and filling them with plants. The plants will grow well and throw interesting shadows.

Curtain-making tips

● Never skimp on curtain fabrics. It's far better to use more of an inexpensive fabric than less of an expensive one. You will need $1\frac{1}{2}$-3 times the window size in fabric, depending on the curtain style, to give an impression of fullness.
● Save some curtain fabric to make matching tie-backs. They hold the curtains away from the window, letting in more light.
● Check that the pattern lies straight on the curtain fabric, otherwise the finished curtains will always look crooked. And don't buy from more than one roll of material – colours can vary from one roll to another.

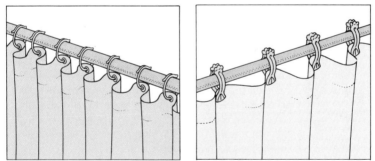

● You can use double-sided adhesive tape and a leather or hole punch to make quick curtain headings. Place a strip of double-sided tape along the top of a piece of lightweight fabric. Fold the material over it to create a hem and sew by hand or with a machine. Punch the holes, thread metal or plastic curtain rings through them and hang the curtain on a pole. Or if you don't like sewing, use brass or chrome clip-on rings.

Dealing with problem windows

Dormer windows You can get special swivel rods for curtains which swing out of the way, allowing in maximum light. Alternatively, fit a pair of louvred shutters to the outside of the window – they're good security too.

Sloping rooflights Use blinds backed with sun-resistant material, suitable for any skylights or conservatory roofs and windows.

Landing curtains Fit a blind or hang curtains inside the window recess – it will stop people brushing into them on a narrow landing.

Cloakroom windows Small, dark windows with no view can be decorated with special stained-glass paints and finished with self-adhesive leading. Alternatively, cover the glass with a special transparent self-adhesive material with a stained-glass pattern.

Arched windows Fit a curtain track well above the arch so you don't lose the effect. Alternatively, use a fan-shaped blind at the top and a second blind fixed to the wooden crosspiece lower down.

Different sized windows To give unity to two windows of different sizes on a wall, hang a pair of curtains to pull across them both.

PUTTING UP CURTAIN TRACK

The area over a window is sometimes hard to drill because a reinforced concrete or steel lintel supports masonry above.

● Use a hammer drill fitted with a sharp masonry drill-bit to punch holes through the plaster and into a concrete lintel.

● If the plaster pulls away because of the vibration, or if you hit a steel lintel, locate the extreme ends of the lintel with a bradawl or drill. Drill and plug the wall beyond the lintel and put up a batten to screw the curtain track to. Apply epoxy adhesive to the batten to help hold it.

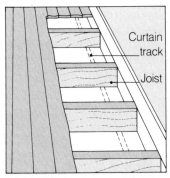

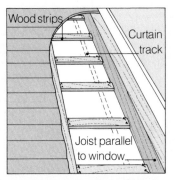

● You can fix most curtain track to the ceiling, using the alternative holes in the fixing brackets. But never rely on the ceiling plaster to take the weight of the curtains. If possible, locate the joists in the same way as locating timber supports in a hollow wall (page 50). If they run at right angles to the track, screw one fixing into each joist (above left).

● If the joists run parallel to the rail, wood strips may have to be laid between joists for the screws to go into (above right). This involves lifting some of the floorboards in the room above, so it's a job to avoid.

FINDING THE RIGHT FURNITURE

Take your time in selecting furniture. Consider your needs carefully, and choose pieces on the grounds of comfort and convenience – if you buy in a hurry, you may have to replace a costly item later.

● Have you got accurate measurements of your front door, internal doors and staircases? Don't forget the headroom on the stairs. Don't waste time and money buying a bed or wardrobe that you can't get up the stairs or into the room.

● What is your family like? Do you have children or pets who might harm delicate furnishings? Choose the most appropriate furniture.

● Are you going to move soon? If so, buy furniture you can take with you – fitted or built-in units will have to stay.

Budget and space-saving ideas

● Brightly coloured folding canvas chairs can be used in teenage bedrooms or living rooms until your budget stretches to something more permanent. Then move the canvas chairs into the garden.
● Round-top patio tables can be covered with floor-length tablecloths and used as side or dining tables during the winter.
● Rather than investing in one large coffee table, four small matching cube tables put together are easier to move around.
● A sofa bed in the spare room might leave enough space for a home office too. Use one in a teenage bedroom for extra seating and overnight stays, or get an upholstered foam block mattress in three sections which will fold up into a spare seat.
● In compact children's rooms, make the most of the space by buying a platform bed with a wardrobe, desk and drawers beneath it.
● In dining/living rooms, a fold-away side table with drop leaves can be extended to seat four to eight people for dinner.
● Folding chairs make excellent extra seating.
● Cane and wicker furniture can go anywhere in the house. It could start off in the living room, and then move into a bedroom when you replace it with something more substantial.

WHEN SHOPPING, YOU WILL NEED . . .

● A comprehensive list of measurements.
● A steel measuring tape.
● A notebook and pencil to make a note of brand names and other information.
● Any samples of furnishing, floorings, fabrics or paints that you want to match.
● A simple floor plan, which shows electrical sockets, plumbing, chimney breasts, doors, windows, radiators and any other major features. It should also show appropriate measurements.

Buying beds: a checklist

Size is important Double beds should be at least 1.4m (4ft 6in) wide, although 1.5-1.7m (5ft-5ft 6in) beds are more comfortable for two. Single beds, for adults or children, should not be less than 900mm (3ft) wide.

Buying a mattress on its own If you already have a slatted wooden base and you're buying the mattress only, test it out on a similar base to your own in the showroom.

'Lie before you buy' Prodding the mattress is not enough – lie on the bed and roll from side to side to make sure you can turn over easily. If possible, take your partner too, so you can see how it suits both of you.

Open or pocket springing? The more springs a mattress has, the more long-lasting it will be. Pocket-sprung mattresses have three times as many springs as open-sprung ones (which tend to creak as they get older) so they tend to have a longer life.

Zip and link mattresses These are good for couples who like mattresses of a different hardness – you can zip together a hard and a soft side with a linking bed base.

629

KEEP AN EYE OUT FOR QUALITY

Wooden furniture
● Does the wood graining match across all the doors and drawers?
● Does the piece stand squarely?
● Are the joints firm and tight?
● Is the finish durable, smooth and evenly applied?
● Does adhesive show around the joints? (It's a sure sign of bad workmanship.)
● Do the drawers fit well, open smoothly and have dust panels?
● Is the wood or hardboard inside the drawers and on the back and underneath smoothly finished?
● Are handles and locks good quality and well fixed?

CAUTION Furniture you assemble yourself is popular and cheap, but the instruction leaflets are often hard to follow, and a large piece can be difficult and time-consuming to put together.

Upholstered furniture
● Is the piece comfortable?
● Is it covered with a closely woven fabric?
● Does the pattern match all the way around; are the seams straight and are the chair skirts lined?
● Do the fabric and fillings match up to British Standards of durability and flammability?
● To check that any foam fillings conform to the latest guidelines on fire-resistance, contact FIRA (page 633). Fillings that don't conform to the latest standards should be avoided, as they could put lives in danger.

Transforming secondhand furniture

● Turn a decorative chest into a coffee table by having a piece of thick glass cut for the top. Remember to get all the edges polished.
● New knobs, handles, locks and hinges improve old whitewood and junk furniture.

● Drape loose fabrics over sofas or chairs for a new effect. Or cover old upholstery with new fabric using a heavy-duty staple gun – it's quick and easy.

● Wobbly furniture? Cut a piece of cork or pencil rubber to the right depth and width and attach it to the bottom of the furniture leg with glue or nails.

● Bulky furniture often looks better painted in a variety of colours and techniques – stippling or sponging, for instance. It can camouflage ugly features.

● If you are making your own dining room suite by buying a table and dining chairs separately, check that there is adequate space for knees between the chair and table.

Covering holes, scorch marks and stains in a sofa or armchair

Using needle and thread

1 Use a piece of fabric of the same age as the piece you are mending, taken from a matching cushion or seam panel. Wash it several times – if it looks too new, it will stand out. The grain and pattern must run in the same direction as the damaged section.

2 Cut a square patch, allowing 40mm (1½in) more than the hole or mark all round.

3 Turn 15mm (½in) under and pin the edges, mitring the corners. Tack the edges of the patch in place and press flat.

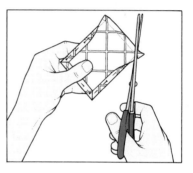

4 Put the patch over the hole, matching the pattern carefully. Stitch into place using a fine thread, and then remove the tacking thread.

Using iron-on adhesive webbing

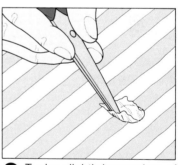

1 Neaten the hole with a pair of scissors and trim a patch to fit and match it exactly.

2 Tuck a slightly larger piece of double-sided adhesive webbing inside the hole.

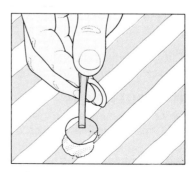

3 Lay the patch in position with the pattern or direction of weave matching the main fabric. Press with a warm iron over a damp cloth until the cloth is dry.

Dyeing and repairing soft furnishings

Professional dyeing Look in the Yellow Pages under 'Dyers – domestic' to find a local firm. The work is expensive, and firms generally won't take faded or stained items unless dyeing black or a dark colour. Dye temperatures are very hot, so be prepared for shrinkage.

Home dyeing in a washing machine Weigh articles carefully and follow the instructions on the dye. Don't skimp on the dye or you will get streaks. Overloading the washing machine will also lead to streaks and patches. Polyester and cotton mixes will dye a light shade only, and acrylic doesn't dye.

Professional sewing repairs Look in the Yellow Pages under 'Upholsterers' for firms that do repairs. You will get the best results on patterned fabrics. If you are having an upholstery job done, or loose covers made, keep at least 1m (3ft) of fabric for later repairs.

CALL IN THE PROFESSIONALS

It's expensive, but the results that you'll get by using professionals for difficult repair and cleaning jobs around the house may be worth it. Check the Yellow Pages for firms that will:
- Dye curtains, bedspreads, tablecloths, towels and sheets.
- Steam-clean carpets and upholstery in your home.
- Dry-clean duvets, pillows, loose covers and curtains.
- Hand-launder delicate linens and lace.
- Reweave furnishing fabrics and torn rugs.
- Recolour and reupholster leather work, including restitching damaged areas.
- Do alterations – relining, shortening and lengthening – to curtains.
- Clean and repair Venetian blinds.

DISPLAYING PAINTINGS

Framing tips

Buy a framing kit This is an inexpensive and quick way of framing prints, posters and photographs. A kit may consist of clips, glass and a backing board, or a complete frame with mount.

Use ready-made cover mounts Cover mounts can be used to alter the shape of a picture and are useful for small or difficult shapes, such as circles or ovals. They are available from specialist art and craft shops.

Pick mounts with a colour theme Pull together a diverse group of paintings by having a colour theme in the mounts. Or use frames and mounts as accent colours in an overall colour scheme.

Choose a mount and frame which complement the picture Mid-grey is the best background for bright pictures as it doesn't distort colours.

Hanging paintings

- It's best to hang paintings away from direct sunlight, strong artificial light, heat and fireplace fumes to prevent the colours changing.
- Use flat plate fixings to hang pictures in narrow spaces such as a hall – conventional wire hangings tip the paintings forward.

● Hang all pictures (and mirrors) with picture wire. It does not rot and is less likely to slip than cord.

● Non-reflective glass is a good choice for oil paintings and water-colours that need protection, but it is not suitable for engravings as it will distort crosshatching.

HOW TO GET YOUR PICTURES LEVEL

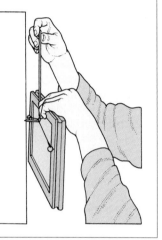

Cut a piece of coat-hanger wire about 250mm (10in) long. Sharpen a point at one end, and make a finger-sized loop at the other end with a pair ot pliers. Measure 10mm ($\frac{3}{8}$in) from the pointed end and bend the wire by 90°. Hang the picture by its wire on the pointed end, and then hold the wire (and the picture) by the loop. Position the picture on the wall, with its full weight on the wire, and press the frame gently in. The wire will make a small mark where the picture hook should go.

How to group paintings

● Single paintings disappear against a bold-patterned wallpaper, so hang them in larger groups (unless you have a very big painting).

● Group paintings in a definite shape, drawing an imaginary top, base or diagonal line through them to give a coherent feel. Or 'centre' a group of pictures by drawing imaginary diagonal lines through the group to find the central point.

● If you are hanging pictures above a seating area, make sure you leave enough clearance in case someone leans backwards.

● Grouping pictures horizontally or vertically can appear to alter the proportions of a room. For low ceilings, try a vertical arrangement; for high ceilings, a horizontal one.

● A large group of similar-sized paintings looks dull. Add one or two interesting objects such as a mask, fan or clock.

Useful addresses

Association of British Picture Restorers
Station Avenue
Kew
Surrey TW9 3QA.
Tel: 081 948 5644.
For information on restorers in your area.

Furnishing Industry Research Association (FIRA)
Maxwell Road
Stevenage
Herts SG1 2EW.
Tel: 0438 313433.
Can provide detailed technical information on materials, kitchen worktops and safety tests.

National Bed Federation
251 Brompton Road
London SW3 2EZ.
Tel: 071 589 4888.
The Federation offers advice to members of the public on all aspects of buying beds and mattresses.

Textile Service Association
7 Churchill Court
58 Station Road
North Harrow
Mddx HA2 7SA.
Tel: 081 863 7755.
Contact the Association for information on delicate household furnishings.

Decorating it yourself

BEFORE YOU START WORK

Successful decorating depends on careful preparation. If you skip essential groundwork, the finished job will suffer.

● Clear and isolate the area you plan to work in as thoroughly as possible. Preparation itself – stripping old wallpaper and sanding down paintwork, for example – can cause a lot of dust and mess which, if you are not careful, can spread into other parts of your home.

● Remove as much as you can from the room. Move the rest to the centre of the room, and cover it with dust sheets.

● Remove curtains. Take up carpets, or protect them with dust sheets.

● Take off lampshades and cover permanent fixtures, such as radiators and fitted units.

● If you take down any wall fittings you'll probably want to know later where the screw holes are. Before you paper the wall, push a matchstick into each hole or wallplug, leaving it sticking out slightly.

When you paper, you can ease the matchsticks through the wallpaper as you are smoothing it.

If the wallpaper is made of vinyl, you'll need to make a small cut with a trimming knife to let each match through.

● Keep a spare pair of shoes or slippers just outside the room you're working in. Change into them when you break off decorating – you won't track paint or dust into the rest of the house.

Choosing wallpaper

If it is your first attempt at hanging wallpaper, choose a good, medium-weight wallpaper. Cheap, thin paper is hard to handle and tears easily. And ready-pasted wallpaper is not necessarily easier to apply. To simplify the job, buy a random pattern which needs no matching.

Ordering paint and wallpapers

● The colour of paint can vary from one batch to another, so make sure all the tins you buy have the same batch number.

HOW MANY ROLLS DO YOU NEED?

Use a leftover roll of wallpaper to calculate how many rolls you'll need to paper another room. Measure the height of the wall and divide the figure into 10m (33ft) – the length of a roll of wallpaper. This tells you how many drops one roll will cover. For example, if the room is 2.3m (7ft 6in) high, you will get four drops per roll. Then use the roll as a measuring stick by holding it horizontally against the wall, moving around the room and counting how many widths are needed. The number of widths divided by the number of drops per roll tells you the number of rolls to buy.

● The same applies to the colouring of wallpapers – always check that the manufacturer's batch number is the same on every one of the rolls that you buy.

● If you are unsure of how many rolls you'll need, order a roll or two extra. Many dealers will take back unwanted rolls – provided they are unopened and you have a receipt.

● If you have to accept a roll with a different batch number, use it in places that won't show, such as behind furniture or in a shadowy area.

● Keep any leftover roll for repair work or for estimating how much paper you'll need for future decorating jobs (see *How many rolls do you need?* facing page).

HOW TO PAPER A ROOM

Removing old wallpaper

It's not advisable to paper over existing wallpaper. The new, wet paste may soften the old, making the previous covering expand or pull away from the wall. So strip it off before redecorating.

Wetting the wall with a garden spray can be quicker than using a sponge, but adjust the spray nozzle to give a fine mist so that you don't have too much water running down the wall.

 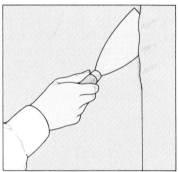

1 Sponge the old paper with warm water to which you've added a squirt of washing-up liquid and a handful of wallpaper paste. The washing-up liquid acts as a wetting agent, while the paste helps to keep water on the wall as the paper soaks. If the wallpaper is painted or washable, first roughen it with coarse abrasive paper on a sanding block.

2 Allow at least five minutes' soaking time, then use a wide stripping knife to lift the paper from the wall. Slide the scraper under a seam, and push it away from you. Be careful not to dig it into the plaster.

3 If the paper won't shift, sponge on more water and allow a longer soak.

TAKING OFF PAPER WITH A STEAM STRIPPER

If there are several layers of paper on a wall, or if the paper has been painted over, it is much easier to get off with a steam wallpaper stripper. Hire one from a tool hire shop which can be found in the Yellow Pages under 'Hire services – tools & equipment'. The stripper gives out steam from a metal plate, softening the paper so that it can be removed.

Caution Be careful when using a steam stripper on plasterboard. It can soften the surface, so use the stripping knife as little as possible.

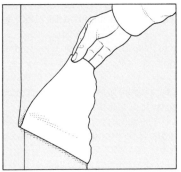

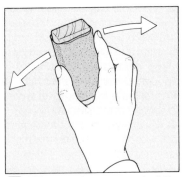

4 Try again with the stripping knife, and if the paper wrinkles pull it upwards from the bottom, away from the wall. If it has been well soaked, it should come away in fairly big pieces.

5 When you've removed all the old wallpaper, allow the wall to dry. Then lightly sand the wall with a medium abrasive paper on a sanding block to remove any little bits of paper.

6 Using a pasting brush, coat the wall either with glue size or diluted wallpaper paste, as directed on the packet. It will seal the surface and make your new wallpaper easier to move about on the wall when you put it up.

Pasting the paper

1 With a steel tape, measure the height of the wall in several places around the room. If it varies, take the largest figure and add 100mm (4in) for trimming at the top and bottom.

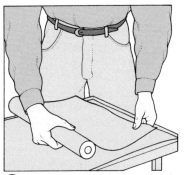

2 Place a roll of paper on the pasting table, pattern side down. Measure off a length and rule a pencil line across it. Then cut off the piece with a pair of paper-hanger's scissors.

3 Use the cut length, pattern side up, to match the pattern with the next length and as a measuring guide. The second piece may be longer because of the pattern match. Then cut the second piece.

A SUPPORT FOR YOUR PASTING BRUSH

Tie a piece of string across the rim of your paste bucket, knotting it at the handle's anchor points. The string provides a useful place to rest your paste brush when you're not using it. And drawing the brush across the string will get rid of excess paste.

4 Repeat this procedure until you have several lengths cut and ready for pasting. Number them on the back so you'll know the hanging order. If the pattern could easily be hung upside-down, write 'Top' on the back at the correct end of each piece.

5 If you're using standard wallpaper, lay the first length pattern down on the pasting table with the surplus paper hanging off the table to the right if you're right handed.

6 Apply the paste from the centre, brushing outwards, herringbone fashion. Make sure edges are well covered. It helps if you line up one edge at a time with the edge of the table as you paste. If you get paste on the table, wipe it off with a damp cloth before doing the next piece.

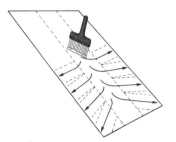

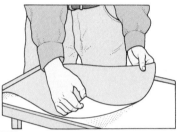

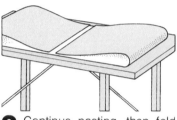

7 Pull more paper onto the table and gently fold over the pasted part, paste to paste. Do not crease it at the fold.

8 Continue pasting, then fold over the other end almost to meet the previous fold. Note which end is the top.

9 Fold again and leave to soak for five to ten minutes, depending on the weight of paper. It's vital to let wallpaper stretch before you hang it. Applying it to the wall too soon will cause bubbles, most of which will be impossible to get rid of. However, vinyl wallpapers don't expand, so you can hang them straight away.

HANGING PRE-PASTED WALLPAPER

If you're putting up pre-pasted paper, submerge the cut length in the water trough that is supplied with the paper. Make sure all the paper is wet, then pull it gently from the trough, allowing the surplus water to drain back in. Apply directly to the wall.

Putting up the paper

Hang the first piece on the wall adjoining the one that has the main window, and work away from the light. If edges overlap, no shadow will be cast by the join. The first length should turn slightly onto the window wall.

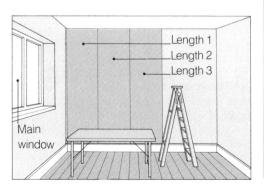

1 Measure a width from the starting point, less 25mm (1in), so that when you hang the paper, it will turn by that amount onto the window wall. Make a pencil mark high on the wall at the measured point.

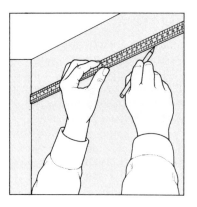

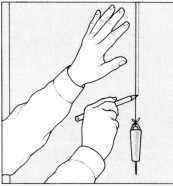

2 Hang a plumb line from the pencil mark. When the line has steadied, get a helper to mark the wall behind the line. You now have a true vertical. A plumb line can be made with a length of string and a small weight.

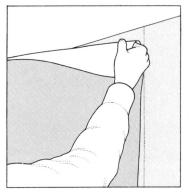

3 Take your first piece of paper, release the top fold and, if you're working to the right of the window, offer the right-hand corner to the wall so it touches the top pencil mark. Leave 50mm (2in) of paper above the top of the wall.

4 Apply the right-hand edge of the paper to the wall so it aligns with the pencil line. If it clings to the wall in the wrong position, carefully pull it away and try again.

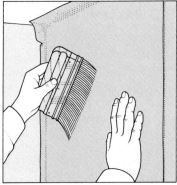

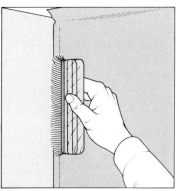

5 Once the right-hand edge is in place, smooth the paper with your hand or a paperhanging brush diagonally up until the top left-hand corner is on the wall.

6 When you're sure it's smooth and correctly aligned, release the bottom fold. Tap the paper into the corner and onto the window wall with the bristles of the brush.

7 Give a final smooth from the centre outwards to ensure the paper is in contact with the wall all over.

638

Trimming the ends

1 Press the paper into the skirting board by tapping it with the bristles of the brush or running the back of the scissors along the junction between the wall and skirting board.

Then, if the paper is strong enough, use a steel straightedge and craft knife with a new blade to trim away the surplus.

If the paper tears easily, pull it away from the wall and trim with scissors along the fold line. The fold mark is easily seen on the back.

Allow a millimetre or two to turn onto the woodwork so that any slight gaps between the wall and the skirting board (or architrave) are hidden.

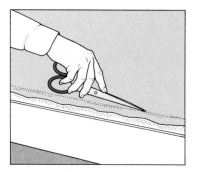

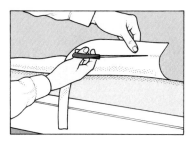

2 When you've finished trimming, press the paper back against the wall with the brush. Wipe any surplus paste from the woodwork with a damp rag while it's still wet.

3 Trim the other end at the ceiling or picture rail – whichever is appropriate – in the same way.

4 Put scraps of trimmed-off paper immediately into a bin liner to avoid mess and to make cleaning up easier.

HOW TO PATCH DAMAGED WALLPAPER

Find a piece of matching wallpaper and tear it into an irregular shape. Don't cut it; the straight edges will show up on the wall. Tear the patch away from you so that the edge is as thin as possible and no white strip is showing. Paste the patch, then stick it over the damaged area, matching the pattern all round.

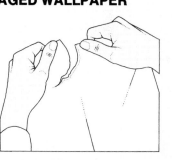

Turning a corner

1 When you get so close to a corner that you can't hang another full width, measure the distance from the last piece to the corner. Take measurements at the top, middle and bottom of the wall. Then add 15mm ($\frac{1}{2}$in) to the longest measurement to allow for a small turn onto the next wall.

2 Cut a length to this width. Keep the offcut piece to use as the first length on the adjoining wall.

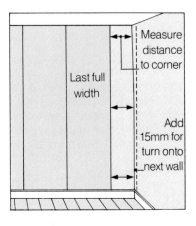

Last full width

Measure distance to corner

Add 15mm for turn onto next wall

3 Paste and hang the first length, using the paperhanger's brush to smooth the paper well into the corner. If you get creases in the corner, tear the paper and overlap the torn pieces so they lie flat (see *Fault-finder guide – Creases in the paper*, facing page).

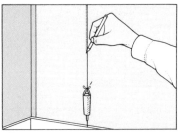 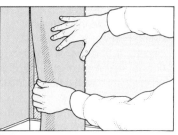

4 Measure the width of the remaining length and, with your plumb line, make a vertical mark that distance away from the corner on the second wall.

5 Hang the second length with its outer edge aligned with the pencil mark. The other edge will overlap the paper that turned from the previous wall.

Papering around switches and sockets

Surface-mounted fixtures

1 Lay the paper over the socket or switch and press on it with your fingers to mark the corners.

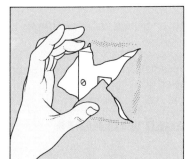 

2 Use small scissors to cut an 'X' from corner to corner across the area. Then press the paper around the socket so that it goes back to the wall.

3 Crease it with the back of the scissors around the four sides of the socket, then trim away the surplus, allowing a millimetre or two to turn onto it.

Flush-set fixtures

1 If the fixture is set flush with the wall, you can treat it in the same way as a surface-mounted one (above), but for a really neat finish the paper can be tucked in under. First, switch off the power at the mains. Then hang the paper from the top of the wall.

2 Using small scissors, cut the paper in an 'X' to the corners of the switch or socket, then unscrew the switch cover until it comes away 5mm ($\frac{1}{4}$in) from the wall.

3 Trim the paper, but leave a good 3mm ($\frac{1}{8}$in) over to tuck under the switch cover.

4 Push the paper behind the cover with a thin piece of wood, such as a lollipop stick. Brush the paper flat against the wall, smoothing out any air bubbles.

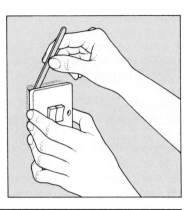

DO NOT use a metal object to push in the paper – even if you have shut off the power.
DO NOT put metallic or foil wall coverings behind any electrical fittings.

Fault-finder guide: wallpapering

Creases in the paper
A crease often means the wall is not flat, or a corner is not true, and there's nowhere for the surplus paper to go.
● Pull the paper away from the wall, preferably while the paste is still wet, and tear it along the line of the crease.
● Paste and press the pieces back in place, making sure the white edge of the tear is underneath. Don't cut the paper – the cut edge will show.

Unsightly blisters
Not allowing sufficient soaking time before you hang the paper is a common cause. Some blisters will dry out, but if they don't there's little you can do. If there are only one or two blisters, cut them open with a razor blade. Fold back the flaps and apply paste, then press the pieces back. If the bubbles are extensive, strip off the piece and replace it.

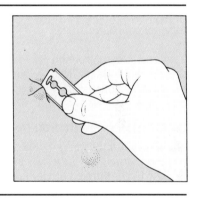

Lifted seams
Usually a problem with vinyls. Let the paste dry, then use a seam adhesive or vinyl overlap adhesive to stick down the seams. Light rolling with a seam roller may also help. But don't put on too much pressure if the covering has a raised pattern; flattened areas will show.

Grubby marks
Discard the crust from some bread, make a ball of the rest, and lightly rub the dirty areas.

DECORATING WITH PAINT

Choosing the paint to use

Follow the manufacturer's advice on the tin. It will tell you what surfaces can be covered, the drying time and covering power. Here are some general guidelines:

Knotting Used for coating resinous patches in new wood, particularly the knots. If knots are not treated, brown stains will eventually come through the paint.

When the knotting is dry, apply an all-over coat of primer, followed by the final coats.

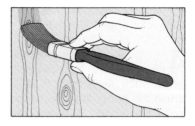

Primer All-purpose primer can be used on plaster, metal and new or exposed wood. It seals pores in surfaces and is a key for other paints.

Undercoat Use on interior and exterior primed surfaces before the gloss topcoat. Also use on dark areas that you want to paint paler or when you are making a strong change of colour.

Oil-based, or synthetic, gloss A topcoat for interior and exterior wood or metalwork. You can also use it on walls and ceilings.

Non-drip jelly A one-coat gloss paint you can use on indoor and outdoor woodwork. Jelly paint is also available as emulsion for ceilings. Combines undercoat and topcoat. Easy for beginners to apply.

Emulsion A quick-drying, water-based paint you can put on walls with a roller. It dries quickly. As it's water based, tools are easy to clean. Doesn't need an undercoat.

Enamel paint A non-toxic paint best for small jobs, such as children's toys and furniture and areas of metalwork. No primer or undercoat needed. Expensive for large areas.

Textured (plastic) coating For indoor walls and ceilings with uneven or unattractive surfaces. Thicker than paint, it is a compound that is difficult to remove. Apply with a shaggy roller unless the instructions say otherwise. Paint with emulsion when dry.

How much paint do you need?

The kind of surface you're painting will affect the amount of paint needed. A highly textured surface may need twice as much paint as a smooth one.

● To work out the area of a large surface, multiply the height by the width to give square metres or square feet. If the area isn't a regular square or rectangle, divide it into rectangular sections, multiply the heights and widths, then add up the total.

● Count windows with mouldings and window bars as a solid area.

● For flat metal windows, do the same but deduct 25 per cent.

● To calculate the area of a moulded door, multiply height by width and add 25 per cent.

Here is a rough guide to coverage on a smooth, prepared surface:

All-purpose primer .... 12sq m (130sq ft) per litre
Undercoat .... 16sq m (170sq ft) per litre
Oil-based, or synthetic, gloss .... 14sq m (150sq ft) per litre
Non-drip/one-coat gloss .... 12sq m (130sq ft) per litre
Emulsion (water-based) paint .... 10-13sq m (108-140sq ft) per litre

Cleaning surfaces before you start

Gloss and emulsion painted surfaces If the surface is sound, wash down with sugar soap and water, then redecorate. In the case of gloss, also rub with a fine flexible sanding pad to flatten down the glaze. Brush off the dust before painting. If there are holes in the surface, fill them with cellulose filler or wood filler and sand down when the filler is dry.

Distempered surfaces Scrub off the chalky barrier formed by distemper with coarse cloth or a nylon pot scourer and water. If the chalky coating is thick, dampen the whole area, then scrape with a stripping knife. Coat any remaining distemper with stabilising solution.

Wallpapered surfaces If the walls you want to paint are covered with old wallpaper, it's advisable to strip them back to the plaster. Painting over old wallpaper can soften the paste and cause bubbling. (See *Removing old wallpaper*, page 635.) If the paper is going to be difficult to get off – perhaps because it has been painted – or if there are several layers, hire a steam wallpaper stripper.

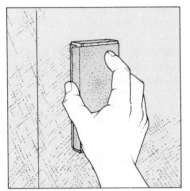

Painted paper If the old wallpaper has been painted over, roughen the surface with course abrasive paper before trying to strip it.

Washable paper If the old covering is washable or a wipe-clean paper, score it with a serrated scraper so water or steam will soak in.

What brushes should you use?

● Spend money on good paintbrushes that have plenty of bristle – cheaper ones tend to have as little as half the amount of bristle, and therefore hold less paint.
● For most work, 12mm ($\frac{1}{2}$in), 25mm (1in) and 50mm (2in) brushes are all you will need.
● For covering large areas, you could buy a 100mm (4in) or a 150mm (6in) width brush, but some people find them tiring to use. For painting walls with water-based paint, a roller or paint pad is much easier.

Paint rollers and paint pads

For large areas, rollers are easier and faster than brushes, but they are best used with water-based paints. Oil-based paints are hard to clean off a roller.

Foam roller Best for general painting, if you don't want a quality finish and if the surface you're painting is smooth.

Mohair roller For fine-finishing, but only effective on smooth surfaces.

Lambswool or nylon roller Use lambswool shaggy pile rollers for textured surfaces, such as embossed wallpapers or textured compounds. You can also get tough nylon shaggy pile rollers which will not be torn by rough walls.

Paint pads As with rollers, the paint pad, or pad brush, is an alternative way of covering large areas quickly – as long as they're smooth and you're using water-based paint that you can clean off with water. Many proprietary paintbrush cleaners affect the bond between the mohair pad and the foam backing, spoiling the tool.

● Choose the largest paint pad you can get for large areas – they come in several sizes, ranging from 25mm (1in) to 180mm (7in) wide.

● The smallest pads can be used to get at awkward spots, such as behind pipes and radiators. Buy one with a long handle.

Using your paintbrushes

● A new brush may shed fine dust and a few bristles, so use it first for primers and undercoats rather than a topcoat.

● Choose a brush to suit the job. Use a 12mm ($\frac{1}{2}$in) brush on frames and beading and 100mm (4in) for doors. For most other jobs, use a 50mm (2in) or a 25mm (1in) brush.

● Work in sections, brushing first in one direction, then at right angles to the first strokes, and finishing with strokes along the longest section. Keep the edges of the painted area wet, especially in warm weather, or you'll get ridges where the paint starts to dry.

Tips for using rollers and pads

● Some paint pads and rollers have hollow handles so you can insert a broom handle, allowing you to reach high walls or a ceiling from floor level. It makes the job easier, particularly if you use solid emulsion paint which can be moved around without spilling.

● Use a brush to finish off around the edges of a wall or ceiling where a pad or roller has missed.

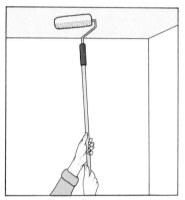

● If you're covering textured surfaces, apply at least two coats of paint. Allow the first to dry, then do the second coat from a different direction.

Painting with a spray can

Small areas – and irregular ones, like wrought iron or Lloyd loom weave – can be painted with an aerosol paint can.

● Make a simple spray booth from cardboard to catch over-spray.

● Read the instructions carefully – you must hold the can the correct distance from the work.

● Always keep the can parallel to the surface being coated as you move the spray around.

● Apply only the thinnest of coats – and build coat upon coat until coverage is complete.

● When you've finished, up-end the can and spray onto newspaper until only propellant comes out. This cleans the nozzle.

PAINT THAT CONTAINS LEAD

Modern domestic paints contain little or no lead. Paints that do have lead must carry a warning. But if you're stripping down paint in an older house, keep in mind that there may be lead in the dust that's created.

● Wear safety glasses and a dust mask, and open the windows.

● Don't strip the paint with a dry scraper. Use a liquid chemical stripper.

● Use dampened wet-and-dry abrasive paper for rubbing down – it will stop dust from forming.

Masking off an area

● To keep paint off the surrounding surfaces while you're decorating, cover them with masking tape. When you're painting the outsides of windows, apply the tape to the glass, leaving a millimetre or so of glass showing. This will ensure that paint seals the join between the putty and the glass.

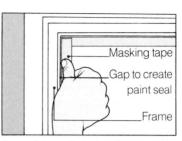

Masking tape

Gap to create paint seal

Frame

● Remove masking tape as soon as the paint starts to harden – at this stage it's easy to remove. If you leave it on for weeks the adhesive hardens.
● Cover odd-shaped items with aluminium foil to protect them. Foil crimps tightly around taps and doorknobs.

Using a paint kettle

● Pour a small amount of paint from the tin into a paint kettle so that the rest stays uncontaminated by grit and dust.
● To save cleaning the kettle each time you switch paints, line it with kitchen foil. When you've finished with one paint, remove and throw away the foil and reline the kettle for the next paint.

Storing paint

● Never store a small amount of leftover paint in a large can. Pour it into a screw-top jar of the right size for the paint to fill. Label the jar with the content. This way the paint will keep for years.
● To prevent skin forming on paint, cut kitchen foil to the approximate inside diameter of the paint tin and rest it on the paint before putting the lid back on.

Painting radiators

Radiator paint is specially formulated to stay white. Other types may be affected by the heat and quickly yellow. If you are painting a radiator to match the walls, use a gloss paint of the same colour.

Taking a break, and cleaning brushes

● The best way to store a brush while you take a break is to load it with paint, then wrap it in kitchen foil to keep out air. The brush will be ready for use when you unwrap it.

● If you are using oil-based paint, you can suspend the brush in white spirit. Drill a small hole through the handle, push a piece of wire through and rest it on a jar.

● Don't rest a brush on its bristles – they will develop a kink which is often impossible to correct.

● Clean brushes used for water-based paints in water as soon as possible. Never stand brushes in water when you take a break from painting – it will swell the wooden handle and rust the metal ferrule.

● Some oil-based paints can be cleaned with detergent and warm water. For others you should use either white spirit or a purpose-made brush cleaner. Instructions are on the can.

● If a brush has splayed out at the tip during cleaning, slip a small elastic band over the tip to hold the bristles close together. Store brushes in a dry place – ideally in polythene bags to keep them clean.

● If a brush has set hard with paint on it, soak it in a brush cleaner and restorer. When the paint has softened, scrape it out of the brush with an old kitchen knife, working from the metal ferrule to the brush tip. When the brush is clean, keep it for priming – never for fine finishes.

Fault-finder guide: painting

Paint problems usually stem from poor surfaces, inadequate preparation or incorrect application. Here are some common problems and their remedies:

Problem	Possible causes	Action/Prevention
Paint won't dry	● The usual cause is a dirty or greasy undersurface.	● Strip back completely. Sand clean or degrease with white spirit before applying primer and redecorating.
Flaking paint	● May be due to an unstable surface, such as old distemper under new emulsion paint. ● Can also be caused by painting straight onto a gloss surface.	● Strip off the new paint, then remove as much as possible of the old material below. Apply a stabilising solution before repainting. ● When painting over old gloss, wash first with sugar soap and rub with a fine flexible sanding pad to flatten down the glaze.
	● Paint flaking off radiators is probably emulsion – not designed for metal.	● Sand it off and repaint with an oil-based paint.
	● Flaking paint on the outside of the house is often caused by air or moisture trapped in the wood.	● Sand down and recoat with microporous paint which 'breathes'.
Wrinkled paint	● An 'orange peel' effect may be caused by applying a topcoat before the undercoat is dry. ● The paints used may be incompatible.	● For large areas, strip off the paint and start again. ● For small areas, sand with wet-and-dry paper used damp, and repaint. ● Next time, choose primers, undercoats and topcoats from the same manufacturer.

Problem	Possible causes	Action/Prevention
Blistered paint	● Usually caused by moisture or air trapped in open-grain wood. The sun's warmth expands the trapped material, which swells the paint into a blister.	● Prick a blister. If moisture comes out, the wood is damp. If there is only air, the wood is dry but the grain needs filling with an epoxy-based wood filler. ● If the blistering is serious, strip back to bare wood, allow to dry and repaint.
Insects settle on paint		● Allow a week for the paint to harden, then rub them off with a clean rag.
Runs and sags	● Caused by applying too much paint.	● Allow to dry hard – it may take some weeks – then sand with damp wet-and-dry paper, and apply a new topcoat. ● If an undercolour is not hidden by one coat, let that coat dry before applying further coats. Never try to cover in one thick coat. It will run.
Surface cracks	● Usually caused by expansion of the wood.	● Occurs with open-grain wood like oak. Strip off the paint, and fill the grain with epoxy-based filler and repaint.
Dull finish on gloss	● Can be caused by applying gloss paint to an unprimed surface.	● Strip off the paint, rub smooth, then prime and undercoat before applying a new topcoat.
Show-through of colour beneath	● Can be caused by relying on only a topcoat to hide the colour underneath, which it usually can't do.	● Make sure the paint is hard-dry. Sand with fine dampened wet-and-dry paper. Apply undercoat until the under-colour is hidden, then topcoat.
Gritty surface	● Grit picked up on a brush and left in the paint, or failure to clean the surface.	● Allow the surface to harden, then sand with damp wet-and-dry paper and apply new paint. ● To avoid this problem, pour a little paint into a paint kettle. If it does get grit in it, you can throw it away, saving the rest in the can. ● If you suspect paint has grit in it, stretch a piece of washed nylon stocking over a clean jar, then pour the paint through it. ● If you're painting a small area, hang the stocking in the paint (left) and dip the brush into the stocking.

TIPS FOR TILE MAINTENANCE

Drilling tiles

To prevent a masonry drill sliding when you're starting to drill into a tile, put a cross of clear adhesive tape over the point to be drilled. The drill tip will then be held by the tape long enough for it to penetrate the glaze. Never use hammer action; it will shatter the tile.

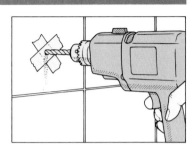

Replacing a damaged tile

1 Protect your eyes and hands with safety goggles and gloves – slivers of tile will fly around the room.

2 Make two or three holes in the centre of the damaged tile using a masonry bit fitted in a power drill.

3 Use a cold chisel (or an old woodworking chisel) and a club hammer to cut away the tile. Work from the centre outwards. That way you won't damage the surrounding tiles.

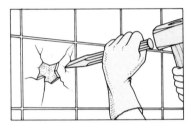

4 Carefully chisel away the old tile adhesive, then apply fresh adhesive to the new tile before pressing it into the vacant space. When the adhesive has dried, renew the grout around the new tile.

Renewing broken grout between tiles

● If you use a combined tile adhesive and grout, remove the surplus material while it's still soft.
● If you use grouting powder, always add the powder to the water to avoid lumpiness. Don't pour the water onto the powder.
● Apply the grout with a small piece of sponge or a rubber squeegee, working it well into the gaps.
● Wipe away surplus grout from the face of the tiles with a clean, damp sponge, then leave to dry before polishing.
● Polishing with a screwed-up ball of newspaper will remove any grout dust from the tiles and give them a nice shine.

Painting tiles

If you want to paint ceramic tiles, you'll get the best effect by using enamel paint. It needs no primer or undercoat, so you'll get a smooth surface. Try to avoid painting the grout lines and, when the enamel is hard, regrout the joints.

New patterns on old tiles

Areas of dull tiling can be brightened with stickers or transfers sold for the purpose. They can also be used in steamy bathrooms.
● Self-adhesive vinyl stickers can be stuck to the tiles, but avoid getting any air trapped under them. It forms bubbles which are extremely hard to remove.
● With waterslide transfers, the transfer is floated on water, then slid in place on the tile. Surplus water is wiped away. They can be fixed to either horizontal or vertical surfaces.

CHOOSING A CONTRACTOR

If you are looking for someone to do work in your house – whether a builder, plumber, roofer or gardener – try and find someone who is personally recommended. Ask friends, neighbours and colleagues if they can help, or if you are new in the area, knock on the doors of properties similar to yours. Get as many recommendations as you can. An architect or surveyor may be able to suggest a reputable firm.

Check that the contractors are members of a trade association before asking for an estimate (not legally binding) or quotation (a firm figure). Never have work done before discussing the price.

Get quotations in writing Ask the contractor to supply as much detail as possible of the work to be undertaken. Where materials such as specific roof tiles are important, these should be specified.

Get more than one quotation for any job Three is a good idea. Don't necessarily accept the cheapest: other factors – time, approach to the job and how much you like the people involved – are also important.

See some previous work Try to look at work a firm has carried out for a previous customer. If they take pride in their work they'll be happy to refer you to someone.

Don't ask for more than originally agreed Don't add in extra tasks, such as a new coat of paint on all the doors, and assume that the original quotation will cover it. If the tradesman suggests extra work that needs doing, either agree a price (in writing) or tell him not to bother.

Drawing up a contract

For a large job, you may want to arrange a specific contract between you and the firm doing the work. If so, consider:
● A time scale. If you want the job done by a particular date and the firm agrees, write it in. You may be able to exact a financial penalty if the date is not met, but they may charge a premium for finishing on time.
● Subcontracting. Check that the firm will be using either its own staff or subcontractors with whom you are happy. Make sure you all know who is responsible if something goes wrong.
● Materials and procedures. Where these are important, agree them in writing with the contractor.

Stage payments

Agree in advance how much and when stage payments should be paid. Beware of being asked to pay for materials unless you have seen both the receipt *and* the arrival of the materials on your premises. Retain a small percentage of the total sum at the end of the work to be paid only after you are satisfied with the standard of work.

Checking standards of work

You can check some things yourself, but others need a professional eye. With easy things – like paint finish or wallpaper hanging – check a contractor's work every day. If you can't judge the work yourself, pay an architect or surveyor to inspect it for you. Remember, if things aren't up to scratch, the contractor has to redo the work at his own expense.

Repairs and emergencies – be prepared

Build up a list of reliable workmen that you can turn to in an emergency. Or join an agency which guarantees you 24 hour coverage on all types of repair – your buildings insurance firm will help you find one.

Moving house without tears

HIRING A REMOVAL FIRM

A professional firm of movers is well worth the extra cost, especially if you have a large household, big or awkward items, or difficult access such as steep stairs, narrow passages or a sloping driveway. Even for a small move, it often pays to hire a removal firm. It is almost always advisable if you work full-time, have small children or are pregnant, elderly or not at the peak of your fitness.

Finding moving companies Friends and neighbours are often a good source of information about movers. Alternatively, look in the Yellow Pages under 'Removals and storage' or contact the British Association of Removers (page 652).

The right price Quotations for moving are usually given free of charge. Unless there is only one company in your area, try to get at least two, or preferably three, estimates before you decide. They can vary enormously. Usually it's best to accept a middle estimate – paying too little may mean that you get a poor job.

Getting an accurate estimate Ask to have someone sent to your home rather than accepting a quotation over the telephone. The figure will be far more accurate if the mover knows exactly how many vanloads and men are needed. Always check that estimates include VAT and read the small print carefully.

Cutting the cost Some movers give discounts to customers who do part of the packing or unpacking themselves, using cases supplied by the mover. If this appeals, discuss it in advance, and ask for two estimates from each firm to see if the saving is worth it. Ask how insurance cover is affected.

When the estimator calls

● Point out any items that may need special packing or handling. Pianos, tropical fish, mirrors, hi-fi equipment, computers, safes, wine, freezers and plants could all present problems if the mover is unprepared.
● Show the estimator any shelves or built-in units that have to be dismantled and reassembled. Show him the contents of attics and sheds.
● If carpets need to be moved, ask if the mover will lift and re-lay them.
● Ask if clothes can be left in drawers and cupboards or if they need to be taken out and packed separately.
● Mention anything that may make access difficult at either end.
● Discuss any parking problems at either address. Most removers will make special arrangements with the local police if you warn them in advance that this is necessary.
● Point out any fragile parquet or tile flooring, and decide who will provide coverings to protect them from heavy furniture.
● Have a written list of all your requirements for the estimator to take away. This will prevent later misunderstandings.

Insurance

A normal home contents insurance policy will not cover your goods while they are being moved. There are three ways to make sure you are protected if anything goes wrong:
● Ask your insurer to extend your policy to cover the increased risks of

moving. This type of insurance is usually only available if you hire a professional moving firm.
● Take out a separate goods-in-transit policy from your insurer.
● Your removal firm may offer removals insurance under the British Association of Removers' policy. Ask for a written statement of exactly what is covered, and any exclusion clauses.

DO-IT-YOURSELF MOVES

Moving yourself is much cheaper than hiring a removal firm, but it can be exhausting, time-consuming and difficult, particularly if there are any problems of access at either end. It also means providing your own boxes, packing materials, string, protective coverings and labels, and usually also finding people who are prepared to help.

Hiring a self-drive van

Where to hire? Firms that hire self-drive vans can be found in the telephone directory or in your local paper. If you drive a large van of 7.5 tons or more, you'll need a HGV licence.

Are you happy to drive a van? Don't consider hiring a van unless you are confident that you will be able to handle an unfamiliar vehicle – and one that is much larger than you are used to.

Working out the number of trips It is not always easy to calculate how many loads you will need. Most people make more journeys than they expected. Remember, overloading is dangerous, and can invalidate your insurance.

Should you hire by the mile? Paying a fixed sum for unlimited mileage may be cheaper than paying a smaller sum and a mileage charge if you have a long way to travel or plan to make many trips. Calculate the approximate distance you'll be driving, and work out which is the better deal. Always ask whether the prices you're quoted include VAT.

In case you're late Moving often takes longer than you think. Ask in advance about extra costs if you return the van late, and let the hire company know as soon as possible if that seems likely.

BEFORE YOU MOVE

● Arrange transfer of gas, water, electricity and telephone accounts.
● Organise disconnection of cooker, washing machine and dishwasher at old address and reconnection at new.
● Change milk and newspaper deliveries to new address.
● Arrange to have carpets cleaned or laid in your new home, if necessary.
● Order change of address cards from a local printer and send them to any banks, building societies, insurance companies or other businesses and organisations that you deal with. The Post Office will also forward letters to your new address for a small fee.
● Arrange contents insurance at the new house from the day you arrive.

Hiring a van and driver

Renting a van that comes with a driver will cost a bit more than a self-drive van, but is worth considering if you're not confident about driving a large

651

vehicle yourself. Another advantage is that the driver may be prepared to help you with the loading and carrying. Check exactly what is on offer before you decide.

ON THE DAY

Keep track of what's packed where Unpacking at the other end will be much easier if you have labelled all boxes and cases. Devise your own system, using colour or letter codes to show which room the contents belong in, and make sure everyone knows what the codes mean. Put the labels on the sides of the boxes rather than on the tops, so that they can be seen when they are stacked on top of one another.

Don't run out of money Have your cheque book and a supply of cash handy for tipping the removal men and in case you need to buy fish and chips for dinner, a bottle of wine to toast the new house, or an emergency supply of light bulbs, matches, or cleaning materials.

Dealing with the movers If you're using a firm of removers, make friends with the foreman as soon as he arrives and then give instructions only to him. Other than that, leave the men to it and stay out of their way. Keep them supplied with tea and coffee – no alcohol.

Before you set off
● Check that you've done everything you agreed with the new owners: heating, mains water supply and handing over the keys, for example.
● Lock all windows and doors and leave the property secure.
● Check that the removal men know exactly where they're going and how to get there. Tell them what they should do if they get there before you and give the foreman a spare key if you can.

At the new address
Before the unloading starts Make sure that carpets in the entrance hall are protected from dirty boots. Give the removal men a plan of the house and make sure that they understand how you've labelled items for different rooms of the house.

Heavy items Check that heavy pieces of furniture are put in the right place and in the right room, so that you don't have to move them later when you're on your own.

Signing the forms When the move is completed, you'll probably be asked to sign that the job has been done as agreed. If you have not yet had time to examine your belongings, write 'unexamined' on the forms.

Dealing with damage If anything has been broken or lost during the move, let the removal firm and your insurers know as soon as possible. If you notice any damage before the removal men leave, write it down immediately and ask the foreman to sign your note.

Useful address
British Association of Removers
3 Churchill Court
58 Station Road
North Harrow
Middlesex HA2 7SA.
Tel: 081 861 3331.

Crisis measures

*W*hen an emergency strikes, you need to take the right action – and take it quickly. Whether someone falls off a ladder and breaks an arm, or water suddenly pours in through the ceiling, this section tells you how to cope with the immediate crisis.

First aid

ANIMAL BITES

Bites from animals or people can cause infection, so wash the area thoroughly and if the skin has been broken see a doctor urgently, particularly if the bite has come from a person. Serious wounds should be treated at the Accident and Emergency Department of a hospital. Report dog bites to the police, as failure to keep a dog under proper control is a legal offence.

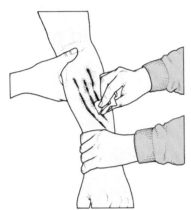

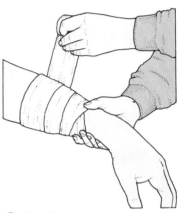

1 Wash the bitten area well with soap and warm water, or a mild antiseptic. Dry the area gently, wiping down and away from the wound. Cover the wound with a dressing, such as a clean handkerchief folded inside-out or a pad of tissues.

2 Bind the dressing in place with a clean piece of cloth or some sticking plaster.

Take the injured person to a doctor, or to your local hospital, because injections against tetanus or a course of antibiotics may be needed.

MAKING A 999 CALL

1 Before making the call, find out where you are. It may seem obvious to you, but the operator will need an address. So you need to know the name of the street, plus a house number or the name of the nearest cross street. The operator will also ask for your telephone number. It will help the emergency services to find you if you are cut off.

2 Call 999. On a pay phone do not put in any coins. In the dark, the 9 is the third button down on the right-hand side. On an old dial phone, the 9 is the second hole to the left of the finger stop.

3 Decide which of the emergency services you want – police, fire or ambulance. If you are in any doubt, ask for the police. They will alert the other services if necessary.

4 Answer all the operator's questions clearly, briefly and as calmly as you can. Do not launch into a long description.

5 Do not hang up until the operator tells you to.

BLEEDING

Even if you cannot stop the bleeding altogether, reducing the flow of blood may be enough to save someone's life.

A deep cut

1 Lay the person down. Remove clothing from around the wound if you can, but don't waste time.
   If possible, raise the wound above the level of the heart to slow the flow of blood.

2 Provided there is no large object embedded in the wound, press down hard on it with a piece of clean, absorbent cloth or paper.
   If the wound is large, squeeze the sides together gently but firmly as you press.

3 Maintain the pressure for five to fifteen minutes. While doing so, place an absorbent pad – such as the inside of a clean, folded handkerchief or pad of tissues – over the wound, and bandage it firmly in place with a scarf or piece of clean linen.

4 If blood seeps through the dressing, do not remove it. Put another dressing on top and bandage it on.

5 Telephone 999 and ask for an ambulance. Alternatively, take the injured person to the Accident and Emergency Department at your local hospital.

A large object in the skin

1 Squeeze the edges of the wound together around the object. Do not try to remove it; it may be plugging the wound.

2 Put a piece of clean cloth, such as a freshly washed handkerchief, over the wound. Then put a pair of raised pads of clean material around the wound (see next page). Try to make the pads higher than the object, to prevent pressure on it.

3 Bandage it with strips of material or adhesive tape. Do not put them over the object if it's protruding above the pads.

4 Telephone 999 and ask for an ambulance. Alternatively, take the injured person directly to the Accident and Emergency Department of your local hospital.

Making a raised pad

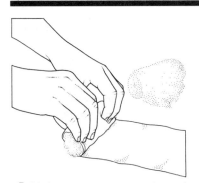

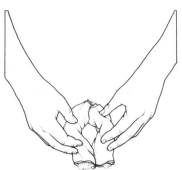

1 Make two sausage-shaped pads by rolling cotton wool or some other material in strips of clean cloth. If possible, make the pads higher than the foreign body in the wound.

2 Bend the pads into curves and place them around the object in the wound. Bandage them on with diagonal strips of cloth, but if the object is higher than the pads, don't cross the bandage over it.

If the bleeding will not stop

A severely bleeding arm As a last resort, press your fingers between the muscles on the underside of the upper arm. This will compress the brachial artery, which roughly follows the seam of the sleeve. Press up and in, pushing the artery against the bone.

DO NOT maintain pressure for longer than ten minutes; it may cause irreparable damage.
DO NOT apply a tourniquet.

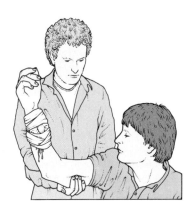

A severely bleeding leg As a last resort, lay the casualty down with the leg bent. Press down in the centre of the fold of the groin with both thumbs, one on top of the other, against the rim of the pelvis. This will compress the femoral artery.

DO NOT maintain pressure for longer than ten minutes; you may cause irreparable damage.
DO NOT apply a tourniquet.

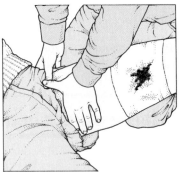

Tell someone to telephone 999 and ask for an ambulance.

When an injured person bleeds from nose, ear or mouth

1 Bleeding from the nose, ear or mouth can be a warning that there is a severe injury to the head or the chest. Put the injured person in a half-sitting position, with the head inclined towards the injured side, to allow the blood to drain.

2 Cover the bleeding point, but do not apply pressure.

3 Telephone 999 and ask for an ambulance.

4 If the person becomes unconscious, put him in the recovery position (page 676).

Puncture wounds

A nail sticking out of a piece of wood, or any other sharp object such as a bicycle spoke or needle, can cause a potentially serious wound.

On the surface the wound may look so small as not to be worth worrying about, and there may be very little blood. However, it may go deep into the flesh, carrying dirt or germs with it and creating a high risk of infection. A puncture wound can also cause serious internal injury to blood vessels and nerves.

Treat all puncture wounds as serious.

1 Stop any bleeding by pressing around the wound with a clean pad, or with your bare hands. Raise the injured part of the body above the level of the heart to help to stem the bleeding.

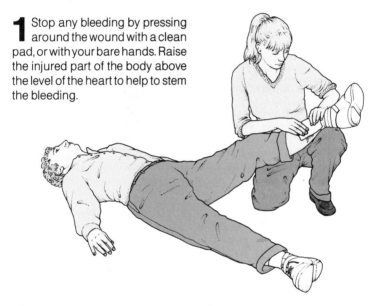

2 Cover the wound with a dressing held on by a bandage (page 475-7).

3 Take the injured person to the Accident and Emergency Department of a hospital.

TETANUS

Puncture wounds, splinters in wounds, burns, animal bites and road accidents all carry a risk of tetanus. This is a dangerous infection which causes acute muscle contractions, particularly in the jaw, giving the disease its other name of lockjaw. It must be treated at the earliest possible moment, so anyone who suffers such a wound and who has not had a tetanus inoculation in the past five years should see a doctor to get a booster injection.

Immunisation programme Children are given three routine injections against tetanus in their first year. They then receive booster injections when they start and leave school. A routine booster is recommended every ten years throughout life (or five years for people working close to animals or the soil).

BACK OR NECK INJURIES

Mishandling a person whose back or neck is broken can cause permanent paralysis or even death. A casualty with a suspected broken back or neck should be left where he is while you call 999 and ask for an ambulance.

When to suspect a broken back

● Loss of feeling and movement below the injured area, or a sensation of having been cut in half.
● Pain at the site of injury.
● A tingling sensation or pins and needles in the hands and feet.
● Inability to move fingers, wrists, toes or ankles when asked to do so, with no symptoms of a broken arm or leg.
● Inability to feel any pain when the skin is gently pinched in the affected area.

BROKEN BONES

Treat all doubtful cases of injured bones as if they are broken. Do not move the casualty unless it is absolutely necessary. Telephone 999 and ask for an ambulance. In the case of a broken arm, it might be reasonable to take the person to hospital in a car.

Deal with any failure to breathe (page 679), unconsciousness (page 676), or severe bleeding (page 655), before doing anything to the broken bone.

Put the casualty in the most comfortable position possible, and provide support for the injured limb with a rolled-up blanket or coat, or with cushions.

Do not move the injured part unnecessarily.

If the ambulance is delayed, or you have to take the person to hospital yourself, the injured limb will need to be immobilised. The simplest way is to secure it to an uninjured part of the body with bandages.

Supporting a broken arm

1 If the arm will bend easily, place it across the chest and put some padding between the site of the injury and the body. Do not bend the arm by force. Strap it to the body in the most comfortable position while you wait for an ambulance.

2 Improvise a sling from a large scarf or other piece of material about 1m (3ft) square, folded diagonally into a triangle.

3 Tie the ends of the sling in the hollow above the collarbone on the injured side. The hand should be just above elbow level.

4 Then strap the arm to the body with a piece of wide material around arm and chest. A tea towel folded diagonally, or a scarf, should do. Tie it on the uninjured side of the body.

Securing an arm that will not bend

Lay the casualty down in the most comfortable position. Put padding between the injury and the body, and strap the arm to the body with three pieces of wide material. Avoid the fractured spot.

Supporting a broken leg

1 A broken leg can be immobilised by bandaging it to the other leg. Move the uninjured leg to it, and put padding in between the two legs, especially at the knees and ankles.

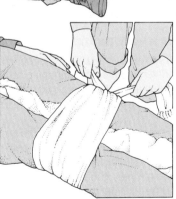

2 Tie the two feet together with a scarf or necktie in a figure of eight. Tie the knot against the outer edge of the shoe on the uninjured leg.

3 Tie the knees together with a wide piece of material knotted on the uninjured side. Tie extra bandages above and below the site of the injury.

659

Broken ribs

A violent blow to the chest, or a heavy fall, can break one of the ribs, causing a sharp chest pain when the injured person attempts to breathe deeply or coughs.

The site of the injury will feel extremely tender and will swell. Pain will increase with movement, including deep breathing or coughing, and there may be a crackling sound from the ribs.

But the injured person is not likely to feel ill and will have no serious difficulty in breathing, even though he may keep his breaths shallow to avoid the pain.

1 Make the person as comfortable as possible by putting the arm on the injured side in an arm sling (page 503).

2 Take him to the Accident and Emergency Department of your local hospital. Use a car if there are no complications (see below).

WHEN TO CALL AN AMBULANCE

A person who has had a severe blow to the chest may have suffered a serious injury if:
● He is unable to breathe properly, and seems to be suffocating.
● Red frothy blood comes from his mouth.
● He becomes restless and thirsty.
If he shows any of these symptoms, telephone 999 at once and ask for an ambulance.

BURNS AND SCALDS

Many burns need medical attention because of the risk of infection and shock. A young child or a sick or old person should always be taken to a doctor.

A burn or scald smaller than a 10p

If possible, remove rings, watch or tight clothing before the burnt area starts to swell.

Is it very painful?

If so, the burn is probably superficial. Put it under slow-running cold water for ten minutes, or longer if pain continues.

Cover the burn with clean, non-fluffy material. A sterile dressing is best, but the inside of a folded handkerchief, held on with cloth, will do.

Is it peeling or charred?

If the skin looks grey, and is peeling or charred and not very painful, the burn may be deep and serious. Cool it under slow-running cold water for ten minutes, then cover it with a dressing such as a clean handkerchief turned inside-out. Take the patient to a doctor or to the Accident and Emergency Department of a hospital.

DO NOT use plasters.
DO NOT apply fat, ointment or lotion.
DO NOT break a blister or touch the burn.

A burn or scald larger than a 10p

1 If possible, remove rings, watch or any constricting clothing before the area starts to swell.

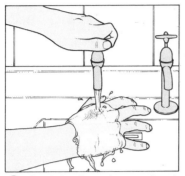

2 Cool the burn by running it under a cold tap for ten minutes, or longer if the pain continues. Cool a large area with a damp, clean cloth, but don't waste time before getting help.

3 Cover the burn with clean, non-fluffy material. A sterile dressing is best, but the inside of a clean folded handkerchief, held on with a scarf or some other piece of cloth, will do.

4 See your own doctor or go straight to the Accident and Emergency Department of your local hospital.

DO NOT use plasters.
DO NOT apply fat, ointment or lotion.
DO NOT break blisters or touch the burn.

A burn or scald covering a large area of the body

A person who receives burns over a large area of the body, such as an arm, thigh, lower leg or chest, needs urgent hospital treatment.

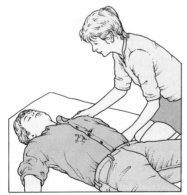

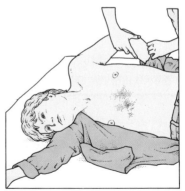

1 Lay the injured person down, preferably on a rug or sheet to prevent the burnt part of the body from touching the ground. Cool the area with cold water on a clean cloth, but don't waste time before getting medical help.

2 If possible, remove rings, watch, shoes or tight clothing before the area begins to swell. Carefully remove clothing soaked in boiling liquid.

Do not remove anything that is sticking to the burn.

3 Telephone 999 and ask for an ambulance, or take the victim to the Accident and Emergency Department of your local hospital.

4 Cover the burn with clean, non-fluffy material, such as a pillowcase. Fix it in place with a scarf or a piece of clean cloth.

DO NOT break blisters.
DO NOT put fat, ointment or lotion on the burn.
DO NOT touch the burn.

For burns to the face, get a clean pillowcase out of the airing cupboard and make a mask by cutting holes for nose, mouth and eyes.

DO NOT break blisters.
DO NOT put fat, ointment or lotion on the burn.
DO NOT touch the burn.

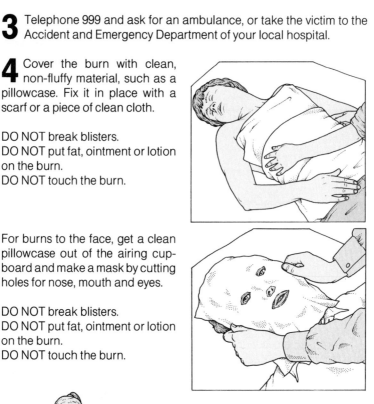

5 If a person with burns on the front becomes unconscious, put him in this recovery position. Turn the head to one side and tilt it back to open the airway. Raise the opposite side of the body on a large cushion or a blanket.

A person with burns on the back should be placed in the normal recovery position (page 676).

CHOKING

If the victim is conscious

1 Remove any food or loose false teeth from the mouth. (Do not try to locate the object with your finger.) Encourage the victim to cough; that may be enough to dislodge the blockage from the air passage.

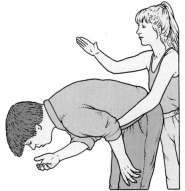

2 If this fails, help the victim to bend over with his head lower than his chest. He can be either sitting or standing. Slap him between the shoulder blades with the heel of the hand up to four times. Each slap should be strong enough to dislodge the blockage.

4 Hold your fist with the other hand and pull both hands towards you with a quick upward-and-inward thrust from the elbows. You are trying to pull the upper abdomen against the bottom of the lungs to drive out the remaining air and force the blockage out of the air passage.

Repeat up to four times. Each thrust must be hard enough to move the blockage.

3 **Abdominal thrusts** If the victim still cannot breathe, stand or kneel behind him. Clench your fist and put it, thumb inwards, between the navel and the bottom of the breastbone.

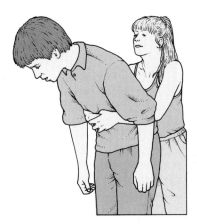

Treating small children

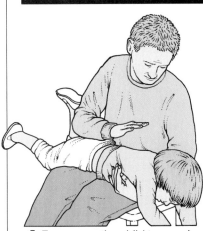

1 Encourage the child to cough. If this fails, lay him over your knee with the head down. Support the chest with one hand and slap him smartly with the heel of the hand up to four times. Each slap should be strong enough to dislodge the blockage.

2 If the child is still choking, sit him on your lap and perform abdominal thrusts (steps 3 and 4 above) – but use only one hand so you don't cause serious injury.

Treating babies

1 Lay the baby head down with the body lying along your forearm, using your hand to support the head and chest.

Slap the baby smartly between the shoulder blades with your fingers up to four times, using much less force than you would for an adult.

2 If the baby still does not start breathing, hold him on his back with the head tilted well back to open up the airway. Apply abdominal thrusts with two fingers of one hand, pressing quickly forwards and downwards just above the navel. Repeat the thrusts up to four times.

If the victim becomes unconscious

1 Start the kiss of life (see page 679).

2 If someone else is with you, tell them to telephone 999 immediately and ask for an ambulance. But if you are on your own, do not stop the kiss of life. Continue until the victim begins breathing normally again.

3 If the kiss of life does not inflate the lungs with the first two breaths, roll the victim onto the side nearest to you, with the chest against your thigh and the head well back. Give up to four strong slaps on the back.

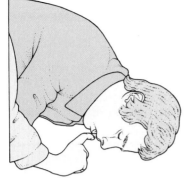

4 Look in the person's mouth to see if the blockage has become dislodged. If it has, hook it out with your finger.

5 If not, turn the victim onto his back and tilt the head well back. Straddle his thighs, or kneel alongside. Put the heel of one hand between the navel and the bottom of the breastbone.

6 Cover your hand with the other hand, and give a quick downward-and-forward thrust with your arms straight. Repeat up to four times.

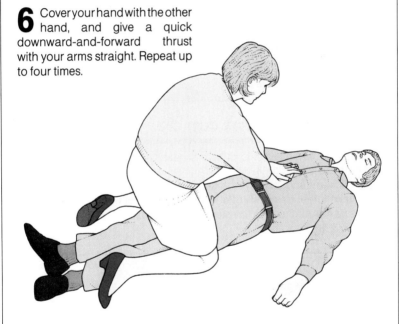

7 Check the victim's mouth to see if the blockage has been dislodged. If it has, hook it out with your finger.

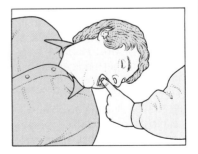

8 If not, resume giving the kiss of life.

9 If the lungs do not expand after two breaths, go back to step 3 on the left-hand page and repeat from there.

DIABETIC COMA

A diabetic who appears to be drunk may be suffering from low blood sugar. The condition is brought on by taking too much insulin or eating too little food. It can also occur after exercise has burnt up the sugar in the blood.

Low blood sugar affects the brain and leads to coma.

The condition can be distinguished from drunkenness by the person's breath, which will have no smell of alcohol.

Symptoms of low blood sugar

● Pale appearance, with sweating, rapid pulse, shallow breathing and possibly trembling.
● Confused state, sometimes resembling drunkenness.
● Faintness, leading to unconsciousness in 15 to 20 minutes.

What you can do

● If a diabetic collapse comes on quickly, you can assume that the patient needs sugar. If he is conscious, give him three or four teaspoons of sugar, some cake or biscuits, jam, chocolate, or a sweet drink.
● If the patient is unconscious, put him in the recovery position (page 676), then telephone 999 and ask for an ambulance.

What the patient can do

A person who is subject to low blood sugar attacks should carry a card or wear a bracelet giving his condition and emergency instructions. This can avoid the danger of being mistaken for being drunk.

A diabetic on insulin should not drive or use dangerous machinery unless he has had food in the previous two hours. Consequently, regular mealtimes are important.

DISLOCATED JOINTS

A bone that is wrenched out of place at a joint is said to be dislocated. The symptoms may include severe pain, swelling and bruising, deformity of the joint and difficulty in moving the joint. Never try to push a dislocated bone back into place, but treat it as though it were broken, and get medical help.

1 Put the injured person into the most comfortable position possible, and support the dislocated joint with pillows or a rolled blanket.

2 Telephone 999 and ask for an ambulance.

3 If the dislocation is in the wrist, you may be able to support it with an arm sling (page 503), and take the victim to hospital.

DRUG OVERDOSE

An overdose of any drug (either an addictive drug or an ordinary medicine) is serious and requires urgent medical treatment. Symptoms of drug overdose may include abnormal dilation or contraction of the pupils of the eyes, vomiting, difficulty in breathing, unconsciousness, sweating and hallucinations.

1 Ask the person what has happened. Get any information you can about the drug as soon as possible. It's likely that the person may become unconscious at any moment.

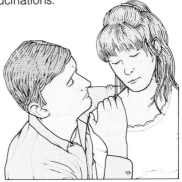

DO NOT try to get the patient to vomit. It wastes time and may also be harmful.

2 If the person becomes unconscious, put her in the recovery position (page 676).

3 Telephone 999 and ask for an ambulance.

4 Put a sample of vomit in a jar or plastic bag. Collect any bottles or pill containers that are near the victim. Send them to hospital with the ambulance men as evidence to assist treatment.

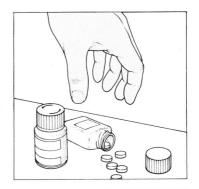

A person who becomes unconscious from alcohol

1 Put him in the recovery position, so that he does not choke on his own vomit (page 676).

2 Telephone 999 and ask for an ambulance.

667

ELECTRIC SHOCK

If someone receives an electric shock, cut off the source of electricity before doing anything else.

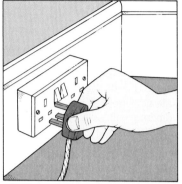

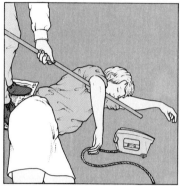

1 Stop the electric current by switching off at the socket or pulling out the plug. If you cannot reach the socket, switch off at the main fuse box.

DO NOT use the switch on the appliance itself. A faulty switch may have been the cause of the accident in the first place.

2 If there is no way to switch off, stand on dry insulating material, such as a thick layer of newspaper, a rubber mat or a wooden box, and push the victim's limbs away from the source with a broom or wooden chair.

DO NOT use anything that is damp or made of metal.

Alternatively, loop a dry towel, a pair of tights or any other dry fabric around the victim's feet or under the arms, and pull her free.

DO NOT touch the victim with your hands.
DO NOT use anything wet, such as a damp towel.

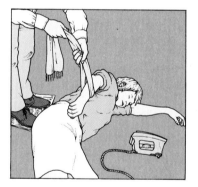

3 If the victim is unconscious but is still breathing, put her in the recovery position (page 676). If she is not breathing, give the kiss of life (page 679) immediately.

4 If the victim has been unconscious, has suffered burns or is unwell, telephone 999 for an ambulance, or drive her to the Accident and Emergency Department of a hospital. Tell the hospital how long she was in contact with the electricity.

INSECT STINGS AND BITES

Stings and bites from bees, wasps and ants can be painful but are not usually dangerous. Only an allergic reaction, or a sting in the throat or mouth, can endanger life.

If the victim has been stung by a bee, the sting will probably still be sticking into the skin. Remove it quickly by scraping it off with a knife or with your fingernail.

Wasps and ants do not leave stings behind.

Apply antihistamine cream to the sting. Or use a solution of 1 teaspoon of bicarbonate of soda in a tumbler of water, or apply a cold compress (page 483).

An allergic reaction

A massive allergic reaction to a sting occurs in a few seconds or minutes, and the casualty will become very weak and feel sick. His chest will feel tight and he will have difficulty breathing. He may be sneezing and his face may swell up. Less often, he may become unconscious, and may even stop breathing.

1 Telephone 999 immediately and ask for an ambulance.

2 Reassure the victim that help is on the way.

3 Lay him on his back. Raise his feet on a cushion or a folded coat. Keep his head low and turn it on one side just in case he should vomit.

4 Keep him warm by covering him with a blanket or rug.

5 Loosen any tight clothing around the victim's neck and waist to help with breathing.

6 Do not give him anything to eat or drink. Do not allow him to smoke, either – it may make breathing more difficult.

7 If he becomes unconscious, or vomiting seems likely, or breathing becomes very difficult, turn him over and put him in the recovery position (page 676).

Stings to the mouth or throat

A sting to the mouth or throat can cause the victim's throat to swell rapidly, blocking the airway.

1 Give the victim an ice cube or some ice cream to suck, or a glass of cold water to sip, to lessen the swelling.

2 If breathing stops, start the kiss of life immediately (page 679).

3 Telephone 999 for an ambulance or take the victim at once to the Accident and Emergency Department of a hospital.

Blood-sucking ticks

Ticks may attach themselves to children who play in woods and grassy areas. Their bodies swell up to hold the blood they feed on.

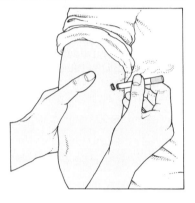

1 Do not try to pull a tick out. Touch it with a cigarette or match and it will fall off. Alternatively, cover it with cooking oil to close its breathing pores. It may fall off at once; if not, leave the oil for half an hour and then remove it carefully with tweezers.

2 Wash the area with soap and water and apply some antihistamine cream.

MOVING AN INJURED PERSON

Injured people should be moved only if they are in immediate danger, as in a burning house, or if they have to be taken to hospital with fairly minor injuries.

Otherwise, leave the person undisturbed and look after him while someone else calls for an ambulance.

TAKE CARE OF YOURSELF

If you must move someone, take care not to injure yourself while you're doing it. Back injuries are easily suffered when moving heavy weights, so keep your backbone straight, your head up, and use the stronger parts of your body to do the lifting – the thigh muscles, the hip and the shoulder. Keep the weight of the injured person as close as possible to your body as you move him.

If other people are on the scene, ask someone to help you. It is always easier for two people to lift a weight than one.

A human crutch

If a person is conscious and able to stand – with a sprained ankle, for example – you can move them by acting as a human crutch.

1 Stand close to the person on the injured side, unless the wound is to the hand, arm or shoulder. In that case, support from the uninjured side. Put your arm around her waist and grip the clothing at the hip.

2 Get her to put her arm around your neck and then take hold of her hand.

3 Take her weight with your body and move forwards with slow, short steps.

Piggyback ride

If the person is small and conscious, get him onto your back and give him a piggyback ride to a safe place.

Dragging a very light casualty

It may be possible to drag a very light person who is unconscious by simply gripping her under the shoulders. Work your way backwards, letting her head rest on your upper arm. If you have to go down stairs, support the head on your thigh.

Dragging a heavier person

If the person is too heavy to drag by the shoulders, or if you have a long way to go, use this method:

1 Turn the injured person onto her back and cross her arms at the wrists.

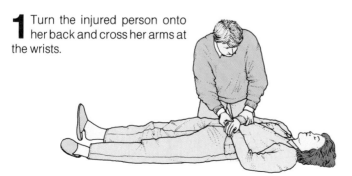

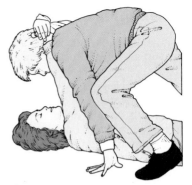

2 Use a belt, tie or scarf to tie the person's wrists together. Wind the material around the wrists tightly, but not so tightly as to impede blood circulation. Tie the ends with a reef knot, and check quickly with your fingers that the knot is completely secure.

3 Kneel astride the person and slip your head through the wrists so they are resting on your shoulders at the base of your neck. Push yourself up into a crouch, and work forwards, using your arms to take the weight. Keep the casualty's head off the ground.

Four-handed seat

A casualty who cannot walk but can use his hands can be carried by two people using a 'four-handed seat'.

1 The helpers grip their left wrist with their right hand, and then grip the other person's right wrist with their free hand (see right).

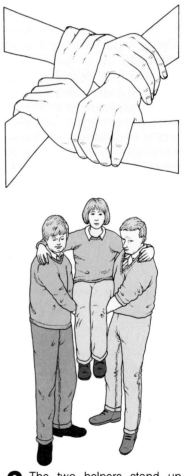

2 The injured person puts an arm around the neck of each helper and sits on the 'seat'.

CARRYING IN A WHEELCHAIR

A disabled person can be carried in a wheelchair, but first put the brakes on. Then stand to one side, with a helper on the other. Hold the fixed parts, not the wheels. Be careful of the arm rests and side supports; they might be removable.

3 The two helpers stand up straight and start walking together with the outside foot.

Chairlift

Using a chair is a good way of carrying an injured person downstairs. But first make sure that the staircase and passage are clear of obstructions, or hazards such as loose rugs or children's toys.

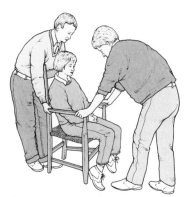

1 Check that the chair is strong enough to take the weight. Sit the casualty well back in it, and stand in front with the other helper behind. Tilt the chair backwards as you lift it.

2 Carry the chair with the casualty facing forwards, so that you go downstairs with the helper at the front backing down. On wide stairs, the two helpers can hold the sides instead.

POISONING

A house contains many substances, such as bleach, insecticides and paint stripper, that are highly dangerous to children. Get medical help quickly if a child swallows one.

Household chemicals

1 If the victim is still conscious, ask her questions to discover what chemical has been swallowed. Remember that she may become unconscious at any moment.

2 If the victim is conscious and has swallowed something that burns, such as bleach, cleaning fluid or paint stripper, give her water or milk to drink slowly.

DO NOT induce vomiting. It wastes time and may be harmful.

3 If the victim becomes unconscious, place her in the recovery position (page 676).

4 Telephone 999 and ask for an ambulance.

5 Give the ambulance men the poison container or a sample of vomit in a jar or plastic bag to help the hospital decide on the best treatment.

Poisonous plant

The most common poisonous plants are the berries of laburnum and deadly or woody nightshade, green potatoes and death cap fungus. Symptoms include vomiting, diarrhoea and stomach pains.

Telephone your doctor or take the child to the Accident and Emergency Department of your local hospital.

Alternatively, telephone 999 and ask for an ambulance. If possible, give a sample of the plant to the hospital or ambulance men.

SPRAINS AND STRAINS

Injuries to the joints and muscles – known as sprains and strains – can be extremely painful. Treatment includes resting the injured part, applying a cold compress, bandaging firmly and raising it above the level of the heart. This all helps to control the internal bleeding.

To make a cold compress, put some ice cubes into a plastic bag, knot the bag and crush the ice with a hammer or heavy saucepan. Then wrap the bag of ice in a towel.

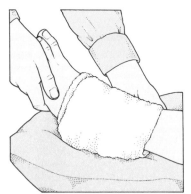

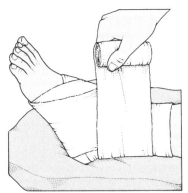

1 Rest in the most comfortable position, and if the sprain has occurred recently, apply a cold compress to it for at least 30 minutes. If no ice is available, soak a small towel in cold water, squeeze out the excess, and wrap it round the injured area. Keep the towel cold by rewetting it.

2 After removing the cold compress, bandage the injured area firmly, but not so tightly as to stop the blood circulation. For an ankle joint, start by making one turn around the ankle. Then go over the instep, under the foot, back across the instep and around the ankle again several times.

3 Raise the injured part above the level of the heart and make it comfortable. Then get medical help if necessary.

674

STROKE OR HEART ATTACK

Stroke symptoms

There may be headache, paralysis down one side, or difficulty swallowing and speaking. Also possibly confusion and unconsciousness.

Heart attack symptoms

Sudden crushing pain in the chest, often spreading to arms, neck and jaw. Possibly breathlessness.

1 **Suspected stroke** If the patient is conscious, lay her down with her head and shoulders slightly raised and supported with a pillow. Place her head on one side to allow saliva to drain from the mouth.

Suspected heart attack If the patient is conscious, place him in a half-sitting position, with his head and shoulders supported with pillows or cushions, and with another cushion placed under his knees.

2 Call the patient's doctor, or telephone 999 and ask them to send an ambulance.

3 Loosen clothing around the neck, chest and waist to help blood circulation and breathing.

DO NOT give the patient anything to eat or drink.
DO NOT allow a heart-attack patient to move unnecessarily.

4 If the patient becomes unconscious, place him in the recovery position (next page).

TOOTH INJURIES

A ll injuries to the teeth should be checked as soon as possible by a dentist or hospital dental department. If there are serious injuries to the mouth, the immediate aim is to ensure that the victim can breathe properly.

● Clear broken teeth and blood from the mouth with your fingers.
● If the casualty is conscious and has no other serious injuries, sit him in a chair with his head tilted forwards over a bowl or basin.
● Telephone 999 for an ambulance, or drive him to your local hospital.
● Never allow a person who is bleeding from the mouth to lie on his back, because he may choke on the blood.

SAVING A KNOCKED-OUT TOOTH

It is sometimes possible to save a tooth that has been knocked out of its socket.

The roots must be kept moist with saliva, so suck a piece of clean gauze or cloth until it is thoroughly damp, or get the casualty to do so. Wrap the tooth in the gauze and put it in a matchbox or other container to take to the hospital or dentist.

UNCONSCIOUSNESS

A person who has become unconscious is in danger of choking to death if he or she is left lying face up.

Vomit, blood or saliva may block the top of the windpipe, or the base of the tongue may slide back over the windpipe. The normal reflexes are not working as they do if the person is asleep.

Deal with the situation in the following sequence.

Is the person breathing?

1 Put your ear to the person's nose and mouth and listen for the sound of breathing. Watch the chest to see if it rises and falls, or rest your hand lightly on the chest to feel for movement. If the casualty is not breathing, start the kiss of life (page 679).

2 If he is breathing, clear the mouth of foreign matter with your finger. Clean up blood around the mouth. Then put him in the recovery position (below) – unless you suspect he has back or neck injuries, in which case he should not be moved at all.

The recovery position

1 Kneel beside the person, about 230mm (9in) away. Turn the head towards you, and tilt it back to open the airway.

2 Lay the nearer arm along the person's side, slightly tucking it under the body and keeping it straight. Place the far ankle over the near ankle. Put the other arm across the chest.

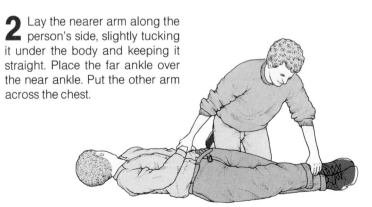

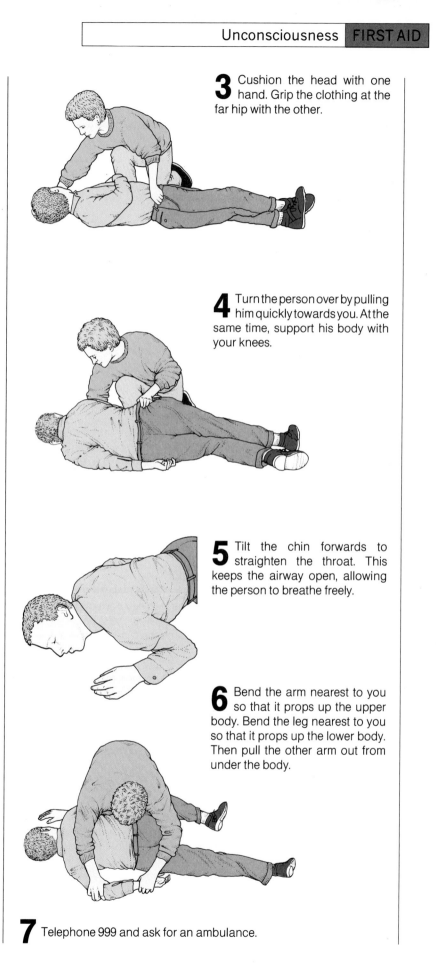

3 Cushion the head with one hand. Grip the clothing at the far hip with the other.

4 Turn the person over by pulling him quickly towards you. At the same time, support his body with your knees.

5 Tilt the chin forwards to straighten the throat. This keeps the airway open, allowing the person to breathe freely.

6 Bend the arm nearest to you so that it props up the upper body. Bend the leg nearest to you so that it props up the lower body. Then pull the other arm out from under the body.

7 Telephone 999 and ask for an ambulance.

677

Turning a heavy person

Grip the clothing at the hip with both hands and roll the body against your knees. If possible, get a second person to support the head while you turn the body.

Alternatively, the helper can kneel facing you and push while you pull.

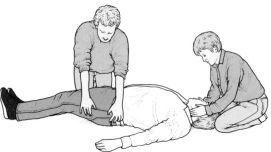

A broken arm or leg

When an arm or leg is broken, or for some other reason cannot be used to prop the casualty in the recovery position, lay a rolled blanket under the casualty's uninjured side. It raises the body on the uninjured side, keeping the airway open.

While you wait for help

1 Once the injured person is safely in the recovery position, loosen any tight clothing at the neck, chest and waist to assist breathing and blood circulation. Provide fresh air by opening a window or door.

2 Check for any other injuries and stop any bleeding (page 655). If possible, get someone to telephone 999 and ask for an ambulance. Then check to see if the injured person is carrying a treatment card – for diabetes, for example.

THREE STAGES OF UNCONSCIOUSNESS

Unconsciousness is not always total insensibility. There are three general stages, and a person may go through all three or may remain in one. They are:

● Drowsiness, in which the injured person is easily roused for a few moments, but then passes back into a sleep-like state. He may be able to give reasonably coherent answers to questions you ask him about his condition.

● Stupor, in which the injured person does not react to questions easily or does so incoherently, giving the impression of being drunk.

● Coma, in which the injured person cannot be roused at all, and is motionless and silent.

THE KISS OF LIFE

Someone who has stopped breathing will probably suffer brain damage after about four minutes. The kiss of life puts air into the lungs until the person can breathe again.

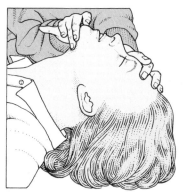

1 With one hand on the forehead and the other under the chin, tilt the head backwards to open the airway. Check if the person is breathing.

2 If not, remove obvious obstructions from the face. With the head to the side, quickly clear the mouth of any foreign material.

3 If the person still doesn't breathe, pinch the nose closed with your fingers and blow into the mouth deeply. Give two full breaths. Do not delay. (For babies and small children, cover both nose and mouth, and breathe gently.)

4 After the two deep breaths, look along the chest to watch it fall. When it does, continue at your normal breathing rate (about 15 breaths per minute). (For babies and small children, breathe slightly more quickly than your normal rate.)

5 When breathing begins, put the casualty into the recovery position (page 676).

Household emergencies

BURST PIPE OR TANK

When water pours through a bedroom ceiling, it is probably coming from a burst pipe in the loft, or from a corroded cold-water tank that has finally sprung a leak.

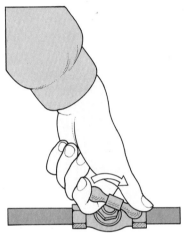

1 Turn off (clockwise) the main stopcock. It is probably under the kitchen sink or in the cellar. In a bungalow it may be in the airing cupboard. This will stop water entering the cold-water tank from the mains.

2 Open all the taps in the house, and flush the toilets, to drain the cold-water tank as quickly as possible. When the water stops flowing from the taps, the flow from the leak will have stopped, or will stop shortly afterwards.

3 If water is running down a light fitting in the ceiling or on the wall, switch off the light and remove the appropriate fuse from the main fuse box.

DO NOT replace the fuse until everything has dried out.

4 If the ceiling plaster is bulging, hold a washing-up bowl beneath the bulge and pierce the plaster with a screwdriver or pair of scissors. Stand out of the way, and have spare buckets ready to catch the water. This will limit ceiling damage to one area.

5 Switch off the water heating on the programmer of a gas or oil-fired boiler, or an immersion heater. Damp down a solid-fuel boiler, but there is no need to put out the fire altogether as the hot-water cylinder will not have emptied.

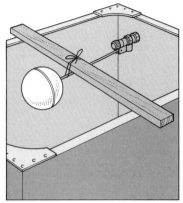 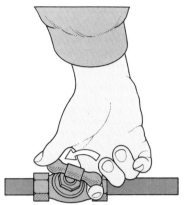

6 Find the source of the leak. If it was from a pipe supplied by the cold-water tank (page 166), or if the tank itself was leaking, tie up the ball valve in the tank to stop it filling up again.

7 If you have tied up the ball valve, turn on the main stop-cock. You will now have cold water for cooking and washing in the kitchen tap. Lavatory cisterns can be filled with a bucket.

8 Contact a plumber.

9 If it looks possible, try to make an emergency repair to any burst pipe (page 175).

ELECTRICAL POWER FAILURE

No electricity in the house

1 If power throughout your house fails and neighbouring houses are also without power, there is a mains supply failure. Report it, using the emergency number under 'Electricity' in your phone book.

2 If the neighbours have power when you have none, the fuse in the sealed unit on your fuseboard may have blown. Report it as described above.

One appliance fails

If one appliance fails, check its plug fuse and renew if necessary. Check that the wires in the plug are firmly fixed to the terminals. If the appliance still fails, try it in a different socket before taking it for repair. If the fault was in the socket, call an electrician.

Several appliances fail

If several appliances on one circuit stop working at once, switch off at the fuse box and check the circuit fuse (page 165). If it is sound, there may be a fault in the circuit cable. Call in an electrician to test it.

FIRE

When fire has taken hold in a house, get out fast. Smoke from plastic-foam upholstery can kill in less than two minutes.

A burning chip pan or frying pan

1 Immediately turn off the heat on the cooker.

2 Cover the pan with a large lid or plate, or with a damp towel or a fire blanket.

DO NOT move the pan.
DO NOT throw water on it.
DO NOT lift the lid off a chip pan for half an hour, even if the flames seem to have died down.

A burning electrical appliance or electric socket

1 Switch off the electricity at the main fuse box.

2 Put out the fire with water or a fire extinguisher, EXCEPT for a TV or computer fire (see below).

DO NOT throw water on a burning appliance or fitting when the electricity is still turned on.
DO NOT touch any switch on a burning appliance or fitting.

3 Have the electrical appliance or the socket checked by a electrician before you try to use it again.

A burning TV or computer

1 Pull out the plug or switch off at the main fuse box.

2 Smother the fire with a blanket or rug, or preferably a fire blanket.

DO NOT use water or a fire extinguisher, because residual electricity may remain in the set.

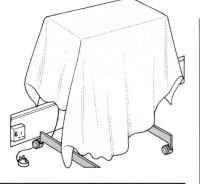

Sparks or smell of burning from an appliance

1 If sparks or a burning smell come from an appliance, turn off the socket switch and pull out the plug.

If it is a fixed appliance with no plug, turn off the main switch at the fuse box. It is then safe to turn off the appliance switch.

2 Get the appliance checked by an electrician.

Sparks or smell of burning from a socket or plug

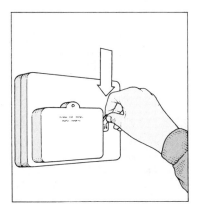

1 If sparks or a smell of burning come from an electrical socket or plug, turn off the main switch at the fuse box.

2 If the plug is hot, carefully remove it from the socket and turn the power back on at the fuse box. Check the plug's connections, including the fuse contacts, and examine the flex for damage. Renew the connections if necessary (page 161).

3 If the socket is hot, remove the appropriate circuit fuse from the fuse box and turn the power back on. Call an electrician.

A burning oil heater

Stand at least 2m (7ft) away, and throw on buckets of water until the flames have totally died out.

Foam furniture catches fire

Burning plastic foam gives off choking black smoke that can kill in less than two minutes. Do not try to put out the fire.

1 Leave the room and close the door to stop smoke spreading.

2 Telephone 999 and ask for the fire brigade.

Someone's clothes catch fire

1 Prevent the victim from rushing about in a panic; the movement will fan the flames and make them worse.

2 Lay the victim down to prevent the flames from rising to her head, and douse the fire with water or other non-flammable liquid (in a kitchen a bottle of milk might be the nearest to hand).

Alternatively, wrap the victim tightly in a heavy coat, curtain, blanket (not the cellular type), or any other thick piece of fabric, and simultaneously lay her down to keep the flames away from the head.

DO NOT use nylon or man-made material to smother the flames.
DO NOT roll the victim along the ground. It can bring the flames into contact with unharmed parts of the body.

3 Treat the injured person according to the extent of the burns (pages 660-2).

You smell burning at night

1 Wake up everybody else in the house.

2 If the fire is too big to deal with safely, get everyone outside. If you think it is well alight in a closed room, don't open the door to find out.

3 Shut all doors behind you to slow down the spread of flames and smoke.

DO NOT go back inside the house.

4 Go immediately to the nearest telephone, dial 999 and ask for the Fire Brigade.

If you are trapped on an upper floor

1 Go to a room at the front of the house, close the door and block up cracks with bedding or clothes.

2 Open the window and call for help.
DO NOT jump out of the window, except as a last resort.

SMOKE INHALATION

If someone is being suffocated by smoke in a burning house, get him out as quickly as possible. Smoke from plastic foam in upholstered chairs and sofas is highly poisonous.

Protect yourself by tying a towel or thick cloth – preferably wet – around your nose and mouth. As you move through the room, keep low because hot, smoky air will rise. Reduce fire risk by closing windows and doors behind you.

Smoke can irritate the throat, causing it to contract in a sudden spasm and close the airway. So someone found in a smoke-filled room may be unconscious and his breathing may have stopped.

DO NOT go into a burning building without telling someone, or if it will place you in danger.

What you should do
● Drag the victim away from the smoke (page 670).
● Once you are both clear of danger, if the victim is unconscious but breathing normally, put him in the recovery position (page 676) until an ambulance arrives.
● If breathing has stopped or is very difficult, begin the kiss of life as soon as possible (page 679).
● Get someone to telephone 999 and ask for an ambulance.

GAS LEAK

Your first priority must always be to cut off the flow of gas.

A strong smell of gas

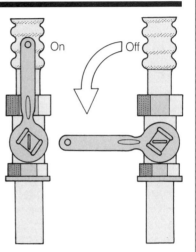

1 Put out cigarettes or naked flames; switch off electric fires. Don't operate light switches.

2 Turn off the main gas tap next to the meter. Put the handle at right angles to the pipe.

3 Open plenty of doors and windows to let out the gas.

4 Get an unconscious person into the open air and put him in the recovery position (page 676). Telephone 999 – preferably from a neighbour's house – and ask for an ambulance.

5 Telephone your local area gas office immediately – day or night. Find it under 'Gas' in the phone book.

DO NOT try to trace the gas leak with any naked flame, such as from a match or cigarette lighter.
DO NOT enter a room or any part of the house where the smell of gas is especially strong. There is a danger that the build-up of fumes may overpower you.

A slight smell of gas

1 Put out cigarettes; extinguish naked flames; switch off any electric fire in the room.

2 Trace the source of the gas immediately. Often the pilot light on a cooker or gas fire has gone out, or a burner on the cooker has blown out in a draught.

3 Turn off the pilot light or burner. If the pilot light does not have a tap, turn off the gas tap next to the meter. Put the handle at right angles to the pipe.

4 Open some doors and windows to let the gas disperse. Wait for the smell to go away.

5 Relight the pilot light or burner.

6 If the smell persists or returns, telephone your local area gas office immediately – day or night. Find it under 'Gas' in the phone book.

DO NOT attempt any gas repairs yourself.

A LEAKING CENTRAL HEATING RADIATOR

I f water is coming out of a central heating radiator for any reason, you need to shut off the radiator at both ends and then get rid of the water inside it.

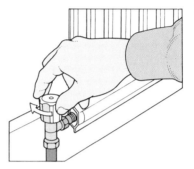

1 Turn off (clockwise) the control valve by hand.

2 Undo the screw on top of the other valve and lift off the cover. Turn off (again clockwise) the valve, using a pair of pliers. Water has now stopped flowing into the radiator.

3 Put a towel and a bowl or dish under one of the valves to catch water, and have a bucket and a second bowl ready.

4 Use a large adjustable spanner or a pipe wrench to unscrew the union nut on the radiator anticlockwise (when looking from the radiator to the valve). If the nut is stiff, there is a danger of bending the pipe, so hold the pipe just below the valve with another pipe wrench to counteract the pressure as you undo the nut.

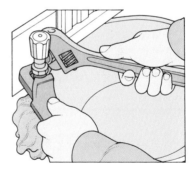

5 When the nut has been undone, some water will probably run out, so be ready to catch it in the bowl.

6 Let air into the radiator by opening the vent at the top with the radiator key (turning it a quarter of a turn anticlockwise). The rest of the water will flow out rapidly, so it's best to have a helper.

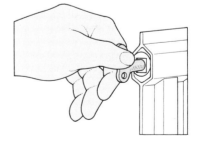

7 Call a plumber to repair the radiator. In the meantime you can still use the central heating.

LEAKING HOT-WATER CYLINDER

1 Turn off (clockwise) the gate valve, if there is one, in the supply pipe from the cold-water tank – which is probably in the loft – to the hot-water cylinder.

Alternatively, turn off the main stopcock and turn on all the taps in the house, and flush the toilets, to drain the cold-water tank.

This will not drain the hot-water cylinder, but will stop water flowing into it.

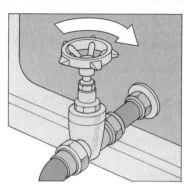

2 Switch off the immersion heater, if there is one.

3 Switch off the boiler, or put out the boiler fire in a solid-fuel system.

4 Connect a garden hose to the cylinder drain cock, if there is one (it will be on the supply pipe from the cold-water tank). Put the other end of the hose into a lavatory or outside drain.

Alternatively, connect the hose to the boiler drain cock (which is on the return pipe near the bottom of the boiler) and direct the other end of the hose to an outside drain.

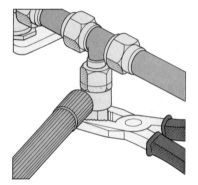

5 Open up the drain cock with a spanner or pair of pliers.

6 Get the hot-water cylinder repaired or replaced by a plumber.

MAIN STOPCOCK IS JAMMED OR BROKEN

● If the stopcock is jammed or if it breaks when you have a burst pipe, turn off the outside stopcock, if you know where it is. If you have no key, try reaching down to turn the tap by hand or with pliers. If you have time, make your own key (page 168).

● For a burst lead pipe in the roof, use a heavy hammer to flatten the pipe between the burst and the tank, where it crosses a roofing timber.

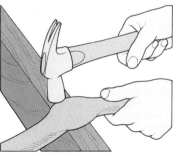

● For a burst copper pipe in the roof space, stuff towelling into the cistern outlet to the pipe, if you can, and raise and tie up the float arm to stop the cistern filling.

● Call an emergency plumber – see Yellow Pages under 'Plumbers'.

A TAP RUNS DRY

1 Turn on the cold tap over the kitchen sink. If no water flows from it, make sure that the main stopcock in the house has not been turned off by mistake. If the stopcock is on (turned fully anti-clockwise), call the regional water authority, which is listed in the phone book under Water. There is probably a problem with the mains.

2 If the kitchen tap is working, look into the cold-water tank. It may have drained because of a jammed ball valve. If it is empty, move the float arm up and down to free the valve, then clean the valve (page 183).

In freezing weather, the rising main is likely to be frozen, probably between the ceiling and the tank.

3 If the tank is filling, check the bathroom taps. If there is no flow from one tap, the supply pipe from the tank is likely to be frozen, probably in the roof-space section. Try to identify the supply pipe which feeds the non-flowing tap.

To thaw a pipe
● Strip off any lagging from the affected part and check for a burst. If the pipe has burst, apply a temporary repair (page 175). Only then should you apply hot-water bottles, or cloths soaked in very hot water and then wrung out. This should melt the ice in the pipe.

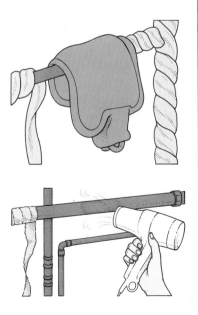

● If a pipe is difficult to get at, blow warm air onto it from a hair dryer. Do not use a blow torch or a hot-air gun – you may set the roof on fire. And keep the hair dryer and its flex well out of any water. A combination of electricity and water is dangerous.

Index

Ammonia
What you can clean with it

Ceramic tiles 65
Chrome 78
Cooker hob surrounds 96
Jewellery 467
Windows 65

Bicarbonate of soda

What you can clean with it

Chrome 82
Fridges and freezers 129
Iron soleplate 139
Laminate worktops 91
Non-stick pans 95
Ovens 98
Plastic furniture 79
Vacuum flasks 96

Bleach

What you can clean with it

Bathroom 88-89
Lavatory 90
Pots and pans 95
Stone fireplaces 83

Borax

What you can clean with it

Aluminium 81
Ceramic tiles 65
Lime scale in lavatory
  bowl 90
Mirrors 89
Windows 65

_C_

Glycerine
What you can clean with it
Food stains 116
Grass and mud stains 116
Old wine stains 72
Unidentified stains 117

Haemorrhoids, *see* Piles 502
Hair care 442-4
Hair removal 438, 448
Halitosis, *see* Bad breath 444,
    474-5
Halls
    flooring 624
    lighting 616-17
    storage space 47
'Hammer' in water pipes
    186-7
Hammer, using 208
Hamsters as pets 384-6,
    407-8
Handbags and purses, care
    465
Hanging baskets 291, 292-3
Hangover 494-5
Hardboard
    bending 213
    flooring 624
Hats 465-6
Hay fever 495
Hazelnuts, preparation 556
Head injuries 495-6
Heart attack 675
Hedges
    growing 322-3
    security risk 218
Herbal baths 453-4
Herbs
    buying 573
    flavouring food 548, 583
    growing 322
    storage 540
Herpes, *see* Cold sores 485
Hessian, cleaning 64
Hiccups 496
Hi-fi 155-7
Hinge bolts 222
Hinge-bound door 198-9
Hire purchase 40, 375
Hiring goods, consumer
    rights 208, 379-80
Hole, cutting an enclosed
    206
Holidays
    arranging family holidays
        358-60
    consumer rights 380-1
    home security 219-20
    preventing freeze-up 190-1
Hollandaise sauce 571, 591
Home decorating, *see*
    Decorating your home

Housework, organising 16-22
Hydrogen peroxide 118
    cleaning with, *see panel*
Hysteria 496-7

Ice cream, storing 543
Icing a cake 563, 564
Illness, coping at home 470-2
Immunising children 338
    See also specific illnesses
India rubber, cleaning
    wallpaper 64
Indigestion 497
Ingrowing toenails 450
Injured person, moving 670-3
Injuries
    arm 658-9
    back 658
    eye 488-9
    head 495-6
    leg 659
    neck 658
    ribs 660
    tooth 675-6
Ink stains 72
Insect pests 100-2, 304, 305-9
    stings and bites 668-70
Insomnia 497-8
Insulating your home 177-8,
    201-4
Insurance
    endowment mortgages 43
    holiday 358
    home and contents 28-29

house move 650-1
    life 30-32
    pet 418
    sickness 30
Investment
    advice 41-42
    devising a savings strategy
        32-35
Iron in the diet 514, 515
Ironing 121-4
Irons 138-40
Ivory, cleaning 84

Jacking up a car 263-4
Jade, cleaning 468
Jams and preserves
    making 586
    stains 72, 116
Jars, tight lids 544
Jet (jewellery), cleaning 468
Jewellery 466-8
    protection in the home
        229-30
Jigsaw, using a 206
Joint of meat or poultry
    carving 578-80
Joints, sprains 674
Joist-and-stud detector 50
Jump-starting a car 259

Kettles, electric 140-1
Keys, security measures 219
Kidney beans 525
Kiss of life 679
Kitchens
    aids for the elderly 365
    creating a kitchen 609
    flooring 624
    hygiene 560
    lighting 616
    storage space 45
Knee, bandaging 475
Knife sharpener, substitute
    566
Knives in kitchen 558-60

Lemon juice
*What you can
clean with it*

Chopping board 92-93
Hands 445
Laminate worktops 91
Microwave oven 98
Rust stains 117
Tarnished brass and
copper 82

Metal polish
*What you can
clean with it*

Acrylic baths 88
Light-switch plates 80
Scratched plastic
furniture 79
White shoes 464
White rings on furniture
75

Methylated spirit

What you can clean with it

Burn marks on worktops 91
Candle-wax stains 64, 115
Glass 84, 95
Grass and mud stains 116
Ink stains 72, 116
Ivory 84
Mirrors 89
Piano keys 76
Shoe-polish stains 72
Stainless steel 83
Windows 65
Windscreens 270

---

pq

n

o

Paraffin

What you can clean with it

Bathroom 87-88
Bronze 82
Chrome 78

r

Turpentine
*What you can
clean with it*

Bathroom 87
Bronze 82
Built-up furniture polish
74
Gilt frames 85
White rings on furniture
75

702

yz

Acknowledgements

The publishers wish to thank the following companies for their help in providing illustrations:

Aid Call plc, Aquaseal (Feb Ltd), Braun (UK) Ltd, Caradon Mira Ltd, Egnell Ameda Ltd, HHS Hire Shops, Ikea Ltd, Keep-Able Ltd, Mothercare (UK) Ltd, Omega Lighting Ltd, Osram-GEC Ltd, Rentokil Ltd, Ulike Ltd, Vacu Products Ltd.

Picture credits

The pictures in HOUSEHOLD HINTS & HANDY TIPS were supplied by the people listed below.

T= top; *C* = centre; *B* = bottom; *R* = right; *L* = left.

10-18 *All* J. Woodcock. **19** *All* S. Pond & W. Giles. **20** *CL* S. Pond & W. Giles, *BL* J. Woodcock. **22** *All* J. Woodcock. **23** *Both* S. Pond & W. Giles. **24** S. Pond & W. Giles. **25** S. Pond & W. Giles. **26** S. Pond & W. Giles. **28** S. Pond & W. Giles. **29** S. Pond & W. Giles. **44** *TL & TR* J. Woodcock, *BR* M. Grey. **45** M. Grey. **46** *TL & TR* J. Woodcock, *CRM.* Grey. **47** *TR* J. Woodcock, *BL & BR* M. Grey. **48** *TR* L. Tucker, *CL & CR* J. Woodcock. **50** *TR* L. Turpin, *CL & CR* J. Woodcock. **51** *All* M. Grey. **52** *TR* L. Tucker, *TR* J. Cummins, *CL & CR* Oxford Illustrators, *BR* Oxford Illustrators. **53** *All* Oxford Illustrators. **54** *TR* Oxford Illustrators, *CL & CR* J. Woodcock, *BL & BR* J. Woodcock. **55** *TR & TL* M. Grey, *CR* M. Grey, *CR* L. Turpin, *B* M. Grey. **56** *All* M. Grey. **57** *All* Kevin Jones. **58** *TR* J. Woodcock, *CR* J. Woodcock, *BR* M. Grey. **63** *TR* L. Turpin, *CL* S. Pond & W. Giles, *CR* M. Grey, *BR* L. Turpin. **66** *TL & TR* M. Grey, *BR* L. Turpin. **68-78** *All* L. Turpin. **79** S. Pond & W. Giles. **80** *TR* S. Pond & W. Giles, *CR* L. Turpin. **81-83** *All* L. Turpin. **84** *TR* S. Pond & W. Giles, *CR* S. Pond & W. Giles, *BR* L. Turpin. **85** J. Woodcock. **86** *Both* L. Turpin. **88** L. Turpin. **89** *CR* M. Grey, *BL & BR* L. Turpin. **90** L. Turpin. **94** *BR* M. Grey. **95-98** *All* L. Turpin. **100-2** *All* S. Pond & W. Giles. **105-9** *All* J. Woodcock. **110** M. Grey. **113** *Both* J. Woodcock. **114** *Both* M. Grey. **117-19** *All* J. Woodcock. **120** *TL* L. Turpin, *TR* J. Woodcock, *CR* S. Pond & W. Giles. **121** L. Turpin. **122** *TL & TR* J. Woodcock, *BR* M. Grey. **123-4** *All* J. Woodcock. **125-7** *All* M. Grey. **129-30** *All* S. Pond & W. Giles. **131** *CL* J. Cummins, *CR* J. Woodcock. **133** *TL* S. Pond & W. Giles, *TR* J. Woodcock. **137** J. Woodcock. **139** *BL* L. Turpin, *BR* M. Grey. **140-2** *All* J. Woodcock. **143** S. Pond & W. Giles. **148-52** *All* M. Grey. **154** N. Hall. **156-9** *All* M. Grey. **161** *TL & TR* L. Turpin, *BR* J. Cummins. **162** *Both* J. Woodcock. **163** *All* J. Cummins. **164** *All* M. Grey. **165** J. Woodcock. **166** M. Grey. **167** *Both* S. Pond & W. Giles. **168** *CL* S. Pond & W. Giles, *CR* M. Grey. **169-70** *All* N. Hall. **171** *Top* N. Hall, *BR* M. Grey. **172** *TL & TR* M. Grey, *CR* M. Grey, *BL & BR* J. Woodcock. **173-4** *All* J. Woodcock. **175** *TL & TR* J. Woodcock, *CL* J. Woodcock, *CR* S. Pond & W. Giles. **176** *TL & TR* J. Woodcock, *CL* J. Woodcock, *BL & BR* S. Pond & W. Giles. **177** *Both* J. Woodcock. **178** *TR* Kevin Jones & Associates, *CL* Kevin Jones & Associates, *CR* M. Grey. **179** J. Woodcock. **180** *CL & CR* J. Woodcock, *BR* M. Grey. **181** *All* J. Woodcock. **182** *All* M. Grey. **183** *Both* J. Woodcock. **184** *TL & TR* J. Woodcock, *CL* J. Woodcock, *CR* S. Pond & W. Giles, *BL & BR* J. Woodcock. **185** *TL & TR* J. Woodcock, *CL & CR* S. Pond & W. Giles. **186** *Both* J. Woodcock. **187** *Both* S. Pond & W. Giles. **188** Kevin Jones & Associates. **190** *TR* Kevin Jones & Associates, *BR* S. Pond & W. Giles. **192-5** *All* S. Pond & W. Giles. **196** *CR* M. Grey, *BR* S. Pond & W. Giles. **197** *TR* N. Hall, *CR* S. Pond & W. Giles, *BR* N. Hall. **198** *All* N. Hall. **199** *CR* S. Pond & W. Giles, *BR* N. Hall. **200** M. Grey. **201** *TL & TR* N. Hall, *BR* M. Grey. **202** M. Grey. **203** *Both* J. Woodcock. **204** *CR* M. Grey, *BR* J. Woodcock. **206** *TL* N. Hall, *TR* M. Grey, *CR* N. Hall. **207** *Both* S. Pond & W. Giles. **208** *CR* J. Cummins, *BR* S. Pond & W. Giles. **209** S. Pond & W. Giles. **210** *CR* S. Pond & W. Giles, *BR* N. Hall. **211** *TL & TR* N. Hall, *CR* N. Hall, *CL* M. Grey, *BL & BR* N. Hall. **212** *TL* J. Woodcock, *TR* N. Hall, *CR* J. Woodcock. **213-14** *All* J. Woodcock. **215** *CL & CR* J. Woodcock, *BL* M. Grey, *BR* J. Woodcock. **216** *TR* M. Grey, *CR* J. Woodcock, *BR* J. Woodcock. **217-19** *All* J. Woodcock. **220-2** *All* M. Grey. **223** *TR* M. Grey, *CR* M. Grey, *BL* N. Hall. **224** *TL* N. Hall, *CL* N. Hall, *B* M. Grey. **225** *Both* M. Grey. **226** *All* J. Woodcock. **227** *TL* J. Woodcock, *TR* J. Cummins, *CL & CR* J. Woodcock, *BL &*

BR J. Woodcock. **228-9** *All* J. Woodcock. **230** *TL & TR* M. Grey, *CL & CR* M. Grey, *BR* S. Pond & W. Giles. **231-5** *All* M. Grey. **236** J. Woodcock. **237-9** *All* M. Grey. **240** *TR* J. Woodcock, *CR* M. Grey. **241-2** *All* S. Pond & W. Giles. **243** Kevin Jones & Associates. **244** *TL* S. Pond & W. Giles, *TR* L. Turpin. **245** *Both* J. Woodcock. **246** Precision Illustrations. **247-50** *All* M. Grey. **252** *CL* M. Grey, *CR* J. Woodcock, *BL* J. Woodcock, *BR* M. Grey. **253** *TL* M. Grey, *TR* J. Woodcock, *CL* M. Grey, *CR* J. Woodcock, *BR* J. Woodcock. **254** *TR* J. Woodcock, *CL* J. Woodcock, *CR* M. Grey, *BR* M. Grey. **255-62** *All* M. Grey. **263** *CR* M. Grey, *BL* J. Cummins, *BR* M. Grey. **264-5** *All* M. Grey. **266** *Both* J. Woodcock. **267** *TR* L. Turpin, *BR* J. Woodcock. **268-9** *All* S. Pond & W. Giles. **270** L. Turpin. **271** *Both* J. Woodcock. **273** M. Grey. **274** L. Turpin. **275** M. Grey. **276** J. Woodcock. **277** *All* L. Turpin. **278** *TL* L. Turpin, *TR* J. Cummins, *BL & BR* S. Pond & W. Giles. **279** M. Grey. **280** J. Woodcock. **281** *Both* H. Haywood. **282** *TL & TR* H. Haywood, *BL* G. Tomblin, *BR* A. Winterbottom. **283** *CL* H. Haywood, *CR* G. Tomblin. **284** *TL & TR* A. Winterbottom, *BR* J. Woodcock. **286-7** *All* J. Woodcock. **288** N. Hall. **289-90** *All* J. Woodcock. **291** *TR* N. Hall, *CL* A. Winterbottom, *CR* G. Tomblin. **292-5** *All* N. Hall. **297-9** *All* S. Pond & W. Giles. **300** *Both* N. Hall. **301** S. Pond & W. Giles. **302** J. Woodcock. **303** *Both* H. Haywood. **304-11** *All* J. Woodcock. **312** *TL & TR* J. Woodcock, *B* G. Tomblin. **313** J. Woodcock. **314** *TR* J. Woodcock, *BR* H. Haywood. **315** *All* S. Pond & W. Giles. **317** G. Tomblin. **319** J. Woodcock. **320-66** *All* S. Pond & W. Giles. **374** J. Cummins. **379** S. Pond & W. Giles. **387-417** *All* N. Hall. **421** *All* J. Woodcock. **422** *TR* J. Woodcock, *BL & BR* R. Surman. **423-5** *All* R. Surman. **426** *TL* A. Bailey, *TR* R. Surman, *BL & BR* R. Surman. **427** *Both* R. Surman. **428** *All* A. Bailey. **429-32** *All* R. Surman. **436-44** *All* S. Pond & W. Giles. **445-7** *All* L. Turpin. **448-9** *Both* S. Pond & W. Giles. **450** *Both* L. Turpin. **451** *TR* S. Pond & W. Giles, *CR* L. Turpin. **452** *All* L. Turpin. **454** *TL* J. Woodcock, *CR* L. Turpin. **457-61** *All* J. Woodcock. **462-6** *All* S. Pond & W. Giles. **467** *TL* S. Pond & W. Giles, *TR* J. Woodcock, *CR* J. Woodcock. **468-79** *All* S. Pond & W. Giles. **481-2** *All* L. Turpin. **483-7** *All* S. Pond & W. Giles. **488-9** *All* J. Woodcock. **490-4** *All* S. Pond & W. Giles. **496-503** *All* N. Hall. **504** *TL & TR* J. Woodcock, *BL & BR* N. Hall. **506** L. Turpin. **507** *TL & TR* L. Turpin, *CR* Precision Illustrations **509-33** *All* S. Pond & W. Giles. **534** *TR* S. Pond & W. Giles, *CR* S. Thomas. **535-7** *All* S. Pond & W. Giles. **538** *TR* Baird Harris, *BR* S. Pond & W. Giles. **539-50** *All* S. Pond & W. Giles. **551** *TL & TR* S. Pond & W. Giles, *CR* S. Thomas, *BR* S. Pond & W. Giles. **552-3** *All* S. Pond & W. Giles. **554** *All* J. Cummins. **555-606** *All* S. Pond & W. Giles. **611** M. Grey. **612** *CL* J. Woodcock, *CR* M. Grey. **613** *TR* J. Woodcock, *CR* M. Grey. **614-15** *All* M. Grey. **616** S. Pond & W. Giles. **617** *Both* M. Grey. **618-19** *Both* J. Woodcock. **621** *All* N. Hall. **622** *CR* N. Hall, *BL* J. Woodcock. **625-8** *All* M. Grey. **630** *Both* J. Woodcock. **631** *TR* M. Grey, *CL & CR* J. Woodcock, *BR* J. Woodcock. **633-7** *All* J. Woodcock. **638** *TR* J. Woodcock, *CL & CR* J. Woodcock, *BL & BR* M. Grey. **639** *TR* J. Woodcock, *CR* J. Woodcock, *BR* M. Grey. **640-2** *All* J. Woodcock. **643** *TL* M. Grey, *TR* J. Woodcock. **644** *TL* M. Grey, *CR* J. Woodcock. **645-7** *All* J. Woodcock. **648** *Both* M. Grey. **654-63** *All* S. Pond & W. Giles. **664-5** *All* N. Hall. **666-79** *All* S. Pond & W. Giles. **680-2** *All* J. Woodcock. **683** *TR* J. Woodcock, *CR* S. Pond & W. Giles, *BR* J. Woodcock. **684** *TL & TR* J. Woodcock, *CL & CR* S. Pond & W. Giles. **685** *All* S. Pond & W. Giles. **686** *TL* S. Pond & W. Giles, *TR* J. Woodcock, *CR* J. Woodcock, *BR* S. Pond & W. Giles. **687-8** *All* J. Woodcock. **689** *TL* S. Pond & W. Giles, *TR* J. Woodcock, *CR* J. Woodcock, *BR* S. Pond & W. Giles.

Separations: Colourscan Overseas Co Pte Ltd, Singapore.
Paper: Townsend Hook Ltd, Snodland.
Printing and Binding: Jarrold & Sons Ltd, Norwich.

40-309-2